THE
CHALLENGE
OF
MODERNITY

—

A READER ON

POST-CONFEDERATION

CANADA

—

IAN MCKAY

Queen's University

Y0-AGL-574

MCGRAW-HILL RYERSON LIMITED

Toronto Montreal New York Auckland Bogotá Caracas Lisbon London Madrid
Mexico Milan New Delhi Paris San Juan Singapore Sydney Tokyo

THE CHALLENGE OF MODERNITY: A READER ON POST-CONFEDERATION CANADA

2 3 4 5 6 7 8 9 0   AP   1 0 9 8 7 6 5 4 3

Printed and bound in Canada

Care has been taken to trace ownership of copyright material contained in this text. The publishers will gladly accept any information that will enable them to rectify any reference or credit in subsequent editions.

SPONSORING EDITOR: CATHERINE O'TOOLE
SENIOR SUPERVISING EDITOR: ROSALYN STEINER
PERMISSIONS EDITOR: NORMA CHRISTENSEN
COVER DESIGN AND TEXT: SHARON MATTHEWS/MATTHEWS COMMUNICATIONS DESIGN

Canadian Cataloguing in Publication Data
Main entry under title:

The Challenge of modernity

Includes bibliographical references.

ISBN 0-07-551150-9

1. Canada–Social conditions–1867-   *
2. Canada–History–1867-   I. McKay, Ian, 1953-

FC85.C53 1991   971.05   C91-095470-4
F1021.C53 1991

CONTENTS

Acknowledgments

My thanks go to Catherine O'Toole of McGraw-Hill Ryerson for suggesting this reader to me and to my students and colleagues at Queen's University for their invaluable, if occasionally rather direct, critiques of this project's early versions. And my thanks to Sally Sharpe for sharing her house with a P.C.B.

INTRODUCTION: ALL THAT IS SOLID
MELTS INTO AIR

This survey reader is an introduction to some of the basic themes of post-Confederation Canadian history. Its 27 readings represent many different perspectives and aspects of the past, presented in ways that range from academic expositions to autobiographical accounts. Unlike many survey readers, this one has a unifying theme: modernity.

What is modernity? "There is a mode of vital experience," the literary critic Marshall Berman argues, in a brilliant book called *All That Is Solid Melts Into Air*,

> —experience of space and time, of the self and others, of life's possibilities and perils—that is shared by men and women all over the world today. I will call this body of experience "modernity." To be modern is to find ourselves in an environment that promises us adventure, power, joy, growth, transformation of ourselves and the world—and, at the same time, that threatens to destroy everything we have, everything we know, everything we are. Modern environments and experiences cut across all boundaries of geography and ethnicity, of class and nationality, of religion and ideology: in this sense, modernity can be said to unite all mankind. But it is a paradoxical unity, a unity of disunity: it pours us all into a maelstrom of perpetual disintegration and renewal, of struggle and contradiction, of ambiguity and anguish. To be modern is to be part of a universe in which, as Marx said, "All that is solid melts into air."[1]

Modernity is the experience of that capitalist revolution that, since the mid-nineteenth century, has transformed the northern half of North America. Here, for perhaps ten thousand years, human beings once structured their interactions with nature and with each other through kinship groups. There were no employers or employed, no nation-states or political parties, no firm boundaries separating religion from science, humanity from the natural world, one community from another. The arrival of Europeans gradually transformed this world. European settlers along the St. Lawrence (and to a lesser extent in the Atlantic region) created a new, "tributary" kind of economy and society, in which those who worked—the peasants—subsidized (through various forms of customary tributes, sometimes called the "feudal burden") those who prayed

---

1. Marshall Berman, *All That Is Solid Melts Into Air: The Experience of Modernity* (New York: Simon and Schuster, 1982), 15.

and governed—a lay and clerical aristocracy. Neither the first form—the "kinship mode of production"—nor the second form—"the tributary mode of production"—was in any sense static or uniform; but both were distinct from modern capitalism.[2] In neither case, down to the late eighteenth century, would we find many people agreeing with Marx that their whole social and economic world had been turned upside down, that all the old truths of religion and social tradition had been thrown into question.

That daunting cultural experience awaited the coming of the third great mode of production in northern North America: capitalism. Capitalism—meaning a system of economic and social life centred on wage-labour, on the ownership of production by a small number of people who derive their profits from the labour of people in other social classes—was the great force that made people think that "all that is solid melts into air." Unlike earlier modes of production, capitalism has built into it a fantastically powerful engine of economic change: competition. This requires the owners of the means of production continually to plow some of the profits derived from the labour of others back into technological change.

Modernity is the lived experience of this unremitting process of rapid change and its social consequences. We are modern because we have learned to expect constant and radical transformation, dramatic growth, development at an ever more rapid rate. We are part of a dynamic social machine, a powerful juggernaut that crushes everything in its path: no traditional kin-ordered "primitive" society, certainly no Berlin Wall, has proven capable of containing the extraordinary power, efficiency, relentless progressiveness of capitalist modernity. It has interacted with all other social forms with the subtlety of an atomic bomb. And we are modern because we can no longer quite remember what this machine was built to do. We serve it because we feel we must to survive. If asked, however, what this machine is *for*, what purpose is served by this unprecedented growth and this unbridled materialism, we fall into silence. Modernity is for, and about, itself. To be modern is thus to be caught "in a vortex where all facts and values are whirled, exploded, decomposed, recombined," to sense "a basic uncertainty about what is basic, what is valuable, even what is real," and to experience a "flaring up of the most radical hopes in the midst of their radical negations."[3]

What began as an economic transformation in the European peninsula

---

2. I am using the useful terms of Eric Woolf, *Europe and the People Without History* (Berkeley: University of California Press, 1982), ch. 3.
3. Ibid., 121.

in about the sixteenth century is now an all-embracing economic, cultural, and political cultural phenomenon. Modernity has become worldwide in its influence. It places humanity in a new position in both time and space, because it involves the "disenchantment" of the world—the replacement of religion and tradition by science and technology. Modernity involves new ways of seeing community and time. One no longer lives among familiars in local locations, but interacts, much of the time, with strangers in a globalized and impersonal world. Humans once considered that their children's lives would be more or less the same as their own, that the future would very much resemble the past. Modern people now see the future as an open realm of possibility, whose outlines can be barely discerned in the present. Modernity is an outlook based on uncertainty. It entails (in the social theorist Anthony Giddens's phrase) "the institutionalization of doubt."[4] Pre-modern societies, lacking our detailed historical awareness and the prospects of an open future, did not need to worry about how or even whether they were to go on. But modern people do have to wonder, for it is precisely this question—"how to go on?"—that we ask again and again as we experience a world without foundations and without guarantees. Modernity involves a significant paradox. Doubt is institutionalized, but so is scientific certainty, precise techniques of surveillance, advanced technologies of power. Such disembodied instruments and bodies of "knowledge" (bureaucracies, professions, economic theories, management sciences) empower small minorities of people. The state is no longer directed primarily by parliamentarians, but by those who speak "words which succeed," who can convince others of their technical expertise in controlling, or at least visualizing, the future.

"Modernity" is the central keyword of this reader. But there are three additional concepts that you may also want to notice if you would like to integrate the wealth of theory and information that these articles contain. These concepts are liberalism, hegemony, and gender.

Liberalism was the political form of modernity in Canada. It came to form the outlook of the governing class in the mid-nineteenth century. Responsible government represented liberalism's first major victory, Confederation and the National Policy its consolidation at the centre, and victory in the western rebellions (and the quieter processes of submission in the North and the East) its continent-wide extension. One way of visualizing post-Confederation Canadian history is as the rise of a liberal

---

4. Anthony Giddens, *The Consequences of Modernity* (Stanford: Stanford University Press, 1990), 176.

empire centred in the Valley of the St. Lawrence, extending its geographical range and intensifying its ideological hold from 1867 to the present by digesting, rearranging, or eliminating alternative ways of ordering society and culture.

Liberalism is often confused with democracy, and in the present day the two political notions have indeed been intertwined. However, the history of the two outlooks suggests they are not the same. Following Anthony Arblaster's important account, we may say that the core of liberalism is individualism, from which all the familiar liberal commitments to freedom, tolerance, and individual rights are derived. Liberalism involves seeing the individual as primary, as more "real" or fundamental than human society and its institutions and structures. It also involves attaching a higher moral value to the individual than to society, or to any collective group.[5]

This individualism has a number of implications. The individual is not only separate from other persons but also from the natural world. Thus, for liberals, it is possible to study the natural world (and this line of thought would later be extended to the society itself) without committing oneself to any particular values. Native thought, and Aristotle, and much of early Christianity regarded values as woven into the fabric of the universe. The individual was not free to pick and choose among them. Liberalism, by contrast, depicts isolated individuals able to separate facts from values in their attempts to maximize their pleasures. For liberalism, individuals are free-standing (whereas for other ways of thinking the individual human being is radically incomplete without his or her social context). It had once been axiomatic that the community was prior to the individual, but for liberalism the opposite axiom held good: "And this fundamental difference of perspective," argues Arblaster, "affects every aspect of liberalism—its conception of human nature, of the relation of man to society, its social goals and political values, and finally its practical policies and specific choices."[6] This is not just a way of thinking about politics, but a tendency to view the entire world as a collection of distinct and separate facts and events. Individuals are essentially self-interested, non-social, and egotistic, and guided by reason in their pursuit of the gratification of desires and appetites, generally in the "free market" (a model that liberals uphold and seek to extend to other social relation-

---

5. Anthony Arblaster, *The Rise and Decline of Western Liberalism* (Oxford: Basil Blackwell, 1984), 15. See as well C. B. Macpherson, *The Political Theory of Possessive Individualism* (Oxford: Oxford University Press, 1962).
6. Arblaster, 23.

ships). The liberal state has a limited job to do: to protect the rights of the individual. Of all the inalienable rights of individuals, the right to private property was central. Private property, no matter how acquired or on what scale, should take precedence as a value over other social goals.

The liberal state's power and authority is limited, not absolute. The basis of legitimate government is consent of the governed; government is to be kept within this framework of legitimacy by the rule of law and the constitution. Thus, although it attached supreme importance to freedom, liberalism classically saw this as *freedom from* rather than *freedom to*. Early nineteenth-century liberals were *not* democrats and could often openly despise the "people" and the very notion of "democracy" (which in many circles sounded as subversive then as "anarchy" or "communism" sound today). For many nineteenth-century liberals, democracy ("mob rule") could imperil individual freedom and right to property. As the nineteenth-century liberals conceived freedom, it was the absence of constraints and restrictions preventing the individual from doing what he wants; democracy, on the other hand, is a matter of how governments are chosen and to whom they must respond. There is no necessary connection between the two issues, and for the greater part of Canadian history, liberals have not been ardent democrats. If we define democracy, minimally, as a political structure in which the vast majority of adult men and women may vote for their political representatives, Canada did not become a democracy until after women were generally enfranchised on both the federal and provincial levels by the 1940s.

That so many liberal notions about humanity and politics strike us as accepted "common sense" ideas testifies to their success as the political ideals of modernity. Although Canadian liberals may have been divided among themselves on important issues—some Canadian "Reformers" wanted low tariffs, while "Liberal Conservatives" often argued for protection—they were not divided on the basis of their respective conceptions of humanity. Defined in this general way, both of the major federal parties, throughout post-Confederation history, have represented varieties of liberalism. Confederation was the moment when possessive individualism solidified a moral consensus and achieved a state presence capable of transforming the northern half of North America. Early nineteenth-century radicals and unreconstructed Tories would both have opposed the liberal vision, in the first case because it did not mean an extension of power to the farmers and other common producers (in fact the victorious reformers actually made the franchise more restrictive in some cases), and in the second because it did not make sufficient allowance for older aristocratic ideals of community, hierarchy, and order.

One way of unifying the diverse history of post-Confederation Canada is to see it as a process of expanding and intensifying this possessive individualism. Bringing small colonial states together for the purpose of commercial expansion and more intense social regulation, Confederation represented an important step toward the achievement of a liberal political and social order. And the order established in 1867 survived, with some significant wartime modifications, down to the Great Depression.[7] Through the use of force as well as persuasion, by rewarding certain standards of behaviour and penalizing others, the liberal state undertook a process of economic, social, and cultural change. On its periphery, it rooted out older ways, overtly calling upon liberal theory in its campaign against the "communism" of native life styles. In its centre, it intensified the campaign to create the new liberal citizen—temperate, industrious, law-abiding—out of the multitude of people crowding the cities and arriving as immigrants on the ships.

One could describe this process of "liberalization" as one of political and cultural hegemony, thereby invoking the reader's second keyword. Hegemony is a word closely associated with the Italian thinker Antonio Gramsci. The idea is this. A successful dominant social class does not rule by force alone, nor just because it controls the economy. There are classes that rule mainly through coercion, but they are not typical of modern states of the West. An effective governing class must create (and keep re-creating over and over again) *consent* to its rule among large numbers of people. Hegemony describes both the process of creating this consent and the (always-up-for-renegotiation) results. A fundamental class (i.e., capital or labour) must first unite itself around a given project. Its members must overcome their immediate individual interests, at least to some extent, and unite in support of a political project that is in the common interest of their class. After this first step, they must then develop a consensual basis for their rule, by developing a political language, a "common sense," which makes their domination seem legitimate in the eyes of those dominated. A truly hegemonic class is able to join the interests of other social groups to its own, through strategic compromise and by developing a kind of "hegemonic principle"—a political force

---

7. Perhaps because so much work in the "new social history" tended to turn away from politics, we do not yet have a major sophisticated attempt to apply neo-Marxist or Gramscian categories to Confederation—although there are a number of rather simplistic analyses that attempt to reduce political ideology in the 1860s to economic interest alone. Here, as elsewhere, the pointless debate between "political" and "social" history may have obscured interesting questions and created false divisions.

analogous to a secular religion. (Liberalism had to say something, for example, to workers and to farmers; and both the traditional parties did.) In short, a hegemonic class exercises moral and intellectual leadership and presents itself convincingly as the "true voice of the people." At the core of hegemony is the ability of a fundamental class, through compromise and the creation of a persuasive political language, to speak to and for the "subaltern" or dominated classes it leads, and to construct a long-term historic bloc through which the rule of a few people in particular social positions comes to seem like the *only* legitimate way a society can be governed. Those who can become liberal citizens are addressed as such by political language. Those who present a greater challenge—workers, immigrants, natives—may be contained through the selective absorption of leaders, or strategic compromises. Hegemony is a subtler and more intricate process than "social control" or "ideological domination": it creates ways of seeing society that seem to arise "spontaneously" out of the governed. Those, finally, who cannot be brought within the liberal fold, who are for some reason unassimilable, are contained, through such devices as negotiating with cultural brokers, the creation of "zones of danger" (such as Chinatown), or even the celebration of difference (as in multiculturalism).

The third keyword, "gender," introduces another dimension to the way we think through the construction of the post-Confederation political and social order. Gender is, according to Joan Scott's influential definition, "the social organization of sexual difference."[8] In her conception, gender does not "reflect" pre-existing biological differences between men and women; instead, gender is a "knowledge" (not absolute or "true" but always relative) that tells us what biological differences "mean" at any given time. Gender varies across cultures; some native societies seem in fact to have had more than two genders. Nothing about the body simply determines how social divisions will be shaped.

Liberalism speaks of "Man." The possessive individual and true citizen is a "he." There is something more going on here than the falsely generic "third person" of the unreformed English language.[9] Male domination was intrinsic to liberal society throughout most of post-Confederation history. Women were not seen as equals. In some respects, they were not even regarded as persons, with full possession of themselves: one of the

---

8. Joan Walloch Scott, *Gender and the Politics of History* (New York: Columbia University Press, 1988), 2.

9. I have not attempted to correct this dated use of the "false generic" in any of the readings that follow.

considerations in the legal treatment of certain nineteenth-century sexual offences against women was the damage done to the man's "property" in his wife. Liberal hegemony and its central emphasis on the individual required the male-dominated family as a key place in which future men and women learned their "proper" roles and in which unequal power relations between women and men were perpetuated. (Some of those who conspicuously failed to learn their proper roles, such as homosexuals, could be condemned to prison.) Women were not invited as participants to the conferences in the 1860s that organized the Canadian constitution, whose key architects are now significantly called the *Fathers* of Confederation."

Many authors in this collection are engaged in developing these concepts in the writing of Canadian history, although there is no unanimity about how to do this. For some feminist authors, gender is the most powerful structuring principle in society and in their arguments; for others, class is primary; yet others are attempting to bring class and gender together in a notion of "dual systems" of social power. For some authors, liberalism is the central problem; for others the liberal order is assumed. Some historians treat "hegemony" apart from considerations of state power, as a cultural or psychological reality; whereas others would argue that it cannot be treated apart from the state. (Feminist scholars have just started to use hegemony as a tool of their analyses.)[10] There is a vast amount of research and debate ahead for those interested in using any one of these concepts, let alone integrating the three of them. The intent of this reader is not to suggest the outline of an emergent orthodoxy but to introduce the student of Canadian history to some of the newer historians who are renegotiating the shape of the Canadian past.

History as a discipline has changed enormously over the past twenty years. My most memorable high school history teacher taught the course on western civilization ("From Plato to NATO," we used to say). He doubled as a gym instructor, and he would drill historical facts into us with the same ferocity he used on the football team. He would bark out historical facts, and you had to fight the temptation to throw yourself on

---

10. I am indebted to Annelee Golz for sharing an unpublished paper with me on this question. See Heather Jon Maroney, "Using Gramsci for Women: Feminism and the Quebec State, 1960–1980," *Resources for Feminist Research*, 17, 3 (September 1988), 26–30; Mary O'Brien, "Hegemony and Superstructure: A Feminist Critique of Neo-Marxism," in Roberta Hamilton and Michele Barrett, eds., *The Politics of Diversity: Feminism, Marxism and Nationalism* (Montreal: Book Centre, 1986), 255–65.

the floor for some serious push-ups. He had a thing about Alexander the Great; or, to be more exact, Alexander the Great's horse, whose name was, year after year, demanded on his final examination. The city in which I grew up was the sort of place that most people left as soon as they were able, fleeing to Toronto, Vancouver, Halifax, even (in one radical case) to Ellesmere Island; and I imagine there must be thousands of us former pupils, well-drilled products of this zealous disciplinarian, anxiously waiting for the moment when, on some television quiz show, or in a game of "Trivial Pursuit," or in some late-night conversation in the High Arctic, we shall be asked to produce the name of Alexander the Great's horse. Surely we did not learn it for nothing?

High school history was facts seemingly without end. History happened to other people far away, and had no direct bearing on the here and now. (This is the sense of history people have when they say, "That's ancient history," or "Well, Barbara, that's a question for the historians to argue over." What they're really saying is, "It's not that important.") These facts were, it is true, not really selected at random. As Plato finally began to give way to NATO, you did start to see where all these data were leading: to a heartwarming tale of progress. Ancient Greece begat Rome, Rome begat Christian Europe, Christian Europe begat the Renaissance, the Renaissance begat the Enlightenment: all culminating in us! Or, to take the Canadian case, heroic French explorers settled an almost empty continent, spreading the benefits of Christianity; then came British civilization; and then—inevitably—Confederation. Our "Canada" was really struggling to be born all along, like the spirit released from the soapstone by an Inuit artist. Canadian history has one major plot line (a "master narrative," literary critics might say) and a (mainly comforting) happy ending—our present happy status quo. Almost everything is for the best in the best of all possible worlds.

This way of thinking history has become a sort of common sense, and it works powerfully in historic sites, television dramas, and contemporary politics. History as "Inevitable Progress" gives many people a sense of belonging (while, of course, excluding many others). It seems to respond to a need, which modernity has rendered painfully acute, for some steadying power, some eternal traditions, some powerful force outside the constant process of change. That force can be described as History, which has a logic of its own. "History" is on our side; "History" has ended, leaving our enemies in the dust; "History" will absolve us. This "History" moves in a certain direction to a foreordained conclusion. This idea of there being one "History," usually the history of the "Nation," to which everything else is secondary, can lead to results that can be both profoundly arrogant and suffocatingly narrow. History is a tale told by one anonymous voice—what documentary producers refer to as "Voice of God" narration—a voice above and beyond the events themselves, who hands out the prizes of historical significance (and the booby prizes of historical oblivion) at the (foreordained) end. This disembodied Voice presumes to tell us what people *meant*; it works at creating the *meaning* of other people's lives.

If you look into it, you'll find that the Voice of History belongs, in Canada, not to some All-Knowing Presence outside or beyond history, but generally to a white, middle-aged man with two kids, a sizable mortgage, and a dental plan. His assumptions, working methods, values, and traditions all contribute to the prizes he hands out at the end of his Tale of History. The anonymous Voice of History can seemingly transform the highly debatable arguments of a small number of people into simple matters of common sense. What has happened in history-writing over the past quarter century is that, gradually, the Voice of History has been challenged, even drowned out, by all those who do not share his comfortable assumptions. The notion that there should be a unified Voice of History is perhaps even more problematical in Canada than it is elsewhere. Canada is an odd country. It never has generated a Voice of History that commands anything close to universal respect. This is because there is no unifying definition of "Canada," no generally accepted vision of what Canada is. (And this, no doubt, tells us something about the weakness as well as the strength of the hegemony of liberalism at the centre.)

According to one approach to the Saga of Canada, Canada was and is a unity, a liberal community with one true, defining essence, a solid permanent core. That essence was that Canadians were, by definition, a British people. Some people even used the image of Canadians holding their land in trusteeship for the British Empire. This insistence on the British character of Canada could be powerfully tied to a sense of geography: the St. Lawrence River, gateway to the continent, and the east–west transportation systems extending from it, constituted a living link to the mother country. There therefore was and is "One Canada," a Canada united as a national community on the basis of its British heritage and its economic history. This was the overwhelming liberal vision in, say, Laurier's Canada, circa 1900.

It was much less hegemonic by 1930. An equally compelling voice told the story of "Two Canadas," whose pact in 1867 had made Confederation possible. This idea seems to have started in the third quarter of the nineteenth century; its influence gained steadily down to the 1970s.

According to this Story of Canada, there were two fundamentally different "races" in Canada (cultural traits were often considered to flow in the blood, almost like red blood cells), the "French" and the "English." These two "races" entered a "pact" at Confederation; and from it one ultimately derived the logic of bilingualism and biculturalism. Two languages, two ways of life, two intertwined but also separate destinies could be discerned in Canada. The theme of duality has played a pivotal role in Canadian historical thought, but the two partners have not always borne the same names: one used to speak of "French Canada" and "English Canada"—a way of getting around the fact that large areas of Quebec, including both Montreal and Quebec City, have at points in their history been dominated by English-speaking majorities—then "Québec" and "English Canada," which raises different complications. ("English Canada" has never quite made it as a phrase, because most of the people who use English as a language are not "English" in origin, including vast numbers of Scots, Irish, and others who immigrated to Canada from the British Isles in the nineteenth century.) From this conceptualization of the country come all the many metaphors based upon marriage—and, in these stormy days, those drawn from the language of divorce. The lens of duality, like the lens of British unity, captures certain aspects of the Canadian reality, but not others.

Would you like One Canada or Two? Unfortunately for people craving tidiness in their histories, there is an equally strong case to be made for many *more* Canadas than that—for a lens open to a bewildering spectrum of colours. The notion of "two founding races" may be handy as a way of preserving our heroic story line of progress and civilization, and having two central collective heroes gives us an opportunity to play around with the potent metaphors of marriage and family. But the natives, who are acutely aware that the land now known as Canada had been settled and "civilized" for perhaps ten thousand years before the arrival of *both* the main sets of imperial colonizers, may be forgiven for seeing in that notion a certain element of white arrogance. On what basis do we exclude natives as "founding peoples"? Then the millions of other Canadians who are descended from neither of the supposed charter "races" have been heard to exclaim, with the natives, "Well, what are we? Chopped liver?" Didn't the Ukrainians homesteading on the Prairies found something too? What about the Chinese who gave up so many thousands of lives building the Canadian Pacific Railway?

Nor is this ethnic argument the only strong point for an approach emphasizing "many Canadas." The geographer R. Cole Harris has raised a very interesting point about patterns of settlement in Canada. Through much of the latter nineteenth century, Canada was losing more people through emigration than it was getting through immigration. (In 1867 the population of the country was about 3.3 million; by 1901, it had grown to only 4 830 000. The country's population would have actually declined had it not been for the high rates of fertility that continued to characterize the Canadian population.) Harris proposes that the most useful image of Canada is that of an archipelago of islands, spread over 4000 miles (6400 km) east to west. Canada was settled in patches, at different times, by different peoples, using different technologies, with different cultures. The patches of land—the islands in the archipelago—capable of sustaining more than a handful of people are separated from each other. These islands of settlement faced geographical limitations. Expanding north, into the Canadian Shield, offered limited possibilities for farming (as many impoverished farmers who went "Back to the Land" in the 1930s learned at great cost). There was, to the South, the United States. When each island of settlement reached the point of acute land scarcity, the people in each faced a difficult choice: to go north, to farm rocks in the Canadian Shield, or to go south, to the amazingly productive United States. Throughout much of their history, Maritimers, Quebeckers, and Ontarians, faced with this choice, went south and became Americans, rather than going west. There was then no continuous, expansive experience with a frontier steadily moving westward; there were patches exporting surplus people to the United States, and thereby retaining their own distinctiveness and apartness from each other. Until the 1880s—well after many of the patches had taken shape as societies—there was no easily accessible West. This pattern could only intensify local identities. The American occupation of the West had the power to mould very different peoples into a relatively homogeneous culture; in Canada, the underlying structure of the population was discontinuous.[11] Regions came to be different from each other in subtle ways—architecture, speech patterns, political traditions, historical memories (one region's hero is another region's forgotten Canadian)—and in more blatant conflicts over resources. Ontario, tending to identify itself with the country as a whole ("Our community is Canada," a true Ontarian will believe), often sees this legacy as one of "parochialism," a disability to be overcome. Outside Ontario, this sounds exactly like Ontario regionalism, and Ontarians, in

---

11. See R. Cole Harris, "The Pattern of Early Canada," in Graeme Wynn, ed., *People Places Patterns Processes: Geographical Perspectives on the Canadian Past* (Toronto: Copp Clark Pitman, 1990), 358–73.

their indifference to, or active contempt for, "regionalism," tend to offend more through their blithe disregard for difference more than any active arrogance. Words sound differently, jokes—Newfie jokes most obviously—work or don't work, depending on where you live and who you are. Who has, or should, exercise the right to rule some "identities" important and worthy of consideration (a status many Ontarians would concede to Quebec) and others obviously of a lower order and unworthy of consideration (a status traditionally accorded both regional and aboriginal loyalties) is by no means clear, either in the historical profession or outside it.

There may in fact be many different kinds of collectivities in Canada, nations or societies originating in kinship networks, regions, bureaucracies, elites, classes; and organizing these into a hierarchy of importance (in which nations are more equal than others) may be a tidy but unproductive procedure. Many identities may defy an easy categorization. Newfoundlanders, for example, once enjoyed Dominion status on a par with Canadians, and have long had a sense of having a very different history than the country they joined in 1949. Do they perhaps constitute a quasi-nation? Attempting to arrange all of these long-established and fiercely defended notions of belonging and identity into a tidy pattern ("English Canada/Quebec") satisfies our need for tidiness, but it may trivialize the complexities and dangers of our history. Perhaps Canada, the land of overlapping and conflicting identities, is the sort of place that defies the rationalists' (and the constitution-makers') desire for precision and order. Therein, perhaps, lie several of our present dilemmas.

What is the alternative to history as the "story of progress"? That alternative, to be blunt, is still under construction. History since 1960 has undergone three great revolutions. First came the working-class revolution of the 1970s. This began with a critique of existing liberal historiography and the development of an alternative view of the Canadian past. In this view, class—defined with reference to ownership in economic production, but also encompassing more broadly conceived class identities and experiences—was one of the key terms. In study after study, historians undermined the tranquil liberal image of a "Peaceable Kingdom" characterized by "Peace, Order, and Good Government" by uncovering violent strikes, political dissent, and a history of political radicalism. Some historians turned to counting people in highly quantitative historical studies modelled on the social sciences; more turned to reconstructing "cultures" in the past. Regional identities also became highly topical, as historians no longer felt obliged to be "nation-builders" in the old sense, but saw themselves more as students of society. From this perspective, a regional or local approach often seemed more appropriate than a Dominion-wide survey.

If conventional history provided people with a reassuring sense of belonging, social history often redescribed society in ways that seemed startling, that seemed to make the familiar strange. Over the past two decades, this new kind of history won hundreds of recruits. A field once preoccupied with documenting the powerful turned to exploring the lives of the powerless. We know more about the lives of ordinary people than one could have imagined was possible two decades ago. New journals— *Histoire Sociale/Social History, Labour/Le Travail, Acadiensis*—and drastically renovated old journals—the *Revue d'histoire de l'Amérique française* and the *Canadian Historical Review*—opened new doors.

Then, in the 1980s, came the feminist revolution, which is still underway. (It was reflected in many of the previously mentioned journals, and in some new ones: *Atlantis, Resources for Feminist Research*, and, internationally, *Gender and History*.) If one started to ask, "But where are the women?" the answer from traditional historiography seemed only too clear: they either did not exist, or they enjoyed at best walk-on parts (driving beleaguered prime ministers to drink, for example). The new working-class history also tended to concentrate on the organized male workers, although there were significant explorations of women involved in waged labour. If feminist scholarship initially focused on the organized women's movement, it gradually widened its focus to include sexuality, women's position within the family, and perceptions of gender. By the 1990s, study of gender and history had broadened still further to consider the ways in which the construction of gender took place in various periods: "masculinity" as well as "femininity" were no longer seen as self-evident qualities, but rather as historical problems, subject to shifting definitions.

Finally, a third transformation became noticeable in the late 1980s, and its outcome is still uncertain: the "linguistic turn." The "linguistic turn" makes the process through which meaning is created a central focus of history. Modern linguistics suggests that language cannot be seen as a kind of mirror of reality; there isn't a one-to-one relationship between the linguistic form and the object to which it intends to refer. Equipped with the insights of modern theories of signs, historians might be able to understand how identities are formed and conceptions of the self "naturalized"—that is, made to seem like simple, straightforward truths. The field of language is immensely complicated and open to a vast range of influences. Systems of meaning are never disconnected from the social or class positions in which speakers are placed, and social groups vie with each other within language. All proponents of the "linguistic turn" think language is far more important as an active shaper of social history than had earlier been suspected. They are by no means a monolithic group, and the implications of the "linguistic turn" for Canadian history are, at the moment, very unclear. It has had a particular appeal for students of gender (who have deftly used linguistic analysis to show how such categories as "homosexuals" and "women" have been used in different ways at different times for different purposes); it has also been fiercely resisted by some Marxists and liberals, who dislike the jargon and suspect the "turn" itself is nothing more than an intellectual fad. The ultimate impact of linguistic theory on Canadian history will probably lie somewhere in between total revolution and complete irrelevance. After tedious post-structuralist nihilist posturing about the end of meaning has become boring and passé, it still seems unlikely that we will be able to go back to thinking about language as the uncomplicated, neutral tool with which we describe "reality."

These phases in the "social history revolution" (and this is a radically oversimplified description, leaving out such important developments as rural and environmental history) have left us with a huge, proliferous realm of possibilities, and a bewildering, eclectic mix of theories with which to analyse them. It has been an exhilarating if often disorienting time to be a Canadian historian. Has the change sometimes perhaps run the risk of throwing some of what was valuable in older approaches out with the elitist bathwater? One of the achievements of traditional political history—and it *does* still have a lot to teach us—was that it strove for an elegant simplicity in expression. Driven by the powerful motor of narrative, it told stories that many people were interested in hearing. The historians of the 1950s thought they were speaking *to*, and sometimes *for*, a much wider public, for *Canada*. Today, as the country enters its most profound political crisis since Confederation, most historians have been too busy to notice; and if they did, it is not clear whether they could still make themselves understood. Whatever their radical, democratic objectives, most social historians are still writing works that will never be read outside the university. An additional disadvantage of some of the new history is that it tends to forget the state. A social history that forgets politics, or a linguistic "new cultural history" that forgets that not all "discourses" circulate equally and that the state is a decisive place in society for making some discourses "truer" than others are both radically incomplete.

Today's historian is expected to apply insights from literary theory, anthropology, sociology, economics, and a dozen other disciplines; to explore every period from a multitude of perspectives; to be alert to questions of gender, class, race, and region. At its most ambitious, the new history presents itself not just as one more discipline, but as the selective integration of all the disciplines in a new, holistic perspective on the past. This new history will seek causes operated over the very long term, as well as those operating in the more familiar pattern of "events." Historians who ask, "Why?" accept that the answer may not be simple. For there is never one cause; there are always causes that work at different levels of analysis to answer different kinds of questions. Today's history (to quote the great French social historian Marc Bloch) "seeks for causal wave-trains and is not afraid, since life shows them to be so, to find them multiple."[12]

This is both an exhilarating and daunting time to be a historian. Exhilarating, because our very concepts of history are changing so quickly, and whole new continents of investigation are being opened up. Daunting, because no human being could possibly live up to the vast interdisciplinary goals of the new social history, and because the more we come to understand how story-telling and language work, the less likely it appears that we will ever come up with that one, complete, neutral, objective, "total" history with which everyone will agree. Most historians are aware that the history they write is a version of the past affected by their own perspectives—how could it be otherwise? Yet most of us are also convinced that by bringing as many versions together, by multiplying the points of view, we can obtain a richer, fuller, better—more accurate and realistic, if you like—sense of the past.

The *past* no longer exists; and *history*, which is how modern western societies try to understand and to "master" the past, is an intellectual activity undertaken in the present. The very ideal of historical objectivity—what was once the core of the historian's craft—has been transformed under pressure into the ideal of refining debate and of the respectful but always imperfect sharing of insights. We can know more and more about the past; but what we could know, and how this might change our understanding of the whole pattern, seems almost infinite. No historian enters the archives, that temple of the primary source, and passively awaits the arrival of "the facts." Historians arrive equipped with preconceptions, hunches, techniques for the evaluation of evidence:

---

12. Marc Bloch, *The Historian's Craft* (New York: Knopf, 1953), 194.

ideally, they arrive with explicitly acknowledged theory. Historians are not the passive recipients of history but, equipped with the tools of modern historical science, its active makers.

The Challenge of Modernity is intended as an introduction to some—but only some—of the questions of post-Confederation Canadian history for students who are meeting the subject for the first time in university. Each topic consists of two or three readings; most have been extensively edited for reasons of space. These are generally from leading authors in the field, but sometimes an excerpt from an original document has been included. The book was prepared for use with *Nation: Canada Since Confederation*; and it has been visualized as a kind of counterpoint, interacting with that text's political narrative by focusing on the social and on the cultural. The Further Readings listed at the end of each topic are *very* selective, listing only a few of the other things a student might read in the area. This book draws on the expertise of scholars in many disciplines (though historians make up the majority of the authors of the readings). I have sought to convey a sense of Canada's social diversity: if about 40 percent of the readings are "national" in scope (which very often means "Ontario-centred" in outlook and research), the remaining 60 percent speak to the other nations, regions, and communities that make up "Canada." We are a formidably diverse people, and Canada is better likened to a multitude of voices rather than to an "identity." Therein lies our perennial confusion, our conflicting stories about what Canadian history means, and the origins of our present crisis. Is the existence of many voices in this conversation, of people who have come to define their identities differently—as First Nations or British Columbians, Québécois or Nova Scotians—a lamentable obstacle to the oneness to which "Canada" must aspire? Is this gathering together of many voices in fact a debate, which will end with a winner and a loser? Then one can bring it to a halt, strike up the national anthem, and silence or marginalize the "Others" by the One Voice of True Canadianism. The "Others" will henceforth be those who have not understood, or who deny, a universal historical truth. Or could the existence of these many Canadas, these many small worlds, be seen as something of value? Could this be visualized as a conversation rather than a debate, whose ultimate result will not be winners and losers but people who have a better, if inevitably partial and tentative, understanding of social and cultural differences? Perhaps in unavoidably having to deal, for so long and in so many ways, with the complementary and conflicting senses of belonging through which overlapping identities have been constructed, some Canadians have come to the intuition that modernity makes all "identities" contingent. Our ways of discussing the radical ethical and political dilemmas of so far-reaching a pluralism could carry implications far beyond the borders of this restless conversation we call Canada.

Canadian history need not be seen as a purgatory, unwillingly served by those who are stuck with the need to fill in their "Canadian content" requirements. The new Canadian history is open to most of the intellectual currents of the late twentieth-century world; and the historian equipped with intellectual curiosity and daring will find it to be an exciting, challenging, and vital field of inquiry. There opens up before the student of Canadian history a vast and mainly unexplored realm, a field of historical possibility extending to the far horizon: a place where, in coming to understand the sense of homelessness that is modernity's inescapable consequence, one may also find that autonomy and creativity and collective possibilities are its underrated and perishable gifts. To explore ourselves through probing the construction of our modernity is the daunting and fascinating challenge of Canadian history.

FURTHER READINGS

Carl Berger, *The Writing of Canadian History* (Toronto: University of Toronto Press, second edition, 1986).

Carl Berger, ed., *Contemporary Approaches to Canadian History* (Toronto: Copp Clark Pitman, 1987).

Marshall Berman, *All That Is Solid Melts Into Air: The Experience of Modernity* (New York: Simon and Schuster, 1982).

Marc Bloch, *The Historian's Craft* (New York: Vintage Books, 1953).

R. Cole Harris, "The Pattern of Early Canada," in Graeme Wynn, ed., *People Places Patterns Processes: Geographical Perspectives on the Canadian Past* (Toronto: Copp Clark Pitman, 1990), 358–73.

Agnes Heller, *A Theory of History* (London: Routledge & Kegan Paul, 1982).

Richard Johnson et al., *Making Histories: Studies in History-Writing and Politics* (London: Hutchinson, 1982).

Joan Walloch Scott, *Gender and the Politics of History* (New York: Columbia University Press, 1988).

TOPIC 1

Conquest and Consolidation: Western Natives and the Cultural Expansion of Canada

B y the time of Confederation, native societies, shaped by a pre-capitalist system of production governed by kinship, had co-existed with white merchants for many decades. Cultural changes, such as the introduction of trade goods, early attempts at Christianization, and the fur trade marriages, were significant, but many of them could be absorbed by native societies without requiring their complete transformation. As the nineteenth century proceeded, however, the cultural balance swung against the natives of the West. Whites were no longer willing to deal with natives as they were. Often armed with doctrines of racism and visions of imperial greatness, whites began to conceptualize the natives not as powerful allies, but as dependants. Ottawa wanted to settle its vast new possessions with white settlers, and through land legislation, massive publicity, the building of the railway, and the new Mounted Police, it strove mightily to develop the West.

This is the terrain mapped by Gerald Friesen in the first reading, an excerpt from his classic study of the Canadian Prairies, in which he suggests the extent to which natives fought tenaciously for recognition within Canadian society. The second reading, Sarah Carter's local Saskatchewan study, suggests the importance of Ottawa's liberal strategy of demolishing the "tribal system" or "communism" of the natives. (Natives were thus caught in a classic modern situation, of being the objects of a *cultural engineering they could not influence.) "We all know that things are changing," the natives of Vancouver Island say in the third reading, attempting to defend long-standing cultural traditions that had been newly defined as "illegal" by the Canadian state. Through war, starvation, treaties, and the creation of new cultural crimes, ways of life founded on kinship were engulfed and culturally subordinated to the triumphant liberal modernity of Empire Canada.*

Prairie Indians, 1840–1900:

The End of Autonomy

GERALD FRIESEN

The last half of the nineteenth century constituted a revolution for most of the native societies of the western interior, particularly those of the plains and parkland. None of the changes in the native way of life in the preceding two centuries could be compared to the extraordinary upheaval of this period, and, what is even more striking, nothing could compare with the speed of the change. A typical Cree youth might have been hunting buffalo and raiding for horses in the 1860s just as his grandfather had done sixty years before; in the 1870s, he might have succumbed to the whisky trade or been struck by an epidemic; almost certainly he would have been removed to a reserve and perhaps even taught the rudiments of agriculture. In the 1880s, some of his children might have been attending school, and he, having faced starvation for three or four years in succession, might have participated in the violence associated with the 1885 uprising. But nothing within his power could alter the circumstances of his life: the buffalo had disappeared, trains and fences and towns now dominated the plains, and the old ways had disappeared beyond recovery. . . .

[Native societies were already in a state of flux by the 1860s. The Ojibwas, especially those living in the woodlands, were already involved in part-time employment as canoemen, cart drivers, and labourers in the fur trade by the 1860s. On the plains, one found sporadic warfare between Blackfoot and Cree-Assiniboine forces, usually with control of the horse trade as object. Tragedy stalked the plains in the deadly decade 1865–75: two devastating epidemics swept through the Cree and Blackfoot camps, whisky traders from Missouri River posts moved north into the Cypress Hills–Oldman River district, dispensing their powerful violence-breeding concoction; and plains wars (culminating in the battle of Oldman River in 1870, which left 200 to 300 Crees and perhaps 40 Blackfeet dead) were immensely destructive. The Cypress Hills Massacre was a brutal reminder of the violence of the frontier and of the treatment Indians might expect in

GERALD FRIESEN, "PRAIRIE INDIANS, 1840–1900: THE END OF AUTONOMY," *THE CANADIAN PRAIRIES: A HISTORY* (TORONTO: UNIVERSITY OF TORONTO PRESS, 1987), 129–61. REPRINTED BY PERMISSION OF UNIVERSITY OF TORONTO PRESS.

3

an uncontrolled confrontation with whites; in late May 1873, about twenty natives were killed, and five native women raped, in a dispute between white hunters and traders and natives. Some of the perpetrators of the crime were eventually arrested, but conflicting testimony and vagueness in details permitted their acquittal. Such unbridled barbarity was never permitted to occur again.]

The violence of the decade after 1865 only made plain what everyone already knew, that the inhabitants of the western interior required new political and judicial arrangements to replace the now irrelevant authority of the Hudson's Bay Company. One of the most pressing issues was the Indian claim to sovereignty. This had not concerned the fur trade companies, but had been of sufficient concern to Lord Selkirk that he had negotiated a treaty with five Cree and Ojibwa chiefs in July 1817. By this agreement, the Indians ceded to the crown strips of land two miles wide on either side of the Red and Assiniboine rivers from Lake Winnipeg to near Grand Forks and the Muskrat River respectively. In exchange, the Indians were to receive 200 pounds of tobacco annually. But this example of Selkirk's scrupulous concern for propriety was the only well-documented case wherein native rights to soil in the northwest had been extinguished. With the transfer of the entire region to Canadian control in 1870, this issue immediately pressed on the federal administration and its agents in the small province of Manitoba, because "Indians, and land reserved for Indians" were matters of federal responsibility under the British North America Act.

The Canadian authorities did not lack for guidance in their deliberations. The basis of Canadian Indian policy had been set out over a century earlier in the British proclamation of 1763, which provided the rules for the administration of the former territories of New France, and in the administrative practices of Sir William Johnson, superintendent of Indian affairs. By this policy, the British acknowledged Indian aboriginal rights to the soil while asserting crown title as well. Thus the crown accepted that it must formally extinguish Indian rights before settlement or other distribution of the land could occur. Only the crown could undertake such negotiations with the Indians, and thus private parties could not legally arrange for their own claims to Indian land; negotiation was to occur at an open assembly before all the people rather than in closed sessions among a few representatives. Treaties of this sort, often with a military alliance in view, were negotiated in the eighteenth century, and, though the object became one of paternalist concern, others were negotiated in the Maritime colonies and Lower Canada in the first half of the nineteenth century. A significant departure in this system occurred in 1850 when the so-called

Robinson treaties were negotiated with the Indians of the Lake Huron and Lake Superior territories. Here, rather than a small acreage required for immediate settlement, as had been the case in the past, the treaties covered huge districts far removed from settled areas. As an example of a carefully organized move by imperial authorities to clear the way for future development, the Robinson treaties set the pattern for the treaties in the western interior in the 1870s.

A treaty was a much more formal and explicit conclusion to an agreement between Indians and Europeans than was the exchange of gifts, medals, or trade goods, but like those earlier and (to Europeans) less binding ceremonies it was a means of cementing a relationship between peoples and setting out the rules by which that relationship would be governed. Though often scorned today as an empty form imposed by a conqueror on the conquered, the treaties of the 1870s should not be dismissed so quickly. The Indians had much less autonomy in the negotiations than would have been the case twenty-five years earlier, but they still negotiated as firmly as they could, won concessions where possible, and produced a settlement that had positive as well as negative features for their group. The Europeans entered the negotiations with limited financial resources to pay for concessions, little military power to enforce their will, and a great deal of nervousness as to what the Indians would accept. Thus the necessity of a treaty was more than a mere formality in the view of the Canadian government. The Indians were a sufficiently powerful military force in the early 1870s to evoke fears in official circles and, if nothing more, to threaten immigration prospects for a generation. The fact that there were 25–35,000 Indians in the western interior in 1870, and another 10,000 metis, and fewer than 2,000 Europeans or Canadians reinforced the government's concern.

The treaties were also sufficiently important to both sides to create a liturgy of their own. The negotiations were accompanied by great pageantry. They featured long and rhetorical statements, often laden with exaggerated metaphors (wherein, for example, the crown and Queen Victoria became the "Great Mother"), and had their own symbols, such as uniforms and peace pipes. They were marked by intense debate, both within the camp of the Europeans and in the deadly serious, often faction-ridden councils of the natives. To our ears, the pompous rhetoric of the mid-Victorian politician rings hollow, whereas the simple nature-based images of the Indians seem to sing of honesty and innocence. However, as in any set of negotiations, one should beware of judging either side simply on the basis of appearances.

The topic of treaties was first raised in the Fort Frances–Rainy River corridor when the Canadian government sought to conciliate the Ojibwas in order to assure the safe passage of the Wolseley expedition to Red River. The response of the Ojibwas was most instructive: they would permit the passage of troops, as well as steamers and even railways, in exchange for appropriate payment (one report said they wanted ten dollars per Indian to relinquish control over the right of passage by immigrants), but they would not permit settlers on their lands. In other words, the treaty concept was not questioned by the Ojibwas, but the proposed terms of the treaty were apparently going to be stiff. As it happened, Wolseley did distribute gifts to the Indians but, probably because of the range of Ojibwa claims, did not conclude a treaty in 1869–70. The Indians around Fort Garry also were prepared to negotiate a treaty as soon as the lieutenant-governor arrived, and presented their case with considerable persistence during Lieutenant-Governor Archibald's first year in Manitoba. At the same time, federal government commissioners opened negotiations with the Ojibwa Indians in the Fort Frances district. The Fort Frances team made no progress in 1870–1. In fact, it was told by one of the Ojibwa leaders: "We want...much that the white man has to give and the white man, on his part wants roads and land. When we meet next summer you must be prepared to tell us where your roads are to pass and what lands you require." The Indians would retain sovereignty, in this view, and the government would acquire corridors running through it. But this was not acceptable to the federal government, which wanted instead to extinguish Indian claims to the territory once and forever. When the commissioner, Wemyss Simpson, member of Parliament for Algoma, presented this proposal to the Ojibwas in 1871, he was unable to win agreement and may even have been insulted by the Indians. Simpson retreated to Winnipeg where, with Lieutenant-Governor Archibald, he began another set of negotiations. Because they were the first to result in a treaty, these latter talks were crucial to the settlement of Indian claims in the west.[1]

Archibald and Simpson convened an assembly of about 1,000 Indians at Lower Fort Garry on 27 July 1871. Government provisions were made available, and liquor was banned. Uniformed troops were present as symbols of the power of the crown. Chiefs and headmen were formally selected by the Indians—in order that the authority of the treaty signato-

---

1. Jean Friesen "My Birthright and Land" unpublished paper presented to Brandon University Native Studies Conference 1981. The prairie treaties are discussed in detail in John Leonard Taylor "The Development of an Indian Policy for the Canadian North-West, 1869–79" PhD dissertation, Queen's University, 1975.

ries could not be questioned—and opening statements were then made. Archibald and Simpson argued that reserves were to be set aside but that these would not be as large as some Indians seemed to assume. The concern of the government was the peace and welfare of its people, Archibald explained:

> Your Great Mother wishes the good of all races under her sway. She wishes her red children to be happy and contented. She wishes them to live in comfort. She would like them to adopt the habits of the whites, to till land and raise food, and store it up against a time of want...Your Great Mother, therefore, will lay aside for you "lots" of land to be used by you and your children forever. She will not allow the white men to intrude upon these lots. She will make rules to keep them for you, so that as long as the sun shall shine, there shall be no Indian who has not a place that he can call his home, where he can go and pitch his camp, or if he chooses, build his house and till his land.[2]

These were memorable words, particularly when seen from the perspective of the land surrenders that occurred in the following half-century, but they were accompanied by an ultimatum that left the Indians little room for manoeuvre. Archibald was offering a treaty in exchange for the cession of all native rights and the grant of land reserves; but, whether the Indians accepted the treaty or not, he was saying, settlement was bound to occur. Given the circumstances, one wonders whether either party had much choice.

The Red River Indians responded with demands that sounded remarkably similar to those of the Fort Frances group. Their fundamental assumption seemed to be that they would retain the bulk of the land—over two-thirds of Manitoba, as Archibald commented later—while relinquishing small portions to the government. This was unacceptable, Archibald replied: "If they thought it better to have no treaty at all, they might do without one, but they must make up their minds; if there was to be a Treaty, it must be on a basis like that offered." The Indians withdrew to reconsider their position and, presumably, to discuss the relative merits of no treaty as against reserves of 160 acres per family of five. Three days later, negotiations resumed, this time not on the contentious issue of reserves but rather on limited matters such as government assistance in education, the provision of farm animals, and the supply of farm implements. After three more days of negotiations—and there was give and take

---

2. Peter A. Cumming and Neil H. Mickenberg eds *Native Rights in Canada* second edition (Toronto 1972) 121-2.

at the sessions—an agreement was reached that satisfied both the Indians (except for Yellow Quill) and the government representatives. The Indians agreed to surrender title to all their territory, to keep the peace, and not to molest the property or persons of Her Majesty's other subjects. In return, they were to receive an immediate gratuity of three dollars each, an annuity of fifteen dollars in cash or goods per family of five, reserves in the amount of 160 acres per family of five, a school on each reserve, and protection from intoxicating liquor. A number of additional items— clothing for the headmen, farm animals, and implements—were not contained in the written text but rather were assented to informally; they were none the less binding. Later, when the government failed to carry out these clauses of the oral agreement, the Indians complained bitterly. After four years of argument, the Ottawa authorities finally acknowledged that these so-called outside promises were indeed part of the treaty. In early August 1871, the negotiations were complete. Pipes were smoked, drums rumbled, shots rang out, and the Lower Fort treaty, treaty 1 as it came to be known, was signed.[3]...[Other prairie treaties—treaty 2, covering the Lake Manitoba area; treaty 3, the Fort Frances–Lake of the Woods Agreement; treaty 4 covering the Ojibwas, Crees, and Assiniboines in the southern prairies between Fort Ellice and the Cypress Hills— differed in substance as well as detail.]

If one prairie treaty stands out from the others it is probably treaty 5. Though future economic development was in part the government's motivation for the treaty, the urgent need of the Indians themselves was also a precipitating factor in its completion. In the territory of Lake Winnipeg and The Pas, employment with the Hudson's Bay Company had dropped with the introduction of steamboats and the use of the American as opposed to the Bay route from England, and the Indians were pressing for the allotment of reserves and supplies in order that they might begin to farm. This Indian concern, coupled with Canadian interest in the timber, mineral, and transportation prospects of the Saskatchewan River–Lake Winnipeg territory, led to the treaty discussions. The negotiations were very rapid; at each of three sites in September 1875, the talks opened and concluded within a single day. Whether these Indians, more distant from the main travelled routes of the plains, understood the implications of the agreement was uncertain. They wanted reserves immediately, and, despite the usual administrative problems, that was achieved. But whether they wanted to bargain away their sovereignty over the territory

---

3. Taylor "Indian Policy" 55–80.

is unknown. In 1876, when a negotiator returned to secure further adhesions to the treaty among bands who had not been present the year before, he encountered Indians at Grand Rapids who claimed that the 1875 talks were merely preparatory to the signing of a treaty. Whatever the sincerity of this misapprehension, it produced little further debate at the time.[4]

The great plains Cree community had been quarrelling with the government and with its Indian enemies since the mid-1860s, and though the war at Oldman River in 1871 had cooled the temper of the warriors the disappearance of the buffalo ensured that they would remain edgy and combative. The dispatch of waves of government observers and of the North-West Mounted Police provided a stream of information on their restlessness, but, for a variety of reasons, the long-promised Saskatchewan treaty negotiations were postponed from season to season to the point where both Lieutenant-Governor Morris and the plains Cree chiefs were angry. In the summer of 1875, the Crees interrupted both the geological survey and the construction of the telegraph line from Winnipeg to Edmonton on the grounds that they would not permit such trespassing until a treaty was completed. These actions were little different in nature or implication from that of the Red River metis who in 1869 stopped a government survey party and thus precipitated the resistance. After four years of sparring, Morris finally received Ottawa's permission to negotiate a treaty at Fort Carlton on the North Saskatchewan River in the summer of 1876. . . .

Once again, the crucial issue in the negotiations was retention of sovereignty. Upon hearing the terms, Poundmaker, then an important man but not yet a great chief, objected to the size of the proposed reserves: " 'The government mentions how much land is to be given us. He says 640 acres one mile square for each band. He will give us, he says,'. . .and in a loud voice, he [Poundmaker] shouted 'This is our land, it isn't a piece of pemmican to be cut off and given in little pieces back to us. It is ours and we will take what we want.' " A wave of approval greeted this protest, and a number of Indians stood up, waving their hands and shouting yes in Cree. Morris was shaken by the incident but took his usual line: because settlement was inevitable, the Indians would be crowded out unless they had reserves. He did not discuss the implied issues of relative size of

---

4. Alexander Morris *The Treaties of Canada with the Indians of Manitoba and the North-West Territories* first pub Toronto 1880 (reprinted Toronto 1971) 143–67 and Taylor "Indian Policy" 185–92.

reserves or of development policy itself. The talks then adjourned. The Indians spent a day in informal discussion and another day in a formal council separate from the Canadians. According to a metis observer, Peter Erasmus, the resistance of Poundmaker and those of his persuasion was overwhelmed by the weighty speeches of two senior chiefs, Star Blanket (Ahtahkakoop) and Big Child (Mistawasis). In the face of rapidly declining food resources, these elders feared that death by starvation was the only alternative to the treaty. As Star Blanket said: "For my part, I think that the Queen Mother has offered us a new way and I have faith in the things my brother Mistawasis has told you...Surely we Indians can learn the ways of living that made the White man strong."[5]

When the Indians returned to the bargaining tent with Lieutenant-Governor Morris on the following day, they devoted their entire attention to the food supply question. "They were not exacting," Morris reported, "but they were very apprehensive of their future, and thankful, as one of them put it, 'a new life was dawning upon them.'" The next day was spent on a list of more precise demands, ranging from farm animals to aid for the blind and lame. This list included a free supply of medicines and, in case of war, exclusion from liability to serve in the military. Morris did agree to provide a medicine chest (a clause that was to return to the courts in modern times), to provide additional aid in the first three years of farming, and to add to the treaty a famine clause indicative of the concerns of the Saskatchewan bands: that is, if famine or pestilence ever struck, the queen would grant assistance "to relieve the Indians from the calamity that shall have befallen them." When Morris had approved the revised terms, Star Blanket called on the people for assent, which they provided by shouting and holding up their hands. But again Poundmaker intervened, saying that he could not see how their children would be clothed and fed on what was promised and that he did not know how to build a house or cultivate the ground. His warnings fell on deaf ears. Mistawasis called Peter Erasmus aside and asked him to ensure that all the promises were actually written into the treaty, but, aside from that precaution, the negotiations were concluded on a basis similar to the others. Some plains Indians, notably Big Bear, refused to sign the treaty, but it was assumed that they, too, would soon come to terms.

The Blackfeet of the Rocky Mountains foothills, whose territory extended from the Missouri to the North Saskatchewan, had had less regular contact with Europeans during the two centuries of fur trade, but

---

5. Cited in Taylor "Indian Policy" 203, 206.

they too had been drawn into the orbit of development in the 1860s. They might have settled on either side of the forty-ninth parallel, depending on the movements of the buffalo and the political situation, had the North-West Mounted Police not arrived in 1874. By suppressing the excesses of the whisky trade and providing a rough but effective judicial system, the Mounted Police acted as a buffer in the times of great trial in 1875-7 when the buffalo hunt failed and thousands of Sioux refugees fled across the border before the American cavalry. The result was that in September 1877 the last of the prairie treaties, number 7, was negotiated at Blackfoot Crossing, with representatives of the units of the Blackfoot confederacy, the Piegans, Bloods, Siksikas (or Blackfoot proper), and Sarcees, as well as a few mountain Assiniboines (Stoney)....

The signing of treaty 7 marked the conclusion of an eight-year debate on Indian–white relations. In the years that followed, a small number of additional bands signed the prairie treaties and separate treaties were negotiated in northern Alberta (treaty 8, 1899) and in northern Saskatchewan and Alberta (treaty 10, 1906-7).[6] The translation of the western interior from aboriginal possession to clear crown land and to private ownership had been accomplished with extraordinary dispatch. The government had achieved title to the soil, according to its view of the law, and the Indians had achieved recognition of their needs and some measure of protection against the seemingly inevitable influx of Canadian settlers. In return for relinquishing sovereignty, the Indians had won a permanent direct relationship with the crown which, they believed, would serve them in case of disputes with local administrators.

To weigh the relative gains and losses of a treaty is a difficult matter. These were not simply imposed settlements as is sometimes suggested. The Indians won more in the negotiations than the government had planned to give, but they lost on the crucial issue of ultimate sovereignty over the land. One might well ask, however, given the time of the discussions and the assumption of rapid development that both parties accepted, whether a better result was possible for either side. Some Indians, perhaps a considerable proportion of the total, particularly among the Ojibwas but also including recognized militants such as Big

---

6. Treaty 8 was not just a repetition of the earlier numbered treaties. Among the significant differences was the provision for "reserves" of land either for an entire band or for families and individuals on the basis of 640 acres per family of five or 160 acres per individual. This treaty also noted Indian concerns about government schools and promised "non-interference with the religion of the Indians"; Richard Daniel "The Spirit and Terms of Treaty Eight" in Richard Price ed *The Spirit of the Alberta Indian Treaties* (Montreal 1980) 47–100.

Bear, wanted to reject the terms. None the less the negotiators were always able to win over the "doves," who could be induced to accept the agreement because of their fears for the future or because they wished help in the process of adjustment. Once some adherents had been obtained, the government negotiators enjoyed the luxury—from the standpoint of a bargaining session—of threatening to settle the deal with those receptive to a compromise while omitting the advocates of a hard line; that is, the government would have been able to extinguish native title and leave the recalcitrants out of the financial arrangements. Indian solidarity was never sufficient to resist this threat because, when forced to make a decision, the greater proportion of Indians—leaders and followers—was persuaded by the case for compromise.

Whether the Indians appreciated that they had agreed in principle to a sweeping change in property relations has been debated ever since. Did the Indians understand the implications of the transfer of sovereignty and, in particular, of the white Canadian perception of private property? Irene Spry has suggested that the Indian notion of property encompassed common property, wherein members of a defined group used an area according to certain rules, and open access, in which the resources were used by everyone as they saw fit. But, she contends, the Indian view did not encompass private property, the actual possession and trade of real estate, and thus the Indians were not capable of appreciating the treaty. They thought they were admitting whites into the territory to share the resources given by the Manitou to all his people, Spry argues; they assumed that in certain parts of this territory—the reserves—resources would belong exclusively to the Indian people and that elsewhere open access would be the rule.[7]

Spry's interpretation corresponds to the Indian perception of property as recorded by Edwin Denig in the mid-nineteenth century:

> None of these...tribes claim a special right to any circumscribed or limited territory...All the...territory in the West [known to them] and now occupied by all the Indians was created by Wakonda [Assiniboine Creator] for their sole use and habitation...Now each nation finds themselves in possession of a portion of these lands, necessary for their preservation. They are therefore determined to keep them from aggression by every means in their power. Should the game fail, they have a right to hunt it in any of their enemies' country, in which they are able to

---

7. Spry "The Great Transformation: The Disappearance of the Commons in Western Canada" in Richard Allen ed *Man and Nature on the Prairies* (Regina 1976) 21–45.

protect themselves. . .It is not land or territory they seek in this but the means of subsistence, which every Indian deems himself entitled to even should he be compelled to destroy his enemies or risk his own life to obtain it.[8]

This argument also supports the view reiterated by Indian elders during this century: Indians gave whites the use of the land for farming purposes, but did not relinquish the water, timber, fish, birds, mountains, or minerals. Such debates must be entered with caution. Not only is there much at stake in the contemporary review of aboriginal rights but also each treaty differs in crucial ways from every other. In treaty 5, of course, the explanations were brief and perhaps incomplete. In treaty 3, the implications of the settlement seem to have been recognized. Jean Friesen argues that the Ojibwas in the latter treaty negotiations knowingly exchanged their property for guarantees of continuing economic and political assistance from the state. In this view, Mawedopenais, a leader of the treaty 3 people, understood very well what the bargain implied: "And now in concluding this treaty I take off my glove and give you my hand and with it my birthright and my land—and in taking your hand I hold fast all the promises you have made as long as the sun rises and the water flows as you have said."[9] There is no short answer to the issue of Indian perception of property relations and sovereignty in the treaties.

There will never be agreement on what the original parties did, let alone what they thought they had done. Nevertheless, it seems clear that a fundamental divergence in Indian and government views of the treaty has marred Indian–white relations from the 1870s to the present. For the crown, the treaty was a single transaction. A price was arrived at, aboriginal title was extinguished, and the two parties had no further claims on each other except as specified in the clauses of the treaty. For the Indians, in contrast, the treaty, like the fur trade exchange, was an alliance. It was subject to renewal each year and implied a continuing relationship between two peoples. The Indian people assumed they had given up their land or birthright, however they understood this concept, and in exchange acquired political protection, economic security, and education not just during the troubled era of transition but forever. As the custom of annual treaty payments recognized, this was not a one-shot

---

8. J. E. Foster "The Saulteaux and the Numbered Treaties: An Aboriginal Rights Position" in Richard Price ed *The Spirit of the Alberta Indian Treaties* (Montreal 1980) 162–3.
9. Friesen "My Birthright and Land."

event, in their eyes, but a relationship that would be reviewed in order that the spirit of the contract, as well as the letter, was maintained.[10]

In the mid-1870s, while the last prairie treaties were being negotiated, while the prairie bands were beginning the process of reserve selection, and while the first white settlers were moving onto the open grasslands to experiment with cereal crops, native apprehension about the new order was slowly growing. Some experienced observers of the region, native and white, assumed that fifty years, a century, perhaps an eternity would pass before the fur trade and the hunt ended. But others feared that hard times were ahead. No one, it can be said with confidence, anticipated just how difficult the next decade would be. Who among the residents of the prairie west imagined a transition that, for most of the sub-districts within the region, was completed within ten years of its start? Adams Archibald, addressing the Indians at the Stone Fort in the negotiation of treaty 1, said that the queen thought it good that the Indians adopt "civilized ways" but would not compel them to do so. They would have to cease hunting over the land as it was settled, but "there will still be plenty of land that is neither tilled nor occupied where you can go and roam and hunt as you have always done, and, if you wish to farm, you will go to your own reserve where you will find a place ready for you to live on and culti-vate."[11] And yet by 1870 there had been no buffalo near Red River for some time; by 1876 there were only a few in the region of Qu'Appelle; and by 1879 even the herds of the Cypress Hills region had melted away. The transition was over, for all intents and purposes, by 1885. This turbulent decade, 1875–85, ended in violence and, it must be said, betrayal of the Indian people.

The heart of the problem was the virtual extinction of the Canadian buffalo herd between 1874 and 1879. No satisfactory explanation, aside from an incredible slaughter by native and white hunters who were supplying the American hide trade, has ever been offered for this sudden destruction of the prairie food supply. A variety of half-hearted conserva-tion measures was considered by the Canadian federal and territorial governments, but no effective limits were adopted in time. Heavy hunting in the mid-1870s depleted the breeding stock, and by 1878 most of the Canadian herd had been driven into Montana. Similar pressure in 1879, allegedly planned by the American authorities to ensure that Sitting Bull

---

10. Jean Friesen "Notes for Treaty 5 Historical Research" unpublished paper prepared for Treaty 5 Chiefs Native Constitutional Conference, Ottawa, March 1983.
11. Morris *Treaties* 29.

and his Sioux soldiers would starve in their Canadian refuges whence they had fled after the Little Big Horn, drove the animals south of the border again just as they were about to make their annual migration into the Saskatchewan country. By the end of 1879, the buffalo had disappeared forever from the Canadian prairies. Though some Indian bands travelled south to the Missouri for another three summers, even those herds were soon destroyed. The plains equestrian way of life, rich and fulfilling as it had been for over a century, had come to an end.[12]

The results were disastrous, especially for the hunters of the western prairies who had relied so completely on the buffalo. The Blackfoot, it was reported, were "selling their Horses for a mere song, eating gophers, mice, and for the first time have hunted the Antelope and nearly killed them all off...Strong young men were now so weak that some of them could hardly walk. Others who last winter were fat and hearty are mere skin and bone."[13] Reports of hardship and of death by starvation were legion during the 1880s. If the government had been slow to react to the destruction of the buffalo, it did move quickly to feed the Indians. Emergency rations, including flour and cattle, were distributed by the federal authorities on numerous occasions.

What is striking, in retrospect, is the government's apparent use of food rations as a means of coercing reluctant Indians into the treaties and, later, as a tool for controlling Indian diplomatic activity. The problem lay with those plains Crees who had not been satisfied by the treaties of 1874 and 1876. Led by Big Bear, Piapot, and Little Pine, these bands had sought vainly to restrict the buffalo hunt to Indians only and then had demanded more generous gifts of food and capital equipment from the government. Though Piapot acceded to treaty 4 in 1875, the other two leaders stayed out of treaty 6 until the food supply crises. Under pressure from his followers, Little Pine gave up in 1879, but Big Bear, who was sustained by the most militant hunters, continued to resist until 1882, when starvation drove him to take the treaty in exchange for food rations. Even after they signed, however, these three leaders struggled to improve on the treaty settlement. Their goal was the creation of contiguous reserves where, as in the Indian territory established by the American reservation system, populous and extensive Indian communities might retain considerable

---

12. Frank Gilbert Roe *The North American Buffalo: A Critical Study of the Species in Its Wild State* first pub 1951 (Toronto 1970).
13. Noel E. Dyck "The Administration of Federal Indian Aid in the North-West Territories 1879–1885" MA thesis, University of Saskatchewan, 1970, 28.

autonomy. This the government could not accept. Indeed, Indian Affairs Commissioner Edgar Dewdney used food rations as a weapon to push Piapot into the Indian Head region and to send the Little Pine and Big Bear bands to Battleford and Fort Pitt respectively. But he could not prevent them from talking. Though separated by 300 miles of prairie, the Indian leaders continued to agitate for revision of the treaties.[14]

Big Bear was a key actor in subsequent events. One of the most independent and influential plains leaders of his generation, he had been consulting native leaders across the region for a decade. He had met [Louis] Riel during a visit to the Missouri valley, had spoken with Sitting Bull after the defeat of General Custer, and had maintained constant contact with militants such as Piapot and moderates such as Crowfoot. W. B. Cameron, who knew him, reported many years later that Big Bear possessed "great natural gifts: courage, a keen intellect, a fine sense of humour, quick perception, splendid native powers of expression and great strength of purpose."[15] In 1884, Big Bear sent runners to all the plains Indians, even the Blackfoot, calling on them to attend a sun dance near Battleford, on the adjoining reserves of Poundmaker and Little Pine, undoubtedly in the expectation that a chiefs' council would follow the religious ceremony. When the great assembly began in June 1884— probably the greatest assembly of plains chiefs in history—a violent confrontation between a starving Indian and a stubborn Canadian farm instructor led to Mounted Police intervention, a near-riot, and, apparently, the temporary discrediting of men such as Little Pine and Big Bear who prevented a slaughter. But Big Bear proceeded to another large assembly at Duck Lake, where, incidentally, Louis Riel spoke to the Indians and where it was agreed that an even bigger council would be held in the summer of 1885. The Indian protest was supported by the Duck Lake people, who drafted a petition detailing government violations of their treaty and accusing the federal commissioners of misleading them in the treaty negotiations. Big Bear's work was nearly complete. With Little Pine and Piapot, he had united the plains Crees and even interested the Blackfoot in the proposed 1885 council where demands for an enlarged "Indian territory" and greater Indian autonomy would be approved and

---

14. For this and the following material, I am indebted to Dr John L. Tobias who permitted me to see "Canada's Subjugation of the Plains Cree 1879–1885" before its publication in the *Canadian Historical Review* 64 (1983) 519–48.
15. William Bleasdell Cameron *The War Trail of Big Bear* (Boston 1927) 243; W. B. Fraser "Big Bear, Indian Patriot" in Donald Swainson ed *Historical Essays on the Prairie Provinces* (Toronto 1970) 71–88; and R. S. Allen "Big Bear" *Saskatchewan History* 25 no 1 (winter 1972) 1–17.

forwarded to Ottawa. A Cree revolt—a political rather than a military uprising—was brewing.

The Canadian authorities were abreast of these developments. Commissioner Dewdney relied on a number of informants, among them the distinguished Cree chief Poundmaker, to follow the course of the Cree diplomatic campaign and to determine his own policy. In the face of this campaign and violent Cree opposition to his threats of ration cuts, Dewdney abandoned his "submit or starve" policy in the summer of 1884. Instead, he would single out the troublemakers and imprison them. "Sheer compulsion," he told Prime Minister Macdonald, was "the only effective course" when handling most Indian bands. In the summer of 1884, as Indian solidarity grew, Dewdney won Macdonald's support for an increase in the size of the Mounted Police force and for an amendment to the Indian Act that would permit the arrest of any Indian who was on another reserve without the approval of Indian Affairs officials. He suggested also that Macdonald contact the stipendiary magistrates in the region to ensure that jail sentences be used wherever possible to remove troublemakers. Dewdney was ready for trouble by the end of 1884, but he did not expect violence.

If government officials had known more about Little Poplar, they might have been less sanguine. This war chief, a member of Big Bear's own band, rejected his leader's long and slow diplomatic campaign for Indian solidarity. Little Poplar advocated violence—execution of Indian agents and government representatives—as a means of restoring Cree independence. He found a sympathetic response among the unruly youths in the Fort Pitt–Frog Lake area. Because of Little Poplar's agitation, Big Bear, whose successes had been achieved at the expense of much time away from his people, was no longer the unchallenged leader of his band. Power among his 500 followers passed to the warrior society—the Rattlers—and to the war chiefs, Little Poplar and Wandering Spirit, and to Big Bear's son Imasees. The militants were spoiling for trouble, and news of a fight between metis and Mounted Police at Duck Lake, over 200 miles east of their camp, pushed them into open warfare. They vented their anger against whites, anger that had been building for a decade, by seizing the Hudson's Bay Company store at Frog Lake on 2 April and killing nine white men in a few brief minutes of rifle fire. Only the company agent and two white women were spared. With news of the "Frog Lake massacre" came the chilling realization in households across the territories that Indians as well as metis were ready to die for the native cause. Among British Canadians, who knew of General Gordon at Khartoum and General Custer at the Little Big Horn, the Frog Lake incident created an atmosphere of terror. As if to make the threat immediate, stores at Fort Pitt, Lac La Biche, Cold Lake, Green Lake, and even the town of Battleford were pillaged by native soldiers. The protest movement had apparently become a general native uprising of the type familiar to every citizen of the empire.[16]

The terror among white settlers and the coincidence of the metis skirmish at Duck Lake with the Cree action at Frog Lake have combined to influence historical interpretations. Inevitably, the "1885 rebellion" is described as a metis and Indian uprising. Inevitably, too, these interpretations have suggested that Big Bear and even Poundmaker were associated with a Cree military movement planned to reinforce the metis under Riel and Dumont. These suggestions are wrong. As John Tobias has argued, the so-called Indian uprising was really the outburst of a few young warriors in each of the Cree and Assiniboine bands in central Saskatchewan. It was not approved by the chiefs and, indeed, did not attract widespread support. But it did offer the government an ideal opportunity to smash the Cree diplomatic campaign for native unity and revision of the treaties. The political goals of Dewdney, the panic of white settlers, and the assumptions of historians have created a concerted Indian–metis war where, in fact, sporadic raids for food and violent acts by a few young Indian rebels happened to coincide with the metis uprising.[17]

Insofar as it was possible, the leading chiefs remained aloof from the battles of 1885. After Frog Lake, Big Bear restored his authority over his band, convinced them to permit the peaceful withdrawal of the police detachment at Fort Pitt, and then headed into the bush country north of the North Saskatchewan where his followers would be far from the action. Beardy, another chief, and his followers refused Riel's invitation to join the metis. Piapot, whose reserve received a special contingent of troops, was never involved. The Blackfoot, likewise, resisted the temptation to strike back at the whites in this time of starvation and of government vulnerability. In their case, perhaps, Dewdney had acted wisely by inviting four chiefs of the Blackfoot confederacy, including Crowfoot, to travel by rail to Regina and Winnipeg in 1884 to view the numbers and achievements of the whites. The tour impressed the chiefs with the futility of defiance. Thus, when their young followers argued that the Blackfoot should join the metis in rebellion, the old chiefs temporized. Two of them, the Blood chief Red Crow, a long-time enemy of the Crees, and Eagle Tail,

---

16. Stuart Hughes ed *The Frog Lake "Massacre": Personal Perspectives on Ethnic Conflict* (Toronto 1976).
17. Tobias "Subjugation."

a Piegan, were adamant in their refusal to join the revolt. Crowfoot was uncertain. In the end, he followed the lead of Red Crow and sought to use his peaceful stance as a bargaining tool to acquire greater concessions from the federal government. Nevertheless, despite his refusal to ally against the whites, Crowfoot provided shelter for all Cree refugees who reached his camp and despised the Canadian military presence. His decision not to take up arms was a measure of his assessment of the military situation, not a statement of loyalty to the federal government.[18]

Poundmaker, whose soldiers were accused of participating in the metis rising, was also responsible for rescuing a portion of the Canadian military force from certain slaughter. In devising a strategy to deal with the vast territory and the confused situation, Canadian authorities had sent three columns of troops north from the newly constructed Canadian Pacific mainline, from Qu'Appelle, Swift Current, and Calgary. The Swift Current group, under Lt-Col William Otter, reached Battleford without difficulty only to discover that the so-called siege was actually a Cree foray in search of food that had escalated into pillage and vandalism. Otter had had the temerity to pursue Poundmaker into his own country, the wooded and hilly land to the west of the village. There, at Cut Knife Hill, famous for a Cree victory over the Sarcees not many years before, Otter's 325 men surprised the Indians early in the morning of 2 May. The Cree soldiers immediately scattered through the bush and coulees surrounding the hill and began to fire at the exposed troops on the bald summit above them. As the morning passed, the troops' position deteriorated, the number of casualties increased, and the Indians almost completely surrounded the hill. Fearing disaster, Otter retreated and, to his surprise, was able to escape without further bloodshed. Little did he know that his men had been saved by Indian kindness. Poundmaker, who had never approved of this war, had ordered his own men to leave the Canadian soldiers in peace. Though he had not participated in the uprising to that date, the battle of Cutknife Hill drove Poundmaker to consider uniting his force with that of Riel. However, the fall of Batoche occurred as Poundmaker was leading his men toward the metis bastion, and, within a week, he too sought terms of peace.[19]

Big Bear's men had remained in their own territory around Fort Pitt,

18. Hugh Dempsey *Crowfoot Chief of the Blackfeet* (Norman, Oklahoma, 1972), 164–70, 189–93.
19. Desmond Morton *The Last War Drum: The Northwest Campaign of 1885* (Toronto 1972) 128–30.

between Edmonton and Battleford, throughout April and had begun to move east toward Poundmaker's camp only in early May and then had stopped to hold a thirst dance in order to restore harmony and confidence among their disparate group of wood and plains Crees. However, when the third military column, Maj-Gen Strange's force from Calgary, reached the Cree camp at Frenchman's Butte, near Fort Pitt, Big Bear's soldiers installed themselves in deep rifle pits above the surrounding plain. A brief Canadian attack was enough to convince Strange that the Indians held a superior position, and so he withdrew to Fort Pitt while the Cree, disturbed by the cannon fire, retreated in the opposite direction. The subsequent pursuit of Big Bear in the bush land west of Battleford was ponderous and extremely taxing—one soldier died of exhaustion after three weeks' march—but the Cree camp was tracked until it broke apart under the weight of internal dissension. Big Bear, ever the plains warrior, turned in his tracks and evaded the troops in a solitary trek to the territory of his birth around Fort Carlton, where he surrendered on 2 July. With the arrest of the leader of the plains Cree diplomatic campaign, the government had achieved its objective. It was the turn of the courts and the law to ensure that Indians acquiesced to Canadian rule.

As in the discussion of the military events of 1885, so in the analysis of the legal proceedings, one must distinguish the whites and metis from the Indians. In the trials, Commissioner Dewdney had an ideal opportunity to break the independence of the Crees. He ensured that over 100 prisoners were processed during the summer of 1885, including 2 whites, 46 metis, and 81 Indians. Most of the trials were for treason-felony, and only a fraction resulted in convictions. The judicial result included the imprisonment of 44 Indians and 7 metis. The bias of the system against the Indians could not be more evident. One experienced legal observer said Poundmaker was "convicted on evidence that, in any ordinary trial, would have ensured his acquittal without the jury leaving the box."[20] Big Bear, Poundmaker, and the other Indians found guilty of serious crimes were transported to the Stony Mountain federal penitentiary, north of Winnipeg, to serve three-year sentences within the stone walls of the fortress. The two chiefs had their long hair cropped, were required to do menial jobs, and, it is clear, were unable to adjust to prison life. Both converted to Roman Catholicism but their perception of this action is not known. Poundmaker was released in the spring of 1886, Big Bear in 1887, both, it is

20. George T. Denison, cited in Peter B. Waite *Canada 1874–1896: Arduous Destiny* (Toronto 1971) 162; also Sandra Estlin Bingaman "The Trials of Poundmaker and Big Bear, 1885" *Saskatchewan History* 28 no 3 (autumn 1975) 81–94.

said, broken in heart and spirit. Neither lived out the year of his release. And the Cree diplomatic movement to create a single large reserve and better treaty terms was decisively defeated.

The events surrounding the treaties and the violence of 1885 have been the chief subjects of historical discussion of prairie Indians in the modern era. The attention is warranted, of course, but it should not obscure the fact that thousands of Indians continued to live in the prairie west after the death of Big Bear and Poundmaker and continued to struggle with government policy, agricultural assistance, and a new educational system. And, despite the undeniable hardships, they retained their sense of themselves as a different people. . . .

The period from the mid-1870s to the mid-1880s had been terribly difficult for the prairie Indians because of the widespread food shortages, but there were other burdens placed on them in this era that were to remain with them for generations to come. The signing of treaties and the establishment of reserves marked the commencement of the process that scholars describe as "directed social change." One social group, in this classic model of social analysis, dominates another, guiding and forcing the latter's adaptation to its culture. In this view, white Canadian expectations and policies would slowly replace the ideas and plans of the Indian people; the social changes in the Indian community would conform increasingly to the rhythms of change in the larger society. Eventually, according to some theorists, there would cease to be a distinguishable native identity. But such enormous changes take time, as students of older societies can attest. School and reserve and administrative fiat would not transform Indians into European Canadians overnight.[21]

The political status of the prairie Indians was actually determined before they negotiated their treaties but was never explained to them or made a subject of negotiation. Instead, unilateral governmental decisions reduced them to the position of minors or wards. The government's Indian policy was a product of its dissatisfaction with native communities as they had evolved in the century after 1760. The Indian settlements, especially those in Upper Canada, had functioned well enough as economic and political units, but the Indians themselves, in the official view, remained distressingly separate from the larger community. To "civilize" them, British authorities concluded, the principles of private property and

---

21. The classic studies of this type are Ralph Linton *Acculturation in Seven American Indian Tribes* (New York 1940) and Melville Herskovits *Acculturation: The Study of Culture Contact* (Gloucester, Mass, 1938).

the franchise would have to be inculcated more effectively. This was the purpose of the Gradual Civilizing Act of 1857. When Indian leaders refused to permit the whittling away of their reserves by the creation of fifty-acre private holdings, and when only a handful of Indians applied for enfranchisement, the new Canadian government, which inherited the British policy and outlook, imposed legal sanctions to control native self-government. By 1876, when the Indian Act was passed, the federal government and its agents had established a system of "wardship, coloni-zation and tutelage" that limited native self-government and even native economic development. Into this situation stepped the native people of the prairie west. They were assumed to possess aboriginal rights when they signed the treaties, to be sure, but they were not informed of the Indian Act's limits on their actions. Rather, only in the years after the treaty did they learn of these restrictions.[22]

The Indian Act, which has governed Canada's Indians since it first consolidated various pieces of legislation in 1876 and, in a more thorough revision, in 1880, requires the government to supervise the economy, politics, education, land, and even many personal decisions of the Indian people. As a former superintendent of Indian affairs once said, "Probably there is no other legislation which deals with so many and varied subjects in a single Act. It may be said to deal with the whole life of a people." The Indian Act is at once protective and coercive. It aims to protect and nurture the Indian people but also to assimilate them into Canadian society. It shows little respect for Indian society and expects few contribu-tions by Indians—as Indians—to the larger community. However, it evinces a respect and concern for Indians as individuals worthy of integration into the Canadian mainstream. The Indian Act, in brief, is an example of the Victorian mind at work in a "missionary" field.

An Indian, according to the act, is someone designated as an Indian. This includes individuals who are members of recognized bands as well as the wives, children, or widows of registered Indians. A white woman who marries an Indian becomes an Indian, as do her children; an Indian woman who marries a white thereupon loses her Indian status, as do her children. Traditional Indian government was superseded in the act by band chiefs and councils whose elections, terms, and powers were carefully set out. Despite the apparent latitude of local band administra-tion, all Indian decisions were reviewed by administrators—usually

---

22. John S. Milloy "The Era of Civilization: British Policy for the Indians of Canada 1830–1860" DPhil thesis, Oxford University, 1978, and John S. Milloy "The Early Indian Acts: Developmental Strategy and Constitutional Change" paper presented to Brandon Native Studies Conference 1981.

whites—at the level of the band and then at regional and national supervisory offices. The bureaucracy was and remains a remarkable case of state direction of a community, as the example of Indian reserve land will illustrate. The purpose of reserves was to permit the Indians to learn European Canadian ways at their own pace; that is, the reserve isolated them from whites in order to integrate them more effectively at some later date. Reserves, by uniting the Indians in close-knit political and social arrangements, actually worked against this end. One important reason for the existence of reserves was officials' fear that if Indians were given individual title to plots of land they might fall prey to white swindlers. To combine the protection of the reserve with the educational virtues of private property, the administrators created "location tickets" or certificates of ownership. By this system, plots of land would remain in the possession of individuals at the pleasure of the band council and the minister of Indian affairs and could not be sold except to the crown. It was an unusual and creative solution but, despite the advantages of this private-public tenure, state power over Indian land, including the power to expropriate, has caused problems. The ultimate goal of the Indian Act was to transform Indians into whites by means of the franchise, which implied not just the right to vote but also the right to hold and produce private property, to use liquor, and to pay full taxes. Enfranchisement, in short, meant that the Indian turned his back on his heritage, left his reserve, and became a non-Indian in the "mainstream" of white society. Few chose this option in the first century of the act.[23]

Another source of friction between government and prairie bands lay in the agricultural policy for the reserves. Because food was the fundamental need of the natives and because training in agriculture seemed an obvious means to "civilize" them, the government placed great hope in its farm policy in the 1880s and 1890s. By hiring white instructors, establishing "model" farms, and employing increasing numbers of agents, the government planned to solve the problem of food supply within just a few years. In order to ensure that Indians did not evade the demands of farm labour, the "pass system" was used to permit only those who had obtained an agent-approved ticket to leave the reserve. Then, when some bands commenced large-scale export agriculture and contracted debts to farm

23. Robert J. Surtees *The Original People* (Toronto 1971); J. D. Leighton "The Development of Federal Indian Policy in Canada 1840–1890" PhD dissertation, University of Western Ontario, 1975; Sally M. Weaver *Making Canadian Indian Policy: The Hidden Agenda 1968–70* (Toronto 1981); Canada Department of Indian and Northern Affairs (Policy Planning and Research Branch) *The Historical Development of the Indian Act* (Ottawa 1975).

implement companies, the government introduced a "permit system" that cut off produce sales beyond the reserve except with the approval of the agent. As this unusual imposition made plain, the Indians were expected to learn individualistic peasant agriculture and to cultivate with hoe and scythe, not to become cash-crop farmers who shared the work and rewards on a collective basis. The spread of the agricultural economy on the reserves was slow, and the returns were poor. By the early twentieth century, the government's native agricultural policy was acknowledged by some officials, particularly by Frank Oliver, minister of the interior 1905–11, to be a failure.[24]

The arrival of hundreds of thousands of immigrants offered an obvious alternative: pressure from settlers, railways, and town site promoters on the "empty" reserve lands could be translated into capital for new Indian development projects. During the next generation, as much as one-half of the reserve land was sold off. In southern Saskatchewan's treaty 4 area alone, 270,000 of 520,000 acres were sold by 1928. There were benefits in such a policy because pools of capital were created for individual bands, but there were great shortcomings, too, as succeeding generations were to discover. An example of relative success was the Blackfoot reserve east of Calgary, where the surrender of 125,000 acres, nearly half the reserve, produced a trust fund of over $1 million by 1920. Henceforth, the reserve could provide its own social security system—weekly food rations, medical care, housing, and some farm equipment. Not all reserves were so fortunate. And, even in this case, the provision of basic material needs did not ensure the satisfaction of the reserve Blackfoot or the avoidance of social problems. As Hugh Dempsey concluded: "Those reserves which surrendered lands showed no noticeable advancement or long-term benefits over those which did not...Rations which should have been used as an inducement to work, had just the opposite effect. The use of firearms was restricted. Travel was limited, and anyone leaving his reserve required a pass. The marketing of grain and hay was strictly regulated, and everywhere an Indian turned, he was greeted by restrictions on his freedom. In the end, it was easier for many to continue the welfare pattern established during the early starvation years than it was to break out of the mold to make a viable living on the reserve."[25]

---

24. Sarah Carter "Agriculture and Agitation on the Oak River Reserve, 1875–1895" *Manitoba History* 6 (fall 1983) 2–9.
25. Hugh Dempsey "One Hundred Years of Treaty Seven" in Ian A. L. Getty and Donald B. Smith eds *One Century Later: Western Canadian Reserve Indians since Treaty 7* (Vancouver 1978); A. J. Looy "The Indian Agent and His Role in the Administration of the North-

The great hope of administrator and missionary alike was that education would break the hold of tradition and create a properly "Canadianized" Indian. As a result of the campaign to "civilize" and "Christianize" Indian children, schools became an issue in native–white relations as early as the 1880s, and native educational institutions, such as the various ceremonies encompassed in the term "sun dance," remained a source of conflict even thirty years later. The goal of white education policy was, of course, to protect Indians from the worst features of white society, to prepare them for the labour market, and to "save" them for the sake of their souls. Church and government co-operated in the provision of three types of institution, the day school on the reserve, the boarding school, and, most elaborate of all, the industrial school. At the latter, children were required to live apart from their families for extended periods in the expectation that Indian attitudes and customs would be forgotten. At the Qu'Appelle Industrial School, for example, the children were expected to learn not only a European language but also European Canadian concepts of time, work discipline, and public order. They spent half their day in trades workshops or in the kitchen, laundry, or dairy and the other half in the classroom. Their recreations were such Canadian pastimes as cricket, football, checkers, and, of course, the brass band. The industrial schools were phased out in the first decades of the twentieth century, partly because they were costly but also because they were failures.[26] The boarding schools continued for another two generations, always under white supervision. Their record has yet to be established by scholarly investigation, but, aside from the predictable academic successes and failures, such schools have been the target of Indian criticism ever since because of their harsh insistence on conformity to Canadian cultural practices.

One reason for the failure of the industrial schools and, by extension, of the government's assimilationist policy was the conscious resistance of

West Superintendency 1876–1893" PhD dissertation, Queen's University, 1977; Esther S. Goldfrank *Changing Configurations in the Social Organization of a Blackfoot Tribe during the Reserve Period* (New York 1945); Lucien M. Hanks Jr and Jane Richardson Hanks *Tribe under Trust: A Study of the Blackfoot Reserve of Alberta* (Toronto 1950); D. J. Hall "Clifford Sifton and Canadian Indian Administration 1896–1905" *Prairie Forum* 2 no 2 (1977) 127–51; Stuart Raby "Indian Land Surrenders in Southern Saskatchewan" *Canadian Geographer* 17 (1973) 36–52.

26. Jacqueline J. Kennedy [Gresko] "Qu'Appelle Industrial School: White 'Rites' for the Indians of the Old North West" MA thesis, Carleton University, 1970; and Jacqueline Gresko "White 'Rites' and Indian 'Rites': Indian Education and Native Responses in the West, 1870–1910" in Anthony W. Rasporich, ed. *Western Canada Past and Present* (Calgary 1975) 163–82.

the Indians themselves. Too often, students of Canadian history have been told that Indian society "collapsed" before a "more advanced" civilization. In fact, prairie Indians did not acquiesce to the pressures for assimilation. Instead, they fought back as best they could, employing passive resistance when their children were recruited into boarding schools and, later, organizing political associations to oppose the excesses of the Indian Act. One of their most important expressions of resistance was the annual summer gathering of the plains communities. This sun or thirsting dance had been the occasion for games, courtship, and visiting as well as for worship in pre-treaty days, and it remained a crucial event in plains Indian life even after the turn of the twentieth century. Despite regular government attempts to proscribe the dancing, it was only when charges were laid that the activity was curtailed. And, even then, the dances remained on the fringes of summer fairs and sports days, illegal and yet all the more powerful for the fact that they were conducted in secret.[27]

Much had occurred in prairie native history during the last half of the nineteenth century. Members of hitherto autonomous hunting bands were confined to reserves in several dozen districts across the west. The Canadian government set the policy for off-reserve travel, for the sale of agricultural goods, for the provision of education, and even for religious worship. It was beyond the power of native leaders to influence the legislation that governed Indian life, the so-called Indian Act. This unhappy circumstance was to remain virtually unchanged for another half-century. Only in the 1940s and 1950s would the two sides begin to address the extraordinary problems that beset this relationship, and only in the 1970s and 1980s would solutions begin to emerge.

27. As note 26.

TWO ACRES AND A COW:

"Peasant" Farming for the Indians of the Northwest, 1889-97

SARAH CARTER

Indian Commissioner Hayter Reed announced in 1889 that a new "approved system of farming" was to be adopted on western Indian reserves.[1] Indian farmers were to emulate "peasants of various countries" who kept their operations small and their implements rudimentary. In Reed's opinion a single acre of wheat, a portion of a second acre of roots and vegetables, and a cow or two could provide sufficiently for an Indian farmer and his family. He argued that it was better for Indians to cultivate a small acreage properly than to attempt to extend the area under cultivation. Moreover, this restricted acreage eliminated any need for labour-saving machinery. Peasants of other countries, Reed contended, farmed successfully with no better implements than the hoe, the rake, cradle, sickle, and flail, and he believed that Indians had to be taught to handle these simple tools. They were to broadcast seed by hand, harvest with scythes, bind by hand with straw, and thresh with flails. In some districts Indians were discouraged from growing wheat altogether in favour of root crops, and this further reduced the need for any machinery. As part of the program, Indians were required to manufacture at home, from materials readily available, many of the items they needed such as harrows, hay forks, hay racks, carts, and ox yokes.

Indian farmers were compelled to comply with the peasant farming policy until 1897, when Reed's career with the department abruptly

SARAH CARTER, "TWO ACRES AND A COW: 'PEASANT' FARMING FOR THE INDIANS OF THE NORTHWEST, 1889–97," *CANADIAN HISTORICAL REVIEW*, VOL. 70, NO. 1 (MARCH 1989), 27–52. THIS IS AN EDITED VERSION REPRINTED BY PERMISSION OF UNIVERSITY OF TORONTO PRESS.

1. Canada, *Sessional Papers*, 1889, no 10, 162. Hayter Reed was born in 1849 in L'Original, Prescott County, Ontario. His early training and career interests were military. In 1871 he served with the Provincial Battalion of Rifles when they were dispatched to Fort Garry as reinforcements during the Fenian scare. Reed was called to the bar of Manitoba in 1872. He retired from military service with the rank of major in 1881. In 1880 he worked out of Winnipeg as "chief land guide" with the Department of the Interior. He was appointed to the position of Indian agent in Battleford in 1881. He had little direct experience with or knowledge of Indians before his first posting. Yet he quickly rose through the ranks of assistant commissioner in 1884, commissioner in 1888, and in 1893 he assumed the position of deputy superintendent general of Indian Affairs. In 1897 he was dismissed by Clifford Sifton, minister of the interior. Reed found employment in 1905 as manager-in-chief of the Canadian Pacific Railway's hotel department.

ended. This policy, along with the permit system and the subdivision survey of portions of reserves into forty-acre plots, had a stultifying effect on Indian farming, nipping reserve agricultural development in the bud. In this article, I will study its impact on the Plains Cree and Plains Saulteaux bands, under the Touchwood Hills, File Hills, Muscowpetung and Crooked Lakes agencies.

Agriculture was not well-established on western Indian reserves by the turn of the century. It has generally been argued that Indians, because they were hunters and warriors, were unable to adapt to farming, and that they could not be transformed into sedentary farmers.[2] The story is far more complex, however. There was an initial positive response to agriculture on the part of many reserve residents which has been overlooked in the literature to date. There were also many difficulties. Some of these problems were those experienced by all early settlers—drought, frost, hail, and prairie fire, an absence of markets, and uncertainties about what to sow, when to sow, and how to sow. There were other problems that were not unique to the Indians but were likely magnified in their case. For example, reserve land often proved to be unsuitable for agriculture. Indian farmers also had limited numbers of oxen, implements, and seed: the treaty provisions for these items were immediately found to be inadequate. Indians were greatly hampered in their work because they lacked apparel, particularly footwear. They were undernourished, resulting in poor physical stamina and vulnerability to infectious diseases.

Indian farmers were also subject to a host of government policies and regulations which hampered agricultural development. If an Indian farmer sought better railway, market, or soil advantages he was not able to pull up stakes and try his luck elsewhere, since an Indian could not take out a homestead under the 1876 Indian Act. Nor could Indians raise outside investment capital; reserve land could not be mortgaged and Indians had difficulty obtaining credit. Freedom to sell their produce and stock and to purchase goods was strictly regulated through a permit system, just as movements off the reserves were rigidly monitored through a pass system.

By the late 1880s Indian farmers of the Qu'Appelle district of Treaty Four had few tangible rewards to show for their years of effort. The decade of the 1880s had been described as a "nightmare" to the early Saskatchewan

---

2. G. F. G. Stanley, *The Birth of Western Canada: A History of the Riel Rebellions* (1936; Toronto 1975), 218.

pioneers, with drought and frost causing homesteaders to desert the district in large numbers.[3] For Indian farmers, however, the 1880s were not totally disastrous. Significant strides had been taken towards alleviating many of the problems which had handicapped reserve farming in the past. For the most part, local officials of the Department of Indian Affairs, the agents and farm instructors, had played a constructive role in facilitating favourable conditions. Steps had been taken to address such problems as the scarcity of milling and threshing facilities. A cattle-on-loan policy helped to assure a larger future supply of work oxen. Farmers on the reserves experimented with such techniques as summer-fallowing and they tested varieties of seed sent from the Central Experimental Farm in Ottawa. Indians participated in the agricultural fairs held annually throughout the Territories, even taking prizes against all competitors for their wheat and cattle. During the 1880s Indian farmers had also begun to acquire some of the equipment necessary to expedite their operations. Mowers and rakes were the most common purchases, and some bands acquired self-binders. Local officials felt that mowers and rakes were essential as stock was increasing, and that self-binders both lessened the danger of the crop being caught by frost during a protracted harvest and reduced the waste experienced in binding with short straw, thus encouraging the farmers to cultivate a larger area.[4] Almost all of this machinery was purchased from the Indians' own earnings, with purchases being made by a band or a number of farmers together and the money coming from the proceeds of crops or from pooled annuities.

Indian farmers of the 1880s, then, were learning the techniques and acquiring the machinery that their farm instructors and agents agreed were essential to dry-land farming. They were not in all cases moving towards conformity with the individualistic model of the independent homesteader; bands pooled their resources for the purchase of implements and on many reserves the fields were tilled in common. Qu'Appelle white farmers remember the year 1890 as "the turn of the tide; after that all went well."[5] All did not go well for Indian farmers, however. Unprece-

---

3. G. Friesen, *The Canadian Prairies: A History* (Toronto 1984), 222.
4. National Archives of Canada (NA), records relating to Indian Affairs, RG 10, vol. 3686, file 13,168, A. McDonald to Edgar Dewdney; 25 June 1884; vol. 3687, file 13,642, John Nicol to Dewdney, 30 May 1884; vol. 3812, file 55,895, W. E. Jones to Hayter Reed; 18 Sept. 1890, vol. 3795, file 46,759, H. L. Reynolds to Indian commissioner, 6 June 1888.
5. *Qu'Appelle: Footprints to Progress: A History of Qu'Appelle and District* (Qu'Appelle Historical Society 1980), 101.

dented administrative control and restriction of their farming activities in the years to 1897 helped ensure that they remained small-scale producers.

The peasant farming policy emerged during an era when the stated priorities of the Department of Indian Affairs were to dismantle what was called the "tribal" or "communist" system and to promote "individualism." After 1885 in particular these goals were undertaken with great vigour and commitment, along with an increased emphasis on the supervision, control, and restriction of the activities and movements of the Indians. Hayter Reed, a major architect of Indian policy in the Northwest in the decade following the 1885 resistance, fully endorsed these goals. Appointed commissioner in 1888 and deputy superintendent general in 1893, Reed was in a position to articulate and compel obedience to his views. He boasted that under his administration "the policy of destroying the tribal or communist system is assailed in every possible way, and every effort made to implant a spirit of individual responsibility instead."[6]...

One way to undermine the tribal system was to subdivide reserves into separate farms. Large fields worked in common fostered the tribal system; according to Reed they did not encourage pride and industry. The individual farmer did not feel it worth his while to improve land significantly when other members of the band also claimed it as their own.[7] With a certificate of ownership, it was believed, the enterprising Indian would be induced to make permanent improvements such as superior cultivation, improved housing, and better fencing, all of which would have the effect of tying the owner to the locality. Reed was also convinced that private property created law-abiding citizens. Property would render the Indians averse to disturbing the existing order of things, as "among them as among white communities, the lawless and revolutionary element is to be found among those who have nothing to lose but may perhaps gain by upsetting law and order."[8]

[This policy of] "severalty" was not a new idea in Canadian Indian policy, nor was Reed the first official to promote the scheme for the Indians of western Canada, but under his administration the program began in earnest. In his annual report for 1888 Reed announced that reserves in the Northwest were to be subdivided into forty-acre plots or quarter quarter sections.[9] Survey work, which began the following spring,

---

6. *Sessional Papers*, 1889, no 12, 165.
7. Ibid., 166.
8. McCord Museum, McGill University, Hayter Reed Papers, address on the aims of the government in its dealings with the Indians, nd, 29.
9. *Sessional Papers*, 1888, no 16, 28.

was done on reserves where farming had met with some success—that is, where the capacity of the land for agriculture had been proven.[10] Reserves with poorer land—such as the File Hills and Touchwood Hills—were not subdivided. The forty-acre plots were located well back of the main-line Canadian Pacific Railway and the new towns along its route, well back of the fine agricultural reserve land that new settlers and townspeople were beginning to covet—the land that was eventually surrendered.

It is clear that what was in the best interests of the agricultural future of these bands was not in the minds of those who devised this policy. When the subdivision surveys were proposed, government and Indian Affairs officials had objectives in mind beyond the establishment of agriculture on an individual model. John A. Macdonald was enthusiastic about severalty, not as a method of promoting individual initiative and private ownership, but as means of defining "surplus" land on reserves that might be sold.[11] If each Indian were allotted the land he would likely require for cultivation, the amount of surplus land available for surrender and sale could be ascertained.

Public opinion appeared to endorse heartily the department's policy of allotment in severalty, as a means of striking at the heart of the "tribal" system. Respected spokesmen such as Father Lacombe agreed that farming Indians could be made more industrious if they were permitted to take up land in severalty.[12]. . .

A letter published in a November 1890 issue of the Ottawa *Citizen* from "Nichie" of Battleford gave a glowing appraisal of the severalty policy in terminology that bore striking similarities to department publications.[13] The author observed that Indians with allotments made worthy efforts to improve and better their condition. He felt this system annulled tribal influence, "the bane of Indian progress," and instead engendered a healthy spirit of rivalry between individuals and bands. Under the system of all things held in common, the industrious worker had to share whatever was harvested with the idle, discontented, and worthless. This was discouraging to progress. The author perceived that the desire to

---

10. On Pasquah's reserve, for example, 164 forty-acre plots were surveyed. Sixteen of these were divided by deep ravines, leaving 148 lots. The population of the reserve was 124, so there was little room for future expansion. This 6560 acres was only a fraction of the 38,496 acres of the reserve. See NA, National Map Collection, 0011553, Pasquah no 179, 1889.
11. Kenneth J. Tyler, "A Tax-eating Proposition: The History of the Passpasschase Indian Reserve" (MA thesis, University of Alberta, 1979), 114.
12. NA, RG 10, deputy superintendent letterbooks, Vankoughnet to Dewdney, Nov. 1889.
13. Ottawa *Citizen*, Nov. 1890.

occupy separate holdings was spreading, particularly among the young men, and he predicted that the time was not far distant when the Indians would no longer be consumers of government "grub" but producers, relieving the government larder.

The peasant farming policy, introduced at the same time as severalty, was also presented as a means of destroying the system of community ownership on reserves and enhancing individualism and self-support. The central rationale advanced in support of the policy was that it was "the manner best calculated to render [the Indians] self-supporting when left to their own resources."[14] Reed repeated many times in his correspondence and public pronouncements that he believed the time was not far distant when the Indians would have to depend entirely upon their own resources. "Our policy," he stated, "is to make each family cultivate such quantity of land as they can manage with such implements as they can alone hope to possess for long enough after being thrown upon their own resources."[15]

The Indians were to aim, not at breaking up large quantities of land, but at cultivating a restricted amount which could be worked solely with the family's own resources. Labour-saving implements, Reed argued, were "likely to be beyond acquisition by the majority of Indians for some time after they may have been thrown upon their own resources."[16] Reed was not pleased that Indians tended to club together to purchase implements because this reinforced the band unit. He wanted to see the Indians become self-sufficient as individuals not as bands. On their own, however, these individuals were not likely to be able to afford machinery. Although Reed conceded that there were individual Indians who were independent of government assistance and could not be restrained from purchasing machinery out of their own earnings, he felt such cases were rare. If Indians received any assistance at all in the way of seed grain, rations, or other goods, then they were not self-sufficient and should not be making payments on machinery. Well-to-do farmers could instead pay for the labour of other Indians.[17] Indian women, Reed hoped, could work in the fields, particularly at harvest time. Agents and inspectors were to cancel the sales of machinery to Indians, even though these were purchased by the Indians and not by the department.

According to Reed, labour-saving machinery was not required by

---

14. *Sessional Papers*, no 10, 162.
15. McCord Museum, Reed Papers, "Address," 28.
16. *Sessional Papers*, 1892, no 14, 48.
17. NA, RG 10, vol. 3964, file 148,285, Reed to Amédée Forget, 24 Aug. 1896.

Indians. They should cultivate root crops rather than concentrate upon extensive grain growing.[18] In Reed's view, root and not cereal crops taught Indian farmers to be diligent and attentive: "I've always advocated growing as many root crops as possible but Indians have to be humoured a good deal in such matters; and as soon as they begin to make some little progress they become fired with an ambition to grow larger quantities of wheat and other cereals [rather than] roots which require working and weeding at the very time they like to be off hunting while the former only require to have cattle kept away by means of a good fence."[19]

The need to go into debt to buy machinery such as self-binders seemed a further reason to halt the use of these implements. Farmers who had to obtain credit were not regarded as self-sufficient. Reed believed the system of purchase on credit of farm machinery had widely and ruinously affected white settlers, and he shared with other department officials the view that Indians were prone to run into debt and were unable or disinclined to discharge their liabilities.[20] It was wiser, he felt, to wait and see whether the climatic conditions of the country warranted the purchase of labour-saving machinery. Machinery, he argued, would not bring prosperity; it had instead been the means of ruining large numbers of settlers.[21]

Another argument Reed forwarded against Indian use of labour-saving machinery was that rudimentary implements afforded *useful* employment for all. The possession of machinery, he believed, allowed the Indians to do nothing but "sit by and smoke their pipes while work was being done for them without exertion on their part," a situation he believed they preferred.[22] In his view the use of such implements was justified only when manual labour was scarce, and this was not the case on Indian reserves.

The same reasons were advanced for the necessity of home manufactures. Gainful employment during spare time prevented the "mischief which emanates from idleness," and trained the Indians for the time when they would be totally thrown upon their own resources.[23] Indian men and women were first encouraged and then required to make an endless list of

---

18. Ibid., vol. 3793, file 46,062, Reed to Dewdney, 11 April 1888.
19. Ibid., vol. 3746, file 29,690-3, Reed to superintendent general, 30 Sept. 1886.
20. Ibid., vol. 3908, file 107,243, Reed to agent Markle, March 1895, and *Sessional Papers*, 1891, no 14, xvii.
21. NA, RG 10, vol. 3964, file 148,285, Reed to Forget, 24 Aug. 1896.
22. *Sessional Papers*, 1889, no 12, 162.
23. Ibid., 1891, no 14, 196.

items "in common use upon a farm."[24] Women's manufactures included mitts, socks, willow baskets, mats, and straw hats. Men were expected to make axe and fork handles, ox collars and harnesses, wooden harrows, bob-sleighs, and Red River carts. Compliance with this policy was readily enforced when requests for the purchase of these items were simply stroked off the estimates.

Reed drew on aspects of an evolutionary argument to support his peasant farming policy. In the late nineteenth century, those who took an evolutionary view of the North American Indian and other "primitive" people believed that there were immutable laws of social evolution.[25] It was thought that man developed progressively through prescribed stages from savagery through barbarism to civilization. These stages could not be skipped, nor could a race or culture be expected to progress at an accelerated rate. The Indians were perceived to be many stages removed from nineteenth-century civilization, and while they could take the next step forward, they could not miss the steps in between.

Reed employed these notions in defending his stand on machinery. He argued that Indians should not make an "unnatural" leap from barbarism to a nineteenth-century environment, including all its appliances.[26] The Indian was "prone to desire to imitate the white man's nineteenth century civilization too hastily and too early."[27] Reed noted this at length in the first of his annual reports outlining the peasant policy: "The fact is often overlooked, that these Indians who, a few years ago, were roaming savages, have been suddenly brought into contact with a civilization which has been the growth of centuries. An ambition has thus been created to emulate in a day what white men have become fitted for through the slow progress of generations."[28]

The ban on labour-saving machinery was something of an about-face for Hayter Reed and the department. Until the peasant program was introduced, the purchase of mowers, horse rakes, threshing machines, and other implements was heralded in the annual reports as evidence of a new spirit of individualism, prosperity, and overall progress. Such purchases were also used as evidence that the Indians were not "squandering" their earnings as many believed they were prone to do.

---

24. Ibid.
25. Brian Dippie, *The Vanishing Indian: White Attitudes to U.S. Indian Policy* (Middletown 1982), 164–71. See also Robert E. Bieder, *Science Encounters the Indian, 1820–1880: The Early Years of American Ethnology* (Norman 1986).
26. NA, RG 10, vol. 3964, file 148,285, Reed to Forget, 24 Aug. 1896.
27. McCord Museum, Reed Papers, "Address," 28.
28. *Sessional Papers*, 1889, no 12, 162.

At the outset of his career as commissioner, Reed was convinced that a means of fostering an independent, proprietary spirit among the Indians was to allow the "industrious" to purchase some property in the way of wagons and implements out of the proceeds of the produce they were allowed to market. If individual Indians were to be allowed to acquire some personal property, their rations should not be suddenly and completely withdrawn once they met with some success, for they would be left wondering whether their exertions were worth the effort.[29] If the industrious were compelled to devote all of their earnings to the purchase of food, while those who produced half the crop received the balance from the government, there would be no incentive to work. The industrious had to be allowed to invest a fair share of their earnings. Reed's policy with regard to the individual enterprising Indian was to continue to assist him for a time so that he could purchase wagons, harnesses and implements. In that way "he develops into the stage of being a property holder, and soon begins to look down upon those whose laziness compels them to seek assistance from the government. Meanwhile what he had purchased secures him the means of assured independence while he has been acquiring the spirit to make it safe to discontinue helping him and his position awakens a spirit of emulation in his less industrious brother."[30] Reed believed that as the farming Indians gained a sense of pride in their prosperity, they would be less inclined to share their produce with "impecunious neighbors," as in the days when "communist" ideas prevailed.[31] This would, he hoped, compel the more reluctant Indians to put themselves into the hands of the government for similar training.

What accounts for the sudden introduction and enforcement of a ban on machinery? Immigrant settlers resented Indian competition for the limited markets of the Northwest. The 1880s saw increasingly strained relations between Indian and white farmers, a situation that was aggravated by the lean times. Local department officials generally came to the defence of the Indians' interests, while more distant officials appeared willing to please the more politically powerful settlers, at the Indians' expense. The recent arrivals believed that everything should be done to encourage their enterprise. They considered themselves the "actual" settlers, the true discoverers and developers of the country's resources. They believed that the government had bought the land from the Indians, and it was now the government's "right and duty to look after the

---

29. Ibid., 1888, no 16, 125.
30. McCord Museum, Reed Papers, "Address," 27.
31. *Sessional Papers*, 1889, no 12, 161.

interests of the settlers, both present and future, for whom the land was bought, and out of whose earnings it is expected ultimately to be paid for."[32]

By the late 1880s, farmers in some areas of the Northwest were complaining loudly about "unfair" competition from Indians in obtaining a share of the markets for farm produce, and a share of contracts for the supply of hay, wood, and other products. They believed that government assistance gave the Indians an unfair advantage, allowing them to under-sell the white farmer. Complaints from the Battleford district were particularly strident as the markets there were strictly limited and local, and competition was intense. In 1888 the residents of that town petitioned their member of parliament, stating that "the Indians are raising so much grain and farm produce that they are taking away the market from the white settlers."[33]

A visit to Battleford that year appears to have had an important impact on Hayter Reed. There he was "assailed" by complaints about the effects of Indian competition.[34] As a Department of the Interior "chief land guide" in Manitoba in 1880-1, Reed had urged settlers to consider points as far west as Battleford.[35] He had given his assurance that despite the absence of a railway, farmers could be guaranteed a market for their produce as the government's demands alone for the Indians, the Mounted Police, surveyors, and other crews would absorb all of a farmer's surplus.[36] If the Indians were able to provide for themselves as well as sell a surplus, the already limited markets were further restricted.

Following his 1888 visit to Battleford, Reed decided that until a railway extended the settlers' opportunities, his department must do what it could to prevent jealous competition.[37] Competition for markets, he claimed, was disastrous to the Indians in any case, as they were so anxious to find purchasers that they would part with their products for a "trifling consideration."[38] Reed arranged with the Battleford citizens to divide up the limited markets in the district. Much of the trade in cordwood was left to the Métis, as this was their mainstay over the winter. The Indians were

---

32. Edmonton *Bulletin*, 17 Jan. 1881.
33. House of Commons, *Debates*, 19 May 1880, 1610. See also Walter Hildebrandt, "From Dominion to Hegemony: A Cultural History of Fort Battleford," unpublished manuscript, 1988, Department of Environment, Parks, Prairie Region.
34. *Sessional Papers*, 1888, no 16, 127.
35. NA, RG 15, records of the Department of the Interior, vol. 245, file 23,563, part 1.
36. Ibid., Hayter Reed, "Canadian and United States Immigration," May 1880.
37. NA, RG 10, vol. 3806, file 52,332, Reed to Vankoughnet, 27 Oct. 1888.
38. Ibid.

allowed to supply wood to the agency and, for one more year, to the industrial school. The sale of grain in the district was left exclusively to the white settlers.

The peasant farming policy, introduced a year after Reed's visit to Battleford, helped eliminate the Indians from effective competition. The permit system was another means of regulating the Indians' participation in the market economy. Under the Indian Act the department could regulate the sale, barter, exchange, or gift of any grain, roots, or other produce grown on reserves.[39] The official rationale for the permit system was that Indians had to be taught to husband their resources. John A. Macdonald stated that "if the Indians had the power of unrestricted sale, they would dispose of their products to the first trader or whisky dealer who came along, and the consequence would be that the Indians would be pensioners on the Government during the next winter."[40] The permit system, however, further precluded the Indians from participation in the market economy as they could not buy, sell, or transact business.

While the peasant policy excluded Indians from effective competition with white farmers, Hayter Reed may have hoped that it might, nonetheless, provide a secure means of subsistence for the Indians. In nineteenth-century liberal economic thought the peasant proprietor gained a new respectability.[41] Among others, John Stuart Mill opposed the concentration of landed property in the hands of a few great estate owners and favoured the creation of a class of peasant proprietors. This it was believed would raise agricultural productivity, lower prices, and reduce urban unemployment. Peasant proprietorship would have social as well as economic consequences as the owner would take a permanent interest in the soil. He would be "thrifty, sober, honest and independent."[42] With a stake in the country, former day labourers would be less inclined to "wanton aggressions," or "mischief," and instead would be interested in preserving tranquility and order. These were exactly the qualities Reed attributed to his peasant proprietors. . . .

Reed was convinced that the independent, subsistence farm could exist on the Canadian prairie, and he was not alone in cherishing the ideal of the self-sufficient farm where the family produced its own food, manufactured at home necessary non-agricultural goods such as clothing and

---

39. *The Historical Development of the Indian Act* (Ottawa 1978), 93.
40. Canada, House of Commons, *Debates*, 24 March 1884, 1063.
41. Clive J. Dewey, "The Rehabilitation of the Peasant Proprietor in Nineteenth-Century Economic Thought," *History of Political Economy* 6 (1) (1974): 17–47.
42. Ibid., 32–47.

furniture, and did not buy or sell. The notion that this was a superior way of life was widespread and persistent, and was reflected in the suspicion of labour-saving machinery and concern about the use of debt and credit. The ideal of the self-sufficient farmer continued to appeal to the general public whereas the concept of agriculture as a market and profit-focused business met with considerable criticism.[43]

Commercial agriculture required new ideas, attitudes, and knowledge. What and how much should be produced on the farm were determined by external market conditions rather than by the family's needs and desires. Under market conditions the farmer made a business decision and had to take into consideration the nature of the soil, the characteristics of commodities, access to markets, and world prices. Commercial farming involved a "rational" approach to technology. Potential profit rather than immediate need led the commercial farmer to purchase expensive implements on credit; payment would in part come from the increased productivity contributed by the new implement. The efficient, profitable management of the farm enterprise thus required new attitudes towards technology, credit, and debt, for immigrant settlers and Indians alike. Hayter Reed felt that Indians were incapable of understanding these concepts, and could not operate farms as business enterprises. His belief in the inability of Indians to manage their own financial affairs, and to handle debt, credit, or the new technology thus precluded commercial farming.

In the United States the ideal of the self-sufficient farm was never more than "a nice dream of a golden age"; nor was Canadian pioneer agriculture ever self-sufficient.[44] Pioneer farmers, economist Vernon Fowke has argued, were "from the beginning tied in with the price system and the urban economy on a national and international basis.[45] . . .

Subsistence farming was not characteristic of the pioneer farms of the prairie west. From the beginning these farms were connected to the local, national, and international economy. Nor did the difficulties of the 1880s imply a need for self-sufficient farms. Large-scale, single-crop farming and the introduction of the techniques and technology of dry farming would be more likely to encourage agricultural prosperity on the plains. Like other western farmers, Indian farmers tended more towards com-

---

43. Rodney C. Loehr, "Self-sufficiency on the Farm," *Agricultural History* 26, (2) (1952): 37, and Clarence Danhof, *Change in Agriculture: The Northern United States, 1820–1870* (Cambridge 1969), 15.
44. Loehr, "Self-sufficiency," 41.
45. Vernon Fowke, *The National Policy and the Wheat Economy* (Toronto 1957), 12.

mercial than subsistence farming, focusing on wheat culture, acquiring machinery to accommodate large acreages, and adopting techniques such as summer-fallowing. In their need to acquire cash, make purchases, and sell products, Indian farmers were just as linked to the larger economy as white settlers. Yet the peasant farming policy required Indian farmers to function in isolation from the rest of western Canadian society.

This attitude was unrealistic. Subsistence farming remained at best a questionable model for the arid Canadian plains, and it may even have been impossible.[46] Western farmers were independent neither of the markets, nor of each other. Settlement of the prairies required mutual assistance and co-operation among neighbours and relatives. Working bees, pooled purchasing, and beef rings were characteristic of the pioneer years. Indians were denounced, however, when they undertook such co-operative action. Indian farmers were expected to conform to the nostalgic ideal of the independent, self-sufficient yeoman.

It soon became clear that peasant farming was a dubious model for reserve agriculture. Farm instructors, Indian agents, inspectors, and Indian farmers all protested the system. Despite this advice, Reed rigidly enforced the policy. As commissioner, he kept a vigilant eye on every kettle and lamp ordered, and he maintained close surveillance as deputy superintendent general. Agents were not allowed to spend a "single copper" without the authority of the commissioner.[47] Reed's replacement as commissioner, Amédée Forget, had very limited powers of expenditure; even the most minute expense had to be sanctioned by Reed. Forget could under no circumstances authorize the purchase, hire, or use of machinery. . . .

During haying and harvest time the full weight of the policy was felt. Agents and instructors were to see that the Indian farmers accomplished these tasks without the aid of any machinery. Even when bands had reapers and self-binders purchased before the policy was adopted, the farmers were to use hand implements. Larger farmers were expected to purchase the labour of others rather than revert to the use of machinery, or were to restrict their acreages to what they could handle with hand implements. "The general principle," Reed explained in 1893, "is not to allow them machinery to save them work which they should with hands

---

46. Irene M. Spry, "The Tragedy of the Loss of the Commons in Western Canada," in Ian A. C. Getty and Antoine S. Lussier, eds., *As Long as the Sun Shines and Water Flows: A Reader in Canadian Native Studies* (Vancouver 1983), 221.

47. NA, RG 10, deputy superintendent general letterbooks, vol. 1115, p. 220, Reed to Forget, 12 June 1894.

available on Reserves, do by help of such implements as are alone likely for long enough, to be within their reach."[48]

Department officials in the field protested the peasant farming policy from its inception. They were dismayed by a policy which appeared to rob the Indians of any potential source of revenue. Their main objection was that the use of hand implements involved much loss in yield at harvest time. Harvesting coincided with haying, and both had to be secured with haste. As the Edmonton agent wrote in 1896: "Personally, I do not see how any band of Indians in this district can ever raise sufficient grain or cattle to become self-supporting as long as they have to work with sickles and scythes only, as the seasons are so very short, haying and harvesting coming together. Perhaps in the south where the seasons are longer the system would work successfully, but up here no whiteman attempts to do so."[49]

Agents throughout the Northwest—even those much further south than Edmonton—agreed that the seasons were too short for the use of hand implements. Once ready to cut, it was vital that grain remain standing for as brief a time as possible. The Carlton agent advised that because the climate brooked no delay with regard to securing grain, conditions in the Northwest could not be equated with the early days of farming in the eastern provinces when hand implements were used.[50] If not harvested as quickly as possible, grain could be lost to frost, hail, dry hot winds, or an excess of moisture. Agent Grant, of the Assiniboine reserve, protested that "the seasons in this country are too short to harvest any quantity of grain, without much waste, with only old-fashioned, and hand-implements to do the work with."[51] . . .

Not surprisingly, there had been very little progress made in reserve farming during the 1890s. There was a modest increase in acreage on some reserves, while on others acreage stayed at about the same level or even decreased. . . . The likelihood of agriculture forming the basis of a stable reserve economy faded even further after 1896, as the new administrators of Indian Affairs promoted land surrender and so further limited the agricultural capacity of reserves. Because much Indian land appeared to be "idle," "unused," or "surplus," the hand of those who clamoured for land surrender was strengthened. Indians were living in some cases in the midst of fine farm land that was not cultivated at all, or was worked with

---

48. NA, Hayter Reed Papers, vol. 14, Reed to T. M. Daly, 10 March 1893.
49. NA, RG 10, vol. 3964, file 148,285, Chas. De Cases to Reed, 19 Nov. 1896.
50. Ibid.
51. Ibid., W. S. Grant to Reed, 1 Oct. 1896.

obsolete methods and technology. Indians appeared to cling stubbornly to the past and remain impervious to "progressive" influences. People concluded that Indians lacked industry and were not natural farmers. These observations, reflected in the histories that have been written until very recently, obscure or overlook the Indians' positive response to agriculture in earlier years. Equally obscured and forgotten has been the role of Canadian government policy in restricting and undermining reserve agriculture in a critical period of agricultural development.

AN APPEAL BY THE INDIANS OF VANCOUVER ISLAND

The following letter addressed by the Indians of northeast Vancouver Island to the Indian Department of Canada throws an interesting light upon their attitude toward their myths and customs:

We have been informed by our Indian Agent that the Government is reconsidering the Indian Act, particularly that part known as Section 149 which deals with our old custom of giving away [potlatch]. The Indian Act makes this an offence punishable by imprisonment and we pray you to reconsider this matter. We have been appointed a committee by our people and we think that if you understood our customs from the beginning that you would amend the law to allow us to go on in our old way. In order to let you know how it was carried on and why it was done we are sending you this letter.

We all know that things are changing. In the old days the only things that counted were such things as food, dried fish, roots, berries and things of that nature. A chief in those days would get possession of all these things and would pass them on to those who had not got any and in many instances would call another tribe and help them out too. We wish to continue this custom. In the old days when feasts were given, those who remained at home were remembered and those who attended would carry stuff home for their wives and children. This is all about our feasts and we want to have the same thing today.

In the old days we got fire from the west coast of the Island; we trained a man known as a deer to go to the west coast for this fire; we split up some pitchwood and gave it to him, so that when this was set on fire he could carry it back to us, that's why we like big fires at our feasts. In the old days Indians specialized in some particular branch of work, some were trained to make canoes, some to hunt, some to catch fish, some to dry fish, some to get material to make our clothes, then we divided this up amongst the others. This was the beginning of our feasts of giving away.

At one time there were no rivers for the fish to come in and there was a

"AN APPEAL BY THE INDIANS OF VANCOUVER ISLAND," *JOURNAL OF AMERICAN FOLKLORE*, 36 (1923), 295–97. BY PERMISSION OF THE *JOURNAL OF AMERICAN FOLKLORE*.

man known by the name of "Omath" (the raven). He was the man who knew the place to get water and he borrowed a sea-lions' bladder; then he walked around where he thought would be a good place for the rivers to run and when he found a suitable place he would break the bladder and let some of the water run. This made all the rivers. He did this so that the salmon would go up for the people to use, so that they could get it to dry and have a feast when they went home to their own places; that's why we want to keep up these feasts.

Men came into the world first as animals and birds and were turned into men, and the things that those men did are what we are still doing today. In the old days these animals and birds had dances like the Cedarbark-dance and they acted a part so that all those who were looking on would understand what they were doing. Omath had a dance called the "Towheet," he was dressed in limbs and cedar brush and we still want to keep up this dance. These things happened, so we have been told by our forefathers, before the flood, and after the flood, these animals and birds were changed into men.

A man by the name of "Kwawnalalase" was asked by the Lord what he wanted to do, did he want to be a big tree? He said "No." Did he want to be a rock? He said "No." Did he want to be a mountain? He said "No, a piece of him might break off, fall down and hurt somebody"; then after thinking a long time he said he would like to be a river so that he might be useful to people in after days so he was changed into the Nimkish River and that is the reason we call it Gwalana, and claim it as ours.

After this a man by the name of "Numcokwistolis" was the first man that lived on a hill called "Kwylque," then there was another man named "Kwunoosala," he was the thunder-bird, he took off his feathers and let them blow up into the air again and left him as a man. There was another man named "Kwakwus," he was from a fish. Omath was the chief over all these and he gathered up all these feathers and tied them into bunches and gave them to his people. After that he got skins such as Marten, Mink, Coon and Beaver, and he sewed them up to make blankets and he invited all his people and gave these things to the people that he invited and he distributed these cedar boards, paddles, Indian wedges, and mats after the fur was given away. He also found out that yellow cedarbark was good to make clothes, so he had his people get the yellow cedarbark and beat it with a club to make it soft and made dresses of it. That is why we use the cedarbark today, when we are giving away.

After this a ship came in with some white men on, we didn't know what the white men were, so we called them "Poopaleepzie"; they bought our furs and gave us in exchange blankets and tobacco and many other things and the chief gave them away to the rest of the tribe, and this is the habit we have kept up ever since.

We now come to the part that affects us most in this custom, not only us, but all the other tribes. In those days people that had sons to marry or maybe wanted a wife himself would hear of another man's daughter and would want to marry her, particularly if she was of a chief's family. When the young couple are married the father of the woman would give to his daughter's husband canoes, food, a name and other different things which have a part in our dances, and a *copper*. This is what a man gets when he is married to a woman and that is what has been passed on until today. The bridegroom would give a feast with what he got and would invite everybody from his own tribe or other tribes to partake of what had been given to him, and we wish to continue this custom as it helps out our old people and young people as well. Each one gets his share and can use it for his own purposes, either to get clothing or other things. The coppers that we got in those days were different from those we got from the white men. These coppers were as they were found only beaten out with a hammer and we have a lot of money invested in them. The copper is the main holder of our customs because the value of them is rising, and as they are passed on to others they increase in value. The copper forms a chief strength of a man who intends giving a feast and he sells the copper and what he gets for it he uses to make a feast. All the other things that we have would be quite useless to us if the copper is thrown out of our custom. It is used in marriages in order to get the things to make a feast. If a father would die and leave the copper to his son no other man could get the copper except the son who would hold it until he thought it time to sell it, he will figure out what it will bring. When he is finished figuring he will call all the people together and will dance for them and give what it is worth and afterwards whatever is given away if any of the other chiefs return it to him as it will be of use to him for many years. These coppers are sold for a large sum of money, and no one will force a person who sells it to give it all away, so that he always has considerable left for his own use. When a man buys a copper he pays a deposit on it and the next man may buy from him and pay a deposit on an increased valuation and so on, it may be through the hands of four or five, and still payment not be completed. If our custom is done away with these coppers will be useless, and will entail a big loss, as all those who have an interest in them will lose all they have put in. Each tribe has its own coppers and each copper has its own value. In the old days there was no money and these coppers were a standard of value but increased in value each time they changed hands. When the white man came and we could earn wages in cash for our labor, we invested our savings in coppers and used them the same as a white man would do with a bank and would always expect more back than we put in. We are giving you a list of the coppers belonging to the Nimkish tribe and their values, other tribes have their own coppers so that you will see a great financial loss would be entailed on us if our custom is suppressed.

We do not want to fight the Government nor do we expect the Government to repay us for the price of our coppers but we do ask to be let alone and left free to follow our men and our old ways, and these coppers represent the chief things in our custom. The way things are now we try not to disobey the Government in any of the criminal laws and we hope the Government will allow us to continue in our old customs so far as they do not come in conflict with the Criminal Law. In the old days and in all villages our forefathers followed this custom and we cannot see any bad results from it. If it suits us and does not interfere with or hurt anyone else, why should we be stopped?

We would ask you therefore to take the matters into consideration and remove from the statute books that part of section 149 relating to our giving away and our feasts and festivals.

FURTHER READINGS FOR TOPIC 1

Robin Fisher and Kenneth Coates, eds., *Out of the Background: Readings on Canadian Native History* (Toronto: Copp Clark Pittman, 1988).

Stuart Hughes, ed., *The Frog Lake "Massacre": Personal Perspectives on Ethnic Conflict* (Toronto: McClelland and Stewart, 1976).

Rolf Knight, *Indians At Work: An Informal History of Native Indian Labour in British Columbia 1858–1930* (Vancouver: New Star Books, 1978).

J. R. Miller, *Skyscrapers Hide The Heavens: A History of Indian–White Relations in Canada* (Toronto: University of Toronto Press, 1989).

D. N. Sprague, "Government Lawlessness in the Administration of Manitoba Land Claims, 1870–1887," *Manitoba Law Journal*, 10, 4 (1980).

Donald Swainson, "Canada Annexes the West: Colonial Status Confirmed," in R. Douglas Francis and Donald B. Smith, eds., *Readings in Canadian History: Post-Confederation* (Toronto: Holt, Rinehart and Winston of Canada, 1986), 64–82.

John L. Tobias, "Canada's Subjugation of the Plains Cree, 1879–1885," *Canadian Historical Review*, 64, 4 (December 1983), 519–48.

T O P I C 2

Working-Class
Arts
of
Survival
in
Urban
Central
Canada,
1870–1900

T*he daunting face of modernity was most clearly seen in the rapidly
expanding nineteenth-century city. Here one found evidence of both
liberal capitalism's stunning achievements and its emergent limitations.
Contemporary books and newspapers focused on the achievements: the
streetlights and water services; the schools and universities; the tramcars
and the telegraphs. Yet the city was also a place where liberalism would be
challenged at its foundations. The liberal view that an individual's property
was at his or her disposal clashed with the new collective realities of urban
life. A state that had no business in the boardroom, that levied no income
tax, that provided no health insurance, that possessed only the rudiments of
a strategy of urban planning, confronted cities that had grown without plan
and without limit, structured by the demands of capital. Workers drawn
from the countryside to the urban factories often lived in the overcrowded,
unhealthy slums. The factory chimney belching smoke might be a
shimmering symbol of progress, duly celebrated in representations of
nineteenth-century cities; it was also a menace to the people who lived
nearby.*

    *These three readings trace the ways in which working-class people
responded to the new challenge of the modern city; two of them focus on
Montreal, Canada's "shock city" of the nineteenth century—the city that*

most graphically demonstrated the social consequences of capitalist modernity. Peter DeLottinville demonstrates how many male workers used a remarkable tavern as a combined centre of recreation, temporary lodging, and employment; at the centre of Bettina Bradbury's account are the working-class women of Montreal, turning to their gardens, animals, boarders, and elsewhere for survival in the impersonal city; and John Bullen's essay introduces us to the child labourers of the day. The working men, women, and children were active shapers of their difficult lives in an urban world turned upside down by industrial capitalism.

Joe Beef of Montreal:

Working-Class Culture and the Tavern, 1869–1889

PETER DeLOTTINVILLE

During the late nineteenth century, Joe Beef's Canteen was a notorious part of that underworld which existed in Victorian Montreal.[1] Located in the centre of the waterfront district, the Canteen was the haunt of sailors and longshoremen, unemployed men and petty thieves. Middle-class Montreal saw this tavern as a moral hazard to all who entered and a threat to social peace. Yet if critics called the Canteen's owner, Charles McKiernan, the "wickedest man" of the city, working-class residents along the waterfront claimed McKiernan as their champion. His tavern was a popular drinking spot, but also a source of aid in times of unemployment, sickness, and hunger. For its patrons, Joe Beef's Canteen was a stronghold for working-class values and a culture which protected them from harsh economic times. . . .

Working-class culture covers a wide range of recreational, social, and job-related activities from labour day parades and trade union picnics to charivaris and the secret ceremonies of the Knights of Labor. While each form of culture can only be understood within its specific time and place, there was a common thread which made particular cultures working-class cultures. As Raymond Williams has stated working-class culture embodies "a basic collective idea and the institutions, manners, habits of thought and intentions which proceed. from this."[2] By assuming an "active mutual responsibility"[3] between workingmen, working-class culture offered an alternative to the individualist, competitive philosophy of the nineteenth-century middle class. Nothing was as common as a tavern

PETER DeLOTTINVILLE, "JOE BEEF OF MONTREAL: WORKING-CLASS CULTURE AND THE TAVERN, 1869–1889," *LABOUR/LE TRAVAIL*, 8/9 (1981/82), 9–40. REPRINTED WITH PERMISSION OF THE EDITOR. © COMMITTEE ON CANADIAN LABOUR HISTORY.

1. This underground Montreal is given a muckraker's treatment in *Montreal by Gaslight* (Montreal 1889), which contains a chapter on Joe Beef's Canteen. Charles McKiernan's landlord, F. X. Beaudry, was closely connected with the local prostitution trade, as his obituary (*Montreal Witness*, 25 March 1885) details. On gambling dens, see *Montreal Witness*, 14 September 1876, and *Montreal Star*, 30 October 1889. The *Star*, 23 January 1872, carries an article on a local cockfight.
2. Raymond Williams, *Culture and Society* (London 1960), 327.
3. Ibid., 330.

in nineteenth-century Montreal, and because of this, working-class taverns probably represented one of the most basic forums of public discussion. Drawing their customers from the neighbouring streets, such meeting places were the first to sense a change in mood, or experience the return of economic prosperity. Joe Beef's Canteen, while attracting a wider clientele than most taverns, was essentially the same type of focal point for the dockyard workers. The uncommon aspect of the Canteen was the remarkable ability of Charles McKiernan, the tavern's owner, to transform this rather commonplace forum into a dynamic force for the working class of Montreal. . . .

Charles McKiernan was born on 4 December 1835, into a Catholic family in Cavan County, Ireland. At a young age, he entered the British Army and, after training at the Woolwich gunnery school, was assigned to the 10th Brigade of the Royal Artillery. In the Crimean War, McKiernan's talent for providing food and shelter earned him the nickname of "Joe Beef," which would stay with him for the rest of his life. In 1864, McKiernan's Brigade was sent to Canada to reinforce the British forces at Quebec. By then a sergeant, McKiernan was put in charge of the military canteens at the Quebec barracks and later on St. Helen's Island. If army life had seemed an alternative to his Irish future, then McKiernan saw better opportunities in North America. In 1868, McKiernan bought his discharge from the Army and with his wife and children settled in Montreal, opening the Crown and Sceptre Tavern on St. Claude Street.[4]

By settling in Montreal, McKiernan joined an established Irish community which accounted for 20 per cent of the total population. Centred in Griffintown, the largely working-class Irish had their own churches, national and charitable societies, political leaders, and businessmen.[5] And as a tavern owner, McKiernan entered a popular profession in a city with a liquor licence for every 150 inhabitants.[6] The increasing number of

---

4. *Montreal Star*, 16 January 1889. See also Edgar A. Collard's *Montreal Yesterdays* (Toronto 1962) for a good general assessment of Charles McKiernan, and the Montreal City Archives clipping file-R. 3654.2 "*Rues, Commune, Rue de la*," for general press coverage of McKiernan by Collard and other Montreal historians.

5. Dorothy Suzanne Cross, "The Irish in Montreal, 1867–1896," (M.A. thesis, McGill University, 1969) gives a general account of the Montreal Irish community. For contemporary descriptions, see John Francis Maguire's *The Irish in America* (Montreal 1868), and Nicholas Flood Davin, *The Irishman in Canada* (Toronto 1877).

6. *Montreal by Gaslight*, 10. Other well known taverns were Tommy Boyle's The Horseshoe, which catered to those who followed prize fighting, and the Suburban which had a reputation for giving the poor man a helping hand. Ibid., 94–105.

taverns caused one temperance advocate to lament that if trends contin-ued Montreal was destined to become "the most drunken city on the continent."[7] The Crown and Sceptre, commonly known as "Joe Beef's Canteen," had a central location with Griffintown and the Lachine Canal to the east and the extensive dockyards stretching out on either side. Business was good for Charles McKiernan.

In spite of the large numbers of taverns, Joe Beef's Canteen had an atmosphere, and a reputation, which was unique. Located in the water-front warehouse district and at night identified only by a dim light outside the door, the Canteen housed a fantastic assortment of the exotic and the commonplace. One visitor described it as, "a museum, a saw mill and a gin mill jumbled together by an earthquake; all was in confusion."[8] The barroom was crudely furnished with wooden tables and chairs, sawdust covering the floor to make cleaning easier. At one end of the bar, great piles of bread, cheese, and beef supplied the customers with a simple meal. Behind the bar a large mirror reflected a general assortment of bottles, cigar boxes, and curios. One bottle preserved for public display a bit of beef which lodged—fatally—in the windpipe of an unfortunate diner. The quick-witted McKiernan served his patrons with an easy manner. An imposing figure with a military bearing and fierce temper, the owner had few problems with rowdyism.[9]

Joe Beef's Canteen had a special type of patron, and McKiernan aptly referred to his establishment as the "Great House of Vulgar People." His clientele was mostly working class. Canal labourers, longshoremen, sailors, and ex-army men like McKiernan himself were the mainstays of the business. Along with these waterfront workers, Joe Beef's Canteen attracted the floating population along the Atlantic coast....McKiernan's tavern was also a well-known *rendez-vous* for the "sun-fish" or "wharf-rats" of the harbour who lived a life of casual employment and poverty. Newspaper reporters often dropped into the tavern to check on petty criminals who mingled with the crowd. Unemployed labourers visited the Canteen in the early morning to look for a day's labour and often remained there throughout the day in the hope of something turning up.

---

7. *Montreal Star*, 14 February 1888. Liquor licences, which included hotels, restaurants, saloons and groceries, increased from 723 in 1879 to 1,273 in 1887. Joe Beef's Canteen had a hotel licence.
8. *Montreal Witness*, 4 April 1881.
9. *Toronto Globe*, 14 April 1876; *Halifax Herald*, 28 June 1880; *Montreal Star*, 3 October 1887.

In all it was not a respectable crowd[10] and, no doubt, was shunned by the more self-respecting artisans of the neighbourhood.

For working-class Montreal, the tavern held attractions beyond the simple comforts of food and drink. With no public parks in the immediate area, and only occasional celebrations by national societies and church groups, their daily recreational activities were centred around places like Joe Beef's Canteen. McKiernan's tavern was exceptionally rich in popular recreations. A menagerie of monkeys, parrots, and wild cats of various kinds were from time to time exhibited in the Canteen, but it was McKiernan's bears which brought in the crowds. Joe Beef's first bear, named Jenny and billed as the "sole captive" of the "courageous" 1869 expedition to the North West, never retired sober during the last three years of her life. One of her cubs inherited the family weakness. Tom, who had a daily consumption of twenty pints of beer, was often as "drunk as a coal heaver" by closing. Indeed, Tom was one of the regulars, usually sitting on his hind quarters and taking his pint between his paws, downing it without spilling a drop. Local temperance men had always pointed out that drink turned men into animals, but in observing Tom's habits Joe Beef could point out this curious reversal of behaviour which the Canteen produced.[11] Other bears were kept in the tavern's cellar and viewed by customers through a trap door in the barroom floor. Occasionally, McKiernan brought up the bears to fight with some of his dogs or play a game of billiards with the proprietor.

The tavern was not an ideal place for animals and one observer remarked on the mangy, dirty, and listless character of the bears.[12] Beatings were often used to rouse the animals into their "naturally" ferocious state. Sometimes McKiernan was mauled during these demonstrations and once a buffalo on exhibit sent him to hospital for a number of

---

10. *Montreal Witness*, 4 April 1881. In an account of Joe Beef's encounter with the census taker, the problems of tracing the transient population were made clear. Of all the one-night guests which the Canteen provided for, only ten men were found by the census taker. Two of these, an Irish musician and a Spanish cook, were probably employees of the tavern. Also listed were an English coachmaker, an Irish blacksmith, an American barber, a Scottish commercial agent, an English (Quaker) leather merchant, an Irish accountant, an English labourer, and an Irish tanner. McKiernan's fifteen-year-old son was listed as a rivet maker and was likely serving an apprenticeship. See Public Archives of Canada, (hereafter PAC), RG 31, Census of Canada, 1881, Manuscript, Montreal, West Ward, Division 3, p. 1.

11. *Toronto Globe*, 14 April 1876.

12. *Montreal by Gaslight*, 115.

days.[13] A Deputy Clerk of the Peace, inspecting the tavern to renew its licence, was bitten by one of Joe Beef's dogs.[14]...

Although lacking formal education, Charles McKiernan considered himself a man of learning and regularly read the *New York Journal*, the *Irish American*, the *Irish World*, and local newspapers. He employed a musician (which was illegal under the terms of his licence) to entertain his customers. Regular patrons played the piano in the tavern. McKiernan, however, led much of the entertainment. Drawing on personal experience and varied readings, McKiernan eagerly debated topics of the day, or amused patrons with humorous poems of his own composition. He had a remarkable ability to ramble on for hours in rhyming couplets. Sometimes to achieve this end, he distorted the accepted English pronunciation beyond recognition. This disgusted some middle-class visitors to the Canteen, but regular customers clearly enjoyed these feats of rhetoric.[15] Behind the bar, two skeletons were hung from the wall and served as props for McKiernan's tales. From time to time, the skeletons represented the mortal remains of McKiernan's first wife, his relatives in Ireland, or the last of an unfortunate temperance lecturer who mistakenly strayed into Joe Beef's Canteen one night.

From the occasional poetry which McKiernan printed in the newspapers, the style and subjects of these evenings can be seen. Concentrating on the figures of authority in the workingman's life, the employer, the Recorder, the landlord, or the local minister, McKiernan's humour allowed his patrons a temporary mastery over the forces which dominated their lives outside the Canteen doors. Inside the Canteen, the rights of the common man always triumphed. On local issues, McKiernan complained about the lack of municipal services for the waterfront community. He demanded,

> Fair play for Sammy, Johnny and Pat as
> well as the Beaver Hall Bogus Aristocrat![16]

Legal authority, most familiar to his patrons through the Recorder's

---

13. *Montreal Star*, 10 September 1883; 11 September 1883; 3 October 1883.
14. *Montreal Witness*, 17 March 1881; 22 March 1881.
15. *Montreal Herald*, 21 April 1880; *Montreal Witness*, 6 August 1875. Jon M. Kingsdale, "The Poor Man's Club: Social Functions of the Urban Working Class Saloon," *American Quarterly*, 25 (1973), 472–89, provides an excellent background to the discussion which follows and demonstrates that many of the Canteen's services were common to nineteenth-century taverns.
16. *La Minerve*, 2 August 1873.

Court, was also denounced, but feared. An engraving of the Recorder looked down on the patrons from above the bar, and wedged into the frame were a number of dollar bills and notes which served as a reserve fund. McKiernan used this fund to pay fines imposed upon his regular customers.[17] Since most depended upon day labour, even a short jail term could spell disaster for the labourers' families. Imprisonment in lieu of fines was a very contentious issue, as the vehemence of the following poem illustrates:

> They have taken me from my father,
> They have taken me from my mother,
> They have taken me from my sister,
> They have taken me from my brothers,
> In this wintry season of woe
> And for the sake of *one* paltry, lousy *Dollar*,
> Down to jail, for to die, like a Dog, amongst *Bugs* and *Vermin*,
> I had to go.
> I died amongst howling and laughter,
> I died howling for a drink of water
> But you living *Tyrants*, and *Two Legged Monsters* take warning and
>   remember that cold, cold Saturday Morning!!!
> For man's vengeance is swift, though God's vengeance is with some,
>   rather slow.[18]

McKiernan himself was no stranger to the Recorder's Court. In July 1867, the tavern keeper faced charges from a disgruntled patron who had been roughly thrown into the street for rowdyism. On different occasions, McKiernan's musician and a former servant complained of beatings they had received for drunkenness on the job.[19] Along with the violations of his liquor licence, such incidents illustrated that Joe Beef's legal opinions were grounded in experience.

Another prominent subject in Joe Beef's Canteen was the economic depression which hovered over Montreal for much of the 1870s. As casual labourers, the Canteen's patrons were severely affected by commercial slumps. In "Joe Beef's Advice to Biddy, the Washerwoman," McKiernan wrote,

---

17. *Toronto Globe*, 14 April 1876; *Halifax Herald*, 28 June 1880; *Montreal Star*, 3 October 1887.
18. *La Minerve*, 20 January 1874.
19. *Montreal Star*, 14 July 1876; *Montreal Witness*, 22 October 1873; 12 November 1877.

> I must tell you that Kingston is dead, Quebec is
> Dying and out of Montreal, Ottawa and Toronto hundreds are flying
> In the country parts unless you can
> Parlez-vous, There is nothing for you to do
> And in John's office it is all the cry
> No Union printers for work need apply
> And if the landlord his rent you cannot
> Pay your sewing machine he will take
> Away. So in the fall God help the
> Poor of Montreal.[20]

The unwillingness of the private and public authorities to provide adequate relief systems also attracted Joe Beef's notice. In a parody of the economic theories of industrialists, McKiernan professed,

> Joe Beef of Montreal, the Son of the People,
> He cares not for the Pope, Priest, Parson or King
> William of the Boyne; all Joe wants is the Coin.
> He trusts in God in the summer time to keep him
> from all harm; when he sees the first frost and
> snow poor old Joe trusts to the Almighty Dollar
> and good maple wood to keep his belly warm....[21]

These were problems which his patrons had little difficulty in understanding.

Central to all of McKiernan's pronouncements was the belief that the common problems of casual labourers and the poor of Montreal should overcome the religious and national differences which separated them. Joe Beef did "not give a damn Whether he is an Indian a Nigger a Cripple a Billy or a Mich"[22] when attempting to help the unemployed. What the unemployed and casual labourer lacked, in McKiernan's opinion, was a common voice. Since no one else was likely to assume that role, Joe Beef became the self-appointed champion of the waterfront workers....And despite his Irish background, Joe Beef had considerable appeal to French

---

20. *La Minerve*, 7 November 1873. John was John Dougall of the *Montreal Witness* who had recently dismissed some union employees. Although the Canteen was a male bastion, McKiernan was not unaware of the growing number of women workers in the Montreal labour force. For the employment of women, see Dorothy Suzanne Cross, "The Neglected Majority: The Changing Role of Women in Nineteenth Century Montreal," *Social History*, 12 (1973), 202–3.
21. *Montreal Yesterdays*, 273–4.
22. *La Minerve*, 28 December 1878.

Canadian workers as well, if one can judge popularity from the coverage Joe Beef received in the French language press. . . .

The most visible service which Joe Beef's Canteen offered was a cheap place to stay for transient and single workers. In the Crown and Sceptre, the barroom was situated next to a dining room and sleeping quarters. The sleeping area contained about 40 wooden sofas which served as beds. At eleven o'clock, boarders deposited ten cents at the bar and were handed a blanket. The men then spread a mattress over the wooden sofa, stripped off all their clothes and went to sleep. McKiernan insisted that all his boarders sleep naked as a matter of cleanliness. Those found dirty were ordered upstairs to use one of the wash tubs. Each boarder also had to have his hair cut short, and those failing to meet the standards were sent to Joe Beef's "inspector of health," or barber, to comply. No conversation was permitted after eleven o'clock and everyone was roused out of bed at seven sharp. These rules were enforced personally by McKiernan in his best British Army sergeant's manner. Three-quarters of the tavern's boarders were boys between the ages of 12 and 14 who earned their living selling newspapers. For 20 cents a day, they received their food and lodging and, although the conditions set down by Joe Beef might be draconian, they were clearly preferred to similar facilities offered by church organizations. Indeed, the Crown and Sceptre proved such a popular place that one of the prime reasons for moving to Common Street in 1876 was the lack of space. His waterfront location had room for 200 men.[23]

Fees for room and board were often waived for those without the means to pay such modest sums. McKiernan's tavern was also close to the sources of casual employment which was an important consideration when a day's work might depend on arriving early on the job site. McKiernan often loaned shovels to men engaged in snow shovelling and other jobs. And as the natural resting place for all types of labourers on the docks, Joe Beef's Canteen was an ideal location to learn who might be hiring in the future. In this way, the tavern allowed transient workers to familiarize themselves with the local labour market and to make a decision whether to stay in Montreal or move on.[24]

---

23. *Toronto Globe*, 14 April 1876.
24. The integration of transient labour into urban centres was very important and a failure to do so is described in Sydney L. Harring's "Class Conflict and the Suppression of Tramps in Buffalo, 1892–1894," *Law and Society Review*, 11 (1977), 873–911. See also James M.

Other social services grew informally as local residents turned to McKiernan for assistance in times of trouble. When a Lachine canal labourer was injured during a blasting operation, fellow workers brought him to Joe Beef's to recuperate. After two men got into a drunken brawl and the loser stripped naked in the street, the crowd brought the man to Joe Beef's for care. A young immigrant who collapsed on the docks also ended up in the tavern for convalescence. While Joe Beef's served as a neighbourhood clinic, McKiernan's folk cures left much to be desired. The young immigrant was treated with a vinegar-soaked towel bound tightly around his head. McKiernan also professed faith in cayenne pepper and whiskey to cure cramps and Canadian cholera. All this in 20 minutes.[25] Still, many people in the nineteenth century attributed medicinal powers to alcohol, and McKiernan did state an intention to take courses at the Montreal General Hospital to improve his knowledge of basic medicine.

These experiences led the tavern owner to lobby established medical institutions to improve health care services for waterfront residents. In December 1879, he set up a collection box in his tavern for the Montreal General Hospital and invited his customers to contribute. Donating one-tenth of his receipts from all his dinners and a similar share of his boarding house income, McKiernan hoped to raise $500 a year. In the following years, McKiernan offered $100 to the Montreal General if they would provide a doctor to attend the poor in their homes. The hospital declined the offer. Unsuccessful in [his search for] a more formal improvement of health care services, McKiernan continued to provide emergency relief. When the body of a suicide was buried in August 1883, the tavern keeper provided a tombstone.[26]

The question of class allegiance was most clearly defined by the incidents of labour unrest which periodically disrupted the city. In December 1877, over 1,000 labourers working on the enlargement of the

Pitsula's "The Treatment of Tramps in Late Nineteenth-Century Toronto," *Historical Papers* (1980), 116–32.

25. *Montreal Star*, 5 February 1877; *Witness*, 2 August 1876; *Star*, 3 October 1879.
26. *Star*, 15 January 1878; 29 December 1879; 27 February 1880; 25 March 1880; 1 April 1880. H. E. MacDermot in his *History of the Montreal General Hospital* (Montreal 1950) wrote that Joe Beef's Canteen was "a particularly staunch supporter, and entries of donations from 'Proceeds of iron box, barroom, of Joe Beef' are frequent, or from 'his own skating Rink,' as well as contributions for the care of special patients." (55) MacDermot's work was cited in Edgar Collard's "All Our Yesterdays," *Montreal Gazette*, 9 January 1960. William Fox Beakbane, who drowned at Allan's wharf on 29 July 1883, was buried in the McKiernan family plot in Mount Royal Cemetery (*Star*, 10 August 1883).

Lachine Canal abandoned their picks and shovels after a reduction in wages. The Irish and French workers paraded behind a tricolour flag along the canal banks and drove off those who refused to participate in the strike. Following a riot at the offices of canal contractor William Davis, during which the strike leader was shot, the Prince of Wales Rifles were called out to protect the canal and those workers who continued to work at reduced wages.[27] The strikers demanded a wage increase to a dollar a day, a nine hour day, regular fortnightly payments, and an end to the "truck system" of payment.[28] Among the Montreal citizens, there appeared to be some sympathy with the poor working conditions of the labourers, notably from the *Montreal Witness* and local MP Bernard Devlin,[29] but the militant behaviour of the strikers was generally condemned.

Strongest support for the strikers came from the waterfront community. Practical in all things, McKiernan realized that strikers, like the army, travel on their stomachs. On the morning of 20 December, he sent 300 loaves of bread, 36 gallons of tea, and a similar quantity of soup. These supplies required two wagons to be delivered. In addition to feeding the strikers, McKiernan took in as many as the Canteen could hold. One night 300 people found shelter under his roof. Throughout the strike McKiernan was observed, "carting loaves and making good, rich soup in mammoth boilers, as if he were a commissary-general with the resources of an army at his back."[30] No doubt his military training was put to the test in maintaining order in his kitchen. That background also made the tavern keeper aware of the awkward position of the Prince of Wales Rifles who had been hastily summoned to guard the canal. To ensure that the soldier ate as well as a striker, McKiernan despatched a wagon of bread to the men on duty. The soldiers saw the humour in Joe Beef's assistance and

---

27. *Witness*, 17 December 1877; 19 December 1877. Strike leader Lucien Pacquette spent several days in hospital recovering from his wound. For contractor William Davis, this was not the first time his workers reacted violently to his labour practices. A year earlier someone tried to blow up the contractor's house and severely damaged the building (*Witness*, 20 December 1877).
28. *Witness*, 17 December 1877.
29. Ibid., 19 December 1877; 20 December 1877. Bernard Devlin (1824–80) came to Quebec in 1844 and published the *Freeman's Journal and Commercial Advertiser*. He ran unsuccessfully for the 1867 Parliament against Thomas D'Arcy McGee who accused Devlin of being secretly in support of the Fenians. Devlin served as a Liberal MP for Montreal West from 1875 to 1878. (DCB, X, 250).
30. *Star*, 20 December 1877; *Witness*, 24 December 1877.

gave most of the bread away to the crowd.[31] Some of the tension between striker and soldier was successfully released. . . .

Besides using his Canteen to take care of the strikers' physical needs, McKiernan also used his skills as an orator to attract public attention to the strikers' demands. By 1877, Joe Beef was a figure of some notoriety in Montreal and the local press found that his exploits made good copy. His support of the strike was reported extensively in Montreal and even in one Ottawa newspaper. The strikers' first meeting took place outside Joe Beef's Canteen and the tavern owner was asked to say a few words. Those nightly discussions in the tavern had given McKiernan a remarkable ease with language, and his talent for speaking in rhyming couplets was not wasted. Most of his speech to the crowd was in rhyming form, which so impressed the *Montreal Witness* reporter that he apologized for only reporting the substance of the speech and not its form as well. McKiernan explained his actions in the following terms.

> I have been brought up among you as one of yourselves since I was a boy running about bare-footed. When I heard of the strike on the Lachine Canal, I thought I would try to help you, for I knew that men employed there had much to put up with. So I sent you bread to help you hold out. I could not send you whiskey, because you might get drunk, and commit yourselves. In this way you might have injured your cause, and perhaps made the volunteers fire on you. (Laughter). . .The greatest philanthropists in the world are in Montreal, and the public here will sympathize with you. They will not see you tyrannized over. But if you are riotous, depend upon it, as sure as you are men before me, the law will take it in hand and crush you. I have nothing against the contractors and you will succeed by speaking rightly to them. You will get your $1 a day for nine hours, or perhaps for eight hours (cheers) or perhaps more (loud cheers). But keep orderly; mind your committee.[32]

The speech was received with "deafening" cheers.

These mass meetings organized by the strike committee were an important part of their efforts to secure better working conditions. Since the canal enlargement was a federal project, Alexander Mackenzie's government was anxious to have it completed before the next election. Failure to live up to this previous election promise would cost the Liberals votes in Montreal.[33] By rallying public support for their cause, the strikers hoped that Ottawa would intervene on their behalf and compel the

---

31. *Star*, 19 December 1877.
32. *Witness*, 21 December 1877.
33. Ibid., 22 December 1877.

contractors to make concessions. As the strike continued, the size of the mass meetings grew. In Chaboillez Square 2,000 people assembled to hear McKiernan and other speakers. Joe Beef lectured on the theme of the "Almighty Dollar."

> My friends, I have come here tonight to address you on "the Almighty Dollar." The very door bells of Montreal ring with the "Almighty Dollar." The wooden-headed bobbies nail you, and you have to sleep on the hard floor provided by the City Fathers, and the next morning the fat Recorder tells you: "Give me the 'Almighty Dollar,' or down you go for eight days." The big-bugs all have their eyes on the "Almighty Dollar," from the Bishop down, and if you die in the hospital, they want the almighty dollar to shave you and keep you from the students. No one can blame you for demanding the "Almighty Dollar" a day. The man who promises 90¢ a day and pays only 80¢ is no man at all. The labourer has his rights.[34]

Public support for the strikers did not alter the fact that the labourers were without income, and after eight days on strike, they returned to the canal at the old wages.[35]

The canal labourers, however, refused to admit defeat. In mid-January, a strike committee went to Ottawa with funds raised by McKiernan and others in order to plead their cause before Alexander Mackenzie. They reduced their demands to the single request that the contractors pay them every fortnight in cash.[36] Mackenzie was sympathetic but non-committal. When the committee returned to Montreal, the mass meetings became overtly political and the problems of the canal labourers were attributed to the inaction of the Liberal government.[37] Meanwhile, Mackenzie had ordered an investigation into the Lachine situation which revealed the widespread use of store payments which considerably reduced the real

---

34. Ibid., 21 December 1877.
35. Ibid., 26 December 1877.
36. *Ottawa Citizen*, 18 January 1878. The *Citizen* carried a copy of a strikers' petition to Mackenzie which was signed by 122 people including McKiernan. Most of the signers were untraceable in local business directories, but some local grocers and dry goods merchants did support the strikers' demands and this suggests some degree of neigh-bourhood support. Original petition in PAC, RG11, B1(a), Vol. 473, pp. 2514–20.
37. *Ottawa Citizen*, 24 January 1878. An admitted weakness of this study is the failure to document the political connections which McKiernan had with municipal politicians. Federally, McKiernan was a Conservative and this no doubt played some part in his attack on Mackenzie. During the 1872 election, McKiernan led a group of sailors into a Liberal polling station and began serenading them with a concertina. When surrounded by an angry crowd, McKiernan pulled out a pistol and fired into the air. In the tumult which followed McKiernan and his companions were beaten and had to be rescued by the police. *Montreal Witness*, 28 August 1872.

wages of the labourers. Sensing a political disaster in the making, the government ordered the contractors to end store payments.[38] All contractors complied immediately and the labourers won a modest victory. McKiernan's efforts, while not the only factor in this outcome, did help the strikers publicize their demands and eased their physical hardships. In doing so, he demonstrated the potential strength of a waterfront community united in a common cause.

The canal labourers' strike was McKiernan's most extensive effort in aiding strikers, but not his only involvement. During a strike against the Allen line, ship labourers used the Canteen as a rallying point and the flag they used in their parades came from the tavern. In April 1880, when the Hochelaga cotton mill workers struck, Joe Beef again assumed his role as people's commissary-general by supplying the strikers with bread.[39] Such incidents illustrated how the working-class culture which centred around the tavern could be mobilized to produce benefits for the Canteen's patrons. But in doing so, McKiernan also attracted the criticism of middle-class reformers who felt that such a culture encouraged workers in a dangerous behaviour which threatened the social stability of Montreal.

During the 1870s, middle-class reformers began to enter into the waterfront community to assist the workingman in overcoming his social and economic poverty. The YMCA, the Salvation Army, as well as local employers and clergy, all found themselves confronted by an existing culture and community services centred around Joe Beef's Canteen. Their response to McKiernan's activities illustrated the immense social differences between the middle and working class of Montreal. One visitor to the city described Joe Beef's Canteen as a "den of robbers and wild beasts" over which McKiernan presided, "serving his infernal majesty in loyal style."[40]. . .

The world of Joe Beef, which developed during the 1870s, continued to function throughout the 1880s, but its dynamic qualities appeared to be on the wane. Joe Beef's public profile certainly declined in the 1880s. The

---

38. PAC, RG11, B1(a), Vol. 473, pp. 2514–69. Not all contractors paid their workers in truck, and those who did argued that the workers benefited from the arrangement. Davis argued that monthly pay periods increased productivity. "On Public Works as a Rule, a large number of men lose time after pay day, and, thereby disarrange and retard the progress of the Works." (Davis to Braun, 21 January 1878, p. 2532). John Dougall of the *Montreal Witness*, however, published an account of the supplies given to a labourer instead of cash. For $1.75 owing in wages, the worker received whiskey, sugar, tobacco, cheese and bread valued at $1.05. The goods were on display throughout the strike at Joe Beef's Canteen (*Witness*, 22 January 1878).
39. *Star*, 17 April 1880; *Witness*, 21 April 1880.
40. *Halifax Herald*, 28 June 1880.

eventual disintegration of this culture cannot be attributed to any single factor either within the working-class community or from some of the larger developments of the decade. A combination of factors, including a decasualization of dockwork, the rise of the Knights of Labor, plus new attitudes towards leisure and urban conditions, made the survival of Joe Beef's Canteen beyond the death of its owner unlikely.

As a waterfront tavern, Joe Beef's Canteen depended upon the patronage of the longshoremen who unloaded and loaded the ships in the Montreal harbour. Longshoremen worked irregular hours, sometimes as long as 36 hours at a stretch. Crews were hired by stevedores who contracted with a ship's captain to unload the vessel for a fixed price and provided the necessary equipment. Longshoremen, therefore, spent long periods of time on the docks either working, or contacting stevedores about the prospects for employment. With between 1,700 and 2,500 men competing for work, individuals had to spend much of their time ensuring that they earned the average wage of $200 per season.[41] Given these job conditions, the attraction of a waterfront tavern where one could eat, sleep, drink, and scout around for employment can not be underestimated.

The nature of employment on the docks began to change in the mid-1880s. H. & A. Allen Company, one of the larger shipping firms in the port, introduced a system of contract labour. Over 100 longshoremen signed contracts directly with the shipping company which guaranteed steady employment for the season. The contract specified that each contract employee would have to pay 1 per cent of his wages towards an accident insurance plan, as well as agree to have 10 per cent of his total wages held back until the end of the season. Any man who left before the term of his contract forfeited claim to these wages. With a rate of 25 cents per hour, the pay of the Allen contract employees was slightly better than regular longshoremen, but these relinquished their traditional rights to refuse work which did not suit them.[42] Longshoremen testifying before the 1889 Royal Commission on the Relations of Capital and Labour were certainly critical of the contract system, which most felt gave the company a guaranteed labour supply without contributing greatly to the welfare of the longshoremen.[43] While the contract system accounted for only a fraction of the total labour force on the docks, the Allen Company's

---

41. Royal Commission on the Relations of Capital and Labour, 1889, Quebec Evidence, Vol. 1, pp. 150–86.
42. Ibid., Testimony of R. A. Smith, 156–60; James Urquhart, 173–5.
43. Ibid., Testimony of Patrick Dalton, 183–5.

desire to "decasualize" their labour force was an indication of the future. Such a system made a convenient tavern unnecessary.

It was no coincidence that the Allen Company attempted to introduce the contract system among longshoreman at the same time that labour organizations appeared on the waterfront. Edmund Tart told the Royal Commission that he belonged to a "secret trades organization" which existed on the docks.[44] Possibly a local of the Knights of Labor, the union had its own benefit plan to offset the Allen Company insurance scheme. Patrick Dalton, a longshoreman for the Allen Company, testified against the contract system. Pointing to the organization of the Quebec City longshoremen, Dalton stressed that only the organization of all longshore-men could guarantee higher wages. Dalton concluded by saying that labour unions were not fundamentally concerned with wages, but with bettering "the condition of the men, socially and morally."[45]

The rise of the Knights of Labor in the mid-1880s produced profound changes in the dynamics of working-class development, and the culture surrounding Joe Beef's Canteen was shaken up by their emergence. Along with lawyers, bankers, and capitalists, the Knights of Labor banned tavern owners from their ranks. Testifying before the Royal Commission on the Liquor Traffic, Louis Z. Boudreau, president of the Montreal Trades and Labour Council, reflected this attitude towards drink when he stated that "people we meet in the Trades and Labor Council are not drinking men as a whole. They are a good class of men."[46] As skilled workers accepted the need for temperance, the unskilled waterfront labourers might also re-examine the benefits of tavern life. This did not signal an alliance between organized labour and the temperance advocates who attacked Joe Beef in the 1870s. Spokesmen for organized labour criticized most of these temperance workers for failing to realize that much of the drunkenness among workingmen resulted from economic hardship. . . .

Outside of the working-class neighbourhoods, other forces were emerging which shaped public attitudes towards Joe Beef's Canteen. Throughout the 1880s, Montreal's middle-class residents grew more critical of the police force's inability to enforce the liquor laws. This new mood was captured by the Law and Order League (also known as the Citizens League of Montreal) which was formed in 1886. The League's purpose was to pressure police to enforce the liquor and public morality laws by publicizing open violations. Operating in co-operation with the

---

44. Ibid., Testimony of Edmund Tart, 175–81.
45. Ibid., Testimony of Patrick Dalton, 186.
46. Royal Commission on the Liquor Traffic, 512.

Royal Society for the Prevention of Cruelty to Animals, the League was able to effect a dramatic increase in the number of prosecutions against tavern owners.[47] Under such pressure, the police were less likely to work informally with Joe Beef on matters of public order.

New attitudes towards leisure activities were also coming to the fore during the 1880s. With the growth of the YMCA and the Amateur Athletic Associations, urban youths were encouraged to spend their time in organized sport and develop the socially useful traits of "teamwork, perseverance, honesty and discipline—true muscular Christianity."[48] As one YMCA lecturer told his audience, recreation had to "invigorate the mind and body, and have nothing to do with questionable company, being regulated by Christian standards."[49] While such campaigns were not designed to recruit former members of street gangs, but rather the middle-class youth and clerks from the new industrial factories, these new approaches to recreation did have an impact on general tolerance of the waterfront culture. Prize fighting, probably a favoured sport of Joe Beef's patrons, was publicly denounced as a barbaric and dangerous sport.[50]. . .

There was also a perceptible shift in public attitudes towards poverty and the city slums. With the reformers' concentration on the physical aspects of their city—clean water, paved streets, public parks, and adequate fire protection—urban slums were no longer seen only as places for poor people to live, but as potential threats to public health. . . .

The rough life along the waterfront had its own hazards and on 15 January 1889 Charles McKiernan died of heart failure in his Canteen while only 54 years of age. His death was received with great sadness in many quarters of the city and the funeral attracted large crowds. As the *Gazette* reporter commented, "Every grade in the social scale was represented in those assembled in front of the 'Canteen.' There were well known merchants, wide awake brokers, hard working mechanics and a big contingent of the genus bum, all jostling one another for a glimpse of the

---

47. *Montreal Star*, 28 January 1886. On the Law and Order League, see *Star* 16 August 1887; 24 January 1889; 16 February 1889; 10 March 1887.

48. Alan Metcalfe, "The Evolution of Organized Physical Recreation in Montreal, 1840–1895," *Social History*, 21 (1978), 153. For the role of the YMCA in the new attitude towards leisure activities, see David Macleod, "A Live Vaccine: The YMCA and Male Adolescence in the United States and Canada, 1870–1920." *Social History*, 21 (1978), 5–25. An excellent study of recreation in England is Peter Bailey, *Leisure and Class in Victorian England* (Toronto 1978).

49. *Montreal Star*, 15 November 1873.

50. For denunciations of prize fighting see *Star*, 4 January 1887; 9 May 1887; 20 May 1887; 23 May 1887; 15 September 1887.

coffin containing what remained of one, whatever may have been his faults, who was always the poor man's friend."[51] After a short Anglican service, McKiernan's body was carried out of the tavern and the procession started for Mount Royal Cemetery. Among those in the procession were representatives from 50 labour societies who acknowledged for the last time Joe Beef's support of the trade union movement. . . .

---

51. *Montreal Gazette*, 19 January 1889.

Pigs, Cows, and Boarders:

Non-Wage Forms of Survival among Montreal Families, 1861–91

BETTINA BRADBURY

"Death to the Pigs" was the dramatic subheading of a disappointingly dry newspaper report on Montreal City Council proceedings in September 1874. Three readings of a bill to prohibit the keeping of pigs in the city were collapsed into one session and the bill quickly passed. One councillor objected that it was "hard if a poor man was to be debarred from keeping a pig or two." Most of the aldermen treated the legislation as an occasion to make "facetious. . .remarks on the species of animal that was to be excluded from living in the metropolis of Canada."[1] The more intelligent and reform-minded councillors no doubt believed that pigs were not simply a nuisance, but also a serious menace to public health. For some of Montreal's working-class families, in contrast, a pig represented a source of cash or of food that would be available in times of unemployment and need—a valuable supplement to a low, unsteady, and irregular wage income. The outlawing of pigs represents one of a complex of changes over the length of a generation that severely curtailed the proletariat's access to means of supplementing their wages. This paper begins an examination of some non-wage-based strategies used by Montreal families living in Ste. Anne and St. Jacques wards between 1861 and 1891.

Over these decades the growth of capitalist industry in Montreal transformed the city from a centre of commerce to the "Workshop of Canada."[2] Starting along the banks of the Lachine Canal, then later in the eastern parts of the city, a new breed of capitalist built workshops and factories. Some employed hundreds of workers by the 1870s and drew on large investments of capital to finance complex arrangements of steam- and water-driven machinery. The newly built railways, notably the Grand Trunk, not only drew trade and passengers into the city, but also provided

Bettina Bradbury, "Pigs, Cows, and Boarders: Non-Wage Forms of Survival among Montreal Families, 1861–91," Labour/Le Travail, 14 (1984), 9–46. Reprinted with permission of the editor. © Committee on Canadian Labour History.

1. *Montreal Daily Witness*, 22 September 1874; Montreal City Council Minutes (hereafter Montreal Minutes), 21 September 1874: Montreal City Bylaw #77.
2. *Montreal Post*, 19 June 1882, cited in S. D. Cross, "The Irish in Montreal, 1867–1896," M.A. thesis, McGill, 1969, 239.

jobs for hundreds of carpenters, carriage makers, blacksmiths, and labourers in their workshops and yards. These and other metal-working industries were one of the major sources of employment for both skilled and unskilled male workers. Montreal's other major industries—clothing, shoemaking, and cigar-making—drew on men, women, and children to work at the newer and less-skilled jobs that the reorganization of production and newly-introduced technology had created.[3]

While workers with specific skills were often in short supply, there was no shortage of unskilled labour for the factories, workshops, and construction projects of the industrializing city. Except in the best of boom periods there were always more people seeking work than jobs available. Tenant farmers from rural Ireland poured into the city both before and after the famine of 1847. Some moved on to establish themselves on the farms and in other cities of British North America. Large numbers stayed, forming the bulk of Montreal's early proletariat.[4]

From the 1840s on, whole families as well as non-inheriting sons and daughters had left the over-exploited, under-capitalized farms of rural Quebec seeking work in the cities of New England and Lower Canada. Between 1851 and 1861 more and more chose to migrate into Montreal. By 1865 the city, which had previously been predominantly anglophone, was in number, though not in economic power, predominantly French-Canadian.[5] From the plain of Montreal and surrounding counties they came

---

3. On Montreal's industrial development during this period, see especially Joanne Burgess, "L'Industrie de la chaussure à Montréal, 1840–1870. Le Passage de l'artisanat à la fabrique," *Revue d'Histoire de l'Amérique Française* (hereafter *RHAF*), 31 (September 1977) 187–210; Paul-André Linteau, "Histoire de la Ville de Maisonneuve, 1883–1918," Ph.D. thesis, Université de Montréal, 1975; John McCallum, *Unequal Beginnings. Agriculture and Economic Development in Quebec and Ontario until 1870* (Toronto 1980); Jean-Claude Robert, "Montréal 1821–1871. Aspects de l'Urbanisation," thesis, 3e Cycle, École des Hautes Études en Sciences Sociales, Paris, 1977 (hereafter "Montréal 1821–1871"); Gerald J. J. Tulchinsky, *The River Barons. Montreal Businessmen and the Growth of Industry and Transportation 1837–1853* (Toronto 1977). On Ste. Anne and St. Jacques specifically, see Bettina Bradbury, "The Family Economy and Work in an Industrialising City, Montreal, 1871," *Historical Papers*, 1979 (hereafter "The Family Economy and Work").

4. H. C. Pentland, "The Development of a Capitalistic Labour Market in Canada," *Canadian Journal of Economics and Political Science*, 25 (1959); Kenneth Duncan, "Irish Famine Immigration and the Social Structure of Canada West," in Michiel Horn and Ronald Sabourin, eds., *Studies in Canadian Social History* (Toronto 1974). Donald H. Akenson in "Ontario: Whatever Happened to the Irish?" *Canadian Papers in Rural History*, III, offers a very powerful critique of the established orthodoxy that all Irish Catholics became wage-labourers.

5. Jean-Claude Robert estimates that 83 per cent of the total growth of Montreal between 1852 and 1861 resulted from the increase in the numbers of French-Canadians. "Urbanisation et population. Le Cas de Montréal en 1861," *RHAF*, 35, (March 1982), 527.

seeking the survival that the land and rural life no longer seemed to offer. In the city they clustered in Ste. Marie and St. Jacques in the rows of housing that were rapidly thrown up by speculators with little regard for either city building codes or basic sanitary measures. They penetrated the once Irish-dominated area of Ste. Anne, forming pockets of French on certain streets in Pointe St. Charles and in the northern section of the ward.[6] In-migrants, immigrants, and natural increase boosted the city's population by 280 per cent between 1851 and 1891, from 57,715 to 219,616. The most dramatic increase—56 per cent—occurred between 1851 and 1861. In the next decade the population grew by only 19 per cent, but in the two following decades, the decades of the Great Depression, growth never dropped below 40 per cent.

In the family economy of this expanding proletariat, wages constituted the major source of support—the "powerful organizing principle of family life."[7] Within the city, family economies were shaped and reshaped to fit the realities of survival on wages. Men whose fathers and grandfathers had worked the land or plied their crafts with the help of their families, now departed from home daily to seek work in the factories, workshops, and construction sites of the city. The wage they earned seemed to repay them for their labour alone. Yet all family members needed the incoming wage to survive. When it was insufficient their children, especially their sons, also sought work for wages. In Montreal, married women's contribution to the family economy lay not in their wage labour, which was infrequent, but in the transformation of the wage of others into sustenance and shelter. The family's standard of living varied both with the amount of wages that could be earned and with the ability of the wife to stretch that wage by careful shopping, cooking, and household management.[8]

It is a mistake, however, to conceive of urban survival solely in terms of waged labour and the management of that wage. Largely new to wage dependence, yet only too aware of its implications, working-class families

---

6. Marcel Bellevance and Jean-Daniel Gronoff, "Les structures de l'espace Montréalais à l'époque de la Confédération," *Cahiers de Géographie du Québec*, 24, 63 (December 1980), Figure 2.

7. Louise A. Tilly, "The Family Wage Economy of a French Textile City: Roubaix, 1872–1906," *Journal of Family History*, 4 (Winter 1979) 381.

8. For an early analysis of the extent of married women's wage-labour in Montreal, see Bettina Bradbury, "The Family Economy and Work," 86–90. In these two wards the percentages and total numbers of wives reporting an occupation between 1861 and 1881 were as follows. In 1861 5.6 per cent of St. Jacques wives reported a job. A decade later only 2.4 per cent did, in 1881 3.3 per cent. In Ste. Anne, 2.2 per cent reported jobs in 1861, 2.4 per cent in 1871 and only 1 per cent in 1881.

sought to retain some element of control over their means of subsistence—
the one area of their life that could be kept autonomous to some extent
from "the dictates of their relations with the ruling class in the sphere of
production."[9] Wives, aided at times by their children, sought ways to
supplement wages and to avoid the purchase of foodstuffs and commodities with much-needed cash. In so doing, they not only helped to cushion
the family against life cycle related poverty, illness, and unemployment,
but also ensured for themselves some measure of the importance that
accompanied the contribution of cash or goods to the family economy. In
the early-nineteenth-century city, non-wage forms of survival were
numerous and diverse, allowing workers to complement wages, or slip in
and out of waged labour. Ragpickers, peddlers, prostitutes, and people
who sieved through discarded cinders for lumps of coal were able to
supplement wages. This paper examines other strategies by which families could and did complement waged labour between 1861 and 1881—
strategies that were largely the responsibility of the women at home. For
to understand the family economy of the working class in this period of
early industrial capitalism, it is necessary to go beyond a simple consideration of the sufficiency of wages, to put aside the equation of work with
waged labour and to examine other ways in which survival could be
ensured or enhanced. To do so is to raise further questions about what was
being done within the home and to begin to identify other types of work
done by the women of the working class. Inevitably this leads to a more
careful, if less tidy picture of the role of the family and women in a period
of transition—indeed to a more complex understanding of the nature of
that transition itself.

Animal raising, gardening, domestic production, the taking in of boarders, and doubling up in living spaces with other families, all represented
methods of retaining an element of self-sufficiency—of producing something that could either be used directly for food or exchanged for cash. All
were not equally important, nor are they equally apparent to the
researcher. The focus here is largely on the raising of animals, the sharing
of space, and the taking in of boarders—all practices which can be
ascertained to some extent from people's responses to the census takers.
Data in the manuscript censuses of 1861 and 1871 enable the historian to
begin to analyze the importance of these forms of survival in the years in

---

9. Wally Seccombe, "Domestic Labour and the Working Class Household," in Bonnie Fox,
ed., *Hidden in the Household. Women's Domestic Labour Under Capitalism* (Toronto 1980),
33.

which they were being undermined by the forces of industrial capitalist production, urban growth, and the beginnings of urban reform.[10]

Over this period, with the exception of boarding and doubling up, such ways of complementing wages were largely eroded. City legislation in Montreal began to curb the keeping of animals, specifically of pigs. Denser housing patterns eliminated most gardens except in areas too far from jobs for workers to live. Home production of cloth, clothing, butter, bread, and wool was gradually and unevenly curtailed as more and more items of consumption were produced not within the household but by capitalist enterprises. Over the length of a generation the Montreal proletariat was largely cut off from access to such means of supplementing their incomes. Wage dependence became almost total by the end of the century.[11]

In mid-nineteenth-century Montreal, people and animals intermingled in a way unimaginable today. Carters and their horses transported their wares from railways and docks to the factories, warehouses, and shops of the city. Montreal's street railway system was pulled by horse until 1892.[12] Personal carriages took the wealthy of the city to and from work or to visit their friends. Cows grazed in backyards and on street verges. Pigs scrounged in courtyards and alleys, and poultry could be heard and seen throughout the city. Cattle, swine, goats, and cows continued to roam at large on city streets throughout the 1870s and 1880s despite bylaws making it a municipal offence. The removal of dead animals was a source

---

10. The major sources for this paper are the manuscript schedules of the 1861 and 1871 censuses for the Ste. Anne and St. Jacques wards of Montreal. Information on animal-keeping, home production, and gardening is based on analysis of all families reporting such practices to the enumerator in those years. Unfortunately, the equivalent schedules for 1881 have been destroyed. Information on families taking in boarders and sharing housing, as well as any basic demographic data is based on a 10 per cent random sample of all households in the two wards from 1861, 1871, and 1881. This data base is complemented by information in the published census and contemporary descriptive material—especially municipal records and reports.

11. John Cooper has argued that by "the end of the fifties the Montreal workingman had little recourse but his wages," in "The Social Structure of Montreal in the 1850's," *Canadian Historical Association Annual Report*, 1956, 63. My evidence suggests that some subsistence production continued into the 70s and 80s. In fact, as the city spread and outer working-class suburbs developed, workers there were able to have gardens, and at times keep animals. Bruno Ramirez stresses the importance of gardens for a later generation of workers—the Italian immigrants—who, nearer the turn of the century, chose specifically to live in parts of the city where they would have access to land for gardens. Bruno Ramirez and Michael Del Balzo, *The Italians of Montreal: From Sojourning to Settlement, 1920-21* (Montreal 1980).

12. Jean Claude Marsan, *Montreal in Evolution* (Don Mills 1981), 183.

of constant concern both to municipal health authorities and residents quite naturally upset by rotting carcasses in their neighbourhoods. In 1883 the police reported removing nearly 1,000 dead animals from the city streets.[13] In a year of peak effort, health authorities and the police combined removed nearly 4,500 carcasses.[14]

Gradually, from the 1850s on, the presence of both live and dead animals began to offend those who sought a cleaner, more sanitary, and orderly city. Bylaws were passed prohibiting the grazing of animals and the driving of stock through certain streets, enforcing the licensing of dogs and eventually outlawing pigs and controlling cows within the city limits. The slaughtering of animals was controlled, and butchers were forced to slaughter in two abbatoirs sanctioned by civic authorities, rather than in their own backyard abbatoirs.[15]

The control of animals—an early element in the imposition of order— represented a major step forward, a progressive move in the eyes of sanitary reformers. There is no doubt that many of the measures helped to make the city a cleaner and safer place to live. Yet at the same time, such legislation struck at the traditional practices and survival strategies of urban families. The impact was harder among the families of the working class and especially the poorer fractions of that class. Their need to supplement unsteady wages was greater, and it was their specific prac- tices that came under attack. It was the "poor man's pig," rather than cows, which were more likely to be kept by the bourgeoisie, that were first outlawed.

Before examining the legislation that curtailed the keeping of animals, it is important to ascertain just which families kept what kind of animals prior to their control. As no animals were illegal in Montreal before 1864, the census returns for 1861 give some idea of their distribution among different families and throughout the city. Unfortunately the census acts as a snapshot as far as property is concerned, relating "solely...to the amount...held at the time for [sic] taking the census."[16] It gives, therefore, little idea of whether families had animals at other times of the year, having sold or eaten them at census time. This is particularly problematic as the 1861 census was taken in January, in the depths of winter, while in

---

13. *Annual Report* of the Chief of Police, 1883. *Montreal Annual Reports*, 1883 (hereafter *MAR*).

14. Ibid., and Annual Report Upon the Sanitary State of Montreal, *MAR*, 1887, 11.

15. Mayor's Inaugural Address, 1885, 6, *MAR*.

16. "Manual Containing Instructions to Officers," Canada, *Sessional Papers*, no. 64, 1871, (hereafter "Instructions to Officers").

subsequent years enumeration took place in the spring. Families may well have slaughtered food animals like pigs, perhaps even sold a cow, to avoid the high fodder and shelter costs of the winter months. The figures for 1861 should, therefore, be viewed as minimal, an underestimate of the extent of animal raising as an urban practice.

In that year there were nearly 3,000 horses in the city of Montreal, 2,160 milk cows, 2,644 pigs, and an indeterminable number of poultry of various kinds (see Table 1). Had these animals been evenly spread among the city's families, this would have represented an average of one animal for every second family. In the previous decade the number of pigs, milk cows, and horses had all increased by approximately 40 per cent, a rate that was only slightly lower than the city's population growth. Legislation

TABLE 1
Animals in Montreal, 1861–1891

		Work Animals		
	Colts & Fillies	Horses over 3 years	Working Oxen	As % of total
1851	n/a	2077	—	37
1861	—	2892		37
1871	72	3458	34	52
1881	67	4412	26	66
1891	118	6633	39	80[1]

				Food Animals					
Milk Cows	Other Horned Animals	Sheep	Pigs	Hens & Chickens	Turkeys	Geese	Ducks	Other Fowl
1528	—	131	1877	—	—	—	—	—
2160	—	91	2644	—	n/a	—	—	—
1837	178	414	831	—	n/a	—	—	—
1658	95	350	180	—	n/a	—	—	—
1290	78	170	92	8353	74	58	179	925

Source: Censuses of Canada, 1851–1891.
Note: In 1851 and 1861 the published tallies were very carelessly counted. The figures here should be viewed as a rough indication of total numbers.
[1]Excluding fowl of all kinds.

in subsequent decades, to which I shall return shortly, would dramatically change this growth pattern. Because pigs, cows, and sheep were food-producing animals and thus a fairly obvious direct alternative to purchases, the following discussion is limited to families holding them. Horses, which were more important as work animals or as part of a person's trade, are ignored, although they too could clearly at times be used to supplement wages.

Animals were not evenly spread throughout the city, nor among all classes and groups. The proportion of families who kept them varied widely across the city depending on the economic base of the area, the size of lots, the availability of free land, and on the class and ethnic structure of the neighbourhood. In the two wards studied in detail, 12 per cent of St. Jacques families and 16 per cent of those of Ste. Anne kept one or more animals other than horses or poultry. In the smaller census subdistricts of these wards the percentage holding such animals varied from as low as 5 to as high as 20 per cent.

Historians have paid little attention to the importance of animals in the family economy of urban residents.[17] When considered, the keeping of stock has been treated either as a survival of rural practice, or as the resort of those in direst poverty. Harvey Graff, for instance, describes stock keeping as "one strategy with which to confront urbanism and poverty" by "adapting older customs to new places."[18] In Montreal, and I suspect elsewhere, such explanations simplify reality. A substantial minority of both bourgeois and working-class families kept stock. There were, however, differences in the kinds of animals they kept and in the role these animals played in the family economy.

In Ste. Anne and St. Jacques two groups of people predominated among the keepers of pigs and cows, the most commonly held stock. Proprietors and professionals were most likely to keep all kinds of animals with about 21 per cent of them doing so in January 1861. Semi- and unskilled workers were next, with approximately 17 per cent of them raising stock in Ste. Anne ward in 1861 and 12 per cent in St. Jacques. Such families were the least likely to be able to afford the costs of keeping animals over the winter. It is possible that had the census been taken at another time of

17. Exceptions include, most importantly, Richard L. Bushman, "Family Security in the Transition from Farm to City, 1750–1850," *Journal of Family History*, 6, (Fall 1981) 238–56; and for an earlier period, Carl Bridenbaugh, *Cities in the Wilderness: The First Century of Urban Life in America, 1625–1742* (New York 1964); and Carl Bridenbaugh, *Cities in Revolt: Urban Life in America, 1743–1776* (London 1971).

18. Richard L. Bushman, "Family Security," 247; Harvey Graff, *The Literacy Myth: Literacy and Social Structure in the Nineteenth Century City* (New York 1979), 94.

year, the proportions of semi- and unskilled families keeping pigs especially may well have been higher.

Pigs and cows clearly offered families different benefits. Small entrepreneurs, especially grocers and traders, kept cows. They were less likely to raise a pig. A few grocers used their cows to produce their own butter and possibly milk for customers. Hotel and innkeepers raised both cows and pigs, using them for their clients. Some bakers kept cows to produce the milk they used in bread and biscuit making.

For families of all classes a cow represented a valuable investment, especially when there were young children in need of a steady, reliable, clean supply of milk. Whereas a pig only produced food or cash once slaughtered, a healthy cow could produce a steady supply of milk for over a year after calving. Many of the families keeping cows had young children. Indeed, a Dr. Grenier, who wrote an informative pamphlet of advice to mothers on how to curtail Montreal's appalling infant mortality rate, recommended using milk—always from the same cow or goat—if breastfeeding or finding a wet nurse were impossible.[19] No families in these wards reported keeping goats in 1861, only three did so a decade later, once pigs were largely illegal. Cows were clearly the preferred milk source. Among the poorer professionals and the working class, the wife or mother would have been in charge of caring for the cows. For the more wealthy, milking the cows was servants' work. "Wanted, a thorough servant," advertised one family living on St. Laurent Street in 1873, "one who can milk a cow; no washing."[20]

Their usefulness made cows the preferred choice of all families. However, access to the capital to purchase a cow and to the greater space necessary to raise one meant that a much greater proportion of proprietors' families than of the working class could afford to own one. Thus, while 16 per cent of the professional and proprietors' families of Ste. Anne owned one or more cows in 1861, only 9 per cent of the semi- and unskilled did. The relative proportions were similar in St. Jacques. That pigs and other stock were used to counteract poverty by the semi- and unskilled is suggested by the fact that the families of skilled workers, who usually could be sure of a higher, if not always a more steady, wage were less likely to keep animals. Twelve and 17 per cent of Ste. Anne and St. Jacques semi- and unskilled families respectively kept some stock, compared to only 9 and 7 per cent of the skilled. Nearly half the pigs, indeed

---

19. Georges Grenier, *Quelques considérations sur les causes de la mortalité des enfants contenant des conseils aux mères sur les soins à donner aux enfants* (Montreal 1871).

20. *Montreal Daily Witness*, 26 March 1873.

half the stock in these two parts of the city, were kept in families headed by the semi- and unskilled, although they constituted only one third of the family heads.[21] For these families, poultry, pigs, and when they could afford it, a cow, represented not a piece of property, but rather a source of food or cash. Pigs cost virtually nothing to raise and were cheaper to purchase than a cow. Pork formed an important component of both French-Canadian and Irish cooking and diet. Pigs might be bought live at market as a piglet or perhaps obtained from relatives in the country. They might also be stolen fairly easily. In the mid-1870s, after pigs had been outlawed in the city, farmers were constantly reporting having their sheep stolen when they stopped for refreshment on the way to market.[22] While roving, pigs scavenged in the courtyards and roadsides—doing cleaning up that firms contracted by the city seldom did efficiently. Once fattened they could be slaughtered and salted to provide meat for several months—or sold to nearby butchers for cash. A pig could sell for as much as $12 to $15 in 1874 at a time when a labourer earned $1 to $1.50 a day and women involved in waged labour earned as little as $2.00 a week. Chickens too probably scrounged, and a few good laying hens could save a family the cost of 24¢ a dozen, or the equivalent of two-thirds of a woman's daily wages in the clothing industry. When hens were first counted by the census takers in 1891, there were over 8,000 of them in the city limits. They were concentrated in Ste. Marie, the poorest of the city's working-class wards.[23]

It thus made good economic sense for the wives of labourers and other unskilled workers to raise whatever fowl or animals they could afford in the backyards, courtyards, and alleys around their homes. And raise them they did, especially among the Irish families of Ste. Anne until new laws and lack of space made it extremely difficult. In 1861 one-quarter of the city's pigs, compared to 14.5 per cent of the population, were to be found in that one ward. There, housing and factories were mixed together. Empty spaces between factories, workshops, and houses, larger corner sections, and as yet scarcely populated areas in the western part of the ward offered extra space for both animals and gardens. St. Jacques, in

---

21. Such families held 46 per cent of all reported stock, excluding horses.
22. *Le Courrier de Montréal*, 16 December 1874.
23. Retail prices are taken from *Le Courrier de Montréal*, 11 November 1874, and Hamelin and Roby, *Histoire Économique du Québec*, Appendix 20; wages are from Canada, Parliament, House of Commons, Select Committee on the Manufacturing Interests of the Dominion, *Report*, Journals, 1874, Appendix 3 (hereafter "Select Committee on the Manufacturing Interests"), 1874.

contrast, was emerging as the most densely populated area of the city. In 1861, 3,854 families were housed in 1,915 households. Around 6 per cent of these families and 12 per cent of the households held animals, compared to 13 and 16 per cent respectively in Ste. Anne. In St. Jacques one-quarter of the cows and pigs were held by small producers—milkmen and butchers who raised their animals and sold their wares in the city. This practice was much less common in Ste. Anne.[24] In both wards the keeping of animals was more common in the least populated areas furthest from the centre of the city—in the western sections of Ste. Anne, and the eastern parts of St. Jacques.

Animal keeping was not limited, however, to families with plenty of space. Even on fairly densely populated streets one finds families living in rear houses and row houses all keeping pigs and cows. A walk along George or Catherine Street in Ste. Anne ward was likely to involve skirting pigs or cows and their droppings. In one small block of the latter street, between Wellington and Ottawa Streets, over twenty families, more than half of them headed by labourers, kept up to nine pigs each. One resident, Elizabeth Martin, the 50-year-old wife of a labourer, reported herself to the census taker as a housewife. Her household duties included mothering four children, housekeeping in their one-storey, frame house and taking care of seven pigs and four cows. A twenty-year-old daughter worked as a servant, and a fifteen-year-old boy as a labourer. Elizabeth kept more animals than most labourers' wives. Most kept no more than three pigs; a minority had a cow as well.[25]

People raised their animals in whatever space they had available. Those with a horse and a stable no doubt used that for other animals as well. Carters who no longer possessed a horse may have sheltered other animals in the remaining stables. Some clearly kept animals inside their houses as it was considered necessary to outlaw this practice in 1875. In the winter months this was the only warm place. A visiting traveller in 1877 remarked with some amusement in his diary that while driving around Montreal in mid-winter he had seen "Two dead pigs trying to climb up the wall of a cottage, frozen of course."[26] . . .

In the city as in the country, raising fowl or animals was the work of

---

24. Canada, *Census*, 1861, Table XVI. *Census*, 1871, Table 1.
25. Mss. Census, Ste. Anne, 1861, fo. 2076.
26. PAC, Henry St. Vincent Ames, "Diary of Travels in North America," MG24 H61, December 1877.

women and children.[27] Children took their animals to graze on the banks of the canal or railway embankment in summer. Some were kept well under control, but stray and lost animals were a constant problem and were often reported in the papers.[28] One particularly sad story was reported of a two-year-old boy in the Pointe St. Charles area who had been attacked by a neighbour's large gander. It knocked him down, pulled at his clothes and "so frightened him that he fell into convulsions, and after lingering a few days in an unconscious condition, died of fright."[29]

Irish and French-Canadian families in Montreal were continuing a practice that derived not simply from a farming background, but from a long tradition of having to supplement low wages. The Irish were over-represented among the keepers of pigs. In Ste. Anne in 1861 they constituted about 50 per cent of the family heads, but nearly 70 per cent of the pig keepers. Among labourers' families, 12 per cent of the Irish kept pigs compared to 7 per cent of French-Canadians. Cultural traditions and class position combined to identify pigs with the Irish. Pig and poultry keeping was much more than a cultural survival, a quaint rural or Irish custom. Although the Irish predominated as keepers of pigs, French-Canadian rural labourers were also used to supplementing waged labour with poultry and pigs, and they continued to do so in urban areas.[30]

Until the late 1860s, the presence of such animals within the city was apparently tolerated by the authorities and the population at large. But, as the city's population increased, as open spaces were filled up between the houses, and as the divisions between workers, the middle classes, and the capitalists became clearer, an assault on animals began.

This attack on the roaming, raising, and slaughtering of animals in the city appears to have coincided with the creation of the Montreal Sanitary Association. In September 1868 they sent a statement to City Council forcibly expressing their opinion that "the keeping of pigs in dense and populated cities is offensive and prejudicial to public health."[31] The Health and Market Committees agreed entirely and suggested that pigs be

---

27. On women's role as chicken and pig keepers in rural areas of Quebec, see Charles Henri Gauldrée-Boileau, "Paysan de Saint-Irenée de Charlevoix en 1861 et 1862," in Pierre Savard, ed., *Paysans et Ouvriers Québécois d'autrefois* (Quebec 1968); on Ireland see Lynn H. Lees, *Exiles of Erin*, 107; and for a later period, Conrad M. Arensberg and Solon T. Kimball, *Family and Community in Ireland* (Cambridge, MA. 1948), 49.

28. *Montreal Post*, 13 May 1886, cited in Suzanne Cross, "The Irish in Montreal," 213.

29. *Montreal Daily Witness*, 3 June 1873.

30. Charles-Henri Philippe Gauldrée-Boileau, "Paysan de Saint Irenée...en 1861 et 1862," 31–2.

31. Minutes, 9 October 1868, 2.

outlawed except in certain limits on the outskirts of the city. In December, the bylaw incorporating this motion was passed and pigs became illegal in all but the western parts of Ste. Anne, the area north of Ste. Catherine St. and in Ste. Marie in the east.[32] More laws followed. In March 1870 a new bylaw stated that "No horse, cattle, swine, hog, sheep, or goat shall be permitted to run at large at any time in the city, or graze, browse, or feed upon any of the streets, squares, lanes, alleys, or public places of this city."

To recover an animal impounded for breaking this law, owners had to pay 10¢ for a sheep, 25¢ for a "gelding, mare, ox or cow," 50¢ for a hog or swine, and $1.00 for "each stallion, bull, boar or ram." Pigs were clearly perceived as a worse evil than much larger animals like horses and cows. In March 1874 they became illegal in all areas of the city. A year later the driving of "any live stock or horned cattle" except on specified streets leading to the markets was outlawed, although "milk cows and their calves" were excepted. Finally, in September 1876, it became illegal to keep any "horse, cow, calf, pig, sheep, goat or fowl in a house or tenement."[33] Outside, all but pigs apparently remained acceptable.

Resistance to the initial bylaw against pigs, while not dramatic, certainly occurred and from two rather different quarters. The first to complain were "certain persons" in Ste. Anne ward—the area where one-quarter of the city's pigs were kept. They requested that the limits within which pigs could be kept be extended and that the time at which the bylaw should take effect be deferred. Deferral would at least have given them time to raise their pigs to a suitable size for slaughtering. The matter was referred back to the Health and Market Committees where it seems to have remained.[34]

The second group of petitioners, the pork butchers of the city, were more successful. In June, the *Montreal Daily Witness* reported that "a great many butchers belonging to the markets in the city" had been brought up before the Recorder for keeping pigs. He deferred any decision for a week, during which time council proposed amending the bylaw so it would not apply to pork butchers or interfere with their trade. Attempts by some councillors at least to regulate the slaughtering of pigs by these butchers so as not to cause a "nuisance in the neighbourhood where the

---

32. Montreal Minutes, 15 December 1868; Montreal City Bylaws #44.
33. Montreal City Bylaws, #43, #77, #223, #105.
34. Montreal Minutes, 25 May 1869, 239.

work is done and subject" them to sanitary regulation failed. The bylaw appears to have been temporarily amended to exclude the butchers.[35] . . .

Between 1861 and 1871, as a result of the bylaw, the number of pigs reported to census takers decreased by over two-thirds (see Table 1). This decrease occurred despite the fact that the former census was taken in mid-winter when many families probably slaughtered their animals. The 1871 census, in contrast, was taken in April, just when pigs might well have been purchased to raise over the summer. Yet, by 1871 not a pig remained in the old part of the city, although people there still kept horses and cows. In St. Louis only 40 pigs remained; in St. Laurent ward a meagre twelve. In St. Jacques, where 160 families had kept nearly 500 pigs in 1861, only five families continued to keep them—or at least to report them to the census taker. One carpenter and his wife kept three pigs along with his horse, three sheep, and three cows. From the latter, the wife produced 411 pounds of butter, sufficient to feed her husband and three young children and to sell some for cash.[36] Such families were exceptions. Most of those able to afford the greater outlay appear to have shifted from keeping pigs to cows, as the number of cows doubled in the 1861–71 decade. Still others raised cattle instead, and sold them to local butchers. In one small area of St. Jacques ward, local carters, grocers, shoemakers, and blacksmiths all reported killing a beef cow during 1870–71. This was an area with at least three butchers running small abbatoirs. These butchers, each working with one assistant, reported slaughtering nearly 3,000 animals between them over the previous year. Included among these must surely have been the 30 or so cattle, pigs, and sheep that locals reported having "killed or sold for slaughter or export." If their contribution to the butcher's income was minor, the cash from slaughtered cattle would, nevertheless, have provided a significant portion of a family's annual income.[37] In Ste. Anne's ward as in the eastern city, pig raising was pushed into the few outer areas where it was still allowed by the 1868 bylaw. There the number of families reporting any pigs dropped from 256 to 70.

Keeping pigs on the city outskirts, raising cattle for local butchers, even keeping cows, all gradually came under fire as unfit practices within a modern, sanitary, industrial-capitalist city. "Have we a City Government?" one irate citizen complained in a letter to the editor in 1868. He described sidewalks "littered every here and there with the droppings of

---

35. *Montreal Daily Witness*, 10 June 1869, 2 July 1869; Montreal Minutes, 15 June 1869, 2 July 1869.
36. Mss. Census, St. Jacques, 1871, Subdistrict 5, 23, line 14.
37. Mss. Census, St. Jacques, 1871, Subdistrict 9, Schedules 1 and 6.

cows, through which Ladies have to pick their way." Any street with grass borders, he pointed out, was especially liable to the nuisance. "Are the streets paid for by the citizens for their own use, or for the use of cows?" he wanted to know. Cows wandered into people's gardens and plots eating vegetables and flowers. The police, he concluded, should impound every roaming cow.[38] In 1881 the *Post* reported that goats were becoming a nuisance. Herds of goats were reported to range around the city. People complained that it was impossible to cultivate a garden without goats devouring all they grew.[39] Unfortunately goats were never counted by the census takers, an omission that is difficult to understand. Certainly goats would have been cheaper to raise than cows and their milk was equally good, if not better for some children. Yet neither goat meat nor goat milk appear to have been a traditional component of the diet of the French-Canadians or the Irish. In the eyes of city councillors goats were not a menace. It was the pigs, the animals of the working class, not the cows or goats that were the first to go.

As more and more housing was built in the area south of the Lachine Canal and to the north of the Grand Trunk Railway yards, some local "proprietors and residents" petitioned council to prevent the keeping of pigs in that neighbourhood too. This was a poor area, where many day labourers and widows lived, keeping cows, pigs, and probably poultry. The Health Committee responded by going even further. They suggested it was time that pigs be prohibited throughout the city. Some initial opposition from city councillors stalled the passage of the bylaw built on this recommendation. By March 1874, however, it was ready for consideration and passed, as we have seen, with only one alderman, the representative for Ste. Anne ward, opposing it on the grounds that it was hard "if a poor man was to be debarred from keeping a pig or two." He succeeded only in having the maximum fine for the offence reduced from the proposed $40 to $20.[40] From then on no person could legally "rear, keep or feed a pig within the limits of the City of Montreal."[41]

Prosecutions again were not vigorous or dramatic. Over the next eight years, only 50 people were found guilty of keeping pigs. Yet the law was apparently successful. The 1881 census reported that only 180 pigs

---

38. *Montreal Daily Witness*, 16 September 1868.
39. *Post*, 13 August 1881.
40. Montreal Minutes, 26 May 1873; Minutes of the Board of Health, 30 May 1873; Montreal Minutes, 2 July 1873; *Montreal Daily Witness*, 22 September 1874; Montreal Minutes, 21 September 1874.
41. Montreal City Bylaw #77.

remained in the city. A decade later the number had halved. Many of these were probably within the walls of the convents and other institutions where self-sufficiency and domestic production continued to exist apparently beyond the reach of the law.

Between 1861 and 1881 the numbers and types of animals kept within the city had changed dramatically. Whereas in 1861 pigs, sheep, and cows, all sources of food, had comprised nearly two-thirds of the animals kept, by 1881 they represented under a third, by 1891 only a fifth. The number of cows decreased slowly and steadily, the number of pigs dramatically to the 92 reported in 1891. Overall, the number of animals apart from pets and poultry decreased and the proportion of work animals to food animals was completely reversed (see Table 1). Within a generation, food production for use within the home and production for sale within the city was severely curtailed. These two decades saw a complex web of regulations erected curtailing the raising, slaughtering, and sale of animals by unlicensed, uninspected, and ordinary citizens.

At a general level the city's role as importer of foodstuffs increased. The division between rural and urban rigidified. Food producers—farmers, milkmen, and butchers—moved to the outer city limits, to other parishes, or joined the proletariat. By the end of the 1880s, the Health Department was euphorically reporting that the number of milkmen resident in the city had diminished and that an increasing number had taken up residence in distant parishes of the island of Montreal. There was, they argued, a "double advantage of economy and healthfulness." By the 1880s the common practice was for milk to be sent into the city every morning to milkmen, who then distributed it to the different families comprising their customers.[42] No longer then did independent milk producers raise their cows and sell the milk in the city. Now one family raised the cows outside the city and the urban milkman had become an intermediary.

Equally important, that proportion of the city's poorer families who had been able to rely on pigs as a source of food or cash had lost one important alternative to paying out cash for their food needs. By 1871 only 4 to 5 per cent of the families in Ste. Anne and St. Jacques ward had any animals apart from horses or fowl, compared to at least 13 per cent in Ste. Anne a decade earlier and 6 per cent in St. Jacques. Furthermore, especially in St. Jacques, the raising of animals had become a bourgeois and petty-bourgeois privilege, with 12 per cent of proprietors' and professionals'

---

42. Report Upon the Sanitary State, *MAR*, 26.

families compared to only 3.5 per cent of the unskilled keeping them. Pigs, which had been kept by 7 per cent of semi- and unskilled families had been effectively eliminated. There the decrease in the number of food animals and their concentration in the hands of the more wealthy were particularly noticeable. For the workers, dependence on waged labour would increase. Women who had once kept a pig, chicken, or cow, and thus helped provide for the family's food, would now have to seek new strategies....

[Gardening, which was cheaper than raising animals, was also resorted to by many working-class families, although incomplete and unclear census returns make its prevalence difficult to determine. Large gardens were concentrated in the hands of the wealthy who were able to afford the land required for them. While some working-class families may well have kept very small patches of gardens and produced some vegetables, the shortness of the growing season, and lack of space and time, meant that most had little alternative to purchasing vegetables and fruits out of the wages of the family's workers. Although some women supplemented wages by making things in the home, either for their families or for sale, home production for use and exchange in Montreal was neither wide-spread nor a major component of a family's support in 1871.]

The taking in of boarders has received more attention from historians than other non-wage aspects of the family economy. Like stock keeping, boarding has been predominantly viewed as a working-class strategy to ward off poverty. John Benson has argued that such strategies can be viewed as aspects of part-time "penny capitalism."[43] Writing at the turn of the century, Margaret Byington described the taking in of lodgers as a deliberate business venture on the part of the family to increase inadequate income from men's earnings.[44] John Modell and Tamara Hareven also describe boarders as one strategy used by American families to solve the problem of the imbalance between income and expenditure.[45] Michael Anderson argues more carefully that in Preston, Lancashire, the poorer

---

43. John Benson, *The Penny-Capitalists: A Study of Nineteenth Century Working Class Entrepreneurial Activity* (Dublin 1983).
44. Margaret Byington, *Homestead; Households of a Mill Town* (Pittsburgh 1974, reprint of 1910 edition), cited in Joan M. Jensen, "Cloth, Butter and Boarders," 20.
45. John Modell and Tamara Hareven, "Urbanization and the Malleable Household: An Examination of Boarding and Lodging in American Families," *Journal of Marriage and the Family* (August 1973), 476.

occupational groups "may have been rather more likely to take in lodgers."[46] Research that explicitly compares working-class with other families is now beginning to support his caution. Between the 1850s and 1880s, in American and Canadian cities, the taking in of boarders does not appear to have predominated among the semi- and unskilled, or the poorest fraction of the population. In Philadelphia in 1880 Michael Haines found that poorer families did not take in boarders in large numbers.[47] Similarly, in Hamilton, Ontario, Michael Katz and Ian Davey report that between 1851 and 1861, boarders did not live most often with those in need of extra income.[48] In Montreal too, while families of all classes did take in boarders, they were more common in the larger homes of those owning their own enterprises, professionals, and skilled workers, rather than among the poorer workers. The semi- and unskilled were more likely to double up, sharing living space with other whole families, than to take in boarders. The following sections examine boarding and the sharing of space as strategies used by different fractions of classes.

A woman taking in several boarders could bring as much cash into the home as she could working for wages. In 1888, women working as bookbinders, or in clothing or shoemaking factories, could expect a wage of between $1.50 and $5.00 a week. Those working at home on clothing or shoes put out by manufacturers made less.[49] Earlier that decade working-class men paid $3.00 to $4.00 a week for board.[50] Taking in one or two boarders then, offered a woman a source of income comparable to a wage, a valuable source of cash that was probably paid directly to her. It could be used to complement her husband's irregular or low wages. However, boarders also entailed expenditures. They had at least to have a bed, linen, and blankets. Most probably expected a separate room. And they had to be fed well enough to keep them in the household. A boarder thus

---

46. Michael Anderson, *Family Structure in Nineteenth Century Lancashire* (Cambridge 1972), 46.

47. Michael Haines, "Poverty, Economic Stress and the Family in a Late Nineteenth Century American City. Whites in Philadelphia, 1880," in Theodore Hershberg, ed., *Philadelphia. Work, Space, Family and Group Experience in the Nineteenth Century* (New York 1981), 244.

48. Michael B. Katz and Ian E. Davey, "Youth and Early Industrialization in a Canadian City," in John Demos and Sarane Spence Books, eds., *Turning Points. Historical and Sociological Essays on the Family* (Supplement to the *American Journal of Sociology*, Vol. 84) S91.

49. Royal Commission on the Relations of Capital and Labour (hereafter RCRLC), Evidence of Henry Morton, Bookbinder, 247; Z. Lapierre, Shoe-manufacturer, 437; Hollis Shorely, Clothing Manufacturer, 285.

50. Canada, *Sessional Papers* 1882, No. 14, Appendix 3, "Annual Report of the Montreal Immigration Agent."

represented not only extra work for the woman of the house, but also extra expenditures and space—resources that were lacking in the poorest families. Thus, it is not surprising that it was among the petty-bourgeois and professional families of Ste. Anne and St. Jacques wards that boarders predominated.[51]

In 1861 over one-quarter of all families in these two wards shared their residences with people who were neither apprentices, servants, or kinfolk. By 1871 and 1881 the proportion had dropped to 14 per cent. This decrease reflects two major factors. Firstly, there was a shortage of housing in Montreal in 1861. The city had increased its population by 75 per cent over the previous decade compared to 18 per cent in the following one. Housing construction had not kept up. The sheer magnitude of population growth placed pressure on housing.[52] So too did the periodic fires that swept through parts of town in the 1850s destroying hundreds of houses at a time. Housing starts could hardly compensate for the lost dwellings, let alone provide for the in-migrants as well.[53]

The particular demographic characteristics of the city's population development also help explain why more families had boarders in 1861 than in later years. In that year only 41 per cent of females and 40 per cent of men aged fifteen to 40 were married, compared to 46 and 48 per cent a decade later.[54] More single people thus needed housing, and they constituted the bulk of boarders.

To discern the class differences in patterns of family augmentation, the figures for the two wards can be examined combined as there was no

---

51. Boarding, subletting, and the doubling up of families to save rent were all common in Montreal. Distinguishing between them on the Canadian Census returns is something of a problem. Boarders in the figures that follow are unmarried individuals or couples whom census takers enumerated as part of a census family. "A family, as understood for the purpose of the Census, may consist of one person living alone, or any number of persons living together under one roof and having their food provided together." Boarders, then, as the last-listed people in each family, probably ate their meals with the family. Relatives were not included as boarders. "Instructions to Officers," Canada *Sessional Papers*, 1871, no. 64, 128. The Canadian Census, like the U.S. one prior to 1880, does not have to identify the relationship of people in the household. I have estimated people's relationships based on the rules set out in Miller (1972). The identification of relatives was verified by crosschecks in the city's parish registers which are especially complete for the Catholic population.

52. W. J. Patterson, *Report of the Trade and Commerce of the City of Montreal for 1863* (Montreal 1864), 4.

53. John C. Weaver and Peter DeLottinville, "The Conflagration and the City: Disaster and Progress in British North America during the Nineteenth Century," *Histoire Sociale/Social History*, 26 (1980), 418.

54. Canada Census, 1861–81.

significant difference between patterns in the two. In 1861, 40 per cent of professionals' and proprietors' wives took in boarders, 34 per cent of skilled workers' wives did, while only 22 per cent of the semi- and unskilled did. Over the next two decades important shifts occurred in the nature of family augmentation. The percentages of families of all groups keeping boarders dropped dramatically. The greatest decrease occurred among professionals and proprietors, who rapidly divested themselves of extra non-family members other than servants, so that by 1881 only 18 per cent reported having boarders. Among the skilled and unskilled the percentage of families having boarders had dropped in half by 1881. Despite the overall decrease, the taking in of boarders continued to predominate in non-working-class families. Before examining the more common working-class strategy—house-sharing—some other characteristics of families taking in boarders and of the boarders themselves need to be explored.

Boarders do not emerge as an alternative to other survival strategies. Almost half the families keeping pigs and cows also took in boarders. While families were generally more likely to take in boarders when there were no children old enough to work, the strategies were not mutually exclusive. Boarders were only slightly less common among families with one or two children at work than among those with none at work. Indeed families with three children at work were as likely to have boarders as those with none. Nor did cultural and ethnic background make much difference to whether boarders were taken in or not. The English appear to have been somewhat less likely to rent out rooms than others after 1861, perhaps as they became wealthier. Groups that represented a minority in their neighbourhood appear to have been more likely to take in boarders than others. This was especially true among the French-Canadian families living in Ste. Anne in 1861, when they were just beginning to move into this largely Irish enclave. That year, 38 per cent of French-Canadian families took in one or more boarders, compared to only 19 per cent of the Irish. In St. Jacques, in contrast, the Irish were slightly more likely to have boarders than French-Canadians. After 1861 major ethnic differences became minimal in both wards. Here we see, I suspect, the important role that boarding could play for migrants new to the city. In 1861, 41 per cent of boarders were born outside Quebec, largely in Ireland. By the 1880s, 80 per cent were native-born. The Quebec countryside, rather than Ireland, Scotland, or England, became the major source of both immigrants and boarders.

Families taking in boarders almost always took people of similar origins and culture. In Ste. Anne ward in 1861, 97 per cent of French-Canadian families with boarders had French-Canadian ones; 92 per cent of the Irish had Irish boarders. Only the Scots were less likely to have Scots than people of other origins. The workplace too was probably a place of recruitment. One-quarter of Ste. Anne families with boarders in 1861 took in people with the same occupations as the household head, although there is no way of knowing whether they actually worked together.

Tamara Hareven and John Modell have argued that the "logic of the life cycle" dominated the "economic squeeze" in explaining the phenomenon of lodgers. Michael Katz, in contrast, found that in Hamilton "the presence of boarders and relatives appears to have been largely accidental."[55] In these two Montreal wards a pattern is observable, if not dramatic. In 1861, when housing was in such short supply, nearly one-third of all households had boarders throughout the life cycle, except for those without children. In 1871 and 1881 a more specific pattern is evident. Around 16 per cent of young married couples took in boarders. Once a baby arrived, however, mothers appear to have avoided the additional work that boarders represented. As children grew older, but were not yet old enough to work for wages, around 15 per cent again took in boarders. This was the critical stage of the family life cycle, when the ratio between consumers and earners was at its most disadvantageous. Thus we find the proportion rising until some children were old enough to work. The pattern diverges in 1871 and 1881. In 1871, a good year when more jobs were available than in either 1861 or 1881, the proportion taking boarders dropped steadily once children reached work age, increasing only after they had all left home. In 1881, in contrast, as children began to leave home, they were replaced by boarders in up to 15 per cent of the households of these wards. Only in that year does the Montreal pattern appear to fit the "social equalization" model suggested by Modell and Hareven, in which economically, if not psychologically, boarders were substituted for departed children in the later stages of the family life cycle.[56]

When a family decided to take in boarders they sought them in a variety of ways. The wealthy advertised in the newspapers of the day. "Furnished Rooms to Let, for Single Gentlemen, in Private Family," read one of fourteen similar advertisements in the *Montreal Daily Witness* of 26 March 1873. "Interested gentlemen" were requested to apply at 28 Union Avenue. More often, and especially among the working class, word of

---

55. John Modell and Tamara Hareven, "Urbanization and the Malleable Household," 476; Michael B. Katz, *The People of Hamilton*, 244.
56. John Modell and Tamara Hareven, "Urbanization and the Malleable Household," 476.

mouth must have constituted the main source of information both for those seeking space and those seeking boarders. Newcomers to the city sought out people from their home counties and villages, whether they came from Ireland or Quebec. If they did not have a space, they would always know someone who did.

The boarders themselves shared certain characteristics, apart from their common origin with the family with whom they lived. The first of these is crucial in understanding why the presence of additional non-family members was not predominant among the poorest families. Less than half the apparent "boarders" reported having jobs at the time the census was taken. Perhaps these household members who were neither kin nor apprentices may not have paid board either. Hence their concentration in the homes of the wealthier.[57] In addition, boarders were overwhelmingly young. Most were between the ages of fifteen and 29. In Ste. Anne in 1861 more were male than female; in St. Jacques the reverse was true. This reflects the different employment opportunities for each sex in each ward. Over the next two decades, women dramatically outnumbered men as boarders. By 1881 three-quarters of the boarders of St. Jacques were women. Young girls hoping to find work or newly-arrived in the city, came to constitute the typical boarder. Seamstresses were always the most likely boarders. They constituted 16 per cent of working boarders in the first two decades. By 1881, they made up nearly 30 per cent of all those listing a job. Some lived in families where they probably helped wives and daughters sewing at home. The other boarders listed a wide variety of occupations. Clerks and construction workers were important in the early period, but less so later.

Boarding, as Michael Katz, John Modell, and Tamara Hareven have pointed out, was a temporary period in a young person's life.[58] It also appears to have often been a very temporary arrangement for the family taking in a boarder. It is impossible to tell how long people remained in any one household. Clearly the ability of the boarder to pay, the compatibility of boarder and family, even the adequacy of the food and lodging, were all important factors. A few glimpses of the potential conflicts that

---

57. Compare this with Sheva Medjuck's research on Moncton, New Brunswick, where virtually all boarders had a job. Moncton's economy offered a majority of male jobs. In 1851 and 1861 boarders there were over 80 per cent male. Sheva Medjuck, "The Importance of Boarding for the Structure of the Household in the Nineteenth Century: Moncton, New Brunswick and Hamilton, Canada West," *Histoire Sociale/Social History*, 25 (1980), 210–11.

58. Michael Katz, *The People of Hamilton*, 264; John Modell and Tamara Hareven, "Urbanization and the Malleable Household," 474.

could arise can be gleaned from the evidence of a court case, which quite coincidentally offered glimpses of boarder–housewife relations. A Madam Gagnon of Montreal reported subletting a room in her house to a Belgian man and his wife, newly arrived in town. The wife appears to have worked as a prostitute. During her residence she convinced her landlady that she was not only vulgar, but also not trustworthy enough to be believed, even under oath. That particular arrangement lasted only two months. Madam Gagnon's next boarders were more acceptable. She took in a Madam Belserre whose husband had "done nothing the last six months after breaking both legs." Whether she was paid or not is unclear, but at the time of her testimony these boarders had remained with her for seven months.[59]

"Doubling up," subletting rooms to other families, or renting one or two rooms from landlords who had divided up their dwellings all helped reduce one of a family's major and most fixed of costs—the rent. Qualitative evidence of this practice is widespread. Dr. Decrow, a Montreal physician who treated infections and contagious diseases among workers' families, testified in 1888 that "about two" families generally occupied a day labourer's house. These houses had only three or four rooms, so that whole families slept in a single bedroom, sharing cooking facilities.[60] "Doubling up" was, he believed, "getting to be the rule with the poorer classes of people" who would rent a "large house for sanitary reasons,... well knowing at the time they took the house that they would have to relet the rest of it" as a result of "the poverty of the family."[61] Five years earlier Montreal's *Daily Star Reporter* had highlighted the overcrowding of families in parts of St. Laurent and St. Jacques wards. In the buildings the reporter visited, families were limited to one room each. In the most depressing case he described, two families, a total of fourteen people, shared a single room.[62] Yet another seeker out of poverty and squalid living conditions, the anonymous author of *Montreal by Gaslight*, found similar conditions shortly after the Royal Commission of 1888. He described a four-storey stone building in Ste. Anne ward near the market. It had once been a hotel, but had been transformed into a "low lodging house":

[W]ithin its four walls and upon its four stories lived at one time no less

---

59. *Montreal Daily Witness*, 28 March 1873.
60. RCRLC, 606.
61. Ibid., 609.
62. *Montreal Daily Star*, 24 December 1883.

than twenty-eight families. In the direst of poverty, in abject want, without air, with no appliances for health and decency, in dirt and filth appalling, over one hundred and ten human beings herded like rats in a pit, barely existing from day to day.[63]

Less sensational evidence of crowding and doubling up is available throughout the reports of the Sanitary Inspectors and in scattered complaints from city officials, especially assessors, about their not being informed about "how many families are under one roof," or of subtenanting arrangements.[64]

Such evidence suggests that the sharing of housing took two distinct forms. Some families rented a house, or in a few cases bought one, then sublet space to one or two other families. In other cases landlords, eager to squeeze as much profit as possible out of their properties, subdivided buildings themselves. It was in the latter situation that one seems to find families confined to a single room.

Determining just how widespread or common either of these practices were is difficult. Ideally, the census enumerators' distinctions between family and household should enable us to discover just how many families were doubled up within a single dwelling unit. Mark Choko, in his study of housing in Montreal, concluded that the numbers of lodgings or households enumerated did closely reflect the number of dwelling units and that the discrepancies observable from 1861 to 1881 therefore indicate a fairly important increase in house-sharing.[65] Initially I made a similar assumption.[66] A closer examination of those families that appeared to be sharing housing, however, suggests that the census enumerators were not always very careful in their distinctions. In attempting to match census returns with both city directories and evaluation rolls, it became clear that some houses that were apparently "shared" by families were actually separate tenements, whose residents were independently assessed by the city for water rates and occasionally even given a separate address in the city directory. Without a full scale and highly detailed study tracing the size and layout of every house, it is impossible to determine exactly which families, or what percentage apparently sharing housing on census day, were actually doing so. Nor is it possible to tell what proportion sublet part of their own dwelling as a survival strategy, and what proportion was

63. Anon., *Montreal By Gaslight* (Montreal 1889), 17.
64. See, for instance, *RCRLC*, Evidence of John W. Grose, Chairman of the Board of Assessors of the City of Montreal, 266; Evidence of Pierre Hubert Morin, Assessor, 552.
65. Marc H. Choko, *Crises du Logement à Montréal (1860–1939)* (Montréal 1980), 16.
66. Bettina Bradbury, "The Family Economy and Work," 92–5.

forced to crowd together in substandard living condition as a result of a landlord's subdivision of space.

The number of families in each "house" does, however, offer some indication of the extent of crowding, if not of the actual sharing of space. A separate house was "to be counted whenever the entrance from the outside is separate, and there is not direct and constant communication in the inside to make it 'one.'"[67]...Between 1871 and 1881, the only years when the categories are strictly comparable, workers' families were more likely to live in what were defined as shared houses than were professionals and proprietors. By 1881 perhaps as many as 40 per cent of semi- and unskilled families, compared to 32 per cent of skilled and 25 per cent of professionals' and proprietors' families were apparently sharing premises with other families. A small percentage shared space and took in boarders.

While the percentage of families sharing housing is probably inflated by the census enumerators' fuzzy distinctions, the pattern is clear enough. Household structure was closely related not only to class position, but also to the family life cycle in a more obvious way than was true of taking in boarders. Couples were most likely to share housing when newly married, or after the birth of one child. As children grew older, and as family size increased, they were more likely to live alone, despite their increased need for extra income. House-sharing was not used to compensate for the life cycle squeeze. The strain of sharing cramped quarters appears to have become intolerable for all but the most needy. It was at this stage that families were more likely to take in boarders who could provide some income without extreme overcrowding. As children left home, women were again likely to share their living space, or to live in small, crowded quarters with both relatives and strangers.

Perhaps we should not be surprised to learn that it was the overcrowding of houses, largely a result of "doubling up," that came under attack during this period, rather than the taking in of one or two boarders. By the mid-1870s health inspectors, ever watchful for contagious diseases, especially smallpox, were attempting to keep a record of the number of rooms and the number of people in them in every house. They were empowered to evict citizens from overcrowded houses. In practice, examination was limited to the working class. "In the case of the poorer classes of tenements," inspectors were specifically warned to "be careful to note the number of inmates occupying each room and to observe whether there is

67. "Instructions to Officers," Canada *Sessional Papers*, no. 64, 1871, 133.

danger of overcrowding."[68] Once again we see reforms touching on those very strategies used by the poorer members of the working class to avoid total dependence on wages.

Actually, evictions for overcrowding were not frequent. The health department had insufficient money to pay a large staff. In a typical year, 1886, only three overcrowded tenements were reported by the Sanitary Police, and the "necessary number of occupants compelled to search for other lodgings."[69] Important however, was the threat of eviction and the power of the local state, through its Sanitary Police, to enter the houses and rooms of the poor to ascertain whether they were living in a suitable manner. The same municipal government that had outlawed pigs and controlled the sale of vegetables, could now move into yet another arena within which the poor could supplement wages—their homes.

"Children aren't pigs you know, for they can't pay the rent," went an old Irish ballad.[70] From the 1870s on, working-class families of all origins increased their dependence on waged labour as pig-raising, gardening, and the production of food and goods at home was curtailed. Children of working age became a source of economic security, the major complement to a parent's inadequate and irregular wage. Children could and did pay the rent. Until they were old enough to do so, those with low and irregular wages faced a period of poverty, which some counteracted by clustering together to spread costs. Even this practice, while not outlawed, came under surveillance as inspectors on the lookout for cases of smallpox and other contagious diseases were empowered to evict excessive numbers from houses.

Keeping animals and gardens was part of the tradition of rural wage-earning families from Ireland and Quebec. Yet it was also an urban tradition. The women who raised pigs and cows in Montreal were not blindly following such traditions. Stock-raising represented a rational and important way of supplementing unsteady wages. Pork formed a major component of the diet of both the Irish and the French-Canadians. Families ceased to keep animals when the law or lack of space prevented them from doing so.

City regulations, surveillance, and urban growth had a very different impact on families in different class positions. The pigs, the working-class animal, were outlawed in this period, not the cow. The inner city areas,

---

68. *Report Upon the Sanitary State of Montreal*, 1881, 7; 1886, 8.
69. *Report Upon the Sanitary State*, 1886, 29.
70. Cited in Lynn H. Lees, *Exiles of Erin*, 22.

where jobs for workers were accessible, became more and more crowded, eliminating garden and animal space. The wealthy, in contrast, could afford homes with sufficient space for gardens, where if they wished, they could raise both vegetables and cows. They also had the space in their homes to take in boarders, if they needed or wanted to do so. Thus extra residents were more prevalent in the families of professional, proprietors, and even skilled workers, while "doubling up" was most common among the semi- and unskilled. While all people were potential victims of smallpox and other infectious diseases, it was the homes of the "poorer classes" that were entered and examined.

As new laws and restructured urban spaces curtailed access to subsistence, the ways in which married working-class women could contribute to the family's survival were narrowed down and altered. Where once she could make or save some money raising animals, making butter, selling eggs or vegetables, now her contribution lay in sharing her living and cooking space with other individuals and families, taking in boarders, or going out to work occasionally for wages herself.

HIDDEN WORKERS:

Child Labour and the Family Economy in Late Nineteenth-Century Urban Ontario

JOHN BULLEN

The secret of a successful farm, wrote Canniff Haight in 1885, lay in "the economy, industry and moderate wants of every member of the household."[1] Haight was simply repeating the conventional wisdom of the age in his recognition that all members of a farm family, including children, contributed to the successful functioning of the household economy. Haight and many of his contemporaries, however, would not have applied the same description to families in urban-industrial centres. The movement of the focus of production from farm to factory, many social analysts believed, decreased the interdependency of the family and offered individual members a greater number of occupational choices.[2] According to this interpretation, a typical urban family relied solely on the wages of a working father and the home management of a mother for its day-to-day survival. This notion of the difference between rural and urban families survived into the twentieth century and surfaced in a number of standard historical works. As late as 1972, for example, Blair Neatby wrote: "The urban family...bears little resemblance to a rural family. On a family farm children can make a direct economic contribution by doing chores and

---

JOHN BULLEN, "CHILD LABOUR AND THE FAMILY ECONOMY IN LATE NINETEENTH-CENTURY URBAN ONTARIO," *LABOUR/LE TRAVAIL*, 18 (1986), 163–87. REPRINTED WITH PERMISSION OF THE EDITOR. © COMMITTEE ON CANADIAN LABOUR HISTORY.

1. Canniff Haight, *Life in Canada Fifty Years Ago* (Toronto 1885). Cited in Michael S. Cross, ed., *The Workingman in the Nineteenth Century* (Toronto 1974), 34.
2. Late-nineteenth-century writers commonly saw their society in transition from a rural-agricultural setting to an urban-industrial one. This simple dichotomy facilitated discussion of new social developments and emphasized the threat to tradition posed by emergent urban-industrial life. Modern historians, taking into account the growth of capitalism and waged labour, have offered a more complex and sophisticated analysis of social change. Michael Katz, Michael Doucet, and Mark Stern, for example, construct a three-stage paradigm which claims that "North America shifted from a peculiar variety of mercantile-peasant economy to an economy dominated by commercial capitalism to one dominated by industrial capitalism." *The Social Organization of Industrial Capitalism* (Cambridge, MA 1982), 364. Despite these more complex undercurrents of social transition, most late-nineteenth-century workers identified with the rural–urban praxis. Historians develop comprehensive theories of social change over time; workers deal with the realities of life from day to day. This paper focuses on the second set of concerns.

helping in many of the farm activities. . . . In the city only the wage-earner brings in money; children. . .become a financial burden who add nothing to the family income."[3] Like many myths of modern civilization, these perceptions of the urban family rested primarily on outward appearances and vague unfounded suppositions.

In the past fifteen years, social historians have uncovered patterns of urban survival which indicate that many working-class families, like their counterparts on the farm, depended on "the economy, industry and moderate wants of every member of the household," including children, to meet the demands of city life. Several well known primary and secondary sources describe in graphic detail the onerous trials of young-sters as wage-earners in the manufacturing and commercial establish-ments of large industrial centres such as Montreal, Toronto, and Hamil-ton.[4] But child labour was by no means limited to factories and shops. Children also performed important economic duties in their homes and on city streets as a regular part of their contribution to the family economy. This article concentrates on youngsters between the ages of seven and fourteen who worked outside of the industrial and commercial main-stream of late nineteenth-century urban Ontario, usually for no wages, but who still contributed in important ways to the day-to-day survival of their families. . . .

Urbanization, like its companion, industrialization, marches to its own

---

3. Blair Neatby, *The Politics of Chaos: Canada in the Thirties* (Toronto 1972), 45. E. P. Thompson writes: "Each stage in industrial differentiation and specialisation struck also at the family economy, disturbing customary relations between man and wife, parents and children, and differentiating more sharply between 'work' and 'life.'. . .Meanwhile the family was roughly torn apart each morning by the factory bell. . . ." *The Making of the English Working Class* (New York 1963), 416.

4. See for example *Report of the Commissioners Appointed to Enquire into the Working of Mills and Factories of the Dominion, and the Labor Employed Therein*, Sessional Papers, 9, XV, no. 42, 1882: *Report of the Royal Commission on the Relations of Capital and Labor in Canada* (Ottawa 1889), (hereafter *Royal Labor Commission*); *Annual Reports* of the Quebec Department of Labour; and *Annual Reports* of the Inspectors of Factories for the Province of Ontario. Among secondary sources, see Terry Copp, *The Anatomy of Poverty: The Condition of the Working Class in Montreal 1897–1929* (Toronto 1974); Bettina Bradbury. "The Family Economy and Work in an Industrializing City: Montreal in the 1870s," *Canadian Historical Association Historical Papers* (1979); Fernand Harvey, "Children of the Industrial Revolution in Quebec," in J. Dufresne, et al., eds., *The Professions: Their Growth or Decline?* (Montreal 1979), reprinted in R. Douglas Francis and Donald B. Smith, eds., *Readings in Canadian History: Post-Confederation* (Toronto 1982); Gregory S. Kealey, *Hogtown: Working Class Toronto at the Turn of the Century* (Toronto 1974), also reprinted in Francis and Smith; Eugene Forsey. *Trade Unions in Canada 1812–1902* (Toronto 1982); Michael J. Piva, *The Condition of the Working Class in Toronto—1900–1921* (Ottawa 1979); and Bryan D. Palmer, *A Culture in Conflict: Skilled Workers and Industrial Capitalism in Hamilton, Ontario, 1860–1914* (Montreal 1979).

rhythm; it does not unfold in carefully planned and even measures. In the latter decades of the nineteenth century, Canada's urban population increased at roughly three times the rate of the general population, a pattern that struck stalwarts of agricultural society with worry and despair.[5] *The Globe* acknowledged the trend in 1894, but conceded: "The complaint about the continual movement of population from country to city is a good deal like a protest against the law of gravitation."[6] Urbanization could take several forms. Many sons and daughters of Ontario farmers, victims of land exhaustion and exclusionary inheritance customs, recognized the diminishing promise of rural life and fled to the cities in search of work and spouses with whom to begin their own families. In other instances, immigrant families, mostly from the cities and countryside of Great Britain and continental Europe, settled in Canadian cities in the hope of escaping poverty and oppression. In the latter case, fathers and older sons often emigrated first and sent for remaining family members once employment and residence had been established.

All newcomers to the city discovered an environment and value system starkly different from rural society. While there is no question that life on the farm rarely resembled the bucolic paradise portrayed by romantic novelists, the city's emphasis on materialism, competition, standardization, and consumption constituted virtual culture shock for many recent arrivals. Skilled and unskilled workers alike adjusted their lives to the vagaries of the factory system, the business cycle, and the seasons, in an attempt to eke out a living above the poverty line. All workers lived in fear of unemployment, which struck especially hard in winter when outdoor work was scarce and the higher costs of food and fuel could wipe out a family's modest savings. Poor families huddled together in crowded and ramshackle rental units that lacked adequate water and sanitation facilities. For some demoralized labourers, the local tavern or pool hall provided the only escape from a working life of long hours, dangerous conditions, and abysmally low wages. In the face of these oppressive conditions, workers instinctively turned to the one institution that had served their ancestors so well for generations—their families. Although old rural traditions did not survive the trip to the city completely unscarred, workers still found their most reliable and effective support

---

5. In 1851, Ontario's rural population stood at 818,541 and its urban population at 133,463. By 1901, at 1,246,969, the rural population was still greater, but the urban population had increased dramatically to 935,978. Source: Canada, Bureau of the Census, *Report on Population*, 1, (1901). In Toronto alone the population increased from 30,775 in 1851 to 144,023 by 1891. Gregory S. Kealey. *Toronto Workers Respond to Industrial Capitalism 1867–1892* (Toronto 1980), 99.

6. *The Globe*, 1 April 1894.

system under their own roofs. Within this scheme, children played a critical role.

In most working-class homes, children assumed domestic responsibilities before they reached the age of eight.[7] Their first duties usually took the form of assisting in the daily upkeep of the home. At any hour of the day, youngsters could be found sweeping steps, washing windows, and scrubbing floors. In neighbourhoods where dirt roads, animals, wood stoves, coal furnaces, and industrial pollution were common features, keeping a home even relatively clean and liveable could require several hands and many hours of labour. In the absence of fathers whose work kept them away from home ten to fifteen hours per day, six days a week, busy mothers frequently called upon children to make minor repairs to poorly constructed houses.

Other common children's chores contributed in a more direct sense to the day-to-day survival and economic status of the family. Youngsters routinely gathered coal and wood for fuel from rail and factory yards, and fetched water from community wells for cooking and washing. To supplement the family's food supply, children cultivated gardens, and raised and slaughtered animals. What home-produced food the family did not consume itself, children could sell to neighbours or at the market for a small profit. In an age when sickness could spell disaster for a family, youngsters provided care for ill family members and sometimes offered themselves as substitute workers. It was also common for older children to assume the duties of a deceased parent, girls frequently taking up mother's responsibilities and boys stepping into father's shoes. On occasion, parents lent their children's services to neighbours in return for nominal remuneration or future favours. Although youngsters who worked in and around their homes did not normally encounter the dangers associated with industrial life, in at least one case a young Ottawa lad who was gathering wood chips outside of a lumber mill succumbed to his youthful curiosity and wandered into the plant only to meet his death on an unguarded mechanical saw.[8] . . .

[Reaching beyond the perimeters of the home, many working-class children participated in street trades. About 700 youngsters polished

---

7. Most of the following examples are drawn from Toronto Board of Education Records, Archives and Museum (hereafter TBERAM), W. C. Wilkinson Diaries, six vols., 1872–74; TBERAM, Management Committee Minutes, 1899–1901; Hamilton Children's Aid Society, Scrapbook of Clippings, vol. 1, 1894–1961, Hamilton Public Library, Special Collections; Susan E. Houston, "The Impetus to Reform"; and Alison Prentice and Susan Houston, eds., *Family, School and Society in Nineteenth Century Canada* (Toronto 1975).
8. Testimony of John Henderson, manager for J. McLaren & Company Lumber Merchants, Ottawa, *Royal Labor Commission*, Ontario evidence, 1137–9.

shoes, sold pencils, fruit or other small wares, or performed on the streets of Toronto in 1887. The most prominent of these workers in urban Ontario were the newsboys.]

Newsboys were serious businessmen, not simply charity cases trying to scrape together a few pennies like the other waifs and strays common to city streets. Some of these lads lived on their own in cheap boarding houses or at the Newsboys' Lodging and Industrial Home in Toronto, or its Catholic counterpart, the St. Nicholas Home. These privately-run institutions attempted to provide independent newsboys with decent accommodation and moral and industrial training. At the Newsboys' Lodging and Industrial Home, 10¢ per day bought supper, bed, and breakfast, while $1.30 per week fetched full room and board. Many free-spirited boys, however, bristled at the home's regular curfew of 7:00 PM, and extended curfew of 9:00 PM two nights a week, and sought its services only during the most desperate of the winter months. The majority of newsboys lived with their parents and pounded the streets daily as part of their contribution to the family economy. A small percentage of boys delivered door to door, but the greater number worked late into the evenings selling on the street. Some lads worked alone, while more experienced boys headed up teams of sellers. A common trick of a newsboy was to approach a customer with a single paper claiming that it was the last one he had to sell before heading home. If the unwary citizen fell for the con, the newsboy then returned to his hidden pile of papers and repeated the trick. Newsboys stationed themselves near the entrance of hotels, where they undersold the stands inside, and always stood out prominently, along with other young street traders, around the train station.[9] A passive visitor to Toronto, unable to resist the persistent overtures of the newsboys, bootblacks, and fruit vendors, would at least leave Union Station well informed, well polished, and well fed.

In some instances, the earnings of a newsboy shielded a poor family from utter destitution. When W. C. Wilkinson inquired into the absence

9. These descriptions of newsboys are drawn primarily from PAC, J. J. Kelso Papers; *Prison Reform Commission*, testimony of J. J. Kelso, 723–9, and George Alfred Barnett, superintendent of the Newsboys' Home, Toronto, 729–30; Ontario *Report of Committee on Child Labor*; "The Tag System Abortive," *The Toronto World*, 22 November 1890; "The Waifs of the Street," *The Globe*, 18 April 1891; "The Industrial School," *The Telegram*, 18 April 1878; "Around Town," *Saturday Night*, 10 (21 November 1896); C. S. Clark, *Of Toronto the Good*; J. J. Kelso, *Protection of Children: Early History of the Humane and Children's Aid Movement in Ontario 1886–1893* (Toronto 1911); and Karl Baedeker, *The Dominion of Canada* (London 1900). I am indebted to David Swayze for bringing this last source to my attention.

from school of fourteen-year-old William Laughlan, the lad's mother told him: "...the boy was the principal support to the house, the father having been ill for a long time. The boy carried out papers morning and evening."[10] This entry from Wilkinson's diary also indicates the importance of children as substitute wage-earners. In his notebooks, newspaper reporter J. J. Kelso speculated that some newsboys, who he estimated earned between 60¢ and $1.00 a day, fully supported their parents.[11] Despite their importance as wage-earners, the vast majority of newsboys, bootblacks, and other street vendors occupied deadend jobs that promised no viable future employment. Although some business skills could be learned on the street, only a tiny percentage of enterprising newsboys managed to climb the professional ladder. Moreover, the "privation, exposure and irregular life" that characterized the street traders' existence frequently led to petty crime and permanent vagrancy.[12] In the estimation of W. H. Howland, the reform mayor of Toronto, "it was ruinous to a boy to become a newsboy, in nine hundred and ninety-nine cases out of a thousand."[13] J. J. Kelso added: "The profession of selling newspapers is in my opinion pernicious right through."[14]

Newsboys and other young street vendors attracted the attention of a new group of middle-class social reformers and self-styled child-savers. These individuals objected to the presence of so many roughly hewn youngsters on public streets and feared that extensive exposure to the harsher elements of city life would turn vulnerable children into vile and irresponsible adults. This, in turn, would place greater burden on the public purse through the maintenance of jails and houses of refuge. In an attempt to ameliorate this situation, J. J. Kelso and other leading philanthropists petitioned the Toronto Police Commission in 1889 to adopt measures to regulate the street traders. Kelso and his cohorts succeeded, and the resultant law, enacted in 1890, required newsboys and other vendors under the age of sixteen to apply for a licence, and forbade boys under eight and girls of any age to participate in the street trade at all. To

---

10. TBERAM, Wilkinson Diaries, vol. 5, entry for 9 December 1873.
11. PAC, J. J. Kelso Papers, vol. 8.
12. Ontario, *Report of Committee on Child Labor*, 11.
13. *Royal Labor Commission*, Ontario evidence, 161.
14. *Prison Reform Commission*, 723. Various police chiefs across Ontario upheld the views of Howland and Kelso. See *Prison Reform Commission*, testimony of W. McVitty, chief constable of Ottawa, 372–3, and Lieut.-Col. H. J. Grasett, chief of police, Toronto, 700. See also Ontario, *Report on Compulsory Education in Canada, Great Britain, Germany and the United States* (Toronto 1891), 89.

qualify for a badge, a boy had to maintain a clean criminal record, avoid associating with thieves, and attend school at least two hours per day. In addition to having their privileges revoked, violators could be fined or sentenced to the industrial school or common jail. Although over 500 boys applied for licences in the first year, the police failed to enforce the regulations rigorously and the law quickly fell into disuse.[15] Two years later, the Toronto Board of Education established special classes for newsboys, but met with little success. In both cases, reformers failed to recognize the enormous distance between controlled orderliness as prescribed by law and the burden of poverty. Irrespective of the intentions of social legislation, many working-class families depended on the contributions of children.[16] Furthermore, the arguments reformers put forward in favour of regulation revealed a deeper concern with public morality and family values than with the economic circumstances of newsboys and their families. This attitude is especially evident in the extra restrictions placed on girls, the future wives and mothers of the nation. Susan Houston's comment on child beggars is equally applicable to newsboys and other young street vendors: "...it was their habits rather than their condition that roused the ire of reformers."[17]...

In private homes and on public streets, children in late nineteenth-century urban Ontario routinely performed a variety of important economic duties that directly contributed to the successful functioning of the family or household economy. Youngsters not only assisted their families in this way, but in many cases provided valuable services to a demanding urban clientele. In working-class neighbourhoods, the widespread practice of child labour exposed the poverty and insecurity that plagued many families which could not rely on industrial wages alone to meet the demands of urban life. At the same time, the use of youngsters as regular or auxiliary workers denoted a family strategy that was both rational and flexible in its response to new and challenging circumstances. In the short term, working-class families could depend on children to add the last necessary ingredient to their formula for survival. In the long term, youngsters paid the price....

---

15. "The Waifs of the Street," *The Globe*, 18 April 1891.
16. Undoubtedly, some newsboys pursued their profession as a matter of personal choice, preferring the small income and independence of the street to the demands and discipline of the school system.
17. Susan E. Houston, "Victorian Origins of Juvenile Delinquency," 86.

FURTHER READINGS FOR TOPIC 2

Herbert Brown Ames, *The City Below The Hill* (Toronto: University of Toronto Press, 1982). [Reprint of 1897 edition.]

Terry Copp, *The Anatomy of Poverty: The Condition of the Working Class in Montreal, 1897–1929* (Toronto: McClelland and Stewart, 1974).

Michael S. Cross, ed., *The Workingman in the Nineteenth Century* (Toronto: Oxford University Press, 1974).

Judith Fingard, *Jack in Port: Sailortowns of Eastern Canada* (Toronto: University of Toronto Press, 1982).

Judith Fingard, *The Dark Side of Life in Victorian Halifax* (Porters Lake, N.S.: Pottersfield Press, 1989).

Gregory S. Kealey, ed., *Canada Investigates Industrialism: The Royal Commission on the Relations of Labour and Capital, 1889* (Toronto: University of Toronto Press, 1979).

Gregory S. Kealey and Bryan D. Palmer, *Dreaming of What Might Be: The Knights of Labor in Ontario, 1880–1900* (Cambridge: Cambridge University Press, 1982).

Bryan D. Palmer, *Working-Class Experience: The Rise and Reconstitution of Canadian Labour, 1880–1980* (Toronto: Butterworths, 1983).

Michael J. Piva, *The Condition of the Working Class in Toronto, 1900–1921* (Ottawa: University of Ottawa Press, 1979).

T O P I C 3

Canadian Mythologies and the Western Frontier

The idea of the frontier has played a complex and ambiguous role in Canadian historical and political thought. In 1893, the American historian Frederick Jackson Turner enunciated the view that the distinctiveness of American development, and in particular the strength and persistence of the democratic tradition, could be explained with reference to the existence of an area of free land, its continuous recession, and the advance of American settlement westward. Some Canadian historians, most notably A. R. M. Lower, the author of an important study of the timber staple, argued that Canadian democracy was "forest-born"; others rejected an emphasis on frontier democracy, and suggested an alternative framework, "metropolitanism," which posited the central significance of the city and trans-Atlantic flows of trade and ideas. Among historical geographers and western Canadian historians, updated (and among the geographers more sophisticated and nuanced) notions of the frontier have proved resilient.

What if one regarded the "frontier" itself, not as something whose existence could be proved or disproved, not as a "factor" or a "place," but rather as a technique for structuring narratives—both the Grand Narratives of Canadian National Development and the humbler, more personal stories people told themselves when trying to make sense of the infinite detail of their own lives? Keith Walden, in the first reading of this section, suggests that the greatest of all the Canadian frontier stories—the Great March of the Mounted Police—can be seen as an instance of modern *myth; Robin Fisher then shows how two very different kinds of "frontierism" animated the brothers Pattullo; and E. R. Forbes suggests that the myth of the western frontier seemed to require the myth of the decadent, conservative East. The frontier may have been most significant as an element in the reconstruction of masculinity, linked powerfully to new concepts of national purpose. As a reassuring myth, the notion of frontier individualism spoke (and still speaks) powerfully to men whose thoroughly modern lives were shaped by interdependence, hierarchy, and bureaucracy—all parts of the "iron cage" of capitalist modernity.*

THE GREAT MARCH OF THE MOUNTED POLICE IN POPULAR LITERATURE, 1873–1973*

KEITH WALDEN

In the popular literature dealing with the Royal Canadian Mounted Police, the achievement of order in various parts of the Dominion was viewed as one of the fundamental accomplishments of the force. Much of the narrative of police history has recounted the way in which the Mounties brought stability and peace to a succession of frontiers, making these formerly wild areas habitable by ordinary settlers or at least amenable to the norms of white civilization. The story of the Klondike provided a classic example and the conclusions of R. L. Neuberger, for one, were typical:

> Dawson was the center of the stampede for gold. Until the Mounties came, it was the wildest and wickedest place in North America. Gamblers and pick pockets and evil women preyed on the miners who had chamois-skin pouches full of gold dust.
> After the arrival of the Mounties, things were different.[1]

Dawson became "as quiet and orderly as a New England hamlet."[2] When historians of the force described the push of the police into the northern interior and the Arctic, their message was the same:

> ...out of seeming chaos emerged order. As an old-timer, a real "sourdough," put it to the writer: "Those Police fellers got a cinch on the

KEITH WALDEN, "THE GREAT MARCH OF THE MOUNTED POLICE IN POPULAR LITERATURE, 1873–1973," *CANADIAN HISTORICAL ASSOCIATION, HISTORICAL PAPERS* (1980), 33–56. BY PERMISSION OF THE PUBLISHER AND AUTHOR. KEITH WALDEN IS A MEMBER OF THE HISTORY DEPARTMENT AT TRENT UNIVERSITY.

* The term "literature" is used here in its wider sense of printed matter generally, rather than simply fiction.

1. Richard L. Neuberger, *Royal Canadian Mounted Police* (New York, 1953), p. 82. Also, Irvin Block, *The Real Book About the Mounties* (Garden City, 1952), p. 78.

2. Jeremiah Lynch, *Three Years in the Klondike* (Chicago, 1967; originally published, 1904), p. 32. See also Nora Kelly and William Kelly, *The Royal Canadian Mounted Police: A Century of History, 1873–1973* (Edmonton, 1973), pp. 90, 99, 101–2; Henry J. Woodside, "Dawson As It Is," *Canadian Magazine*, XVII (September 1901), p. 408; Muriel Denison *Susannah of the Yukon* (New York, 1937), p. 29.

country from the word go, an' they never let-up. They ran the place, sir, like an all-fired day and night school. . . ."[3]

The Canadian North, as a result, was "as close to being crimeless as any place on earth."[4]

[The tale of the triumph of order in the far North merely continued the lessons taught by the force's experiences in the prairie West. The Northwest of myth was wilderness, a vast tract of empty, threatening, unknown land, the "great lone land." The setting added dignity, grandeur, and exoticism to the task of the young force. But the great land was not as "lone" as it first appeared. Some people did inhabit the West, and they were felt to be creating a great deal of trouble. Natives, in the minds of the historians of the force, represented one element of disorder. Typically historians suggested that the key to the force's success in bringing order to the West lay not in exercises of raw power, but rather in demonstrations of their fairness and consistency. For many historians, the clarity of the law and the uniformity of its application went a long way to explain how the force had transformed the West so dramatically. But this process was also accomplished quickly, because natives intuitively discerned that the mounted police were a force for good. Commentators on the force assumed that, because they came from a superior and more powerful culture and were fair and consistent in all their dealings, the Mounties were able to work a veritable miracle. These assumptions had a heavy cultural bias, and several of them were naive.]

What people, no matter how badly off, so willingly accept the intrusion of outsiders into their affairs or the disruption of their traditional customs? What human beings could really have been as altruistic, as humane, as consistent as the Mounties were made out to be? Or again, does it seem plausible that such a small group of men could master so quickly and so completely such a large territory and one, moreover, which was completely new to all of them? These things do not make sense. Any immigrant experience involves a long, subtle process of adaptation to a new environment and of interaction with the existing inhabitants of the new region. Such subtlety was completely missing from the traditional

---

3. A. L. Haydon, *The Riders of the Plains: A Record of the Royal North-West Mounted Police of Canada, 1873–1910* (Toronto, 1912; reprint ed., Edmonton, 1973), p. 227. Also R. C. Fetherstonhaugh, *The Royal Canadian Mounted Police* (New York, 1938), p. 132.

4. Douglas Spettigue, *The Friendly Force* (Toronto, New York, London, n.d.), p. 89. See also T. C. Bridges and H. H. Tiltman, *More Heroes of Modern Adventure* (London, 1931), pp. 215–6; Fetherstonhaugh, p. 94.

accounts of police history....The conventional explanations of how the police brought order to the West just do not ring true, either to real human psychology or genuine frontier experience. They do ring true to myth.

The story of how the police brought order to the West occupied a large place in the annals of the North-West Mounted Police. Historians of the force realized, however, that before the public could believe that the men in scarlet had imposed order on the external world, it was necessary to prove that they had imposed order on themselves. Integral to this western success story was the description of the primal event in the formation of the famous corps. The great march to the West in 1874 from Dufferin, Manitoba, to Fort Whoop-Up in the shadow of the Rockies was, in the minds of those who wrote the history of the force, clearly central to an understanding of its inner spirit and achievements. By comprehending the deeper significance of the great march in their minds, it may be easier to understand why the distorted image of this early period was so largely unquestioned.

As S. W. Horrall has pointed out, the great march to the West has always had a special place in the traditions of the force: "Over the years, the March West has occupied the thoughts of the members of the Force more than any other event in its history."[5] This is interesting in view of the fact that the march was by no means a glorious triumph. It has suffered, wrote Ronald Atkin,

> ...embarrassing exaggerations and has invariably been hailed as an epic. It was certainly an epic of endurance and determination; but it was also epic in its lack of organization, in the poor way in which it was conducted and in its incredibly close brush with disaster....long before the end survival had overtaken success as the main aim of the expedition.[6]

That survival, it might also be pointed out, was to a large extent dependent on the very whiskey traders the force had been sent to control in the first place.[7]

A few writers disregarded the problems of the march and blandly assumed that it was a complete and unqualified success. Norma Sluman,

---

5. S. W. Horrall, "The March West," in H. A. Dempsey, ed., *Men in Scarlet* (Calgary, n.d.), p. 14.
6. Ronald Atkin, *Maintain the Right: The Early History of the North-West Mounted Police, 1873–1900* (London, Toronto, 1973), p. 60.
7. Roderick Charles Macleod, *The North-West Mounted Police and Law Enforcement, 1873–1905* (Toronto, Buffalo, 1967), p. 23.

for example, described the police at the end of the trek as being in high spirits and "dressed splendidly."[8] A little research would have indicated that, in fact, many of the men were sick and exhausted, and that their uniforms were in tatters. Most writers, however, even though they were not as critical as they might have been, did not try to hide the difficulties of the march. Indeed, it was the hardships and trials, successfully endured, which in their view gave its participants a claim to fame.

If the mounted police had been the first to venture into the unknown West, this interpretation might make some sense. However, in light of the fact that similar, largely unheralded journeys had been made previously and been made much more competently—most notably perhaps by the boundary survey group—it seems odd that the great march of the mounted police should have earned so much attention and glory. Though observers of the force claimed that the actual march was significant, it is obvious that its historical importance, in their view, was to be derived from an appreciation of the force itself, an appreciation which made more sense in light of its later accomplishments. It was natural that those who admired the force would look back to its earliest days and expect to find there some explanation for what they felt to be its magnificent record. Not surprisingly, they found what they were looking for. In their minds, the great march was the mechanism which transformed a group of ordinary young men into a remarkable frontier corps. In their hands, the great march became an account of the creation of heroes.

Anthropologists, literary critics, psychologists, and many others have long been interested in the general phenomenon of hero myths. From their labours to record and understand the stories told by all human societies, it has become clear that almost all legends of heroes share a strikingly similar pattern. Some people, pointing to such things as dreams and rites-of-passage rituals, have even suggested that this is a universal structure fundamental to human perceptions of the meaning of life. Joseph Campbell in *The Hero with a Thousand Faces* charted what he called the "monomyth" of the hero and his analysis of this seemingly archetypal structure confirmed and clarified the conclusions drawn by other scholars.[9] Campbell distinguished three basic stages in the hero

---

8. Norma Sluman, *Blackfoot Crossing* (Toronto, 1959), p. 228. See also *New York Times*, 6 August 1933.

9. See Joseph Campbell, *The Hero with a Thousand Faces* (Princeton, 1972); [Fitzroy Richard Somerset] Lord Raglan, *The Hero: A Study in Tradition, Myth and Drama* (London, 1949), pp. 177–99; Otto Rank, *The Myth of the Birth of the Hero and Other Writings* (New York, 1964), pp. 3–96. Also interesting are A. van Gennep, *The Rites of Passage* (London, 1960); and Wendell C. Beane and William G. Doty, eds., *Myths, Rites, Symbols: A Mircea Eliade*

myth and within each stage identified various recurring motifs. In the first stage, "the call to adventure," the hero or the collective hero is summoned from ordinary life to "the threshold of adventure," the point at which he must leave the normal world and his commonplace previous existence to take up an unusual but vital task. The hero may be lured away or forced away from his former state, or he may leave voluntarily, but either way he moves towards a state of existence clearly differentiated from the usual. In this stage, he may be given aid or advice or charms by some cosmic helper who understands, even if the hero does not, the essential purpose and importance of his mission. When the hero arrives at the "threshold of adventure" and crosses into the supranormal realm, the event is marked by a happening of obvious import. Whether he is crucified, attacked by a dragon, or placed in a boat to drift on the oceans, he is subjected to an experience which clearly indicates that he has crossed a boundary into another world. Once he breaks across this threshold, "the hero journeys through a world of unfamiliar yet strangely intimate forces," some of which threaten him, some of which give him aid. If he successfully deals with these powers, if he triumphs over the supreme ordeal which he must face in the nether world, he gains a reward. This may be symbolized by a sexual union, by the acquisition of some valuable device or elixir, or by a transformation in himself. Whatever it is, it is something remote and highly esteemed by humankind. Once this point has been reached, the hero is ready to return to the ordinary world. Again, at the threshold between the two realms there is a struggle as the forces of darkness make one last attempt to keep the hero in thrall. When he does finally win re-entry into the normal sphere, he is equipped to bestow on it advantages which have accrued to him from the successful completion of his ordeal. This is the essential pattern of the hero myth and, as Campbell has so aptly demonstrated, it can be found in every hero tale from the legends of the Buddha to the stories of Horatio Alger and beyond. More surprisingly, perhaps, it can as well be found in the supposedly factual history of the great march of the mounted police.

The typical myth of the hero begins with the call to adventure, which in this case, clearly, was the announcement that the government intended to open the West. In some myths, the hero has to be coerced or seduced into undertaking his mission. This was not so with the mounted police. As the

---

Reader, two volumes, (New York and Toronto, 1976), 1, pp. 164–7. It should be emphasized that there are disagreements about the meaning of this pattern, but its existence is not questioned.

historians made clear, they were not reluctant voyagers. Irvin Block, for example, described the reaction of the men to Colonel French's address to them on the eve of the march:

> Trumpeter Bagley's voice rang out clearly, "Ready, sir—ready to follow you anywhere!" Bagley looked about and blushed. He had called out without thinking—he had not been able to control himself.
> But his blush of embarrassment turned to a radiant glow as the ranks of grinning men took up his shout. Three hundred Mounties stood in their stirrups, lifted their snow-white helmets and heaved them into the air so that it seemed the sky above them was thronged with swooping white gulls.
> "Ready!" was the word that was shouted by three hundred throats. "Ready!" filled the valley. "Ready! Ready! Ready to go!"[10]

T. M. Longstreth was equally insistent about the enthusiasm of the men. The policemen

> ...were now facing the unknown with an elation that can come to a man hardly oftener than once a lifetime. As they headed into that unpeopled vacancy of golden summer, the light-drenched distances before them formed a fit setting for their unbounded spirits.[11]

Of course, there were some problems. Not all recruits looked forward to the arduous nature of the task, and it had to be admitted that a substantial number had deserted across the American border. Colonel French, according to the story, conscious that a large portion of his force might drift away even before its work had begun, countered this threat by calling a full-dress parade. With the whole corps assembled, he proceeded to outline the dangers and discomforts which could be expected on the journey and then suggested that those not willing to face these trials might leave the force immediately without penalty. Accounts vary as to whether any men took up his offer,[12] but there was complete agreement that this marked a significant point in the history of the police.

Though it is seldom possible to name with assurance the moment when

---

10. Block, p. 24.
11. T. M. Longstreth, *The Silent Force: The Making of the Mounted Police* (New York 1927), p. 27.
12. Spettigue, Longstreth, and Block, for example, claimed that no men accepted French's offer; Phillips and Nora and William Kelly suggested that a few did leave.

the traditions of a military force are born, it would seem that on the day of Lieutenant-Colonel French's appeal the North-West Mounted Police came into its own.[13]

At this point, it was felt, the misfits had been weeded out. "The weak had already been separated from the strong, the timid from the brave."[14] The work of the force required men of heroic stature and not all men were heroes. Those who were not, understandably refused the call to adventure. Their desertions were to be expected. The remainder took up the call willingly and prepared to "meet the unknown out there where grass merged with sky."[15] They willingly chose to become, as Longstreth so appropriately put it, "the confidant of mystery."[16]

Those who genuinely belonged in the mounted police, the true heroes, accepted the call to adventure without hesitation. Their confidence was well founded for they, like most heroes, had a helper of such stature and potency that their mission could hardly fail. That helper was none other than Sir John Alexander Macdonald. The first prime minister, it was emphasized, was the founder of the force, the man who had dreamed it into being. The police "were one of Macdonald's inspirations,"[17] and he moulded them to the vision he had in his mind's eye.[18] Nor did he abandon them after the creation: they were his "pet scheme"[19] and he made sure that they "always remained under his eye."[20]

> ...in all his administrations the Premier kept the control of the Force in his own hands; it was, in a sense, his own pet scheme, and he saw to it that both in its military and civil capacities the corps maintained its efficiency and smartness in the highest degree. Thanks to his guidance the North-West Mounted Police passed through their early stormy years to a place in the country's regard which few were found to cavil at.[21]

One writer even went so far as to claim that Macdonald "initiated the idea

---

13. Fetherstonhaugh, pp. 12–3.
14. Spettigue, p. 6. See also Block, p. 25; Kelly and Kelly, p. 28; Haydon, p. 22.
15. Longstreth, *The Silent Force*, p. 20.
16. Ibid., p. 26.
17. J. G. A. Creighton, "The Northwest Mounted Police of Canada," *Scribner's Magazine*, XIV (October 1893), p. 399.
18. Haydon, p. 18. See also Kelly and Kelly, p. 14; T. M. Longstreth, *The Scarlet Force, The Making of the Mounted Police* (Toronto, 1953), p. 4.
19. Agnes Deans Cameron, "The Riders of the Plains," *Cornhill Magazine*, n.s., XXXIV (January 1913), pp. 90–1.
20. Creighton, p. 399. Also, Fetherstonhaugh, p. 64.
21. Haydon, p. 170.

of a special police force for the Yukon and the allied Territories."[22] If he did, it must have been from beyond the grave.

It is obvious why so many writers wanted to see such a close association between Macdonald and the mounted police. By linking the two, it was natural to think that the vision which brought the force into being was part and parcel of the vision which had inspired Canada itself. Macdonald's interest seemed to imply that the formation of this dedicated corps was part of the act of national creation. The force, therefore, was an instrument of national growth and not a repressive, negating element in Canadian life. It was central to the Canadian experience and an essential element in the ongoing success of the nation.

Like any good mythological helper, Macdonald not only pushed his heroes gently on their way; he was also credited with giving them a number of devices and aids to help them in their quest. For one thing, he decided that the new body would be called a police force rather than a military corps. In the realm of myth, names are important and this one was designed to soften the image of the new body and so reduce the chance of hostility towards it by both the Americans and the Indians. It was a device that offered protection from two powerful enemies.[23] As well, Macdonald decided that the uniform of the force would be as simple as possible. There would be no "frills and feathers," no unnecessary encumbrances which would detract from the completion of the task. The wise, old sage knew that the renown of the true hero came from what was inside, not from what was tacked on to the exterior. The uniform of the troopers would be as simple as their motives were pure. Finally, Macdonald decided that the uniforms of the force would be red in colour. Knowing that red was identified by the Indians with the fairness and friendship of Queen Victoria and the British Empire, he wrapped his initiates in clothing with magical powers to protect them from the hostile forces they would encounter. These were all powerful aids. They did not guarantee the success of the mission—in myth, of course, that depends on the inner resources of the heroes themselves—but they were a tremendous help nonetheless.

Having accepted the call to adventure and having been prepared for the ordeal by their cosmic helper, the police, like all heroes, were ready to

---

22. J. B. Kennedy, "Scarlet of the Mounted," *The Mentor*, XXVI (March 1928), p. 4.
23. Captain Ernest J. Chambers, *The Royal Northwest Mounted Police* (Montreal, 1906; facsimile ed., 1972), p. 18; Longstreth, *The Silent Force*, p. 8; Neuberger, p. 36; Phillips, p. 282.

begin their task. The date of 19 June 1874 was one of great significance in the history of the force. On that day the three newest divisions of the North-West Mounted Police arrived at Fort Dufferin from Toronto and were united there with the three older divisions. This was the first time the force as a whole had been together. That evening a storm erupted in the night. It was, said A. L. Haydon, "one of the most dreadful thunder-storms ever witnessed in the country."[24] Longstreth's account of it and its effects provides the essential details:

> The thunderstorm which fell on the Force the night after the arrival, secured for itself a permanent place in history. It nearly wrecked the expedition. An enclosure had been made for the horses by means of stakes and a long cable; outside these horse-lines the wagons were arranged in a ring, a single passage having been left at the corner. The first gusts of wind ripped open the canvas wagon-covers, whose flap-pings kept up a fusillade of cracking and roaring. Lightning filled the sky and glittered from the hail, coming closer and closer, finally striking, by the camp. The terrific thunder, the rush and impact of the rain, and the destructive wind crazed the horses. Panic was multiplied by numbers. Senseless, climbing one another's backs, leaping through overturned wagons to the noise of broken wood and shouting men, some of who were being trampled, they burst the barrier and streamed southward on the only way they knew. Thus were the new-comers initiated into their wild and hoped-for West.[25]

Longstreth's description emphasizes well the two important mythic motifs at work here. One is the thunder. As a symbol, the thunderbolt often represents the action of the higher world on the lower. It is a sign of supreme creative power. The lightning concomitant with thunder is usually related to dawn and illumination: it is "symbolic of the spring principle and of the initial stage of every cycle."[26] The other element is the corral. A corral is generally a circle, a circumference, and a circumference, besides being a sign of perfection and oneness, is a symbol of "the manifest world, of the precise and the regular."[27] The symbol of the corral, then, represents the ability of man to establish successfully some protec-tive order and unity in the face of a natural world that is essentially

---

24. Haydon, p. 23.
25. Longstreth, *The Silent Force*, p. 24. See also Longstreth, *The Scarlet Force*, pp. 14, 18–9; Kelly and Kelly, p. 26; Spettigue, p. 6; Fetherstonhaugh, p. 11; Turner, I, p. 119; Steele, pp. 63–4. Interesting as well is the illustration by H. Julien originally published in the *Canadian Illustrated News* in 1874 and reprinted in Dempsey, p. 29.
26. J. E. Cirlot, *A Dictionary of Symbols* (London and Henley, 1976), p. 342.
27. Ibid., p. 48.

chaotic, the ability to sustain over time in some systematic way a control over potentially disruptive cosmic forces which continually threaten society from within and without. The corral represents the power of known civilization.

Having left Fort Dufferin, the last outpost of civilization, the Mounties attempted to recreate the traditional structures which provided shelter. There was no reason to doubt the effectiveness of the wagons and wire in confining the horses. Obviously, though, they were not enough. What the famous thunderstorm of the great march indicated, was that in the realm about to be entered by the mounted police the protection offered by the known order was not enough. They were entering a sphere clearly differentiated from the normal world. They were beginning to trespass in an environment where the full creative powers of the cosmos held sway and those powers, though they held out the promise of eventual illumination, would not lightly admit any intruders. The thunderstorm marked a transition from one world to another. It indicated that ordinary existence had been left behind. Though shaken by the experience as heroes usually are, the mounted police had been fully initiated into the trials that lay in store for them. The threshold of adventure had been crossed.

Beyond the threshold, according to the archetypal pattern of the hero myth, lies a mysterious world full of strange yet familiar forces. It is a confusing, threatening, sinister environment capable of terrifying the irresolute with the unknown or seducing the unwary into peril through a false aura of normalcy. It is a place palpable with danger. In the histories of the mounted police, the plains over which the force marched in 1874 were described in very much these terms. Irvin Block pictured the prairie as a "treeless brown ocean that rolled across hundreds of miles of barren continent." Its earth was "dry and cracked," locusts had descended on it "like a black storm cloud and had devoured every blade of grass so that the land looked naked," and buffalo "lurched over the parched mounds until they staggered to their knees in a dried out wallow and died." The area was, he concluded, "a terrible, silent, death-haunted place."[28] For Alan Phillips as well, death and uncertainty were everywhere: "Heat lightning flickered in the awesome expanse of sky and thunder echoed ominously. Everywhere they saw bleached bones of buffalo."[29] Longstreth's description was fuller, but its essential features were the same:

---

28. Block, p. 26, also, p. 18.
29. Phillips, p. 284.

Mirage tantalized the men, but not one actual bush relieved the eye. The sky was brazen, the earth brown, and the sight dwelt on vacancy. Hope was parched into a semblance of fatalism. The emptiness of the land weighed on them like a mechanical power.[30]

This was not a world made for ordinary men.

Not only was the land itself portrayed in these narratives of the great march as the usual desolate, eerie, nether world of myth, it was also peopled with the destructive and hostile forces usually found there. The whiskey dealers, by the very nature of their trade, were violent, malicious, and mercurial. The Indians, with an equal potential for violence, were just as unpredictable and all-pervasive. Even the Métis guides hired by the police to pilot them to the West were sometimes accused of deceitfully leading the force astray.[31] In the stories of the great march, it was emphasized that nothing about the land or its indigenous inhabitants could be taken for granted. According to William and Nora Kelly, even the buffalo were a dangerous menace.[32]

Not only were the police portrayed as being surrounded by hostile and shadowy elements, it was also made clear that they were subjected to the hero's usual "road of trials."[33] "Dufferin has barely disappeared behind the horizon," wrote R. L. Neuberger, "before the difficulties of the trek begin to be evident."

Water holes are few and far between. The horses gasp and choke in the midsummer prairie heat of 100 degrees. Troopers are miserably uncomfortable in their uniforms which fit like glue. When a creek is reached, the horses must drink first. The water is a muddy gumbo by the time the men can quench their thirst.

Dysentery breaks out. The Constables retch in their saddles and sway weakly, trying to hold on to the reins of the horses. Grasshoppers settle on the carts and wagons in a dark cloud, devouring quantities of the precious food supplies. Prairie cholera attacks some of the men who drank too greedily of alkali water. They lose weight rapidly. All food sickens them.[34]

---

30. Longstreth, *The Silent Force*, p. 35. Also Fetherstonhaugh, pp. 18–9; Donalda Dickie, *The Canadian West* (Toronto, 1927), p. 238.
31. Longstreth, *The Silent Force*, p. 35; Phillips, p. 285; Kelly and Kelly, p. 38. See also Haydon, (p. 29) who described how the Métis exaggerated the threat posed by the whiskey traders, and Block, (p. 29) who emphasized the general threat of Métis violence.
32. Kelly and Kelly, pp. 37–8.
33. Campbell, p. 97.
34. Neuberger, p. 42.

Neuberger might also have mentioned dust, hail, wind storms, autumn cold, a lack of wood for cooking, a scarcity of grass to feed the horses, lice, mosquitoes, prairie fires, broken carts, and worn-out boots. Other writers did.[35] The catalogue of suffering was long, but it was entirely within the keeping of the normal hero's journey. Through it all, boasted the storytellers, these adventurers did what heroes have to do: "with dogged determination, they carried through the service required of them."[36] . . .

It is. . .interesting to note that, in many myths, the successful completion of the hero's task depends on strict adherence to a rigidly prescribed order of activities. His discipline stands in contrast to the chaos around him. In the case of the police as well, the emphasis on the deliberate arrangement of the troopers does suggest that this was a protective device to shield them from the disorderly forces which surrounded them. . . .

The great march, it was believed, had turned the young troopers into rugged westerners. John Peter Turner believed that "readiness to make the best of every situation had become an essential part of duty: and the western frontier within the limits of a single month, had marked for its own many a daring and resourceful recruit."[37] T. Morris Longstreth concurred. "That sight, that sense of space and glory, that smell of living air caught them up, marked them for life, branded them as sons of those plains from which they would wish never to return."[38] They had begun the trek as inexperienced novices from the East; they ended it as "lean, tanned, hard young soldiers,"[39] at home in the West.

The march was credited by some people, however, with doing much more than transforming the men into hardy plainsmen. It was also seen to be the mechanism by which the isolated individuals who comprised the force were fused into a single, effective unit. It was the furnace in which the soul of the force was fired. Those who were "weak and recreant,"[40] those who lacked heroic character, were described, as has been seen, as dropping out even before the journey began. With the sluggards gone, "the force took on new life."[41] As they began their journey along the road of trials, as the powers of darkness hurled their worst against the

---

35. See Kelly and Kelly, pp. 36–8; Spettigue, p. 7; Phillips, p. 284; Block, p. 28.

36. Haydon, p. 33. (He was quoting Colonel French.)

37. John Peter Turner, "When the Mounted Police Went West—Part I," *Canadian Geographical Journal*, X (February 1935), p. 61.

38. Longstreth, *The Silent Force*, p. 40.

39. Ibid. See also Spettigue, p. 8.

40. Turner, "When the Mounted Police Went West—Part I," p. 55; also Norman Fergus Black, *History of Saskatchewan and the Old North-West* (Regina, 1913), p. 575.

41. Kelly and Kelly, p. 28.

vulnerable wanderers, the chronicles of the march record how the men responded with what was best in themselves. "As signs of settlement disappeared," wrote Turner, "love of daring and adventure stirred the resolute."[42] In the face of danger and suffering, the young policemen were described as telling stories, singing, dancing, and laughing.[43] The tests of the march, it was said, brought the men together and gave them a new sense of who they were:

> ...in the autumn darkness and chill, surrounded by dangers known and unknown, and 700 miles from help, the men of the Northwest Mounted Police became conscious of themselves as a new unity. It was the first coming to life of a pride in their outfit. The months of training in obedience held all hands together now in a spirit of co-operation. They respected their leaders, trusted each other and themselves.[44]

Indeed, to some commentators, the march created an almost magical bond of union among the men. One novelist, describing its finish, suggested that

> These last few days had done something to the force that everyone felt— a strange welding of spirit which brought every man in the train to a common bond. . . . The force was becoming as one man now, and pride was high.[45]

The march had truly effected, in the eyes of many admirers of the police, a profound transformation.

It is difficult to say whether this famous journey was as successful in uniting the force as it was made out to be. There is some evidence to suggest the claims have been distorted. One account of the march written by a rank-and-file participant casts doubt on the assertions that men had complete confidence in their officers and that harmony prevailed. Commissioner French, according to this witness, "showed great want of ability as Commander-in-Chief," and, he reported, among the officers serious conflict existed.[46] Moreover, the phenomenal desertion rate which

---

42. Turner, "When the Mounted Police Went West—Part I," p. 55.

43. Harwood Steele, *Spirit of Iron: An Authentic Novel of the North-West Mounted Police* (Toronto, 1923), p. 26; Block, p. 27; Turner, "When the Mounted Police Went West— Part I," p. 61; Illustration for *Canadian Illustrated News* of 1874 by H. Julien, reproduced in Dempsey, p. 32.

44. Longstreth, *The Silent Force*, p. 38. See also Longstreth, *The Scarlet Force*, p. 39; Phillips, p. 288.

45. John F. Hayes, *Bugles in the Hills* (Toronto, 1955), p. 228. Also Turner, "When the Mounted Police Went West—Part II," p. 114.

46. Jean D'Artigue, *Six Years in the Canadian Northwest* (Toronto, 1882; facsimile ed., Belleville, 1972), pp. 35, 44. Also Atkin, p. 62.

plagued the force during its early years in the West invites speculation as to how strong the bonds actually were among those who had allegedly been welded into one unit. Similarly, in the same period, the force seems to have had major problems with illness, which again leads to some questioning about how successful the Mounties were in adapting quickly to the western environment.[47]

However, if the popular accounts of the march do not precisely conform to what actually happened, they do conform to the typical hero myth. As Campbell pointed out, when a hero enters into the realm of adventure,

> ...he undergoes a supreme ordeal and gains his reward. The triumph may be represented as the hero's sexual union with the goddess-mother of the world (sacred marriage), his recognition by the father-creator (father atonement), his own divinization (apotheosis), or again—if the powers have remained unfriendly to him—his theft of the boon he came to gain (bride-theft, fire-theft); intrinsically it is an expansion of consciousness and herewith of being (illumination, transfiguration, freedom).[48]

To learn, then, that in successfully undergoing the rigours of the great march, the police had been transformed so completely is not surprising. As is usually the case, their reward involved an expansion of their powers and of their consciousness of who they were. No hero could expect less.

Once transformation has been achieved, according to the mythic framework, the adventurer is ready to leave the underworld and return to the normal realm. He is ready to bring to mankind the benefits of the struggle which he has undergone. But, in order to return, he must meet one last challenge: he must recross the threshold of adventure between the nether world and the ordinary world. The powers he has confronted will not easily relinquish him from their grasp. In light of this pattern, the accounts of the conclusion of the long march take on a new significance.

The destination of the Mounties in the West was the notorious haunt of the whiskey traders, Fort Whoop-Up. With Jerry Potts guiding them, the story goes, the police found the disreputable post and drew up in front of it. It was an ominous scene, as the description of T. M. Longstreth suggested: "The dark palisade of the fortress hid the main stronghold behind. The American flag presumptuously flapped in the wind. Whoop-

---

47. See E. C. Morgan, "The North-West Mounted Police: Internal Problems and Public Criticism, 1874–1883," *Saskatchewan History*, XXVI (1973), pp. 41–62; and also Atkin, p. 62.
48. Campbell, p. 246.

Up was silent, too!"[49] Many historians emphasized the rumours which indicated that Whoop-Up was well armed with cannon, had extensive underground tunnels for defence, and was determined to fight any intruders.[50] As the police approached, however, there was no sign of life. Macleod, after positioning his field gun and placing his troops around the fort, approached its entrance with only Jerry Potts at his side. He rapped on the heavy gate. Minutes passed. "Finally, it swung open. A tall angular man with sharp eyes, a long nose and a brown pointed goatee drawled, 'Walk in, General. Walk in, General, make yourself at home.'"[51] As in hundreds of myths and folktales, a lone hero had approached a dangerous and guarded gate, only to be met at the threshold by a decrepit-looking old man. Whoop-Up offered no resistance.

Some observers lamented the fact that the fort was captured so easily. Observed Longstreth: "It was not to their liking that without a shot, without a flurry, the stronghold of the desperadoes had fallen."[52] Nevertheless, in terms of myth, the outcome was not unusual. As the noted historian of religions, Mircea Eliade, has pointed out, in many stories which recount initiatory activities, expected danger disappears when the ordeal itself is successfully undergone.[53] By confronting danger, it is banished. When the final threat to the successful completion of the great march evaporated at the entrance to the lonely fort, therefore, it was a sign that the underworld adventures of the police were about to end.

If the moment of separation from the normal realm came with the destruction of the corral during the thunderstorm outside Dufferin, the moment of return came when the police occupied Whoop-Up. In crossing its threshold, they were recrossing the threshold of adventure. The transformation they had undergone was symbolized by the fact that they could now maintain the kind of civilizing structure which in their uninitiated state was easily destroyed by the cosmic powers. Not only could they master the pre-existing structures of that hostile environment, they could now successfully erect their own. The first major action of the men after their capture of Whoop-Up, according to most histories, was the construction of Fort Macleod, the western headquarters of the force.[54] If additional

---

49. Longstreth, *The Scarlet Force*, p. 40.
50. Haydon, p. 29; Neuberger, p. 52; Turner, I, p. 165.
51. Phillips, p. 287. Longstreth, *The Silent Force*, p. 48; Kelly and Kelly, p. 41; Neuberger, p. 52; Turner, I, p. 165.
52. Longstreth, *The Silent Force*, p. 48.
53. Beane and Doty, II, p. 411.
54. See for example, Haydon, p. 34; Turner, I, pp. 190–1; Fetherstonhaugh, *Royal Canadian Mounted Police*, p. 23; Dickie, p. 239.

proof were needed to show that the force had been changed, it could be found in the return march of Colonel French and some of the troopers back across the prairie to Manitoba where they were to establish their main headquarters. This time, as the same men crossed the same territory, they experienced few problems. "Nothing eventful occurred during the march," wrote Haydon.[55] With the capture of Fort Whoop-Up, the prairies, it seems, no longer constituted a kingdom of dread. They had been redeemed for normal human habitation.[56]

In myth, when the hero returns from the transcendental darkness, "the boon that he brings restores the world."[57] The fruits that he has won from his ordeal are generously spread for the rest of humankind. As the histories of the police make clear, their actions after the capture of the whiskey post were the actions of typical heroes. One of the first things they did was to take active steps to suppress the liquor trade. Many histories recounted the story of how the police, literally within hours of arriving at the site of what was to become Fort Macleod, captured a party of whiskey traders, confiscated their pelts, and poured their vile liquor into the ground.[58] With this kind of efficiency, the suggestion that the men in scarlet had quickly eliminated the whiskey trade from their territory was not to be wondered at. As well, said most observers, the police took immediate steps to pacify the warlike Indians. This involved explaining the law and the intentions of the force to the tribes and indicating what was and was not acceptable behaviour. As has been seen, these were the very things which were felt to be necessary to bring order to the West. The elimination of illegal activities and evil men, the subjugation of chaotic

---

55. Haydon, p. 32. Also Longstreth, *The Silent Force*, p. 43. Even those writers who suggested that the returning troops encountered continuous difficulties did not elaborate, leaving the impression that these difficulties were easily dealt with. See Kelly and Kelly, p. 41; Fetherstonhaugh, *Royal Canadian Mounted Police*, p. 21. In light of the strong linear character of the descriptions of the actual march, the breakup of the force at its end, and indeed the earlier separation of "A" Division which left the main column at La Roche Percee and went to Edmonton, it is interesting to note Eliade's observation that "in innumerable mythologies, the world came from the cutting up of a primeval monster, often serpentine in form." See Beane and Doty, I, p. 24.
56. The point made by Campbell should be kept in mind. "The hero adventures out of the land we know into darkness; there he accomplishes his adventure, or again is simply lost to us, imprisoned, or in danger; and his return is described as a coming back out of that yonder zone. Nevertheless—and here is a great key to the understanding of myth and symbol—the two kingdoms are actually one. The realm of the gods is a forgotten dimension of the world we know." See p. 217.
57. Campbell, p. 246.
58. See MacBeth, *Policing the Plains*, pp. 59–60; Block, p. 30; Haydon, pp. 36–7; Neuberger, pp. 45–9; Kelly and Kelly, pp. 44–5.

forces, the establishment of order—these were the changes wrought by the mounted police. However, such beneficial results did not accrue simply because the men journeyed to the far West. It was not simply their presence which brought the possibility of civilization to this new frontier. Rather, this was a gift bestowed on humanity by a group of heroes who, having braved the terrors of the kingdom of darkness, had the special powers necessary to effect such a change. No ordinary beings could have accomplished such deeds.

Like all heroes and successful initiates, the mounted police deserved explicit public recognition for their accomplishments. Historians of the force made sure they got it. In their hands, the meeting between Macleod and Crowfoot became not only a symbolic ceremony to confirm the passing of the old ways and to acknowledge the superiority of the new, but also a formal rite to honour the mounted police for their noble deeds. Some indication of the imaginative significance of the meeting can be gained from a painting by R. Lindmere, reproduced in R. C. Fetherstonhaugh's history of the force.[59] Lindmere placed the encounter outside Fort Macleod. In the foreground of the panel, about to shake hands, stand the two great protagonists. Macleod is pictured in his full dress uniform. Crowfoot is clothed in what appears to be a frock coat, modestly decorated with native designs. It is an Indian version of statesmen's garb. Although the policeman wears a high-plumed helmet which makes him appear taller, both men are about the same height. Clearly, in stature and presence, the two are equal. Crowfoot, the leader of the western tribes, a true "redskin statesman"[60] widely known for his bravery and wisdom, represents the natural man, the noble savage who can see beneath surface glitter to the true state of things beneath:

> The Queen meant nothing to him; but this man, her representative, did, and he had to assess him correctly. That he was a good man and passionately sincere, Crowfoot could not doubt. The stamp of him was plainly upon him.[61]

In the painting, Crowfoot offered his hand to a man of obvious honesty and goodness and strength—to a man with the qualities of a hero.

If the Blackfoot chief represented natural man and his instinctive knowledge, he was also a symbol of the spirits of place. He encompassed the strength and wisdom of all the forces that inhabited the plains. It was

---

59. See Fetherstonhaugh, *Royal Canadian Mounted Police*, p. 24.
60. Longstreth, *The Scarlet Force*, pp. 52-3.
61. Sluman, p. 238.

he who was best able to evaluate the accomplishment of the dashing troopers:

> He, more than anyone, knew what this handful of young men in the gay scarlet had dared when they penetrated to the heart of his realm uninvited. His own young men, even when incited by the war drums to prove their valour by the number of scalps taken could have shown no more courage than this.[62]

When Macleod grasped the hand of Crowfoot, he did so to accept his investiture into the ranks of the heroes. The powers that be had acknowledged his greatness and his right to impose virtue and order on the rest of the population. It was truly a cosmic moment, "one of the great hours in the history of Canada."[63] It was as if "civilization stood still for one brief instant."[64] Only those close to the gods can make such things happen.

It is not surprising that the great march was given such a central place in the history of the force. It was an epic which told of the coming of order to a frontier wilderness and its subsequent transformation into a garden of man. Canadians, interested in the way in which their country developed; Anglo-Saxons, fascinated with the expansion of the British race or with the "westward course of empire"; indeed, all groups which professed to believe in the concept of progress, were bound to feel that the march was an event of some significance. It had brought order to an important part of the globe. Order was the foundation, the first principle of civilization. Those who furthered civilization were enlarging the possibilities of all humankind. The world stood in their debt and the record of their activities naturally became the focus of much interest. To a society deeply involved in a questioning of the ultimate possibility of order, such heroes and such an event had a special attractiveness and appeal.

However, it was not simply the importance of the changes it purportedly accomplished which explains the popularity of the story of the great march. This also rested on the fact that the trek of 1874 was told as a chronicle of the heroes. All the elements of the typical hero adventure were present: the call to adventure, the cosmic helpers, the journey through the underworld and the trials at its thresholds, the ordeals and tests of the kingdom of darkness, the return to the normal world. The story of the great march was appealing because it was structured on an age-old and universal pattern of romance. Although obviously some

---

62. Longstreth, *The Scarlet Force*, p. 51.
63. Ibid., pp. 52-3.
64. Turner, I, p. 193.

people were more interested in the specific cultural context, almost anyone, anywhere, could respond to a framework of archetypal significance. The essentials of the tale were so basic that they were readily accepted and digested by those who read. Here, there were no complicated and confusing principles of causation to deal with, no subtle and complex analyses of hows, whats, and whys. Instead the reader or listener discovered a success story so well known in its outline that he or she might tingle in pleasurable anticipation of the familiar.

The structure of the story, however, dictated many of the conclusions that were drawn about the mounted police character and the accomplishments of the force. In accepting that structure, most people also accepted the validity of those conclusions. Even if on the surface what was said about the force seemed fantastic or extravagant, the way in which the story was cast made it seem reasonable and correct. Because they had successfully undergone the ordeal of heroes, it was logical to assume that the policemen did indeed have the characters of heroes as well. Similarly, according to the archetypal mythic structure at work here, the noble adventurer, by virtue of his triumphs in the underworld, conveyed benefits of inestimable value to the general population on his return. Therefore, by putting the march in this context, it seemed entirely believable that the police could have subdued the West so quickly and completely, and that they were the only agents in its transformation. It was not necessary to take into account the impact of the Hudson's Bay Company or the presence of the Métis, the options and alternatives of the Indian tribes (conditioned as they were by a knowledge of events on the American frontier), or anything else. The existence of order in the Canadian West was a boon conferred by the police, whose heroic apotheosis had transformed them into superior beings capable of performing such deeds. Having done it once, it was obviously an easy matter for them to do it again in the Yukon and again in the Arctic.

Because the story of the initiation of the force was cast in these terms, its popularity is understandable. However, this conclusion only invites a more difficult question. Why did the chronicle of the great march have this structure? Why did historians of the force describe the event as a typical hero myth? Such a pattern might be expected in a purely imaginative work, but the great march, surely, was not invented out of thin air. Historians of the trek did not invent such things as the thunderstorm outside Dufferin or the capture of Fort Whoop-Up to ensure that their story conformed to the archetypal pattern. These things happened and the historians believed they were describing them accurately and honestly. Even where licence was taken to imagine conversations or reactions, the authors involved did not feel they were distorting the essential truth of what went on. Certainly they did not conjure up the basic events of the march.

While the pattern was not a fabrication, neither was it simply a factual accounting of a sequence of events. The optimism of Lord Acton that "ultimate history" could be written has vanished and in its place has come a realization that fact and interpretation do not exist independently of each other. Whether a particular fact or event is seen to have significance is determined by preconceived cultural assumptions. Probably there was more than one thunderstorm endured by the police during the march, yet the others were not deemed worthy of consideration. Why have the historians emphasized those events which make the story a typical hero myth?[65] There is no clear answer to this.

Inevitably a discussion of the relation of myth and history raises many questions for which there are no clear answers. Perhaps there never can be. Does all written history rest ultimately on such universal mythic frameworks? Are all our perceptions of what is important determined by archetypal structures in our minds? Are events which seem to conform to these patterns deemed to have a significance which other events do not? Is this how we determine what is important historically? Or do historians arrange basically shapeless material into preconceived configurations? To what extent do these structures dictate assumptions and conclusions about the characters and actions of historical participants?...

---

65. It could be argued that the historians were merely restating what the actual participants in the march said and wrote at the time. The historians, therefore, did not make any assumptions. But this contention only carries the problem back to an earlier stage. How did the policemen at the time decide which events had more significance than others and why?

DUFF AND GEORGE GO WEST:

A Tale of Two Frontiers

ROBIN FISHER

This is the story of two brothers, two frontiers, and the evolution of two political cultures. When they were young men, Thomas Dufferin and George Robson Pattullo left their birthplace in southern Ontario and headed west. But they went in different directions to two very different frontiers: one to the Canadian west and the other to the United States. Their frontier experiences were a major influence on their later lives, particularly on their political ideas. By the 1930s they had moved to opposite ends of the political spectrum within two increasingly divergent federal systems.

Duff and George grew up amid politics and discussion of politics. They were born in Woodstock, Ontario, in 1873 and 1879, respectively. The younger brother was named after their father, who was an important influence on their early lives. George Pattullo, senior, was a prominent Liberal party organizer, and so from the cradle the Pattullo boys were nurtured in late nineteenth-century Canadian Liberalism. A portrait of Wilfrid Laurier, who Duff and George later agreed was the greatest Canadian who had ever lived, hung in the family living room. Prominent Liberals of the day, from both the federal and provincial cabinets, were frequent guests in the Pattullo home. The Pattullos were acquainted with another Liberal family living in nearby Berlin whose eldest son, a year younger than Duff, was named William Lyon Mackenzie King. As the editor of a Liberal newspaper and the chief party bagman in Oxford County, Pattullo senior was most closely associated with the provincial Liberal party and the Ontario government of Oliver Mowat. During his premiership from 1872 to 1896, Mowat moved the Liberals away from the old laissez-faire individualism of an earlier generation, appealing instead to the Reform tradition within the party. He was a strong advocate of provincial rights who showed some inclination to use the power of the state to regulate social and economic development.[1] When Mowat with-

---

ROBIN FISHER, "DUFF AND GEORGE GO WEST: A TALE OF TWO FRONTIERS," CANADIAN HISTORICAL REVIEW, 48 (DECEMBER 1987), 501–28. REPRINTED BY PERMISSION OF UNIVERSITY OF TORONTO PRESS.

1. For a general summary of Mowat's policies see A. Margaret Evans, "Oliver Mowat: Nineteenth Century Liberal," in Donald Swainson, ed., *Oliver Mowat's Ontario: Papers Presented to the Oliver Mowat Colloquium Queen's University, November 25–26, 1970*

drew from provincial politics in 1896, it was Duff and George's uncle, Andrew Pattullo, who replaced the former premier as the Liberal member for North Oxford. Politics seemed to be inbred in the Pattullos, and in later years the brothers would represent, among other things, the two tendencies—interventionist and individualist—of Canadian Liberalism.

But neither Duff nor George immediately re-enacted the family tradition of political involvement. In earlier generations, other members of the Pattullo family had gone west both to the California and British Columbia gold fields, and it was the footsteps of these forebears that the two boys followed. As their ancestors had done, Duff and George went to two widely separated and quite different frontiers. Duff Pattullo went to the Canadian northwest: to Dawson City at the height of the Klondike gold rush. George went to the American southwest: to the cattle ranches of the Texas, New Mexico, and Arizona borderlands.

Joining the stampede in 1897, Duff Pattullo went west to the Klondike during the madness of the last great gold rush. He did not, however, go to moil for gold on the banks of Bonanza or Eldorado Creek, but to begin a career in the offices and back rooms of the federal civil service. He was appointed secretary to Major J. M. Walsh, the first commissioner of the Yukon Territory, getting the job more through political patronage than individual initiative. His father's considerable Liberal party connections landed him the position with the federal government expedition that was sent out from Ottawa to impose Canadian law and order on a potentially unruly gold mining frontier. The leader of the party, Major Walsh, was a former inspector in the North-West Mounted Police and the hero of earlier dealings with Sitting Bull when the Sioux leader sought sanctuary in Canada following the battle of the Little Big Horn.[2] Now Walsh was sent to the Yukon to replace the American pattern of frontier administration with the Canadian system. Prior to the gold rush the Canadian government had done little to establish its jurisdiction in the Yukon, and the small and largely American population of miners had set up a grass-roots system of administration through the institution of the miner's meeting. This was a form of local democracy in the best tradition of the American

---

(Toronto 1972), 34–51; on his assertion of provincial rights see Christopher Armstrong, "The Mowat Heritage in Federal-Provincial Relations," in ibid., 93–118; and for a more critical look at his policies on resource development see H. V. Nelles, *The Politics of Development: Forests, Mines & Hydro-Electric Power in Ontario, 1849–1941* (Toronto 1974), esp. 27, 102–3.

2. See Gary Pennanen, "Sitting Bull: Indian Without a Country," *Canadian Historical Review* 51 (June 1970): 123–40.

frontier as described by Frederick Jackson Turner.[3] With the influx of thousands of miners in 1897, however, Canada introduced its own system of frontier management in the Yukon. The Walsh Party and the North-West Mounted Police were sent to Canada's farthest frontier to impose the authority of the federal government, from the top down. It was as a part of this process that Duff went west.

Although he left the east as an agent of metropolitan authority, Duff Pattullo nevertheless felt invigorated by the new land in the west that was opening up to settlement. He was impressed by the optimism and energy of the people who were founding a new society on the prairies. He was moved by the wild grandeur of the Rocky Mountains, and recognized that he had come to a place that was very different from the small towns and gentle countryside of his boyhood in southern Ontario. After sailing up the west coast, he approached the infamous Chilkoot pass in the teeth of a gale and experienced the exhilaration of facing the elements and achieving the height of land. Pattullo, along with most of the Walsh party, did not reach Dawson City until the spring of 1898, but the journey had been one of self-discovery that had instilled in him the naive belief that hard work and determination were sufficient to overcome any Chilkoot.[4] For many of the stampeders of 1897, simply getting to the Klondike was enough and, having reached the objective, they turned around and went home again. But Duff Pattullo stayed, for the next twenty years living in the small towns of the northern frontier.

While westering in a new land may have been a regenerative experience for individuals like Pattullo, at a more general level Canada's historians have seen the west as a place where old values were imposed rather than new ones created. They tend to refer to the periphery as the hinterland rather than the frontier. Rejecting the Turnerian idea of the creative role of the frontier, they argue instead that the metropolitan centre asserted control over the hinterland and shaped the new society in

---

3. The point is made by William R. Morrison, *Showing the Flag: The Mounted Police and Canadian Sovereignty in the North, 1894–1925* (Vancouver 1985), 13. Turner's classic exposition of the nature of the American frontier is, of course, to be found in Frederick Jackson Turner, "The Significance of the Frontier in American History," in *The Frontier in American History* (New York 1962), 1–38.

4. In later life his favourite book about the Yukon was one that emphasized that the true adventure of the north was the psychological search for one's self. See Mary Lee Davis, *Sourdough Gold: The Log of a Yukon Adventure* (Boston 1933), 197, 342; Provincial Archives of British Columbia (PABC), Thomas Dufferin Pattullo Papers (PP), Add. MS 3, vol. 32, file 3, M. L. Davis to T. D. Pattullo, 15 Jan. 1938.

an old image.[5] Established tradition was a stronger force than the new environment. Even on frontiers where one might have expected a significant American influence north of the forty-ninth parallel, there was little inclination to develop distinctive local institutions. Thus British Columbia during the gold rush era has been described as a "counterfrontier" of metropolitan dominance, while the ranching frontier of southern Alberta was characteristically Canadian in the deference shown to established authority by a population confident in its own tradition.[6] The most important distinction between the American and Canadian west was the fact that in Canada there was no "free land." There was "Crown land as opposed to public land."[7] Instead of being free for the taking, the land was owned, and access to it was controlled, by government. By virtue of its ownership of land, the Canadian government could regulate any frontier development, whether it be mining or ranching. The most effective instrument of federal power in western Canada was the North-West Mounted Police and the clearest example of the role of the police was their work in the Yukon during the gold rush.[8] They made their name by imposing tight control over the frontier. The Yukon was virtually a police state that was governed by remote control from the Department of the Interior in Ottawa.

Duff Pattullo had come to a frontier that was dominated by powerful outside forces. As a civil servant and later a businessman and local politician, he recognized the extent to which the periphery was subordinate to metropolitan political and economic interests. The Canadian west has been described as a "colony of a colony,"[9] and as in other colonies there was a propensity to turn to government for solutions. Pattullo soon learned, however, that the outside could not be relied upon to solve local problems and, partly because of the power of metropolitan forces, there

---

5. See, as a recent example, Gerald Friesen, *The Canadian Prairies: A History* (Toronto and London 1984), 170–1.
6. Barry M. Gough, "The Character of the British Columbia Frontier," *BC Studies* 32 (winter 1976–7): 38–9; David H. Breen, "The Turner Thesis and the Canadian West: A Closer Look at the Ranching Frontier," in Lewis H. Thomas, ed., *Essays on Western History* (Edmonton 1976), 145–56.
7. Breen, "The Turner Thesis," 151.
8. See R. C. Macleod, "Canadianizing the West: The North-West Mounted Police as Agents of the National Policy, 1873–1905," in Thomas, ed., *Essays*, 99–110; and on the police role in the Yukon see Morrison, *Showing the Flag*, 28–49.
9. W. L. Morton, "Clio in Canada: The Interpretation of Canadian History," in A. B. McKillop, ed., *Contexts of Canada's Past: Selected Essays of W. L. Morton* (Toronto 1980), 109.

was a need for some grass roots initiative. But asserting the interests of the periphery did not mean establishing new institutions. When federal agencies failed to deliver, local ones were called upon even though they were based on national models. So that while the form of western institutions may have been imposed by the east, they were increasingly used to express regional grievance.

As Duff Pattullo became involved in Liberal party and local politics on the periphery, his views were not necessarily those of the party leaders in Ottawa. In 1904 as a member of the Dawson City council and the executive of the Dawson Liberal club, he was a vocal opponent of the Federally appointed commissioner of the Yukon, Frederick T. Congdon. In the midst of some bitter party infighting, Pattullo made it plain to both Wilfrid Laurier and Clifford Sifton that he was not impressed with their unwillingness to bring Congdon to heel and, in the process, acquired a reputation in Ottawa as a political maverick.[10] Later as alderman and mayor in the northern company town of Prince Rupert, he urged the city government to resist the domination of outside forces. Believing that the city, and not the Grand Trunk Pacific Railway, should control the development of the town, he insisted that the railway company's substantial land holdings be taxed at a rate that was high enough to enable the council to finance city services. He also worked to limit private enterprise by ensuring that utilities in Prince Rupert were publicly rather than privately owned. He suggested that the city set up a rudimentary system of arbitration to deal with labour disputes. As mayor of Prince Rupert he advocated large-scale deficit spending on public works in order to attract development. In 1913 he tried to sell city debentures on the depressed money markets of eastern Canada and Great Britain. He was, however, completely unsuccessful.[11] Local politicians like Pattullo might take the initiative, but in Canada the periphery remained subject to its context.

While Duff Pattullo was learning these political lessons on the Canadian frontier of government control, his brother George went to the American frontier of the myth of self-made man. George Pattullo initially pursued a career as a newspaper reporter, first in Montreal and London, then in Boston. By 1908 he was Sunday editor for the Boston *Herald*. But

---

10. Public Archives of Canada (PAC), Sir Clifford Sifton Papers, MG 27, II D 15, vol. 169, T. D. Pattullo to Sifton, 3 July 1904; PAC, Sir Wilfrid Laurier Papers, MG 26 G, vol. 327, T. D. Pattullo to Laurier, 8 July 1904, and Laurier to T. D. Pattullo, 25 July 1904.
11. I have developed these points in more detail in "T. D. Pattullo and the North: The Significance of the Periphery in British Columbia Politics," in Kenneth Coates and William R. Morrison, eds., *For the Purpose of Dominion* (North York 1989).

he was fed up with working long hours for little money and no prospects, and when he met Erwin Evans Smith, a young photographer whose ranching scenes were exhibited in Boston, he felt the call of the west. Erwin Smith was to the American cowboy what Edward Curtis was to the North American Indian. Like Curtis, Smith believed that he was engaged in salvage ethnography by photographing a culture that was about to disappear. He also put a great deal of time and effort into staging his shots carefully in order to contrive a particular image of reality.[12] George Pattullo was deeply moved by Smith's scenes of cowboy life and work. In an article in the Boston *Sunday Herald*, Pattullo wrote that Smith's pictures of range life were unique and authentic because the photographer had "caught and felt the nameless, indefinable spirit of the vast cattle country."[13] The two became friends, and in the summer of 1908 they left the cities of the east for the ranching frontier of the southwest.

George Pattullo went west with two purposes in mind: "to get back my health and become a magazine writer"; as he later succinctly put it, "I succeeded in both."[14] In search of material for stories, Pattullo spent the next few years playing at being a cowboy. He worked as a regular range hand on the big outfits of the southwest: the J A, Matador, and Spur ranches in Texas; the Bar W and Blocks in New Mexico; the O R and Wagon Rods in Arizona; and the R O and Turkey Track in Old Mexico.[15] He shared the daily work of the cowhands and he met and interviewed big ranch owners such as Charles Goodnight. He was well aware that he was experiencing a frontier that was already passing away. Just as the Klondike was the last of the great gold stampedes, by the turn of the century the heyday of the large cattle ranches and the American cowboy was over. As some of Pattullo's own stories indicate, nesters were already moving in the last of the cattle country and the huge ranches were breaking up as the longhorn was replaced by the more profitable hereford.[16] That the cowboy

---

12. On Smith's photography see Eldon S. Branda, "Portrait of the Cowboy as a Young Artist," *Southwestern Historical Quarterly*, 71 (July 1967): 69, and J. Evetts Haley, *Life on the Texas Range* (Austin 1952). Haley's book includes many of Smith's photographs and George Pattullo appears in a number of them.
13. George Pattullo, "From Bronco Buster to Boston Art Student," *Sunday Herald*, Boston, 12 Jan. 1908, 1.
14. George Pattullo, *Era of Infamy* (San Antonio 1952), 179.
15. Laurier Papers, vol. 654, George Pattullo to Frank Pedley, 17 Dec. 1910.
16. See, for example, George Pattullo, "The Nester Parson," *Saturday Evening Post* 181 (2 Jan. 1909): 8–9, 29–30.

era was almost over was one of the reasons why Pattullo wanted to record it.

George quickly became a well known and prolific writer of western stories. His first, called "Blackie, a Texas Night Horse," appeared in the *Saturday Evening Post* in July 1908.[17] He had met George Horace Lorimer, the editor of the *Post*, whom he admired as "the ablest and most forceful man I have ever met."[18] Lorimer also thought highly of George Pattullo, and so with the encouragement of its editor, Pattullo published dozens of stories in the *Post* over the next few years.[19] He also wrote for *Collier's*, *McClure's*, and *Sunset Magazine*. Several of his early stories were about animals and one of them, "Corazón," was illustrated by the western artist Charles M. Russell, who thought that it was the best rangehorse story he had ever read.[20] He also wrote one western novel entitled *The Sheriff of Badger* and many of his stories were collected and published in three separate volumes.[21] George must have particularly liked the title of one of his stories since he used it again for one of these collected volumes, and *A Good Rooster Crows Everywhere* seems also to have been a credo that he personally followed. On one occasion the *Douglas Daily International* reported that George Pattullo, "probably the foremost writer of western fiction in this country," had blown into town to absorb some local colour for a series of border articles that he was writing for *Collier's*. The Arizona newspaper continued in its fulsome way by noting that Pattullo "is about the finest looking fellow that ever landed in Douglas and if he was not a writer of excellent short stories he could make a hit in art circles as a sculptor's model." George clipped the article and sent it to his father with the comment that it was "the only impartial and absolutely accurate estimate of myself I have ever seen."[22]

Critical evaluation of George Pattullo's writing has been somewhat

---

17. George Pattullo, "Blackie, a Texas Night Horse," ibid. (4 July 1980): 16–17, 22.
18. PABC, G. R. Pattullo Papers, file 3, George Pattullo to Wynnie (Ethelwyn Ballantyne), 29 June (1910?).
19. On the basis of the accounts that Pattullo later wrote on the First World War, Lorimer described him as "the best correspondent in America." George Lorimer to Lucile Pattullo, 19 April 1919, cited in D. H. Stewart, "George Pattullo: Western Writer," *Southwestern American Literature* 12 (fall 1986): 13.
20. George Pattullo, "Corazón," *McClure's Magazine* 35 (July 1910): 300–7; Stewart, "Pattullo," 17.
21. The novel was *The Sheriff of Badger: A Tale of the Southwest Borderland* (New York 1912); and the stories were published in *The Untamed: Range Life in the Southwest* (New York 1911), *A Good Rooset Crows Everywhere* (New York 1939), and *Horrors of Moonlight* (New York 1939).
22. PABC, G. R. Pattullo Papers, file 9, clipping from *Douglas Daily International*, 31 March 1916.

more restrained. James K. Folsom has noted that for some reason "Pattullo's western fiction has never achieved the recognition it deserves," and suggests that it is because his stories are not as sensational and do not portray as much violent action as those of the more popular writers of the genre.[23] Certainly there are not many gunfights in George Pattullo's stories. But, like many other western writers, he also churned out too many stories too quickly for any of them to be more than average in the literary sense. Although he wrote for slick magazines rather than the pulps, he was subject to the demands of the medium in which he published. The success of magazines like the *Post* depended on satisfying the advertisers and the audience, and editors expected their writers to produce stories made to order. Some of the more creative western storytellers tested these constraints, but Pattullo was not concerned about his independence as an author.[24] He was writing for a livelihood rather than as an artistic endeavour, and was more concerned with quantity than quality.

Besides having no great literary merit, George Pattullo's stories exhibited some other characteristics of the formula western of the era. He was among the first generation of western writers.[25] Owen Wister's *The Virginian*, which many see as the classic cowboy novel, appeared in 1902, and Zane Grey published his best-known work, *Riders of the Purple Sage*, in 1912.[26]. . .

In Pattullo's stories, new arrivals in the west who were prepared to adopt its ways were accepted and successful, while outsiders who did not conform to frontier values remained out of place. In a story called "Never Say Die," an Italian peddler comes to the town of Badger "from that vague region which Badgerites called the East." Pasquale Amati is welcomed with a beating by the town bully, but through hard work and sobriety he builds up a business, ruins his rival, and marries the girl.[27] "Frenchy: He

---

23. J. K. F. (James K. Folsom), "George Pattullo," in Howard Lamar, ed., *A Reader's Encyclopedia of the American West* (New York 1977), 896. For other assessments of Pattullo's writing see James K. Folsom, "George Pattullo," in James Vinson, ed., *Twentieth Century Western Writers* (London 1982), 602–3; and Joe B. Frantz and Julian Ernest Choate, Jr., *The American Cowboy: The Myth and the Reality* (Norman 1962), 168–9.

24. For a discussion of the distinction between slicks and pulps and the demands that the magazines made on western writers see Christine Bold, *Selling the Wild West: Popular Western Fiction 1860–1960* (Bloomington and Indianapolis 1987), xiv, 77–9, and passim.

25. For a rough periodization of western fiction see Richard W. Etulain, "The Historical Development of the Western," *Journal of Popular Culture* 7 (winter 1973): 718–24.

26. Owen Wister, *The Virginian* (New York 1902); Zane Grey, *Riders of the Purple Sage* (New York 1912).

27. George Pattullo, "Never Say Die!" *Saturday Evening Post* 184 (8 June 1912): 8–9, 28–30.

Makes Good with the Outfit" is an account of how a Frenchman is educated in the ways of the cowboy.[28] A tenderfoot who was willing to learn was an admirable man, whereas those who came west merely to take what they could and then leave were despised; and all the more so if they continued to believe in the superiority of eastern manners. Thus in "The Better Man," an English aristocrat, Lord Dunster, arrives at the Lazy L Ranch planning to marry the young and wealthy owner in order to shore up the family fortune back home. But in the end it is the taciturn, outwardly awkward, but highly capable range boss who wins the girl. The Englishman finally acknowledges that the cowboy "is the better man . . . and as good a gentleman."[29] This picture of the American west as a place where the frontier imposes its norms on the newcomer is very different from the view that Canadian historians have taken of the ranching frontier of southern Alberta, where there was an emphasis on British and eastern Canadian social patterns.[30]

George Pattullo was, of course, writing mythology rather than history. He was just one of the long list of "hands" that signed on to ride with Owen Wister and who, as one historian has put it, dished up the Turner thesis to the reading masses on a fictional platter.[31] Some historians still argue that the cattle-ranching frontier in the United States was one of free men living on free land; that, unless it was specifically in their self-interest, the cowboys and cattle kings resented any form of government interference and, accordingly, government did not "exert any heavy pressure in favour of conformity." According to this view, the ranchers saw themselves as "rugged individualists who opposed government paternalism." Indeed, since the availability of free grazing land was fundamental to their survival, they defied the government in order to maintain their hold on public land.[32]

But the era of the big ranches was a fleeting one, and American historians no longer believe in the Turner thesis any more than Canadian historians do. More than thirty years ago Earl Pomeroy urged a "reorien-

---

28. George Pattullo, "Frenchy: He Makes Good with the Outfit," ibid. 181 (20 Feb. 1909): 10–11, 34–7.
29. George Pattullo, "The Better Man," ibid. 182 (23 April 1910): 14–15, 59–60.
30. Breen, "The Turner Thesis," 152–6; and David H. Breen, *The Canadian Prairie West and the Ranching Frontier, 1874–1924* (Toronto 1983), 30–2.
31. Robert G. Athearn, *The Mythic West in Twentieth-Century America* (Lawrence, Kansas 1986), 168–9. Athearn's comments are particularly about Zane Grey, but they apply as well to Pattullo.
32. These points are made by Atherton, *Cattle Kings*, 102–10.

tation in western history" by suggesting that the development of the American west was characterized by conservatism, imitation, and dependency.[33] Since then the revision of Turner has continued apace. Historians have described the role of the army in the exploration of the American west and examined the contribution that federal government agencies made to the survey and improvement of transportation routes.[34] The hardy pioneers who followed the wagon roads west to the new promised land took along their well-established notions of law and order and continued to apply them.[35] The ranching frontier depended, as Gene Gressley has pointed out, as much on investment capital from the east as it did on free land in the west.[36] Even the western writers themselves can be seen as the hired hands of eastern publishers who perpetuated a view of the frontier that meant more to readers on the Atlantic seaboard than it did to drifters on the high plains.[37] For the American west was not necessarily settled by pioneers who, having cut loose from the restraints of the east, rediscovered freedom and democracy in the wilderness. While the frontier was seen as the land of opportunity, it always required support from the outside.

And yet the myth persists. The cult of the unfettered individual and self-made man was not unique to the cattle kingdom of the American west, but it did flourish there and through the medium of western fiction it was disseminated across the nation. Although they were not universally true, it was certainly these attributes of the ranching frontier that Pattullo admired and wrote about. His stories, along with those of other western writers, contributed to the development of a national mystique that was based on an idealized view of a west that perhaps had never existed, and certainly had passed away. In the United States there was sharpening discord between the myth of the west and the reality of the frontier. Canadians, by contrast, have never looked expectantly west for the

33. See Earl Pomeroy's influential article, "Toward a Reorientation of Western History: Continuity and Environment," *Mississippi Valley Historical Review* 41 (March 1955): 579–600.

34. William H. Goetzmann, *Army Exploration in the American West, 1803–1863* (New Haven 1959); W. Turrentine Jackson, *Wagon Roads West: A Study of Federal Road Surveys and Construction in the Trans-Mississippi West, 1846–1869* (New Haven and London 1965).

35. John Phillip Reid, *Law for the Elephant: Property and Social Behaviour on the Overland Trail* (San Marino, California 1980).

36. Gene M. Gressley, *Bankers and Cattlemen* (New York 1966).

37. Athearn, *Mythic West*, 175.

origins of a national identity. To the extent that there is a Canadian myth of the frontier, it is more in keeping with historical reality. In fiction, as in history, the mounted police force is a symbol of stability and order.[38]

It was, therefore, undoubtedly significant that George Pattullo once tried to gain access to the Canadian frontier, but without success. He wrote to the federal government to ask if he could live and work for a while, incognito if possible, with the North-West Mounted Police as the basis for writing some stories about the force. He allowed as how he would be no trouble to anyone, having "lived among cowboys of the Texas variety so much, any ordinary hardships of chuck, exposure, fatigue etc. are luxuries to me." The police, he continued, "probably have some horses they can spare; if they be not outlaws, I can handle them, as I've had to top some rare snorters and have mingled with the scenery often, acquiring the knack." But George probably did not help his chances of getting into the mounted police by quipping that "If necessary, I can rustle some horses too."[39] The Ottawa bureaucrats no doubt were somewhat mystified by all this nonsense and inevitably Pattullo's request was denied. While earlier in its history the North-West Mounted Police may have encouraged writers and journalists who wanted to publicize their activities,[40] clearly the Canadian government did not want any free-lance Texas cowboy investigating the agency of the national policy. For his part, Duff Pattullo did visit his brother in Texas, but there is no evidence that he was ever tempted to move to the American west.

During the First World War, however, both Duff and George left their respective frontiers, as they pursued different careers through the second decade of the century. Although they moved on to other places, their extended sojourn on the frontier remained an important influence on their lives, and the lessons they had learned were not forgotten. By the 1920s the frontier no longer existed as a place in North America, but it certainly persisted as an idea. Indeed, the very fact that the frontier had passed away as a place led many, particularly in the United States, to call for a reassertion of the values and ideals that the frontier was held to have represented.[41] There was also some tendency in Canada, in that uncertain decade, to turn to the land that was lost as the source of national

---

38. See Keith Walden, *Visions of Order* (Toronto 1982), 212–13.
39. Laurier Papers, vol. 658, George Pattullo to Frank Pedley, 17 Dec. 1910.
40. R. C. Macleod, *The NWMP and Law Enforcement, 1873–1905* (Toronto and Buffalo 1976), 30–1.
41. See Roderick Nash, *The Nervous Generation: American Thought, 1917–1930* (Chicago 1970), 77–90; Athearn, *Mythic West*, 43–77.

distinctiveness.[42] But Canadians had not explored the west of the mind and the spirit as Americans had, and there was no cowboy legend to remind them of an ideal frontier that was no longer there. As the subsequent careers of Duff and George were to show, two very different frontier traditions had emerged in the two nations.

Duff Pattullo continued his political career. Elected to represent Prince Rupert as a member of the British Columbia Legislative Assembly in 1916, he was immediately made minister of lands in a new, reformist Liberal government. He came to the provincial legislature as a representative of the northern periphery. Throughout his political career he drew on his early northern experience when he formulated policy, and he was a constant advocate of frontier development. In the years immediately after the war he was involved in providing government assistance to returned soldiers wanting to establish themselves on the land. He introduced legislation to enable the Department of Lands to intervene and finance the rebuilding of the irrigation systems in the Okanagan Valley. Private enterprise had failed to maintain the irrigation works and fruit farmers were not getting the water they needed. Pattullo argued that only government could solve the problem. As provincial minister of lands, Duff Pattullo also made an effort to press the advantages of crown ownership of forest lands to impose government regulation on the forest companies. Forestry had gone through a period of rapid and largely uncontrolled development, and by the 1920s it had become British Columbia's largest industry. Pattullo felt that it was now time to strengthen public regulation of the industry in the interests of long-term management. As elsewhere in Canada, however, this effort was not entirely successful. In his chapter entitled "A Frontier of Monarchy," H. V. Nelles has shown how crown ownership of lands naturally led to the notion of an interventionist government in the Ontario resource sector, but then goes on to detail a process whereby government became the client of big business.[43] There was a similar development in British Columbia in the 1920s. In the economic uncertainties of that decade, Pattullo's initiatives in the forestry sector were undermined by the short-term priorities of private enterprise and the government's need for income.[44]

By the second half of the decade it was clear that much of the reformist

---

42. John Herd Thompson with Allen Seager, *Canada 1922–1939: Decades of Discord* (Toronto 1985), 161–2.
43. Nelles, *Politics of Development*, 1–47 and passim.
44. See Stephen Gray, "Forest Policy and Administration in British Columbia, 1912–1928," MA thesis, Simon Fraser University, 1982, 48 and passim.

steam had gone out of the Liberal government and it was defeated at the polls in 1928. Soon after the electoral defeat, Duff Pattullo was made party leader. Over the next few years he worked to reinvigorate the party organization. He built up an efficient party machine that owed him considerable loyalty as leader. At the same time, he was an effective leader of the opposition in the legislature. The Conservative party had been in power for a little over a year when the stock market crash of October 1929 heralded the beginning of the Great Depression. Like all depressions, the collapse of the 1930s hit the vulnerable British Columbia economy particularly hard. As things went from bad to worse, Pattullo became more and more scathing in his criticism of the Conservative government's apparent ineffectiveness in the face of the economic and social crisis. He wrote to his brother in the United States to tell him that he "was looking for a pretty fierce fight" at the next election and he was not counting any chickens, but the smart money was on his party.[45]

George had problems of his own with the coming of the Depression for, while Duff remained in politics, he had gone into business. With the outbreak of the First World War, George Lorimer had persuaded him to report on the war effort in France for the *Saturday Evening Post*. He had discussed his writing habits in an earlier letter to his father in which he explained that he intended to avoid pretentious and ponderous prose. Instead, he would cultivate that chatty writing style which, he claimed, was the secret of Boswell's success. Thus his first war article was not a "highbrow effort; but it has swing and punch." It ran in the *Post* under the title "Fightin' Sons of Guns."[46] Another story, called "The Second Elder Gives Battle," introduced readers to a new American myth named Alvin C. York. Pattullo's story provided the basis for Gary Cooper's portrayal of Sergeant York in the later movie.[47] But George had never been particularly interested in artistic achievement and he wrote war items, as he had done his western stories, primarily to make money. His writing brought a reasonable return and, in 1913, he had married into a wealthy Texas family that had made a fortune in ranching and oil. It was on his own account in the 1920s that George was really successful in business. By 1922 he had accumulated enough capital to buy a flour mill in partnership

45. PP, vol. 47, file 6, T. D. Pattullo to George Pattullo, 17 Dec. 1932.
46. PABC, G. R. Pattullo Papers, files 3 and 4, George Pattullo to George R. Pattullo, 19 Dec. 1911 and 18 Sept. 1917; George Pattullo, "Fightin' Sons-of-Guns," *Saturday Evening Post* 190 (10 Nov. 1917): 3–4, 90, 93–4, 97–8.
47. George Pattullo, "The Second Elder Gives Battle," *Saturday Evening Post* 191 (26 April 1919): 3–4, 71, 73–4.

with a cousin from Woodstock. The business expanded, they bought more mills, and then patented a flour-bleaching process that produced enormous profits. By the end of the decade George had lived the myth of the self-made man and believed it to be true. He was extremely wealthy. When he was not travelling, he resided in an opulent apartment in the Carlyle Hotel in New York, he had a large private yacht in Florida, and he rented a river for sport fishing in Norway.

Duff Pattullo had never been financially successful, so it was not surprising that he should turn to George at a time of need. In 1931, when he was opposing a government with a three to one majority and trying to rebuild his own party, he wrote to George to ask if he would like to contribute to the British Columbia Liberal party. Duff explained to his brother that he was trying to establish an independent provincial Liberal party that was not beholden to the few who usually controlled Liberal finances. They always wanted to run things in the interests of the federal wing of the party. So Pattullo was financing the provincial organization out of his own pocket. Badly in need of some help, he wrote to George, asking for a reply to his home address by registered letter.[48] George declined the invitation to contribute to the party, saying that it would be improper for an American citizen to provide financial support to a Canadian political party. He did feel that it was a mistake for Duff to attempt to finance the party on his own and therefore wondered if there was not "any honest Liberal money out there which won't expect the favours demanded by the big fellows with whom you are very properly declining to traffic?"[49] When he replied to George's letter, Duff did not answer that question. Instead he argued that a contribution by George to the British Columbia Liberals would not be read amiss by the public, but would merely be taken as evidence of "fraternal feeling."[50] Subsequently, although George remained adamant about political contributions, he did give Duff the occasional modest "Christmas present."

George was freer with advice than he was with his money. An election was finally called in British Columbia in 1933 and, while Duff was in the thick of the fray, his brother drew on his experience in the southwest and sent a suggestion that was surely unique in the annals of Canadian electoral history. George wished Duff good luck in the coming campaign, and then told him a cockfighting yarn from Mexico. "In America," he alleged, "when a cock gets a numbing wallop, his handlers revive him by

---

48. PP, vol. 41, file 19, T. D. Pattullo to George Pattullo, 9 March 1931.
49. PP, vol. 41, file 19, George Pattullo to T. D. Pattullo, 18 March 1931.
50. PP, vol. 41, file 19, T. D. Pattullo to George Pattullo, 24 March 1931.

sticking his head into a pan of water. The technique is better in Mexico; there the handlers fill their mouths with water, up-end the cock's tail feathers and spray his testicles. And that rooster gets up on his hind legs, shakes his head and just wades into the fight again to beat hell. I mention this as a friendly gesture," George concluded, "to the end that you may always carry along with you a short length of rubber hose."[51]

With such advice Duff could hardly lose, and indeed he did not. When the dust settled on election night, British Columbia had a new Liberal government and Thomas Dufferin Pattullo was premier of the province. He received an enthusiastic letter of congratulation from George, whose only regret was that their father was not alive to enjoy Duff's triumph.[52] George's limited financial and substantial moral support of his brother's campaign was somewhat ironic in retrospect, because the two were soon to be poles apart in their political points of view.

Duff Pattullo came to the premiership of British Columbia as a Liberal reformer. That is, while he advocated a series of thoroughgoing reforms to deal with the problems of the Depression, he did not propose a radical upheaval of the capitalist system. During the election campaign he had talked about "socialized capitalism," by which he meant that capital would have to "recognise both the duty and the desirability of giving larger consideration to the needs and welfare of society generally."[53] He believed that capitalism could only be preserved by a redistribution of wealth, and that only the state had the power to effect such a redistribution. In an increasingly complex society there had to be some influence that could reconcile conflicting interests in the general good. Such reconciliation could only be achieved "through collective authority and that authority is the state." So he argued that the level of state intervention should increase, but his critique of capitalism did not mean that he was advocating socialism. On the contrary, state intervention was the means of maintaining capitalism and individual liberty. Thus it was "essential for industry itself as well as for the people at large that there shall be governmental regulation and control."[54] Duff explained his ideas to George with an analogy that they both understood. "The trouble is that everybody has been playing poker and the chips have gravitated to one

---

51. PP, vol. 51, file 27, George Pattullo to T. D. Pattullo, 18 Sept. 1933.
52. PP, vol. 52, file 16, George Pattullo to T. D. Pattullo, 3 Nov. 1933.
53. PP, vol. 64, file 5, T. D. Pattullo to editor, *Financial Post*, 30 Jan. 1936.
54. PP, vol. 65, file 1b, T. D. Pattullo, address at the University of British Columbia, 9 May 1935, and radio address, 20 Sept. 1935.

source. Some way there must be a redistribution of the chips if the game is to continue."[55] Government, said Duff, would have to deal a new hand.

As premier of British Columbia through the 1930s, Pattullo introduced a series of reformist measures. He believed in drawing on academic expertise, and appointed an economic council to investigate social and economic problems and advise the government on policy. Early in his government's mandate there was a flurry of legislation dealing with such matters as minimum wages and maximum hours of work, and providing for the collective marketing of agricultural products. Programs were established to provide financial help for the mining and fishing industries, forestry training camps, and to grubstake young men to go prospecting in the north. Spending on education was increased and the school system was reformed. Pattullo tried to persuade the federal government to introduce unemployment insurance and to improve old-age pensions, and he committed himself to bringing in government health insurance in British Columbia. But the long suit in Pattullo's deck of policies to deal with the Depression was public works. He advocated massive government spending on large-scale public works that he hoped would prime the economic pump as well as provide jobs for the unemployed. There would also be other spin-off benefits: building roads and bridges, for example, would open up new parts of the province for development and encourage more tourists to come to British Columbia. Partly because of its activist approach, the Liberal government of British Columbia was one of the few in Canada to be re-elected during the Depression. After the provincial election of 1937, Pattullo became more cautious, but his government was still the first in Canada to attempt to impose thoroughgoing regulation on the multinational oil companies.[56]

As a game plan to end the Depression, Pattullo's policy of redistribution at the provincial level failed to allow for the fact that the federal government held most of the chips. His program was predicated on the assumption that Ottawa would be willing to provide much of the funding to enable him to carry out his schemes, but whenever he turned to the federal government for assistance he encountered a stone wall of fiscal conservatism. The Conservative prime minister, R. B. Bennett, was prepared to provide small amounts of financial relief when he was absolutely

---

55. PP, vol. 47, file 6, T. D. Pattullo to George Pattullo, 19 Oct. 1932.
56. See Robin Fisher, "Regulating Fuels in the Depression: The Coal and Petroleum Control Board of British Columbia," *BC Studies* 66 (summer 1985): 3–27.

convinced that the British Columbia government had hit the bottom line of the ledger. When the Liberals were returned to power in 1935 the old family friend, Mackenzie King, was even less responsive than Bennett. He believed that in tight economic times the public treasury should be carefully guarded rather than expended and he resented the easy confidence with which Pattullo advocated expansive and expensive policies.[57] During his premiership, Pattullo became increasingly frustrated with the lack of co-operation from Ottawa and more and more convinced that, instead of a new deal to end the Depression, British Columbia was getting a raw deal out of Confederation.

Both Pattullo and his policies actually had more in common with Franklin D. Roosevelt and the New Deal in the United States than they did with any other Canadian politician or government. The Liberal government of British Columbia was the most activist in Canada during the 1930s, Pattullo and Roosevelt had similar personalities and related well to each other when they met, and both advocated moderate reform. The New Deal example was not seriously taken up by federal politicians in Canada, but Pattullo was struck by the similarities between his policies and those being followed in the United States. He wrote to George to ask if he had heard Roosevelt's inaugural address, because when he listened to it he thought that the American president "must have been previously reading the [British Columbia] Liberal platform and some of our speeches in amplification of it."[58] Duff Pattullo was only half serious, but he did take great exception to the suggestion that he had borrowed his ideas from Roosevelt. In the end he was "content to think that it was a natural coincidence of viewpoint in the light of existing conditions."[59]

At the same time as Premier Pattullo advocated policies that were similar to Roosevelt's, his brother in the United States became an increasingly strident opponent of the New Deal. At first George hoped that Roosevelt might do something about the mess that, in his opinion, the United States had got itself into. Although he was a Republican, he was disillusioned with Herbert Hoover, "that bright Boy Wonder" who had "been blah-blahing for four years about efficiency in government and cutting down expenses" while "in fact, governmental expense had gone up." He complained that, even though revenue from his business was increasing, he was not making any more money because the government took away any profit through increased taxes. He also claimed that the

---

57. PAC, W. L. M. King Papers, MG 26, J 13, Diary, 26 Feb. and 18 Oct. 1937.
58. PP, vol. 51, file 27, T. D. Pattullo to George Pattullo, 6 March 1933.
59. PP, vol. 64, file 5, T. D. Pattullo to editor, *Macleans*, 7 Nov. 1936.

country was being bled to death by financiers, and the rightward trend in his thinking was clear enough when he declared that if he were a Mussolini, "I would take a round dozen of big bankers of New York and stand them up against a wall as traitors to the country."[60] George had decided that Hoover, who he called the "Great White Feather," was incapable of vigorous measures and, although he did not really trust Democrats, he hoped that Roosevelt would have the courage to come to grips with the problems that faced the country. When Roosevelt did take action, however, George was not pleased, and his denunciations of the president became more and more vitriolic.

He objected even to the modest New Deal efforts to redistribute wealth because, he argued, business was being crippled by high taxes in order to fund wasteful government programs that were dreamed up by woolly headed bureaucrats who had not been elected by the people. In 1936 George Lorimer asked Pattullo to write a piece for the *Post* for old times' sake. Pattullo agreed and he used the article, called "Our Sentimentalists," as an opportunity to denounce the humanitarian give-aways that were sapping the true spirit of the nation. He acknowledged that the greed of big business was partly responsible for the Depression, but when New Deal defenders "solemnly declaimed that the only remedy is to turn management of finance and industry over to the Government," Pattullo thought that it was laughable. "So far as I know," he wrote, "history has yet to record that driving out one crowd merely to install a greedier has ever improved a situation." And so it was that, under the New Deal, "Campaigns which started out with the laudable objective of affording relief to the stricken presently developed into wholesale raids on the national purse."[61] To the end of his days, George Pattullo remained a bitter opponent of the "prodigal spending and waste" of the New Deal because he believed that it led to the "destruction of the self-reliance of our people."[62]

George's criticisms of the New Deal also revealed clearly the fascist tendencies of right-wing opinion in the United States. Roosevelt's policies were objectionable to Pattullo, as they were to others on the right, because they were taking the United States in the direction of communism. Even worse, the Roosevelt administration, like the international banking community, was dominated by Jews. . . .

---

60. PP, vol. 47, file 6, George Pattullo to Wee Wee [Ethelwyn Ballantyne], 30 March 1932.
61. George Pattullo, "Our Sentimentalists," *Saturday Evening Post* 209 (28 Oct. 1936): 69.
62. George Pattullo, *All Our Yesterdays* (San Antonio 1948), 262, 273.

The two frontier traditions exemplified by Duff and George Pattullo, their different ideas about how to deal with the Depression, and the western opposition to the Ottawa and Washington governments that the brothers reflected were all major factors in the divergent development of Canadian and American federalism in the twentieth century. From their distinctive perspectives the two Pattullos strongly objected to the way their federal governments responded to the economic and social crisis of the Great Depression. In each case, the regional discontent that they represented was firmly grounded in the frontier past. But the nature of the tension between the periphery and the centre was very different in Canada and the United States, and these distinctions do much to explain why the two federal systems were evolving in opposite directions.

In Canada, Duff Pattullo represented a western tradition of government activism that, by the 1930s, was opposed to a laissez-faire government in Ottawa. The political response to the Depression at the federal level in Canada was minimal. Whether the government in Ottawa was Conservative or Liberal, very little money was spent on the west and, as far as Pattullo was concerned, Mackenzie King was no better than R. B. Bennett on that score. On one notable occasion, therefore, Duff Pattullo persuaded Franklin Roosevelt to spend some New Deal money in British Columbia on building the Alaska highway. But this scheme was quickly vetoed by the federal government because it constituted a threat to Canadian sovereignty.[63] The west got little satisfaction out of the federal system in the 1930s, and the provinces continued to flex their constitutional muscles. Because they negotiated from a position of economic weakness, they made no headway during the depression decade, but in the boom times after the Second World War, as they continued to press their case, the provinces became more powerful in relation to the federal government. Having failed to buy off regional discontent in the 1930s, Ottawa still had to deal with boisterous western governments and the process continued whereby the provinces of Canada became much more powerful than the founders of confederation ever intended.

In the United States, George Pattullo represented a western tradition of individualism and free enterprise that, by the 1930s, was opposed to an activist government in Washington. There was a vigorous federal response to the Depression in America, and the west did disproportionately well out of New Deal spending. As federal money flowed

---

63. Robin Fisher, "T. D. Pattullo and the British Columbia to Alaska Highway," in Kenneth Coates, ed., *The Alaska Highway: Papers of the 40th Anniversary Symposium* (Vancouver 1985), 14–15.

westward, the region became a "planned promised land."[64] It was federal spending that allowed the economy of the American west to take off and so "the New Deal was largely responsible for the development of a great industrial and agricultural empire in the West in the post-war years." The American west moved "from pioneering to planning" through the impetus of the New Deal and its agencies,[65] but federal spending also brought increased centralization. The states became weaker and the federal government more powerful. Comparatively little reform emanated from the western states because New Deal ideas did not mesh with frontier individualism. Although the myth of west was assailed when the Depression clearly showed that rugged individualism had not worked, the trust that many westerners placed in the ideal was not entirely erased by the experience of the 1930s. They continued to believe that regional planning was undesirable because it was associated with the Depression, and the hardliners among the conservative, anti-government forces were often the cattle men. But individualism has always been a hindrance to gaining regional leverage in the United States.[66] So the process was continued whereby the states became much weaker within the federation than those who established the United States of America ever intended.

And what of George and Duff? They both held to the beliefs that were nurtured by their western experience. Duff Pattullo was defeated as premier of British Columbia in 1941. As a backbencher until 1945 and later in retirement, he continued to defend the achievements of his administration. He protested most loudly when other politicians dismantled the regulatory agencies that he had established. With the decline of his ideals, George became a rather bitter old man. He castigated President Harry Truman as the inheritor of the New Deal mantle and he published a number of autobiographical volumes in the 1950s that continued to bemoan the passing of the true American spirit.[67] In the context of the cold war he felt that the United States was weakly abrogating its responsibilities in the face of international communism. He told Duff that "one thinks of the Roosevelt–Truman New Deal era as dirt that will gradually wash

---

64. Richard Lowitt, *The New Deal and the West* (Bloomington 1984), xvi and passim; Leonard J. Arrington, "The Sagebrush Resurrection: New Deal Expenditures in the Western States, 1933–1939," *Pacific Historical Review* 52 (Feb. 1983): 1–16.
65. Lowitt, *New Deal*, 225 and chap. 14.
66. These points are made by Gene M. Gressley, "Regionalism and the Twentieth-Century West," in Jerome O. Steffen, ed., *The American West: New Perspectives, New Dimensions* (Norman 1979), 199–201, 223; and Athearn, *Mythic West*, 100–5.
67. George Pattullo, *Era of Infamy* (San Antonio 1952); George Pattullo, *Morning After Commeth* (San Antonio 1954); George Pattullo, *Giant Afraid* (San Antonio 1957).

from the souls and minds of decent citizens.[68] Both of them wrote verse in their old age. Duff, in spite of his achievements, wrote about loneliness and unfulfilled ambition. George knocked off little ditties of political commentary such as:

> Once I was a Democrat, happy and free
> Now I wish I were a dog and Truman a tree.[69]

Needless to say, James Boswell was still unavailable for comment on George Pattullo's writing style.

Throughout their lives, Duff and George maintained the beliefs that they had formed on the frontier. The views that they, and others like them, held had a major impact on the politics of the depression era and the development of two federal systems. The differences between the two frontier traditions were, of course, not absolute. The myth of the self-made man has not been absent from Canadian thought, just as westerners in the United States often talk about the colonial status of the region and the extent to which it has been put upon by the east.[70] But the careers of Duff and George reveal two distinct currents of thought that flowed out from the two wellsprings on the western frontiers. There was arguably a higher level of government involvement in the early development of the Canadian west than there was in the United States. Certainly Duff Pattullo represented a tradition of government intervention that, in part at least, had its origins in frontier conditions. While Duff was involved in the west of practical politics and government, George believed in the frontier of the spirit and imagination. In the United States the myth of the frontier was less clearly related to the reality of the west. Those like George Pattullo who had fostered the development of the cowboy legend had great difficulty coping with the growing discrepancy between myth and reality in the twentieth century. Most of all, perhaps, the careers of the two brothers show the extent to which frontier ideas continued to influence the development of the two nations long after the frontier as a place had passed away.

---

68. Collection of letters in the possession of Mrs D. Collison, George Pattullo to "Big Un" [T. D. Pattullo], undated.
69. Collection of letters in the possession of Mrs D. Collison, George Pattullo to "Wynnie" [Ethelwyn Ballantyne], undated.
70. On Canada see Allan Smith, "The Myth of the Self-made Man in English Canada, 1850–1914," *Canadian Historical Review* 59 (June 1978): 189–219; and on the American west see Athearn, *Mythic West*, 106–9; Gressley, "Regionalism," 197.

In Search of a Post-Confederation Maritime Historiography, 1900–1967

E. R. FORBES

This paper began as a critical review from a Maritime perspective of Professor Carl Berger's *The Writing of Canadian History: Aspects of English-Canadian Historical Writing, 1900–1970* (Toronto, 1976). I had initially envisioned it as a contribution to a kind of Carl Berger "roast." The approach had its appeal for had not this work received the highest award to which a Canadian historian might aspire? And had not the author supped with the gods, or at least the governor-general? Obviously some good-natured raillery and honest criticism would be in order to restore the author's status as a fallible human being. To this end one could point out that in *The Writing of Canadian History*, Professor Berger did not mention a single major historical work on the Maritimes for the period after Confederation. Surely this was a shocking display of regional bias! But upon reflection, this author too was unable to name any books dealing primarily with aspects of post-Confederation Maritime history written in English by a professional historian in the first century after Confederation. Thus the paper turned into an examination of the deficiencies of Maritime post-Confederation historiography. In fact, this is the story of two failures: the failure of mainstream Canadian historians to pursue themes which readily included the Maritimes, or to include the Maritimes in the themes which they did pursue, and the failure of academics residing in the region to respond effectively to the Maritimes' own obvious, and sometimes desperate, search for a historical perspective which would help them to understand their plight in a modern world. Neglect and stereotype left the Maritime student with a version of Canadian history to which he was unable to relate and seriously distorted the national picture. . . .

The frontier approach, which diverted attention away from the Maritimes in the modern era, paradoxically contributed to the image of the region which did emerge. Frederick Jackson Turner's essay of 1893 set out

E. R. Forbes, "In Search of a Post-Confederation Maritime Historiography, 1900-1967," *Acadiensis*, VIII, 1 (Autumn 1978), 3–21. Used by permission. This is an edited version of the aforementioned text.

the hypothesis of a frontier moving in stages westward through the United States with the availability of free land. This frontier provided a "crucible" in which "immigrants were Americanized, liberated, and fused into a mixed race." The ideas of social stratification were sloughed off with other cultural baggage and from this process came a dynamic for social and material progress, democracy and nationalism.[1] It was a thesis, which with a few adjustments for differences in westward development, could readily be applied to Canada.[2] The thesis had tremendous appeal to those who could still see themselves or their region as close to the frontier stage. After all, it implied that they were progressive, democratic and represented the true essence of the nation. But it was difficult for Maritimers to perceive themselves as part of a frontier society. The Maritimes were the only provinces lacking huge territories in the process of settlement or other forms of primitive development. And even a cursory examination suggested that here the process of cultural fusion was neither rapid or complete. In short, the frontierist approach implied that for an understanding of the progressive dynamic animating Canada in the late 19th and early 20th centuries, one should look westward to Ontario, to the Prairies, to British Columbia and to the North. The Maritimes were of interest only as a foil against which to demonstrate the validity of the frontier approach; simple logic suggested that, if the frontier encouraged progressive, egalitarian and democratic attitudes, then that part of the country furthest removed from the frontier stage must be conservative, socially stratified and unprogressive.

It would be simplistic, however, to attribute the pervasive frontierist influence in Canadian writing merely to a conscious acceptance of the theories outlined by Turner. In 1970 Michael Cross commented that "an avowed 'frontierist' is hardly to be found in a day's walk. Yet evidence of the frontier approach is to be discovered in the writings of a great many historians, many of whom would take umbrage at having this fact drawn to their attention."[3] Perhaps the latter were unaware of any debt to Turner because they were influenced more by the popular ideas in which Turner's work had its roots. Often the "greatest" and certainly the most popular historians are those who express clearly ideas and emotions

---

1. *The Early Writings of Frederick Jackson Turner*, Essay Index Reprint Series (Freeport, N.Y., 1938), p. 211.
2. Chester Martin, *Foundations of Canadian Nationhood* (Toronto, 1955), pp. 271–75.
3. M. S. Cross, ed., *The Frontier Thesis and the Canadas* (Toronto, 1970), p. 1.

implicit in the local folk culture.[4] Henry Nash Smith in *Virgin Land: The American West as Symbol and Myth* suggested such a role for Turner. The principal ingredients of Turner's hypothesis—the focus on the West, pride in democracy, the provision for new opportunities and the emphasis on agricultural settlement—were already very much a part of the Americans' view of their country when Turner presented his paper. Canadians too developed a myth of the West similar in essence to that of the Americans. Professor Gerald Friesen has outlined the principal ingredients of that myth, which portrayed the West as a source of individualism, new opportunities, virility, co-operative ideals, democracy, cultural fusion and material and social progress.[5] Undoubtedly Turner's contribution to the formulation and articulation of this myth was significant; one suspects, however, in view of the all-pervasive expression of these ideas in popular culture and the emotional satisfaction which they provided for so many Canadians, that a similar myth would have evolved even had Turner remained a journalist.[6]

In any case, the "myth of the West," as Professor Friesen has noted, "captured" English Canada before the end of the First World War. The popular view that western development and the wheat economy were the keys to Canada's current and future prosperity suggests an underlying economic motive in the myth's triumph. In a bid for immigrants, government, railway and board of trade propaganda portrayed Canada as a frontier community. The ideals of the western myth—democracy, cultural fusion, agrarianism and progress—had become so firmly rooted in British, American and Canadian traditions that most English-Canadians delighted in ascribing them to their country.[7] The popular literature of the day, including the work of Canadians Ralph Connor and R. J. C. Stead, and

---

4. H. N. Smith, *Virgin Land: The American West as Symbol and Myth* (New York, 1950), p. 293. In *Frederick Jackson Turner, Historian, Scholar, Teacher* (New York, 1973) Turner's biographer, R. A. Billington, stresses the "indelible impressions" made by Turner's boyhood experiences in a frontier community and outlines the conjunction of circumstances which made his work popular. Not the least of these was the revolt of the mid-west against the cultural domination of New England (pp. 17, 112). To these factors Richard Hofstadter added the emotional needs of the progressives. "At last the democratic middle-class reformers, especially those rooted in the agrarian traditions of the Middle West, were beginning to find a historical basis for their politics." *The Progressive Historians* (New York, 1968), p. 86.

5. G. A. Friesen, "Studies in the Development of Western Regional Consciousness," Ph.D. thesis, University of Toronto, 1973, p. 110.

6. In 1919, Turner conceded the same point regarding the United States. Quoted in Billington, *Frederick Jackson Turner*, p. 112.

7. Friesen, "Studies in the Development of Western Regional Consciousness," p. 109.

Americans widely-read in Canada, such as Zane Grey, trumpeted the virtues of the frontier *ad nauseam* .[8]

In the western myth's capture of Canadian historians the key factor was probably the personal contact with the Prairies. Westerners espoused their myth with a passion and commitment that was contagious. In the early decades of the 20th century those who took their news from the Winnipeg *Free Press*, attended the sermons of a William Ivens, J. S. Woodsworth, or other Prairie social gospel preachers, and rubbed shoulders with the enthusiasts of the graingrower co-operatives could hardly have avoided a warm glow of satisfaction that they too were involved in a dynamic experiment which would lead the way to a prosperous and morally superior nation. One of the striking facts revealed in Berger's survey was the number of Canada's leading historians of the first half of the century who taught on the Prairies at the formative stages of their careers. These included Chester Martin, Frank Underhill, A. R. M. Lower, W. A. MacIntosh, D. C. Masters and sociologist S. D. Clark. Not surprisingly, some of the leading Canadian exponents of frontierism came from this group. Both Frank Underhill, who lectured at the University of Saskatchewan from 1914 to 1926, with only a brief interruption, and A. R. M. Lower, who taught at Wesley College in Winnipeg until his call to Queen's in 1947, proclaimed a version of Canadian history in which the ideas of Turner and the western myth were prominently featured, and a version of Canadian history in which the Maritimes virtually ceased to exist after the union. As Underhill succinctly put it, "As for the Maritime provinces, nothing, of course, ever happens down there."[9] A. R. M. Lower, who had enthusiastically espoused the Turner thesis from the beginning of the 1930s, made the same point more subtly by entirely ignoring this period of Maritime history in his *Canadians in the Making*. Although Lower was already showing interest in the role of the metropolis when this text appeared in 1958, the following excerpt reveals his continued commitment to the myth of the West and his disdain for the Maritimes:

There is an ocean of difference between the relatively mature localism

---

8. See for examples, Ralph Connor, *The Man From Glengarry* (London, 1901); R. J. C. Stead, *The Cowpuncher* (Toronto, 1918); Zane Grey, *The Light of the Western Stars* (New York, 1913); Zane Grey's more than two dozen novels, many of which explicitly developed the theme of superiority and reforming influence of the western frontier, were available from T. Eaton catalogues on into the 1950s.
9. F. H. Underhill, *The Image of Confederation* (Toronto, 1964), p. 63; also cited in G. A. Rawlyk, "A New Golden Age of Maritime Historiography?" *Queen's Quarterly*, LXXVI (Spring 1969), p. 55.

of a secondary urban community and the air that blows through the national capital, Ottawa. This air begins to blow at Montreal, where the meeting of the two cultures makes for unwilling breath. It strengthens in Ottawa, whose major reason for existence is the duty of seeing in all directions. A current from it runs down to Toronto and the western peninsula of Ontario (only three chapters ago this was "western Canada"), both of which are rescued from parochialism by the scope of their economic activities. But it is at the head of the lakes that the air begins to blow strong, for with Port Arthur the traveller is in another world, the West. From the Lakehead to the Pacific coast, the same air blows. The same kind of observation could be made as one goes northward, for here too there is another world. The atmosphere is similar to that of the West. It has the geographical emancipation, the hope, energy, lack of convention, readiness to accept all comers and on equal terms that mark new societies wherein, the old moulds having been broken, the pieces are set loose and shaken up into new patterns.[10]. . .

Logically deducible from the frontier thesis, the popular stereotype of regional conservatism had received a strong boost from the Prairie's disappointment at the Maritimes' rejection of their leadership in the Progressive movement. Refusing to admit that Maritime interests differed in any way from their own, Prairie Progressives ascribed their failure in the region to one factor—the innate conservatism and traditional partisanship of the people.[11] Residents of the Central Canadian metropolises were also happy to attribute the destruction of the Maritime economy to the generally unprogressive nature of the Maritime character—a cause for which they could in no way be held responsible. According to R. L. Calder, a Montreal barrister, instead of trying to help themselves, Maritimers preferred "to sit on the country store steps. . .chew apples and talk politics." Or, as Harold Cunningham put it in an article in *Maclean's Magazine*, the Maritime provinces were like a housewife who having

---

10. A. R. M. Lower, *Canadians in the Making* (Toronto, 1958), p. 358. In his autobiography Lower was more explicit. The Maritimes were "the most conservative parts of English Canada. . . .It is in the less restless, less dynamic nature of their society that Maritimers differ from other parts of English Canada." *My First Seventy-Five Years* (Toronto, 1967), p. 226.
11. E. R. Forbes, "Never the Twain Did Meet: Prairie-Maritime Relations, 1910–27," *CHR*, LIX (1978), p. 28. The terms "conservative" and "conservatism" as employed by contemporaries and later historians, are negative and critical epithets equivalent to "backward," "cynical," "timid" or "unprogressive"; any resemblance to any political or social philosophy living or dead is probably coincidental.

married for money which failed to materialize "neglected her housework, went down to the seashore. . .watched the ships go by and pouted."[12]

While it is not surprising in view of the paucity of research, that contemporary stereotypes should provide historians with explanations for Maritime behaviour, it is ironic that one of those who relied on the stereotype was W. L. Morton who stressed distinct regional perspectives in his 1946 critique of the Laurentian school of Canadian historians. In 1950 Morton himself gave an effective affirmation of the Prairie regional perspective in his *Progressive Party in Canada* (Toronto, 1950). But in this and in his later works he appeared to draw his interpretations of Maritime behaviour from the Winnipeg *Free Press*. Having established the Progressive Party as the product of a unique economic base—the "political expression of the monolithic wheat economy"—he then explained its failure in the far east by a wholly gratuitous invocation of Maritime conservatism.[13] His oft-cited article, "The Bias of Prairie Politics," minimized the effectiveness of separate political movements by exaggerating Maritime gains from working within the traditional party framework—an exaggeration which was the standard ploy by the Prairie press and politicians in demanding more for their region.[14] The shaky foundations of Morton's generalizations about the modern Maritimes are most clearly revealed, however, in a highly misleading statement in the *Kingdom of Canada*, where he informs the reader that in the 1920s "Maritimers refrained from protest or talk of secession as in the past. They generally put their faith in the Liberal party and followed the veteran Fielding and the young J. L. Ralston in seeking relief by pressure on that party. In 1926 they were rewarded by the appointment of a royal commission on Maritime claims."[15] This, of course, was the period of the Maritime Rights Movement, the secession resolution of H. W. Corning and the overwhelming Conservative victories in the region in three provincial and two federal elections.

Similar distortions can be found in other monographic literature. In 1950 Catherine Cleverdon's *Woman Suffrage Movement in Canada* provided a more balanced regional study of a nation-wide movement. Each of the traditional regions received a separate chapter. But despite the

---

12. Quebec *Telegraph*, 12 October 1926; *Maclean's Magazine*, 15 October 1926.
13. W. L. Morton, "Clio in Canada: The Interpretation of Canadian History" in Carl Berger, ed., *Approaches to Canadian History* (Toronto, 1967).
14. W. L. Morton, "The Bias of Prairie Politics," in Donald Swainson, ed., *Historical Essays on the Prairie Provinces* (reprinted Toronto, 1970), p. 296.
15. W. L. Morton, *The Kingdom of Canada* (Toronto, 1963), p. 445.

regional approach, the traditional myth of the frontier and the Maritime stereotype continued to dominate. The overriding thesis was apparent in the chapter subheadings. Ontario was the "Pioneer" which "bore the brunt of pioneering for women's rights." Then the Prairies, which represented "Democracy's Grass Roots," took the lead in giving full political privileges to women, an action "typical of western progressiveness." The Maritimes, "Stronghold of Conservatism," afflicted by the "weight of indifference" and an "atmosphere of conservatism," brought up the rear, at least for English Canada.[16] Cleverdon's Maritime chapter is a classic example of begging the question and using emotive language to support a weak thesis. The suffrage movement in Canada, as Cleverdon portrays it, was a narrow middle class crusade involving no more than a tiny minority of women in each province. This fact is mentioned as a neutral piece of information in the chapters on each of the other regions, but in the Maritimes the non-involvement of the majority of women becomes a critical factor in demonstrating regional conservatism. In her discussions of New Brunswick and Nova Scotia women, Cleverdon manages to use the words "indifference" or "indifferent" nine times, "conservative" or "conservatism" eight times and adds, perhaps for stylistic variation, the terms "disinterest," "apathy," "hostility," "contempt" and "ultraconservative."

What evidence is there to justify the thesis of a greater Maritime conservatism in women's rights? For New Brunswick and Nova Scotia before 1912 there seems to be none at all. Indeed, Maritime women appear to have led the agitation for admission to universities. In 1846 a pamphlet by a Halifax lady scathingly asked: "Who gave you men the right to establish Colleges, and Universities, at which to educate your sons, in all the substantial sciences. . .while woman, hedged about on every hand by the guardianship of the governess, is taught. . .the whole science of composing and scrawling billetdoux after the most approved method. . .?"[17] A later pamphlet berated Joseph Howe for his failure to take up the

---

16. C. L. Cleverdon, *The Woman Suffrage Movement in Canada* (reprinted Toronto, 1974). See esp. pp. 24, 44, 49 and ch. 6. In his introduction, Professor Ramsay Cook did not help to correct the stereotype when he disenfranchised the women of New Brunswick and Nova Scotia until the "early 1920s" and then sought new reasons to explain their conservatism. Ibid., p. xv.

17. *Essays on the Future Destiny of Nova Scotia, Improvement of Female Education and on Peace* (Halifax, 1846). A subsequent essay ascribed to "An Anonymous Lady" had written immediately thereunder with a quill pen the inscription "by an insane female." Unfortunately this pamphlet, which the author read in the open stacks of the Dalhousie University Library in 1965, can no longer be located.

cause and in 1859 Mount Allison University admitted its first women students to a degree programme. Most other Maritime universities soon followed. Cleverdon portrayed E. H. Stowe of Toronto as the heroic pioneer of the Canadian feminist movement, citing particularly her influence in securing the admission of women to the University of Toronto in 1886. This "triumph" came 11 years after Mount Allison had granted the first Bachelor of Science degree awarded to a woman in the British Empire.[18] For Halifax, at least, the suffrage movement of the 1880s and 1890s marked the culmination of nearly half a century of vigorous debate on women's place in society.[19] And for those two decades the agitation in the two larger Maritime provinces followed a pattern similar to that of the other provinces—a pattern characterized by a plethora of bills, supported by a comparable number of petitions and meeting an identical lack of success. Defeated in every province by the end of the 1890s, the movement entered what Cleverdon called a "breathing period" from which it would not emerge until 1912. The tardiness by two or three years of Nova Scotia and New Brunswick women in actually securing the vote hardly justifies the image of an all-pervasive indifference or hostility to the feminist movement arising from an innate regional conservatism.

Morton and Cleverdon were but the first of many historians to invoke the stereotype as the explanation of supposedly deviant behaviour by Maritimers. Sometimes the evolution of the stereotype involved a co-operative effort by several historians. This seems to be the case in the field of labour history. A multi-volume series on Social Credit included D. C. Masters' study of the Winnipeg General Strike which suggested a greater militancy and radicalism among labour in Western Canada. S. D. Clark's "forward" took the process a step further by setting the One Big Union in "the tradition of America frontier radicalism."[20] With the West more radical than Ontario all that was needed was a conservative Maritimes to round out the familiar frontier model. In his survey of labour unrest in Canada S. M. Jamieson initially shied away from the Western myth by stressing the importance of the industries involved rather than the regions in which they were located. But when he came to the Maritimes he

---

18. R. S. Harris, *A History of Higher Education in Canada, 1663–1960* (Toronto, 1976), p. 11; V. J. Strong-Boag, *The Parliament of Women: The National Council of Women in Canada 1893–1929* (Ottawa, 1976), pp. 12–3.

19. Robert Sedgewick, *The Proper Sphere and Influence of Women in Christian Society* (Halifax, 1856); John Munro, *The Place and Work of Women in the Church* (Halifax, 1877); J. S. David, *A Reply to the "The Place and Work of Women in the Church"* [Halifax, n.d.]; *Debates and Proceedings of the House of Assembly of Nova Scotia,* 1886, p. 506.

20. D. C. Masters, *The Winnipeg General Strike* (Toronto, 1950), p. viii.

reverted to the traditional pattern. Since there was no research to indicate radical labour activity in the Maritimes outside of the coal mining areas, he readily concluded that there was none. Maritime labour was "exceedingly conservative in political and other orientations."[21] Certainly if he knew anything about Amherst's version of the One Big Union or the T.L.C.'s expulsion of the Nova Scotia Federation of Labour in the reaction against industrial unionism, he made no mention of them.[22] British Columbia's Martin Robin took the final step and excluded even the coal miners on the assumption that nothing radical of a political nature involving labour had ever developed in the conservative Maritimes. Thus his *Radical Politics and Canadian Labour* omitted all mention of the protracted struggles between the "radicals" and the "progressives" for control of District 26 of the United Mine Workers of America, the largest geographically cohesive bloc of organized labour in the country. In 1922 the radicals endorsed a programme which included the statement that "we proclaim openly to all the world that we are out for the complete overthrow of the capitalist system and capitalist state, peaceable if we may, forceable if we must" and elected their slate of candidates to the executive by majorities of more than four to one.[23] That the radicals did not succeed in their goal of linking up with the Red International and ultimately succumbed to a concerted effort of repression from the U.M.W. International, the British Empire Steel Corporation and the local government does not erase the significance of their victory. Labour in the Maritimes did not achieve a revolution, or even come close, but then where in North America did they do so?

Accumulated ignorance also contributed to the stereotype of religious conservatism in the Maritimes. First, the author of a University of Toronto M.A. thesis on the social gospel in the Methodist church suggested, without any reference to Maritime sources, that the social gospel had little impact on the church there. Stewart Crysdale and E. A. Christie noted the hostile response by the Halifax Presbyterian *Witness* to labour's tactics in the Winnipeg General Strike. Apparently guided by such comments, the Western myth and the overriding stereotype of Maritime conservatism, Richard Allen rashly concluded that the Maritimes was "a part of the

---

21. S. M. Jamieson, *Times of Trouble: Labour Unrest and Industrial Conflict in Canada, 1900–66* (Ottawa, 1968), pp. 25, 100.
22. Nolan Reilly, "The Origins of the Amherst General Strike, 1890–1919" (paper presented to the annual meeting of the Canadian Historical Association, 1977).
23. Martin Robin, *Radical Politics and Canadian Labour* (Kingston, 1968); *The Workers Weekly* (Stellarton), 30 June, 25 August 1922.

nation where the social gospel had made virtually no impact whatso-ever."[24] Not only was this conclusion inconsistent with Allen's own thesis that the movement in Canada was a product of broad intellectual currents, but it ignored the fact that the major Protestant denominations in the Maritimes formally endorsed social gospel principles and that clergymen from the Maritimes were active in the movement at the national level.[25]...

It is not the purpose of this paper to develop a new myth of a dynamic and progressive Maritimes. What the paper is trying to show is that we really know very little about the Maritimes in the post-Confederation period. Much of the so-called "knowledge" we do have is highly suspect, having in many cases been deduced from the frontier myth supported by contemporary attitudes, or a repetition of the stereotype seized upon as a convenience by the researcher, who boggled at the task of having to open a neglected field as only a small part of a major study. With repetition in so many books on so many topics, the stereotype has become an accepted historical "fact." It should not be necessary to point out the danger of dealing in stereotypes, be they regional, racial or national. It is not that the stereotype is entirely false, although on occasion, that may be the case. The danger lies in an acceptance of a point of view in which fact and fiction are jumbled together without critical analysis. The term "conserva-tive" is particularly unfortunate since it is a comparative term which has little meaning unless the point of comparison is clearly indicated. In many cases "conservative" was used by Maritimers themselves to compare the Maritimes, less to some other region, than to their own ideal of what their region should be. That appears to be the way it was used in the various comments of Maritimers employed as evidence by Cleverdon. One suspects that there was also an element of social criticism in Beck's ringing indictment of Nova Scotia's leaders for their excessive caution in domestic legislation and their failure to protect regional interests at the federal level.

Another danger of the stereotype, towards which historians in particu-lar should be alert, is its static image which does not allow for chronologi-cal variation. Perhaps there were periods in the Maritimes' history when a

---

24. M. V. Royce, "The Contribution of the Methodist Church to Social Welfare in Canada," M.A. thesis, University of Toronto, 1940, p. 238; E. A. Christie, "The Presbyterian Church in Canada and its Official Attitude Towards Public Affairs and Social Problems," M.A. thesis, University of Toronto, 1955; Stewart Crysdale, *The Industrial Struggle and the Protestant Ethic in Canada* (Toronto, 1961), p. 83.
25. Richard Allen, *The Social Passion: Religion and Social Reform in Canada, 1914–28* (Toronto, 1973) p. 110.

careful and specific comparison with other regions would show them to be more conservative in certain respects. By the end of the 1930s, for example, the Maritimes had endured two decades of depression—one more than the rest of the country. Successive attempts at political and social protest had failed.[26] Their people had reason to be pragmatic, cautious and sceptical—especially of the ready solutions to their problems offered by outsiders. Thus it is not surprising that some Maritimers who lived through this period have been quick to brand people of their region as conservative and have found it difficult to imagine the optimism of an earlier age. Perhaps too it explains the comments of some visitors to the region in this period. Although here one has to be careful that "conservative" does not merely mean "different"—something the outsider may in his arrogance not fully understand. . . .

FURTHER READINGS FOR TOPIC 3

Carl Berger, *The Writing of Canadian History: Aspects of English-Canadian Historical Writing Since 1900* (Toronto: University of Toronto Press, second edition, 1986).

J. M. S. Careless, "Frontierism, Metropolitanism, and Canadian History," in Carl Berger, ed., *Approaches to Canadian History* (Toronto: University of Toronto Press, 1967), 63–83.

Michael S. Cross, ed., *The Frontier Thesis and the Canadas: The Debate on the Impact of the Canadian Environment* (Toronto: Copp Clark, 1970).

David Laycock, *Populism and Democratic Thought in the Canadian Prairies, 1910 to 1945* (Toronto: University of Toronto Press, 1990).

Jeffrey M. Taylor, "The Language of Agrarianism in Manitoba, 1890–1925," *Labour/Le Travail*, 23 (Spring 1989), 91–118.

Graeme Wynn, ed., *People Places Patterns Processes: Geographical Perspectives on the Canadian Past* (Toronto: Copp Clark Pitman, 1990).

---

26. E. R. Forbes, *The Maritime Rights Movement: A Study in Canadian Regionalism* (Montreal and Kingston, 1978).

Topic 4

*The
Mysterious
Other:
Immigrants,
the
New
Labour
Market,
and
the
Construction
of
Ethnicity*

*Perhaps immigrants, as they pushed into a strange world in which they
were often treated as little more than numbers and muscle-power, had
more cause than anyone to feel that with modernity, "all that is solid melts
into air." Immigrants were drawn from the four quarters of the globe by the
brilliant propaganda and administration of a renovated Department of the
Interior and its key architect, Clifford Sifton (aided by the often
disreputable tactics of various immigration agents); by the country's
reputation for prosperity and rapid growth, at a time when the
international economy seemed to smile upon Canada's prospects; by the
rise of the prairie wheat economy, which created its own demands for
labour and sent abroad the heady promise of cheap and fertile land; and by
an intensified demand for industrial workers, in a country that was
building two new transcontinental railway lines. Perhaps as many as
900 000 unskilled and skilled workers arrived in search of industrial
employment between 1907 and 1930. The immigrants were not only pulled*

to Canada, but also pushed out of Europe and Asia, by the forces of modernity: by rising population, by land scarcity and rural exploitation, by perceptions of religious and ethnic discrimination.

The three readings in this section show three starkly different faces of the experience of immigration. Kay Anderson's study goes beyond the familiar denunciations of prejudice in British Columbia to explore the dynamics through which white cultural hegemony was maintained by constructing a "Chinatown" in the imagination; Robert Harney's compelling portrait of an Italian merchant of labour power puts a human face on the international capitalist labour market and dramatizes the position of the Italian "sojourner," for whom Canada was not a prospective home but a temporary job-site; and Joy Parr illustrates the gendered complexities of immigration in the case of one small industrial Ontario town. Victims or architects of modernity? Immigrants were clearly both.

The Idea of Chinatown:

The Power of Place and Institutional Practice in the Making of a Racial Category

KAY J. ANDERSON

They come from southern China...with customs, habits and modes of life fixed and unalterable, resulting from an ancient and effete civilization. They form, on their arrival, a community within a community, separate and apart, a foreign substance within but not of our body politic, with no love for our laws or institutions; a people that cannot assimilate and become an integral part of our race and nation. With their habits of overcrowding, and an utter disregard for all sanitary laws, they are a continual menace to health. From a moral and social point of view, living as they do without home life, schools or churches, and so nearly approaching a servile class, their effect upon the rest of the community is bad....Upon this point there was entire unanimity (Canada 1902, 278).

It would be easy to interpret the words of Royal Commissioners Clute, Munn, and Foley in 1902 as further evidence, if more were needed, of the weight of racial discrimination in British Columbia during the stern years of the late nineteenth and early twentieth centuries. Like many other official utterances at the turn of the century, their words strengthen the claim that the Chinese, because of their distinctiveness, were subjected to many forms of victimization at the hands of a vigorously nativistic white community. Largely in response to that prejudice, overseas Chinese formed Chinatowns, or so a tradition of liberal discrimination studies has held. Chinatown has been a victimized colony of the East in the West.

Neighborhoods of Chinese settlement in Western societies have been extensively studied throughout the twentieth century. Subjected to hostile receptions, Chinatowns serve as commentaries on the attitudes and behavior of their host societies (e.g., G. Barth 1964; Lyman 1974; Palmer 1982; Price 1974; Roy 1980a; Ward 1978). They have also been an entry point to many research questions in sociology and anthropology about

KAY J. ANDERSON, "THE IDEA OF CHINATOWN: THE POWER OF PLACE AND INSTITUTIONAL PRACTICE IN THE MAKING OF A RACIAL CATEGORY," ANNALS OF THE ASSOCIATION OF AMERICAN GEOGRAPHERS, 77, 4 (1987), 580–98. A COMPLETE VERSION OF THIS PAPER, INCLUDING MAPS AND ILLUSTRATIONS, APPEARS IN THIS PUBLICATION. BY PERMISSION OF THE ASSOCIATION OF AMERICAN GEOGRAPHERS AND THE AUTHOR.

cultural transfer overseas and the dynamics of social organization and community stratification in new environments (e.g., Crissman 1967; Hoe 1976; Nee and Nee 1974; Weiss 1974; Wickberg et al. 1982; Wong 1982). A recent history of Toronto's Chinatown, for example, examines the transformation from "the homogeneous population of the traditional period" to "the diverse heterogeneous Chinese population today" (Thompson 1979, 361). In social geography, Chinatown has been conceptualized as a launching point in the assimilation of Chinese immigrants, as an urban village pitted against encroaching land uses, as a product of segregation on the basis of race or ethnicity, and as a Chinese architectural form (e.g., Cho and Leigh 1972; Cybriwsky 1986; Lai 1973; Salter 1978). Chinatown has been viewed as either a ghettoized, minority community or as an "ethnic" community. One geographer summarizes the common social science conceptualization in his words: "Chinatown in North America is characterized by a concentration of Chinese people and economic activities in one or more city blocks which forms a unique component of the urban fabric. It is basically an idiosyncratic oriental community amidst an occidental urban environment" (Lai 1973, 101).

It is possible, however, to adopt a different point of departure to the study of Chinatown, one that does not rely upon a discrete "Chineseness" as an implicit explanatory principle. "Chinatown" is not "Chinatown" only because the "Chinese," whether by choice or constraint live there. Rather, one might argue that Chinatown is a social construction with a cultural history and a tradition of imagery and institutional practice that has given it a cognitive and material reality in and for the West. It is, as Ley (1977) describes the elements of human apprehension, an object for a subject. For if we do not assume that the term "Chinese" expresses an unproblematic relationship to biological or cultural constants but is in one sense a classification, it becomes apparent that the study of the Chinese and their turf is also a study of our categories, our practices, and our interests. Only secondarily is the study about host society attitudes; primarily it concerns the ideology that shaped the attitudes contained in the opening quotation. This step beyond "white" attitudes is critical because it is not prejudice that has explanatory value but the racial ideology that informs it. Such an argument is not unimportant for the conceptualization of Chinatown. Indeed it requires a more fundamental epistemological critique of the twin ideas of "Chinese" and "Chinatown," of race and place.

It is not possible to investigate in one brief article the process of the classification of identity and place in the numerous contexts where the race idea has been institutionalized. Rather, my aim here is to argue the case for a new conceptualization of Chinatown as a white European idea with reference to one context, that of Vancouver, British Columbia. There, one of the largest Chinatowns in North America stands to this day, in part as an expression of the cultural abstractions of those who have been in command of "the power of definition," to use Western's (1981, 8) valuable phrase. But the thrust of the paper is not limited to the study of ideas. Indeed the significance of "Chinatown" is not simply that it has been a representation perceived in certain ways, but that it has been, like race, an idea with remarkable social force and material effect—one that for more than a century has shaped and justified the practices of powerful institutions toward it and toward people of Chinese origin.

The brevity of a paper also precludes attention to the century-long workings of the race definition process in Vancouver. Such a process has operated from the time Chinatown was reviled as Vancouver's public nuisance, promoted in the mid-1930s as its "Little Corner of the Far East," reconstructed in the 1950s and 1960s as a "slum," and finally under the aegis of multiculturalism courted by the state in the 1970s precisely for its perceived "Chineseness" (Anderson 1986). I thus confine the historical focus to Vancouver's Chinatown in the late nineteenth and early twentieth centuries, when its social definition was sweeping in both cause and effect. I thereby attempt to uncover the broader relationship between place, power, racial discourse, and institutional practice....Such an interpretation of Chinatown might be equally relevant to the making of other racial categories in Vancouver, to "Chinese" and "Chinatowns" in other settings, and to other racially defined people in other settings.

I begin by providing a brief outline of the geographical site of the subject of this paper. Following that sketch, I discuss the conceptualization of Chinatown as a Western landscape type and then present empirical material from the Vancouver example.

A SKETCH OF THE SETTLEMENT AT DUPONT STREET, 1886–1900

By the time the City of Vancouver was incorporated in 1886, Chinese settlement in the city was severely proscribed. The senior levels of state had already intervened in the "Chinese question" and ensured that by the mid-1880s, there would be limits on the participation of Chinese-origin people in political life,[1] their access to Crown land,[2] and their employment on public works.[3] In 1885, after the completion of the Canadian Pacific Railway, the federal government in Ottawa took a decisive step by imposing a head tax on Chinese entrants, and in 1903 Wilfrid Laurier's administration raised it to an almost prohibitive level of $500. Thus by the time of Vancouver's first municipal election in May 1886, when 60 Chinese-origin men were chased from the polls and denied the vote (Morley 1961, 73), a culture of race was fully respected in separate statutory provisions for "Chinese" by the provincial and federal administrations.

From the late 1850s, when gold was first discovered in British Columbia, people from China lived and worked on Burrard Inlet. Most were men employed in unskilled jobs at the Hastings and Moodyville sawmills, but a minority opened stores to service the mill employees. By 1884, the population of Chinese on the inlet was 114 (Morton 1977, 144) and a number of settlements had been established. One of these was built in the vicinity of Dupont Street where woods and a rocky outcrop afforded protection (Yip 1936, 11) and where nearby industries on False Creek offered employment opportunities. Other small settlements of Chinese pioneers existed on the road to New Westminster, in Stanley Park, and the West End.

One such camp on the Brighouse Estate in the West End was particularly provocative to Vancouver's early European residents. Resentment was intense against the laborers who cleared land there at low cost, and on the night of February 24, 1887 some 300 rioters decided to escalate their intimidation strategies. Unimpeded by local police, they raided and destroyed the camps of Chinese laborers; they then attacked the washhouses, stores, shacks, and other structures in the vicinity of Dupont Street ("Outbreak against the Chinese" 1887). The day after, some 90 Chinese from that area were moved to New Westminster ("The Chinese leaving" 1887). So lax were the local authorities in controlling the violence

---

1. In 1875, the jurisdictional competence of the Province to deny the franchise to people of Chinese origin was affirmed (British Columbia, *Statutes*, 35 Vict., 1875, ch. 26, s. 22).
2. Clause 122 of the Land Act deemed it unlawful "for a commissioner to issue a preemption record of any Crown land, or to sell any portion thereof to any Chinese" (British Columbia, *Statutes*, 51 Vict., 1884, ch. 16).
3. By 1900, an anti-Chinese clause was introduced in government contracts that refused provincial aid to public works contractors who employed "Orientals" (British Columbia, *Journals of the Legislative Assembly*, 1900, vol. 29, p. 125).

that the Smithe administration in Victoria, hardly known for its sympathy to Chinese, annulled Vancouver's judicial powers and dispatched special constables to take charge of what the attorney general described as Vancouver's decline into "mob rule" (Roy 1976; "Their drastic measures" 1887; "The Robson regime" 1887).

In the context of such hostility the Chinese returned to Vancouver and re-established a highly concentrated pattern of residence. Most of those who had fled returned directly to the original Dupont Street settlement, which also attracted many of the West End laborers after they completed the Brighouse Estate contract. It was a swampy district, with an adverse physical quality that paralleled the peripheral legal, political, social, and economic status of the pioneers it housed. Some lived more comfortably than others, however. Laborers mostly resided in wooden shacks, in conditions a Chinese statesman found "distressed and cramped" on his visit in 1903 (Ma 1983, 34), but merchants usually lived in elevated brick structures on the north and south sides of Dupont Street.

By the turn of the century, the total population of the settlement was 2,053 men (of whom 143 were merchants and the rest workers), 27 women (16 of whom were wives of merchants), and 26 children (Canada 1902, 13). Family life was the preserve of a small economic and political elite, some members of which established a property base in the area from the 1890s (see Yee 1984). As W. A. Cumyow, a British Columbia–born court interpreter testified in 1901, "a large proportion of them would bring their families here were it not for the unfriendly reception...which creates an unsettled feeling" (Canada 1902, 236). Such was the marginal turf from which the Chinese launched their contested claim to Canadian life in the twentieth century.

CHINATOWN AS A WESTERN LANDSCAPE TYPE

How was it that the streets of Dupont, Carrall, and Columbia in Vancouver became apprehended as "Chinatown"? Whose term, indeed in one sense whose place was this? No corresponding term—"Anglo town"—existed in local parlance, nor were the residents of the likes of Vancouver's West End known as "Occidentals." Why then was the home of the pioneers known and intelligible as "Chinatown"? Consistent with the prevailing conceptualization of Chinatown as an "ethnic neighborhood," we might anticipate the response that Chinese people—a racially visible and culturally distinct minority—settled and made their lives there through some combination of push and pull forces. One view, then, might be that the East lives on in the West and Chinatown expresses the values and experiences of its residents.

That people of Chinese origin, like other pioneers to North America, brought with them particular traditions that shaped their activities and choices in the new setting can hardly be disputed. Indeed an important tradition of scholarship has outlined the significance of such traditions for North American Chinatowns as overseas Chinese colonies. Needless to say, Chinese residents were active agents in their own "place making" as were the British-origin residents in Vancouver's Shaughnessy. My decision not to give primary attention to the residents' sense of place then is not to deny them an active role in building their neighborhood nor of any consciousness they may have had as Chinese. Some merchants from China might have even been eager to limit contact with non-Chinese, just as China had obviated contact with Western "barbarians" over the centuries. Others, given a choice, might have quickly assimilated.

But the multiple reality of place invites another equally important but neglected viewpoint. The phenomenon of "John Chinaman's" overseas home was well-known to late nineteenth-century North Americans of European origin, whatever definitions of place the residents themselves might have held. Regardless of how each of the residents of such settlements defined themselves and each other—whether by class, occupation, ethnicity, region of origin in China, surname, generation, gender, or place of birth—the settlement was apprehended and targeted by European society through that society's cognitive categories. Without needing the acknowledgment or acceptance of the residents, Chinatown's representers constructed in their own minds a boundary between "their" territory and "our" territory.

In his important discussion of "imaginative geographies" such as Europe's "Orient," Edward Said (1978, 55) argued that this distinction is one that "helps the mind to intensify its own sense of itself by dramatizing the distance and difference between what is close and what is far away." This process suggests the argument that although North America's Chinese settlements have often been deliberately isolated, "Chinatown" has been an arbitrary classification of space, a regionalization that has belonged to European society. Like race, Chinatown has been a historically specific idea, a social space that has been rooted in the language and ethos of its representers and conferred upon the likes of Vancouver's Dupont Street settlement.

The word "arbitrary" is not unimportant here. "Chinese" have been residentially segregated and socially apprehended in North America on capricious grounds. Such a claim rests on the view that any classification of the world's populations into so-called "races" is arbitrary and imperfect. Despite the biological fact that systematic differences in gene frequencies exist among geographically or culturally isolated inbreeding populations, most contemporary biologists agree that genetic variability between the populations of Asia, Europe, and Africa is considerably less than that within those populations (e.g., Farish 1978; Lewontin, Rose, and Kamin 1984; Montagu 1964). Apart from the visible characteristics of skin, hair, and bone by which we have been socialized to "see" what is popularly called a difference of "race," there are, as Appiah (1985, 22) notes, "few genetic characteristics to be found in the population of England that are not found in similar proportions in Zaire or China." The important point is that because genetic variation is continuous, "racial" difference cannot be conceptualized as absolute. "Racial categories form a continuum of gradual change, not a set of sharply demarcated types" (Marger 1985, 12), a point that leads biologists Lewontin, Rose, and Kamin (1984, 127) to argue: "Any use of 'racial' categories must take its justification from some other source than biology."

A growing literature in ethnic studies would also suggest that categorizations such as "black," "white," "Oriental," or "Hispanic" are not rooted in an unproblematic difference of ancestral culture or ethnicity either. Fredrick Barth (1969, 14) began the critique in anthropology over 20 years ago when he claimed "we can assume no simple one-to-one relationship between ethnic units and cultural similarities and differences." There is by now a convincing critique of the tradition of cultural relativism in North American ethnic studies, where ethnicity was accepted as an innate property of culture-bearing groups (e.g., Jackson 1981; Peach 1984; Perrin 1983; Steinberg 1981; Watson 1981). According to the more recent argument, ethnic groups are created socially by internal rules of exclusion and inclusion around idioms of actual or perceived common descent such as language and religion. Territory may also be a symbol and resource around which ethnic boundaries are negotiated (Suttles 1968).

Clearly, there is a distancing in such a perspective from a reified notion of ancestral culture as an external system of values and practices. "Chineseness" is not an entity that is imbibed across generation and context by a person of Chinese origin in Hong Kong, a third generation Chinese-origin resident of Malaysia, a Chinese in mainland China, a person of Chinese descent in South Africa, and a fourth generation "Chinese-Canadian" of Vancouver. Of course a subjective sense of ethnic identity can be strong in the absence of binding cultural traditions, but the important point here is that an analytical distinction must be drawn between self (or emic) definitions of identity and those etic classifications that are conferred from without. The former are predicated upon subjective or inclusive processes, whereas the latter are based upon exclusive processes (Banton 1983, 104; Cohen 1978).

Clearly, I do not assume that race and racial categories are discretely given facts with their own descriptive and analytical utility. In itself, "race," and the prejudice it is often ipso facto assumed to inspire, explains nothing. For the purposes of social science, the concept of race must be located strictly in the realm of ideology. Of course other social scientists, including Western (1981) in geography, have recognized race as problematic, but there have been few attempts to confront the epistemological implications of this in substantive research.[4] Almost no attention has been given to the process by which racial categories are themselves constructed, institutionalized, and transmitted over time and space. Banton (1977, 19) suggests as much in his statement: "Though much has been said about the evils associated with racial classification, there has been little systematic study of the process."

Chinatown has not been incidental to the structuring of this process in the example of the classification "Chinese" or "Oriental." Indeed by situating one such place "in process, in time" (Abrams 1982), it is possible to demonstrate that as a Western idea and a concrete form Chinatown has been a critical nexus through which a system of racial classification has been continuously constructed. Racial ideology has been materially embedded in space...and it is through "place" that it has been given a local referent, become a social fact, and aided its own reproduction.

In itself, the idea of Chinatown would not be so important or enduring but for the fact it has been legitimized by government agents who make cognitive categories stand as the official definition of a people and place. In the Vancouver case, "Chinatown" accrued a certain field of meaning that became the justification for recurring rounds of government practice in the ongoing construction of both the place and the racial category. Indeed the state has played a particularly pivotal role in the making of a symbolic (and material) order around the idiom of race in Western societies. By sanctioning the arbitrary boundaries of insider and outsider and the idea of mainstream society as "white," the levels of the state have both "enforced" and "propagated" a white European hegemony.[5]...

---

4. One edited volume by Husband (1982) addresses aspects of the culture of race in contemporary Britain. The literature on labeling may be relevant here. For original statements on mental illness, see Goffman (1963) and on crime, see Matza (1969).

5. The words "enforced" and "propagated" are borrowed from MacLaughlin and Agnew's (1986) discussion of the state and socially based hegemonies. On the state's role in South Africa, see Pirie (1984) and Western (1981).

"CHINATOWN" IN INTELLECTUAL CONTEXT: THE AGE OF THE RACE IDEA

Since classical times, Europeans have shared with other cultural traditions a tendency to generalize about the world's different populations.[6] Aristotle, for one, referred to his own "Hellenic race" around 300 B.C. as "high spirited and intelligent," while "Asiatics" were "inventive" but "wanting in spirit" (March 1974, 23–24). Indeed well before the birth of capitalism and colonialism, a European worldview made evaluative distinctions of "East" and "West," Christian and heathen, civilized and uncivilized. There was also a classical color sensitivity that became heightened during the spread of Christianity from the tenth to thirteenth centuries (Bastide 1967). In subsequent centuries, European explorers relied upon, reinforced, and extended this early cognitive package. The Portuguese slave traffic in Africa in the fifteenth century (Boxer 1963) and, by 1650, slavery in the American colonies (Jordan 1968) sealed the outlook with the stamp of phenotype, and British imperialism from the late eighteenth century consolidated all of the we/they distinctions into an ideological structure of formidable rigidity.

During the nineteenth century a transformation from ethnocentrism to a radical biological determinism took place, facilitated by a major theoretical effort in the new biological sciences. Certainly by the time immigrants from China arrived in British Columbia, the leap from color to a fundamental difference of "race" had been solidly made by the scientific community of Britain, North America, and Western Europe. Environmental explanations for human variation had been abandoned, and the focus of scientific attention had become fixed upon discrete types. Skull sizes and shapes were outward signs of innate biological and cultural differences, and a generation of physical anthropologists measured them despite the nagging problem that features such as skin color, facial angle, and cranial shape did not covary in a systematic way (Stepan 1982; Gould 1981). Nor did Charles Darwin's evolutionary and environmental theory prompt people to question their beliefs about absolute differences.[7]

---

6. See Tuan's (1974, 38) figure of traditional Chinese worldviews with zones of increasing barbarism away from the Chinese court. On the universality of the categorization process, see also Berger and Luckmann (1966).

7. In geography, Griffith Taylor's (1927) "migration-zone theory" of cultural evolution challenged the assumptions of the day, arguing that environmental pressures were more critical than were biological constants in shaping human destiny. Like Darwin himself, however, Taylor remained locked within the old race science because he assumed that the racial type was the unit upon which evolutionary processes operated. Only by the 1940s,

Indeed biologists, social scientists, and the populace at large made their own interpretation of *The Descent of Man*, taking it as confirmation that discrete races of variable "fitness" were governed by impersonal laws and engaged in an inexorable struggle (see Jones 1980).

The early nineteenth-century discovery of the vast stretch of geologic time seemed to confirm the European view that human history was a kind of natural progression from barbarism to civilization. Like the transformation of the earth, the evolution of humanity was a formidably slow process in which savages might become "Caucasians," but the latter were thousands of years "ahead" of the other races (Harris 1972, 266). For all contemporary purposes, the races were immutably separate. "John Chinaman," for example, possessed properties that permitted him to achieve only a semicivilized, despotic state. His race was so retarded, claimed Judge J. Gray of the British Columbia Supreme Court, that he could see no reason why "the strong, broad shouldered superior race, superior physically and mentally, sprung from the highest types of the old world and the new world, [should be] expressing a fear of competition with a diminutive, inferior, and comparatively speaking, feminine race" (Canada 1885, 69). More often, however, the evolutionary doctrine was taken as a warning that the higher "races" were vulnerable to contamination from immigration and "hybridization" with those who would pass along their deficiencies.

According to this nineteenth-century worldview, Vancouver's Dupont Street settlement would be a generically "Chinese" or "Oriental" phenomenon. It would be *their* home, *their* evil—evidence, in itself, of a different capacity for achieving civilization. Even before a "Chinatown" had been identified as such in Vancouver, Secretary of State Chapleau conveyed the connotation of the term: "Their custom of living in quarters of their own—in Chinatowns—is attended with evils, such as the depreciation of property, and owing to their habits of lodging crowded quarters and accumulating filth, is offensive if not likely to breed disease" (Canada 1885, 130). Clearly, "Chinatown" would be an evaluative classification. Chapleau had formed his opinion from an investigation in California in 1884 when many witnesses referred to Chinatown and told British Columbians what to expect. "The Chinaman seems to be the same everywhere," Chapleau concluded (Canada 1885, 128); and his China-

---

did a new theory of heredity enable scientists to integrate Darwin's work into a view of human evolution that emphasized genotypic variation of populations rather than the anatomy of immutable types.

town was "an ulcer lodged like a piece of wood in the tissues of the human body, which unless treated must cause disease in the places around it and ultimately to the whole body" (Canada, House of Commons, *Debates*, July 2, 1885, 3010).

With this diagnosis, how did respective Vancouver officials confront the district of pioneers from China? How did they justify the idea of Chinatown and invest it with the authority of some "natural" truth? The rest of the paper is devoted to answering that question and is divided into two sections; the first concerns the image of Chinatown as an unsanitary sink, and the second deals with the perception of Chinatown as a morally aberrant community....

THE "CELESTIAL CESSPOOL": SANITARY DIMENSIONS OF THE CHINATOWN IDEA, 1886–1920

Shortly before the anti-Chinese riot of 1887, a reporter for the *Vancouver News* wrote: "The China Town where the Celestials congregate is an eyesore to civilization" and if the City could be "aroused to the necessity of checking the abuse of sanitary laws which is invariably a concomitant of the Chinese, [it] will help materially in preventing the Mongolian settlement from becoming permanent" ("Progress of the agitation" 1887). Four months later, a row of "hateful haunts" on Carrall Street was specifically singled out for the attention of Council. There, warned the *News*, "in the nucleus of the pest-producing Chinese quarter...strict surveillance by the City will be necessary to prevent the spread of this curse" ("Slave labor" 1887).

True to Chapleau's image of the "ulcer," it was the "ordinary Chinese washhouse scattered over the city" (CVA, *In Correspondence*, Vol. 6, July 4, 1893, 5275) that was an early target of civic concern. For a "race" so dirty, there was certainly plenty of work in the business of cleanliness, and by 1889 as many as 10 of the 13 laundries owned by merchants from China were located outside Dupont Street (Henderson's 1889, 426). One medical health officer found the spread so fearful as to condemn the washhouse "an unmixed evil, an unmitigated nuisance" (CVA, *In Correspondence*, Vol. 17, November 26, 1900, 13301) and from the late nineteenth century, Council sought means of keeping the "Chinese" laundry in its proper place.

Important judicial limits hampered the City of Vancouver, however. For one, Vancouver's municipal charter...did not grant legal competence to Council to deny business licenses to "particular nationalities or individuals."[8] The city's challenge was to circumvent such legal restrictions on its political will, and in the case of the "Chinese" laundry, numerous indirect strategies were devised. One alderman, for example, arrived at an artful solution. According to his 1893 bylaw, no washhouse or laundry in Vancouver could be erected outside specified spatial limits, "that is to say beyond Dupont Street and 120 feet on Columbia Avenue and Carrall Street, southerly from Hastings" (CVA, *Bylaws* 1893).

During the late nineteenth century, an equally vigorous assault was launched in the name of sanitary reform on the wooden shacks of the Dupont Street settlement. In 1890, fear of cholera gripped the city and the local press demanded the city take action against "the people of Dupont Street" given that "in Chinese style...they will not fall into line for the purpose of maintaining cleanliness" ("Preserve the public health" 1890). Fear of contamination from "the degraded humanity from the Orient" (McDonald 1893) was widespread in Vancouver society, and it was customary for letters to the editor to argue that although the "white" race was superior, "Oriental" afflictions would eventually subvert it.

The city fully shared this twist of Darwinist logic and in the mid-1890s—in a significant act of neighborhood definition—Council formally designated "Chinatown" an official entity in the medical health officer rounds and health committee reports (see CVA, *Health Committee Minutes*, 1899–1906). Along with water, sewerage, scavenging, infectious disease, slaughter houses, and pig ranches, Chinatown was listed as a separate category and appointed "a special officer to supervise [it] under the bylaws" (CVA, *In Correspondence*, Vol. 17, November 26, 1900, 13292). One officer reported the following impressions in 1895:

> In my inspections of Chinatown this year, I have not observed any improvement in the cleanliness of the dwellings and surroundings. The former are becoming increasingly dilapidated and filthy and the latter, together with the shores of False Creek, are more and more saturated with manurial refuse and garbage....All the cabins on the foreshore should be condemned and destroyed. In no other way is it possible to

---

8. There were other legal limits on the ability of agents within the divided Canadian polity to implement their will. At the provincial level, anti-Chinese legislation that contravened the division of powers laid down by the British North America Act was routinely disallowed by Ottawa (see La Forest 1955). At the municipal level, an important precedent was set in 1888 when M. Fee of Victoria successfully appealed to the Supreme Court of B.C. the refusal of the City of Victoria to renew his pawnbroker's license (*Regina v. Corporation of Victoria*, [1888] B.C.R. 331).

abate the nuisance arising from the constant deposition of filth and refuse by the occupants. At present they cannot be other than a standing menace to public health (CVA, *In Correspondence*, Vol. 17, November 26, 1900, 13291).

In response to this and similar descriptions, four rows of shacks and cottages were destroyed by the city in the latter part of the decade (CVA, *In Correspondence*, Vol. 10, August 15, 1896, 8522). In 1897, Medical Health Officer Thomas recommended the destruction of more shacks on Dupont Street because "they are dangerous to the health of the city" (CVA, *In Correspondence*, Vol. 11, March 9, 1897, 9296), and two years later, Health Inspector Marrion served notices under the newly enacted Boarding House Bylaw after a visit by a number of City officials, including Mayor Garden (CVA, *In Correspondence*, Vol. 14, December 10, 1899, 10696). The bylaw had been passed, without being so framed, as another attempt "to secure better regulation and supervision in the case of Chinese dwelling places" (CVA, *In Correspondence*, Vol. 17, November 26, 1900, 13299).

Marrion adopted a firm stance toward Chinatown from the time of his appointment in 1893. "The Chinese method of living is totally different to that of white people," he claimed in 1902. "The Japs try to obey the laws, but the Chinese are always on the lookout to evade them" ("Chinese defy city by-laws" 1902). The living conditions the health inspector perceived along Dupont Street therefore had little to do with constraints on Chinese family settlement, job and pay discrimination, or the physical condition of the industrial inlet. Rather they were a product of "the difficulty to get Chinese people to adopt sanitary methods....Even where every convenience is provided...Chinese are generally dirtier than whites" (Canada 1902, 14). Though blunt, Marrion's statements were entirely conformist for his day; he spoke not out of irrational prejudice but rather in the accepted vocabulary for discovering and characterizing the district that housed these pioneers to Vancouver. Identity and place were inextricably conflated, and the process of racial classification was corroborated with every official expedition.

Given this nearly universal scheme by which "Chinatown" was comprehended,[9] it was remarkable for a non-Chinese to argue: "It would

---

9. There are difficulties with reducing majority perceptions to the constant of a singular "white" European viewpoint. The ideas of race and Chinatown enjoyed a popularity, however, that overrode any idiosyncrasies that might have existed in the British, American, and Canadian perceptions. Although no origin classifications are available from the 1891 or 1901 census, early Vancouver society was made up of predominantly British immigrants and their Canadian-born descendents (Roy 1980b, 28).

be extremely difficult, if not impossible, even in the worst Chinese quarter, to parallel the state of affairs revealed amongst some white men in our city not so long ago in some of the cabins behind the Imperial Opera House" (CYMRA 1893). Other evidence reveals that the bias of the municipal authorities' attention to sanitary matters in Dupont Street stemmed from their respect for the race idea. For example, the "Chinese" disease-bearing capacity was never borne out by actual disease or epidemic outbreaks recorded in the health inspector's reports or in the local press.[10]

At the same time, a number of Chinese-origin merchants made known their willingness to establish an amenable environment for business and residence. At odds with the typifications projected on the area, some merchants complained to Council about the poor condition of Dupont Street and its sidewalks (CVA, *Council Minutes*, Vol. 7, January 20, 1896, 4); in 1899, 24 firms requested Dupont Street be sprinkled twice daily in the summer and back lanes be repaired (CVA, *In Correspondence*, Vol. 14, June 14, 1899, 10433); and in 1905, a group of businessmen asked the Board of Works to pave Shanghai Alley (CVA, *Council Minutes*, Vol. 13, May 22, 1905, 395). Far from passive victims steeped in some fixed standard of living, or for that matter, hapless victims of "white" prejudice, the entrepreneurial sector of Chinatown effectively used its understanding of civic politics to try to elevate the physical condition and social profile of the neighborhood. The Lim Dat Company was so dissatisfied with the City's refuse collection in the area that in 1906 it applied for a license to conduct its own street cleaning operation ("To do their own work" 1906).

The local unit of knowledge called "Chinatown" was carried forward in government practice and rhetoric well into the new century. In the same month as the riot of 1907 in Chinatown, Inspector Marrion could describe the neighborhood in no more original terms than its "fowls, refuse, filth, dead dogs, and offal" ("Dirty Chinese are fined" 1907). Whether or not the image of Chinatown as unsanitary was accurate, the perceptions of image makers intent on characterizing the area as alien were the ones that continued to have consequences.[11] Certainly the city was not prepared to

---

10. The solicitor for the Chinese Board of Trade, A. Taylor, told the commissioners in 1901: "No instance is given of the origin of any contagious disease in the Chinatown of either city [Vancouver or Victoria]." Using City statistics, he submitted "there is no evidence that the presence of the Chinese is in any way a menace to health" (Canada 1902, 297).

11. Foucault has said that "the problem is not one of drawing the line between that in a discourse which falls under the category of scientificity or truth, and that which comes under some other category, but with seeing historically how effects of truth are produced

compromise its idea of some essentially "Chinese" Chinatown in the face of challenges to its authority from the courts. Such obstructions served only to provoke new strategies, so assured were city officials of the integrity of their mission. By 1910, for example, a circle of city officials including Mayor Telford and Chief of Police Chamberlain, sought to achieve "full control of conditions in Chinatown." They hoped to "reform" the area with wider powers of bylaw enforcement that would stifle "Chinamen [who] manage to fight bylaws by successful applications for injunctions" ("City powers to be widened" 1910; "Dealing with the Chinese" 1910). Fortunately for the residents, the provincial government was not inclined to concede such powers to the city.

It was not as if other districts in Vancouver, of actual or perceived marginal sanitary status, did not exist. In 1914, Inspector Hynes visited a district in Vancouver's East End that was home to a number of residents from Italy and found conditions "sickening in the extreme"; as "abominable" as the Chinese quarter ("Cleaning up starts..." 1914). But only the Dupont (by this time Pender) Street settlement was publicly known as a social and spatial unit according to putatively immutable "racial" qualities. Even the much-disliked settlement of pioneers from Japan on Powell Street appears to have escaped the crude neighborhood characterization that gave "Chinatown" its name in the early decades of this century. In part this can be explained by the widely held view that, although the Japanese were also a foreign "race," their homeland was not only a world power of some import in Britain's eyes, but the Japanese seemed to possess a conception of progress and civilization more assimilable to the European cultural tradition than was that of Japan's more mysterious "Oriental" neighbor. (Such a generous view gave way to extreme forms of discrimination by World War II.)

The distilled vision that was Vancouver's Chinatown was, for the city, a pressing mandate, and its actions reinforced both the vision and the reality of a neighborhood and a people apart. Almost immediately after the alleged murder of the wife of a well-known West End railway administrator by her "China-boy" in 1914 ("City acts on agitation" 1914), Council led the clamor to have Chinese removed from the schools. Based solely on the fact that the "boy" was educated in the school system, Council stated its "grave apprehension" at

the prevailing practice of the School Board in permitting children and

---

within discourses which in themselves are neither true or false" (cited in Rabinow 1984, 60).

young men of Oriental race to attend our public schools. . . . By being indiscriminately thrown into contact with Orientals. . . our children are wantonly exposed to Oriental vices at an age when revolting incidents may be indelibly stamped upon their minds. Furthermore the health of our children is endangered by such close association with Oriental children, many of whom hail from habitations where reasonable sanitation and cleanliness are not only despised but utterly disregarded. In some cases, these Orientals come into our public school classrooms with their apparel polluted with the fumes of noxious drugs and germs of loathesome diseases on their persons (CVA, *Council Minutes*, Vol. 20, April 8, 1914, 122).

Although Council's request to Victoria for school segregation foundered on legal obstacles, the city continued to wield its own power tirelessly. In the following year, the local press described "Chinatown" as no less than "besieged." "Lined up on this side," wrote the *Sun*,

is the civic authority led by the medical health officer, the building inspector and the chairman of the health committee supported by the City aldermen. This great civic force has as its ally the law in the form of health bylaws, building regulations, police officers and penalties. Arrayed against this seemingly formidable army is the wily Oriental with his fondness for defying the civic powers. . . . Civic regulations are dust to the Chinaman ("Aldermen and Chinese. . ." 1915).

Clearly, the idea of "Chinatown" was being inherited by successive rounds of officials who adopted the conceptual schemes of their predecessors. The health committee of Council described the area as a "propagating ground for disease" in 1919, and, true to old remedies, an inspection team was set up to monitor the area despite the fact that still no concrete evidence confirmed that Chinatown was a threat to public health (CVA, *Council Minutes*, Vol. 22, May 19, 1919, 488). Within ten months, the owners of more than 20 lodgings were threatened with orders to condemn their buildings, including the Chinese Hospital at 106 Pender Street East (*Chinese Times*, January 24, 1920). Indeed, well into the 1920s the city operated assertively in the idiom of race, indiscriminately raiding Chinatown and harassing residents about bylaw compliance (e.g., *Chinese Times*, March 4, 8, April 5, 1921).

In translating racial ideology into official practice, the civic authorities of Vancouver performed an important legitimizing role in the social construction of Chinatown in the late nineteenth and early twentieth centuries. Chinatown was not simply an idea. It had a concrete referent in the form of a concentrated community whose physical presence propped up the vision of identity and place we have been examining. Furthermore, the circumstances of Chinese immigration to Canada probably encouraged objectively poor living conditions in many sectors of the community. In that sense, the material reality of the district justified and fulfilled the prophecy of Chapleau's "Chinatown." But it was the mutually reinforcing ideas of race and place, and their scope and influence in British Columbian culture, that gave the district its coherence as a discrete place in the social consciousness of its representers. In the eyes of successive civic officials, "Chinatown" signified no less than the encounter between "West" and "East"; it distinguished and testified to the vast asymmetry between two "races." As such, Chinatown was not a benign cultural abstraction but a political projection, through which a divisive system of racial classification was being structured and institutionalized.

VICE-TOWN: MORAL DIMENSIONS OF THE CHINATOWN IDEA, 1886–1920

Much as the "West" has defined the "Orient" (Said 1978), Vancouver's "Chinatown" was a collection of essences that seemed to set the Chinese fundamentally apart. Above all, it was nonwhite, non-Christian, uncivilized, and amoral. It was something of a "counter-idea," into which were concentrated qualities thought to be in opposition to the European ingroup (see Voegelin 1940). Matters of hygiene were only part of the vocabulary out of which this idea was being constructed. Equally significant and perhaps more effective were moral associations. Because the "Chinese" were inveterate gamblers, "Chinatown" was lawless; as opium addicted, Chinatown was a pestilential den; as evil and inscrutable, Chinatown was a prostitution base where white women were lured as slaves. "Is there harm in the Chinaman?" Reverend Fraser asked a meeting of the Asiatic Exclusion League in 1907. "In this city," he said, "that would be answered with one word, 'Chinatown,' with its wickedness unmentionable" ("Greed at bottom. . ." 1907).

Two city hardliners, Police Magistrate Alexander and Chief of Police Chamberlain, legitimized a particular vision of Chinatown in their everyday business. As the home of the "racial other,"[12] Chinatown signified many impulses that Europeans feared and attempted to repress in them-

---

12. See Gates (1985) and other essays in the volume. The phrase refers to the metaphorical negation of the European in Western language use and is derived from the more general notion that consciousness of the self involves distancing from the Other (Laing 1961).

selves....Only those aspects of Chinese living that conformed to the categorization "Chinese" were being filtered by members of the governing body of Vancouver, as they were by European communities throughout North America.[13]

Why did the municipal officials of Vancouver reach the conclusions they did when describing and managing Chinatown? How was it that Chamberlain and Alexander were concerned with a few elements...and not others? The relevance of this question has been obscured by the familiar prejudice framework for the study of race relations. That perspective has tended to explain away such systems of imagery and indeed racial categories themselves, in some unproblematic "white" predisposition toward nonwhites.[14] In particular, the explanatory focus upon prejudice and discrimination (attitudes and behavior) has obscured the deeper process by which classifications have themselves been built around the concept of race.

Or again, economic competition was a major rallying point for anti-Chinese sentiment in British Columbia, as it was in other areas of Chinese settlement (e.g., Hill 1973; Roy 1979; Saxton 1971). But it, too, has been less a primary cause of such sentiment than an outcome of the more decisive role that must be accorded collective conceptions about the "Chinese" as a category in the European cultural tradition. Of course racial ideology did not alone cause a segregated occupational order in British Columbia, and another paper might examine the relationship between racial ideology and the development of a capitalist economy in that province.[15] The point here is that ideological formulations have made their own powerful and distinct contribution to such structures of inequality and must be examined on their own terms (see also Prager 1982). Were it not for ideas about

---

13. That it was more the white European view that was the "same everywhere" and less Chapleau's "Chinaman," see for example Light (1974), Paupst (1977), Salter (1984), Steiner (1979, Ch. 15). Some of the themes are common to descriptions of other racially defined outgroups such as "blacks" in America (e.g., Ley 1974, Ch. 1) and "East Indians" in Canada (e.g., Ley 1983, 268).

14. Ward (1978, 169) explains anti-Chinese sentiment in terms of "that psychological tension which *inhered* in the racially plural condition" (emphasis added). In reifying race as something external to the situation under investigation, he treats as an explanation that which itself must be explained. Within the white racism thesis, there are more precise analyses, such as Jordan (1968, Ch. 1) who emphasizes the culture of early English colonists to America in his account of tensions between "blacks" and "whites."

15. For an attempt to locate racial ideology within the field of capitalist social relations in early British Columbia, see Creese (1984). Boswell (1986) develops the argument on the American context. Split labor market theory emphasizes the economic sources of conflict between groups distinguished by color under conditions of unequal labor costs. It is less successful in explaining why Chinese laborers were underpaid in the first place.

"race"—myths that were readily exploited by owners of capital in British Columbia (see the testimony of capitalists in the Royal Commission of 1885) and by the Dominion Government during the construction of the Canadian Pacific Railway (see, e.g., Chan 1983)—so-called "coolie" labor might not have been so cheap; nor might the entry of labor from China have been considered anything but "natural." Certainly there would have been no logical basis on which to charge and penalize the Chinese as a category with collectively undermining the standard of living and the bargaining power of the "white" worker.

What then were the features of the language, imagery, and rhetoric with which the "West" interpreted China in the late eighteenth and nineteenth centuries?...

"The Heathen Chinee"

The desire of Westerners to measure China against an idealized vision of themselves dates as far back as the thirteenth century when travelers, imbued with the Greek dualisms of "Europe" and "Asia," "East" and "West," "Orientis" and "Occidentis," set out to uncover the unknown (March 1974). Consistent with the Greek conception of "Asia" as the oldest, richest, and most populous of civilizations, medieval travelers such as Marco Polo were captivated by China's opulent ruler, the abundance of silks, rugs, and porcelains, and the splendor and size of Chinese cities. China was the vast, farthest shore of the East, the most marginal, isolated, and ipso facto most Oriental of all of Asia, and it was this romantic view that lingered in the European consciousness for more than three centuries (Dawson 1967).

By the late seventeenth and certainly by the early eighteenth century, Europe's emerging image of itself as imperial, industrial, enlightened, and progressive provided the benchmark for different perceptions of "the Middle Kingdom." A new construction upon China's antiquity began to be articulated that focused relationally upon its changelessness, homogeneity, and uniformity—"the despotism of Custom"—as John Stuart Mill wrote in his mid-nineteenth century essay *On Liberty* (March 1974, 40–41). With British military power in ascendancy, the European image of China began to darken. The Chinese became "a people of eternal standstill," or as Mr. Chapleau put it: "Races change slowly but the stationariness of the Chinese seems phenomenal" (Canada 1885, 98). In so conceiving China, and more generally "Asia" as a negative—that is, non-European—construct, scholars have argued that Europe was giving force to its own idea of itself (Dawson 1967; Hay 1966; Said 1978).

Miller (1969) traces this decline in China's image from the time of its first trade with America in 1785. It was around that time that frustrated traders, diplomats, and missionaries sent home the message of China's resistance to their commercial and evangelical entreaties. From the records of 50 traders to China from 1785 to 1840, Miller identifies the following themes: China's technological and scientific backwardness; its military ineptitude, from which many traders deduced a national coward-ice; the venality of the Chinese character, as revealed by their devotion to gambling and their "diabolical cunning"; and their peculiarity, for which one had only to look to their theater, music, insistence on writing up and down the page, slant eyes, and their propensity for eating birds' nests.

The diplomats' memoirs and accounts—from Lord Macartney's in 1792 to the embassy sent by President Jackson in 1892—were more important than were the traders' reports in shaping American public opinion. Despite some nostalgia for Marco Polo's Old Cathay, most memoirs were contemptuous of the backwardness and vice that China's despotism was thought to inspire. Military impotence, infanticide, depravity, and addic-tion to "pernicious" drugs were all construed as signs of a civilization in decline.

As opinion makers, however, it was the nineteenth century Protestant missionaries, armed with their own press, who commanded the widest audience in America. Unlike the Jesuits, who had seen valuable prepara-tion in Confucianism for Christian teachings, Protestant missionaries to China in the nineteenth century were scathing critics. For them, there could be no more damning evidence against Confucianism than the rampant idolatry, infanticide, slavery in women, polygamy, opium obses-sion, noonday orgies, treachery, and endemic gambling. So puny was the record of conversions in fact, that some missionaries concluded that the wily Chinese were conscious agents of Satan who deliberately humiliated God with acts of immorality.

Discovering "The Heathen Chinee"

In February 1912, a newspaper feature on Vancouver's Chinatown began:

> Conditions prevailing in the cities of China are familiar topics of the returned missionary, who will dwell at length upon the awful condition of the slums, the armies of the unwashed, and the prevalence of vice in the shape of opium smoking and gambling, in the empire across the seas. Would you believe that the same condition of affairs is in existence in the city of Vancouver in our Chinatown, which constitutes a consid-

erable quarter on Pender street between Canton and Shanghai alleys? ("Vancouver's Chinatown..." 1912).

Yet how else, we might ask, could Pender Street be known?

The plight of the fallen woman disappearing into the clutches of procurors in segregated "Oriental" vice districts was, from the turn of the century, a pressing concern of Vancouver's moral reform groups (Roy 1980b, 82). Not surprisingly, therefore, anxiety was heightened in Vancouver by the location of the "restricted area" (where prostitution was tolerated by the police) right next to the Chinese quarter from the time the city was incorporated. But the reform groups' worst fears were realized in 1906 when prostitutes moved en masse to Shanghai Alley following a Council request for their eviction from the prior location (CVA, *In Correspondence*, Vol. 22, September 1906, 17480). No police protection like that offered the residents of Mount Pleasant (the area that was expected to receive the dislodged prostitutes) was extended to Chinatown, and for some time it became the new "restricted area" for prostitution in Vancouver. Later, in the face of much local protest about the unhappy combination of prostitutes and "Chinamen" in the one location, the restricted area was moved to other areas in the East End (Nilsen 1976, Ch. 3).

Of these various niches where prostitution enjoyed a blind eye in Vancouver, an especially evil construction was cast upon the practice only in "Chinatown." Wrote one indignant citizen about the "almond-eyed lawbreakers" in 1908: "A regular traffic in women is conducted by the Chinese in Vancouver. The Chinese are the most persistent criminals against the person of any woman of any class in this country...all this goes on in a Christian community" ("In the sunset glow" 1908). Most often, petitions to Council concerning prostitution dwelt on the risk to property values; however in Chinatown, the voice of the nineteenth-century Protestant missionary reverberated. One resident contended: "It is a disgrace to our city to have *that* evil in *that* location" (cited in Nilsen 1976, 37).

Stamped with the weight of a typification, Chinatown was intelligible only in terms of a few (unflattering) criteria. Class distinctions paled beneath the more influential racial characterization. Indeed Council simply ignored a 1906 petition from the Chinese Board of Trade, which, in protesting the unimpeded movement of prostitutes into Shanghai Alley and Canton Street, reflected concerns not far removed from the most traditional of Christian mission ministers in Chinatown. "We the undersigned (30) merchants and others," the Board wrote, beg leave to respectfully call your attention to the fact that several of the women of ill repute...are moving into Shanghai Alley and Canton Streets. This we consider most undesirable. It is our desire to have our children grow up learning what is best in Western civilization and not to have them forced into daily contact with its worst phases (Shum Moon 1908).

Some Chinese merchants mounted a campaign in Vancouver against another perceived vice out of which the non-Chinese concept of place was constructed. In 1908, the merchants' anti-opium league sent a petition to Ottawa asking the federal government to "decisively exercise its authority and powers to prohibit the importation, manufacture and sale of opium into Canada so that the social, physical, and moral condition of both Chinese and Europeans may be vastly improved" ("Seek to check opium..." 1908). But try as some merchants did to counter the idea of Chinatown, the drug that Britain had introduced to China in the 1840s was now a powerful metaphor for neighborhood definition. In 1899, a newspaper reporter who accompanied Marrion on one of his tours of Chinatown's bachelor shacks, remarked that "the luxury of smoking opium is beyond comprehension in such tight boxes" ("Unsanitary Chinese" 1899). Another in 1908 noted the fine access that such tight quarters provided to "bargain-rate heaven" ("How Two Lung Lee goes to heaven" 1908). And like the construction put upon "white" participation in Chinatown's bawdy houses, the large extent of non-Chinese use of opium that the Minister for Labor, Mackenzie King, uncovered in his 1908 investigation (Canada, *Sessional Papers*, 1908, No. 36b, 13) only confirmed the belief that Chinatown was a menace to civilized life. White drug use did not prejudice, but rather validated, the more comforting racial and spatial category.

Once the image of "Chinatown" as an opium den was consolidated, no amount of counter-evidence could acquit it and all manner of accusations could be adduced, especially by politicians, to support the neighborhood image. By the 1920s, when the race idea was being feverishly exploited in British Columbia, the old opium image fed and was assimilated into an image of Chinatown as a narcotics base and "Chinese" as dangerous drug distributors. In March 1920, for example an editorial warned: "The traffic in habit-forming drugs centres in Chinatown" and "if the only way to save our children is to abolish Chinatown, then Chinatown must and will go, and quickly" ("Chinatown—or drug traffic?" March 22, 1920).

In the context of rising anti-Chinese sentiment in the House of Commons, Consul General Yip and the Chinese Benevolent Association of

Vancouver formed a Self Improvement Committee to try to elevate the reputation of their neighborhood (*Chinese Times*, April 15, 1921). Cumyow (by this time president of the Chinese Benevolent Association) also spoke out against the *Sun's* vendetta, calling attention to "the suggestion of Police Commissioner Buckworth that Chinese vendors are merely conveniently used and that the traffic is controlled by persons other than Chinese" (Cumyow 1920). But the irrepressibly anti-Chinese Member of Parliament for Vancouver Centre, H. Stevens (also secretary of the Vancouver Moral Reform Association) was not to be deterred, and in a series of speeches in the House of Commons in the early 1920s, he transmitted these most recent charges against Vancouver's Chinatown to the senior level of government. "The basis of the pernicious drug habit on the Pacific Coast is Asiatic," said Stevens in 1921. "We have seen in Vancouver almost innumerable cases of clean, decent, respectable young women from some of the best homes dragged down by the dope traffic and very, very largely through the medium of the opium dens in the Chinese quarter" (Canada, House of Commons, *Debates*, April 26, 1921, 2598).

A more lurid tale of Chinatown's "snow parties" was told for Parliament in 1922 by L. Ladner of Vancouver South. Within months, the federal authorities amended the Opium and Narcotic Drug Act to provide for the deportation of aliens found guilty of any drug offense (Canada, *Statutes*, 12–13 Geo. 5, 1922, c. 35). In 1923, the language of race was conferred its most extreme official seal when Canada's door was effectively closed to immigrants from China for 25 years (Canada, *Statutes*, 13–14 Geo. 5, 1923, c. 38). With considerable consequences, then, local definitions of place continuously influenced rounds of legislative activity at all levels of government in the ongoing construction of this category of outsiders.

Known to police for "inveterate" gambling, the "heathen Chinee" was actively pursued by officers of the Vancouver police force from the 1890s to the late 1940s. By that time, the extent of the harassment had become embarrassingly transparent even to the city. Until then, however, it was rare to find a year that the *Chinese Times* and the local press did not report a raid on Chinatown's gambling quarters. Cumyow saw the record as more telling of the enforcement practices of the police than of any intrinsic "Oriental" proclivity to gamble, as he told the Royal Commission in 1901:

> There is proportionately a large amount of gambling among the Chinese. Some do gamble for large amounts, but more commonly, the play is for amusement only and for small sums to pass the time as this is done

in the common room of the boarding house. If a police raid is made and any are caught playing, all are arrested for gambling and looking on. If the same course were pursued in relation to white men, gamblers could be caught in barrooms and of course all who were at the bar would be arrested as onlookers (Canada 1902, 236).

Just as the opium den raids vindicated widespread assumptions about the moral laxity of the Chinese, the formidable scrutiny that Chinatown experienced from the City for gambling sprang from and confirmed popular assumptions about a generically addicted "Chinaman." And one vice bred another, as Alderman McIntosh observed in 1915. Gambling and opium in Chinatown required constant civic vigilance, he claimed, because they were associated with tuberculosis and slavery in women ("Urge enforcement..." 1915).

Yet gambling was not restricted to the Pender Street area. One letter to the editor in 1900, appealing for greater control of gambling in the city, said: "Everyone knows that gambling goes on promiscuously all over Vancouver, in clubs, in hotels, in saloons, in rooms connected with saloons and in private houses" ("A lover of the truth", 1900). But only in "Chinatown" was a neighborhood image built around both its practice and the attempts of police—confronted by "ingenious Oriental systems of spring doors and getaway rat tunnels" ("Burrows under Chinatown" 1915)—to suppress it. So perturbed were Chinese merchants by this harassment that in 1905, the Chinese Board of Trade protested:

> The members of our board are law abiding citizens. Many of them have been residents of this country for a number of years and are large holders of real estate, payers of taxes and other civic assessments. The members...have been constantly annoyed by what we believe to be an unjustifiable intrusion of certain members of the Vancouver Police Force...in the habit of going into our stores and rooms where our families live, showing no warrant whatsoever, nor do they claim any business with us....We are subjected to indignities and discriminating treatment to which no other class would submit and to which *your* laws, we are advised, we are not required to submit (Young 1976, 65).

CONCLUSION

I have argued that "Chinatown" was a social construct that belonged to Vancouver's "white" European society, who, like their contemporaries throughout North America, perceived the district of Chinese settlement according to an influential culture of race. From the vantage point of the

European, Chinatown signified all those features that seemed to set the Chinese irrevocably apart—their appearance, lack of Christian faith, opium and gambling addiction, their strange eating habits, and odd graveyard practices. That is, it embodied the white Europeans' sense of difference between immigrants from China and themselves, between the East and the West. This not to argue that Chinatown was a fiction of the European imagination; nor can there be any denying that gambling, opium use and unsanitary conditions were present in the district where Chinese settled. The point is that "Chinatown" was a shared characterization—one constructed and distributed by and for Europeans, who, in arbitrarily conferring outsider status on these pioneers to British Columbia, were affirming their own identity and privilege. That they directed that purpose in large part through the medium of Chinatown attests to the importance of place in the making of a system of racial classification....

Perhaps not all places are as heavily laden with a cultural and political baggage as "Chinatown." But Chinatown is important in pointing up once again the more general principle that a negotiated social and historical process lies behind the apparently neutral-looking taxonomic systems of census districts.[16] More importantly perhaps, the manipulation of racial ideology by institutions is additional testimony to the fact that a set of power relations may underpin and keep alive our social and spatial categories.

The importance of these "imaginative geographies" cannot be underestimated because, as we have seen, they organize social action and political practices....In the course of its evolution, Chinatown reflected the race definition process, but it also informed and institutionalized it, providing a context and justification for its reproduction. Pender Street has been the home of the overseas Chinese to be sure, but "Chinatown" is a story, which, in disclosing the categories and consequences of white European cultural hegemony, reveals more the insider than it does the outsider.

REFERENCES

Abrams, P. 1982. *Historical sociology*. Bath: Pitman Press.

Aldermen and Chinese having royal battle. 1915. *Sun*, May 24, p. 14.

---

16. See also Lowman's (1986) argument that crime maps may be mental maps reflecting more the images of the city and the activities of control agents than the inherently criminogenic nature of "problem" areas. Ley (1983, 293–94) discusses the labeling practices of institutions.

Anderson, K. 1986. "East" as "West": Place, state and the institutionalization of myth in Vancouver's Chinatown, 1880–1980. Ph.D. thesis, Department of Geography, University of British Columbia, Vancouver.

Appiah, A. 1985. The uncompleted argument: Du Bois and the illusion of race. *Critical Inquiry* 12(1):21–37.

Banton, M. 1977. *The idea of race*. London: Tavistock.

————. 1983. *Ethnic and racial competition*. Cambridge: Cambridge University Press.

Barth, F. 1969. *Ethnic groups and ethnic boundaries: The social organization of cultural difference*. Boston: Little, Brown.

Barth, G. 1964. *Bitter strength: A history of the Chinese in the United States, 1850–70*. Cambridge, Mass.: Harvard University Press.

Bastide, R. 1967. Color, racism and Christianity. *Daedalus* 96:312–27.

Berger, P., and Luckmann, T. 1966. *The social construction of reality*. Garden City, N.Y.: Doubleday.

Boswell, T. 1986. A split labor market analysis of discrimination against Chinese immigrants, 1850–82. *American Sociological Review* 51:352–71.

Boxer, C. 1963. *Race relations in the Portuguese colonial empire, 1415–1825*. Oxford: Clarendon Press.

British Columbia. 1900. *Journals of the Legislative Assembly of the Province of British Columbia*. Victoria: R. Wolfenden, Government Printer.

British Columbia Law Reports. 1888.

Burrows under Chinatown. 1915. *Sun*, June 19, p. 10.

Canada. 1885. *Report of the Royal Commission on Chinese Immigration*. Ottawa: Printed by Order of the Commission.

————. 1902. *Report of the Royal Commission on Chinese and Japanese Immigration*. Printed by S. E. Dawson.

Chan, A. 1983. *Gold mountain*. Vancouver: New Star Books.

Chinatown—or drug traffic. 1920. *Sun*, March 22, p. 6.

Chinese, The. 1893. *Vancouver Daily World*. March 23, p. 4.

Chinese defy city bylaws. 1902. *Province*, June 18, p. 1.

Chinese leaving, The. 1887. *Vancouver News*, February 26, p. 1.

Cho, G., and Leigh, R. 1972. Patterns of residence of the Chinese in Vancouver. In *Peoples of the living land*, ed. J. Minghi, pp. 67–84. Geographical Series, No. 15. Vancouver: Tantalus.

City acts upon Oriental agitation. 1914. *Province*, April 7, p. 3.

City of Vancouver Archives (CVA). City of Vancouver, RG2-B1. *Council Minutes*. miscellaneous years, 1886–1920.

————. City of Vancouver, RG2-A1. *City Clerk's In Correspondence*. miscellaneous years, 1886–1920.

————. 1899–1906. *Health Committee Minutes*. Vol. 2, Chairman's report.

————. Office of the City Clerk. 1893. *Bylaws*. Vol. 1, No. 176, May 15, pp. 1044–45.

City powers to be widened. 1910. *Province*, January 27, p. 28.

Clark, G., and Dear, M. 1984. *State apparatus*. London: Allen and Unwin.

Cleaning up starts in foreign quarters. 1914. *Sun*, March 31, p. 3.

Cohen, R. 1978. Ethnicity: Problem and focus in anthropology. *Annual Review of Anthropology* 7:379–403.

Creese, G. 1984. Immigration policies and the creation of an ethnically segmented working class in British Columbia, 1880–1923. *Alternate Routes* 17:1–34.

Crissman, L. 1967. The segmentary structure of urban overseas Chinese communities. *Man* 2(2):185–204.

Cumyow, W. A. 1920. In defence of Chinatown. *Sun*, March 24, p. 6.

Cybriwsky, R. 1986. The community response to downtown redevelopment: The case of Philadelphia's Chinatown. Paper presented at the Association of American Geographers Conference, Minneapolis.

CYMRA. 1893. Shall the Chinese go? *Vancouver Daily World*, July 6, p. 3.

Dawson, R. 1967. *The Chinese chameleon: An analysis of European conceptions of Chinese civilization*. London: Oxford University Press.

Dealing with Chinese. 1910. *Times*, January 29, p. 18.

Dirty Chinese are fined. 1907. *Province*, September 16, p. 16.

Farish, D. 1978. *Biology: The human perspective*. New York: Harper and Row.

Gates, H. 1985. Writing "race" and the difference it makes. *Critical Inquiry* 12(1):1–20.

Geertz, C. 1973. *The interpretation of cultures*. New York: Basic Books.

Goffman, E. 1963. *Stigma*. Englewood Cliffs, N.J.: Prentice-Hall.

Gould, S. 1981. *The mismeasure of man*. New York: W.W. Norton and Co.

Greed at bottom of importation of Orientals. 1907. *Province*, October 7, p. 2.

Harris, M. 1972. Race. In *International encyclopedia of the social sciences*. New York: Macmillan.

Hay, D. 1966. *Europe: The emergence of an idea*. New York: Harper and Row.

Henderson's B.C. Directory. 1889. Victoria: L. G. Henderson.

Hill, H. 1973. Anti-Oriental agitation and the rise of working class racism. *Society* 10(2):43–54.

Hoe, B. 1976. *Structural changes of two Chinese communities in Alberta, Canada*. National Museum of Man Mercury Series, Paper No. 19. Ottawa: National Museum of Man.

How Two Lung Lee goes to heaven. 1908. *Province*, September 26, p. 25.

Husband, C., ed. 1982. *"Race" in Britain: Continuity and change*. London: Hutchinson.

In the sunset glow. 1908. *The Saturday Sunset*, October 10, p. 1.

Jackson, P. 1981. A transactional approach in Puerto Rican culture. *Review/Revista Interamericana* 11:53–68.

Jones, G. 1980. *Social Darwinism and English thought*. Sussex: Harvester Press.

Jordan, W. 1968. *White over black: American attitudes toward the Negro, 1555–1812*. Baltimore: Penguin.

La Forest, G. 1955. *Disallowance and reservation of the provincial legislation*. Ottawa: Department of Justice.

Lai, D. 1973. Socio-economic structures and the viability of Chinatown. In *Residential and neighborhood studies*, ed. C. Forward, pp. 101–29. Western Geographical Series, No. 5. Victoria: University of Victoria.

Laing, R. 1961. *Self and others*. London: Tavistock.

Lewontin, R.; Rose, S.; and Kamin, L. 1984. *Not in our genes: Biology, ideology and human nature*. New York: Pantheon Books.

Ley, D. 1974. *The black inner city as frontier outpost*. Monograph No. 7. Washington, D.C.: Association of American Geographers.

————. 1977. Social geography and the taken-for-granted-world. *Transactions of the Institute of British Geographers* n.s. 2:498–512.

————. 1983. *A social geography of the city*. New York: Harper and Row.

Light, I. 1974. From vice district to tourist attraction: The moral career of American Chinatowns, 1880–1940. *Pacific Historical Review* 43:367–94.

Lover of the truth, A. 1900. The curse of gambling. *Province*, January 30, p. 10.

Lowman, J. 1986. Conceptual issues in the geography of crime: Toward a geography of social control. *Annals of the Association of American Geographers* 76:81–94.

Lyman, S. 1974. *Chinese Americans*. New York: Random House.

Ma, L. 1983. A Chinese statesman in Canada, 1903: Translated from the travel journal of Liang Ch'ich'ao. *B.C. Studies* 59:28–43.

March, A. 1974. *The idea of China: Myth and theory in geographic thought*. New York: Prager.

MacLaughlin, J., and Agnew, J. 1986. Hegemony and the regional question: The political geography of regional industrial policy in Northern Ireland, 1945–72. *Annals of the Association of American Geographers* 76:247–61.

Marger, M. 1985. *Race and ethnic relations*. Belmont, Calif.: Wadsworth.

Matza, D. 1969. *Becoming deviant*. Englewood Cliffs, N.J.: Prentice-Hall.

McDonald, W. 1893. The degraded Oriental. *Vancouver Daily World*, March 23, p. 4.

Miller, S. 1969. *The unwelcome immigrant: The American image of the Chinese, 1785–1882*. Berkeley: University of California Press.

Montagu, A., ed. 1964. *The concept of race*. New York: The Free Press.

Morley, A. 1961. *Vancouver: From milltown to metropolis*. Vancouver: Mitchell Press.

Morton, J. 1977. *In the sea of sterile mountains*. Vancouver: J.J. Douglas.

Nee, V., and Nee, B. 1974. *Longtime Californ'*. Boston: Houghton Mifflin.

Nilsen, D. 1976. The "social evil": Prostitution in Vancouver, 1900–20. B.A. Honors essay, Department of History, University of British Columbia, Vancouver.

Outbreak against the Chinese. 1887. *Vancouver News*, February 25, p. 1.

Paupst, K. 1977. A note on anti-Chinese sentiment in Toronto before the First World War. *Canadian Ethnic Studies* 9(1):54–59.

Palmer, H. 1982. *Patterns of prejudice: A history of nativism in Alberta*. Toronto: McClelland and Stewart.

Peach, C. 1984. The force of West Indian island identity in Britain. In *Geography and ethnic pluralism*, ed. C. Clarke, D. Ley, and C. Peach, pp. 214–30. London: George Allen and Unwin.

Perrin, R. 1983. Clio as an ethnic: The third force in Canadian historiography. *Canadian Historical Review* 64(4):441–67.

Pirie, G. 1984. Race zoning in South Africa: Board, court, parliament, public. *Political Geography Quarterly* 3:207–21.

Prager, J. 1982. American racial ideology as collective representation. *Ethnic and Racial Studies* 5(1):99–119.

Preserve the public health. 1890. *Vancouver Daily World*, August 30, p. 4.

Price, C. 1974. *The great white walls are built: Restrictive immigration to North America and Australia, 1836–1888*. Canberra: Australian National University Press.

Progress of the agitation. 1887. *Vancouver News*, January 13, p. 2.

Rabinow, P., ed. 1984. *The Foucault reader*. New York: Pantheon Books.

Robson regime, The. 1887. *Vancouver News*, March 16, p. 1.

Roy, P. 1976. The preservation of peace in Vancouver: The aftermath of the anti-Chinese riot of 1887. *B.C. Studies* 31:44–59.

———. 1979. White Canada forever: Two generations of studies. *Canadian Ethnic Studies* 11:97–109.

———. 1980a. British Columbia's fear of Asians, 1900–50. *Social History* 13(25):161–72.

————. 1980b. *Vancouver: An illustrated history*. Ontario: James Lorimer.

Said, E. 1978. *Orientalism*. New York: Vintage Books.

Salter, C. 1978. *San Francisco's Chinatown: How Chinese a town?* San Francisco: R. & E. Research Associates.

————. 1984. Urban imagery and the Chinese of Los Angeles. *Urban Review* 1:15–20, 28.

Saunders, P. 1979. *Urban politics: A sociological interpretation*. London: Hutchinson.

Saxton, A. 1971. *The indispensable enemy: Labor and the anti-Chinese movement in California*. Berkeley: University of California Press.

Seek to check opium manufacture. 1908. *Province*, July 3, p. 3.

Shum Moon. 1908. Chinese deny responsibility. *Province*, February 3, p. 16.

Slave labor. 1887. *Vancouver News*, May 1, p. 4.

Steinberg, S. 1981. *The ethnic myth: Race, ethnicity, and class in America*. New York: Atheneum.

Steiner, S. 1979. *Fusang: The Chinese who built America*. New York: Harper and Row.

Stepan, N. 1982. *The idea of race in science: Great Britain, 1800–1960*. London: Macmillan.

Suttles, G. 1968. *The social order of the slum*. Chicago: University of Chicago Press.

Taylor, G. 1927. *Environment and race*. London: Oxford University Press.

Their drastic measures. 1887. *Vancouver News*, March 2, p. 1.

Thompson, R. 1979. The state and the ethnic community: The changing social organization of Toronto's Chinatown. Ph.D. thesis, University of Michigan, Ann Arbor.

To do their own work. 1906. *Province*, February 9, p. 15.

Tuan, Y-F. 1974. *Topophilia*. Englewood Cliffs, N.J.: Prentice-Hall.

Unanswerable argument, The. 1907. *The Saturday Sunset*, August 10, p. 1.

Unsanitary Chinese. 1899. *World*, April 28, p. 4.

Urge enforcement of health bylaws. 1915. *Province*, January 26, p. 5.

Vancouver must keep this team. 1908. *The Saturday Sunset*, February 1, p. 1.

Vancouver's Chinatown has become plague spot. 1912. *World*, February 10, p. 6.

Voegelin, E. 1940. The growth of the race idea. *Review of Politics* 2(3):283–317.

Ward, P. 1978. *White Canada forever: Popular attitudes and public policy toward Orientals in British Columbia*. Montreal: McGill-Queen's University Press.

Watson, G. 1981. The reification of ethnicity and its political consequences in the north. *The Canadian Review of Sociology and Anthropology* 18(4):453–69.

Weiss, M. 1974. *Valley City: A Chinese community in America*. Cambridge, Mass.: Shenkman.

Western, J. 1981. *Outcast Capetown*. Minneapolis: University of Minnesota Press.

Wickberg, E.; Con, H.; Johnson, G.; and Willmott, W. E. 1982. *From China to Canada: A history of the Chinese communities in Canada*. Toronto: McClelland and Stewart.

Williams' Illustrated Official British Columbia Directory. 1892. Victoria: R. Williams.

Wong, B. 1982. *Chinatown: Economic adaptation and ethnic identity of the Chinese*. New York: Holt and Co.

Yee, P. 1984. Business devices from two worlds: The Chinese in early Vancouver. *B.C. Studies* 62:44–67.

Yip, Q. 1936. *Vancouver's Chinatown*. Vancouver: Pacific Printers.

Young, D. 1976. The Vancouver police force, 1886–1914. B.A. Honors essay, Department of History, University of British Columbia, Vancouver.

Montreal's King of Italian Labour:

A Case Study of Padronism

ROBERT F. HARNEY

On 23 January 1904, more than 2,000 Italian labourers paraded through the streets of Montreal. They were there to fête Antonio Cordasco, steamship agent, *banchista* [banker] and director of a labour bureau. Two foremen presented him with a crown "in a shape not unlike that worn by the King of Italy." The crown was later displayed in a glass case along with a souvenir sheet containing eleven columns of Italian names and entitled "In Memory of the Great Parade of January, 1904, in honour of Signor Antonio Cordasco, proclaimed King of the Workers." During February, *caposquadri* and *sub-bossi* (foremen) organized a banquet for Cordasco. Invitations to the banquet bore a seal suspiciously like the Royal Crest of Italy, and Cordasco's kept newspaper, the *Corriere del Canada*, reported the occasion in detail.[1]

Four months later, in June and July 1904, the "King of Italian labour" was under investigation by the Deputy Minister of Labour, about to be the centre of a Royal Commission inquiry into fraudulent business practices, and excoriated by officials of the Italian Immigrant Aid Society. What emerges from the reports, testimony and newspaper accounts about the activity of Cordasco and his competitors in Montreal is not just the picture of an exploitive and dishonest broker but of a man truly in between— willing enough to put his boot into those beneath him, such as the greenhorns who depended upon him for jobs, but also forced to tug his forelock and to anticipate the wishes of the English-speaking businessmen and employers whom he served. It was these men upon whom the labour agent depended in his delicate task of wedding North American capitalist needs to seasonal labour. Cordasco's career and the public assault upon

---

ROBERT F. HARNEY, "MONTREAL'S KING OF ITALIAN LABOUR: A CASE STUDY OF PADRONISM,"*LABOUR/LE TRAVAILLEUR* 4 (1979), 57–84. REPRINTED WITH PERMISSION OF THE EDITOR. © COMMITTEE ON CANADIAN LABOUR HISTORY. THIS IS AN EDITED VERSION OF THE AFOREMENTIONED TEXT.

1. The chief source for this essay is the *Royal Commission appointed to inquire into the Immigration of Italian Labourers to Montreal and the alleged Fraudulent Practices of Employment Agencies* (Ottawa 1905). The Commission produced a 41 page report and 170 pages of testimony. The Commission's report is generally marred as a source by an undercurrent of nativism, ignorance of Italian ways, and a view of free enterprise as part of the divine plan. Henceforth cited as *Royal Commission 1904*.

him affords us a rare entry into the world of the *padrone*, the exploitive Italian brokers who were stock—but little understood—villains in the drama of immigration.[2]

Antonio Cordasco, the protagonist of our story, appears in the end as a nearly perfect Italian parody of the "negro king,"...a puppet who serves those who really control the society and the economy.[3] In 1904, Cordasco's stupidity and avarice combined with circumstance—a late thaw, high unemployment in the United States, and pressure from the Montreal Italian Immigrant Aid Society and his chief competitor, Alberto Dini—to expose him to public scrutiny. He proved to be a man whose new crown rested uneasily; he had to threaten and cajole his *sub-bossi*, placate his capitalist overlords, hide from irate workers, and scheme to destroy competitors who aspired to his throne. Moreover, he carried on a complex foreign policy with *padroni* in other cities and with steamship and emigration agents in Italy and on Italy's borders. Cordasco stood astride a free enterprise system that brought Italian migrant labour into contact with North American job opportunity. His power lay in his control of the communications network between labour and capital, and that was not an easy position from which to carve an empire. Like the "negro king," he had neither the affection of his people, the migrant Italian labourers, nor the trust of his Wasp masters, but he served them both as intermediary and spared them both from dealing directly with the mysterious other....

[Cordasco rode to power on a commerce in migration which grew up in the late nineteenth century. The need for manual labour at remote northern work sites, the attitudes of Canadian big business and of European village labourers, the climate, the difficulty of transportation, and the xenophobic immigration policy of the government, made a "sojourning" (or seasonal guest worker) system inevitable. The Canadian employer received the work of a docile and mobile work force, free from

---

2. The word *padrone* does not appear in the testimony. Mackenzie King, chief investigator for the Dept. of Labour and future Prime Minister of Canada, probably knew the word and its connotations from his American experience. I have used the word throughout the paper as a convenient label for the chief intermediaries but do so on the understanding that the reader has a wary and sophisticated approach to its use. I have dealt more historiographically with the padrone in North America in an earlier article. See R. F. Harney, "The Padrone and the Immigrant, *Canadian Review of American Studies*, 5 (1974), 101–118.

3. The expression was popularized in Canada by André Laurendeau (1912–1968), the editor of Montreal's *Le Devoir*. Laurendeau claimed that Quebec was governed by "les rois negres"—the equivalent of those puppet rulers in Africa through whom the British authorities found it convenient to wield power....

the taint of unionism. Although the Canadian government preferred northern European immigrants, such employers as the railways, mines and smelting interests preferred southern Europeans, who could be relied upon to feel alien in the new land, not to jump track, not to wish too far, and to be transient or sojourning in their frame of mind. Such employers circumvented government policy and used steamship agents to draw such labourers to Canada. Workers, for their part, reached job sites without undue delay or hardship, and after a single season's work might have enough money to send home; by staying several seasons, they might make a nest-egg so that they would never have to come back again. Despite Italian laws against foreign recruitment of labour, the intermediaries, who brought the two sides together, reaped rich profits from the arrangement.

Competition was rife in the *commercio di carne umana* (white slave trade) which emerged in the early twentieth century. For every *padrone* in Montreal or Boston, there were one or two steamship sub-agents in an Italian town, who earned their way by the bounty paid for each migrant recruited for steamship passage. Such sub-agents were often well-connected local notables and officials. Antonio Cordasco rose to be the "king of Italian labour" by virtue of the decision of the Canadian Pacific Railway, which elevated the small-time hustler into a *padrone* by regarding him as their sole agent. It was George Burns, the company's chief hiring agent, who made Cordasco the "negro king," because he regarded him as a reliable supplier of labour. This benefited Cordasco, but it also often left him in an awkward position. Having advertised the benefits of Canada in his newspaper, the *Corriere del Canada*, Cordasco was blamed when conditions were not as promised. The *padrone* system ultimately depended on the support of the migrants who were both consumers and commodities in the trade in human labour.]

Cordasco himself sometimes sensed that he was a man dangling between forces which could manipulate him. There is a painful and a plaintive quality in a letter to a contact in Udine expressing his annoyance at the demands made upon him by workers: "I am not responsible for the extremely cold season that prevents the companies from starting work." The labour practices for which he was being criticized in 1904...had begun in 1901...with the approval of the Canadian Pacific Railway. Cordasco described to the commissioners the situation in that year when three officials of the railway came to him, saying they wanted labourers and asking if he had any Italian labour to supply to the Canadian Pacific. At the beginning he could find only 400 or 500 men, and the company offered him no fee or salary, probably because they assumed that Cordasco himself would charge the labourers as would a regular employment agency. However, when the strike began later in 1901, they offered to pay him a dollar a man, and with that as an incentive, Cordasco rounded up about 2,000 men from throughout North America.... He devised a system in which each winter he registered both workers and foremen in a work book with his agency, charging a dollar apiece for workers and more for foremen, and assuring them that they would receive work in the spring from the railway contractors on the basis of their place on that list. What appeared to be a simple and sensible registration system, however, turned out to be a form of bounty not unlike that charged by the steamship agents. By over-inscribing workers and then failing to cope with a late thaw and the possibility that there would be less work than expected, Cordasco brought himself and his monarchy to the brink of economic and personal ruin in spring 1904.

In many ways the crisis in padronism was atypical because the *padrone's* profit and power, his relationship to the local "Little Italy," was based on a system far more complex than that of simply collecting bounty. The *intermediarismo* (brokerage) that he practised extended both into many aspects of Italian life in Canada and, as we have seen, along the communications network between European labour and North American industry. Cordasco's activities conveniently divide into those which, remembering our analogy to monarchy, we might call his foreign policy... and his domestic policy.... By extension, he helped to shape the Italian community itself.

Cordasco's foreign policy had the Chiasso Connection as its linchpin but it also included his relations with the various *padroni* and labour agents in the American "Little Italies" and his relations with the major steamship companies. The official report of the Royal Commission listed some of the methods Cordasco used to make contact with the labour supply in Europe. The investigators admitted that they could only infer from the correspondence a conspiracy to mislead workers. Mackenzie King, the chief investigator, had remarked that "there is no business relation existing between himself [Cordasco] and these agents but I think there can be no doubt as to their acting in direct accordance with an understood arrangement which he has with them."[4]...

The nature of the *padrone* connection, the nature of *vincolismo* (complex linkage), led North American investigators like Mackenzie King and Marcus Braun to hint suspiciously of crime, when, in fact, padronism was

---

4. Report in *Labour Gazette* (June 1906), 1350.

a business—albeit the business of pre-industrial men. . . . The agents may have seemed *strozzini* (sharks) to those outside the ethnic group, but a system of honour existed among them that depended on hand shakes, ascriptive encounters, kinship, mutual trust, and respect. In every major city the leading labour bureaus and *padroni* had a shared interest in controlling and regulating their relations with one another, so that too many new competitors, upstart foremen who had learned a bit of English, could not successfully compete.

The memoranda of understanding and letters of agreement that passed between Cordasco and his peers were callous documents reflecting the tenor of the commerce in human flesh. But steamship agents and labour agents of every ethnic background dealt with migrants thus, and the line between the clever use of the free enterprise system and fraud is more discernible to us now than it was then. . . .

When we first encountered Cordasco at his mock coronation, we were watching a media event. The parade and banquet took up most of a special issue of the *Corriere del Canada* and that special issue was printed and sent to many Italian towns. With touching modesty and some *campanilismo* (localism) Cordasco himself claimed that he never sent any newspapers abroad except to his own village. But it seems obvious from the testimony of trapped migrants to the Commission that issues of *Corriere del Canada* were used as an advertising device to encourage labour to come to Canada from throughout Italy. For example, a witness from Reggio Calabria said that he had seen many circulars and newspapers, and that, at about the same time, a man had come to his village with packets of Cordasco's business card. Cordasco had also sent business cards. . . to almost everybody who addressed inquiries to him. Although hardly grounds upon which to base a charge of conspiracy to defraud, the flow of business cards back and forth seems a fitting image for describing the network that existed between *padroni* and emigration agents. It served the steamship agent in Italy well to be able to give the migrant Cordasco's card and to direct him to Cordasco, as if the *padrone* were but a runner for the steamship agent himself, and it obviously served Cordasco to have the fish directed into his net as they came toward Montreal. . . .

Both Cordasco and [Alberto] Dini [Cordasco's competitor] were evasive in their testimony about their use of newspaper advertising. Dini's advertisements were mostly printed in *La Patria Italiana*; Cordasco's in the *Corriere del Canada*. These newspapers may have existed as more than advertising devices for the *padroni*—Dini and Cordasco were careful not to claim any direct relationship to the papers, and each paper had an editor who tried to be independent and to create an Italian cultural *ambiente* (ambience) in Montreal—but several curious letters bring the editors' independence into question. For example, Cordasco wrote to Luigi Scarrone, a newspaperman in Toronto, describing himself "as the capitalist administrator of the *Corriere del Canada*." Cordasco asked Scarrone, as a favour, to write an article about the *padroni*, since he could not do it himself, because "if I should place this before the readers they will say that I sing my own praise or that I order others to praise me. So you can, (and I thank you for that) send articles on the work and solidity of the Canadian Pacific Railway but do not tell the readers that I belong to this newspaper."[5]

The *padrone* was an ethnic entrepreneur involved in many businesses. In his testimony, Dini told the judge, "I have got an employment office, banker is name known to Italians." Earlier in his testimony, he had also pointed out that he was the steamship agent for North German Lloyd's Line, Hamburg-American Anchor Line, and two Italian lines, including La Velocce. Cordasco in turn had extracted a promise from Mr. Burns of the CPR when he helped find strike breakers in 1901, that the CPR would help him become the agent for their steamship line, for Compagnie Générale Transatlantique and for several others. Like Dini, he referred to himself as a banker and his newspaper announcement to the labourers in 1904 began:

> To the army of the pick and shovel Italian labourers, bosses do not show a double face, do not be false but only one. Be true. Have a soldier's courage, apply to the elegant and solid Italian bank of Antonio Cordasco, if you do not want to weep over your misfortunes in the spring when the shipments of men will begin.[6]

Both men described themselves as bankers, perhaps as steamship agents and employment agents, but would not have used the word *padrone*. They specialized in performing as brokers between labour and capital, as transmitters of remittances and pre-paid tickets, and as steamship agents, while engaging, because of the migrants' dependence on them, in many other businesses.

Cordasco's banking, for example, included lending money to foremen so that they could pay the registration fee of a dollar a head for their work gangs. Often the faith of the workers in the *banchista* was touchingly

---

5. Letter from Cordasco to L. P. Scarrone (9 February 1904), *Royal Commission 1904*, 103.
6. Notice in *La Patria Italiana, Royal Commission 1904*, 106.

naive. A 1903 letter reads, "We the undersigned, signed with a cross mark because we cannot write or read, both of us, we authorize Mr. A. Cordasco to draw our wages for work done in the month of October last, 1903. And we both authorize the Canadian Pacific Railway Company to pay over our wages to Mr. Cordasco at 375 St. James Street." Cordasco himself understood the complex nature of his *intermediarismo*. An advertisement appearing in *La Patria Italiana* showed a rather charming, if dangerous and old-fashioned, sense of the word *patronato*: "If you want to be respected and protected either on the work or in case of accident or other annoyances which may be easily met, apply personally or address letters or telegrams to Antonio Cordasco."[7] It was protection that the *padrone* offered, protection against undue delay, protection against fraud by others, protection against all the dangers of an unknown world, of a world where the labourer could not cope for himself because of lack of education, lack of language skills and lack of time to stand and fight when his cash supply was threatened.

Mr. Skinner, Mr. Burns' assistant, showed a certain sympathy for Cordasco, for the *padrone* who had to deal with what Skinner seemed to see as the child-like qualities of the labourers:

> He has lots of trouble. He keeps an office with a waiting room, and they are the resorts where these people spend all winter. They come to smoke, he keeps all sorts of conveniences for them.[8]

In a strange way, the chief power of the intermediary, just as in the old country, lay in his literacy. Cordasco's clerk on the witness stand mentioned writing over 87 letters a month. When Dini was pressed as to what he actually did when people came to him seeking work, he answered, "I write to several contractors, to employers, to Grand Trunk if they want labourers and if they want them I'll ship them quickly." He was asked how many contractors he represented, and replied, ten or twenty. "When the contractors want labourers, they have my address, they write or telegraph me, if I have any Italians to send them." So it was their ability to correspond and to communicate with the American employer which made *padroni* powerful. They played a role no different from that played by the bourgeoisie of the small towns of the Italian south and northeast, a role in which literacy was a form of capital and the basis of the brokerage

---

7. *La Patria Italiana* (20 February 1904), *Royal Commission 1904*, 107.
8. Testimony of CPR agent Skinner, *Royal Commission 1904*, 26.

system itself. Men who would have been brokers between the well-born and the peasantry or between government and peasantry in Europe, found themselves brokers between sojourners and English-speaking employers.[9]

There is no doubt that Cordasco made a profit from both the employer and labourer. That was only fitting since he served both groups. The amount of the profit, however, was outrageous by any standard. At one point, it became clear from the testimony that Cordasco was buying from his own supplier near Windsor Station and supplying most of the canned anchovies and bread for labourers at different Canadian Pacific sites across northern Ontario. He made 150% profit on a can of sardines, the bread was often moldy and he clearly made a high profit on it as well. In one season he cleared $3800 as a provisioner. The figure of a dollar a head for registration of men pales in comparison. . . . The foremen who came to the stand to testify against him pointed out that they had been forced to raise the money for the banquet that had been held in his honour and that some of that money had also mysteriously disappeared into Cordasco's pocket.[10]

If the investigators had understood the system a little better, had understood the degree to which the foremen and labourers were also consumers, they would have noticed that the anger of those who came to the stand was not over the fact that they had to pay tribute to Cordasco or that they had to register seasonally for work with him, but that he had not found jobs for them or for their gangs that year. The foremen, particularly, since they too were men in between, were galled by the fact that they had promised their gangs work, that they had often raised the dollar a head for Cordasco from their gangs. . . . One foreman, Michael Tisi, was pressed on the witness stand about the fact that he had paid ten dollars to be foreman of a gang of 100 men and that each of the men had paid two dollars. He admitted paying that, but he felt that he had no grievance against Cordasco. He answered simply, "They went to work. I'm not complaining about that."[11]

It has always seemed illogical to speak about a large scale broker like Cordasco controlling thousands of men through ties of paesanism, kinship

---

9. See Harney, "Commerce of Migration," *Canadian Ethnic Studies*, 9 (1977), 42–53, on the concept of the *borghesia mediatrice*. See G. Dore, *La Democrazia italiana e l'emigrazione in America* (Brescia 1964).
10. Testimony of Pompeo Bianco, foreman, *Royal Commission 1904*, 163.
11. Testimony of Michele Tisi, foreman, *Royal Commission 1904*, 33.

or even through shared ethnicity. In 1903, the CPR hired over 3500 Italians. Cordasco could not have known them all. They came from all over Italy, from the Veneto to Sicily; few, if any, were his *paesani* (fellow townsmen), let alone his friends and relatives. It was the *sub-bossi* who organized and controlled the work gangs. Sometimes those gangs were made up of *paesani* but not always. The testimony of the *caposquadri* (foremen) partially explains one aspect of the padrone's power. One foreman, Sal Mollo, in his testimony pointed out to the Commission that his "men don't know him [Cordasco] at all. They know me. When I went there to his bank he would not hear me." Another foreman, Pompeo Bianco, claimed to know all of his gang of 104 men brought from the United States, except for perhaps 12.[12]

Loyalty to the bosses was functional; it had to do with their ability to operate as secondary intermediaries, in this instance between the men and Cordasco, but usually between the men and the section bosses of the CPR. If that loyalty was sometimes based on regional allegiances, such as the whole gang and the boss being Calabrese or being Venetian, it was still not synonymous with paesanism.

From the ranks of these foremen however, as well as from other small entrepreneurs, individuals came forth to try to compete with Dini and Cordasco in the lucrative trade in migrants. If Cordasco was the *generone* (*haut bourgeois*) then these were the *generetti* (*petit bourgeoisie*) nipping at his heels. Whatever the true basis of loyalty between *sub-bosse* and gangs, Cordasco was able to control thousands of men from his Montreal office without going into the field; it could depend not just on his own immediate employees but on the *sub-bossi* as vassals.

The veil did lift enough for us to see how the *padrone* ultimately depended on his Anglo-Saxon master, the employer of labourers. Cordasco saw Burns or his assistant Skinner almost daily....Much of Cordasco's power over his Italian migrant labourer clientele derived from his right to advertise himself as the only acting agent for the CPR....On the stand, Burns admitted readily that he had given Cordasco a monopoly: "You have always stated that Mr. Cordasco was labour agent for the CPR. Answer: I have said that he was sole agent to hire Italians." From the phrasing, one senses that Burns really did find the ways of the migrant Italians mysterious and needed Cordasco's help. He remarked of Cor-

---

12. Testimony of Salvatore Mollo, foreman, *Royal Commission 1904*, 34; testimony of Pompeo Bianco, foreman, *Royal Commission 1904*, 29.

dasco's runners, "these men have connections down there [the States] and they pick out forces of men, pay a lot of expenses, railway fare and two or three dollars a day."[13] He had been so impressed by Cordasco's energy and ingenuity in finding strike breakers in 1901 that he remained committed to him through the 1904 crisis.

Burns contributed directly to the expansion of Cordasco's role from that of a minor employment agent into a *banchista*. The commerce of migration led inevitably to a variety of entrepreneurial possibilities and the CPR's agent gave his blessing:

> The way it came about was this. He only had a regular office and was doing a large business but he had no steamship agencies. And of course when these Italians come back from work most of them have a good deal of money which they want to send over to their relatives and friends, some for their wives and children and they buy these steamship pre-paid tickets. Cordasco is desirous of getting a line of these tickets on the different steamship agencies. And he came to me about the matter and I told him he could easily get agencies if he made the proper representation to the agents that were in New York. Question: You recommended him? Answer: I took some steps to get these agencies for him.[14]

So from his castle in Windsor Station, George Burns protected his vassal from both do-gooders and the competition of lesser brokers because the railway found the *padrone* system efficient and flexible. A delegation from the Italian Immigration Aid Society had approached Burns offering to provide him with Italian labourers directly from Italy through the good offices of the Italian government. Burns replied to them,

> I have taken up the question of the employment of labour with the proper authorities and have to advise you that it is not the intention of this company to change the arrangements of the employment of Italian immigrant labour which have been in effect during the past few years. Our present system has given entire satisfaction so far and I therefore

---

13. Testimony of Burns, *Royal Commission 1904*, 61. It is important to note that Burns stressed that Cordasco was sole agent for Italian labour; he had in that sense an ethnic monopoly but not a franchise for hiring all track crews. As Burns pointed out (52), Italian labour had a specific purpose—"The Italians on our line are used to replace these men who have been employed earlier in the season on contracts, and to whom at this time of year, July and August, when the harvest starts, the farmer offers high wages and they jump their jobs, and the work is left behind, and we have to rely on anything we can get."

14. Testimony of Burns, *Royal Commission 1904*, 41.

regret I shall be unable to place direct with your Society any specific order for any number of men.[15]

Cordasco's sway over Italian migrant labour had the approval of the company. For example, at the famous banquet in the *padrone's* honour, most of the foremen in attendance were impressed by the presence of the chief superintendent of the CPR's Vancouver division. After all, that gentleman would be hiring 5000 or 6000 Italians during the coming spring, and he seemed to be there honouring his friend Cordasco.

In 1904, company support, even though it showed the limits of Cordasco's independence, enabled him to thwart attacks upon his monopoly. That support came in at least four ways. First, at no point in their testimony did Skinner or Burns speak explicitly enough to compromise Cordasco. Second, they maintained throughout his exclusive right to hire Italians for the railway rather than turning to aspiring *sub-bossi*. Third, they had refused to order manpower from Alberto Dini, Cordasco's main competitor. Fourth, Burns did his best to discredit or ignore the Italian Immigrant Aid Society.

With his overlords to protect him...Cordasco seemed as safe as a *padrone* could be. To raise money for the banquet in his honour he warned any man who hesitated to donate five dollars to the cause that he would publish his photograph upside down on the souvenir sheet. The real threat was that "anyone who refused to pay will go out of my office," that is, would be eliminated from the hiring register. In an address to labourers printed in *La Patria Italiana* Cordasco flaunted his monopoly:

> If you do not want to weep over your misfortune in the spring when the shipment of men will begin you will do business with me. Do not believe that with your dollar that you will be able to get work like your comrades who have been faithful. Those who had signed the book earlier. We will inspect our books and money orders and our passage ticket books and those who will not have their names in them will in their despair tear out their hair and will call Mr. Cordasco, Lordship Don Antonio, "Let me go to work." "No, never," will be answered to them. "Go to those to whom you have sent your money away..." Forewarned is a forearmed man.[16]

Despite this unintentional parody of Christ's monopoly over salvation

---

15. Letter from Burns to C. Mariotti, Secretary of the Italian Immigration Aid Society (16 March 1903) *Royal Commission 1904*, 3.
16. *La Patria Italiana*, advertisement (20 February 1904), *Royal Commission 1904*, 106.

Cordasco could not stifle all the competition. The same entrepreneurial spirit that brought so many of the migrants to North America led a certain number of men to see in Cordasco or Dini models for action. One could almost say that an infernal spirit of capitalism had begun to inject itself into his feudal system. Foremen, *sub-bossi* and *caposquadri* who had been in America for a number of seasons—especially if they spoke English well—must have seen advantage in eliminating Cordasco as intermediary even if they did not aspire to a brokerage status for themselves. The *sub-bossi* were...at once in a feudal and capitalist relationship with the padrone. The *sub-bossi* gave Cordasco his power; he gave them theirs. Each could claim to provide work to those below them. If one of the *generetti* tried to by-pass Cordasco and deal directly with the employer, Cordasco could only hope that the employer would not take advantage of the situation to undermine him.

As we have seen, George Burns of the CPR did not take advantage of the situation. He found it easier to have one reliable *padrone* and to turn a blind eye to his corruption and unfair exactions. By 1904, with the help of the company, Cordasco had defeated non-Italian suppliers of labour and had excluded Dini from the CPR system, while he himself cut into Dini's commerce with the Grand Trunk Railway. From the *padrone's* correspondence, we can see how he used Burns and the sub-contractors' fear of anarchy in the supply system to thwart emerging competitors. Cordasco went so far at one point as to write a letter to Boston interfering in the recruitment of labourers there and in the competition between the Bianco Stabili Company and Torchia and Company. He warned Messieurs Torchia that there was no point in recruiting people for the CPR in British Columbia because he, Cordasco, was the sole agent for that railway and he would only order manpower through Stabili. He ended his letter thus, "No shipment of men will be recognized but those made through Stabili and Company.[17]...

The greatest challenge to Cordasco's pre-eminence in the commerce of migration arose from the changing attitude toward protecting labourers in Italy. If it was Montreal civic authorities who precipitated the Royal Commission inquiry into Italian migrant workers, it was the city's Italian Immigrant Aid Society, acting for the new Commissariat of Emigration in Rome, which tried to pounce upon the unfortunate situation in order to destroy the *padrone* system, or at least to discredit Antonio Cordasco.[18]

---

17. Letter from Cordasco to M. Torchia & Co. (12 March 1904), *Royal Commission 1904*, 89.
18. With the passage of new legislation on immigration in Italy during 1901, the Society had changed from a private Montreal charitable agency to an adjunct of the Italian consulate

The Society, even though it had existed as a local private organization for a number of years, was incorporated under Canadian law only during winter 1902. Its leadership was a compound of Italian government officials, local professionals of Italian descent and the *notabili* from among older Italian settlers of Montreal. Among the Society's officers were Honoré Catelli, director of the city's largest pasta manufactury, and—unfortunately for the Society's image—Alberto Dini, Cordasco's principal rival as Italian banker, travel agent and employment broker.

From the outset, the Society did not seem as intent upon solving the problems that arose from clandestine Italian migration to Canada as it did upon usurping Cordasco from his position in the network. Long before the Royal Commission hearings, the Society had tried unsuccessfully to undermine the Canadian Pacific Railway's support for Cordasco. Special agent Burns admitted on the stand that he had been informed of a number of incidents in which the Society accused the *padrone* of cheating workers. A letter to Burns' immediate superior in 1903 hinted darkly that Cordasco was hoodwinking the railway, implying that Burns was in collusion with him. The letter came from the Society's offices:

> We suppose it never came to your knowledge that certain people, possibly authorized to deal with your company, engaged Italian labourers to work on your roads, only on payment of a commission of $3.00 each, and refused to engage those who cannot afford to pay such commission. . . . We wish to stop an abuse of charging $3.00 pr more to poor men, whose children are perhaps starving.[19]

For his part, Cordasco never treated the Society as other than a rival intermediary and labour brokerage. Dini's presence on the group's board of directors lent some credence to Cordasco's claim that there was no ethical difference between the services he rendered or the fees he charged to sojourners and those that the Society wished to substitute. Cordasco, with characteristically clumsy malice, tried to discredit the Society as well. In winter 1903–1904, he had written to the editor of an Italian newspaper on Mulberry Street in New York City. Paying him for advertis-

---

funded by the Italian government. Its papers of incorporation listed as the Society's purpose: "1. the assisting of Italian immigrants to reach Canada; 2. assisting Italians to obtain employment; 3. assisting Italian immigrants to obtain land for settlement. . .; 4. assisting Italian immigrants in every possible way; 5. enabling persons in Canada in want of labourers, artisans or servants to get from Italy desirable citizens." (Incorporation 10 November 1902.)

19. Letter from Italian Immigration Aid Society to D. McNicoll, General Manager Canadian Pacific Railway (26 March 1903), *Royal Commission 1904*, 73.

ing space, the Montreal *padrone* added, "please make an article speaking about the negligence of this Consul and the Italian Immigrant Aid Society."[20] And, even though he had written earlier to the CPR agent to warn him that the best labourers were being siphoned off by other companies, Cordasco reacted to the first public outcry against the number of Italian migrants loitering in Montreal in spring 1904 by telling Burns that it was the Society who had, by providing shelter and sending notices about agricultural possibilities in Canada to Italy, caused the embarrassing glut of greenhorns in the labour pool:

> Sure will be disgraceful [*sic*] for these poor emigrants with the old ones which they put up here all winter, and Italian Consul with his Society are to be blamed and they should be crushed to peace [*sic*].[21]

Because of Dini's presence on the Society's board, Cordasco and his lawyers were able to deflect the struggle away from the point that the Italian government would have preferred, that is, that regulation (and *patronato*) should replace exploitation and the *padrone* system. However honest the practices of Dini and his companions, he was a *banchista* and a rival broker; his presence on the board of directors brought the Society's integrity, or at least its good sense, into question. . . .

Candori, the Secretary of the Society, boasted from the witness stand that the Society had drawn to Canada a better class of Italian workers from Venetia, "picked men, and any railway company would be glad to have these men because they are strong and even good looking."[22] Both the Society and Canadian immigration authorities tended to use words like "class" and "type," when in fact they meant race. The Society's intervention against the *padroni* was ineffective because it misunderstood the temper of Canadian officialdom and even more the distinction between the government's desire to find agriculturalists for the prairies and the desire of the major employers of unskilled labour to find men who would not settle down. In a letter to the CPR authorities, the Society boasted that they would bring over men who, after working on the railway, would settle on the land and "make industrious Canadian citizens."[23] Such a promise pleased neither those who preferred the workers to think like sojourners nor those who preferred to people the prairies with northwest European stock. A line from the Society's bulle-

20. Letter from Cordasco to V. Capparelli, editor of *L'Operari* (28 January 1904), *Royal Commission 1904*, 139.
21. Letter from Cordasco to Burns (10 May 1904), *Royal Commission 1904*, 57.
22. Testimony of Candori, Society secretary, *Royal Commission 1904*, 13.
23. Letter from Mariotti to McNicoll, *Royal Commission 1904*, 13.

tin—"Look at the splendid results that the Italian agriculturists have had in South America, and especially in Argentina. Why should you not have the same result in Canada?"—must have elicited the answering shudder that Canada was a protestant, northerly, British colony, not a potential Argentina.[24]

In the end, the Commission was unwilling to attack directly the major companies involved in employing Italian sojourners, and those companies refused to desert their intermediaries, so the *padrone* system came through the 1904 crisis unscathed. There is little evidence for the claim that more honest brokers began to compete successfully with the chief *padroni* after 1904, even though a limit was placed on how much a labour bureau could charge to register a worker.[25] Neither Cordasco's nor Dini's power declined after the hearings, and both passed quietly from being *padroni* to *notabili*, their prominence measured by stained glass windows in parish churches and by their presence on Montreal Italian civil committees.

The employers such as the Canadian Pacific Railway section bosses had the means to resist revolt. When Italians at Crow's Nest Pass in British Columbia refused $1.50 a day, they were simply dismissed and the local labour agent began "filling orders with Galicians from the North."[26] On the other hand, Cordasco had no protection from the caprice or anger of Italian workers; he faced physical attack and verbal abuse. If men he gathered were dismissed or left a job site disgruntled, he could only plead

---

24. The phrase about Argentina was contained in one of the Society's bulletins, *Royal Commission 1904*, 15. Block settlement in the Canadian West did resemble the Argentine experience, but Italians were not encouraged by the authorities. The Minister of the Interior himself wrote to an aide that "no steps are to be taken to assist or encourage Italian immigration to Canada..." Sifton papers, quoted in D. Avery, "Canadian Immigration Policy and the Foreign Navvy, 1874–1914," *Historical Papers* (1972), 135–156. The Italian consul in Montreal reported in 1901 that not a single Italian migrant interviewed in the city wished to settle. All were sojourners or seasonal labourers looking for ready cash. *Immigration Branch* 1901, File 28885. "As a matter of fact Mr. Solimbergo [the consul] found out that out of all Italian emigrants who were already in Canada, not one thought it of any use to become a colonial." Emigration of Italian peasants to Canada, enquiry of *Corriere della Sera* (June 1901), typescript translation of newspaper article.

25. See A. V. Spada, *Italians in Canada* (Montreal, 1969), 89. The Commission recommended finally that Montreal pass a by-law, like Toronto's which required licensing for labour bureaus and a scale of fees for registering workers for employment. *Labour Gazette* (June 1905), 1348. Cordasco in the end, made restitution to registered workers who got no work under $3,000 and resumed his business without using a registration fee system. As we have seen that was not the chief source of his income and power anyway.

26. Letter from Burns to Cordasco, *Royal Commission 1904*, 113. Burns also informed the Italian Immigration Aid Society of this matter.

for patience from *sub-bossi* or for patronage from other employers. So the consumer power of the migrants—before they were acclimatized or turned to North American unionism—was turned against the *padrone*, not the employer. In this, as in every aspect of the system, a *padrone* like Cordasco was the man in between. Not only did he face the anger of workmen and treason from his vassals, but he ran the risk of being seen as an unreliable broker by big business because he supplied troublesome men.

Cordasco then was probably a nasty man and certainly did not deserve the excess profits he exacted from the migrant labour force, but he did, except perhaps in spring 1904, do his job. The historical literature has too often assumed that the male sojourners of the 1890s and 1900s were helpless victims of the system, potential settlers held in thrall by the *padroni* and condemned to exploitation and to transience by his machinations. At least in the Canadian case, that was simply not so.

The sojourners accepted the *padrone* because they reckoned that he provided them the best alternative in their search for cash; their commitment to the system, like their avoidance of unionism or agricultural work, reflected their desire to return home as quickly as possible with cash and with as little North American encumbrance as possible. When an official of the Commissariat asked Italian labourers in the Niagara Peninsula why they hadn't taken up some of the rich farm lands in that region, the answer was simple: "We have to think about our families in Italy."[27] In 1900, the Canadian Consul in Montreal had reported that of all the trapped migrants interviewed there, none had come to Canada to settle. Agricultural work did not bring in the cash which was the goal of the sojourning family member. . . .

B. Attolico, in 1912, met a Calabrese youth in the bush "at a little station four hours away from Lake Superior."[28] The youngster complained to him about missing his village but he had wintered over in a bunkhouse because he did not want to go to Port Arthur and spend his salary on *madamigella* ("the ladies"). The boy had already sent 350 lire—the equivalent of a half year's wages—to his mother back in his home town and had been in Canada less than three months when Attolico encountered him. He did not mind the deprivation but he kept repeating that, while there were many other Calabrese about, he was the only one from

---

27. B. Attolico, "L'agricoltura e l'immigrazione nell'Canada" in the *Bollettino* #5 (Anno 1912) Commissariat of Emigration, Rome, 547.
28. B. Attolico, "Sui campi di lavoro della nuova ferrovia transcontinentale canadese" in the *Bollettino* #1 (Anno 1913) Commissariat of Emigration, Rome, 7.

Mammole and had no one for company but God. Since the young Calabrese section hand worked for the Canadian Pacific Railway, he was mistaken if he thought the deity was his only companion. The latter might have heard his prayers, but it was Cordasco or one of his successors who had found him his job, remitted his money to his mother, delivered her letters to him, and would handle pre-paid tickets for kinfolk or for his passage home later on. It was a *padrone*, not God and not the free flow of labour to capital, who had brought a man from the hills of Calabria to the northern Ontario bush. . . .

The Skilled Emigrant and Her Kin:

Gender, Culture, and Labour Recruitment

JOY PARR

Emigration is generally understood as a gendered process, beginning for men with a solitary experiment in distant lands, for women with a long interlude between two worlds while they wait for word that it is safe to follow. For men the journey is seen as a response to international differentials in the labour market, for women as a way to begin or consolidate a married life. Emigration usually seems to cast men in active roles and women in adaptive roles, men being part of a structured system, and women living out the consequences of subjective choices.[1] These characterizations probably miss the mark, even for emigration within marriage. As descriptions of female migration outside marriage (and probably also within it for all but women of independent wealth), these depictions omit several essentials.

Single female emigrants have not been uncommon historically. Typically they left home in early adulthood, at a marriageable age, although, as Charlotte Macdonald reminds us, the fact that emigration and marriage have similar locations in many life cycles does not establish that young women, any more than young men, left home in order to marry. Most working-class women understood that marriage, either before or after emigration, would not end their experience with wage work. Female emigrants had their eye on the job market, both short and long term.[2] In Canada even young women recruited for their domestic skills often remained for many years in the labour force before marriage.[3] In the

Joy Parr, "The Skilled Emigrant and Her Kin: Gender, Culture, and Labour Recruitment," *Canadian Historical Review*, 68, 4 (1987), 529–51. Reprinted by permission of University of Toronto Press.

I am grateful to Shula Marks, Alice Kessler-Harris, and the members of the Queen's University Seminar in National and International Development for thoughtful commentaries on this paper.

1. Sheila Allen, *New Minorities, Old Conflicts: Asian and West Indian Migrants in Britain* (New York 1971), 29; Mirjana Morokvasic, "Why Women Emigrate? Towards Understanding of the Sex-Selectivity of the Migratory Movements of Labour," *Studi Emigrazione* 20 (June 1983): 133; Elizabeth Ewen, *Immigrant Women in the Land of Dollars* (New York 1985), chap 3.
2. Charlotte J. Macdonald, "Ellen Silk and her sisters: Female emigration to the New World," in London Feminist History Group, *The Sexual Dynamics of History* (London 1983), 82–5.
3. Varpu Lindstrom-Best, "'I Won't Be A Slave': Finnish Domestics in Canada," 36, 44–50, and Marilyn Barber, "Sunny Ontario for British Girls," 55–71, in Jean Burnet, ed., *Looking Into My Sister's Eyes: An Exploration in Women's History* (Toronto 1986).

twentieth century, emigration frequently has been a flight from marriage rather than a strategy to pursue it, a way either to evade or escape conjugality.[4]

Emigration is a sex-selective process experienced differently by women and men. It is also part of a wider social existence in which gender is perceptible only as it is confounded by time, class, and place. Emigration can be the product of sex imbalances; it also forms them, both in the old country and the new. By its sex-selectivity, emigration creates social groupings in which women and men are present in radically unequal numbers. Gill Burke describes the two such communities created by miners' emigration from nineteenth-century Cornwall—the women's world of the Cornish villages, the male society of overseas mining territories.[5] As large emigrant flows alter the economies at both source and destination, they also change the demography and create communities in which same-sex bonds are especially important. Sometimes this heightened homosociability is an unintended and unwanted consequence of the move. In other instances it may be an integral part of the decision to emigrate for both the emigrants and the non-emigrating kin.[6] Emigration has offered a release from domestic tensions as well as an escape from economic deprivation. For skilled wage-earning women, anomalies in both the factory and the family circle, the recruiter's promise of a "Golden Land,"[7] suggested new lives in more than a material sense.

This paper considers the relationships among gender solidarities, wage work, and the reconstitution of family in a community to which many women emigrated when preference or circumstance led them to lives without men. It deals with the particular case of approximately 700 British hosiery workers, principally from the east midlands, whom Penman's Company, then the largest Canadian knit-goods firm, assisted to emigrate

---

4. Annie Phizacklea makes this point, based on the unpublished work of Mirjana Morokvasic, in her introduction to *One Way Ticket, Migration and Female Labour* (London 1983), 7.

5. Charlotte Macdonald in "Ellen Silk" argues for closer study of communities characterized by sex imbalances, 81. Gill Burke's "The Cornish Diaspora of the Nineteenth Century" in Shula Marks and Peter Richardson, eds., *International Labour Migration, Historical Perspectives* (London 1984), 57–75 describes such communities.

6. This seems to be the case for many of the non-migrant wives of Turkish emigrants to northern Europe described by Lenie Brouwer and Marijke Priester, "Living In Between: Turkish Women in their Homeland and the Netherlands," in Phizacklea, *One Way Ticket*, 113–30.

7. In the context of British immigration to Canada in the first quarter of this century, this term is most closely associated with the illustrated book for popular audiences by Arthur Copping, *The Golden Land* (London 1911). It is a phrase frequently used by Penman's emigrants when they remembered their encounters with recruiters.

to Paris, Ontario, population 4000,[8] between 1907 and 1928. This is a study of the reasons for their emigration, their relationships with the networks of female kin who followed them to Canada, and the reasoning and rituals that characterized the women's culture forged by life-long mill work in one Canadian hosiery community. It is about female British wage workers whom Canadian managers sought out and whose emigration they financed. It examines the life these women thought they were choosing when they accepted an offer to go to a community where their future in the workforce was much more certain than their prospects as wives.

The Penman's emigrants were selected because they were accomplished hosiery workers. The contradictions between being female and being financially independent did not exist for the recruiter while he was recruiting them. Rather, he assiduously searched out skilled female wage earners for the very combination of attributes that complicated their lives at home. He was looking for female wage earners simply because they were wage earners, promising steady long-term employment; but his offer presented these emigrants with a social possibility as alluring as the expected hike in pay.

The period was one of considerable British emigration to Canada. Although government advertising was directed towards agriculturalist and domestic servants, and the Canadian Manufacturers' Association more frequently sought out male industrial workers for its members, the recruitment of female factory operatives did occur. The British Women's Emigration Association sponsored a factory scheme from 1904, publicizing requests from Canadian employers, principally in textiles and garment manufacture, among Girls' Clubs in industrial cities, and arranging for the extension of assisted passages to young women who decided to go abroad.[9] Penman's used Canadian Manufacturers' Association representatives and hired their own recruiters to work through the commercial emigration bureaux associated with shipping offices, advertising in the local press and labour exchanges for experienced help.[10]

---

8. Census of Canada, 1911, 1921.

9. Fawcett Library, British Women's Emigration Association, Vol. III, "Factory Scheme Subcommittee," Jan–Nov. 1904; *Imperial Colonist*, "History of the Factory Workers Fund," Oct. 1905, Nov. 1906, July 1909, May 1910, Nov. 1911, 404, Dec. 1919, 424.

10. *Hosiery Trade Journal* (HTJ), June 1907, 223. The *Leicester Mercury* through the spring of 1908 ran a specific advertising section, "Emigration," directly following the "Hosiery Hands Wanted" listings. I am grateful to Dr Ian Keil, Department of Economic History, University of Loughborough, for arranging for me to have access to the department's collection of Leicestershire newspapers. See also HTJ, April 1910, 137.

The knit-goods industry in Canada grew rapidly between 1907 and 1928. Labourers building two new transcontinental railways and opening mines in the Rockies and the northern shield wore Penman's underwear and sweaters. Wartime contracts followed the completion of the railways, and the postwar fashion for knitwear prolonged strong demand until the late 1920s. Paris was a small town in a prosperous agricultural district, and even in the nineteenth century the mill's demand for female labour had exceeded the local supply. As the firm grew after a major financial reorganization in 1906, the labour shortage became acute.

Raw recruits could be found nearer to hand than Leicestershire. "Skilled and experienced workers, those able to earn the highest wages" were what the firm specified in British advertisements. The demand was greatest for operators with machine-specific skills on equipment traditionally run by women. Penman's purchased knitting and looping machines from midlands builders, and on occasion arranged for both mechanics and operatives who knew a new technology to come to Canada with the equipment. More generally, the firm wanted that combination of judgment and dexterity which allowed a worker simultaneously to maximize volume of production and quality, to make the most efficient use of the equipment and generate the fewest possible seconds. The smallest flaw, of no significance in woven fabric, easily spread the length of a knitted garment. A firm selling under trade mark needed operatives who knew the machines they were running well enough to diagnose imperfections, and a cadre of meticulous inspectors and menders who reliably detected and stabilized seconds. A male Penman's manager called these "limited skills," comparing the specific expertise of the female immigrants with the all-round knowledge of the trade he had gained in a midlands technical apprenticeship. (Might he, in considering males, have said specialized?) The healthy profitability of the firm, however, depended on these limited proficiencies, depended upon them sufficiently to justify the inconvenience of offshore recruitment and the risk of extending pre-paid passages. The midlands was considered a reservoir of such skill, with a population so long engaged in the trade that "expert hosiery production [had become] an instinct."[11]

---

11. *Imperial Colonist*, July 1904, 75; Sept. 1904; May 1910; HTJ, April 1910, 137, 158; *Canadian Textile Journal*, "Immigration of Skilled Workmen," Jan. 1917, 3; Richard Gurnham, *A History of the Trade Union Movement in the Hosiery and Knitwear Industry, 1776–1976* (Leicester 1976), 112; Nottingham Local Studies Library, Oral History Collection, Interview A19, a male knitter born in 1919. I am grateful to Judy Kingscott, Oral History Coordinator, for assistance in using this collection. The quote from the Penman's technical expert is in Paris Industrial History Project (PIHP), Charles Harrison, 11. The names cited

The east midlands hosiery was not experiencing the gradual sectoral extinction which had expelled earlier agricultural and mining immigrants to the Canadas and other colonies. Relative to the woven cloth trade, in fact, the knit-goods industry fared relatively well in the first third of this century. There were, however, certain general and gender-specific economic reasons for midlands hosiery workers to consider emigration. When Penman's began their Nottinghamshire and Leicestershire recruiting in 1907–9, times were slack in the British trade. It was in the spring of 1910, in the wake of these hard times, that Canadian agents had their greatest prewar success in encouraging hosiery workers to consider Canada. This activity was not well regarded by midlands hosiery manufacturers, who wondered in print about the improbability of British hosiery hands departing "old England for the land of the maple leaf—and snow" and who suggested suspiciously that "whoever has succeeded in persuading so many workpeople to leave these shores must be given credit for a rare fund of tact, energy and persistence," given the "extreme briskness of the English hosiery trade." When Penman's recruiters used the Leicester and Nottingham labour exchanges to secure a contingent of 130 female hosiery emigrants in 1910, the editor of the *Hosiery Trade*

---

are the pseudonyms assigned on the transcripts. On the "instinctual knowledge" of midlands hosiery workers see H. Wignall, "The Economics of the Hosiery Industry," HTJ, April 1936, 42. Of the female immigrants from whom data on earnings was available, 147 of 267 were earning wages sufficiently high from the day they began work in Canada to repay their fares at the maximum rate. Paris Historical Society (PHS), Penman's Imported Help Books, 3 volumes.

The definition of skill is problematical. Royden Harrison has suggested that skill be considered as an "active relationship" among "a hard won set of judgments and dexterities," their "worth" as defined by their "scarcity," and the "organizational prowess" of those who hold them to maintain for themselves a social ascription as skilled. Harrison, "Introduction," in Royden Harrison and Jonathon Zeitlin, *Divisions of Labour* (Brighton 1985) 1, 8–9. The female emigrants meet only the first two of these criteria. In neither the midlands nor Ontario were they organized to claim equal standing with male mechanics. See Joy Parr, "Disaggregating the Sexual Division of Labour: A Transatlantic Case Study," *Comparative Studies in Society and History* (forthcoming). Craig Heron and Robert Storey have argued against too strenuous an assumption of deskilling following upon mechanization; they note that machine operators, while lacking the "all-round knowledge of the whole production process" assumed of craftsmen, by "care, attention and familiarity" with the equipment produced at premium levels which made employers loathe to lose them. Introduction in Heron and Storey, eds., *On the Job: Confronting the Labour Process in Canada* (Montreal 1986), 14–15. John Benson argues similarly in "Work," in Benson, ed., *The Working-Class in England* (London 1985), 78. Heron and Storey call such workers "semi-skilled" using the artisan as a reference point. In the context of twentieth-century workplaces, specialized skill seems to me a more apt characterization of both the competence and the market power such workers could claim.

Journal protested that the exchanges "were certainly not intended to find skilled labour for competitors even though they may be colonials."[12] The deportation of one of the May 1910 parties, after a week's detention in Quebec, was widely publicized as a cautionary tale for "poor knitting folk" who might be tempted to break up their homes and hazard their fortunes to colonial "red-tapism."[13] The warnings went largely unheeded. Penman's June and July 1910 parties proceeded to Canada without incident.

After the war there was a brief fillip in the industry, and then, beginning in 1921, a stretch of years in which union officials reported "uncertainty in the trade," "bad trade," and then a "general slump." Unemployment in the hosiery averaged 8200 in 1923 and 6700 in 1927. Many of these redundancies were caused by productivity-enhancing technological changes, and were unlikely to be reduced even when demand recovered. Heightening external tariffs in Germany and Canada, among other jurisdictions, limited Britain's traditionally vigorous export markets for knit goods. In this sense, the emigration to Canada was part of a new international division of labour.[14]

Within the new regime, women's prospects in particular were better in

---

12. HTJ, June 1907, 223; "Nottingham News," 158, and "Editorial," 137, in HTJ, April 1910; May 1910, 206.
13. HTJ, "Notes and News," July 1910, 302; Aug. 1910, 350. The party from Derbyshire and Nottingham was detained and then deported because the Penman's agent had not arrived with sufficient funds to meet the £5 in hand requirement for entry of each non-agricultural immigrant. This regulation was an attempt by the Laurier Liberal government to appease its organized labour constituency that was concerned that immigrants were becoming public dependents and undercutting wages.
14. United Kingdom, Board of Trade, *Working Party on the Hosiery*, 1946, 9; HTJ, May 1909, 202, April 1910, 136. For statistics on 1920s' unemployment in the industry see HTJ, March 1928, 94, following the Hosiery Trade Enquiry; also HTJ, May 1926, 96, and June 1926, 46; Leicestershire Record Office (LRO), National Union of Hosiery and Knitwear Workers (NUHKW), Leicester DE 1655/2/7, secretary's half-yearly report, S. Bassford, 9 May 1925; DE 1655/2/8, secretary's half-yearly report, H. Moulden, July 1928; Hinckley DE 1655/3/3, 1 Feb. 1921; Loughborough DE 1655/7/1 27 Aug. 1923, 30 Aug. 1928; NLSL Oral History Collection, interview A 19 9–10. F. A. Wells *Hosiery and Knitwear Industry* (Newton Abbott 1972), 169, but he bases his discussion on production figures. Union officials were reporting on declines in employment which accompanied technological change. Technological change in the hosiery industry is discussed in more detail in "Disaggregating the Sexual Division of Labour." See also an interesting series of papers by Harriet Bradley, including "Technological Change, Management Strategies, and the Development of Gender-based Job Segregation in the Labour Process," and "Gender: Authority and the Division of Labour in the Workplace," Department of Sociology, University of Durham. On overseas tariffs see HTJ, July 1926, "British Hosiery Trades Future," 34; LRO, NUHKW, DE 1655/2/7 9 May 1925.

Canada than in Britain. As the number of jobs in British knit-goods firms was reduced, the hosiery unions moved, cautiously but deliberately, to protect men's jobs to the detriment of women's and to redraw gender divisions in the industry so as to favour men. In Canada, because the hosiery industry was not unionized until the late 1940s as well as for many other reasons,[15] jobs in knitting, countering, and shading, which remained or were becoming increasingly men's work in the midlands, were open to women. Besides more jobs, Canadian recruiters could promise, and deliver, better paying and more steady work. Travellers between Paris and the midlands reported women's wages 50 per cent higher in Canada in both 1908 and 1923.[16] Because capital in the Canadian industry was highly concentrated, Penman's and the small number of companion firms with which it colluded in the market could work to inventory rather than to order, running their plants at a reasonably steady rate year round. The promise of regular work was especially inviting to employees of small midlands firms which had always produced seasonally and which, in the 1920s, quickly assimilated the advantages of the new Unemployment Insurance Act, "using the people whilst it was necessary and then giving them their cards."[17]

Many midlands immigrants came to Paris independently, using their own savings or tickets sent back to them by kin already established in town. The first English hosiery workers arrived in the 1870s, soon after the small Penman's partnership began factory production. Others came with state support, having declared their intention to farm, and then reached Paris by way of Saskatchewan or Alberta, some directed to the town by their children who found the picture of Penman's mills in their primary school geography book. There were a few mill families in town headed by male spinners or mechanics who had been to Australia, New England, the

---

15. The difference in the arrays of sex labels for hosiery jobs in the east midlands and Ontario is analysed in detail in "Disaggregating the Sexual Division of Labour."
16. H. W. Hill, a midlands hosiery expert who visited Canada frequently, reported a 50 per cent wage differential in 1908. HTJ, March 1908, "Hosiery Trade in Canada," 122; George Wooler, a midlands emigrant to Paris in 1910, reported the same spread during an extended visit home in 1923. *Paris (Ont.) Star*, 15 Aug. 1923.
17. On seasonality in the Nottingham trade see F. A. Wells, "Nottingham industries," in J. D. Chambers, *A Century of Nottingham History* (Nottingham 1952), 34. Jeremy Crump made the same point for Leicester in his paper, "Leisure and Non-work in Leicester," given at History Workshop 16, Nov. 1984, in Leicester. The promise of "steady" work was prominent in publicity directed towards female industrial emigrants from early in the century. See *Imperial Colonist*, Sept. 1904, "Report of Miss Vernon," 101, and *Imperial Colonist*, Nov. 1906, similarly. The quote linking seasonality and the Unemployment Insurance Act is from NLSL, Oral History Collection, transcript A 17a, Reginald Smith.

American west, and back to England again before they settled on Paris.[18]
The core of the mill-workers community in town, however, consisted of
the 700 persons assisted by the firm to emigrate in the twenty years after
1907, along with their kin.[19]

Of the assisted emigrants, at least three-quarters were female, four-
fifths of them unmarried.[20] In Britain they were given tickets covering
their rail fares and their transatlantic passage and, in some cases, small
cash advances. They travelled in parties, accompanied by a Penman's
agent. On arrival in Paris they were required to sign a contract agreeing to
repay the sum advanced at a rate of 50 cents per week while earning less
than $6.00 per week and $1.00 per week while earning more, the unpaid
sum "at all times constituting first lien" on their wages, the whole unpaid
balance becoming due immediately should they leave the company's
employ. Most immigrants arrived owing Penman's about $60 in 1910 and
$110 in 1928, sums which throughout the period took between twelve and
eighteen months to repay.[21]

Contract labour schemes such as this were usually failures in both the

---

18. There were numerous local newspaper reports on midlands emigrants to Paris in the
1880s. See *Paris (Ont.) Star* 8 Feb. 1934, Golden wedding announcement of Mr and Mrs
T. Bishop; 25 April 1935 obituary for Mrs Robert Etherington; 25 July 1936 obituary for
Thomas Watson English. For accounts of peripatetic skilled emigrants see Charles
Harrison, Ida Glass, PIHP; for agricultural immigrants, Ida Pelton, Jean Hubbard, Elwood
Bain, May Phillips, Doris Ashley, Lottie Keen, PIHP; *Paris (Ont.) Star*, 23 Aug. 1922,
obituary for George Edward Taylor; on skilled male workers see Charles Harrison,
Thomas Blaney, Horace Timpson, PIHP.

19. Registers for the assisted emigration are incomplete. The Paris Historical Society has
"Imported Help" books for thirteen of the twenty years in which recruitment is known
to have taken place, including World War I but excluding 1907–8 and 1919–23. The
indexes in these registers list 442 names, but the volumes are in poor condition and only
378 collection sheets recording biweekly repayments remain. From oral evidence it
seems reasonable to assume that at least as many immigrants arrived in the seven years
for which records are gone as in those thirteen for which the registers remain, hence the
estimate of approximately seven hundred. The statistics which follow are based on the
378 emigrants for whom repayment schedules exist in the Paris Historical Society
collection.

20. Names in the registers appear in two forms, initials and last name alone, or full Christian
name and surname preceded by "Miss" or "Mrs." All those listed by initial only were
assumed to be men, a convention which biases the test against the assumption that most
assisted emigrants were women, as several identified by initial were later discovered in
the personnel files to be female. By this convention, 285 of the 378 emigrants for whom
repayment schedules exist were assumed to be female; 227 of these were identified as
"Miss" rather than "Mrs.," or 80 per cent of the 285.

21. PHS, Imported Help Books. Ticket vouchers and copies of several contracts are inter-
leaved with the registers. The sum extended and the date the loan was made appear on
each repayment schedule.

settler dominions and the United States. Workers simply decamped, leaving their ticket stubs behind them, to find jobs where their wages would be their own. In Paris, by contrast, most assisted immigrants faithfully repaid their loans. It was the Depression of the 1930s rather than defaulting debtors that caused the firm to discontinue overseas recruitment. One in four of the "imported help" left before the loan was entirely repaid, but in most cases the sum remaining on the firm's books was small.[22] The majority stayed for the rest of their lives in town, for most of their years as employees of the mill.

It was not a keen sense of contract which kept them. As Philip Corrigan has noted from Marx, there are "chains" in capitalism apart from the law.[23] The distinction between bound and free labour is to be found in the "conditions of work" and in the social relations that accompanied it. For migrants, as Colin Newbury has argued, the distinction lies between those "allowed to enjoy a measure of vertical mobility and participation in the organization of a political economy, and those whose entry into such economies was partial, peripheral and without political influence."[24]

In a sense the Penman's immigrants, as skilled female wage-earners, had no place to go. Among the emigrant parties, those who began at the Paris mills as lower-paid workers were most likely to quit before their loans were repaid, partly because they were discharging the debt at a much slower rate but also because they had much less to leave.[25] Those

---

22. One hundred (27.1 per cent) of the 369 immigrants for whom clear schedules exist defaulted before the full debt was repaid.
23. Philip Corrigan, "Feudal Relics or Capitalist Monuments? Notes on the Sociology of Unfree Labour," *Sociology* 11 (1977): 450, citing Karl Marx, *Capital* (London 1967), I, 641.
24. Colin Newbury, "The Imperial Workplace: Competitive and Coerced Labour Systems in New Zealand, Northern Nigeria and Australian New Guinea," in Marks and Richardson, eds., *International Labour Migration*, 226.
25.

Table 1

Penman's Imported Help: Repayment or Default on Loans by Earning Levels

Earning Level*	Repaid	Defaulted	Total
Low	100	82	182
(row %)	(54.9)	(45.0)	(52)
(col %)	(40)	(82)	
High	150	18	168
(row %)	(89.2)	(10.7)	(48)
(col %)	(60)	(18)	
Total	250	100	350
(%)	(71.4)	(28.6)	

* Low earnings levels were those of less than $6.00 per week. High levels were $6.00 per week or more. Those earning more than $6.00 repaid twice as much per week on their passage debts as those earning less.

who found other jobs in town quickly confronted the loyalty and hierarchy among local capitalists, and had their wages at their new employment docked for remission to the "masters of the mill." Having arrived without savings, set down in a small community in a strange country, even those without ties in town and willing to take any job were likely to linger through most of the repayment schedule accumulating the cash and information with which to make a move. For skilled workers, leaving was less attractive. They were unlikely to be able to get good hosiery work and to evade their debt. The fraternity among the few Canadian knit-goods manufacturers was close, and those who, in applying for new jobs, had to explain themselves to new employers found their obligation to Penman's followed them.[26] More importantly, they would be leaving behind a range of other advantages which, as skilled female wage-earners, they were less likely to secure elsewhere. Paris was a place where they were at the centre of the local economy, where community social relations were organized around wage-earning women, where they were not an anomaly.

Penman's recruiters went to the east midlands not only because it was a reservoir of skill in the hosiery trade but also because, particularly in Leicestershire, there was an accepted tradition of life-long female wage work, a tradition that was lacking in the surrounding Ontario community. In searching out women such as Miss Florrie Morris, born 1895, emigrated to Paris 1912, retired from Penman's in 1970 at the age of seventy-five, and Mrs Annie Smith, born 1890, emigrated to Paris 1913, retired from Penman's at the age of seventy-nine in 1969, managers were seeking both skill and stability in their workforce. Overseas recruitment was a way to overcome what Charlotte Erickson has called the "social obstacles" that existed locally to the labour system the firm wished to sustain. In this conjuncture was a social setting that female mill workers made their own. Florrie Morris and Annie Smith were exceptional in their length of service at the mills, and exceptions to the common Canadian story about the passing of an adult woman's days and years, but they were not as life-long wage workers considered oddities in Paris by either the community or the firm. That acceptance, and the range of possibilities of which it was a part, drew several skilled female immigrants back to Paris from confinement on

---

26. PHS, Imported Help Books. Clara Fox, emigrated 30 March 1910, had the balance of her debt collected by Mr Isaacs at the Canadian Hotel, Paris. Miss G. Eley, emigrated January 1912, repaid her passage through her employer at the New Royal Hotel. The T. Eaton Company, Toronto, docked the wages of Mrs Morley, emigrated from Ilkeston July 1912, at the rate of $3 per month. The Ellis Company, Hamilton, collected Penman's loan from Mrs Pemberton, emigrated October 1910, for a year after she left Paris.

the margins of the mainstream economy in larger centres (and also to discharge the debts which remained unlapsed on Penman's books).[27]

The midlands tradition of life-long female wage work was as anxious and self-denying as it was persistent. There are enough affirmations in the record that married women's employment should not exist to convince a careful scholar that indeed it did not.[28] As female seamers and menders were brought from domestic workshops into the factories in the 1890s, industrialists argued against mothers' wage work "on moral and humanitarian grounds" that children were thereby "persistently neglected" and "very, very poorly cared for." Yet they continued to employ wives during all but the first month after child birth—"on business grounds...some of them are the best workers we have, and we should be sorry to lose them." Unionists worried that married women with husbands at work would undercut the wages of single women and men.[29] But both the oral history and the wage-book evidence is clear. Large numbers of married women were employed in the east midlands hosiery industry through the first half of this century.[30] In 1919 "hundreds" of these workers struck in Hinckley,

---

27. PHS, Penman's Imported Help Books, F. A. Morris, 32; Mrs Albert Smith, 186. The work history data comes from the personnel cards in the Penman's Archives, Cambridge, Ontario. I am grateful to Fred Bemrose and Gordon Parsons for helping me to locate and use these records. Charlotte Erickson, "Why Did Contract Labour Not Work in the Nineteenth Century United States?" in Marks and Richardson, eds., *International Labour Migration*, 35. Among female emigrants who left and later returned to Paris see PHS, Imported Help Books, May Barker, emigrated September 1913, left Paris December 1914, returned and balance paid September 1919; Lily Russell, emigrated August 1912, left Paris May 1913 for Hamilton, returned December 1914, debt discharged June 1915. Olive Cavan, Alice Russell, PIHP.

28. See Sandra Taylor, "The Effect of Marriage on Job Possibilities for Women and the Ideology of the Home: Nottingham 1890–1930," *Oral History* 5 (1977): 46–61.

29. Royal Commission on Labour 1892 [c. 6795-VI], XXXVI Pt 2, Second Report of the Minutes of Evidence, Group C, vol. II, testimony of B. C. Wates, president, Leicester Chamber of Commerce, questioned by A. J. Mundella, 533, and James Holmes, Midlands Counties Hosiery Federation, questioned by Mundella, 541.

30. Note the Essex Oral History interview with Mrs Randall, born 1910, whose mother, a knitter, did not work after marriage. Randall herself, however, was employed as a winder and knitter throughout her married life. Essex tape no 157 in Nottingham Local Studies Library. See also NLSL, Oral History Collection, A53, interview with Mrs Fretwell, born Shaw 1883, an overlocker and mender.

Few hosiery wage books remain but two collections in the Leicestershire Record Office are of interest. The Jersey Wage Books, 1924–6, for Samuel Davis and Sons, Hinckley, show more than a third of employees as married, DE 2544/30. The J. Lewin and Company records, 1865–1937, also include wage books. The 1946 Board of Trade, *Working Party on the Hosiery*, found that "the hosiery industry retains a large proportion of its women employees after marriage. This applies more particularly to the long-established centres of Leicester and Hinckley," 95.

"determined their custom continue of going in at 9 AM instead of 8," presumably so as to have time for their home duties before reporting for wage work. Male union officials were both individually conflicted and organizationally divided on the issue of married women's employment. Although they recognized that question as one to be handled "very delicately" since "married women had the same rights as members" as all others in the union, they worked steadily to shift the boundaries between men's and women's work in favour of men. There are examples of women themselves, while largely supporting their households, struggling to maintain for their children the illusion of the husband as breadwinner.[31]

A wage-earning woman existed in the thralls of an awkward and unsatisfactory negotiation, not only to retain the right to work and to be employed on schedules that made wage-earning tenable, but also to reconcile social ideology with her own experience. In other communities, women were employed for a time in their teens and twenties and perhaps returned to the labour force later in life when their children were grown, so that wage work was scripted to a safe place as a contingency, to be pursued only when it would not collide with primary obligations as mother and wife.[32] Where the labour force tradition was different, where daughters followed mothers in patterns of life-long wage work in the presence of a patriarchal culture that declared these patterns pathogenic, a safe place was more difficult to secure. The antipathies between female wage work and heterosexual conjugality called for a different resolution. There are signs of these negotiations in textile towns: the later age at marriage, the greater incidence of non-marriage, the commercial provision of food preparation and laundry services elsewhere labelled wives' work, and the more intense networks for labour exchanges among households.

These struggles to reconcile material sustenance and domestic satisfaction pose questions about consciousness of gender and the experience of security in same- and cross-gender connections. Like Ross and Rapp's parsing of the relationships of inheritance patterns through nuptiality to sexuality, these indications take us towards an emerging social possibil-

---

31. LRO, NUHKW, Leicester Trades, DE 1655/2/7, minutes of 17 May 1919; Hinckley minutes on meeting of the Hosiery Federation on the married woman question, DE 1655 3/3, 22 June 1921. On the devices through which a Nottingham chevenner's husband who was irregularly employed maintained his familial standing as breadwinner see Thea Thompson, *Edwardian Childhoods* (London 1981), 69, 71, 74.
32. The best discussion of this process of negotiation and resolution is Sarah Eisenstein, *Give Us Bread, But Give Us Roses* (London and New York 1983), esp. 47–52.

ity.[33] Could it not be that, for some, wage work came to be understood as the continuity, and marriage the contingency in the unfolding of an adult woman's life?

Were this the case, how would one come to acknowledge it as a social existence rather than as a personal happenstance? There must have been many routes through which this process of "self-discovery" as a group developed, and as many paths at which it was blocked. For Penman's mill households, emigration was a section in one of the open routes. Midland women workers were coming from wage work to wage work, making the decision to emigrate based on the gains they could achieve as wage workers. The emigrant group was dominated by widows with families, veterans of troubled marriages, women alone, single women with children, and pairs of women friends. For many, marriage was not an active post-emigration consideration. Emigration by congregating numbers of women who were living without men clarified this cultural alternative. They came with common experience of wage work and the domestic dilemmas female employment engendered to a women's town, a place where the prevailing wage form did not require a male breadwinner or give precedence to households which included men, where the numerical dominance of female wage-earners offered a certain psychic and physical protection, a shelter for a woman-centred culture.

Among widows the domestic provocations for emigration were most plain. For older women whose spouses had died, especially those with several daughters, emigration was a way to keep the family solvent and together. Mary Cavan and a female cousin came to Paris in 1912 and returned to Glasgow in 1914 to fetch her widowed mother, a younger sister, and one of her two brothers. Maud Chappell, her three sisters, and widowed mother arrived in Paris in 1913. All but Maud had worked previously in lace and box-making in Nottingham. Her first week in Canada, fifteen-year-old Maud began her twenty-nine year career in the mill. Anne Hedley and her sister were urged to emigrate by their mother when their coal-miner father died, so that they could make a home together rather than live separately in domestic service. Each of these households became the nucleus of a spreading mill family in Paris, bound

---

33. Diana Gittins, *Fair Sex: Family Size and Structure, 1900–1939* (London 1982); Gittins, "Marital Status, Work and Kinship, 1850–1930," in Jane Lewis, eds., *Labour and Love* (Oxford 1986); Patricia Connelly and Martha MacDonald, "Women's Work: Domestic and Wage Labour in a Nova Scotia Community," *Studies in Political Economy* 10 (winter 1983); Ellen Ross and Rayna Rapp, "Sex and Society: A Research Note from Social History and Anthropology," in Ann Snitow, Christine Stansell, and Sharon Thompson, eds., *Powers of Desire: The Politics of Sexuality* (New York 1983), 56, 68, and 117.

together by strong female kin ties. In each of these cases, and characteristic of midland families in town, links with male siblings attenuated. There were brothers in the Cavan, Chappell, and Hedley emigrant groups, but all left town and lost close connection with the family circle. On several occasions it fell to daughters to assume their brothers' passage debts as family obligations when sons lost patience with their widowed mother's choice of destination overseas.

Atypically of chain migrations, males among the Paris emigrants were frequently the last rather than the first in kin groups to go abroad, reluctantly following the initiative of female family members. Betty Shaw's widowed mother, a lace-maker, went to Paris alone in 1913, leaving two-year-old Betty in the care of her grandparents and returning later to persuade them to join her overseas. Betty's grandfather, a coal miner, did a youngster's work as chore-boy in the mills in Paris, but the earnings of several skilled women in the household carried them through until 1949, when, to a woman, they were fired as militants in a long local strike.[34] Their husbands' deaths made widows consider emigration to a place where they and their children might be self-supporting. The widow's initiative gave her household independence, drawing daughters together, but frequently cast sons and male kin in dependent roles.

For women in troubled marriages, as for widows, emigration to skilled work overseas offered an opportunity to overcome the wrecked promises of conjugality. Edith Elliott's grandmother summoned all her children and shepherded them to Paris; as Elliott recalled, "the whole family came out, except the father and he stayed back because he worked in the coal mines over there and they came here." The Elliott family became prominent in the mill community, proprietors of a large boarding house, where grandmother Elliott might supervise her daughters' courtships with lodgers and arrange for aunts to initiate their nieces into the better jobs at the mill. Hilda Sharp's mother had come to Canada at the urging of female kin already established in Paris. Her husband had been invalided after the South African War; she may have seen the move as a way to reduce the domestic tensions arising from his limited earnings. The household prospered in Paris, turning its female members' domestic and hosiery

---

34. Mary Cavan, Anne Hedley, Maud Chappell, Betty Shaw, Frances Randall, PIHP; *Paris (Ont.) Star*, 17 Dec. 1936, obituary for Rebecca Fisher; PHS, Imported Help Books: Olive Adcock emigrated 30 March 1910; Mrs Fanny Adcock, Doris Adcock, Albert Adcock emigrated 17 October 1910; Violet Kelford and Gladys Kelford paying for Rupert Kelford, emigrated 19 July 1912. Annie, Eunice, and Lillian Woods repaid the debt of their father, Thomas Woods, emigrated 20 September 1912.

skills into accumulations of real estate, earning the respect of the mill community as boarding-house keepers and mid-wives. Mr Sharp, however, saw none of this, having early returned to his old job in Ilkeston. Ida Pelton's father stayed with her mother in Paris, but emigration consolidated a change in their household relationships. Her father's family had come to Paris at the turn of the century from Bulwell, Notts. He stayed behind, employed by an uncle in a declining trade: "in those days they had horses not cars, and they had funerals and weddings and they had all the outfits for them, that's what he did. My Dad had to go to war and he was in Germany a year after the war ended and when he was away my Mother had read in the paper where people like us, we could come to Canada...so she told my Dad this when he came home and...it was all fixed for us to come." Ida's mother earned good money as a mender at Penman's; Ida became a looper, a job which paid high piece rates. Together they managed, pooling their earnings and sharing domestic labour, although none of Ida's three brothers stayed in town, and neither her father nor husband was regularly employed. For Ida and her mother, as for many others, Paris offered a certain refuge to those for whom the scripted plan of stable marriage to a male breadwinner had gone awry.[35]

Within the mill community the intertwining of emotional and economic reasons for emigration was commonly experienced and understood. Emigration offered a resolution to domestic tensions which poverty, legality, and convention made otherwise unresolvable. Among women, so long as there was no harm done to others, an accepting discretion surrounded the paternity of youngsters and the mortal and marital state or whereabouts of spouses. A line between discretion and the countenancing of deception was, however, maintained by group scrutiny. Sam Horsley, a midland knitter active in the mill community but exceptional in town as a mature unattached male, found himself vexed by "false stories being circulated around town that I am a married man, and have left a wife and children in England"; to counter the rumours, he posted a $100 reward in the local paper in 1926 to "be paid to anyone bringing forward the slightest evidence that these stories are true," and threatened action "against any person making such false statements." In the case of Margaret Etherington, the local gossip turned out to be true. Etherington had emigrated from a textile town in Yorkshire to work in the local flannel factory. She declared herself a widow and in December 1923 married Bert

---

35. Edith Elliott, Ida Pelton, May Phillips, PIHP. Paris Public Library, *Historical Perspectives*, Hilda Sharp Scott.

Raynes, a knitter mechanic at the hosiery mill. Something seven years later made Raynes enlist the aid of the local police in Paris to inquire into her past. Word came back from the chief constable in Burnley that her husband, Frank Etherington, was alive in Earby, Yorkshire. He had commenced divorce proceedings twelve years previously, "but being short of money was unable to go forward with the case." Raynes chose to resolve the matter by full disclosure, declaiming in the press, "she is still his wife and I give this notice that the public may know that I have no lawful wife."[36]

In most early twentieth-century communities the respectability of young unmarried women was closely scrutinized, female factory workers with, perhaps, more public flourish than any others. The majority of the Penman's assisted emigrants were single women; few travelled abroad by themselves. Most came with friends or female kin, many to join relatives already established in Paris.

For single mothers with children the demographics in town were sheltering. In 1936 more than a quarter of Penman's female employees lived in single-headed households, the majority of which included children. Ann Wilson had been a winder in Nottingham. In a slack season she and a woman with whom she worked in the hosiery encountered a Penman's recruiter and decided to emigrate, Ann bringing with her Gordon, her pre-school-aged son. They set up housekeeping together and worked side by side in the knitting mill. In time Ann's friend's daughter joined them. The community had developed housing forms, work schedules, and child-care arrangements that accommodated wage-earning mothers. Among others whose household form was similar, at a distance from past personal events, widows, deserted wives, and single mothers shared the dilemmas of wage work and childrearing outside conjugality. Frances Randall, a child born out of wedlock in Bulwell, came to Paris at the age of fourteen to join her maternal kin in a community where, although her early circumstances were known, they distinguished her less than they might have in the town of her birth.[37]

---

36. *Paris (Ont.) Star*, 13 Jan. 1926, advertisement signed S. G. W. Horsley; 17 April 1930, letter from Bert Raynes.

37. Lillian Watson, Frances Randall, PIHP. The statistics are for the Penman's workforce as a whole rather than the immigrant group separately. They were derived by linking the firm's personnel records, now in the Penman's Archives, Cambridge, Ontario, with the municipal tax rolls, housed in the Town Hall, Paris. These rolls list all adult household members, the numbers of school-aged children, and household size. Of the women located in the tax rolls in 1936 47 of 170 were living in single-headed households; 30 of these households included children.

Emigration and the help of female kin did not resolve all the problems of being single and alone. In December 1919 Christina Addison joined her sister, Mrs Ireland, in the comfortable boarding house she ran on Elm Street near the Grand River and took a job in the mill. Her family noted her melancholy but could not assuage it. In April she rose one morning, instructed the postmaster to destroy all further correspondence, walked to the mill race, set her hat by the dam, and jumped to her death. But the community of single women was large in town; in 1936 28 per cent of Penman's women workers entered middle age unmarried, and the female society of the boarding houses smoothed the emigrant transition. The acceptance that women should live as well as work together, organizing community events and convening festive gatherings in their homes, extended through the Penman's Pleasure Club and the company-owned YWCA to the churches, the Maids and Daughters of England, and the Ladies Auxiliary of the British Empire Service League. All female house-holds composed of sisters and friends were among the most vigorous social centres in the mill community and their members unselfconsciously claimed the scrupulous and attentive acknowledgment their domestic milestones were due. When the local paper reported in May 1935 that a "friendship of seventeen years had been severed" by the death of Miss Susan Baldwin in the house she shared with Lottie Trueman on Yeo Street, the editors were obliged to publish a correction noting that the two women "had been friends for 35 years, and came to Canada together 23 years ago, during seventeen of which Miss Baldwin was an invalid." Susan Baldwin was survived by five sisters in England but had remained through years of heart trouble in her Canadian home with her friend.[38]

It was rare for single emigrants to wed within their first eighteen months in Canada. Paris was probably not the easiest place in which to find a spouse, if one were looking, there being relatively few jobs to attract or keep unattached men in town. However, combining wage work with marriage was common in the community. In 1936, 40 percent of Penman's

---

38. The Addison suicide is reported in the *Paris (Ont.) Star*, 14 April 1920. The obituary for Susan Baldwin appeared in 30 May 1935 and the correction 6 June 1935. For instances of women's households as centres for community social activities see *Paris (Ont.) Star*, 12 Sept. 1923, Lily Cotton and her sisters; 26 Dec. 1923 and 10 Aug. 1927, the Misses Barlow; obituary for Alexandrine Patterson, 6 April 1933. Ida Glass, PIHP. The activities of the Maids and Daughters of England and the Pleasure Club were regularly reported in the local paper through the 1920s. Of the ninety-four single women located in the personnel files as employed in 1936, twenty-six or 27.7 per cent, were older than age thirty-six.

female employees were wives.[39] Among the skilled emigrant women who had come to Canada as wage-earners and commanded the highest piece rates as knitters, loopers, shaders, and finishers, continuing on at the mill after marriage was especially common. Coping with employment, marriage, and motherhood simultaneously rather than sequentially required adaptations in domestic gender divisions and household boundaries that the midland emigrants shared with couples in the mill community generally.[40] But there were some ways of signalling symbolically the rules which must govern marriage between wage-earning spouses that were unique to the east midlands emigrants.[41]

Most intriguing of these rituals were the mock weddings which Sallie Westwood describes as continuing in Leicester to this day. The midlands origins of the mock wedding are unclear. Today in Leicester factories where men's and women's occupations are strictly segregated and men command the best-paying manufacturing and mechanical jobs, mock weddings are women's rituals. Brides are to wear pornographic costumes designed by female co-workers and are left by their women friends tied to the factory fence in a frightening public display of bondage, as "a celebration of their own oppression in marriage." The rites mark changes in a woman's intimate life, acknowledging that she now will be sexually available to her husband and that, in accord with the appropriate power relationships of marriage, her sexuality will be "crucially mediated by men." These bridal rituals take place on the shop-floor and around the factory gate, but they are not about the particular imminent dilemmas of wage-earning wives.[42]

As practised among the east midlands emigrants in Paris in the 1920s and 1930s, mock weddings had very different functions. As pantomimes of gender roles they ridiculed conventions of patriarchal hierarchy within marriage; as celebrations among co-workers who would continue to be

39. PHS, Imported Help Books. Only 26 of the 227 single women for whom passage repayment schedules remain married before their debts to the firm were extinguished. Of the 168 women traced in the personnel records as employed in 1936, 68 were married.
40. The adaptations of households to life-long wage work among women are treated in detail in my "Rethinking Work and Kinship in a Canadian Hosiery Town, 1910–1950," *Feminist Studies* 13 (spring 1987), 137–62.
41. I am grateful to H. V. Nelles of York University, Toronto, for alerting me to the clear group limits on this practice within the mill community.
42. Sallie Westwood, *All Day Every Day: Factory and Family in the Making of Women's Lives* (London 1984), 111–19. The characterization of the costumes as pornographic is on page 117; the interpretation of the brides' rites, 118–19.

employed together, they warned the couple that the intense commitment they were about to make to each other must be exclusively domestic and not privilege their relationship on the shop floor.

It was in the mixed-gender knitting, spinning, and cutting rooms, and when both spouses worked in the mill, that mock weddings were most common. On these elaborately costumed occasions, sex and age roles were reversed, the bride being a senior male skilled worker or foreman, the clergyman a young girl, the groom an older married woman, the best man one of her peers. The games were raucous parodies of domestic life. Sam Horsley, the machinist who a decade earlier had taken to the press to refute rumours concerning his own marital state, organized a mock wedding in 1937 at the home of a male co-worker in the shadow of the hosiery mill. Horsley himself was the bride, "charmingly dressed in black and pink velvet, carrying a bouquet of roses and sweet peas." Mrs Crump from the finishing room "took the part of the groom dressed in evening suit and top hat." Mrs Alice Russell, a sixty-year-old winder, was the bridesmaid, "dressed in pink and silver lace, carrying a spray of forget-me-nots. The flower girl was Miss Williamson and the best man Miss Raycraft. The ceremony was ably performed by Miss F. McLaughlin. After the service Mr. J. Raycraft and Mr. S. Horsley rendered the beautiful duet 'Love's Sweet Dream' accompanied on the guitar by Miss M. Williamson...Mr. C. Williams executed on an old fashioned clog dance to 'Bye Bye Blues.'"[43] The workplace parity between male and female co-workers in mixed departments (the bride in this case, Violet Jones, was a skilled burson knitter) carried over into sociability. The ritual affirmed that these conventions must influence marital politics as well if the bride were to continue effectively in her job. The inversion of the mock wedding played upon the suppleness of gender boundaries. The common laughter affirmed that equality among co-workers did not imply sameness in marital partners.

Because most women from midlands emigrant families worked in the mills after they were married and for many years after they had children as well, the politics of mill and domestic life were interdependent and intertwined. When Jean Elliott, the granddaughter of a woman who had brought her family from Nottinghamshire, married her foreman in 1938, the mock wedding took place in their department in the hosiery mill. Here the significance of the role reversals was especially marked. Co-workers

---

43. *Paris (Ont.) Star*, 29 April 1937; see similarly, 31 Aug. 1939, 8 Aug. 1935, 2 March 1927. In the latter report Mrs Bert Raynes, soon to be denounced as a bigamist, was the bridegroom.

used the occasion to emphasize that nepotism must not intrude after the marriage, prejudicing the fair distribution of work in the room. The topic of mock weddings came up in this interview while we were talking about workplace tensions, rather than marriage:

> John: She was just another worker there; I could love her up at home but not at work. If there was a choice of a good bag for this one and a bad one for that one, she would get the bad one.
> Edith: Wasn't that nice.

Then John came to the question of mock weddings:

> John: You couldn't play favorites—people would be looking for that type of thing. They had a mock wedding for us—the whole mill up to the department, over a hundred people. It was something I tell you, the old pot that goes under the bed, they had that all tied up in ribbons and I know I blushed too. I wish we had pictures of it but we didn't.

The mock wedding had achieved its purpose, reminding the foreman of his vulnerability before shopfloor consensus and of the limits on his authority as both husband and boss.[44]

The lives of the female skilled workers and their kin in Paris were formed by a series of common transatlantic experiences passed down as family lore and neighborhood reminiscence to daughters and grand-daughters. The women from the east midlands were recruited for their workplace proficiencies with hosiery machinery and knitted fabric and their community traditions of life-long female wage work. In English hosiery districts these traditions were embattled. They were fortified by manufacturers' preferences for experienced, lower-waged women employees and long-standing community acceptance of the jointly constituted household rather than the individually garnered, male-breadwinner wage. They were challenged by the male-dominated hosiery unions who claimed wage-earning wives were complicit in pay cuts and who feared long-serving female employees as competitors with men for the declining pool of skilled jobs in the knit-goods industry. For all parties to the convention, life-long female wage work existed in awkward contradiction to the prevailing social ideology governing gender roles. For skilled women workers, emigration mitigated these conflicts by offering steady and well-paid employment and anonymous distance from the domestic tensions

---

44. Edith Elliott, PIHP.

their English circumstances had conditioned. Emigration brought together women experienced in wage work, selected because of their workplace skills, and congregated them in a community where their prospects as wage earners were brighter than their likely fortunes as wives. Among the female emigrants and their kin, the economic and emotional reasons for leaving Britain were recounted as of a piece. Emigration, by offering women in one generation a way to evade or escape conjugality, opened a social possibility that wage work rather than marriage would be the continuity in an adult woman's life. In the community in which women were at both a numerical and an economic advantage, life after emigration was characterized by stronger bonds between women, weakened links with male kin, a more comfortable social acknowledgment of variously constituted female-headed households, and a greater willingness, at least within the emigrant community, to use group pressure to reinforce marital relations that would facilitate life-long female wage work.

FURTHER READINGS FOR TOPIC 4

Donald Avery, *"Dangerous Foreigners": European Immigrant Workers and Labour Radicalism* (Toronto: McClelland and Stewart, 1979).

Hugh Johnston, *The Voyage of the Komagata Maru* (Vancouver: University of British Columbia Press, 1989; first published 1979).

Howard Palmer, *Patterns of Prejudice* (Toronto: McClelland and Stewart, 1982).

Roberto Perrin, "Clio as an Ethnic: The Third Force in Canadian Historiography," *Canadian Historical Review*, 64, 4 (1983), 441–67.

Bruno Ramirez and Michael Del Balso, *The Italians of Montreal: From Sojourning to Settlement 1900–1921* (Montreal: Editions Du Courant, 1980).

Patricia E. Roy, *A White Man's Province: British Columbia Politicians and Chinese and Japanese Immigrants, 1858–1914* (Vancouver: University of British Columbia Press, 1989).

John E. Zucchi, *Italians in Toronto: Development of a National Identity, 1875–1935* (Kingston and Montreal: McGill-Queen's University Press, 1990).

TOPIC 5

The Mysterious East: Or, The Strange Death of Dreams

In the 1920s the Maritime provinces were ushered into their twentieth-century role in modern Canada: one of dependence and underdevelopment, out-migration and unemployment, political marginality and cultural exclusion. In the same decade, Newfoundland, an independent Dominion, entered into a cycle of political and economic crisis culminating in mass riots and the suspension of responsible government in 1934. The rural decline, out-migration, and social decay engendered by massive economic changes—particularly the consolidation of capital in far fewer and larger firms—was not in itself an eastern phenomenon. Elsewhere, however, there were countervailing tendencies (such as the massive American investment that underwrote so much of Ontario's economic expansion) missing in the East. Maritimers uprooted from their farms or whose industries were "merged" with those of central Canada, and dispossessed fishers from Newfoundland, often left the Atlantic region altogether. Out-migration had started as early as the late nineteenth century, but only in the 1920s did it reach a level of absolute and severe crisis, a crisis from which the region has never really recovered.

David Alexander surveys the economic history of Newfoundland, in a balanced appraisal of internal and external forces leading to economic crisis; John Reid surveys the impact of the 1920s, in an assessment of the *strengths and weaknesses of the region's protest tradition; and David Frank focuses on the coal miners' dramatic struggles. All three balance "internal" explanations of regional decline and crisis (which focus on the deficiencies of regional society and economy) and "external" explanations (such as political disadvantages within Confederation and economic exploitation by outside interests). The debate over the causes of, and remedies for, Canada's Atlantic tragedy remains a burning issue in Canadian history.*

Newfoundland's Traditional Economy and Development to 1934

DAVID ALEXANDER

The price of being a country is willingness to bear a cross. For Germany it is the cross of beastliness; for Russia it is stolidity; the United States must rise above material wealth; and Canada is required to find a national identity. The burden which Newfoundland has carried is to justify that it should have any people. From the Western Adventurers of the seventeenth century to Canadian economists in the twentieth, there has been a continuing debate as to how many, if any, people should live in Newfoundland. The consensus has normally been that there should be fewer Newfoundlanders—a conclusion reached in the seventeenth century when there were only some 2,000 inhabitants, and one which is drawn today when there are over 500,000.

Newfoundland's economic history has centred on valuation of its natural resource endowment in relation to the size of its population. The particular object of debate has been (and still is) the size and well-being of the traditional or rural economy, and the likelihood that it could expand extensively at acceptable standards of life, or that other sectors can be developed to absorb labour exports from the traditional sector. The economic characteristics of a traditional economy can be stated simply enough. Labour and natural resources, or "land," are the most important factors of production, and capital plays a very minor role. If it is assumed that land is a constant, then the average output of labour is a simple function of the ratio of labour to land. Thus, if the population expands and the ratio increases, then average per capita output falls; that is, standards of living fall. If it is further assumed that the economy is closed to emigration, then the prospects are those of deteriorating standards to a very low level of physical security and comfort. To make matters still more depressing, a once-and-for-all technical improvement in the traditional economy (say the introduction of the cod trap) which shifts average per capita output upwards, is of little long-term benefit, for the gains in

David Alexander, "Newfoundland's Traditional Economy and Development to 1934," *Acadiensis*, V, 2 (Spring 1976), 56–78.
This is an edited version of the original text. The tables and some of the supporting data have been edited out of this version as well.

living standards will be eaten away by the likelihood of strengthened population growth: one ends up with a larger economy, but not necessarily a more prosperous one. The only routes to a long-run improvement in living standards are a widening resource base and technical change (including organizational changes such as the growth of domestic and international market activity).[1] These assumptions imply a movement away from the traditional economy with capital growth (both reproducible and human) defining the growth of total and per capita income.

The stark features of this simple model obviously fail to capture accurately the complexities of Newfoundland's economic history. Yet it does identify some realities of its economic problems and, what is just as important, perceptions of the problems. When Newfoundland's traditional economy reached an apparent limit to extensive expansion in the second half of the nineteenth century, a struggle was waged to expand the resource base and modernize both the structure of production and the composition of output. This campaign ended in collapse and that collapse led directly to union with Canada. In 1949 the effort to "develop" was resumed under new constitutional dress. But the historical record sketched in this essay suggests that confederation did not introduce any especially new perceptions of Newfoundland's economic problems and potential, and some might argue that it simply reinforced a depressing tendency to neglect the province's most obvious natural resource— the sea.

At the time of its discovery Newfoundland's fishery was an international open-access resource, exploited by fleets from France, Portugal, and Spain. At this time (unlike today) the volume of factors of production available to exploit the resource, the primitive techniques, and the size of the markets meant the resource base was in no danger of overexploitation in the sense of significant reductions in maximum sustainable yield. For the continental countries, the adoption of a "green cure" (transport in salt bulk) meant the issue of settling Newfoundland did not arise, since the island was mainly a convenient watering and repair station. But this was not the case with the west of England fishery, which developed in the second half of the sixteenth century.[2] Whether in response to relatively high costs of salt or to local tradition, the West Country fisherman pursued a light-salted, sun-dried fishery at Newfoundland. Land

---

1. See C. H. Fei and Gustav Ranis, "Economic Development in Historical Perspective," *American Economic Review* 59 (1969): 386–400.
2. On this point see Keith Matthews, "A History of the West of England–Newfoundland Fishery" (unpublished D Phil thesis, Oxford 1968).

resources were consequently important to the Westcountrymen, as wood was needed for flakes and stages, and shore facilities for drying. The consequences of this technology were two-fold: first, an undignified annual rush by the west of England fishing boats to Newfoundland to claim *seasonal* property rights over the best fishing "rooms"; and secondly, opposition to establishment of "plantations" or any other settlement of the island, whether by Englishmen or foreigners, which would prejudice seasonal claims to ownership over essential land inputs.

The short fishing season and poor winter employment opportunities in Newfoundland, as well as the grim agricultural potential, favoured a migratory fishery; but very slowly in the course of the seventeenth and eighteenth centuries the difference in the rates of return between a migratory and a settled fishery shifted in favour of the latter. Rising European shipping costs and the development of regular and lower cost supplies of food and other imports from the North American colonies were critical factors in this shift. Nonetheless the growth of a resident population was painfully slow. In 1650 it was around 2,000 and by 1750, with sharp fluctuations, reached only 6,000. The turning point came in the second half of the eighteenth century. The French fishery declined after the Seven Years' War and the New England fishery following the American revolution, and neither fully recovered until the end of the Napoleonic Wars. By the end of the century the West Country merchants had translated an international migratory fishery at Newfoundland into a colonial industry in Newfoundland. Between 1750 and 1804 Newfoundland's population grew at an annual rate of 2.3 per cent reaching over 20,000 and in the next twelve years doubled to 40,000, implying a high growth rate per annum.[3]

The transition from a British fishery at Newfoundland to a Newfoundland fishery was significant in two ways. It meant the foundation of a new country in the world, for while it is customary (at least in Newfoundland) to claim a history of many hundreds of years, it is more realistic to view Newfoundland as one of the nineteenth-century countries of European settlement. Secondly, while there was always a possibility (however remote up to the nineteenth century) that an expanding migratory fishery would deplete an open-access resource, there was now a better possibility that a settled traditional economy would expand to the point of impoverishing a country.

---

3. Calculated from figures in Shannon Ryan, "Collection of CO 194 Statistics" (unpublished manuscript, Centre for Newfoundland Studies, Memorial University, 1970).

The inshore salt cod industry dominated Newfoundland's economic history in the nineteenth century and continued to be the single most important source of employment and market income well into the twentieth.....[I]n terms of the gross value of (export) production, prices, and physical output, there were three long cycles running between 1815 and 1934: the first covering 1815/19 to 1850/4, the second between 1855/9 to 1895/9, and a third between 1900/4 to 1930/4. Mean volumes, prices, and export values tended to be higher in each period, but...fluctuations around the means were extreme, especially with respect to prices and export values. It is clear that prices were more volatile than physical production, and that on a quinquennial basis gross export values were less stable than either output or prices. The industry was obviously an unstable one upon which to found a country's external earnings and such a large fraction of its national income, and it is hardly surprising that with responsible government politicians launched an effort to widen the country's production base....

Between the grant of responsible government in 1855 and the mid-1880s, Newfoundland's basic industry flourished, although there were always bad years, frequently coupled with indifferent ones. But prices grew by 1.17 per cent per annum in 1850/4–1880/4 and were above the trend referred to earlier in every quinquennia. Volumes grew by 1.25 per cent per annum and were above trend in four out of six quinquennia. Accordingly, over the same interval, export values grew by 2.14 per cent per annum and were above the trend in each quinquennia. Over the period 1857/84 population growth decelerated to an annual rate slightly over 1.7 per cent. Furthermore, while according to the censuses the labour force (occupied population) was growing at just over 2 per cent per annum, the male fishing labour force grew by only 1.7 per cent. Thus, the industry's share in total employment fell from 90 per cent in 1857 to 82 per cent in 1884, and the implication (under the assumption of constant factor proportions) is a modest growth in total productivity. The trend in living standards, however, is unclear. The U.S. wholesale price index for farm products rose sharply from 83 in 1856/60 to 117 and 130 in the two quinquennia of the 1860s, then fell to 86 in 1880/4. The U.K. merchandise export price index moved in the same direction, rising from 110 in 1856/60 to a plateau of about 126 in the three quinquennia between 1861 and 1875 and then falling off to 93 in 1881/5. But whatever the implications of the terms of trade for living standards, behind the growth rates for the fishing economy an alarming situation was emerging. The absolute level of employment in the fishing industry grew from some 38,500 men in 1857 to around 60,400 in 1884, and fishing rooms in use expanded from some

6,000 to around 10,500.[4] This meant that the average volume of production per fisherman was falling from around 30 quintals in the 1850s and 60s to a low of some 23 quintals in the late 1880s, after which there was a modest recovery.[5] We know little about trends in man-hours among fishermen and the growth of employed capital, and it is therefore difficult to be certain about changes in labour and total factor productivity. But contemporaries were convinced that the traditional fishing economy had reached a limit to extensive growth.

The size of national income produced by this traditional economy is impossible to estimate precisely. In 1884 the value of all exports was $6.6 million and almost all of this was accounted for by fish products—notably salt codfish and oil, while the remainder consisted of mineral and other primary product shipments.[6] Primary employment (the export sector) accounted for 87 per cent of the labour force, the secondary sector some 10 per cent and the service sector some 3 per cent.[7] If we assume that the value of output in the secondary and tertiary sectors was a proportional fraction of their labour forces to the *realized* output of the primary sector, then the realized national income would be around $7.5 million.[8] There was a great deal of production in rural Newfoundland, however, that did not move through markets. In the late 1930s it was estimated that income in kind amounted to some 55 per cent of the value of fish exports.[9] If the same proportion of non-market income was produced in 1884, then this would add some $4.1 million to the realized national income, for a total national income of some $11.6 million and a per capita income of around $60. Probably this is a low estimate. . . .

Newfoundland's traditional economy underwent a crisis in the late 1880s and 1890s. Export prices for salt codfish sank from $3.82 a quintal in 1880/4 to $2.89 in 1895/9—a collapse of around 32 per cent. Production volumes also fell from about 1.5 million quintals in 1880/4 to some 1.2 million in 1895/9—a 20 per cent decline. Accordingly, industry gross

---

4. *Tenth Census of Newfoundland and Labrador*, 1935, pt I, vol. 2, 87.
5. Calculated from ibid.
6. Parzival Copes, "Role of the Fishing Industry in the Economic Development of Newfoundland" (unpublished manuscript, Centre for Newfoundland Studies 1970), table 3.
7. Calculated from *Tenth Census of Newfoundland*.
8. By "realized" output is meant that fraction which enters into markets. For estimates of "National Cash Income" in this period see Steven D. Antler, "Colonialism as a Factor in the Economic Stagnation of Nineteenth Century Newfoundland: Some Preliminary Notes" (unpublished manuscript, Centre for Newfoundland Studies 1973), table 3.
9. R. A. MacKay (ed.), *Newfoundland: Economic, Diplomatic and Strategic Studies* (Toronto 1946), appendix B.

earnings sagged from $5.6 million to $3.6 million—a decline of 36 per cent.[10] But the impact on the real level of national income and per capita consumption was probably less severe than these figures suggest. . . . The terms of trade actually moved in Newfoundland's favour in the two quinquennia 1884–94 relative to the 1870s and first half of the 1880s, although there was a sharp deterioration during 1895–9. But the point remains that employment levels reached in 1884 could not be maintained, quite apart from the additional burden of absorbing into the traditional economy increments from natural increase. The male labour force engaged in catching and curing fish fell back from an historic peak of 60,000 in 1884 to just under 37,000 in 1891. Employment inched up again during the prosperous first decade of this century and reached almost 44,000 in 1911; but then it began a slow decline to some 35,000 in 1935.[11]

The sharp decline in employment in the traditional economy after 1884, and its relative stability during the first half of this century, was achieved in part through the absorption of labour into other sectors; but a major contribution also came through slower rates of growth of population and labour force. Whereas in 1874–84 population grew at a rate of 2.1 per cent per annum, it was close to stationary in 1885–91 at 0.3 per cent and remained below 1 per cent per annum until World War II.[12] Deceleration of population growth was not principally a function of changes in fertility or mortality. The crude birth rate was around 30 per thousand in 1884, 33 in 1891, and 35 in 1901. The crude death rate, which was 14 per thousand in 1884, rose to 22 in 1891 and fell back to 15 in 1901.[13] Throughout the 1920s and 1930s the crude birth rate was above 20 per thousand—in the high twenties during the relatively prosperous 1920s and the low twenties during the depression—while the crude death rate fluctuated around 12 per thousand.[14] It follows that population and labour force growth could only have been held down by substantial net emigration. Trends in net migration can be estimated by noting population levels at census periods and imputing what the population would have been with no migration at the estimated rate of natural increase. By this method, net immigration at an annual average of less than 1,000 prevailed between 1869 and 1884. But

---

10. Calculated from Government of Newfoundland, *Historical Statistics of Newfoundland and Labrador* (St. John's 1970) vol. I, table K-7.

11. Calculated from *Tenth Census of Newfoundland.*

12. *Historical Statistics of Newfoundland*, table A-I.

13. Calculated from *Census of Newfoundland*, 1901, table J, 17. The sharp increase in the death rate in 1891 may represent an unusual year or a weakness in the census.

14. Dominion Bureau of Statistics (hereafter DBS), *Province of Newfoundland, Statistical Background* (Ottawa 1949), tables 21, 22.

from 1884 to 1935 a large flow of emigrants began. Between 1884 and 1901 it probably ranged between 1,500 to 2,500 per year, and from 1901 to 1945 between 1,000 to 1,500 per year.[15]

It is clear that the 1880s is an important benchmark in Newfoundland's economic history. The traditional economy reached a limit to its extensive growth and further development was perceived as a function of the emergence of modern resource industries, with emigration acting as a mechanism to balance a labour force growing faster than employment opportunities. Since the acquisition of responsible government in 1855, the ever pressing task which confronted ministries was to raise market incomes in the traditional sector and to substitute domestic job creation for the humiliating, costly, and enervating mechanism of emigration. Indeed, during the decades when the traditional economy was approaching its maximum extensive growth, government had begun to search for a development strategy which would reduce the rate of inshore fishery expansion and initiate its relative decline. The most famous statement of this goal was the report of the committee headed by William Whiteway,[16] which declared that "no material increase of means is to be looked for from our fisheries, and...we must direct our attention to the growing requirements of the country."[17] The strategy the committee proposed contained the essential features of the national development policy pursued by all nineteenth-century territories of European settlement.[18] Through railway technology the country would be shaken free from dependence upon coastal resources, and a moving frontier of inland settlement would open export sectors in agriculture and minerals— resources whose existence in Newfoundland was confirmed by geological survey. There was also a hint in the committee's report that St John's would provide a market for country products, and, presumably with the growth of the latter, would emerge as a centre of domestic manufacturing. At one stroke, a blow was dealt to the one-product export economy and the income leakages resulting from high foreign trade dependence. In

---

15. Sources for these estimates are the *Census of Newfoundland*, 1901, 1911, and 1935; and DBS, *Newfoundland, Statistical Background*, table 23. Michael Staveley, "Migration and Mobility in Newfoundland and Labrador: A Study in Population Geography" (unpublished PhD thesis, University of Alberta 1973), 71, also concludes that a flood of emigration began around 1884.

16. William Whiteway, born Devon, 1828; lawyer and politician; entered politics as a Conservative in 1859; premier, 1878–85, 1889–94, 1895–7; died St. John's 1908.

17. "Report of the Select Committee to Consider and Report upon the Construction of a Railway," *JHA*, 1880, 126.

18. For a discussion of this point see A. J. Youngson, "The Opening up of New Territories," *Cambridge Economic History* (Cambridge 1966), vol. 6, pt I, ch. 3.

general, Newfoundland's economic problem was seen not as an actual or approaching overabundance of labour relative to resources, but of labour relative to resources currently being exploited.

In the latter part of the nineteenth century this strategy was pursued with a legislative ferocity which took second place to no developing country. In 1873 a Homestead Law was passed to encourage "Agriculture and the more speedy settlement of the Wilderness" and the Companies Corporation Act provided the legal framework for establishing limited liability companies in manufacturing, mining and commerce. In 1875 a system of bounties was introduced to speed up land clearance and cultivation. Two years later there was an "Act for the Encouragement of Manufacturing" providing subsidies on imports of flax, cotton, and wool used in fishing gear and textiles. An Act of 1880 offered large blocks of land to licensees who would settle farming families. In the same year the receiver general was authorized to issue debentures for construction of a railway from St. John's to Notre Dame Bay, and in the next year the first railway contract was brought down for a line to Halls Bay with branches to Conception Bay. The 1880 session also introduced one of many bounty schemes to encourage ship-building for the bank fishery, and legislation was passed in 1882 providing assistance to New York promoters to establish the Newfoundland Dock Company—the railway and drydock being the two great infrastructure investments of the late nineteenth century.[19]

The 1882 session included a flight of fancy, in legislation for the "Great American and European Short Line Railway." It provided the promoters with incentives to build a southern line from St. John's to the southwest coast, there to link up by steamer with railways to be built or running rights to be acquired, through eastern Canada and the United States—a scheme perhaps no more ridiculous in its historical context than the Canadian dream of an imperial transportation link between Europe and the Orient. In any case, it was an early manifestation of Newfoundland's continuing fascination with its supposed locational advantages in the North Atlantic. In 1884 an act closely modeled on Canadian legislation provided for the survey of Newfoundland into townships, sections, and quartersections, with further development of homesteading, mining, and forestry law. This was followed two years later by an "Act for the Promotion of Agriculture" which established agricultural districts under

---

19. For the statutes embodying these provisions see *Statutes of Newfoundland*, 36 Vict., c.7, c.8;38 Vict., c.18;40 Vict., c.10;43 Vict., c.3., c.4;44 Vict., c.2;43 Vict., c.5; and 45 Vict., c.3.

the direction of a superintendent and staff to direct settlement, road building and other public works as well as the promotion of scientific agriculture. In 1889 these measures were supplemented by the establishment of a Board of Agriculture to supervise local agriculture societies, and found a model farm to introduce improved stock, seeds, and farm equipment.[20] In 1896 the trans-insular railway was completed, but the decade saw the projection of fresh schemes, including a line from the Canadian border to the Labrador coast.

Throughout the late nineteenth century the St. John's newspapers followed the progress of secondary manufacturing, giving close attention to technical accomplishments, the level of employment, and the likelihood of staunching imports. Gaden's Ginger Ale Factory was applauded for beating out imported mineral waters. The carriage factory of Messrs W. R. Oke and Sons was hailed for developing a wooden tricycle for the French consul which could be marketed at a quarter the cost of steel models. Archibald's Tobacco Works, employing some 120 people, produced a Newfoundland plug tobacco. Stained glass, with designs in a national idiom, was made by the Newfoundland Glass Embossing Company. Newfoundland fruit was bottled in a new factory on Mundy Pond Road and samples were sent to the queen with the hope of acquiring a royal appointment. Boots and shoes were turned out in a plant at Riverhead in St John's employing close to 150 people, and since its work could "compare more than favourable with work turned out in any part of the world" it was anticipated that imports would be reduced.[21] The seriousness with which manufacturing development was viewed was symbolized by a government decision in 1891 to fund an industrial exhibition at St John's "for the encouragement of the national and mechanical products of this colony."[22]

Like Canada's National Policy, Newfoundland's first development strategy envisioned a moving frontier of agricultural settlement (facilitated by investments in inland transportation) linked to an initially protected and subsidized industrial sector. The results were disappointing. Improved acreage doubled from 36,000 acres in 1874 to 86,000 in 1901, but on a per capita basis this meant a growth from only 0.28 acres to

---

20. See ibid., 45 Vict., c.4;47 Vict., c.2;49 Vict., c.3; and 52 Vict., c.8.
21. I am grateful to Mrs B. Robertson of the Newfoundland Historical Society for drawing my attention to these references. See *Daily Colonist* (St John's), 1 April, 13 Sept. 1886; 9 July 1887; 8 Oct. 1888; 4 June 1889.
22. 54 Vict., c.10.

0.32.[23] Similarly, there was modest growth in the livestock population—
from 90,000 cows and cattle to 148,000, and from 180,000 sheep to
350,000—but the country had hardly made a dent in its domestic import
bill and certainly had not emerged as one of the world's frontiers of
agricultural investment.[24] In the industrial sector the value of factory
output per capita grew from only $10 in 1884 to $12 in 1901 and $14 in
1911.[25] It is, accordingly, a reasonable conclusion that agriculture and
secondary manufacturing developments brought no important shifts in
the composition of output. Nonetheless, the structure of employment in
the country was significantly different in 1911 compared with 1884....
Between these dates almost 30 per cent of the labour force—a growing
labour force—was shifted out of fishing and into other occupations. Over
half of this 30 per cent represented small gains to defined primary,
secondary, and service occupations, while the other 13 per cent was
accounted for by the census aggregate "others." This category likely
included workers in a variety of personal service occupations, although
the sharp increase in the category between 1884 and 1891 suggests
another analysis which supports its allocation to secondary employment.
Between 1884 and 1891 railway construction and a number of urban
service projects got underway, and the upswing in the category "others"
probably reflects the emergence of a large labour force in transportation,
communications, public utilities, and construction. If this is so, then a
large share of employment diversification in this period was secured by a
flow of public, and largely foreign private funds, into capital projects.
Indeed it was two of the largest of these investments—the Bell Island iron
mine and the Harmsworth newsprint plant at Grand Falls—which
accounted for the decline in fish products as a percentage of exports
(despite rising values from 1900) from over 90 per cent in the 1880s to less
than 70 per cent by the opening of the war.

It is very probable that gross domestic product grew substantially in
real terms between the mid-1880s and 1911. But the gains to gross national
product and to personal incomes would be less dramatic; for both the
railway, the new resource industries, and the expanding urban services
must have increased the gross investment ratio and introduced for the first

---

23. Calculated from *Census of Newfoundland*, 1911, vol.I, table 21.
24. Ibid., table 22.
25. Ibid., table 23. Some large firms, however, did not report, such as Reid-Newfoundland,
    Angel Engineering, and A. Harvey.

time into the Newfoundland economy substantial payments abroad for technology, capital, and entrepreneurship.

The assumptions guiding Newfoundland's first development strategy were akin to those shaping the nineteenth-century territories of settlement. The weight of development was to be assumed by Newfoundlanders—native born and immigrants—accumulating capital and absorbing modern technology through the formation and expansion of small agricultural and industrial enterprises. Their efforts would be complemented by footloose entrepreneurs who, with government backing, would tackle large and complex capital investments. These assumptions began to give way by the beginning of the twentieth century. It is true that interest in native Newfoundland enterprise remained strong in the St John's newspapers. For example, in 1912 excitement built up over the prospect of a rubber goods factory employing "all local capital," but it was abandoned when it was found that "the smallest plant which could be established...would produce enough stock in about four to five weeks to accommodate the demand."[26] It was also suggested at various times that factory hands should boycott merchants who carried imported lines when local products were available.[27] But the bulk of development legislation from the turn of the century was devoted not to the stimulation of local enterprise, but to a search for foreign direct investment firms to develop modern resource industries through a package of advanced management and technology.

The reasons for this shift are clear. The original development strategy had failed. The high cost of land clearance and fertilization of an acidic soil made the land marginal to Newfoundlanders and the European migrants who flooded into the prairie lands of Australia and South and North America. With manufacturing, the size of the domestic market doomed firms to suboptimal scale, and the absence of an industrial tradition in the country among capitalists and workers made it unlikely that Newfoundland firms would overcome the difficulties of entering foreign markets to achieve optimum scale. The remaining avenue to development was primary manufacturing industries, where possession of a scarce natural resource provided cost advantages for entry into international markets. Unlike the fishing industry, however, the minimum size of the firm in modern resource-based manufacturing was large, and Newfoundland,

---

26. *Daily News* (St John's), 16 Jan. 1912.
27. *Evening Telegram* (St John's), 9 July 1908.

with its tiny national income, had neither the savings, the entrepreneurs, nor the skilled workers to launch and control such developments.

The resulting wedding between Newfoundland and the international corporation can be traced back to the nineteenth-century contracts for railways, the drydock, and the Bell Island mines. But the volume of such contracts accelerated with the successful Anglo-Newfoundland Development Company agreement in 1905 for a paper-mill at Grand Falls. In the following year the Marconi Company was given a monopoly over telegraphy in return for a commitment to improve the island's communications. In 1910 the "Coal Development Act" provided the Newfoundland Exploration Syndicate with tariff guarantees on coal imports if the company established a commercial mine. A similar inducement was given in 1910 to the Newfoundland Oil Fields Limited of London. In 1911 the British-Canadian Explosives Company, also of London, was offered protection to establish a manufacturing plant of sufficient capacity at least to supply local demand. In the same year an agreement was reached with the International Carbonizing Company to manufacture peat fuel, and two Maine promoters were offered various inducements to build five cold storage plants for fish products. In the next year the American-Newfoundland Pulp and Paper Company of Grand Rapids, Michigan, entered into an agreement for a pulp- and paper-mill at Deer Lake. In 1913 the Orr Newfoundland Company was empowered to construct five reduction plants to manufacture glue and fertilizer from dogfish, while the Canadian North Atlantic Corporation revived an old vision of a railway from Quebec City to the Labrador coast.[28]

The war years slowed down but did not staunch the flood of industrial promotions. In 1915 the Newfoundland-American Packing Company received concessions for cold storage facilities to pack freshwater fish, fruits, and berries, and the Newfoundland Products Corporation was launched to manufacture fertilizers on the Humber. In the first year of peace the St George's Coal Fields Company revived the prospect of domestic coal supplies. In 1920 the St Lawrence Timber, Pulp and Steamship Company offered prospects for the development of pulp mills on Bonne Bay, while the Terra Nova Sulphite Company was planning a similar facility at Alexander Bay. In 1921 the D'Arcy Exploration Company was granted leases for oil exploration, while the Pulp and Paper Corporation of America proposed mills in Labrador—probably only to

---

28. See *Statutes of Newfoundland*, 5 Ed. VII, c.9, c.8; 10 Ed. VII, c.23, c.24; I Geo. V, c.11, c.20, c.22; 2 Geo. V, c.8, c.14.

acquire rights to export pulpwood and pit-props. In 1923 an agreement with the Newfoundland Power and Paper Corporation resulted in the mill at Corner Brook—one concrete success. In 1924 the Newfoundland Milling Company was founded to mill cereals with a guarantee of a twenty-year monopoly and tariff protection. In 1929 the Newfoundland Mines and Smelters Limited was granted concessions over a large part of the Avalon to mine and process lead, copper, zinc, and other ores. In 1930 one of the most imaginative—and enduring—schemes was launched by the Great Lakes-Atlantic Newfoundland Company for a transshipment port at Mortier Bay. In the last years, as the edifice of responsible government slipped away, the Terra Nova Oils Company was granted privileges to distil for export.[29]

Each of the agreements had common threads. Any provision for Newfoundland equity participation, either public or private, was absent. The Newfoundland government provided concessions in the form of crown land grants, drawbacks on duties on new construction materials, machinery, and raw materials, tax holidays, and where applicable, the promise of protective tariffs. In return for these privileges, the companies promised to employ Newfoundland labour wherever possible and to invest certain minimum amounts over specified time periods—a guarantee which was commonly extended for further grace periods by amending legislation. But for all the hopes and efforts embodied in these agreements, few resulted in any investment and still fewer in any permanent additions to the country's productive capacity.

In contrast to the late nineteenth century, legislation involving Newfoundland entrepreneurship was remarkably scarce and, with two exceptions, unoriginal. In 1908 the Model Farm Act provided for an agricultural experimental station to undertake original and applied research. In 1917 the Newfoundland Knitting Mills and the Riverside Woolen Mills, both apparently Newfoundland firms, were given relief from import duties on machinery and raw materials and a limited subsidy for fifteen years. In 1928 a Harbour Grace merchant was given a three-year monopoly to establish a shark oil industry—a trade perhaps better fitted to some of the foreign concessionaires. A more promising direction was offered in the Tourist Commission Act of 1927 which established a public corporation drawing revenues from a tax on hotels, steamships,

---

29. Ibid., 6 Geo. V, c.3, c.4; 9 & 10 Geo. V, c.25; 11 Geo. V, c.2, c.6; 12 Geo. V, c.8, c.9; 14 Geo. V, c.1; 15 Geo. V, c.1; 20 Geo. V, c.12; 21 Geo. V, c.6; 22 Geo. V, c.5; 23 & 24 Geo. V, c.5.

and similar enterprises to promote a tourist traffic and a "wider knowledge of the colony's natural resources." Undoubtedly the most important legislation in these years seeking to upgrade the efficiency and returns to Newfoundland enterprise was the two acts which made up the Coaker Regulations.[30] The acts established national quality controls in the production of saltfish and an organized approach in the markets for all Newfoundland output. Regrettably, the regulations foundered on divisions within the trade and were repealed in the following year.[31] It was not until the economic collapse of the 1930s, when prospects of attracting foreign capital for resource development dried up, that attention to fishery legislation revived. In the interval Newfoundland's position as the world's largest exporter of salt cod weakened in the face of a growing competitiveness in Scandinavia and the development of national fishing fleets in traditional importing countries.[32]

"No colony of the British Empire," it was stated in 1910, "has made such progress in recent years as has Newfoundland." It was "one of the most progressive states in the Western hemisphere" and "no people in the world maintain a more comfortable and contented existence than the Newfoundland fishermen...."[33] Twenty years later, on the eve of Newfoundland's economic and political collapse, Joseph Smallwood wrote at length of the country as a budding industrial Michigan set down in a North Atlantic Arcadia.[34] But the structural transformation, so often planned, predicted, and seen, had not in fact arrived. Between 1911 and 1935 Newfoundland's population grew from 243,000 to 290,000, an annual rate of 0.8 per cent as compared with about 1.7 per cent in Canada. As a consequence of emigration, the labour force grew more slowly than population at an annual rate of 0.3 per cent whereas in Canada it grew faster than population at slightly over 1.8 per cent.[35] In other words, the

30. Ibid., 8 Ed. VII, c.7; 8 Geo. V, c.1., c.2; 18 Geo. V, c.1; 11 Geo. V, c.25., c.27.
31. See Ian McDonald, "Coaker the Reformer: A Brief Biographical Introduction," in J. R. Smallwood (ed.), *The Book of Newfoundland*, vol. 6 (St John's 1975), 71–96.
32. See G. M. Gerhardsen and L. P. D. Gertenbach, *Salt Cod and Related Species* (Rome: Food and Agricultural Organization 1949).
33. "The Golden Age of Newfoundland's Advancement" (1910), I, 8. Internal evidence suggests this to be a Harmsworth promotional pamphlet.
34. J. R. Smallwood, *The New Newfoundland* (New York 1931).
35. The Canadian rate is calculated for the employed population, 1911–31. The dependency ratio was not, however, remarkably different. Both countries had heavy child dependency ratios of 35 per cent in Newfoundland in 1935 and 31 percent in Canada for 1931. That the Newfoundland ratio was not more unfavourable may be attributable to the apparently higher infant mortality rate (see DBS, *Newfoundland, Statistical Background*, table 24) and differing marriage and fertility patterns. Whatever the explanation, the

demographic trends were not those of a country which had surmounted a development hump into modern economic growth.

The foreign trade statistics appeared, superficially, to indicate considerable growth and diversification. Exports and re-exports grew from $11.7 million in 1906/10 to a peak of $40.0 million in 1929/30, or from about $50 per capita to around $135, while fishery products fell from some 80 per cent to 40 per cent of total exports.[36] Indeed, per capita exports from Newfoundland were higher than in Canada, which stood at $40 in 1911 and $115 in 1929. But given the small volume of domestic production for home consumption, Newfoundland needed very high levels of exports per capita to emulate the North American pattern of consumption which, as Smallwood noted, was increasingly emulated and desired.[37] Moreover, the gains to levels of consumption from rising per capita exports could not have been very great since...the export price indices of countries from which Newfoundland drew most of her imports rose by 40 to 60 per cent between the immediate pre-war years and the second half of the 1920s. Secondly, duties as a percentage of imports rose from around 20 per cent to 28 per cent over the period,[38] and expenditures for servicing foreign debt rose from 20 per cent of revenue in 1919–20 to 35 per cent in 1929–30.[39] Thirdly, the per capita value of exports in pre-war Newfoundland reflected much more realistically returns for consumption to factors of production in Newfoundland than was the case by the late 1920s. The new resource industries in mining and forest products, which accounted for over 55 per cent of the value of exports in 1929–30, required substantial payments out of the gross value of sales for capital depreciation, payments to foreign suppliers of intermediate inputs and non-resident management and ownership. For the same reason, the apparent diversification of the economy is misleading. Newfoundland had progressed from a domestically owned one-product export economy to a substantially foreign owned three-product export economy, for in 1929–30 some 98 per cent of exports were accounted for by fish, forest, and mineral products.

Diversification of output for the export economy had no dramatic impact on the distribution of the labour force....[T]he apparently strong growth in service employment and the decline in secondary shares

---

occupied labour force was 34 percent of the population in 1911 and only 30 per cent in 1935.

36. DBS, *Newfoundland, Statistical Background*, table 97.
37. Smallwood, *New Newfoundland*, 211.
38. DBS, *Newfoundland, Statistical Background*, table 97.
39. Dominions Office, Newfoundland Royal Commission, *Report*, 1933 (Cmd. 4480), 57, 63.

between 1911 and 1935 is largely a statistical illusion arising either from a failure to enumerate personal service before 1935, or its allocation to "others" in earlier periods....Relative to the labour force, primary employment was declining, service employment was increasing, but secondary employment was stabilizing at around 20 to 25 per cent of labour force. This was the share reached in the 1890s when the modern transportation, communications, and construction labour force began to emerge. Fishing and lumbering in 1935 continued to employ almost half the labour force, while factory and shop employment, despite the paper-mills and electrical power stations, still employed only about 7 per cent, while all occupations in the service sector showed small relative gains. The modern resource industries attracted to Newfoundland since the turn of the century had had a much greater impact on the composition of domestic product than on the structure of the labour force. The *trends* in labour's sectoral allocation were the same as those affecting other countries in the western world,[40] but the strength of demand for labour in Newfoundland's non-primary sectors and the growth of labour productivity in the primary sector had generated a much slower pace of transition than elsewhere. Thus, while the employment trends were toward the "modern" allocation, at each date the secondary sector and, to a lesser degree, the service sector were more weakly developed....

...The critical fact is that the economy as a whole could not provide sufficient employment for the growing population and potential labour force, necessitating emigration from *both* urban and rural sectors. With stronger growth in secondary and tertiary sectors the level of emigration would have fallen, but it would have required a massive boom in demand for secondary and service output and a correspondingly sharp rise in per capita earnings in those sectors to have attracted large amounts of labour out of the primary sector.

The Newfoundland government struggled with the prospect of bankruptcy during the early years of the depression, and finally surrendered independence and dominion status early in 1934. The commission appointed from Britain a year earlier to review the causes of impending collapse attributed it largely to the irresponsibility of politicians in the management of public funds.[41] But from its own evidence it is difficult to make the case that there was a riot of spending. Revenues grew steadily from $8.4 million in 1920/21 to $11.6 million in 1929/30, but current

---

40. See Simon Kuznets, *Modern Economic Growth* (New Haven 1966), ch. 3.
41. 1933 Commission *Report*, 43.

expenditures actually declined from $8.9 million to $7.2 million and in every year between were under $7 million.[42] It is true that the budget was in surplus only in 1924/5, whereas it was in surplus in every year after 1922 in Canada; but the great development expenditures of the Canadian government were over by the 1920s, whereas in the twenty-eight years between 1885 and 1913 the Canadian budget had been in deficit in all but six of those years.[43] In 1933 the per capita public debt in Newfoundland stood at around $344 compared with $540 for all levels of government in Canada,[44] which given relative income levels implied a heavier burden in Newfoundland.[45] Analysis of the Newfoundland public debt in 1933 shows that 35 per cent was attributable to development of the railway; 60 per cent was accounted for by the railway and other development expenditures on fisheries, agriculture, schools, roads, urban development, and similar accounts; that over 70 per cent was chargeable to these and the war debt; and finally that the lion's share of borrowings made to cover budget deficits was in order to keep the railway operating.[46]

Whatever the peccadillos of its politicians, Newfoundland's collapse was not the result of corruption or even unwise, as distinct from unfruitful, spending of public funds. With the grant of responsible government, Newfoundland had set out to replicate the economic performance of its continental neighbours. The levels and patterns of North American consumption were the goal, and it is not surprising that development strategies to achieve it were imported as well. From hindsight, some of the reasons for failure are apparent. The matter of scale was crucial, for it was only by the output of massive volumes of several primary products and the simultaneous enlargement of domestic markets that servicing of development expenditures could be covered, a measure of isolation from the swings of international prices secured, and dependence upon external capital markets reduced. Newfoundland was unfortunate. The economy was too narrowly based to benefit from war demand in 1914–18 and at best only a small commodity trade surplus was achieved. Moreover,

---

42. Ibid., 57, 63.
43. Calculated from *Historical Statistics of Canada*, series 621–4 and 626–44.
44. Calculated from 1933 Commission *Report*, 253; *Historical Statistics of Newfoundland*, table A-I, and *Historical Statistics of Canada*, series 696–710.
45. In Canada in 1933 debt charges of all governments as a percentage of revenues amounted to 40 per cent as compared with 63 per cent for Newfoundland in 1932–3. Calculated from *Historical Statistics of Canada*, series 662–82, 683–710, and 1933 Commission *Report*, 57, 63.
46. Calculated from 1933 Commission *Report*, 253.

unlike Canada, Newfoundland had to finance much of her war effort by borrowing in London and New York. The economy emerged from the war without a sharply diversified structure or increased capacity, with a casualty-ridden labour force, and an increased external debt.

In the 1920s weak primary product prices offered no relief, and unlike Canada the country could not escape from the treadmill of external borrowing to service existing debt and to seek the elusive breakthrough into modern economic growth and structure. Hence the country was extremely vulnerable in the face of the international economic crisis which was steadily building throughout the 1920s. Newfoundland's export earnings dropped by 22 per cent in 1930/1–1934/5 over their level in 1925/6–1929/30—a rather modest decline compared with the almost 50 per cent collapse in Canada's foreign earnings in 1931–5 over 1925–9.[47] But the smaller percentage decline had a much greater impact on Newfoundland since a larger share of national income was derived from foreign trade, the fishing industry (which was the most important in terms of payment to resident factors) was most severely hit, and government revenues, out of which payments on development capital had to be met, were almost entirely derived from customs.

Emulation of the style of life and the development strategies by which the new continental countries had achieved it resulted in ruin for Small-wood's "New Newfoundland." For the impatient public servants of the 1933 royal commission, it was a case of a "people misled into the acceptance of false standards" and a "country sunk in waste and extravagance."[48] A blunter conclusion was reached in the 1940s by MacKay and Saunders: "the Newfoundland economy cannot, in normal times, provide the revenue required to supply the Island with the public services demanded by a Western people."[49] . . .

E. H. Carr has suggested that history rarely repeats itself because man is conscious of the past.[50] But in Newfoundland the past has not been well understood and the range of choice has been severely restricted. After the 1934 collapse succeeding decades have brought a repetition of earlier development cycles. During commission government in the 1930s and 1940s, attention reverted to improving the efficiency and expanding the capacity of indigenous enterprise; in the 1950s and 1960s, as a province of Canada, there was a further round on "infrastructure" investment and

---

47. Calculated from DBS, *Newfoundland, Statistical Background*, table 97, and *Historical Statistics of Canada*, series F242–5.
48. 1933 Commission *Report*, 43.
49. MacKay, *Newfoundland*, 190.
50. *What is History?* (New York 1972), 84–9.

strenuous efforts to woo international capital and corporations. In the 1970s the province confronted the highest per capita debt and burden of taxation and the lowest credit rating in Canada. Almost half of provincial revenues are transfers from the federal government, and consumer expenditure and private investment is heavily supported by direct and indirect federal expenditures and transfers. The level of unemployment hovers around 20 per cent of a labour force with a low participation rate, and many of the province's hard-won industrial projects, such as the electric reduction plant, the linerboard mill and the oil refinery, are either heavily subsidized or operating at a loss. The Labrador mineral and hydro-electric projects have not generated major returns to the province and their prospect for further expansion is now dim. On the island and coastal Labrador a large rural population remains, reluctant to move to the mainland, and dependent upon the tattered remnants of a once great fishing industry wrecked by unfavourable trends in the international economy and hopelessly ineffective national trade and fisheries policies.[51] As Newfoundlanders once hoped that paper and mining companies would finally bring prosperity, they now await the discoveries of international oil companies on the Labrador coast.

If there are lessons from the past, however, they suggest that the province's natural potential lies on the sea, not the land, and that international resource corporations will not effect the economic transformation so long awaited. It might be wiser for Newfoundland to define and accept more modest goals and expectations, or perhaps more accurately, different ones. The development which a country achieves is not simply a quantitative measure of real output, but a qualitative valuation of the levels and patterns of consumption secured with that output, and its mental independence from valuations made by other influential countries. A tropical island will be poor no matter how much fish, fruit, sunshine, and leisure its economy can provide, if its people want, or are persuaded to want, cars and apartment towers. It is possible Newfoundland could develop a more prosperous economy and more self-confident society if its people adjusted to a pattern of consumption somewhat different from that of the mainland, and its labour and capital were more effectively linked to its obvious natural endowment.

---

51. See David Alexander, *The Decay of Trade: An Economic History of the Newfoundland Saltfish Trade, 1935–1965* (St John's 1977), and below.

THE 1920s: DECADE OF STRUGGLE

JOHN G. REID

During the 1920s, the Maritime provinces faced economic disaster. It was in this decade that it became clear that the industrialization of the late nineteenth century had not provided any guarantee of future economic stability. It was in this decade that the foundations were laid for the Maritimes' status as a "have-not" region of Canada. For much of the rest of the country the Great Depression was a phenomenon only of the 1930s. In the Maritimes it began in the summer of 1920 and lasted for a full generation. It was not accepted passively. In settings as diverse as in the mines of Cape Breton, in the small-town universities of the region, in newspaper offices, and in the lobbies of Parliament, the effects of economic decline were resisted with skill and tenacity, though not with success.

There is a myth that portrays Maritimers as docile, quiescent, slow to generate any kind of collective emotion. The events of the 1920s amply demonstrate the falsity of that image. Lacking wealth by comparison with other regions of Canada, losing population whenever there were jobs to be found in more prosperous areas, the Maritimes would henceforth find more difficulty than before in asserting national leadership in political, social, or cultural fields. "As for the Maritime provinces," one of Canada's most prominent historians felt able to remark in 1963 on CBC radio, "nothing, of course, ever happens down there."[1]

Much did happen in the Maritimes in the 1920s, and much has happened since. However, all that has happened since has been influenced by the fact that the economic forces besetting the region in the 1920s were ultimately too strong for those who resisted them.

As the 1920s began the Maritime provinces—like the rest of Canada—were still recovering from the traumas of the First World War. The adjustment to peacetime conditions, in fact, had worldwide implications, economic as well as social and political. The war had been enormously expensive and yet had stimulated industrial development in all the countries involved. Demand for iron and steel products, as well as for other commodities that had war uses, had been high. As a result the

---

JOHN G. REID, "THE 1920S: DECADE OF STRUGGLE," SIX CRUCIAL DECADES: TIMES OF CHANGE IN THE HISTORY OF THE MARITIMES (HALIFAX: NIMBUS, 1987). PUBLISHED WITH PERMISSION, NIMBUS PUBLISHING, HALIFAX, NOVA SCOTIA.

1. Frank H. Underhill, *The Image of Confederation* (Toronto, 1964), p. 63.

industrialized world emerged from the conflict with more industrial capacity than would be needed in peacetime. This was true in Canada as elsewhere. After a short period of post-war boom, fuelled by the renewed production of peacetime goods, the reality of surplus capacity had to be faced by early 1920.

Furthermore, world trade patterns had been disrupted by the war. Traditional European markets for Newfoundland fish, for example, had been effectively cut off during the war years and were not fully recovered afterwards. One result was that Newfoundland fish exports began increasingly to compete in traditional Nova Scotia markets, such as in the Caribbean. The issue was complicated by the uncertainties of the Caribbean economy, which depended heavily on exports of cane sugar. These exports had been in high demand during the war years, when European beet sugar production had been sharply reduced. Now, beet sugar returned to the world market, and prices declined: as they did, so too did Caribbean purchasing power for Maritime products. Another trade shift, though not so directly connected with the war, was in international markets for timber. Here, the old-established Maritime lumber producers met increasing competition from the newly-opened forest resources of British Columbia. Decreased demand for Maritime sawn lumber was partly offset by developments in pulp and paper, but the overall result was decline.[2]

In grappling with worldwide industrial and trading problems after the First World War, the Maritime provinces were not alone. All major economies of the world were affected. In the Maritimes, however, there were certain factors that made this region's experience unique in Canada. First of all, major changes in industrial organization had taken place since the 1880s. "By 1914," the historian T. W. Acheson has written, "the Maritimes had become a branch-plant economy."[3] The failure to develop an adequate financial structure within the region during the 1880s had led to major takeovers by Montreal and Toronto financiers. In 1881, there had been 274 branch businesses in the Maritimes; the number had grown to 416 by 1901, and to 950 by 1921.[4] Not all of these branches resulted from takeovers. Some represented the construction of new plants by national firms, while others were essentially distribution networks for products

---

2. S. A. Saunders, *The Economic History of the Maritime Provinces*, 2nd edition, (Fredericton, 1984), pp. 37–42.
3. T. W. Acheson, "The Maritimes and 'Empire Canada,'" in David J. Bercuson, ed., *Canada and the Burden of Unity* (Toronto, 1977), p. 95.
4. L. D. McCann, "Metropolitanism and Branch Businesses in the Maritimes, 1881–1931," *Acadiensis*, 13 (Autumn 1983), pp. 112–13.

manufactured in central Canada. Yet the dramatic increase in the number of branch businesses between 1901 and 1921 did include takeovers in important manufacturing industries, an example being the 1909 amalgamation of the Rhodes, Curry Company of Amherst—one of Canada's leading producers of railway cars—with two Montreal companies to form the Montreal-controlled Canadian Car and Foundry Company.

In stable economic times, outside control might make little obvious difference to the economy. In bad times, such as the early 1920s, branch plants became prime candidates for cutbacks or closure, as companies attempted to cope with excess capacity and reduced demand. Matters were further complicated by the particular difficulties of the Nova Scotia steel industry, which played a key role in the wider regional economy as a consumer of coal and as a supplier of manufacturers of secondary steel products. Chemical and metallurgical problems in the coal and iron ore resources of the region led to increased production costs, which offset the advantage of having these resources close at hand. Also the industry had depended heavily before the First World War on railway expansion, with its demand for products such as rails and axles. Now railway expansion had levelled off, and the age of steam and steel was itself being overtaken by technological changes. These factors made Maritime industries all the more vulnerable to takeovers and to possible eventual retrenchment in favour of plants more centrally located in Canada.[5]

Yet even all of this might not have led to an economic debacle had it not been for another factor entirely: the political decline of the Maritimes as a region within Canada, and the economic consequences of that decline. When Nova Scotia and New Brunswick had entered Confederation in 1867, they had been two of four provinces, and had contained (to use 1871 census figures) 18.7 percent of the Canadian population. By 1891 the Maritime provinces were three out of seven, with 18.2 percent of the overall population. By 1921 they were three of nine, with only 11.4 percent of the national population.[6] This relative decline was faithfully reflected in the number of parliamentary seats allocated to the Maritimes, which were reduced after each census, despite equally regular protests by the provincial governments of the region.[7] As a result, it became increasingly difficult

---

5. L. D. McCann, "The Mercantile-Industrial Transition in the Metal Towns of Pictou County, 1857–1931," *Acadiensis* 10 (Spring 1981), pp. 50–61; K. Inwood, "A Merger Bid Which Failed: the 1910 Raid on Scotia," paper presented to Canadian Historical Association Annual Meeting, Winnipeg, 1986, pp. 13–17.

6. F. H. Leacy, ed., *Historical Statistics of Canada* (2nd ed.; Ottawa, 1983), series A2–14.

7. Ernest R. Forbes, *The Maritime Rights Movement, 1919–1927: A Study in Canadian Regionalism* (Montreal, 1979), pp. 13–17.

for Maritime political leaders to sustain the region's interests effectively at the federal level. An early indicator of what was to come was a change in 1907 in the National Policy tariff on imports of coal. Already reduced in 1897 from 60 cents per ton to 53 cents per ton, the tariff was now eliminated in cases where coal was used "for the smelting of metals."[8] The tariff had helped Maritime coal to find a ready market in central Canada, and had also encouraged manufacturing firms to locate close to the coalfield. Now, however, it would be easy for iron and steel firms in central Canada to import from the United States, rather than buy from Nova Scotia and New Brunswick.

An even more serious setback for Maritime industry occurred between 1912 and 1923. The freight rate structure of the Intercolonial Railway had always been favourable to shipments of Maritime-produced goods travelling west. Regarded in the Maritimes as a right, and in fact as the only way in which the National Policy could be made to work fairly for the eastern as well as the central areas of Canada, these freight rates nevertheless came under criticism in the early part of the twentieth century. Central Canadian complaints about discrimination in favour of the Maritimes brought about the abolition of the east–west differential in 1912. Western complaints about the general low level of the Intercolonial's freight rates—despite which, the company managed to make a profit more often than not—led to attempts in 1917 to have rates raised to western levels. Ultimately, in a process spanning the years from 1917 to 1923, the Intercolonial was amalgamated with four other railways in different parts of Canada to form the Canadian National Railways. In the same space of time, freight rates in the Maritimes rose between 140 and 216 percent, depending on commodity. The issue had been complicated by disputes within the region, notably between the ports of Halifax and Saint John, as to whether the Intercolonial had favoured some local interests over others. Nevertheless, the result was that the competitive position of all Maritime producers trying to sell in central Canadian markets was effectively undercut.[9]

In the years immediately following the First World War, the Maritime economy suffered a series of heavy blows. In part the problems were

---

8. E. R. Forbes, *Aspects of Maritime Regionalism, 1867–1927* (Ottawa, Canadian Historical Association, 1983), p. 13; David Frank, "The Cape Breton Coal Industry and the Rise and Fall of the British Empire Steel Corporation," *Acadiensis*, 7 (Autumn 1977), p. 9.

9. E. R. Forbes, "Misguided Symmetry: The Destruction of Regional Transportation Policy for the Maritimes," in David J. Bercuson, ed., *Canada and the Burden of Unity* (Toronto, 1977), p. 70; Ken Cruikshank, "The People's Railway: The Intercolonial Railway and the Canadian Public Enterprise Experience," *Acadiensis*, 16 (Autumn 1986), pp. 92–4, 98–100.

worldwide. In the Maritimes, however, the effects of these wider trends were transformed into a major crisis by complicating factors that originated within Canada: outside control of the regional economy, and the inability of outnumbered political representatives to put up an effective defence of regional interests in such crucial areas as tariffs and freight rates. The results were disastrous. In the years between 1920 and 1926, some 42 percent of the manufacturing jobs in the region simply disappeared.[10] Meanwhile, as deindustrialization proceeded, non-manufacturing sectors such as fisheries, lumber, and agriculture had to deal with world trade disruption and severe competition in uncertain markets. There were exceptions. In Nova Scotia, for example, the decline in exports of salt cod was offset for a time by increased output of fresh and frozen fish for the New England market. In New Brunswick, and especially in Prince Edward Island, exports of seed potatoes prospered as successful efforts were made to produce disease-free stock at a time when other North American growing areas were encountering potato blights. Also in Prince Edward Island, the 1920s saw fox-farming reach its height, as the market value of silver-fox pelts steadily increased. Yet even in Prince Edward Island population declined in the 1920s, and rural population declined more rapidly than urban. There, as in the other two provinces, many decided to leave—perhaps as much as one-fifth of the entire population of the region. Those who remained had to find ways of dealing with the new, harsh economic climate.[11]

The first group to be directly threatened was the industrial working class. During the early years of the 1920s, industrial Cape Breton became a battlefield as workers resisted wage cuts and layoffs. There were good reasons why this part of the Maritimes would see the most dramatic labour-capital struggle of the decade. The reasons were partly economic, in that the steel and coal production of Cape Breton depended to a large extent on central Canadian markets, and so these industries were acutely sensitive to any alterations in the National Policy as it related to tariffs and freight rates. The 1907 abolition of the import tariff on foreign coal used

---

10. Forbes, *Aspects of Maritime Regionalism*, p. 18.
11. Saunders, *Economic History*, pp. 42, 64–5; *Report of the Royal Commission Investigating the Fisheries of the Maritime Provinces and the Magdalen Islands* (Ottawa, 1928), p. 9; Andrew Hill Clark, *Three Centuries and the Island: A Historical Geography of Settlement and Agriculture in Prince Edward Island, Canada* (Toronto, 1959), pp. 121, 128, 150, 172; Gene Barrett, "Capitalism and the Fisheries of Atlantic Canada to 1940" (unpublished manuscript), pp. 35–40; Kennedy Wells, *The Fishery of Prince Edward Island* (Charlottetown, 1986), pp. 159–60.

for metal-smelting was an obvious blow to both coal and steel in Cape Breton. The later increase in freight rates compounded the effect. . . .

Labour-capital conflict was not new in the Maritimes in the 1920s. The years between the turn of the century and the First World War had seen increased union militancy at the same time as the ownership of industry was becoming increasingly concentrated, and a strike such as the 22-month Springhill miners' strike in 1909–11 was exceptional only in its length.[12] As recently as in 1919, a general strike in Amherst had pitted the Amherst Federation of Labour against major employers of the town, in the wake of layoffs at the Canadian Car and Foundry Company and protests against the higher wages and more regular work being offered to the company's Montreal employees. The results of the three-week strike were inconclusive, and in the years to come Amherst's economy was devastated by branch-plant closures. Nevertheless, the strike had been an early indication that the crisis following the First World War would be met forcefully by organized labour.[13]

In Cape Breton the most serious phase of the crisis began in early 1922, when BESCO [British Empire Steel Corporation] announced a wage cut of 37.5 percent; a bitter coal strike ensued. . . .[See the following reading by David Frank.]

There was resistance also in the more formal settings of provincial and federal politics. In the immediate aftermath of the First World War, it had seemed that both political levels might be transformed by the intervention of new parties. Farmers' and labour movements sprang up throughout Canada and enjoyed varying degrees of success as pressure groups and political parties. In the Maritimes the province least affected was Prince Edward Island, where the industrial working class was small, while the concerns of farmers were so important that they were central to the policies of the existing political parties. The Island farmers' movement formed in early 1921, therefore, found itself confined for the most part to marginal issues in attempting to assert a distinctive identity.[14]

The New Brunswick experience was different, with the United Farmers fielding successful candidates in both federal and provincial elections. Their president, T. W. Caldwell, won a federal seat on behalf of the newly-

---

12. Ian McKay, "Strikes in the Maritimes, 1901–1914," *Acadiensis*, 13 (Autumn 1983), pp. 3–46.
13. Nolan Reilly, "The General Strike in Amherst, Nova Scotia, 1919," *Acadiensis*, 9 (Spring 1980), pp. 56–77.
14. Forbes, *Maritime Rights*, p. 45.

formed Progressive party in the Victoria-Carleton by-election of November 1919, and in a provincial general election the following year, the farmers won six seats out of 48. The allied Labour party won two, to complete a respectable showing. In Nova Scotia, earlier in the year, farmers' and labour parties failed to arrive at an agreement to cooperate formally, but still seven farmers won seats in the 43-seat house, and four labour candidates, with a combined popular vote of 30.9 percent.[15]

Yet 1920 proved to be the high-water mark of farmer-labour success in the region. Caldwell narrowly gained re-election in the federal election of 1921, but no others joined him. . . . Instead, the great majority of Maritime seats—25 out of 31—went to the Liberal party of Mackenzie King, which ousted the existing Conservative government of Arthur Meighen in this election. Regional issues had dominated the campaign. Throughout 1920 the three Maritime provincial governments had coordinated representations to Ottawa on transportation and other issues, emphasizing the disastrous implications of rising freight rates. They had met with scant response, and one Conservative party statement went so far as to brand Maritime claims to lower freight rates as "rank sectionalism."[16] To such an attitude, the Progressive party could offer no satisfactory alternative, since most of its supporters in the west, who were much more numerous than in the Maritimes, favoured tariff and freight rates policies directly opposite to those that were in the Maritimes' best interests. The Liberals were the beneficiaries of the shortcomings of the other two parties.

Ironically, the election of 25 members of the governing party did not help to advance regional interests significantly. The King government was in a minority position, and depended for its survival on not offending the 64 Progressives, of whom the majority represented western constituencies. King, as Prime Minister, tended now to be more sympathetic to western than to Maritime interests, and yet of course continued to demand the party allegiance of the Maritime Liberal members.[17]

This impasse, again a consequence of the political decline of the Maritimes as a region within Confederation, could not readily be resolved within the existing Parliament. The years from 1922 to 1925 therefore saw the growth of an extra-parliamentary political movement for "Maritime

---

15. Ibid., p. 47; Arthur T. Doyle, *Front Benches and Back Rooms: A Story of Corruption, Muckraking, Raw Partisanship and Intrigue in New Brunswick* (Toronto, 1976), pp. 212–16; Anthony Mackenzie, "The Rise and Fall of the Farmer Labor Party in Nova Scotia" (M.A. thesis; Dalhousie University, 1969), passim.
16. Quoted in Forbes, *Maritime Rights*, p. 80.
17. Forbes, *Maritime Rights*, p. 87; John Herd Thompson with Allen Seager, *Canada, 1922–1939: Decades of Discord* (Toronto, 1985), pp. 14–17.

Rights." The mood had also changed. While provincial governments and business interests had initially argued against freight rate alterations on the basis of the potential harm they could do, it was now clear that the time of warding off a future threat was gone. The damage was done, and the crisis was real.

The Maritime Rights movement was not monolithic. It drew support from boards of trade in towns and cities, from newspapers such as the Halifax *Herald* and the Saint John *Telegraph-Journal*, and from some provincial politicians, including the Liberal premier of New Brunswick, P. J. Veniot. Its goals ranged from general to specific. A general aim was to explain the Maritimes' grievances plainly to other Canadians. For that purpose, speakers were sent to centres throughout Canada, the leading exponent of the movement being H. S. Congdon, a Dartmouth journalist who proved adept at explaining why "it will not pay Canada to have these provinces destroyed...."[18] More specifically, leaders of the movement argued for revisions in freight rates, for use of Maritime ports rather than Portland, Maine, for shipping of Canadian goods, and for measures to stimulate immigration to the Maritime provinces, among other issues.

The climax of the initial phase of the Maritime Rights movement was reached in February 1925 when the Saint John board of trade sponsored a large delegation to Ottawa, intended to include a representative from every incorporated community in the region. Although that ideal was not reached, some 300 delegates did make the trip. Despite some confusion as to the exact arguments to be put to Prime Minister King on the morning of the 25th, the meeting was dominated by an effective and impassioned speech from the mayor of Saint John, John Murphy, who denounced the restrictions put upon the economic development of the region by federal policy. Mackenzie King was not impressed, and said so. His unwillingness to concede that the Maritimes had a case was consistent with the policy of the government since the election of 1921. In the new election of October 1925, the response of the voters was clear. The Conservatives won 23 seats, almost entirely reversing the Liberal tide of 1921. Whatever else the Maritime Rights movement may or may not have achieved, it had established its importance in regional electoral politics.[19]

The Maritime response to the conditions of the 1920s was not confined to the areas of politics and industrial relations. With industrial areas suffer-

---

18. H. S. Congdon to J. V. Mackenzie, 31 October 1923, quoted in Forbes, *Maritime Rights*, p. 107.
19. Forbes, *Maritime Rights*, chapters vi, vii.

ing from plant closures and slowdowns, and rural areas from decay and out-migration, the economic malaise of the region was a matter for general concern. As in the political arena, reform movements that immediately followed the First World War were transformed during the 1920s into instruments by which Maritimers put up what defence they could against economic pressures. Nowhere was this more true than in the area of higher education.

By 1920, higher education in the Maritime provinces was the responsibility of nine degree-granting colleges and universities, as well as professional training colleges and junior colleges. Many of the institutions were small, and the majority were associated with religious denominations. Most had no government funding, and had to be financed on the basis of tuition fees, church subsidies, and private donations. Increasingly in the early part of the twentieth century, they had turned to United States-based private foundations for assistance. The Carnegie Corporation of New York, one of the largest of these philanthropic organizations, decided in 1921 to commission a major study of higher education in the region, as a guide for future donations. The two commissioners, William S. Learned and Kenneth C. M. Sills, were senior academic administrators in the U.S., and in late 1921 they visited the Maritimes on an inspection tour.

Their recommendations, published in 1922, were potentially far-reaching. The most important was that six of the universities—Acadia, Dalhousie, King's, Mount Allison, the University of New Brunswick, and St. Francis Xavier—should join together in Halifax to form a federated University of the Maritime Provinces. By forming one large university to replace several small ones, the commissioners believed that higher academic quality would be achieved.[20] The scheme eventually failed to be realized, except that the University of King's College moved from its original site in Windsor, Nova Scotia, to a new location in Halifax, in close association with Dalhousie. With that exception, even the promise of a subsidy of $3 million from the Carnegie Corporation could not persuade the various institutions to comply.

More significant than the ultimate failure of the scheme, however, was the way in which it was discussed. From the beginning, the Carnegie commissioners had been aware that the decline of the Maritimes as a region within Confederation was a current political concern. Noting the

---

20. William S. Learned and Kenneth C. M. Sills, *Education in the Maritime Provinces of Canada* (New York, 1922), passim.

Maritimes' "feeling of comparative poverty," they noted that "the adjustment of this inequality is now an issue in Canadian politics, or at least in
that aspect of it that especially interests the Maritime Provinces."[21] This
theme was taken up by the supporters of their proposals. "We talk about
'Maritime rights,'" remarked President A. S. Mackenzie of Dalhousie, and
yet "even the Western Universities, which are so much newer, have
already gone way beyond us." James J. Tompkins, vice-president of St.
Francis Xavier University, put the matter more bluntly by declaring that
what was at issue was "justice for the Maritime Provinces in matters
educational."[22] . . .

The larger struggle continued also in Ottawa. The 23 Conservative
members of Parliament elected in the Maritimes in 1925 soon found
themselves in the midst of a constitutional crisis. The 1925 election
reduced the governing Liberals to only 99 seats out of 245. The 116
Conservatives could not claim a majority, however, and Prime Minister
King attempted to soldier on with the acquiesence of the 24 Progressives.
When this arrangement collapsed in June 1926, King asked the governor-
general, Lord Byng, to call a new election. Byng refused. Instead, he called
on Arthur Meighen's Conservatives to form a government. Only when
Meighen also proved unable to command the confidence of the House of
Commons was a general election called for September. This time Mackenzie King's Liberals, loudly proclaiming that the "King-Byng Affair" had
been an example of a British governor-general thwarting the legitimate
advice of a Canadian prime minister, were returned convincingly to
power. Their 128 seats represented a clear majority.[23]

Two points arose from this episode which had especial significance for
the Maritime provinces. First, that at a time when every vote was
important, Mackenzie King finally recognized the political force of Maritime Rights advocacy. In early 1926, the King minority government
announced the appointment of a federal royal commission to look into
Maritime demands. Headed by the British lawyer Sir Andrew Rae Duncan,
who had also headed the provincial royal commission on the Nova Scotia

---

21. Ibid., p. 5.
22. A. S. Mackenzie to G. J. Trueman, 30 April 1926, Dalhousie University Archives,
    DAL/MS/1/3. J. J. Tompkins to W. S. Learned, 2 April 1922, Carnegie Corporation
    Archives, Maritime Provinces Educational Federation Files; cited by permission of the
    Carnegie Corporation of New York.
23. Thompson and Seager, *Canada, 1922–1939*, pp. 114–27, 334–5.

coal industry in the previous year, the commission began its hearings in July 1926.[24] The second point to emerge was that the Maritime electorate, however much the appointment of the Duncan commission may have been welcomed, was still in no mood to place its trust in the Liberal party. In the 1926 election the Liberals succeeded in winning back three New Brunswick seats, but still the Conservatives elected members in 20 of the 29 Maritime constituencies. The problem was, of course, that they would now sit in opposition rather than in government.[25]

The Duncan commission completed its report speedily. Although the full text did not appear until near the end of 1926, a preliminary version was delivered to Mackenzie King on 23 September, just over a week after his election victory. The report was forthright in conveying the Maritime provinces' sense of crisis and injustice. "It is not possible to exaggerate," declared one passage, "the dismay and depression with which some communities in Cape Breton look upon the approach of the winter season, in view of the distress arising through the irregularity of employment that is then experienced." In general, Duncan argued that a bright future was possible for the Maritime provinces, but with an important proviso: "if they are relieved of the disabilities under which they have been suffering and are enabled to approach their problems with renewed vigour." The commission had specific recommendations as to how this could be achieved. Its major proposals included a 20 per cent reduction in railway freight rates, increases in federal subsidies to the provincial governments so as to bring them into line with those paid to the central and western provinces, measures to promote port development in Halifax and Saint John, a subsidy to steel producers using locally-mined coal so as to compensate for lack of tariff protection, and upgrading of the Prince Edward Island ferry service.[26]

The Duncan report was described by the Halifax *Herald* as the "Magna Charta of the Maritimes."[27] However trite the phrase, there was no doubt that Duncan had made a serious effort to come to grips with the Maritime grievances. Had the report been implemented in an equally serious spirit, genuine change might have come about. By King and the cabinet, however, it was mined for politically expedient measures and then set aside. As summarized by E. R. Forbes, the historian of the Maritime Rights movement, "the cabinet. . .changed Duncan's program for Maritime reha-

---

24. Forbes, *Maritime Rights*, p. 149.
25. Thompson and Seager, *Canada, 1922–1939*, pp. 124–8, 335.
26. *Report of the Royal Commission on Maritime Claims* (Ottawa, 1926), pp. 36, 44, and passim.
27. *Halifax Herald*, 11 December 1926.

bilitation into a plan for Maritime pacification—a pacification to be achieved with the fewest possible concessions."[28] Of the major recommendations, the reduction in freight rates was implemented. So was the increase in provincial subsidies, but only on a temporary basis. National harbours boards were created for Halifax and Saint John, and incentives given for coking plants to use Canadian coal.

Many Maritime Rights leaders now declared that victory had been won. Only later did it become evident that those of Duncan's recommendations that had supposedly been deferred for further study had in fact been dropped entirely, and that even those implemented—such as the freight rate reduction—were to be subjected to narrow interpretations that would destroy much of their value.[29] For the moment the Maritime economy began in 1927 to experience an apparent revival. Pulp and paper markets were healthy, while the prosperity of other parts of North America led to significant growth in the tourist industry. Together with investment in new facilities at the major ports, these developments and related construction activity gave a temporary brightness to the economic picture. Yet the reality was that the Maritime provinces were left with no effective defence against the renewal of depression in 1929. . . .

---

28. Forbes, *Maritime Rights*, p. 176.
29. Ibid., pp. 182–91.

CLASS CONFLICT IN THE COAL INDUSTRY: CAPE BRETON, 1922

DAVID FRANK

Suddenly the whole country was watching. Alarming reports were coming out of "the Canadian Far East." Sabotage seemed to stalk the eastern edge of the country. Then came Sovietism. Soon the coal mines were shut down, and Nova Scotia was "simply bristling with dangerous possibilities." By the late summer of 1922 more than one-quarter of Canada's army was boarding eastbound trains, fully equipped for battle.[1]

What was happening among the coal miners of Nova Scotia? In March the Minister of Labour denounced them as "un-British, un-Canadian and cowardly." In June the miners proclaimed themselves "out for the complete overthrow of the capitalist system and the capitalist state, peaceably if we may, forcibly, if we must," and all Canadian workers were invited to join in the attempt. In August the coal miners closed the mines, and their disciplined strike became "the most remarkable possibly in the history of Canadian labour disputes." In left-wing circles the coal miners were acclaimed for placing themselves "in the forefront of the radical forces in North America"; in business circles the cry went up for prompt military action to put down a red uprising in the east. What had happened in Nova Scotia's major coal-field? It was "the most menacing industrial crisis" in the province's history, worried the *Halifax Herald*. "Never before since coal mining began in this province has a like mental attitude existed among the workers." "The idea of a class war, rather than a partnership in industry, had taken possession of the mining towns," commented another observer. But perhaps it was J. S. Woodsworth who suggested the most useful way of looking at events in Cape Breton. "What is the root of all this trouble in Nova Scotia?" he wrote, "Bolshevism among the foreign miners? No, that is not an adequate answer, though an easy way of disposing of any industrial difficulty. The miners in Nova Scotia are chiefly of Scotch-Canadian stock and there was similar trouble

DAVID FRANK, "CLASS CONFLICT IN THE COAL INDUSTRY: CAPE BRETON, 1922," IN GREGORY S. KEALEY AND PETER WARRIAN, EDS., *Essays in Canadian Working-Class History* (Toronto: McClelland and Stewart, 1976). Used by permission of the publisher.

1. *The Worker*, August 1, 1922: *Halifax Herald*, September 2, 1922; King Papers, Public Archives of Canada (PAC), J4, Vol. 130, file no. 1027.

long before Lenin came upon the international stage. No case can be summed up in a word, yet there is one word that is much nearer than Bolshevism: that is 'Besco'—the common sobriquet of the British Empire Steel Corporation. For years we have been studying the miners and are puzzled because we cannot find a solution to the trouble. Suppose we devote our attention to the other factor. Better still, suppose we study the relations of the two factors."[2]

Under industrial capitalism class relationships are broadly similar from time to time and place to place. But they are never just the same—and they do not have just the same results. For instance, the explosive confrontation between labour and capital in Cape Breton in 1922 emerged from the specific circumstances in the coal industry at the end of the First World War. Two historical cycles intersected. The coal miners harboured their highest expectations at a time when the coal industry teetered dangerously on the edge of collapse. A rejuvenated and aggressive labour movement clashed head on with the anxious new captains of a weakened coal industry. For reasons of their own, each side urgently wanted to change the terms on which labour power was bought and sold in the coal industry. Neither side was willing to yield, and the course of events in the 1920s demonstrated this common stubbornness and tested the comparative strength of the two sides. The confrontation of 1922 showed the effectiveness of several sources of strength available to the working class and introduced one of the most sustained episodes of open class conflict in Canadian history.[3]

The First World War was a decisive turning point in the history of the coal industry. The period of rapid expansion ended with the war and the

---

2. *Debates of the House of Commons, 1922*, Ottawa 1922, pp. 512–514: *Maritime Labour Herald*, July 1, 1922; *Halifax Herald*, September 2, 1922; *The Worker*, August 1, 1922; *Halifax Herald*, August 19, 1922; *Mining Record*, September 13, 1922; *The Canadian Forum*, IV, March 1924, p. 169.

3. The present account draws heavily on this writer's "Coal Masters and Coal Miners: The 1922 Strike and the Roots of Class Conflict in the Cape Breton Coal Industry," M.A. Thesis, Dalhousie University, 1974. Useful surveys of the coal industry and the coal miners are Eugene Forsey, *Economic and Social Aspects of the Nova Scotia Coal Industry* (Montreal, 1926); S. A. Saunders, *The Economic Welfare of the Maritime Provinces* (Wolfville, 1932), pp. 30–46; David Schwartzman "Mergers in the Nova Scotia Coal Fields: A History of the Dominion Coal Company, 1893–1940," Ph.D. Thesis, University of California, Berkeley, 1952–1953; P. S. Mifflen "A History of Trade Unionism in the Coal Mines of Nova Scotia," M.A. Thesis, Catholic University of America, 1951; C. B. Wade "History of District 26, United Mine Workers of America, 1919–1941," unpublished ms., 1950; Don Macgillivray "Industrial Unrest in Cape Breton, 1919–1925," M.A. Thesis, University of New Brunswick, 1971.

industry began its long decline. The crisis was rooted in the uneven development between regions which characterized the growth of industrial capitalism in Canada. Two aspects of this process shaped the history of the coal industry in Nova Scotia. The division of labour between regions established the Nova Scotia coal industry as a staple exporting industry for the use of central Canada, rather than as an engine of local industrial development. At the same time, the concentration and centralization of economic power delivered control of the industry into the hands of Boston, Toronto, Montreal and London financiers, for whom the fate of the coal industry was only one of a hundred considerations of rates of profit. As a result the Nova Scotia coal industry suffered from two historic weaknesses: distant and unstable markets, and external corporate control. Each contributed heavily to the crisis in the coal industry at the end of the First World War.[4]

The National Policy established central Canada as the main marketplace for the Nova Scotia coal trade, but it did this in an ambiguous and incomplete way. The tariff was never high enough to let Canadian coal compete against imported American coal in the industrial heartland of Ontario. And in Quebec, its major market, Nova Scotia coal faced a continual threat from American producers. Transportation added another handicap: though the water route was relatively cheap, navigation on the St. Lawrence was subject to various natural hazards, including the annual freeze-up. The disruption of commercial shipping during the war completely closed the Quebec market to Nova Scotia coal; the alternative of rail shipments was uneconomic. Wartime demands for coal from the local steel industry and the British fleet compensated for the closing of the Quebec market. But after the war recovery of the Quebec market was slow and inadequate. Overproduction in the American fields led to increased exports to Canada at unusually low prices, and the Nova Scotia coal operators seemed to find the prospect of temporary gains in overseas markets more attractive than a difficult campaign against their traditional rival in the Quebec market. By 1921 sales in Quebec were about 60 per

---

4. It is often said that the human costs of "developing" the coal industry have been excessive, yet it may be argued that the costs were all the greater because "underdevelopment" took place. This is the interpretation in Frank, pp. 5–32. For discussions of uneven development between regions see Bruce Archibald, "The Development of Underdevelopment in the Atlantic Provinces," M.A. Thesis, Dalhousie University, 1971; Andre Gunder Frank, "The Development of Underdevelopment," *Monthly Review*, Vol. 18, No. 4, pp. 17–31; Ernest Mandel, *Capitalism and Regional Disparities* (Toronto, 1970); Karl Marx *Capital* (New York, n.d.), Chapter XXV.

cent less than in 1914. The industry's second major customer, the local steel industry, offered no consolation, for it was undergoing its own economic calamities and working far below capacity. Under the impact of this crisis of markets, coal production and man-days worked by the coal miners fell by one-third between 1917 and 1921.[5]

Meanwhile a second crisis further weakened the coal industry. By early 1921 an ambitious Montreal shipper and financier, Roy M. Wolvin, had skilfully merged his latest personal promotion, Halifax Shipyards, with the whole of the province's inactive steel industry and practically the entire coal industry. The resulting merger, the British Empire Steel Corporation (Besco), at once earned the jibe that it was formed with hydrants instead of hyphens. Large blocks of "watered" stock represented idle or grossly overvalued assets, no new capital was raised, no provision was made for rehabilitation of the war-weary coal and steel industries, and market prospects were painted in deceptively optimistic terms. To still doubts about its flimsy financial structure, to demonstrate the corporation's viability, and to attract new investors, Besco needed to show an ability to return high dividends on its top-heavy capitalization. Within Wolvin's ramshackle merger the coal industry, despite its crisis of markets, remained the strongest and only profit-making sector; as a result the coal industry was assigned the urgent task of generating sufficient earnings to support Besco's unrealistic financial structure. Given the crisis of markets, higher coal prices could not meet this need. And increased productivity was unlikely in an industry which needed development work and suffered from a shortage of experienced miners. In an industry where wages made up about 60 per cent of production costs, the easiest answer seemed to be to reduce wages and increase the margin of profit on the coal operations. Squeezed between falling markets and a rising need for profits, Besco during the 1920s desperately attempted to stave off financial collapse at the expense of the working class in the coal industry. To solve this crisis of corporate welfare, when Besco began discussing its first contract with 12,000 coal mining employees in 1921, the corporation proposed that the wage scale be reduced by one-third.[6]

In the coal industry, as elsewhere, the working class emerged from the

5. Saunders, pp. 30–46; Forsey, pp. 43–46; Frank, pp. 9–18, 231, 235.
6. Forsey, 34–42; Schwartzman, pp. 151–204; *Report of the Royal Commission Respecting the Coal Mines of the Province of Nova Scotia, 1925* (Duncan Report), (Halifax 1926), pp. 52–56; N. W. Rowell to E. H. Armstrong, May 9, May 12, 1921, Armstrong Papers, Public Archives of Nova Scotia (PANS); Frank, pp. 18–24, 100–106.

First World War with hopes for substantial improvements in their standard of living and with a growing interest in the possibilities of social reconstruction. The longstanding poverty of the mining communities was aggravated by rising prices and unsteady employment at the end of the war. Living conditions in the coal towns drew statements of anger and disbelief from outside investigators and sparked strong demands from the miners' union for better housing and sanitary living conditions. And demands for stricter enforcement of safety regulations and for improvements in working conditions in the mines occupied a large part of union energies at the end of the war. The miners' resistance to the proposed wage reduction became a symbol of protest against all of these conditions and expressed the miners' view that the time had passed when "anything was good enough for a miner."[7]

The establishment of effective collective bargaining in the coal industry provided a suitable instrument for pursuing these goals. In 1917 the formation of the Amalgamated Mine Workers of Nova Scotia, encouraged in wartime by the federal and provincial governments, ended the divisive rivalry between the indigenous Provincial Workmen's Association (PWA), which had been established in 1879, and the more militant international union, the United Mine Workers of America (UMWA), who began to challenge the PWA after the turn of the century. In 1919 the coal miners linked their popular new organization to the UMWA and became District 26 of the international union. Through their union the coal miners almost doubled their wage scale between 1916 and 1921. But in a time of rising prices this was not enough: the miners found they were barely keeping up to the cost of living and often they were falling behind. "We want a better standard to build on than the conditions in 1914," argued union president Robert Baxter in July 1920, when the miners' real wages were 11 per cent less than in 1913. "When we have comfortable conditions in which to live, then we shall have something to keep up to." And he added a warning: "If things do not improve, then we will have the same result as they have had in Russia. It might very easily happen if we do not get what we are asking for."[8]

As the remark implied, the end of the war saw the growth of labour

---

7. Royal Commission to Inquire into Coal Mining Operations in Nova Scotia and New Brunswick, "Minutes of the Royal Commission on Mining, Sitting at Halifax, August 9, 1920 and Following Days," p. 6, Department of Labour Records. PAC, Vol. 141–142.
8. Royal Commission to Inquire into Coal Mining Operations in Nova Scotia and New Brunswick, "Proceedings of Conference at Glace Bay, July 20–21, 1920," p. 33. Department of Labour Records, Vol. 141–142.

radicalism in the mining districts. The tragedy of the war generated hopes that society might be reconstructed on a sound moral and economic basis, with cooperation replacing profit as the ruling principle in society. "Yes, we have come to the turn of the road," announced the Sydney *Labour Leader* in 1919; "the wagon has been jarred, and, at last the workers are awake. They will not go to sleep again until the day's work is done." A vocal labour press spread radical ideas and encouraged working class political action. The miners elected labour candidates to their town councils, sent four labour members to the provincial legislature in 1920, and enthusiastically supported their secretary-treasurer, James B. McLachlan, when he attempted to win election as a labour candidate to the House of Commons in 1921. The Russian Revolution and the Winnipeg General Strike inspired wide interest and sympathy among the miners. "Bolshevik" ideas were popularized for instance, by Glace Bay writer and poet Dawn Fraser:

> In every contest between labour and capital, I am with labour and against capital, first, last, and all the time. And if you ask me what percentage of the actual product of labour capital should receive? I cry loudly none. Damn it. None. But be assured that I class all worthy effort as labour, and summed up my contention simply is: That any person who does not work at all, should not eat at all. Excepting of course invalids and children.

The arrest of leaders of the Winnipeg Strike drew protests and support from the coal miners, and strike leaders toured the coal district. One dramatic indication of the miners' increasingly militant mood came on May 1, 1920, when, in response to an appeal from Winnipeg for demonstrations of support for the arrested leaders, the coal miners closed the mines for a one-day general strike.[9]

The flow of life in the coal mining communities of Cape Breton promoted a spirit of interdependence and cohesion among the population. United in "the largest compact industrial community in Canada," dependent on a single employer, facing common hardships and enjoying common recreations, the coal communities "had what was a togetherness, and one's trouble was the other, one's joy was the other. They were

---

9. *Labour Leader*, January 18, 1919; A. A. Mackenzie "The Rise and Fall of the Farmer-Labour Party in Nova Scotia," M.A. Thesis, Dalhousie University, 1969; Nova Scotia *Journals of the House of Assembly* (JHA), 1921, Appendix No. 32, pp. 5–11; Canada House of Commons, *Sessional Papers*, 1922, No. 13, pp. 310–312; Dawn Fraser *Songs of Siberia and Rhymes of the Road* Glace Bay, n.d., p. 176.

a very close knit people." Culturally the population was strongly homogeneous, and the traditions of Scottish culture and history offered a common bond. The basic pre-industrial Highland stock contributed a scale of moral values against which the "tyranny" and "slavery" of workaday life was measured, as in the words of a Gaelic song written in Glace Bay in 1922:

> Oh isn't it a shame for a healthy Gael living in this place to be a slave from Monday to Saturday under the heels of tyrants, when he could be happy on a handsome spreading farm with milk-cows, white sheep, hens, horses, and perhaps a car, and clean work on the surface of the earth rather than in the black pit of misery.

The migration of experienced mineworkers from the Scottish Lowlands at the turn of the century added the ginger of militant trade unionism. With an eloquent blend of Burns, Carlyle, and Hardie, of "scotchie talk," "pit talk," and "clan spirit," leaders like Robert Baxter and James B. McLachlan, who had learned their class consciousness and socialism in the Scottish coalfields, effectively rallied the community around the miners' common concerns. The mining towns themselves were another focus for working class consciousness. These were no simple "coal patches," for with so much of the coal resource lying under the ocean floor the major towns enjoyed a unique permanence as beachheads for the assault on the undersea seams; nor were they simple "company towns," for by the 1920s the town councils habitually challenged the coal operators on various civic issues and in times of crisis actively took the miners' side. Against this community solidarity it was difficult for a corporation to make way. The community regarded the parade of successive absentee coal owners as a "floating element," one local writer explained,

> . . .the industrial population is settled; Cape Breton is its home. Every man has relatives and friends and neighbours. The entire population is with him. The managing operator is the floater. He shifts every three or four years and sees only the dollar in the vision. He has no stake in the community; no love for the people.

Or, as another local observer wrote:

> We in Glace Bay are unfortunate in being a one-industry town. Close or suspend operations at the mines and we starve. But before dying we put up a fight, and that is exactly what has happened in this mining area.[10]

---

10. *The Canadian Forum*, III January 1923, p. 106; Archie McIntyre Interview, on tape at the Miners' Memorial Museum, Glace Bay; quoted by C. W. Dunn *Highland Settler, A Portrait of the Scottish Gael in Nova Scotia* (Toronto, 1953), pp. 131–132; F. W. Gray "The Future

An important source of working class unity lay below ground too, in the unusual physical conditions which make up the everyday work of most miners: the wet, the dirt and the darkness, the coal dust and stale air, the ever-present danger and the back-breaking hard work. Robert Drummond, a founder of the PWA in 1879 and an unsympathetic witness to the labour militancy of the 1920s, wrote that the coal miner has "an interesting personality":

> Daily he has to face perils of one kind or another. But he is not flustered, he is without neither hope nor consolation. He derives satisfaction from the knowledge that he is the autocrat of industry. He squares his shoulders and declares that a live collier is better than a dead cardinal. Knowing his power and position he may at times be inclined to be somewhat impulsive. His continual tussle in the mine, with the forces of nature, and the bosses, and out of it with the General Manager, give him an independence which at times is embarrassing to his leaders, his employers and the community.

The hardship and the peril connected with coal mining bred an endemic "radicalism" among the coal miners: "blood on the coal" helped shape the miners' attitudes to the coal operators and helped set the market price of their labour power. The miners' union aspired to win "compensation fully compatible with the dangers of our occupation." Between 1871 and 1939 more than 1,600 men were killed in the Nova Scotia coal mines, an average of about twenty-three deaths per year, but in the years 1914–1921 the average annual fatality rate was more than twice as high, mainly as a result of major mine disasters in 1917 and 1918, which killed 153 men. Pressing the case for nationalization of the mines in 1925, McLachlan opposed any form of compensation for the owners: "The workers have put too much into these mines...more than all the millions they [the operators] have put in. Over a period of years they have put the money in, the workers have put their blood in it."[11]

---

of the Sydney Coalfield," *Dalhousie Review*, XXI (1941), pp. 178–183; Stuart McCawley *Standing the Gaff: The Soreness of the Soul of Cape Breton* (Glace Bay, 1925), p. 23; Dawn Fraser, *If We Saw Ourselves as Others See Us: The Truth About Glace Bay and Other Mining Communities* (Glace Bay, n.d.), p. 12.

11. Robert Drummond, *Recollections and Reflections of a Former Trades Union Leader* (n.p., n.d.), p. 251; *Constitution and Preamble of District No. 26, United Mine Workers of America, Nova Scotia* (Halifax, 1909); Nova Scotia, Royal Commission on Coal Mining Industry, "Minutes of Evidence," mimeo., 1925, p. 1175. The fatality rate per thousand workers in the Nova Scotia mines was comparable to that in the United States, but almost three times greater than in Britain. See C. Ochiltree Macdonald, *The Coal and Iron Industries of Nova Scotia* (Halifax, 1909), pp. 190–191; JHA, 1940, Appendix No. 9, p. 140;

The organization of work underground also set the miners apart and helps explain the sense of "power and position" and "independence" described by Drummond. Though machine cutting grew significantly after the 1890s, bringing some new tensions into the workplace, by the early 1920s the traditional organization of work remained basically unchanged. Coal mining was still a labour-intensive industry conducted within the traditional room and pillar geography of the underground coal mine. Before the introduction into Cape Breton in the late 1920s of longwall mining, a rough version of the mechanized assembly line in the coal mines, the coal industry largely escaped the rigorous work discipline associated with the growth of industrial capitalism. In 1922 about half the underground workers did the actual mining and shovelling of coal, about one quarter transported coal within the mines, and another quarter were engaged in ventilation, pumping, roadmaking, and timbering work. In the extensive honey-combed interior of the room and pillar mine, most men seldom saw their supervisors. The actual miners and their helpers worked in distant, isolated locations, while drivers, timbermen, and roadmakers were constantly on the move within the mines. As a result, like the "autonomous workman" in the disappearing crafts, the mineworker himself retained a considerable degree of control over his work and his workplace. "We built up a certain pride," recalled one miner, "This is *my* mine. This is my *section* of the mine. And you prided on that." In important ways the coal miners continued to regard themselves as "their own men," and felt less responsible to the coal operators than to their own pride in their work, their own ideas about how long and hard a "normal day's work" should be, and their responsibilities towards other underground workers. For about one-third of the miners this independence retained formal expression in the payment of a tonnage rate rather than a daily wage for the coal they mined. In the absence of close supervision underground the miners generated their own rules of suitable underground behaviour to enforce safety, fairness and efficiency in mine operations. The miners also developed a spirited tradition of conversation and debate in the mines. A break in the work—and groups of miners would gather to air common complaints, send grievances to the mine managers, discuss the conduct of operations in the mines, or debate topical issues. The end of the day was one such occasion, one coal miner recalled:

Special Committee of the House of Commons on the Future Fuel Supply of Canada, *Official Report of Evidence*, (Fuel Supply Hearings) (Ottawa, 1921), p. 128; Frank, pp. 45–46.

You'd be sitting down waiting for what they call the trips—a trip of empties, empty boxes or empty cars. They're always talking about McLachlan [the union leader], and this and that, strikes, and so on, always. . . .It was the way since I can remember, and so it was the way with us young fellows too. We had our own interests. . .and we'd be thinking of our own way. But nevertheless we'd be listening, and we'd be following them. . . .We'd be getting our political education from them.

Such talk has always been a basic ingredient in trade union traditions, and together with other aspects of the coal miners' work gave the working class tradition strength and meaning at the workplace as well as at union meetings or in the community at large. Indeed it is not surprising to find the emergence of strong trade union traditions in work situations where the workers had some amount of independent control over the production process.[12]

The buying and selling of labour power causes an ongoing quarrel over the price of labour power in this transaction. As one early writer about working class problems in the Maritimes observed, the price "will lie somewhere between the subjective estimates of the buyer and the subjective estimates of the seller."[13] In the Cape Breton coal industry by 1921 the "buyer's estimate" was shaped by a crisis of restricted markets for coal and a crisis of corporate welfare within Besco. On the other hand, the "seller's estimate" was shaped by enhanced working class hopes and growing labour militancy and radicalism, which both found strong sources of support in the pattern of life and work in the coal communities. In 1920 the inflationary price cycle ended. Prices fell sharply until the middle of 1921 and remained fairly stable at this reduced level for the rest

12. D. J. MacDonald Interview, on tape at the Miners' Memorial Museum, Glace Bay; Murdoch Clarke Interview by this writer; Frank, pp. 47–54, 69–71, 79–87. Carter Goodrich *The Miner's Freedom* (Boston, 1925) found the coal miner to be a "remarkably unbossed workman," "an isolated piece worker, on a rough sort of craft work, who sees his boss less often than once a day." Noting the unusual blend of individual independence and collective discipline among the coal miners, Goodrich suggested that resistance to the erosion of the "traditional freedom of the miners" through the "onward sweep of machine production" might take the form of "increasing workers' control,—a demand, that is, for a miners' freedom to take the place of the miner's freedom they are losing in the change." A mining engineer brings his stopwatch into the mines and finds the time for scientific management long overdue, in Hugh Archibald, *The Four Hour Day in Coal* (New York, 1923). The importance of the relationship between the organization of work and the working class tradition is also pointed out by B. Soffer, "A Theory of Trade Union Development: The Role of the 'Autonomous Workman'" *Labor History* I, pp. 141–163.
13. John Davidson, *The Bargain Theory of Wages* (New York, 1898), p. 257.

of the decade. Pointing to this sudden change in price levels, in 1921 the coal operators demanded that the miners accept a one-third reduction in their wage scale, a measure which threatened to reduce the miners' real wages to the pre-war level.

But from the miners' point of view, the drop in prices provided a windfall gain in real wages: if the wage scale could be defended against excessive reductions, the miners would win a permanent improvement in their standard of living. In the past it had been the policy of the PWA that the wage scale "must accommodate itself to the state of the trade" and to the ebb and flow of prices, but by 1921 the miners were no longer willing to follow this philosophy. Nor did the miners accept the corporation's argument that lower wages would bring larger markets for their coal. The miners argued that coal prices could be lowered by placing the burden on accumulated surpluses and existing profit margins, not on the wage scale. Production costs might be reduced through elimination of needless officials and exorbitant executive salaries, greater efficiency in mine operations, and a more concerted campaign to recover the Quebec market. Indeed, they pointed out, in a country which imported half its coal supplies, adequate protection of the coal industry by the federal government could easily stabilize the domestic coal industry. In short, the miners refused to offer their wage scale as "economic cannon fodder"; they wanted a "new code of morality" to distribute more fairly the burdens of economic problems in the coal industry. Wages and not profits, they argued repeatedly during 1922, should be the first charge upon the earnings of the coal industry. Also, Besco's notorious financial structure, Wolvin's precarious position in the Canadian financial community, and the corporation's refusal to discuss production costs and profit margins with the miners, all reinforced suspicions that Besco wanted to cut wages for the good of a sickly corporation, not for the health of the coal industry itself. To earn profits on "watered stock and idle junk," the miners' wages were attacked. As it turned out, these suspicions were justified. The Duncan Commission, which closely audited Besco's books in 1925, discovered that in spite of "hard times" the coal mines returned handsome profits and "the operators were not justified in insisting on a reduction of wages in 1922, even in spite of the change which they estimated had come over the market and future prospects by the end of 1921."[14]

---

14. H. A. Logan, *The History of Trade Union Organization in Canada* (Chicago, 1928), pp. 82, 99; Robert Baxter to Arthur Meighen, August 2, 1921, Meighen Papers, PAC; *Maritime Labour Herald*, January 28, 1922; *Labour Gazette* (February, 1922), p. 178: J. B.

No settlement of the dispute was reached before the standing agreement expired at the end of 1921, and the corporation introduced the full one-third wage reduction on January 1, 1922. The union protested that because a conciliation board was being formed to hear the dispute, this unilateral step violated the provisions of the Industrial Disputes Investigation Act. One Nova Scotia Supreme Court Justice agreed and issued an injunction forbidding the wage cut, but the full court swiftly reinstated the reduction before the first payday arrived. In January and again in May conciliation boards supported the corporation's case for substantial reductions; both times the board agreed to take confidential evidence from the coal operators and then ruled two-to-one against the miners, the employers' representative and the government-appointed chairman voting together against the union appointee. By the summer the corporation had modified the original wage cut to some extent, but the miners' resistance had stiffened in the meanwhile and there was still no settlement. When the miners went on strike in August, some 1200 troops poured into the Cape Breton coalfield. More troops and a special provincial police force were held in readiness.

Despite this intimidating display of power and influence on the part of the corporation during 1922, Besco did not triumph in the conflict. The corporation was forced repeatedly to change its terms during the year. The outstanding feature of the coal miners' response to the wage reduction in 1922 was its unanimity. After the first conciliation board's disappointing report, the miners voted only 486 in favour and 10,305 against its recommendations. In March, when union leaders obtained some concessions and urged that a contract be signed, the miners voted 1,352 in favour of settlement and 8,109 against. Even a last-minute compromise, agreed to by the union officers on the eve of the August strike, was repudiated by the miners. By September, the miners had managed to transform an average 33.6 per cent reduction in their wage scale into a more acceptable 18.9 per cent average reduction. By resisting the initial wage reduction the miners raised their real wage scale from an average index of 102.0 in January (1913 = 100.0) to 134.7 in September, thus defeating the corpora-

---

McLachlan to Members of the House of Commons, March 20, 1922. Meighen Papers; Duncan Report, p. 31. The Duncan Report, pp. 27–30, established Dominion Coal's gross profit on invested capital at 9.7 per cent for 1913, 13.2 per cent for the year ending March 1921, 10.8 per cent for the remainder of 1921, 8.1 per cent for 1922. Profits fell sharply in 1923 and 1924, and the Commission thought later wage reductions justified. These calculations were based on the elimination of hidden subsidies to the unprofitable sectors of the corporation; for the purpose of regulating the miners' wages, the Commission held that accounts of the coal operations should be kept "separate and distinct."

tion's attempt to restore real wages to the pre-war level.[15] Moreover, the miners preserved their union at a time when some leaders feared the miners' intransigence would lead to the collapse of collective bargaining in the coal industry. Though they might have accepted a smaller wage cut, the vast majority of the miners plainly found the one-third reduction intolerable. But how were they to enforce this opinion? What were the sources of working class effectiveness in this confrontation?

With sharply reduced rates in effect and working time even shorter than usual during the winter months, the coal miners and their families quickly felt the pinch of necessity in January, 1922. Union locals distributed their savings as relief, and the company stores advanced goods on credit. One local resolution warned that if the government "wishes to avoid any riot, revolution or upheaval on the part of labour, then they had better provide our idle members with that which is necessary for the upkeep in comfort and decency as becomes a British subject." Strong words were matched with action. When an unemployed miner with nine children was denied credit at the New Aberdeen company store on January 21, the prevailing bitterness in the Glace Bay district erupted in a series of raids on the store. The first was a spontaneous reaction to the denial of credit to the one miner; the men present ordered the store manager aside and "took what they needed. There was no disorder. Only food was taken." In the evening a large crowd gathered, tossed snowballs at the company policeman on duty, then smashed the windows and looted the store. The next night a crowd of some 4,000 people surrounded the store. When several hundred men rushed forward with a shout and attacked the store, a squad of company policemen fired in the air and retreated. A fourth raid was averted by the town police with drawn pistols. The raids did not continue or spread, nor did they recur until 1925. Community opinion distinguished carefully between those who raided "for need" and those who raided "for gain" and regarded this form of

15. In 1922 Besco reduced wages 25 per cent below the prevailing scale of early 1920, which was itself 12.5 per cent below the 1921 rates. As a result the wage cut became popularly known as a 37.5 per cent reduction. The miners' struggle in 1922 basically eliminated the "25 per cent" part of the general reduction for the lower paid workers, and somewhat less for the better paid men. For instance, the lowest daily wage at the mines, for surface labourers, went from $3.25 in 1920 to $3.80 in 1921, down to $2.44 on January 1, 1922 and then back up to $3.25 by September. An index of real wages was obtained by comparing representative nominal daily wage rates to the changing cost of living in industrial Cape Breton, as collected by the federal government. The figures of course refer to rates, not earnings: they do not tell us how often how many miners earned these rates; and in an industry with some 300 wage classifications, they give only a rough average picture. We lack adequate records for a more accurate series. For details, Frank, pp. 90–97, 120, 193–195, 234.

direct action as an unfortunate symptom of the deepening distress rather than as an attractive or effective solution to the miners' serious plight.[16]

As the crisis sharpened during the next two months, spokesmen for the coal communities articulated their support for the miners' resistance to the wage reduction. New Waterford Mayor James Ling served as the miners' representative on the first conciliation board, though with no effect on the majority decision. And in March the town councils in four mining towns launched a joint appeal to Ottawa on the miners' behalf. They argued that the miners' wages were too meagre "to provide even the necessities of life for themselves and their families" and noted that malnutrition, sickness and inadequate clothing among children were causing more absenteeism from school "than ever before in the history of the mining towns in this district." The mayors complained that the conciliation board had failed to investigate the impact of its decisions "in the lives of tens of thousands of human beings" and called for appointment of a "competent, independent commission" to visit the mining districts and see "with their own eyes the conditions under which these people are expected to live and bring up healthy families." A solution must be found, they warned, for "matters, too long drifting, may break out into open hostilities. . . ." Petition in hand, the mayors of Glace Bay, Dominion, New Waterford and Springhill arrived in Ottawa at the end of March.[17]

But it was mainly through their union that the miners tried to express their response to the wage reduction. The alternative of going on strike, however, was unattractive, for without adequate financial backing a strike would only invite more hardship and deprivation into the miners' homes. Unfortunately, the UMWA offered no hope of substantial aid for a strike, though this was a major attraction of membership in the international union. In early 1922 the UMWA was bracing for its own fight to maintain the 1921 rates in the American fields and was unwilling to commit resources to a difficult preliminary skirmish in an outlying district. Setting these facts before the miners' convention in late February, union president Robert Baxter concluded that the "whole question resolves itself into one of force."[18] And the miners apparently had little "force" at their

---

16. *Maritime Labour Herald*, January 21, January 28, 1922. In the end 13 men received prison terms for their part in the raids, but the miner who first sparked the raids received a suspended sentence, as did five other culprits.

17. "Memo re Request for Appointment of Commission to Investigate Conditions in Coal Mining Industry of Nova Scotia," March, 1922, Meighen Papers.

18. *Proceedings of the 29th Consecutive and Sixth Biennial Convention of the United Mine Workers of America* (Indianapolis, 1924), I, pp. 446, 445–452. In 1922 the UMWA

disposal. The union executive travelled to Montreal, met corporation officials, and despite sharp differences among themselves, decided to refer a proposed settlement back to the membership. When it came to a vote on March 14, the "Montreal Agreement" was soundly defeated. Apparently the miners had a different opinion than their president about how much "force" was at their disposal.

The ensuing events demonstrated that wage disputes are not decided across the bargaining table alone. Under various names and in various forms, restriction of output, or striking on the job, has been a recurrent form of protest among the working class. In the Scottish mineworkers' tradition it persisted in the form of the "wee darg," as R. Page Arnot has explained:

> It had long been the custom amongst the colliers to meet a reduction of wages or other worsening of conditions by a reduction of output, called the "wee darg." The "wee darg" recurred for another generation after 1837, and, though in an altered form, could be found till nearly the present day whenever conditions called it forth. The "wee darg" was a normal, "instinctive" reaction to any unfair bargain, especially when trade unions were repressed or not recognized, so that collective bargaining could not take place.

In so complex an industry as coal mining, the notion of a "normal day's work"—"the darg"—was as difficult to measure as it was to enforce. The size of the "darg" was a matter of custom—and of dispute, never more so than when the miners objected to the coal operators' policies. Then came the time to "ca' canny"—go slow—and substitute the "wee darg" for the normal "master's darg." Rooted in the Scottish working class tradition and made possible by the special conditions of underground work, restriction of output came readily to hand as a suitable device for the Cape Breton miners to use.[19]

---

successfully defended its "no backward step" policy in the union fields. In western Canada District 18 successfully resisted the coal operators' attempt to impose a 35 per cent reduction. There the conciliation process aided the coal miners. First the cut was reduced to 15 per cent, and then, in line with the American outcome, it was entirely eliminated.

19. R. Page Arnot, *A History of the Scottish Coal Miners from the Earliest Times* (London, 1955), p. 17. The "darg" is "a day's work," "a set task," "the amount of coal put out by a miner in a day," "the set amount of coal to be mined in a shift," and "ca'canny" means "to proceed warily," "to be moderate," or according to Ramsay Macdonald, "a magnificently organized system of passive resistance," William Grant, ed. *The Scottish National Dictionary* (Edinburgh, 1931), III, 22; II, 6. The device appears under many names, with various connotations: slacking, shirking, soldiering, loafing, going easy, the passive

In January and February 1922 the idea of striking on the job became the tacit alternative to normal strike action. The device answered the need of the moment: unprepared to walk off the job, the miners could still register an effective protest. Moreover, at a time when demand for coal was short, a slowdown would "spread the work around" and help reduce idleness. In January the tactic enjoyed some success at one mine where underground drivers who had been demoted from contract rates to daily wages decided that a "fair day's work" ought to be somewhat less than before this change in their status and earning power. The tactic also gained support as a response to the general wage reduction. In February, a Halifax reporter finally broke the silence about what had been taking place unadvertised for at least a month. "Fabian tactics," he reported,

> had spontaneous growth, arising with the men themselves as their method of expressing dissatisfaction with the wages now in force, and with the same wages in force it is likely that the practice will continue. Beyond question, it has operated to cut down production, in some mines by something like 50 per cent...

After rejection of the "Montreal Agreement" on March 14, striking on the job became an open strategy. Its purpose was to put pressure on the corporation by raising production costs and lowering profits, and at the same time, to dramatize the miners' plight, make their cause a public issue and compel the government to intervene on their behalf. On March 16 the tactic acquired a dynamic public spokesman in the person of James B. McLachlan, the union's fiery secretary-treasurer, who circulated a formal appeal. "War is on, class war," his declaration began; the plan of attack was outlined in detail:

> War is on, and it is up to the workers in the mines of the British Empire Steel Corporation to carry that war into the "country" of the enemy. . . . Every contract man who voted against acceptance of the wage agreement last Tuesday should at once cut down his production to a point where he can get about the same wage as the low paid men in the mine, and at the same time see to it that every day paid man takes the full eight hours to land his reduced output on the surface.

---

strike, conscientious withdrawal of efficiency. Restriction of output appears in many historical contexts, as an informal protest and as an organized tactic, among organized and unorganized workers. The Webbs discuss the use of the tactic among coal miners and other British workers in the 1890s. *Industrial Democracy* (London, 1920), pp. 446–450, 307–309. For other discussions see "Regulation and Restriction of Output," *Eleventh Special Report of the Commissioner of Labour* (Washington, 1904); S. B. Mathewson, *Restriction of Output Among Unorganized Workers* (Carbondale, Illinois, 1969).

As the plan suggests, striking on the job was well suited to conditions in the mines. The chain operations started at the coal face, and if the coal cutters would "work with their shirts on" and "walk about between whiles," then the pace of work throughout the mines could easily be slowed, especially among the loaders and drivers, the other two major groups of mineworkers. Only the contract miners, who were paid by the tonnage of coal they produced, needed to suffer reduced earnings through the slowdown, but as the best paid workers in the mine, they could afford to sacrifice one-third of their rate. Most mineworkers could "go slow" and still collect their daily wages as strike pay. The appeal of the tactic also had a certain logical neatness: a fair day's work supposed a fair day's pay, if wages were cut one-third then profits should be cut one-third, if the corporation could water their stock then the miners could water their labour.[20]

In the first three months of 1922 coal production was one-fifth less than in the same months of 1921 and one-third less than in 1923, but the significance of this is not clear. We lack adequate records to attempt an exact measure of how widely restriction of output was practised. McLachlan soon after stated that striking on the job achieved dramatic results at Dominion No. 2 and No. 4, where output was said to have tumbled by two-thirds or more and the tactic to have been "down to a perfect science." From here, McLachlan claimed, the campaign "spread to the other mines like wildfire." In 1925 Besco's superintendent of coal mines, Alex S. McNeil, gave a similar estimate to the Duncan Commission: "He thought that the 'strike-on-the-job policy' had been followed 'pretty generally' throughout Nova Scotia, but added that it had been followed most consistently at Dominion's Nos. 4 and 2." The local press was uniformly hostile to the "monstrous proposal," claiming that it was imported from the Old Country or from the IWW [Industrial Workers of the World] and associating the tactic with vandalism and sabotage. The daily newspapers played upon the miners' traditional distrust of shirkers and appealed to their "reputation for honesty and square dealing," and such appeals probably reflected ambiguous feelings among many miners about the morality of the tactic. The local president at Dominion No. 1 resigned because he opposed the general support for the tactic at that mine. But he was the only reported public critic among the miners; it seems that disagreements were suppressed, and it was only after the episode was over that Baxter and McLachlan openly debated the morality

---

20. *Halifax Herald*, February 27, March 20, 1922; *Maritime Labour Herald*, March 18, 1922.

and effectiveness of "ca'canny methods." Striking on the job found no reported support at the five mines in the Sydney Mines district, but carried great appeal in the larger south Cape Breton field.

At six of the 13 operating mines in this area, including three of the largest producers, there is strong evidence of support for the slowdown strike. Joint meetings of locals in the Glace Bay and New Waterford districts endorsed the policy, and after a stormy debate the union executive officially endorsed the strike on the job on March 23. These endorsements no doubt increased the spread of the tactic among the miners. Given the hostility of the press, the elusive nature of the size of a "normal day's work" and the semi-conspiratorial style of the strike, much support went unproclaimed and undiscovered. Probably restriction of output was supported at least to some extent by most of the more than 8,000 men who rejected the corporation's latest offer on March 14.[21]

Whatever its actual extent, the tactic brought results. Though the corporation failed to yield, the political pressure created by the dramatic protest was successful. Twice McLachlan addressed open letters to the members of the House of Commons pointing out the desperate tactics the miners were forced to use against Besco. His furious telegraphic duel with James Murdock, Mackenzie King's novice Minister of Labour, rivetted the country's attention on the controversial dispute. Himself a former labour official, Murdock judged the miners "un-British, un-Canadian and cowardly to pretend to be working for a wage rate in effect while declaring to the world that only partial and grudging service will be given." McLachlan retorted that in the absence of any wage agreement there was "nothing dishonest about it....Our method of fighting this unjust wage reduction is effective and within the law." Their words flew back and forth; the whole country was watching. Spurred on by the growing crisis in the coalfields, the delegation of mayors from the mining towns arrived in Ottawa. But their appeal to the cabinet for a new public inquiry into the miners' case was dismissed. A different story unfolded on the floor of the House of

---

21. Dominion Bureau of Statistics, *Coal Statistics for Canada*, 1925 (Ottawa, 1926) p. 39. Debates of the House of Commons, 1922, p. 513; *The Worker*, May 1, 1922; *Canadian Mining Journal*, December 18, 1925, p. 1158; *Nova Scotian and Weekly Chronicle*, March 24, 1922. Baxter, who opposed the tactic in the union executive sessions, later argued "ca'canny methods" had been given a fair trial and proved ineffective; McLachlan argued the tactic was effective and won sympathy because it had "a moral purpose"; *Maritime Labour Herald*, April 15, April 22, 1922. Though vehemently opposed to the strike on the job and unwilling to report its spread, the daily press does reveal support for the tactic among the miners at Dominion Nos. 1, 2, 4, 5, 10 and 14. At No. 9 there was considerable unrest at the beginning of the year, but this mine was closed in February.

Commons. On March 30 William Irvine, the Calgary labour MP, launched an emergency debate on the crisis in Nova Scotia. The debate revealed considerable sympathy in Parliament for the strike on the job. Murdock defended his earlier views, J. S. Woodsworth, the second labour MP, defended the miners' actions and, as a student of society and sometime longshoreman, informed the House that restriction of output was a "natural, recognized mode of procedure" in Canada, in business, on the farm, and at the workplace. Conservative leader Arthur Meighen condoned the miners' tactic and scolded the government for refusing to reopen their case. And Progressive leader T. A. Crerar suggested the conciliation board be sent to make a more thorough study of conditions in the coalfields. Faced with this united opposition, the minority Liberal government accepted Crerar's plan, with the implicit condition that in return the miners end their slowdown. On April 4 the union executive accepted this solution. The decision on March 30 represented success for the imaginative tactic. By dramatizing their resistance to the wage reduction through the strike on the job, the miners had won national attention, and though the delegation of mayors was brushed aside, the miners' own protest could not be ignored.[22]

An uneasy peace settled over the coalfields. With the resumption of shipping in the spring and the shutdown of the American coal industry by the UMWA's strike there, the condition of the coal trade improved. The miners enjoyed full shifts and steady wages, in sharp contrast to the harsh winter months. When the original conciliation board refused to reconvene, a new board was established. Its hearings were markedly sympathetic to conditions in the mining districts, but the plea for a "living wage" in the form of the 1921 wage scale was no more successful than earlier in the year. Despite critical comments about living and working conditions among the coal miners, the board's majority report recommended almost exactly the same wage scale which the miners had rejected so unanimously in their referendum on March 14. Relying again on undisclosed evidence, the board held that the corporation could afford to pay no more. For his part, the miners' representative stood by the principle that "dividends should be sacrificed before the worker should be compelled to accept less than living wages." Less restrained were the words of the *Maritime Labour Herald*, which reached back to the warrior traditions of

22. McLachlan to Members of the House of Commons, March 20, 1922, Meighen Papers; *Maritime Labour Herald*, April 1, 1922; Debates of the House of Commons, 1922, pp. 497–545; W. L. M. King to R. M. Wolvin, April 1, 1922, King Papers, PAC; W. F. Carroll to E. H. Armstrong, April 4, 1922, Armstrong Papers.

the Highlands for its response: the award of the conciliation board "takes the place of the cross dipped in blood as the signal of war. The fight is not against another clan. The fight is directed against as bold a band of cutthroat robbers as ever disgraced a country. So the miners gather to the fight, with weapons the profit gluttons little dream of."[23]

The test of strength was renewed. In June delegates from the union locals met in convention and discussed a policy report which offered a choice between two courses of action:

(a) accept the present conditions with all their humiliation and poverty, and repudiate the sacred obligations which every sire owes to his son; or

(b) reject and fight with all the power that is in us the present conditions and make one bold attempt to hand down to our children something better than a slave's portion.[24]

The miners chose the second course, resolving to sign no contract for less than the 1921 wage rates. By late July, encouraged by the apparent success of the American strike for the 1921 rates, and prodded by the international union not to continue working without an agreement, the miners' locals voted almost unanimously to strike on August 15 unless the 1921 wage scale was restored by that date. The brisk condition of the coal trade now enhanced the prospects of a successful strike against Besco, and the miners prepared enthusiastically for the forthcoming shutdown. Last minute negotiations produced a compromise settlement which the union executive tried to refer to the miners for a vote, but their attempt to postpone the strike on August 14 failed, and the walkout took place as planned.

The strike closed all Besco's collieries in Nova Scotia. Moreover, it was a "100 per cent" strike, a term the miners used to describe the removal of every last union member from the mines, including the maintenance workers. This not only halted production, but it also added the threat of mounting accumulations of gas and water in the mines. Though the tactic was not used in the mines of Pictou County, where high gas levels made it unattractive to the miners, the "100 per cent" strike was universally adopted in Cape Breton. In the wetter mines of this district the corporation predicted the imminent destruction of several collieries and denounced the whole strike as "an insurgent move by men who have

23. *Labour Gazette*, June, 1922, p. 589; *Maritime Labour Herald*, June 10, 1922.
24. *Maritime Labour Herald*, July 1, 1922.

overridden law and order."[25] The miners argued that only inconvenience but no permanent damage would result from the mounting water levels in the mines. The tactic expressed the miners' determination to win a suitable settlement—and the threat of flooding promised a short, decisive confrontation.

Armed force was the coal operators' main reply to the outbreak of the strike, a course of action Wolvin had planned the week before the strike began. When the strike started on August 15, Glace Bay's labour mayor, D. W. Morrison, a war veteran and a former miner, twice rejected requests that he requisition troops to deal with the strike, pointing out that there was "absolutely no disorder, much less violence" and troops were "totally unnecessary." But later in the day County Court Judge Duncan Finlayson made the necessary application to the military authorities, and that night troops began embarking at Halifax and Quebec City for the Sydney coalfield. Jeers and stones greeted the first troop train the next afternoon. But although the troops were fully armed and equipped for battle down to the last bayonet and chinstrap, on the whole it was a remarkably peaceful invasion. Except for three people killed at a level crossing by one of the unscheduled special trains en route to the coal district, there were no casualties during the strike. The 1,200 troops occupied the vital Dominion No. 2 colliery, the largest producing mine and the site of the power station for the Glace Bay area mines. Under strict orders from Ottawa to refrain from "active measures. . .likely to precipitate trouble," such as escorting strikebreakers, they remained under canvas and made no attempt to replace pickets or take control of other mines. If the troops were supposed to preserve law and order, there was no disorder to command their attention. The use of troops only strengthened the miners' solidarity and marshalled the entire community against the invasion.[26]

A remarkable order reigned in the south Cape Breton field. Some 200 miners and war veterans were sworn in as special town police by Mayor Morrison. Prohibition was never more strictly enforced: the "lid was on tight" as squads of union men raided illegal drinking spots and searched all incoming traffic, including the troop trains, for illicit "scabs and booze." On the road from Sydney the miners erected a barrier across the

---

25. *Montreal Star*, August 16, 1922.

26. Roy M. Wolvin to King, August 6, 1922, King to Wolvin, August 9, August 15, 1922, King Papers; D. W. Morrison to King, August 17, 1922, King Papers; similar protests came from the mayors of Sydney Mines and New Waterford also; "Memo of Communications Ottawa-Halifax (GOC, MD#6)," August, 1922, King Papers. On this and other episodes see Don Macgillivray "Military Aid to the Civil Power: The Cape Breton Experience in the 1920s," *Acadiensis*, III (1973–4), pp. 45–64.

highway, and all cars were stopped and searched before they were allowed to enter the strike zone. At the mines themselves access was controlled by shifts of union pickets, organized in semi-military picket companies with elected captains. As the strike progressed, the military discipline grew more overt, and a bugle would sound each morning in the streets of New Waterford to rouse the men for picket duty. Nor was all seriousness: on occasion bagpipes played in the street, and the miners took advantage of a rare summer vacation to visit the prolific blueberry barrens. Except for one short altercation between soldiers and pickets on the night of August 16, no clashes took place between the rival camps at Dominion No. 2; both sides hung over the fences and talked. Reporting the strike for a Halifax newspaper, Dalhousie philosophy professor H. L. Stewart was amazed that "the order preserved by a leaderless multitude has been so perfect. No looting, no drinking, no rioting!" But behind the orderliness he found a "distinctly fierce mood." "This is too quiet," worried another visitor, who sensed something "ominous" about the "deliberate, organized quality" of the strike discipline.[27]

On August 18 the only mass demonstration of the strike took place in the form of a silent semi-military parade of four or five thousand men through the streets of Glace Bay: "no chanting, no disorder, no impressive features apart from the impressiveness of a vast body of men moving methodically and purposefully through the streets of the town." After displaying their marching precision to the troops at No. 2, they completed manoeuvres at the ballgrounds with resolutions of protest against the presence of troops. Meanwhile a flood of other resolutions coursed into King's office in Ottawa. Among them, the Great War Veterans' Association in Glace Bay censured the Prime Minister for "helping Wolvin make a fortune out of starving miners and their families" and appealed for national support for the miners' "fight for a living wage, home and children against stocks, bonds and dividends."[28]

Though Wolvin and the local military authorities appealed for additional troops, naval forces and an air squadron, the federal government denied these requests. In Halifax, however, E. H. Armstrong, the Minister

---

27. *Halifax Herald*, August 21, September 2, 1922.
28. *Halifax Herald*, August 18, 1922: Harry Spracklin, Robert Ferguson, Great War Veteran's Association, Glace Bay to King, August 19, 1922, King Papers. The veterans called "the attention of the people of Canada to the stand Premier William Lyon Mackenzie King takes today on the side of tyranny against the people as compared with the courageous stand his grandfather William Lyon Mackenzie took in bygone days on behalf of the people against tyranny."

of Mines and Public Works, announced plans for a special 1,000-man provincial police force to wrest control of the mines from the union pickets. But this force was not used in 1922. The intervention of Premier George H. Murray resulted in the corporation's agreement to resume negotiations if the "100 per cent" aspect of the strike was ended, and the maintenance workers returned to the mines on the sixth and seventh days of the strike. Strike discipline continued until the miners ten days later endorsed a new agreement with the coal operators, 7,768 in favour, 2,920 against. Work resumed on September 5. The agreement did not restore the 1921 rates, but it did eliminate a large part of the original wage reduction, especially for the lower paid workers, and the long sixteen-month contract represented a substantial victory for the coal miners. Relying on the general support of the mining communities and on their own latent ability to control production by restricting output or by closing the mines, the coal miners had regularly refused to compromise their demand for a "living wage." Weakened by lack of support from the international union and disappointed by the wavering of a divided leadership at home, the rank and file of the miners themselves provided the main inspiration for the continuing resistance to the wage reduction in 1922. What the Halifax *Citizen* said of the "most unique strike in Canada's history" was true of the whole process of events leading up to the August strike: it was "a solid strike, with leaders ordered to take orders from the rank and file or get off the job."[29] Without this militant pressure from below, exerted on both the coal operators and the union leaders, the issue of the miners' wages would likely have been settled sooner and with poorer results for the coal miners.

The events of 1922 were primarily a campaign of resistance against the wage reduction, but the conflict was also a struggle over the future of the coal industry. The growth of the coal and steel industries in Nova Scotia was "a case of development from without," Harold Innis noted a few years later, and "resistance came, not from the industries as such, but from the workers to whom they gave employment." The miners' resistance to lower wages grew into a challenge to private ownership and control of the coal industry. By August 1922 Prof. Stewart could observe that the miners saw the coal mines as a "high public utility, not owned by any corporation, but owned by the province as a whole, and thus the intimate concern of every taxpayer"; they believed the corporation was betraying this public trust when it placed the good of Besco ahead of the

29. *The Citizen*, August 18, 1922.

miners' welfare. Wolvin's Besco was never a popular corporation. Attacks on Besco's absentee management and "autocratic methods" were mounted by the local Tory press, and this helped deepen the miners' distrust of the corporation. For instance, in January 1922 the *Sydney Post* complained: "Who ever heard of an efficient management being located 1,000 miles away from the actual base of operations? With such absentee management, even an intelligent discussion of reformed industrial relations is impossible." From the beginning Besco was frowned upon in Canada's best financial circles, and during the 1920s a concerted move was afoot to oust Wolvin from control of the coal and steel industries and install Royal Bank President Sir Herbert Holt in his place. The first open skirmish of this ultimately successful campaign came at Besco's annual board meeting in June 1922, where Wolvin repulsed the attempt by securing increased British backing and reorganizing the board of directors. But the months of visible crisis, manoeuvring and suspense highlighted Besco's instability and undermined Wolvin's authority.[30]

"Cost of production," the *Post* observed in February, "is the pinch of the whole dispute"; only through "co-operation, mutual trust and open dealing" could the miners ever be led to accept "costs of production" as a satisfactory reason for reducing wages. But the corporation stubbornly refused to discuss costs or profits. No presentation of the miners' views at this time was complete without reference to the substantial accumulated surpluses of the coal industry in the years since the war. And when Besco published its first annual report in May 1922, revealing earnings of more than $4.4 million in the last nine months of 1921, resentment grew. Distrust of the corporation's candour led to demands for seats on the Dominion Coal Company's board of directors, in harmony with an early Besco promise to put "Workers on the Directorate." When the conciliation board rejected the miners' arguments that wages should be the first charge on the industry's earnings, a spate of new proposals followed from the union locals, declaring that the only way to free the coal industry from "incompetent private management and overcapitalization" was to cancel Besco's coal leases and have the province run the mines "for the benefit of the people." In February the miners' convention unanimously adopted a demand that the province take over the mines and run them with the participation of the coal miners. In Halifax labour MLA Forman Waye

---

30. *Cambridge History of the British Empire* (Cambridge, 1930), VI, p. 665; *Halifax Herald*, August 21, 1922; *Sydney Post*, January 25, 1922.

tried to introduce a bill for nationalization of the coal industry should Besco continue to deny "a decent Canadian standard of living."[31]

The proposals circulating in the labour press and debated at union meetings were vaguer and less developed than those in parallel campaigns among British and American miners at this time, but they did reflect the same view that private ownership of the coal mines was wasteful to the country and harmful to the wellbeing of the coal miners. The proposals reflected a growing opinion that it was wrong to assume, as the *Maritime Labour Herald* put it, that "labour will go on labouring, and capital will go on capitalizing, and labour will be willing to go on short rations in order to allow capital to continue augmenting their revenues." By the time the second conciliation board met in May, many miners were inclined to agree with McLachlan when he declared: "the miners are going to get a living out of this industry and there will be no peace until they do..." A long time socialist, McLachlan argued that "if this system of production and distribution cannot give to the toilers human living conditions—then we are wasting our time discussing wages and hours of labour; we should be discussing the route to a new and better system." In June the miners' convention adopted a policy document which condemned "the pretty state existing among coal miners in Nova Scotia as a result of the efforts of 'captains of industry' to run the coal business." The miners' delegates then adopted a series of radical resolutions, including an appeal for allies in their campaign "to secure for our class...the working class of Canada, a living and free access to all means of life in this country." They concluded with the soon notorious declaration:

> That we proclaim openly to all the world that we are out for the complete overthrow of the capitalist system and capitalist state, peace-

---

31. *Sydney Post*, February 15, 1922; Fuel Supply Hearings, 490; *Labour Gazette*, February, 1922, p. 181; *Press Opinions of Empire Steel*, n.p. (Besco) 1920, p. 7; *Maritime Labour Herald*, January 21, January 28, 1922; *Labour Gazette*, March, 1922, pp. 308–309. In 1925 the Trades and Labour Congress of Canada endorsed nationalization of the coal mines in Canada. In parallel agitations British miners sought implementation of a 1919 royal commission report recommending nationalization. In 1919 the UMWA called for nationalization of the coal mines in the U.S. and Canada; in 1921–1922 the union's Nationalization Research Committee prepared and published a practical proposal for the takeover of the American coal industry. For an important discussion of the growth of "direct action" and "workers' control" struggles among the American working class in this period, see David Montgomery, "The 'New Unionism' and the Transformation of Workers' Consciousness in America, 1909–1922," *Journal of Social History*, VII, (Summer, 1974), pp. 509–535.

ably if we may, forcibly, if we must, and we call on all workers, soldiers and minor law officers to join us in liberating labour.

Bold in its language, the declaration was far from an irrational or gratuitous outcry, for it was firmly rooted in the miners' search for ways to replace private control of the coal industry with social control.[32]

By 1922 the appeal of radical ideas among the coal miners was twofold. Partly it was a tactical appeal: the threat that dire consequences like "Bolshevism" would follow if the miners' just demands were not met. As one local resolution protested early in the year, "Bolshevism is the effect of oppression and tyranny on the part of those in control. . . . Bolshevism finds no soil to grow in a community of working people who have employment at an adequate wage." And partly the appeal was a strategic one: the feeling that if society could not provide men with a "living wage," then it deserved to be rebuilt more soundly. Under the impact of economic and social crisis in the coalfields after the First World War, hopes for social transformation continued to grow and acquire new meaning among the coal miners. As "oppression and tyranny" continued to deprive the miners of a "living wage," the radicalism of the coal miners became less a symbol of protest and more a conscious policy. In the wake of the radical declarations of the June convention, the coal miners showed they were willing to support radical policies and leaders. At the convention the union's divided executive resigned, and the new election in August brought a decisive victory for the "radical" candidates. For the post of secretary-treasurer the miners re-elected McLachlan by a vote of 6,192 to 2,250, and for the presidency they chose a McLachlan ally, Dan Livingstone, over Baxter by a vote of 7,170 to 1,695. The election of the "red executive" marked a clear "left turn" in the miners' affairs. On May 1, 1923, some 5,000 coal miners, headed by their union officers, marched through the streets of Glace Bay behind the "biggest red flag in Canada"

---

32. *Maritime Labour Herald*, April 1, 1922; *Sydney Record*, May 9, 1922; *The Worker*, June 15, 1922; *Maritime Labour Herald*, July 1, 1922. The encounter of "radicalism" and "revolutionism" in the coalfields in the 1920s was partly the meeting of the coal miners and the newly-formed Workers' Party of Canada. Spokesmen for the WPC visited the district in May and June 1922, and by early 1923 McLachlan and other prominent radicals had joined the WPC. But the militancy of the coal miners in 1922 cannot be attributed to the work of outside agitators. The radical declarations of June 1922, especially the decision to apply for membership in the Red International of Labour Unions, show some WPC influence, but they mainly represented the working out of an indigenous working class tradition, with deep roots in the British experience. For instance the very phrase "peaceably if we may, forcibly, if we must" came from the Chartists.

emblazoned with the words "Long live Communism." And in the summer of 1923 the coal miners risked their hard-won contract to mount a sympathetic strike to support the Sydney steelworkers and protest the renewed use of troops in industrial Cape Breton. In 1922 the coal miners' campaign was "a fight of patriotic, loyal citizens against industrial tyranny," their goal was an ill-defined "industrial democracy," and one of their rallying cries was "Rule Britannia, Britons never shall be slaves!" But the process of radicalization which had begun was no less authentic for that.[33]

Unlike other factors of production, labour power is not easily regulated by the laws of the marketplace. "Labor, in spite of sentimental objections, is undoubtedly a commodity which is bought and sold," explained University of New Brunswick political economist John Davidson in 1898, "...but it is not therefore true that labor is a commodity resembling in all essential respects every other commodity in the market. Labor differs from most, if not all, other commodities in retaining, even under modern industrial conditions, its subjective value to the seller. We cannot separate the labor and the laborer." As E. P. Thompson has pointed out, coal miners have had particular trouble in "comprehending the simplest of propositions as to the market regulation of wages, and they have always clung tenaciously to unscientific notions such as 'justice' and 'fair play.'" Caught in a crisis of markets and a crisis of corporate welfare, the owners of the coal industry in Cape Breton attempted to ensure the survival of Besco at the expense of the coal miners, and repeatedly attempted to reduce the miners' wages. When the first of these assaults came in 1922, the coal miners defied the economic orthodoxy that when prices fell wages should fall in step. Instead they asserted a new regulatory principle:

> The miners' wages and working conditions have been determined largely by the kind of organization the miners had and whether the tactics applied by that organization were those taught the miners by the coal operators and businessmen or were developed by themselves from their own economic necessities and surroundings.

In applying this guideline and organizing their resistance to the wage reduction in 1922, the miners expressed the cohesion of life in the coal mining communities and the strength of working class solidarity among the coal miners. United against an outside corporation and its allies, the

---

33. *Industrial Canada*, March, 1922, p. 71; *The Worker*, May 16, 1923; *Maritime Labour Herald*, March 18, June 17, 1922; *Halifax Herald*, April 1, 1922.

working class found their most effective tactics in the assertion of a latent workers' control over the production process, earning key victories through the strike on the job and the "100 per cent" strike. Agreeing that the coal industry was in poor health, the miners also launched a search for solutions which would promote the prosperity of both the coal industry and the coal miners at the same time. This led them to challenge private control of the coal industry, to propose nationalization and democratic control as the alternative, and to question the capitalist system in general.[34]

What would be the miners' next step? After 1922 it remained to be seen whether the coal miners would again be able to resist renewed corporate assaults on their wage levels in 1924 and 1925. And to what extent would the miners continue to follow the "left turn" they began in 1922? Would the miners complete the transition from their spontaneous radicalism to the establishment of an effective form of radical trade unionism in the coalfields? And to what extent would the government, the corporation and the international union, all alarmed by the events of 1922, allow the attempt to take place?

Ultimately there were no victors in the dramatic and tragic events of the 1920s in Cape Breton. In 1923 the coal miners' union was seriously weakened by the intervention of the international union, the suspension of district autonomy, and the removal of the district's strongest leaders; after the long and traumatic strike of 1925 the union remained largely ineffective until the 1940s. In 1926 the flimsy structure of the British Empire Steel Corporation began finally to collapse; Wolvin was ousted in 1928 and a new coal and steel corporation replaced Besco. The coal industry, propped up by growing government aid after 1927, continued its long decline. The 1920s brought lasting victories for neither the coal industry, the corporation, nor the coal miners. But, as E. P. Thompson writes, it is never safe to assume that any of our history is altogether dead. It tends to accumulate as a form of "stored cultural energy," and from time to time moments of cultural transmission and illumination take place.[35] As the history of the coal miners' revolt against industrial capitalism in Canada is written, we shall find much to learn.

---

34. Davidson, p. 156; E. P. Thompson, "A Special Case," *New Society*, February 24, 1973, pp. 402–403; *Maritime Labour Herald*, February 18, 1922.
35. Thompson, "A Special Case," p. 404.

FURTHER READINGS FOR TOPIC 5

T. W. Acheson, "The Maritimes and 'Empire Canada,' " in David J. Bercuson, ed., *Canada and the Burden of Unity* (Toronto: Macmillan, 1977).

P. A. Buckner and David Frank, eds., *Atlantic Canada After Confederation: The Acadiensis Reader*, Vol. II (Fredericton: Acadiensis Press, 1985).

Gary Burrill and Ian McKay, *People, Resources, and Power: Critical Perspectives on Underdevelopment and Resource Industries in the Atlantic Region* (Fredericton: Gorsebrook Research Institute and Acadiensis Press, 1987).

E. R. Forbes, *Challenging the Regional Stereotype* (Fredericton: Acadiensis Press, 1989).

E. R. Forbes, *Maritime Rights: The Maritime Rights Movement, 1919–1927: A Study in Canadian Regionalism* (Montreal: McGill-Queen's University Press, 1979).

E. R. Forbes and Del Muise, eds., *The Maritimes in Confederation* (Toronto: University of Toronto Press, forthcoming).

David Frank, "The Cape Breton Coal Industry and the Rise and Fall of the British Empire Steel Corporation," *Acadiensis*, 7, 1 (Autumn 1977), 3–34.

Peter Neary, *Newfoundland in the North Atlantic World, 1929–1949* (Kingston and Montreal: McGill-Queen's University Press, 1988).

TOPIC 6

The
Politics
of
Reproduction

*F*ewer *modern questions raise deeper controversies than the shifting
terrain of human reproduction. Who has the primary responsibility for
raising children? What rules should govern sexual relations? What should
sexuality mean? How should children be raised? Issues of sexuality and
reproduction are never just "biological"; they are constructed within
cultural frameworks, and these in turn interact with the changing
structures of social and economic life. Although there has probably never
been a consensus in Canada about the politics of reproduction, throughout
much of the nineteenth century, respectable common sense and morality
held that sexuality should be confined to marriage and aimed principally at
reproduction. A deeply entrenched double standard gave men much greater
sexual freedom than women, and placed women at risk of sexual assault.
Even as society became more secular, this "reproductive matrix" of values,
laws, and traditions held firm.*

*Modernity changed this pattern, in ways we are only beginning to
understand. As Andrée Lévesque's moving description of the single mothers
of Montreal reveals, women who defied the reproductive matrix in interwar
Quebec were shamed as deviants; facing social disgrace of such power,
many women continued to turn to infanticide, abortifacients (the wide
array of folk and commercial remedies, many of them advertised in the
public press, for procuring abortions), and the backstreet abortionist. As
Angus McLaren notes in the second reading, however, a secular movement,
seemingly more based upon "science," and intent upon reforming the
politics of reproduction through the state, was redrawing the lines
separating the "private" and the "public." Finally, the writings of*

Mrs. Donald Shaw of Halifax document the arguments of a sexual traditionalist. They suggest both the vigour with which such views were held, and their new vulnerability, under modernity, to debate, criticism, and eventual marginalization.

DEVIANT ANONYMOUS:

Single Mothers at the Hôpital de la Miséricorde in Montreal, 1929-1939

ANDRÉE LÉVESQUE

Historians and sociologists have stressed the prominence of the Catholic patriarchal family in Quebec society, women's role within that institution and the paramount importance of motherhood within marriage. Few scholars have so far studied the experience of women who did not fit the conventional model of married mothers at home. Childbearing was particularly honoured in Catholic society; yet women who were reproductive outside the bounds of marriage had no visible place in Quebec. The *revanche des berceaux* [the "revenge of the cradles"—the idea that French Canadians would, through their high birth rates, avenge the Conquest] so valued by the church and by Catholic nationalists, was to take place within the family. Illegitimacy* violated the moral and cultural ideal of the family defined by church and society. Consequently women who transgressed societal and familial norms disrupted the stability of the family and brought shame upon themselves, their immediate family and their kinship network. This shame had to be hidden, and single pregnant women who could not go to private maternity homes or be sent to distant friends or relatives concealed their condition amongst other women, nuns, who had themselves renounced family life, sexuality and motherhood for the higher calling of religious life. The hospitals provided by the nuns give us a microcosm of the world of the single mother: the conduct of

ANDRÉE LÉVESQUE, "DEVIANT ANONYMOUS: SINGLE MOTHERS AT THE HÔPITAL DE LA MISÉRICORDE IN MONTREAL, 1929-1939," *HISTORICAL PAPERS/COMMUNICATIONS HISTORIQUES* (CANADIAN HISTORICAL ASSOCIATION), 1984, 168-83. ALSO IN KATHERINE ARNUP, ANDRÉE LÉVESQUE, AND RUTH ROACH PIERSON, *DELIVERING MOTHERHOOD* (LONDON AND NEW YORK: ROUTLEDGE, 1990). BY PERMISSION OF AUTHOR AND PUBLISHER.

I WOULD LIKE TO THANK BETTINA BRADBURY, BARBARA BROOKS, GEOFFREY EWEN, PAUL LACHANCE, JANE LEWIS, AND SUSAN MANN TROFIMENKOFF FOR THEIR HELPFUL COMMENTS AND SUGGESTIONS. I, OF COURSE, CLAIM FULL RESPONSIBILITY FOR ERRORS OF FACTS OR INTERPRETATIONS. I AM ALSO VERY GRATEFUL TO ODETTE VINCENT DOWNEY AND JACQUES DOWNEY FOR THEIR INVALUABLE HELP IN UNRAVELLING THE INTRICACIES OF WORD PROCESSING. I AM FOREVER IN DEBT TO NICOLE LAFERTE FOR HAVING GRANTED ME ACCESS TO THE ARCHIVES OF THE HÔPITAL DE LA MISÉRICORDE AND WITHOUT WHOSE HELP THIS STUDY WOULD NOT HAVE BEEN POSSIBLE.

* Throughout this article I have used the expression "illegitimate" to refer to births to single mothers. I understand that this term is obsolete and even insulting, but for the sake of convenience I have used it in its historical context.

the pregnancy, the conditions of stay, the submission and rebellion of the women and the contradictory demands of society regarding her child.

Each year, from 1929 to 1939, there were between 2,335 (1934) to 2,668 (1939) children born out of wedlock in Quebec.[1] Roughly 20 percent of these (an annual average of 560), were born at the Hôpital de la Miséricorde in Montreal.[2] There are no statistics for pregnancies out-of-wedlock but they were surely more numerous given the number of miscarriages and abortions. The reported illegitimacy rate in Quebec was slightly lower than the national average by .3 to .7 percent. According to federal statistics, from 2.9 to 3.4 percent of total live births were to single mothers in Quebec.[3]

The Hôpital de la Miséricorde had been performing a service to single mothers and illegitimate children since the mid-19th century. In 1840, Mgr. Bourget asked widow Rosalie Jetté, née Cadron, to take a young single pregnant woman into her home. This request was followed by others until he asked her to leave her own children, rent a house and manage it as a home for unmarried pregnant women. This was the beginning of the Refuge Ste-Pélagie in 1845. Three years later, Rosalie Cadron Jetté and seven other women founded the Congregation of the Sisters of Misericordia to look after women who "needed to hide."[4] The babies were then looked after by the Grey Nuns. This arrangement lasted until 1889 when the Sisters of Misericordia set up their own crèches. By 1920 the hospital had a school of nursing and was used by the students of the school of medicine at the University of Montreal for their training in obstetrics.[5]

As long as some women had to conceal their pregnancies, the hospital fulfilled a genuine need. Single pregnant women's imperative to hide their

1. Province de Québec, *Rapport annuel du ministère de la Santé et du Bien-être social pour les années 1935 à 1941* (Québec, 1944), p. 204.
2. Compiled from the registers of the Hôpital de la Miséricorde, in Archives de l'Hôpital de la Miséricorde, Montreal (hereafter AHM).
3. *Recensement du Canada*, 1931, Vol. XII; M. E. Fleming and M. MacGillivray, *Fécondité de la femme canadienne* (Ottawa, 1936), p. 262.
4. Sr. Saint-Jean-Vianney, s.m., M.S.S., "Un peu d'histoire," paper presented at the Journée d'étude tenue à l'occasion du 10e anniversaire de l'incorporation du service social de la Miséricorde, le 17 novembre, 1955, pp. 4–5.
5. *L'Union médicale*, Vol. LXI (1932), pp. 179–80. In Quebec City, the Hôpital de la Miséricorde, under the direction of the Soeurs du Bon Pasteur, performed the same function as its homologue in Montreal and recorded an average of 457 deliveries a year between 1929 and 1933; see Albert Jobin, "Hôpitaux de la Miséricorde et de la Crèche St-Vincent-de-Paul," *Bulletin de la Société Médicale des Hôpitaux Universitaires de Québec* (1934), p. 304.

condition highlighted society's orthodox view of the role of women, a role they had failed to follow. In the interwar period the clergy, the politicians and the doctors all entertained a rigidly polarised view of lay women: they were either mothers-at-home, or their antithesis, prostitutes.[6] The woman who found herself a prospective mother, after exercising her sexuality outside the bounds of matrimony, literally had no place in this dichotomised representation. She was an outcast from the time her condition was obvious; her chance of regaining a place in her milieu was linked to the success with which her fault could be concealed from those around her.

The woman who registered at the Dorchester Street hospital was usually French Canadian and Catholic; only exceptionally was an Italian, an Irish or a Lithuanian woman admitted. A close female relative, her mother, aunt or cousin, was likely to accompany her to the admission. Often an orphan, since 27.7 percent of single mothers had lost their own mothers and 25.8 percent their fathers,[7] she was usually a young domestic servant. Statistics show that 60 percent of the women were between 18 and 22. Before their admission, 47 percent were domestic servants and 31 percent lived with their family. Only 5.7 percent worked in factories or in offices. Occasionally a schoolgirl, a nurse or a school teacher sought admission.[8]

The occupations entered in the register may give us a false impression regarding the number of domestic servants: the women may have come to Montreal to work as servants once they became pregnant, or they may already have been domestics when they became pregnant. Similar problems concern the place of residence: of all the women who gave Montreal as their last address, some had only been there a short time. The medical records contain information concerning the patients' health. The figure

---

6. For the medical discourse and prescriptions on women, see A. Lévesque, "Mères ou malades," *RHAF*, Vol. 38 (été, 1984), pp. 23–37.
7. Statistics compiled from AHM register, 1929–39.
8. Ibid. Given the small percentage of women who entered La Miséricorde, it does not seem that illegitimacy was linked to industrial work. It is not the purpose of this article to add one more footnote to the modernization debate. E. Shorter's hypothesis has been answered by J. Scott and L. Tilly, and J. Gillis has analyzed the pregnancy of servants in London. A study of the social origins of the patients at La Miséricorde as well as the father of their children will be the subject of another article. E. Shorter, "Illegitimacy, Sexual Revolution, and Social Change in Modern Europe," *AHA*, 1970, in *The Family in History*, eds. T. K. Rabb and R. I. Rotberg (New York, 1971), pp. 48–84; J. W. Scott and L. Tilly, "Women's Work and the Family in Nineteenth Century Europe," *Comparative Studies in Society and History*, Vol. XVII (1975), pp. 36–64; J. Gillis, "Servants, Sexual Relations and the Risks of Illegitimacy in London. 1908–1900," *Feminist Studies*, Vol. 5 (Spring, 1979), pp. 142–73.

for weight is meaningless because it was taken when the women were pregnant and we are not given their usual weight. A large number had bad teeth that necessitated extraction in the hospital. During the whole decade, an average of 30 percent had gonorrhea and 3.7 percent a positive Wasserman test indicating syphilis. For 16 percent of the women this was not their first pregnancy.[9] Undoubtedly, the stay at the hospital gave many inmates an opportunity of obtaining a diagnosis and some treatment.

During the period of isolation at Miséricorde, a period which could last as long as a year, the new boarder was to assume a new identity. The first step, upon registration, was to receive an "imposed name" from an existing bank of names.[10] The names were not ordinary ones but highly unusual and sometimes conveyed a meaning, such as Humiliane or Fructueuse! The names were assigned in alphabetical order and when the list was exhausted, after many months, the process started over again. Along with her new name, the boarder acquired, at the cost of $2, a uniform. In exceptional cases, some paying boarders occupying a private room would be veiled for the length of their stay to ensure greater secrecy. From the moment of registration until her departure, the *repentante*, or penitent, as she was to be known, was shut off from the world and could trust that the nuns would ensure complete discretion. Except during Lent or Advent, she could receive visitors at the parlour once a week, but those visitors had to be close relatives who were given a card with the "imposed name" of the boarder on it. Without this card no visit was permitted, as in the case of one out-of-town mother who could ill-afford the transportation costs and had left her card at home.[11] Discretion was assured even in the case of a mother enquiring whether her thirty-four-year old daughter was a patient. Sister Tharcisius, in charge of the women, answered: "If the young girl was always good, why fear or doubt?"[12]

The anonymity extended to the child from the moment of her/his birth. It seems that the mother had little say in the name given her child. The

---

9. Ibid. While no conclusion regarding the health of the mother can be drawn from her weight statistics, neither can any be drawn from the infant weight since it was seldom recorded. Lack of adequate data prevents us from making a comparison with Patricia Ward and Peter Ward's findings in "Infant Birth Weight and Nutrition in Industrializing Montreal," *American Historical Review* 89, 2 (April 1984), 324–45.

10. AHM. Here are just a few of these unusual names: Héraïs, Calithène, Potamie, Rogata, Macédonie, Gemelle, Nymphodore, Extasie, or Symphorose.

11. Information taken from the correspondence found in a patient's files will be identified by the date or the registration number.

12. AHM, 1932.

surname was the same for all babies born each month; it might be that of a nurse or an intern on duty. As for the first names, they were attributed in alphabetical order. To a mother who asked for a note in order to see her child in the crèche in Trois-Rivières and who inquired about the god-parents' names, Sister Tharcisius wrote that their names were not required; "Anyway, they are pure strangers, a nurse and one of our interns."[13]

La Miséricorde was a peculiar institution in that boarders usually entered voluntarily—if we ignore social pressures for the moment—but once inside they lived in a state of sequestration. They were not free to leave at will and they were subject to strict discipline. A short, one-page prospectus described the terms of admission, the cost for single or double rooms or wards ($90, $60 or $8 a month) and $155, $130 or $120 for adoption fees and the cost of the delivery.[14] The new boarder was told that she would have to spend six months of service at the hospital after the birth of the child and after her two-week period of recuperation. Only thus could she refund the costs of delivery and treatment and the adoption fees. Any time spent working at the hospital before the delivery could be deducted from the six months term of service. Death of the child at birth or later did not change the conditions of admission; indeed a sepulchre charge of $25 was added to the amount owing.[15] Even though the terms were explained at admission, the length of time to be served surprised many, particularly if the baby died.

Although 47 percent of the women were under the age of 21, all boarders whatever their age were considered minors. Visits were con-trolled and mail was censured. Letters could be written only on Sunday and not during Lent or Advent. If a patient tried to escape she was brought back by a detective. In fact, the status of pregnant single women was similar not only to that of children but also to that of criminals: the father of the child was referred to as "the accomplice" by the nuns.[16] Deemed to have committed an offence, some of the women were themselves the victims of crime. In about 3 percent of the cases when the young woman was under sixteen, "and of previously chaste character," according to section 301 of the Criminal Code, the baby's father was guilty of seduction and subject to five years imprisonment. If the woman was 16 or 17 years

---

13. AHM, Sr. Tharcisius to A., 12637.
14. AHM. *Prospectus*, Hôpital Catholique de la Maternité de Montréal, sous la direction des Soeurs de la Miséricorde.
15. AHM, Sr. Tharcisius, 30 September 1935; 21 October 1935; 7 November 1935.
16. AHM, 32653, 32771.

old, as 11 percent were, "and of previously chaste character," he could receive a maximum of two years in prison. If the man were over 21 and the woman under 21 and he promised to marry her, he was nonetheless guilty of seduction punishable by one year in prison under Section 210 of the Criminal Code.[17] Very few of the cases of seduction which were brought to court each year resulted in a conviction.[18] It was also a crime to seduce a feeble-minded woman or an employee but one can only guess at the number of single mothers who were victims of these crimes or of incest.

Whatever the circumstances surrounding the pregnancy of the single woman, great care was taken to preserve the outside world from her presence. Some patients' mothers begged the hospital to let their daughters go before their six months were up because people would start talking if their daughters were missing for too long. In another case, the mother argued that if the father came down from the shanties and realised that his daughter had been gone for so long he might guess the cause of her absence.[19] Younger siblings had to be protected from the truth since their sister was an object of scandal.[20] A father wrote that he could not telephone the hospital and did not want the nuns to contact him to announce the birth of his grandchild since people listened on the party line he shared with twenty families. He also requested that letters not bear the hospital's return address as the staff at the post office would then "find out."[21] One patient is known to have left the hospital immediately when she recognised a new boarder.[22]

While the world was protected from her presence, the single mother went through a state of infantilism or "minorisation." Depending on her behaviour she could earn good marks which could shorten her stay by as much as two weeks, or bad marks, which had the opposite effect. Attempts to smuggle letters out of the hospital resulted in bad grades.[23] One patient was kept an extra month for having hit a child and having kept a pacifier for her own child.[24] The parents of another inmate came

---

17. Canada, Public Archives, MG30 E256, Vol. 20, John Kerrey, "The Legal Status of the Unmarried Mother and Her Child in the Province of Quebec," 1926.
18. Montréal, Archives judiciaires, Cour des Sessions, Cour du Banc du Roi, 1929–39.
19. AHM, Sr. Tharcisius refused the request. 24 July 1937.
20. AHM, 1933.
21. 20 June 1936. A mother also wrote, "nous avons des parents de prêtre, des cousines religieuses dans plusieurs communautés à Montréal aussi ne donnez de réponse à personne, ni prêtre, ni religieuse." 2 March 1933.
22. AHM, 35181, 10 May 1937.
23. When caught, a patient had to serve an extra month; altogether she worked seven months after her delivery: 34502, 30 March 1936.
24. AHM, 32542, 1933.

from out-of-town only to find that their daughter was being kept an extra fortnight.[25] Marks were earned by giving a blood transfusion to one's own child, or by breastfeeding several babies.[26] Good behaviour was also rewarded with responsibilities such as supervising a ward. Such activity could in turn be transformed into good points toward an early release.

The image of the single mother justified this treatment. She was considered weak and ignorant, strong-minded and wicked, or simple-minded. Perhaps because mentally handicapped women were more vulnerable to abuse, single mothers were often believed to be of inferior intelligence. A doctor writing in a Quebec medical journal in 1932 stated that "natural [i.e. illegitimate] children seem particularly exposed to madness....It is probable, in fact, that the parents of a natural child are often abnormal."[27] In the register, one finds such comments as "stupid" or "idiot" written in by the nuns. The nuns may have been exaggerating at times but one cannot rule out passive resistance from the women who wanted to be expelled before their term was up or, if brought in forcibly by their parents, before their delivery.

Even if it was recognized that many of the women had been abused, sometimes by a relative—while recommending a patient, the parish priest would occasionally make a point of writing that she came from a very poor but good family and had been taken advantage of—most were deemed to have fallen and hence needed to repent. This feeling was sometimes shared by the inmates' mothers. One wrote that she hoped that her daughter's stay of one year and three months would be a good lesson for her.[28] In a few cases, the parents or the parish priest requested that a young woman be kept after her six months until the age of 21, or even later, working in return for room and board as well as protection from the outside world and her own weakness.[29] These cases were referred to the Sisters du Bon Pasteur d'Angers who had a home for young delinquent women. Some of them were taken there most reluctantly.[30]

---

25. As a mother from St.-Hyacinthe put it, "je ne voudrait pas voyager pour rien le temps est trop dur." [sic] AHM, 32000, 1933.
26. The blood transfusion was assessed at $20 or one month of service; AHM, 32537.
27. C. A. Décary, "Maladies mentales," *Annales Médico-chirurgicales de l'Hôpital Ste-Justine*, Vol. 1 (mai 1932), p. 126.
28. AHM, 1939.
29. A curé wrote Sr. Tharcisius, "que je serais content pour les parents et leur fille Y., si vous pouviez décider cette dernière à demeurer chez-vous comme une autre des soeurs, parmi les filles repentantes. Là seul elle serait sauvegardée contre de nouveaux malheurs qui la guettent chez elle, j'en ai la ferme conviction." 17 October 1933, 32760. Similar requests from the patients' mothers are in 32357, 17 October 1933, and 32578, 19 November 1933.
30. AHM, 32509, May 1937; a 17 year old "fait une scène pour ne pas rester, prétend être amenée de force."

The women were confined not only to avoid causing scandal but also to reform. Attendance at chapel was required three times a day. The whole atmosphere was designed to induce humility, repentance and penance. Sr. Tharcisius, for instance, wrote to a woman coming back for the second time: "Poor lamb wounded on the thorns along the path, you will have no reproach if you show yourself to be repentant, submissive and humble."[31]

The work the single mothers performed at La Miséricorde was both a means of atonement for sin and an economic necessity. The avowed purpose of the six months of service was to refund the cost of the delivery and medicine and to pay for the child who was *abandonné*. If the baby was placed and adopted, the service was reduced to three months. If the baby died, six months work remained owing to pay for the cost of sepulchre. If the child was kept in the crèche, the daily board was $1. The work was assessed at $20 a month, but days of sickness were not counted.[32] Clearly it was not simply economic considerations that dictated the length of service; the good or bad marks also affected the time spent in the institution. . . .A letter from the parish priest, if it could be obtained, proved the surest way of getting an early dismissal. Women who had nowhere to go went on serving the nuns for many months, sometimes years, in return for room and board. They thus had the spiritual and material benefits of living in a religious community without being committed to vows.

There were other instances, however, when women had to work against their will to pay off a nonexistent debt. Someone who cared for the patient, in some cases a priest, or another nun from her home town, sent money but asked that the inmate not be told "so that she can prolong her time for a complete recovery if possible."[33] Recovery here seems to mean moral recovery. When the father of an eighteen-year-old patient successfully sued the baby's father, the hospital got $300 but the family was not refunded the account of $126.50 for the woman's board before delivery, $50 for abandoning the child, and $44 for doctor's fees and treatment.[34]

Whether for penance or to refund a debt, service in the hospital consisted of general housework, such as washing furniture; kitchen work,

---

31. AHM, Sr. Tharcisius, 10 August 1938.
32. AHM, Sr. Tharcisius, 30 September 1935, 21 October 1935, 15 October 1937.
33. AHM, 3 November 1937. Even women over the age of 21 were sometimes kept against their will. To a hotel keeper who had brought his 27 year-old employee, an orphan, to the hospital Sr. Tharcisius wrote, "she wants to leave the hospital at all costs. . .she believes she is in prison. . . .If we keep her here it is only in answer to your desire which you have expressed so clearly already." 12 April 1932, 31557.
34. AHM, 32460 and 35175, May 1937 who had an account of $97.

like peeling potatoes; laundry work, diapers being the most arduous; and work in the nursery or the crèche: feeding, supervising and changing the babies or children. One mother breastfed three or four babies and exhausted herself to the point of anemia and then was discharged because she was incapable of doing her work. A few days before delivering, a boarder wrote: "I spend all day ironing."[35] The doctor asked that an inmate who had developed a skin irritation washing furniture should stop work for forty days. She was then given damp clothes to fold and the doctor told her to stop if she felt weak and to take her tonic three times a day.[36] It is difficult to argue that this kind of work was solely for moral reform when women in private rooms were exempt from all work before their delivery (nor did they work afterwards since they paid the fees) except for "des ouvrages de fantaisie pour elles-mêmes, des lectures...."[37] And yet, one Protestant woman was discharged after three months of service because "puisque protestante ne peut tirer aucun profit spirituel."[38]

The penitents were also the objects of rescue work. The most devout could join the Madelon, named after St. Mary Magdelen, and become Oblates. The condition of admission, according to Sr. Tharcisius, was good health and good will. After spending a few months as a Daughter of St. Marguerite, the candidate was issued a uniform and given a new name; she then entered the order on 22 July, feast day of St. Mary Magdelen. The Oblates did not have the strict discipline of the ordained nuns: they did not have to fast, but they could not go out and had parlour only once a month. They worked for the nuns, the stronger ones in the kitchen, the others sewing or performing housework.[39] Thus they would atone for their sins for the rest of their life. At least one mother wrote advising her daughter to expiate her fault by renouncing her life and entering the order.[40]

A very small number entered the Madelon. Those who did not hear a religious calling had to deal with the immediate responsibility for their

---

35. AHM, 32662, 1932. In 1938, a twenty-year-old anglophone of Lithuanian origin was "acquitted" after four months as a wetnurse. In a note to Sr. Tharcisius, she wrote, "my mother thinks I only do 6 babies, she doesn't know I have been doing 13 babies for 3 months, washing them, feeding them and scrubbing." How many was she breastfeeding? 35436, 1938.
36. AHM, 1932.
37. AHM, Sr. Tharcisius to the curé of Ste-Justine-de-Dorchester, 18 April 1939.
38. AHM, 33660, 2 October 1935.
39. AHM, St. Tharcisius to E.P., 15 July 1937.
40. AHM, 2 March 1933.

offspring. Single mothers were generally encouraged to keep their child. Already in 1915, the Women's Directory of Montreal, engaged in reform work for single mothers, aimed at keeping mother and child together to encourage breastfeeding, partly in order to cut down on infant mortality.[41] In 1931, the feminist Idola Saint-Jean recommended to the Royal Commission on Social Services (the Montpetit Commission), that the single mother keep her child "as a safeguard for her." She also argued that it would not only be beneficial for the mother but would also allow children to enjoy the warmth and maternal care that no institution could provide.[42] While the experts recommended that mothers keep their child either for their own or for the child's welfare, only 14.6 percent of patients actually did leave the hospital with their child. Legally, the so-called illegitimate child was the mother's responsibility; it was a crime for her to neglect or abandon her offspring. She was bound to support it, though the law allowed her to avail herself of adoption.[43]

By leaving her child at La Miséricorde a mother indicated that she wished it to be adopted. The mother would pay a lump sum of at least $50 for the unkeep of the child at the crèche until adopted. If, instead of leaving the child to be adopted, she could afford the daily fee of $1, she could keep her child at the crèche and retain visiting rights on the first Thursday of the month.[44] A number of women intended to look after their child when their financial situation improved or if they married. They would send money for months, sometimes years, although they usually stopped gradually when personal circumstances changed. In some cases, the child was indeed claimed after the mother married. In other cases, the babies left the hospital with their grandmother, but a large number were destined to spend their childhood in institutions.

The nuns exercised great powers over the relations between the mother and her child. The hospital's desire to avoid a new infant charge led the nun to trace a patient who had deserted, placing the baby in her arms and sending both on their way after extracting a promise from the mother to send the payments.[45] Another woman came back to get her child, but she was refused on the advice of a priest and the Children's Aid Bureau.[46]

---

41. *First Annual Report of the Women's Directory of Montreal* (Montreal, 1915).
42. *La Presse*, 13 January 1931.
43. Kerry, pp. 9–10.
44. Parlour on a week day was very inconvenient for working mothers, especially if they lived out of town. AHM, 4 July 1940.
45. AHM, 30590, 4 October 1930. Also 33919, 2 September 1935.
46. AHM, 33296, July 1934.

Mothers who left their children at the crèche often wrote to inquire about their health and wellbeing: "Let her take fresh air outside. I would so much like her to enjoy good health."[47] Many sent money for photographs to be taken and one mother, noticing that her child had bandy legs, sent money for a pair of boots.[48] Even three years after she had left the hospital, one mother was encouraged to come and pick up her child. An anglophone patient wrote: "If your answer to me would be that my baby had died and God had taken him to Heaven, I would be so much happier. I am so lonesome for him."[49]

For over a third of the mothers, long-term responsibilities for the care of their child did not pose a problem since it died during its first year. At the beginning of the decade, Montreal had the unfortunate reputation of having one of the highest infant mortality rates in Canada if not in the western world: it fell from 12.5 percent in 1931 to 7.2 percent in 1938.[50] At La Miséricorde, 37.7 percent of the infants born between 1929 and 1939 died in their first year, mostly from preventable diseases such as gastroenteritis or pulmonary infections.[51] For the sisters and some mothers, the death of a child was almost a cause for rejoicing since the infant would be spared a life of misery. To a mother who wrote that she could not forget her child and wanted to know its complete name, Sr. Tharcisius answered, "Our good Mother in Heaven has taken care herself of little Adrien. She came and got him last May. It is a little Angel who is up there watching over his maman." This was written in November, six months after Adrien's death.[52] In the same vein, the sister wrote to a grandfather: "Dear Sir: We regret to say that the baby born to E.C. is dead. Thank God for this great favour."[53]

To concerned mothers, the sisters gave news regarding the child's weight and behaviour. Sometimes this information appears to have

---

47. AHM, 1935.
48. AHM, 1937.
49. AHM, 27 June 1940 when the child was one year old.
50. Province de Québec. Ministère des Affaires Municipales, de l'Industrie et du Commerce. *Annuaire Statistique du Québec,* 1930–40 (Québec: Imprimeur de Sa Majesté le Roi, 1931–1941.)
51. Statistics compiled from AHM, the registry, 1929–39.
52. AHM, 27 November 1939.
53. AHM, 1934. A 19 year-old who left the hospital just two weeks after her child's birth, wrote Sr. Tharcisius, "Si le bon Dieu venait la chercher pour faire un petit ange au ciel à que je serais heureuse car qui dit plus tard qu'elle n'aura pas de misère, je sais qu'elle me maudira peut-être un jour, mais il me faut subir mon sort que j'ai voulue [sic]." She need not have feared being damned one day, as the baby died at nineteen days. 35065.

referred to the wrong child. One mother asked whether her child was dead so that she could stop worrying. In April, she was informed that "elle va bien et est toujours gracieuse"; shortly after this, she was notified that the child had died the previous December.[54]

While Sr. Tharcisius personally encouraged mothers to keep their child, most of them could not do so and a large number left the hospital to take up a position as a domestic. It was a special favour to be chosen by a doctor to serve his family.[55] Many left for another city, as far away as Ottawa, to make a new start and forget their past. Others tried to save money in order to claim their child one day and kept in touch even when they had signed the "abandonment" form.

There are difficulties in assessing the changes that took place during the period under study. The number of admissions was limited by the number of beds; yet we know that the total number of births from single women in Quebec rose from 2.9 percent of live births in 1931 to 3.4 percent in 1939, that is a 17 percent increase.[56] In 1933, both the Miséricorde in Montreal and the one in Quebec City were full and turning women away. In Montreal, La Miséricorde began to restrict admission to women from the city in their seventh month of pregnancy or later. Was there an increase in illicit sex? The illegitimacy rate did go up from 3 percent in 1932 to 3.2 percent in 1933, but the main reason for the rise in demand for admission was that, in both cities, private maternity homes were closing because of the depression and the overflow was going to the Miséricorde hospitals.[57]

What did decrease during the period were the rates of syphilis and of infant mortality. The rate of positive Wasserman tests which was 8 percent in 1930, never went above 6 percent after January 1936.[58] An active anti-veneral disease campaign had been launched in the early twenties, but Prime Minister Bennett's government had cut the federal funds in 1931. More refined studies are needed to provide a satisfactory explanation for the decreasing rate of syphilis. The drop in infant mortality, from 43 percent in 1930 to 27 percent in 1939,[59] follows the trend in

---

54. AHM, 32634, April 1934 and 9 September 1934.
55. AHM, 32192, April 1933.
56. Province de Québec, *Rapport annuel du ministère de la Santé et du Bien-être social pour les années 1935 à 1941* (Quebec, 1944), p.204.
57. Ibid. AHM, C. Joncas to Sr. Tharcisius, 20 February 1933. Sr. Tharcisius to the curé B., January 1933.
58. Statistics compiled from AHM, the register, 1929–39.
59. Mortality rate of infants born at the Hôpital de la Miséricorde: 1929: 39.6 percent; 1930: 43 percent; 1931: 44 percent; 1932: 51 percent; 1933: 59 percent; 1934: 37 percent; 1935: 34 percent; 1936: 35 percent; 1937: 29 percent; 1938: 17 percent; 1939: 27 percent. Statistics from AHM, the register, 1929–1939.

Quebec and Canada. As physical conditions inside the institutions did not change noticeably, the decrease can only be attributed to traditional causes which have been identified by other historians: better nutrition and a better understanding and application of measures of hygiene.[60]

The treatment of single mothers at the Hôpital de la Miséricorde raises a number of questions. The letters intercepted and kept in the dossiers may give us a biased picture of the living conditions since the majority were written by dissatisfied boarders. There were, however, some letters from grateful ex-patients to Sr. Tharcisius. Besides the correspondence, comments written in the patients' records by the supervisors provide some insights into the reaction of the boarders, the extent of submissiveness or rebellion. While the nuns commented on the patients' stubbornness or insubordination, inmates' letters repeatedly mention tears, tiredness, suicidal thoughts and general depression. Unhappiness was expected by the authorities and interpreted as a sign of repentance. Sr. Tharcisius wrote to an ex-boarder with whom she kept up a warm correspondence and who planned to come to Montreal for a visit: "Il vous sera sans doute agréable de revoir la chapelle où vous avez tant de fois prié et pleuré."[61]

Except for women who had nowhere to go, with no family or friends, and for whom the hospital was indeed a haven from a corrupt world,[62] we can assume that most women were anxious to leave as soon as possible. The majority appeared to be resigned, some trying to get good marks in order to be let out early, others begging their parents, relatives or boyfriend to find some money to pay off their debt.

Comments by the nuns would lead us to believe that some silent sabotage and passive resistance occurred. One patient was deemed not to be very bright because she took so long getting her work done. Yet her intercepted letters are very coherent and show no signs of dimness of wit. Out of desperation, some women threw letters out of windows, attempted to smuggle them out with visitors or entrusted them to companions leaving the institution. We only know of those who got caught.[63] The supervisors reported misdemeanours, but were all cases detected and reported? We know that some 4 percent of the women were discharged

---

60. See Terry Copp, "The Health of the People: Montreal in the Depression Years," in *Norman Bethune, his time and his legacy, son époque et son message*, eds. David A. E. Shepard and Andrée Lévesque (Ottawa, 1982), pp. 129–31.
61. AHM, 34378 stayed a year and a half.
62. AHM, 24 June 1937.
63. Having tried to send a letter "en cachette," 34502 had to work an extra month in the nursery; altogether she had already served seven months after her delivery. AHM, 32771; 35217, 29 May 1937; 35840, 14 May 1938, were also caught and punished.

for being insubordinate, stubborn or vulgar.[64] The best way to get expelled quickly was to be an object of scandal, to use foul language and hold conversations on scandalous subjects.[65] At least one young woman may have tried to injure herself voluntarily since she needed an operation on a finger "infected by guilty negligence."[66] A small minority managed to escape without being brought back. . . .

Open rebellion, at great risk, was only the most overt manifestation of resistance. In most cases, even passive resistance was out of the question. Depressed women, often coping with the trauma of having been deserted by their lover and being cast out from their familiar surroundings, busy all day and bearing the discomforts of pregnancy, had little energy left for rebellion. Like their mothers, most would have internalized the religious, traditional and patriarchal values which justified their punishment. Society's rules had been transgressed by them and their child's father. They, and later their child, were to pay the price.

Women had to come to terms with the social consequences of out-of-wedlock pregnancies. Given the contradictory demands made on single mothers—to hide their shame and to keep their child—anonymity provided an escape route if the child died or if, transgressing the usual prescription, the mother left it with the nuns. This dissimulation, during and after pregnancy, could only be accomplished with the complicity of other women, nuns or mothers. Nuns offered shelter, discretion, correction and rehabilitation. Mothers had to protect their daughters from the danger of losing their honour. Yet in many cases mothers were not there since over a quarter of single mothers had lost their own mothers. As this seems higher than for the majority of women their age, their mothers' absence may have been in part responsible for their situation. Mothers of single mothers showed their concern for their daughters, suffered great grief and often blamed themselves for their children's faults. This feeling of guilt was reinforced by some popular writings of the time. In a collection of morality tales, the chaplain of the Hôpital de la Miséricorde in Quebec City, Father V. Germain, maintained that if a single women became pregnant it was usually a sign that her own mother had previously sinned either by having had an illicit love affair before her marriage, or by practising birth control.[67] Not only did the inmates' mothers take moral responsibility for their daughters but, within their means, they also

---

64. Statistics compiled from AHM, the register, 1929–39.
65. AHM, 33275, 1934.
66. AHM, May 1939.
67. V. Germain, *Contes de la crèche* (Québec, 1939).

showed concern for their material well-being. They sewed clothes for their daughters, wrote them letters and covered up for them. Of the patients who had a mother—this applied to 72 percent—5 percent took charge of their grandchildren, usually adopting them.[68]

Confronted with an unwanted pregnancy many women attempted some form of abortive procedure, from taking hot mustard baths to inserting an instrument into the cervix. Presumably not all of them admitted this to the examining doctor at the hospital, but this information appears on 5.1 percent of medical records.[69] Short of aborting, the surest way of escaping the social consequence of single motherhood was to marry the father. Canada and Quebec do not keep statistics on births occurring within six months of marriage and, except by consulting parish records, we cannot estimate the incidence of extramarital pregnancies. The correspondence found in the hospital reveals that some fathers claimed that they intended to marry the mother when their financial situation allowed it, when they found a job for instance. Some kept their word and the child was claimed later on. Some parents forbade their daughter to keep in contact with her lover and their mail was intercepted even when the woman was over 21 years of age.[70] The nuns took note of at least one woman who married a drunk she did not love only to give her child a name.[71] A few times a year women married in the chapel of the hospital, either before the birth or, more often, upon leaving with her child.[72] If the father was acceptable, both the parents and the nuns viewed marriage as the best solution short of entering the convent.[73] Thus the woman could reenter society in the role prescribed for her, that of a married mother.

Starting anew as if nothing had happened was the other route back into "the World." The woman faced a paradox here: the best way to hide her past was to hide her child. Yet the law, the experts and the nuns all made

---

68. Statistics compiled from AHM, the register, 1929–39.

69. Ibid.

70. AHM, 36523, 9 October 1939. John Gillis has already shown that, in 19th century London, men who might have considered caring for their girlfriends and their children were often prevented by circumstances from doing so. Gillis, pp. 157–63.

71. AHM, 30377.

72. Statistics compiled from AHM, the register, 1929–39.

73. To a patient's mother who asked some advice as to whether her daughter should correspond with the young man who promised to marry her, Sr. Tharcicius answered, "le meilleur conseil est de la laisser marier puisque le jeune homme le désire....c'est son désir aussi....Ce serait la meilleure solution car elle ne montre pas d'attrait pour le couvent. Et le travail est très difficile à trouver." Ibid., 19 November 1933. AHM, 32578.

the mother responsible for her child. This contradiction could only engender feelings of guilt and inadequacy.[74]

In order to survive economically and socially, the single mother had little choice but to abandon her child. Jobs were difficult to get during the depression and domestic service was the main occupation for single women. Few employers were willing to hire a woman and her child. In 1937, single mothers who tried to subsist on welfare were denied this means of survival in Montreal when the city, to comply with orders from the Quebec government, cut single mothers off the relief lists.[75] Economic conditions forced many mothers to institutionalize their children and make them available for adoption. An institutionalized illegitimate child had a minimal chance of being adopted during these years of depression when adoption rates were dwindling.[76] The social stigma attached to illegitimacy would pursue such a child for the rest of her/his life. The label was in the parish registers and some religious orders did not accept bastards, hence denying them the highest aspiration of a Catholic. A mother could well feel guilty for condemning her child to a life of discrimination by putting her own welfare first. In this context, the expressions of relief at the death of the child are not surprising. As one grandmother wrote Sr. Tharcisius, "we are satisfied. The baby is dead, the past erased."[77] But the past was erased only after the single mother had undergone a period of anonymity, in isolation, in penance, as atonement for her sin and just retribution for her delinquent behaviour.

---

74. Seventeen years later, parents wrote enquiring about their child, adding: "plus nous vieillissons, plus nous y pensons, sa ne se passe pas [sic]." Ibid., 17 December 1956, AHM 36571.
75. *Le Devoir*, 18 May 1937.
76. AHM, C. Joncas to Sr. Tharcisius, 20 February 1933.
77. Ibid., 31541, April 1932.

The Creation of a Haven for "Human Thoroughbreds":

The Sterilization of the Feeble-Minded and the Mentally Ill in British Columbia

ANGUS McLAREN

In 1933 the *Canadian Medical Association Journal* reprinted an address that Dr H. A. Bruce, lieutenant-governor of Ontario, had given to the Hamilton Canadian Club. In it, Bruce, a respected surgeon, wandered far from his own area of professional expertise into the nightmare world of eugenic speculation. Between 1871 and 1931, he informed his audience, the general population had doubled but that of the mentally ill had increased six-fold. Fifty per cent of the latter were produced by feeble-minded parents, who were far more prolific than the normal. Bruce warned that if some steps were not taken to stem this tide, in seventy-five years one-half of the population would be condemned to labour to support the other half that would be institutionalized. Since the segregation of the subnormal had clearly not restricted their multiplication, the only answer was to embark on a policy of sterilization.[1]

Bruce's comments did not go unanswered. Dr W. D. Cornwall of Port Dalhousie, Ontario, retorted that Bruce was patently apologizing for the faults of capitalism inasmuch as he attributed mental illness solely to innate genetic faults and glossed over the impact of social deprivation. It was, asserted Cornwall, obvious that in a capitalist society, generous, altruistic, socially minded traits were not valued....one were truly inter-

ANGUS McLAREN, "THE CREATION OF A HAVEN FOR 'HUMAN THOROUGHBREDS': THE STERILIZATION OF THE FEEBLE-MINDED AND THE MENTALLY ILL IN BRITISH COLUMBIA," *CANADIAN HISTORICAL REVIEW*, 67, 2 (1986), 127–50. REPRINTED BY PERMISSION OF UNIVERSITY OF TORONTO PRESS. THROUGHOUT THE ARTICLE, THE EXPRESSIONS "RETARDED," "FEEBLE-MINDED," "SUBNORMAL," AND "MENTALLY ILL" ARE USED BECAUSE THESE WERE THE TERMS USED BY CONTEMPORARIES. IN THE CONTINUING DEBATE OVER THESE ISSUES, ALL FOUR HAVE BEEN ATTACKED AS VALUE-LADEN TERMS OF ENCLUSION.

1. *Canadian Medical Association Journal* [CMAJ], XXIX, 1933, 260. It is true that if both parents are retarded there is a good chance their offspring will also be retarded. Recent studies have suggested if both parents have an IQ of less than 70, 40 per cent of the offspring will be retarded; if only one parent, 15 per cent of the offspring will be retarded; and if both parents are normal, 1 per cent of the offspring will be retarded. But this still means that 83 per cent of the retarded have normal parents. If sterilization were going to be employed to eliminate the retarded it would be necessary to sterilize the normal. See Michael Craft, ed., *Tredgold's Mental Retardation*, 12th ed. (London 1979), 367–8.

ested in eliminating the marginalized and the misfit, the task would be to improve the environment rather than attempt to control breeding.[2]

Both sides of the sterilization debate were aired in the *Canadian Medical Association Journal* but those of Cornwall's opinion were very much in the minority. The pro-sterilization camp was led by such well-known medical figures as CMAJ editor A. G. Nichols, its assistant editor H. E. MacDermott, Dr C. M. Hincks of the National Committee on Mental Hygiene, Dr C. B. Farrar of the Toronto Psychiatric Hospital, Dr W. L. Hutton, president of the Canadian Eugenics Society, and Professor Madge Thurlow Macklin of the University of Western Ontario. The general thrust of their argument was that the struggle for survival had been reversed by the advances of medicine. A resulting problem was that the unfit, who once would have perished, were now able to survive and reproduce.[3] Indeed, Dr Hutton asserted that figures drawn from the asylum at Orillia suggested that the families of the feeble-minded had on average eight children while the normal had only three. Society was thus caught in the quandary of the feeble-minded having excessively large families while the intelligent employed birth control to limit the reproduction of fit stock. The question, said Hutton, was how "sound stock" could prevent "its dilution and pollution with the blood of the feeble-minded and the sufferers from the hereditary diseases."[4] The answer offered by his colleagues was that since doctors had helped to create the problem, they had a responsibility to solve it. Medical intervention in the form of sterilization was needed to counter the surge of mental deficiency created by earlier forms of intervention. To the objection that individual freedoms might be violated as a result, A. G. Nichols responded that to spread disease purposely was considered by all a crime. Surely it followed, he argued, that, "to bring into the world another individual grievously handicapped for the struggle of life, one who may in addition prove a menace to his fellows, is as much to be deprecated as murder."[5] If such "crimes" could not be punished they could at least be prevented. A "police state" already existed inasmuch as vaccinations and quarantines were enforced by law to deal with infectious diseases. A similarly aggressive attack on the roots of mental illness was justified by the same concerns for the well-being of the community.

---

2. CMAJ, XXIX, 1933, 443–5; see also CMAJ, XXX, 1934, 210.
3. CMAJ, XI, 1921, 823–5; XVI, 1926, 1233–8; XVII, 1927, 1526–8; XIX, 1928, 586; XXIX, 1933, 306, 657; XXX, 1934, 190, 195.
4. CMAJ, XXX, 1934, 77; see also CMAJ, XXXIII, 1935, 192.
5. CMAJ, XXI, 1929, 72–4; see also CMAJ, XXII, 1930, 91.

It comes as somewhat of a surprise to find in a medical journal an impassioned debate over the merits of capitalism and socialism and the police state. The discussion of sterilization of the feeble-minded was, however, an issue that inextricably entangled medical, moral, and political issues. Many doctors were naturally enough attracted to the notion of a biologically based program of reform. Such a program would inevitably have to draw on their expertise and highlight the social importance of the profession. Convinced that the same objectivity that they employed in the medical laboratory could be sustained when dealing with public policy, they were accordingly angered and alarmed when mavericks like Cornwall accused them of social bias and prejudice.

The year 1933 was the highwater mark of the debate over sterilization. In that year British Columbia followed Alberta in becoming the second province in Canada to pass legislation permitting the sterilization of the mentally ill and retarded.[6] The act empowered an Eugenics Board, consisting of a psychiatrist, a judge, and a social worker, to order the sterilization of any inmate of a provincial institution who "would be likely to beget or bear children who by reason of inheritance would have a tendency to serious mental disease or mental deficiency."[7] But 1933 was also the year in which Manitoba rejected similar legislation and in the later 1930s Ontario, despite the goadings of Bruce, similarly refused to follow the lead of Alberta and British Columbia.[8]

Given the fact that 1933 was the same year in which the Nazis began their own campaign for racial hygiene in Germany,[9] it might well be asked if British Columbia's sterilization law indicates that Canada also harboured fascistic sentiments and programs. An analysis of the sterilization debate in British Columbia reveals that eugenically based racial concerns were all-pervasive in interwar Canadian society and the most extreme policies tended to be advanced by progressive and scientifically minded

---

6. On Alberta see Terry L. Chapman, "The Early Eugenics Movement in Western Canada," *Alberta History*, XXV, 1977, 9–17; K. G. McWhirter and J. Weijer, "The Alberta Sterilization Act: A Genetic Critique," *University of Toronto Law Journal*, XIX, 1969, 424–31; Timothy J. Christian, "The Mentally Ill and Human Rights in Alberta: A Study of the Alberta Sexual Sterilization Act" (Unpublished paper, University of Alberta, nd).

7. Statutes of the Province of British Columbia, 1933, "An Act Respecting Sexual Sterilization," chap. 59, 7 April 1933.

8. On Manitoba see Brian L. Ross, "An Unusual Defeat: The Manitoba Controversy over Eugenical Sterilization in 1933" (unpublished paper, Institute for the History and Philosophy of Science and Technology, University of Toronto, 1981); on Ontario see Harvey G. Simmons, *From Asylum to Welfare* (Downsview, Ont. 1982), 114–17.

9. *The Law for the Prevention of Hereditarily Diseased Offspring* (Berlin 1935).

groups rather than by conservatives.[10] The 1933 sexual sterilization bill was of importance, not because it reflected the concerns of radical fringe groups, but because it represented the optimistic belief of respectable members of the helping professions. They asserted that many of the apparently new and menacing social problems of the twentieth century could be contained by medical intervention. What was rarely appreciated at the time was that professionals were calling for policies, such as the sterilization of the retarded, to counter a spectre that the professionals had themselves conjured up—that of a dangerous surge in the numbers of the mentally deficient. The sterilization debate in British Columbia can help us to understand how this "problem" forced itself upon public consciousness, and why the medical profession responded as it did.

In British Columbia, as in the rest of Canada, the "feeble-minded" were in effect "created" as a category at the turn of the century when education was made free and compulsory.[11] There had, of course, always been some members of society who, because of their mental or physical handicaps, had been perceived by their neighbours as somehow deficient. With the emergence of a modern, centralized, mass form of education, however, one entered a new world. To an unprecedented extent enormous numbers of children were subjected to common tests, examinations, and medical inspections. Those who met the new norms were declared "normal"; those who did not were labelled as inadequate.

The medicalization of the British Columbia school system began in 1907 with school medical inspection instituted throughout Vancouver.[12] In 1910 a full-time nurse was hired and Dr F. W. Brydone-Jack appointed as Vancouver's school medical officer. Josephine Dauphinée, who became supervisor of special classes, established in 1910 the first class for the "subnormal." In 1918 Martha Lindley, who had worked with H. H. Goddard of the Vineland Training School for Feeble-Minded Girls and

---

10. See William L. Morton, *The Progressive Party in Canada* (Toronto 1950); for the international context see D. Pickens, *Eugenics and the Progressives* (Nashville 1969), Richard Hofstadter, *The Progressive Movement* (Englewood Cliffs, NJ 1963), and Michael Freeden, "Eugenics and Progressive Thought: A Study in Ideological Affinity," *Historical Journal*, XXII, 1979, 645–71.

11. Patricia Rooke and R. L. Schnell, *Discarding the Asylum: From Child Rescue to the Welfare State in Canada (1800–1960)* (New York 1983), 278–81; see also John Gabbay and Charles Webster, eds., "Mental Handicap and Education," *Oxford Review of Education*, IX, 3, 1983.

12. Norah Lewis, "Physical Perfection for Spiritual Welfare: Health Care for the Urban Child," in Patricia Rooke and R. L. Schnell, eds., *Studies in Childhood History: A Canadian Perspective* (Calgary 1982), 138–50; Diane L. Matters, "Public Welfare Vancouver Style, 1910–1920," *Journal of Canadian Studies*, XIV, 1979, 3–15.

Boys in New Jersey, was appointed Vancouver's first full-time school psychiatrist.[13] Goddard had popularized Binet's IQ test in America; Lindley in turn employed the Goddard or Terman revision of the Binet-Simon IQ scale in British Columbia.[14]

The IQ tests to which students were subjected naturally relied on "cultural experiences and the verbal skills and practices" of the cultural elite.[15] As a social product of the middle class they necessarily confused innate intelligence with an appreciation of bourgeois norms. And, if tests and examinations did not single out problem children, deviant behaviour could. Teachers, by attributing behaviour problems to retardation rather than to the child's environment, unwittingly participated in fostering the idea of an increase in the numbers of the feeble-minded.

We know today that "so-called mental retardation" is higher between school entry and leaving age.[16] Compulsory education not only reveals cases of retardation, but, in effect, creates them by subjecting many children to completely new and frightening demands for systematic intellectual functioning. But such apparent retardation often disappears once the individual is freed of the restraints of the institution and allowed to pursue his or her interests. The reason why the feeble-minded appeared to be increasing after the turn of the century was because the community's demands on children were increasing. Larger and larger numbers of children were labelled as incapable of being educated because they failed to respond adequately to a specific form of education that they were compelled to experience.

But in the first decades of this century teachers and doctors interpreted the findings to mean that only because examinations and inspections were now being carried out systematically was the "true" extent of feeble-mindedness evident. The problem as they saw it was that only the school population was being surveyed; an accurate account of the ways in which mental retardation contributed to rending the fabric of society, and a gauge of the extent to which "racial degeneration" had spread, awaited investigation of all public institutions.

In the British empire the fear of racial degeneration was sparked during the Boer War when it was discovered that vast numbers of potential

---

13. On Dauphinée and Lindley see Canadian National Committee for Mental Hygiene [CNCMH], *Mental Hygiene Survey of the Province of British Columbia* (Toronto 1920), 19.
14. On Goddard see Stephen Jay Gould, *The Mismeasure of Man* (New York 1981), 158–74.
15. Law Reform Commission of Canada [LRCC], *Sterilization: Implications for Mentally Retarded and Mentally Ill Persons*, Working Paper 24 (Ottawa 1980), 10.
16. LRCC, *Sterilization*, 16.

recruits were either physically or mentally unfit to serve their country overseas. In Canada there was, in addition, the Anglo-Saxon concern that the nation was being swamped by waves of new immigrants.[17] Moreover, the First World War cut a swathe through the generation of young men on which the country set its hopes. Canadian authorities expressed their concerns that the postwar nation would have to shoulder the burden not only of the handicapped at home but also of the returning veterans, including over 5000 shell-shock victims. It was in this context that Dr J. D. Maclean, the Liberal provincial secretary of British Columbia in 1919, called on Dr C. M. Hincks of the Canadian National Committee on Mental Hygiene to carry out a survey of the feeble-minded in the province.[18] The first such Canadian survey had been held in Ontario in 1906; between 1918 and 1922 the CNCMH carried out similar investigations in seven provinces. Hincks had already surveyed the New Westminster Hospital for the Insane in December 1918, and in 1919 he extended his scope to include public schools, industrial schools, detention homes, and orphanages. Hincks reported not only that the extent of feeble-mindedness was high, but that it posed a serious threat to society inasmuch as it was a primary cause of poverty, crime, and prostitution.[19] What measures should the province take to protect itself from the internal and external threat of the reproduction of the feeble-minded?[20]

Until the turn of the century the main way in which the feeble-minded were controlled and prevented from reproducing was by segregating them in asylums. The early twentieth century brought the criticism that segregation had proved both expensive and inefficient. The sterilization of the feeble-minded, it was argued, would prove to be a far more effective,

---

17. James S. Woodsworth played a central role in popularizing eugenic fears in a series of articles he wrote for the *Winnipeg Free Press*, 11 Oct. 1916, 9; 1 Nov. 1916, 9; 8 Nov. 1916, 11; 15 Nov. 1916, 11. In the last article he stated: "Sterilization has been proposed. But general sentiment is so strong against such a radical measure that its adoption is not practicable." See also Zlata Godler, "Doctors and the New Immigrants," *Canadian Ethnic Studies*, IX, 1977, 6–18.
18. On Hincks see Dr J. G. Fitzgerald and Dr Grant Fleming, *Report of a Survey Made of the Canadian National Committee for Mental Hygiene in 1932* (Ottawa 1932).
19. Hincks reported that 3.56 per cent of the Vancouver school population was "mentally abnormal," and 72 per cent of the asylum population foreign born. CNCMH, *Mental Hygiene*, 14–18, 48–50.
20. On Hincks's continued campaign to arouse the Canadian public to the danger of feeblemindedness see "Mental Hygiene Provisions in Public Health Programs," *Canadian Journal of Public Health*, XXXVI, 1945, 89–95; "Man's Last Spectre," *Proceedings of the Royal Canadian Institute*, 1936, 65–75.

humane, and cheap method of restricting their breeding.[21] The stimulus for this response came first from the defenders of eugenic arguments. Francis Galton had coined the term "eugenics" in 1883 to mean well-born.[22] He argued that the Darwinian struggle for survival had recently been reversed by medical advances that allowed the unfit to survive and multiply and by the employment of birth control by the fit that permitted them to restrict their fertility. If, as it appeared, a policy of "positive eugenics" to encourage the fertility of the superior stock proved unworkable, at the very least government could employ a policy of "negative eugenics" to prevent the multiplication of the inferior. In so doing, feeble-mindedness would be eliminated, along with the violence, vice, and misery to which it gave rise. The fact that safe, surgical methods of sterilization were now available made the suggestion eminently feasible.[23]

In North America the first bill in favour of sterilization was introduced in Michigan in 1897; the first to be enacted was in Indiana in 1907 and the second in British Columbia's neighbour to the south, Washington, in 1910. Eventually, thirty-one states and two Canadian provinces (Alberta and British Columbia) would enact similar legislation.[24]

In British Columbia the earliest and most vigorous proponents of sterilization were the members of the various women's movements. It would appear that the first public declaration in support of sterilization was carried in a 1914 edition of the British Columbia suffragist paper *The Champion*.[25] To understand why the same women who were campaigning for political freedoms should have given support to a policy that limited the rights of the handicapped requires that we recall the ethos of the early women's movement. It was very much marked by what has been called an

---

21. The phrase "sterilization of the unfit" entered the vocabulary in 1888–9; see, F. B. Smith, *The People's Health, 1830–1910* (London 1979), 120.
22. C. P. Blacker, *Eugenics: Galton and After* (London 1952); Karl Pearson, *The Life of Francis Galton* (London 1914–30); Mark Haller, *Eugenics: Hereditarian Attitudes in American Thought, 1870–1930* (New Brunswick, NJ 1963); Charles Webster, ed., *Biology, Medicine and Society* (Cambridge 1981).
23. As early as 1861 Joseph Workman of the Toronto Asylum had written: "Insanity would die out if the sane avoided intermarrying with insane stock"; *American Journal of Insanity*, Jan. 1861, 314, cited in Norman Dain, *Concepts of Insanity in the United States, 1789–1865* (New Brunswick, NJ 1964), 241. R. W. Bruce was among the first in Canada to refer to the need for "asexualization" to supplement segregation; "Mental Sanitation," *Canada Lancet*, XL, 1906–7, 976.
24. J. H. Landman, *Human Sterilization: The History of the Sexual Sterilization Movement* (New York 1932).
25. *The Champion*, Jan. 1914, 11–12; see also Feb. 1914, 6.

ideology of "maternal feminism."[26] Women demanded the vote so that they could more adequately defend their home and their children. The war helped focus even greater attention on health and population issues. Accordingly, after the vote was attained, a good deal of the attention of the various women's groups in the 1920s was devoted to developing programs to protect their children. Baby welfare centres, better baby contests, and well-baby clinics proliferated. Maternal feminists rallied support for a series of campaigns in favour of preventative medical attacks on tuberculosis, venereal disease, and influenza.[27] Mothers' pension and juvenile courts were similarly demanded in order to shore up the family.

Unfortunately, the defence of these progressive measures was often accompanied by statements that revealed the siege mentality of many of their proponents. If Canada were to be healthy and happy it was necessary to prevent the entry of immigrants who, they asserted, were overrepresented by the feeble-minded, the epileptic, the idiotic, the tubercular, the dumb, the blind, the illiterate, the criminal, and the anarchistic.[28] And if normal Canadian children were to receive a healthy upbringing and a decent education they would have to be protected from disruptive and potentially degrading associations with the abnormal. In 1915 the National Council of Women asked Prime Minister Borden to appoint a royal commission on mental defectives; in 1925 the NCW came out in favour of sterilization.[29] The strongest support in the provinces came from Alberta and British Columbia, with such luminaries as Nellie McClung, Emily Murphy, Henrietta Edwards, and Helen Gregory MacGill providing public backing.[30]

The *Western Women's Weekly*, which served as a mouthpiece for the main women's group and the Child Welfare Association of British Colum-

---

26. Carol Bacchi, "Race Regeneration and Social Purity: A Study of the Social Attitudes of Canada's English Speaking Suffragists," *Histoire sociale/Social History*, XI, 1978, 460–74; Gillian Weiss, "'As Women and as Citizens': Clubwomen in Vancouver, 1910–1928" (PH D thesis, University of British Columbia, 1983).

27. Veronica Strong-Boag, *The Parliament of Women: The National Council of Women of Canada, 1893–1924* (Ottawa 1976), 353–70.

28. The United Farm Women of Alberta were the most outspoken proponents of sterilization and curbs on immigration. See, for example, *United Farmers of Alberta*, 1 Dec. 1923, 8; 26 Feb. 1924, 12.

29. Strong-Boag, *Parliament of Women*, 318.

30. Nellie L. McClung, *The Stream Runs Fast: My Own Story* (Toronto 1945), 177–80; Byrne Hope Sanders, *Emily Murphy: Crusader* (Toronto 1945), 186–8; Elsie Gregory MacGill, *My Mother the Judge* (Toronto 1955), 216; Howard Palmer, *Patterns of Prejudice: A History of Nativism in Alberta* (Toronto 1982), 112–13.

bia, led the campaign for sterilization in the province. It informed its readers that 51 per cent of the feeble-minded were new immigrants, that certificates of "normality" should have to be obtained before marriages were allowed, that mentally defective girls in particular presented a "social and moral menace."[31] The most authoritative statements were made by Josephine Dauphinée: 80 per cent of feeble-mindedness, she wrote, was due to hereditary causes; the portion of feeble-minded in the community had doubled in the past two decades because of their prolificity; and the feeble-minded in turn formed the core of "the poverty stricken, criminal and degenerate classes."[32] Sterilization was the only way in which society could protect itself from such scourges at home. But what of threats from abroad? Dauphinée conjured up the following lurid portrayal of new immigrants: "Here we see two brothers from sunny Italy, lazy, degenerate, dissolute and mentally deficient; no challenge halts them; the port of entry is not barred—Canada is theirs for the taking."[33] To counter such threats, the women's groups sought more stringent screening of immigrants.

The women's movement in British Columbia had direct access to the Legislative Assembly as Mrs M. E. Smith, a contributor to the *Western Women's Weekly*, was MLA for South Vancouver. Smith, who had sat as the first woman cabinet member in the British empire in John Oliver's 1921 Liberal government, was a vigorous supporter of several programs aimed at protecting women and children. It was in light of just these concerns that she rose in the assembly in December 1925 to call for both more restrictive legislation on immigration and a sterilization bill similar to that of Washington State. The press reported her stating that, "if this were done, the English speaking peoples would maintain their position of supremacy on which the peace and prosperity of the world depend."[34]

In fact, the previous month provincial secretary William Sloan had received the unanimous support of the Legislative Assembly to establish a select committee to investigate mental retardation in the province. In introducing his motion, Sloan had given three reasons for such an enquiry. The first was the alarming growth of mental illness and mental retardation. In 1872 there were only two mental cases for every 2265 citizens; in

---

31. *Western Women's Weekly*, 8 Feb. 1919, 8; 8 March 1919, 1; 6 Dec. 1919, 1; 3 June 1922, 4.
32. Ibid., 10 Jan. 1918, 2.
33. Ibid., 6 Aug. 1921, 8. Explicitly anti-Asian sentiment was expressed by the British Progressive League; see ibid., 14 Oct. 1922, 2.
34. Victoria *Daily Times*, 2 Dec. 1925, 2; Vancouver *Sun*, 2 Dec. 1925, 20.

1924 there was 1 for every 293.[35] This growth was in part due to the fact that, as Dr. H. C. Steeves, superintendent of Essondale had indicated, in 70 per cent of cases of manic depression, dementia praecox, epilepsy, idiocy, and imbecility the hereditary factor predominated. Only in 30 per cent of cases such as those relating to syphilis, senility, and psychosis following illness could the physical factor be found to predominate.[36] Sloan's second reason for alarm was that British Columbia was becoming a dumping ground for foreign misfits. He reported that an analysis of the inmate population found that a bare 10 per cent were from British Columbia and only 30 per cent from the rest of Canada; a full 60 per cent were foreigners. And this in turn led to Sloan's third preoccupation, the cost of supporting the existing system of segregation which amounted to $750,000 per year.[37] Speaking in support of the enquiry, Drs Wrinch and Rothwell agreed that new policies were required, but that years of education were needed before the public would see the wisdom of sterilizing the feeble-minded and placing restrictions on marriage and immigration.[38]

The Royal Commission on Mental Hygiene of 1925 consisted of its chairman Dr E. J. Rothwell, Brigadier-General V. W. Odlum, Reginald Hayward, W. A. Mackenzie, and Paul Harrison. It held open sessions in Victoria and Vancouver where it received briefs and evidence. It also received material from experts from eastern Canada and the United States. The commission was mandated to investigate the reason for the growth in the numbers of the mentally deficient, examine the causes and prevention of lunacy, gauge the extent of entry into the province of the deficient, and determine the level of care currently available for the subnormal.[39]

In its 1927 report the commission responded to the first issue by noting that the growth of mental problems was not as alarming as had been thought; the extent was simply more accurately reported because of the larger number of facilities available for the care of the subnormal. British Columbia's rate of increase was on about a par with the rest of Canada.[40] Overcrowding did exist in the available institutions, however, so that

---

35. *Journal of the Legislative Assembly* (Session 1925), LV, 37; see also Vancouver *Sun*, 19 Nov. 1925, 2.
36. On the investigations of Dr H. C. Steeves see *Bulletin of the Vancouver Medical Association*, 1 March 1926, 12–16.
37. On the history of institutional care and its growth in British Columbia see *Report of the Mental Health Services, Sessional Papers: British Columbia*, II, 1953–4, 15–22.
38. Victoria *Daily Times*, 19 Nov. 1925, 16.
39. E. J. Rothwell, *Report of the Royal Commission on Mental Hygiene* (Victoria 1927).
40. Ibid., CC 9.

concerns about added growth did have some foundation. The entry of defective immigrants into British Columbia was the special concern of Dr Henry Young, secretary of the Provincial Board of Health, and Dr A. G. Price, Victoria's city medical officer. The commission agreed that a disproportionate percentage of asylum inmates were foreign born and called for some form of screening process to be instituted.[41]

The evidence received by the commission on the causes of mental deficiency was conflicting. Dr J. G. McKay, founder of the Hollywood Sanitarium at New Westminster and one of the most active participants in the commission's hearings, asserted that 60 to 70 per cent of all mental problems were inherited. He was supported in the main by the evidence of Herbert W. Collier, superintendent of the detention home and chief probation officer of Victoria, Dr George Hall of the Victoria Medical Society, Vancouver police magistrate J. S. Jamieson, Dr Mackintosh, the Burnaby medical officer, and J. Williams of the Child Welfare Association.[42] Doctors such as K. D. Panton and W. A. Dobson who were attracted to a psychodynamic approach to mental health problems were sceptical of the claims of the hereditarians.[43] They were in turn supported by Dr Helen P. Davidson of Stanford University whose statistical analysis was included in the Royal Commission's Appendix G.[44] She reported that only 11 to 30 per cent of mental defects were related to hereditary transmission. Most of the outside witnesses were, however, convinced of the primary importance of heredity and accordingly prone to support a policy of sterilization. They included Dr C. M. Hincks of the Canadian National Committee on Mental Hygiene, Dr C. B. Farrar of the Toronto Psychopathic Hospital, and Paul Popenhoe of the Human Betterment Foundation of Pasadena, California.[45] Moreover, even those doctors who must have been aware of the distinctions that separated feeble-mindedness from mental illness

---

41. Victoria *Daily Times*, 17 April 1926, 1–2.
42. Vancouver *Daily Province*, 14 April 1926, 17.
43. Rothwell, *Report*, CC 17; see also Victoria *Daily Times*, 23 April 1926, 13; Vancouver *Daily Province*, 14 April 1926, 17.
44. Rothwell, *Report*, CC 53.
45. Ibid., CC 9–10. A special submission of Paul Popenhoe was included in the *Final Report of the Royal Commission on Mental Hygiene* (Victoria 1928), Appendix H. Because sterilization was compulsory in California, over 7500 operations (more than half of the entire country) were by 1932 performed in the state. See Harry H. Laughlin, *Eugenical Sterilization: 1926* (New Haven 1926); E. S. Gosney and Paul Popenhoe, *Sterilization for Human Betterment* (New York 1929); F. O. Butler, "A Quarter Century's Experience in Sterilization of Mental Defectives in California," *American Journal of Mental Deficiency*, LI, 1945, 1–6.

tended to lump together the problems posed by both imbeciles and psychotics.

The commission heard a number of suggestions on how the care and prevention of mental illness could be improved. Mrs Emily May Schofield of the Victoria Local Council of Women wanted the institution of marriage certificates and special classes for the retarded. Miss Olive Snyder of the Victoria Social Service League called, as did Mrs Schofield, for child guidance clinics.[46] Drs Hincks and Dobson also expressed support for early treatment in preventative clinics. The preventive measure that received the most attention, however, was sterilization. The commission reported that seven of its nine medical witnesses and the Local Councils of Women were in favour of sterilization.[47]

Amongst the arguments marshalled in defence of the policy of sterilization, the first was that the prevention of mental deficiency and its accompanying evils had become an economic necessity. Helen MacMurchy of the federal government's Ministry of Health summed up the thesis in her 1934 study of the subject: "We are beginning to see that our troubles and burdens are caused by a very small proportion of our people. Out of every thousand of us there are about ten who are the chief causes of our present enormous expenditures for institutions and other forms of relief and care."[48] Since there existed for the moment no cure for most forms of mental deficiency, the choice was between society's carrying ever higher institutional costs or taking a preventive measure that would both limit the reproduction of the subnormal and lower the cost of their care by allowing some to be released.

The second argument in favour of sterilization was that feeble-mindedness and mental illness were hereditary complaints. Although the figures advanced to support this notion tended to vary over time, the adherents of this view were convinced that "like begat like" and that the mentally deficient exacerbated the problem by being more prolific than the normal. The Canadian National Committee on Mental Hygiene asserted that heredity was the biggest factor in mental deficiency and it and other groups could point to the purported sixteen years of success in California

46. Victoria *Daily Times*, 17 April 1926, 1–2. On the establishment of new services see Richard James Clark, "Care of the Mentally Ill in British Columbia" (Master of Social Work thesis, University of British Columbia, 1947), 87–90.
47. On the lobbying of the Local Councils of Women see Provincial Archives of British Columbia [PABC], Provincial Council of Women Papers, Add. MSS 1961, box 1, file 1, 147, 171, 175; file 2, 5–9–10. See also Vancouver *Sun*, 30 Sept. 1926, 24.
48. Helen MacMurchy, *Sterilization? Birth Control? A Book for Family Welfare and Safety* (Toronto 1934), 3.

as reported by Popenhoe to back up the argument for sterilization. To those who argued that some feeble-minded parents could nevertheless give birth to "normal" children, the hereditarians, switching to an environmental tack, responded that such children would eventually be damaged because inadequately parented and so also should be prevented from being born.[49]

The third set of arguments in favour of sterilization was based on moral preoccupations. Some saw sterilization as a form of "discipline" that the abnormal required for their own good and for the good of the community. To liberals who might protest against such therapeutic intervention, the sponsors of sterilization responded that segregation was itself a denial of liberty. Sterilization would, it was claimed, result in greater liberty because it would permit the feeble-minded to leave their institutions and marry without running the danger of reproducing.[50] The argument that the sterilized might be even more promiscuous and degenerate because they no longer had to fear pregnancy was one to which proponents of the operation were especially sensitive. They indignantly replied, although not always with any factual backing, that sterilization resulted in greater order and self-control. It was apparent that many proponents who argued that the operation was a humane act also saw it as a sort of punishment. Indeed, some confused sterilization with castration and wanted sex offenders and habitual criminals[51] to be sterilized.

Taking all these arguments into account, the commission supported in its *Report*: "Sterilization of such individuals in mental institutions as, following treatment or training, or both, might safely be recommended for parole from the institution and trial return to community life, if the danger of procreation with its attendant risk of multiplication of the evil by transmission of the disability to progeny were eliminated."[52] Written consent was to be given by the patient or spouse, parent or guardian, or minister of the department, and only after recommendation by the superintendent of the institution and approval of the Board of Control.

It says something of the seriousness with which mental deficiency was viewed in the interwar period that the British Columbia Legislative Assembly was specially adjourned on 6 March, 1928 to allow the MLAS to

---

49. Rothwell, *Report*, CC 9.
50. Rothwell, *Final Report*, Appendix H.
51. UBC Special Collections, Vancouver Local Council of Women box 1, files 2–3; box 4. On similar sentiments in Alberta see *United Farmers of Alberta*, 1 Feb. 1926, 20.
52. Rothwell, *Report*, CC 25.

hear Dr D. M. Lebourdais give a lecture on mental defectives.[53] The Final Report of the Royal Commission on Mental Hygiene was submitted on 14 March. No immediate action was taken, because Dr John Maclean, who had commissioned the Hincks survey in 1919 and led the government when the commission was carrying out its investigations, was replaced as premier by the Conservative Simon Fraser Tolmie in August 1928.

Between 1928 when the commission's final report was filed and 1933 when the sterilization bill was introduced, public and private pressure in favour of the policy slowly built. To an extent there was a simple continuation of the sort of lobbying which a federal commission had noted in 1926. Sterilization in British Columbia was gaining support, it reported, because "the Women's Council of Vancouver is endeavouring to create public opinion for the establishment of this measure. The department of neglected and dependent children is strongly in favour of such a measure, and is bringing the question before the public whenever possible through various organizations."[54] In September 1926 the New Westminster Local Council of Women sponsored a resolution in favour of sterilization. Individuals such as Dr Irene Bastow Hudson and Mrs Schofield of Victoria voiced opposition but the Local Councils of Women, at their provincial gathering in the fall, passed the resolution.[55]

Feminist support for the policy was indicated by a series of articles Emily Murphy wrote as "Janey Canuck" in the Vancouver *Sun*. In "Sterilization of the Insane" she argued that to protect women and children from sexual attack, to end the crippling expenses of incarceration, and to promote the mental and physical betterment of the race, sterilization of the unfit was required. "Human thoroughbreds" were what Canada wanted, but at the moment the nation was burdened by 25 000 lunatics, a disproportionate number in Catholic Quebec where religious and political partisanship opposed progressive legislation.[56] In "Should the Unfit Wed," Murphy asserted that they should, but only if sterilized so that insanity, venereal disease, tuberculosis, and epilepsy could be contained. "We protect the public against the offal of human-

---

53. Vancouver *Morning Star*, 7 March 1928, 1.
54. *Mental Defect and Social Welfare: Joint Report of the Committees on the Family and Child Welfare of the Social Service Council of Canada* (Ottawa 1926), 27.
55. Schofield called the resolution "the most unthought out piece of legislation ever asked for"; Victoria *Daily Times*, 30 Sept. 1926, 6. See also ibid., 17 April 1926, 1–2; 12 Oct. 1926, 6.
56. Vancouver *Sun*, 3 Sept. 1932, 3.

ity."[57] And not content with having likened the abnormal to animals, Murphy proceeded to compare them to plants, asserting that sterilization was no more unnatural than pruning a tree.[58]

Murphy was in some ways a "typical" progressive inasmuch as she favoured a whole series of reforms aimed at improving the health of the family.[59] She was as concerned with birth control and marriage health certificates as she was with sterilization. The response of other eugenically minded commentators to birth control was ambivalent. The more conservative believed that the restriction of fertility by the fit was dysgenic because it deprived the community of sound stock.[60] The progressives tended to accept birth control as a fact of life among the intelligent. It did not have to be socially harmful as long as the reduction of the birth rate of superior types by contraception was balanced by the restriction of the inferior by sterilization. The Canadian Birth Control League, formed in Vancouver by A. M. Stephen in 1923 after a visit to the city by Margaret Sanger, listed as its goals both the establishment of clinics where mothers could be instructed in the use of contraceptives and the sterilization of the unfit.[61] The latter's reckless breeding resulted, according to Stephen, in the healthy having to pay crushing taxes to support the offspring of the diseased and criminal. Dr George Hall of the Victoria Medical Society, while testifying before the Rothwell Commission in 1926, called on the one hand for "the sterilization of persons unfit for marriage," but on the other urged "that scientific methods of birth control should be known more widely."[62] Similarly, Dr L. E. Borden of Victoria was quoted by the Vancouver *Sun* in 1932 as backing both policies. " 'Birth control is the most important issue in Canada,' he said, emphasizing not only the economic cost imposed upon governments, but the wastage of human life involved in perpetuating the unfit."[63]

Murphy's defence of sterilization was perhaps the most outlandish in its extravagant claims, but almost every discussion of sterilization carried by the British Columbia press was equally one-sided. The Vancouver *Sun* in

---

57. Ibid., 10 Sept. 1932, 4.
58. Ibid., 17 Sept. 1932, 2.
59. Ibid., 27 Aug. 1932, 5; 24 Sept. 1932, 5.
60. So, for example, the 1922 National Convention of Local Councils of Women discussed an issue of the *Birth Control Review* under the topic of "objectionable printed matter and films." *Western Women's Weekly*, 21 Oct. 1922, 2.
61. *B. C. Federationist*, 21 Nov. 1924, 1; 26 Dec. 1924, 1.
62. Victoria *Daily Times*, 17 April 1926, 1–2.
63. Vancouver *Sun*, 6 April 1932, 1.

1926 quoted a noted Viennese surgeon: "In saving the weak of mind from the hazards of a hard and selfish world, by prolonging the lives of the constitutionally weak persons with hereditary tendencies towards mental and physical disease, we are allowing more and more of the poorer human stock to survive and reproduce."[64] In 1927 the *Sun* heralded Oliver Wendell Holmes's judgment in the American Supreme Court that sterilization was not unconstitutional since it was "the only reasonable way of protecting the strains from which the world must draw its leaders." The *Sun's* editorialist concluded that Canada should follow the Americans "the sooner the better."[65] In November of the same year the *Sun* returned to the subject, making the wild claim that "It is an admitted fact in every civilized country of the world today that the unfit are multiplying at a rate something like double of the fit. Thus, for every child born with mental, physical and moral ability to maintain and promote civilization, two are born with the instincts to flout the essential discipline of civilization and tear civilization down."[66] Readers of the British Columbia press were informed that there were "millions" of unfit stock whose reproduction was "a crime against humanity" in that it represented "the greatest burden" on civilization.[67]

On 1 April 1933, Conservative provincial secretary S. L. Howe asked the Legislative Assembly if it were prepared to consider a sexual sterilization bill. The house unanimously agreed. Reginald Hayward, who had sat on the 1925 Rothwell Commission, declared that many members had long been in favour of such a policy but remained silent because of concerns that an uneducated public would be hostile to such a measure.[68] Hayward's statement was somewhat curious; what impresses one most in the literature on sterilization in the 1920s and 1930s is the scarcity of views hostile to the program. Prior to 1933 the only vocal opponents of sterilization in British Columbia appeared to be Alan and Ada Muir. This couple had been active in left-wing political circles in Winnipeg up until the First World War. In the postwar period they moved to Vancouver and established a Peoples League for Health and an Anti-Vaccination and Medical League.[69] They were interested in herbal medicine, astrology, Rosicrucianism, and mental telepathy; regular medicine they viewed with suspi-

---

64. Ibid., 24 Nov. 1926, 16.
65. Ibid., 25 May 1927, 8.
66. Ibid., 8 Nov. 1927, 8; see also 31 Dec. 1928, 8.
67. Ibid., 3 April 1933, 4.
68. Victoria *Daily Times*, 1 April 1933, 5.
69. *Labour Statesman*, 20 Feb. 1925, 3.

cion. When a Vancouver *Sun* editorial lauded the sterilization laws of America, Alan Muir replied that no one had the right to judge the fit or unfit. Going further, he claimed that doctors in their ravenous pursuit of power were doing the dirty work of the capitalists in exterminating labour leaders in prisons and asylums.[70] In March 1929 Muir cast his net wider in claiming that operations on tonsils, adenoids, and appendixes were all evidence of "medical sadism," that the giving of iodine to school children was a way of creating drug dependency, and that sterilization was equivalent to murder.[71] All of these policies were manifestations, in Muir's mind, of the extent to which doctors were controlling government. The fact that the only vocal opposition to sterilization in British Columbia came from health cultists like the Muirs highlights the extent to which the policy had the support of the professional classes. But though sterilization had been called for in the early 1920s, it was only introduced to the legislature in 1933. Clearly the "advanced" members of the middle class were initially concerned that the mass of the population would be hostile to the idea and would have to be slowly enlightened as to the benefits of the policy. By 1933 the politicians assumed that this education was complete.

The bill, introduced on 1 April and passed on 7 April, received only cursory debate in the Legislative Assembly. Tolmie's government was in the process of falling apart. The sexual sterilization bill, along with a motley collection of other measures, was rushed through three readings in the last week of the government's life.[72] At first it appeared that there would be no debate whatsoever. The leader of the opposition, T. D. Pattullo, agreed that since segregation had resulted in "whole colonies of the mentally unfit" being created, some radical therapeutic measure was required. Pattullo mysteriously boasted that he himself had long supported sterilization despite the fact that his life had been threatened three times for taking such a stand.[73] Even Tom Uphill, the independent member from Fernie who had in the past been critical of the medical profession, fell into line; it was reported he "apologized for his opposition of the past five years and would support such a bill."[74] At the second

---

70. Vancouver *Sun*, 1 June 1927, 8.
71. Ibid., 21 March 1929, 8. For other left-wing attacks on eugenics see the *One Big Union Bulletin*, 28 May 1931, 2; *Canadian Tribune*, 27 April 1940, 2.
72. *Journal of the Legislative Assembly* (Session 1933), LXII, 101–15.
73. Victoria *Daily Colonist*, 1 April 1933, 2.
74. Vancouver *Daily Province*, 1 April 1933, 3.

reading, however, opposition emerged on the liberal side of the House. Dr W. H. Sutherland asserted that the bill was meaningless because doctors were already providing sterilizations for the mentally ill who provided their consent. Dr J. J. Gillis, an active Catholic, opposed the bill on the grounds that mental problems should not be responded to with surgical solutions.[75] He argued that tuberculosis once had been thought to be hereditary; mental deficiency would also likely prove to be a far more complex problem than the eugenicists imagined. Though twenty-three American states introduced sterilization, he pointed out, only four continued to employ it.[76] To the anger and surprise of the government even Pattullo did a volte face and now claimed that because of religious and moral objections he was opposed to the legislation. The support that he had expressed only a few days previously had, he brazenly claimed, been misinterpreted.[77]

Pattullo was obviously responding to the belated protests of the Catholic church in British Columbia. Why the church had kept its silence for so long is unclear. Only after the bill was actually introduced did Catholics begin to organize any opposition.[78] And only after the bill was actually passed did Archbishop W. M. Duke formally condemn it. Speaking for the province's 90 000 Catholics, the archbishop declared the bill malicious in intent: "The bill savours of that unfortunate country where the state tries to control everything, even the conscience of its citizens, and where man's private property and inherent rights and religious convictions are confiscated in the name of social progress and economy and hygiene…It will work an injustice especially on the poor and unfortunate whom we are bound in charity, before God, not to injure permanently, but to protect effectively even at legitimate expense."[79] Politics makes strange bedfellows. In addition to the Catholics, the only public protesters of the bill were the indefatigable Muirs. Once the legislation was in place, Alan Muir

---

75. Vancouver *Sun*, 6 April 1933, 1, 5.
76. Ibid., 7 April 1933, 12.
77. Vancouver *Daily Province*, 7 April 1933, 13; Victoria *Daily Colonist*, 7 April 1933, 5.
78. On the protests of the Catholic Women's League and the Knights of Columbus see the Vancouver *Sun*, 6 April 1933, 1; 25 May 1933, 14.
79. Ibid., 24 April 1933, 9; Vancouver *Daily Province*, 23 April 1933, 2. Pius XI had condemned sterilization in 1930: "Public magistrates have no direct power over the bodies of their subjects. Therefore, where no crime has taken place and there is no cause present for grave punishment, they can never directly harm or tamper with the integrity of the body, either for the reason of eugenics or for other reason." Cited in MacMurchy, *Sterilization*, 16. See also Dr Letitia Fairchild, *The Case against Sterilization* (London, nd).

warned that with such processes the Nazi could turn on the Jew or the capitalist on the labourer.[80]

British Columbia was, of all the provinces in Canada, the one in which Catholics formed the smallest percentage of the population. The weakness of the church in the West clearly simplified the passage of the sterilization bill. Professionals and progressives right across the country were interested in enacting similar statutes, but it was only in British Columbia and Alberta, where there was on the one hand a large immigrant presence that raised hereditarian concerns and on the other little effective Catholic opposition, that eugenic measures could be confidently advanced. In those regions of the country where Catholics predominated such measures would not be broached; in Ontario and Manitoba the Catholic minority was large enough to ensure that they would be beaten back.

Despite the beginnings of some opposition, the sexual sterilization act passed without a formal division in the Legislative Assembly. The act called for a Board of Eugenics made up of a judge, a psychiatrist, and a social worker. Section 4, subsection (1) provided that: "Where it appears to the Superintendent of any institution within the scope of this Act (i.e. any public hospital for the insane, the Industrial Home for Girls or the Industrial Home for Boys) that any inmate of that institution, if discharged therefrom without being subjected to an operation for sexual sterilization would be likely to beget or bear children who by reason of inheritance would have a tendency to serious mental disease or mental deficiency, the Superintendent may submit to the Board of Eugenics a recommendation that a surgical operation be performed upon the inmate for sexual sterilization."[81] The consent of the subject was required if capable of being given or that of spouse, parent, guardian, or Provincial Secretary.

At the beginning of the paper it was noted that the sterilization issue indicated the extent to which biologically based programs of reform gained credibility in the twentieth century. It should be further stressed that doctors not only assisted in the formulation of such programs; they also helped legislate them into being. In the 1926 Legislative Assembly five of the forty-eight MLAs were doctors, including J. D. Maclean who called for the first survey of the feeble-minded and E. J. Rothwell who chaired the 1925 Commission on Mental Hygiene. The 1928 assembly

---

80. Vancouver *Sun*, 15 Feb. 1934, 6.
81. "An Act Respecting Sexual Sterilization," chap. 59, 7 April 1933.

included six doctors and a druggist. Tolmie as a stock-breeder could also be considered as expert in matters of heredity. The North American eugenics movement in fact began as an offshoot of the American Breeders' Association and so it was altogether fitting that it was with Tolmie as premier and in a legislature which included a pharmacist and seven doctors (the highest number of medical men ever to occupy seats in the Legislative Assembly) that the province's Board of Eugenics was established.[82] In the press, Drs J. G. McKay, R. E. McKechnie, Edwin Carter, and Frederic Brodie all expressed support for the bill, and W. B. Burnett asserted that every doctor in the province was of the same opinion.[83] Opposing views were certainly scarce but it should be recalled that in the legislature such opposition as there was had been voiced by Drs Gillis and Sutherland.

Did the sexual sterilization act accomplish what its proponents claimed it would? This question does not admit of a simple answer because in fact sterilization had been proposed for a variety of not always consistent reasons. The bill came into force in July 1933 but only in November was a Board of Eugenics established. It was made up of Judge H. B. Robertson, Dr J. G. McKay, who had campaigned long for such a board, and Laura Holland.[84] In January 1934 the press began to complain that the board had as yet done nothing, in part because its powers were limited by the consent requirement.[85] Indeed, during the debate over the bill Drs Burnett and Borden had wanted the legislation extended along the lines of the California legislation which sanctioned compulsory sterilization. Such demands were taken up in 1934 by the Nanaimo Local Council of Women which wanted criminals forcibly sterilized.[86]

In British Columbia the act was not frequently employed. In Alberta between 1928 and 1971, 4725 cases were proposed for sterilization and 2822 approved. In British Columbia it is difficult to determine the total number sterilized but it was not more than a few hundred.[87] This was because of the narrower provisions of the British Columbia act. In Alberta sterilization was approved if a patient's reproduction involved the risk of hereditary taint; in British Columbia sterilization was only allowed if such a taint was likely to result. Moreover, in Alberta sterilization was not

---

82. See the *Canadian Parliamentary Guide* for the appropriate years.
83. Vancouver *Daily News*, 3 April 1933, 6.
84. Vancouver *Daily Province*, 1 Nov. 1933, 22.
85. Victoria *Daily Times*, 6 Jan. 1934, 1–2.
86. Vancouver *Sun*, 20 June 1934, 9.
87. LRCC, *Sterilization*, 27–8. See also A. E. Grauer, *Hygiène publique: étude preparée pour la commission royale des relations entre le dominion et les provinces* (Ottawa 1939), 54, 120.

limited, as in British Columbia, to inmates of institutions, but was also proposed for clients of the Mental Hygiene Clinic.

If it is difficult to determine the full extent of the use of the British Columbia legislation, it is even more difficult to determine the "success" of sterilization. An attempt was made in 1945 by M. Stewart in a report entitled "Some Aspects of Eugenical Sterilization in British Columbia with Special Reference to Patients Sterilized from Essondale Provincial Hospital since 1935."[88] To determine if the sixty-four cases of sterilization at Essondale had had the desired results, Stewart essayed a full history of each patient; this was not always possible because, once discharged, many simply disappeared from view. In the main it was those who had awkward economic adjustments to face and came to the attention of Social Service Exchange who could be traced. But even with its gaps the Stewart report is revealing, inasmuch as it shows that sterilization was not carried out in random fashion. There was a marked sexual division. Of the sixty-four sterilized, seven were men (six married and one single) and fifty-seven were women (eleven married and forty-six single). Six of the seven men operated on were over the age of twenty-five; thirty-three of the fifty-seven women were under twenty-five and in fact three were under fifteen. The one single male had no children whereas the forty-six single women had had thirty-three illegitimate children. Even the diagnoses differed along sex lines. Of the males six were declared psychotic and one an imbecile; of the females eighteen were psychotic, eighteen imbeciles, and twenty-one morons. Six of the seven men were discharged after the operation but only forty-one of the fifty-seven women. In short, the picture that emerges of the "typical" sterilized patient was of a young unwed mother who had been diagnosed as mentally retarded.

What was the effect of the operation?[89] Of the sixty-four sterilized, only forty-seven were discharged. Fourteen remained in care, two died while in care, and one died as a result of the operation. The fourteen who were not discharged can certainly not be counted as "successful" cases; in fact, since sterilization was supposed to be carried out only to permit a return to the community, it is not clear why they were operated on in the first place. Of the remaining forty-seven, Stewart had follow-up information on twenty-seven; he optimistically assumed that a lack of subsequent

---

88. PABC, Provincial Secretary, Mental Health Services, GR 542, box 14, "Sterilization" [GR 542]. The report was prepared by M. Stewart for A. L. Crease, the superintendent of Essondale, who forwarded it to deputy provincial secretary P. Walker on the assumption that sterilization would be discussed in the 1946 session of the legislature. Most of the medical diagnoses in the report were provided by Dr E. J. Ryan.

89. Sterilization was by vasectomy for males and by salpengectomy for females.

reports could be taken as a sign that major problems had not ensued. The report classed the twenty-seven remaining as thirteen "successes," twelve "doubtfuls," and only two failures.

To reappraise the supposed success or failure of the operation, it has to be recalled that sterilization was defended by those who wanted to eliminate hereditary taints, decarcerate inmates and so save the province money, improve the life of the mentally deficient, and facilitate moral improvement. The perfect case would have presumably been one in which all four goals were attained, but these results were in fact rarities.

Although a Board of Eugenics was established with the purported purpose of supervising a policy based on the theory of hereditary taints, the board did not include a geneticist and did not show any great interest in the subject. Only in sixteen of the sixty-four cases was any mention made of kin having histories of mental problems. Instead of hard data on genetically linked complaints, the Stewart report fell back on reference to incarcerated kin, siblings seen at Child Guidance Clinics, cases of incest and suicide, and the pat phrase the "family history is not good" as sufficient evidence of hereditary taints. The point that the issue of heredity was slighted in the board's discussions was made by one of its own members, Isobel Harvey, who wrote to E. W. Griffith, the assistant deputy provincial secretary in 1944. Harvey complained that another member, Judge Manson, was too busy to attend to the board's duties. "His mind [was] never on eugenics," she stated, and he had no idea of the patient's problems.[90] Harvey wanted Manson replaced; as it turned out she was removed and the board's luke-warm interest in eugenics continued.[91]

Those interested in the economic savings that sterilization was to bring could at least argue that by removing forty-seven inmates from the asylum the province was saving money.[92] Such an argument was countered in the Stewart report itself, however, in its depiction of the mentally handicapped who had been simply abandoned to the support of the community or family. For example, case number 38 was reported a "success" despite the admission that this imbecile with an IQ of 39 was now living in wretched conditions and her two illegitimate children were in care. It was not so

---

90. GR 542, Isobel Harvey to E. W. Griffith, 18 March 1944.
91. Ibid., A. L. Crease to P. Walker, 9 May 1944.
92. On the costs of the provincial mental health system see *British Columbia in the Canadian Confederation; A Submission to the Royal Commission on Dominion-Provincial Relations by the Government of British Columbia* (Victoria 1938), 92.

much a question of money being saved as shifting the responsibility from the province to the local community.

The argument that sterilization actually improved the life of patients appeared to be only fully borne out in two cases.[93] In each case a manic-depressive married woman was diagnosed as suffering from breakdowns following pregnancies (puerperal psychosis). The operation, in removing the threat of subsequent conceptions, allowed these women to have normal lives. In the other female cases, however, "success" was assumed if the woman simply married or found employment as a domestic. These women had been all diagnosed as imbeciles or morons; the fact that they had been shunted from institutional care into an appropriate female role meant that, whatever their living conditions, they would be recorded on the credit side of the ledger. As regards those cases in which males were reported to have been successfully reintegrated into the larger society, it is of interest that three of the six ended up in the armed forces: an imbecile and a paranoidal schizophrenic in the army and a manic-depressive in the navy.[94] How sterilization contributed to their ability to serve the nation in wartime was not made clear.

Did sterilization result in moral improvement? The Stewart report makes it obvious that the operation was frequently carried out for the purposes of preventing illegitimate births. As noted earlier, forty-six of the fifty-seven women sterilized were single. In running over the reasons given for their sterilization we read that case 36 has a "sexual colouring" to her ideas, that case 12 has "sexual inclinations," that case 28 is "easily led," that case 31 had an abortion, that case 32 had "sex difficulties," that case 37 was "too friendly," that case 41's "sexual propensities are quite marked," and that case 49 was from a family in which incest had taken place. Sterilization obviously ended the possibility of these women having children. Indeed, the report even indicates that three of the women were provided with abortions for pregnancies that were already under way. What was never satisfactorily explained, however, was how sterilization was, as its defenders claimed, supposed to curb promiscuity. Dr Gillis and others hostile to sterilization pointed out that it would be just as reasonable to assume that once free of the danger of pregnancy the released patient would be more promiscuous than ever.

Defenders of sterilization might still defend the morality of the opera-

---

93. Cases 9 and 14.
94. Cases 5, 21, and 26.

tion, however, on the grounds that at least it was carried out only after the patient's consent or that of a guardian had been obtained. Dr A. L. Crease, the superintendent of Essondale, in a letter accompanying a copy of the 1933 act to an Ontario colleague, asserted: "About all our Bill has accomplished is to make legal what has been done for years, that is, sterilization where it was requested. . . . You and I know that sterilization and the removing of the ovaries has gone on in the gyneacological services, and no particular reports with regard to the subject have been kept. People do not seem to object to this at all but when sterilization for males comes up there is quite a stir."[95] Crease's comments on the extent of unreported sterilizations is important because it indicates that prior to the legislative enactment such operations had been carried out. But what Crease and others failed to appreciate is that even with the new law which required the patient's consent to the operation, such consent could hardly be considered freely given when it was the price that had to be paid to obtain release from an institution. Moreover, the doctor who performed sterilizations was placed in a curious moral position. It has to be recalled that surgeons who sterilized the sane were liable to prosecution as having helped persons "maim" themselves.[96] The 1933 act provided legal immunity to doctors who provided the same operation for asylum inmates on the grounds of serious hereditary defects. As the records indicate, however, there were few cases in which there was convincing evidence of such defects. A reappraisal of the data available on sterilization in British Columbia leads to the conclusion that this long-sought legislation was infrequently and chaotically employed. There is little evidence that any of its eugenic, economic, humanitarian, or moral goals were achieved.

The importance of the sexual sterilization act lay not in what it accomplished but in what it symbolized. It came into being because in the interwar period sterilization won the support of a large number of professionals who were convinced that a concern for the well-being of the community justified radical therapeutic intervention in the lives of the handicapped. Doctors obviously played a key role in advancing such an argument. They campaigned in favour of sterilization, they helped in obtaining its legislative passage, and they directly carried out the administration of the act. But despite the extent of medical input into the debate,

---

95. GR 542, A. L. Crease to B. T. McGhie, director of hospital services, Ontario, 1 May 1933.
96. See the circular sent out to British Columbia doctors by J. MacLachan, registrar of the College of Physicians and Surgeons of British Columbia, 26 Oct. 1945, GR 542; and see also CMAJ, XL, 1939, 205–6.

sterilization was, as has been noted, rarely carried out for strictly medical reasons. Indeed, the act was passed just as advanced medical opinion was turning against sterilization. As early as 1926 A. F. Tredgold, the eminent British authority on retardation, had co-authored a letter to the *Times* of London which stated that sterilization would have "very little effect on the prevention of mental deficiency, and it would certainly lead to serious social evils and it would be inimical to defectives and to the community were it adopted."[97] This line of argument was followed in the 1934 Brock report made to the British government which, while defending the right of the feeble-minded to voluntarily seek sterilization, opposed compulsory sterilization because it could not be justified on hereditarian grounds, would not in any event displace the need for institutional care, and would lower mental institutions in the public esteem.[98] A Committee of the American Neurological Association established in 1934 reported that the purported growth in numbers and high fertility of the feeble-minded were myths, and thus further undermined belief in the efficacy of sterilization.[99] The more geneticists learnt about the importance of recessive characteristics, the more sceptical they became of the crude social engineering sought by the eugenicists.[100]

The sterilization law was passed to deal with social problems, not medical problems. Given the Board of Eugenics' ignorance of genetics, it is clear that it was the deviant behaviour of the patient—as defined by middle-class professionals—and not any proof of genetic failure that led to sterilization. In place of medical diagnosis the board relied heavily on the social criteria of what represented "normal" morality, sexuality, and work habits to classify its charges.[101] In so doing the board was reflecting

---

97. Cited in Simmons, *Asylum*, 117.
98. Jonas Robitscher, ed., *Eugenic Sterilization* (Springfield, Ill. 1973), 100; Fairchild, *Sterilization*, 28.
99. *Canadian Journal of Public Health*, XXVIII, 1937, 152.
100. See, for example, the anti-eugenic attacks of Raymond Pearl as cited in Charles Rosenberg, *No Other Gods: On Science and American Social Thought* (Baltimore 1976), 96. The labelling process of the eugenicists also was subjected to closer scrutiny; Goddard estimated in 1914 that 55 per cent of criminals were defective; a 1940 study established the rate at 2.4 per cent. See L. S. Penrose, *The Biology of Mental Defect* (1949; London 1963), 260.
101. Craft, ed., *Tredgold's Mental Retardation*, 4–8; Penrose, *Biology*, 288–90; R. C. Scheerenberger, *A History of Mental Retardation* (Baltimore 1983), 154–6. British Columbia's Sexual Sterilization Bill was finally repealed in 1972 by the province's first New Democratic Party government.

the state of mind of that generation of Canadian progressives who embraced the dangerous notion—a notion pushed to its logical conclusion in Nazi Germany—that the social and economic challenges of the twentieth century could be resolved by recourse to a biological solution.

Debating Sexuality in Halifax, 1920:

Mrs. Donald Shaw and Others

Introduction

Although Halifax—as a port city and a garrison town—has always had a bit of a reputation for sinfulness, it was probably not that unusual in conducting a major debate over sexual morality, birth control, and motherhood in the years following the Great War. The debate came after many decades of uneasy co-existence between the city's middle class and the "upper streets" of brothels and bars, which defied the best efforts of various nineteenth-century reformers to root out the "social evil." In 1912, the "Social and Moral Reform Association"—an umbrella group of middle-class, mainly Protestant, progressive reformers—declared war on the red-light district at the foot of the city's famous Citadel. The City Council came on side; there were police raids and exposés in the press; and by the end of the year, the Halifax *Herald*—a violently sensationalist newspaper that served as the city's chief voice of militant middle-class progressivism—proclaimed the battle over. The red-light district had been demolished! Just four months later, however, the moral reformers ruefully admitted that prostitution had not been vanquished: it had merely changed locations. For the working-class writers in the *Eastern Labor News*, that development would have been no surprise: "Vice," the left-wing newspaper argued, "will never be eliminated by raids and arrests, investigations and reports. We have reported and raided for the past three thousand years. We are making the old, old mistake of trying to get rid of bad results without stopping detrimental sources....We can build a hundred rescue homes in every city and vice will still be with us. We can increase our reform schools a hundred-fold but vice will be with us until we remove the cause of vice. The main causes of vice are economic and social. Morality depends more on a living wage than on rescue homes." Perhaps so, but in the course of the Great War, which affected Halifax more powerfully than any other Canadian city, prostitution and the tavern were targeted once again by the reformers, who now could link moral depravity to low morale among the troops. Once again the key

The excerpts in this article appeared in the Halifax *Herald* in the 1920s.

instruments were the police and the courts, but there were also some revealingly new weapons: public lectures on venereal disease, and showings of a film, "Damaged Goods," designed to scare audiences (segregated by sex) into good behaviour during wartime.

The 1920 debate over morality occurred in the Halifax *Herald*, a conservative but rabble-rousing newspaper, long the scourge of the prostitute, the corrupt politician, and the liquor-seller. The newspaper would shamelessly boost its circulation by marketing scandal, then editorially deplore the shocking depravity of modern life—a formula found coast to coast in Canadian journalism. During the war, it stepped up its attack on bars and prostitutes. A "Carnival of Indecency" in suburban Halifax was exposed to the eyes of its readers; the criminal prosecution of a dive evocatively named "Dreamland" made for columns of delicious copy. And although high-ranking Canadian police officers complained that lurid and unfounded tales of the "White Slave Trade"—the luring away of innocent Canadian girls to the big cities of the United States, sometimes with the implication of their being entrapped by orientals or blacks—were causing panic, the *Herald* continued to make good mileage out of the "very grave menace," warning that "to fall into the clutches of these human vultures is a fate too terrible to contemplate." It was a safe way of handling a pervasive climate of sexual uncertainty. Until recent times, in fact, there has been little acknowledgment that family members, friends, and neighbours represented a far greater risk of sexual violence to women than did the mythified "Foreigner" who stalked the pages of the popular press—focusing on the drooling "Foreigner" obscured the magnitude of abuse within the nuclear family.

The debate that broke out in the *Herald* in 1920 over questions of sexuality thus fit within the newspaper's sensationalist trajectory. The editors knew that people in 1920 were keen to read about the future of marriage and the family. Later in 1920, they appointed a "Marriage Editor" who opened the columns of the newspaper to scores of correspondents who wanted to discuss the question, "Is Marriage A Success?" (Wrote "Discouraged Wife": "How can a woman say marriage is a success when she has a husband that has a grouch on five days out of a week?") But the heart of the *Herald's* new interest in debating sexual morality was undoubtedly Mrs. Donald Shaw's articles, seemingly prompted by a reprinted article entitled "Women's Wild Oats," a plea for recognition of couples outside the formal marriage state. When Mrs. Donald Shaw answered this scandalous defence of "living together," she was part of something old and something new. Her position, accepting as an absolute guide Christian moral teaching, is traditional; her situation is new, in that she has been called upon to defend something that had hitherto gone without saying. Most modern minds will find Mrs. Shaw's argument unpersuasive, her tone shrill, her apocalyptic predictions unfounded. Yet, in her desperate attempt to salvage her traditions in the face of modernity, in her sense of a world suddenly turned upside down, and in her attempts, admittedly rather scattergun, to respond to the fragmenting secularization of modernity with her own fierce insistence on absolute and timeless moral standards, is she not responding to moral predicaments very much like the ones we too face, decades later?

* * *

WOMEN'S WILD OATS

Halifax Herald, *2 April 1920 [reprinting the* Weekly Despatch *of London]*

When people do not understand and thoroughly fear a proposition it is inevitable that they will misinterpret it. In particular, I think, will they conceive violent prejudices against any attempt to reform sexual conduct. Cover up the sin, pretend it is not there, but do not try to find out the truth about it; above all, make no effort to mix and remove the cause of the sin, for that will make everyone uncomfortable. We have, most of us, grown up from childhood morally blind and deaf—deadened to the truth by our sexual dishonesties. The greatest trouble arises from our secretiveness and our fear.

Today much of our civilization has revealed itself as a monstrous sham, more dangerously indecent because of its pretence of decency. Unfortunately, we are just too civilized to face this, and our timidity reacts in fear against any honest dealing with the gravest problems of life.

When, therefore, in my latest book, "Women's Wild Oats," published a few days ago by T. Werner Laurie, I advocated an open recognition of passionate friendships, regulated associations between women and men, not necessarily permanent, but honorably entered into between those who do not wish for the binding ties of children and of home-making, I expected to be misunderstood.

In the earlier essays of the book I have done my uttermost to say that it is the accepted relationships of husband and wife, of parent to child, by which the greatest human possibilities and happiness are developed. I have said that expectation of pleasure, more or less refined, of self-gratification from love, is a great delusion of modern societies. Certainly the contract partnerships I have suggested will be powerless against the truer ideal of wedded love, of which the child is the glorious symbol.

My proposal is for a recognized relationship additional to marriage, not less respected, but distinctly intended for weaker women and men, more selfish, less capable of the permanent life. . . .

. . . I do not protest . . . on account of myself, which would not trouble me at all, but for the sake of the cause for which I so deeply care, against the statement which has been made that my proposals "have a suspicious resemblance to the old immorality."

I deny this charge. Such an explanation is absolutely false to all I would teach. For mark this: to be immoral is to act without truth, contrary to the duties which men and women owe to each other.

Now, this is exactly the sort of conduct that I want to prevent. I insist upon truth. Better to know ourselves as sinners than to be virtuous in falsehood. I would fasten responsibility, shackle profligates and wantons to their duty, without leaving loopholes for easy escape. I connive at no concealments, which make wrong-doing easy and honorable conduct difficult.

Marriage cannot longer be supported on the rotten old props of vice and wild love. I am up in furious conflict against secret relationship, either for men or for women.

Nothing that is known and done openly can ever be as terrible as when it is hidden, for then the hideousness will come to be forgotten and men and women will accept sin as a matter of course.

An honorable recognition of unions outside of marriage, in my opinion would act more strongly than anything else in the cause of morality and healthy living, by preventing the escape on the part of so many men—and also women—from responsible action in their sexual life. It is because I believe this, believe that honesty is a first necessary step in right living, that I advocate recognition of honorable partnerships outside of marriage.

I affirm without hesitation, that such a proposal has no connection "with the old immorality." It will not make sin easy, rather it will make the way of the sinner much harder, by fixing duties and imposing obligations where none exist.

Do let us make an effort to see this matter without hypocrisy. Our society is parched for honesty, and we cannot, I am certain, suffer the continuance of an increase of secret vice that has lately been tolerated among us. Conditions have become so bad that action is imperative. We shall have, I am sure, to set up wider conventions, establish fresh sanctions, and accept new interpretations of what is right conduct and what is wrong. We have to rebuild our broken ramparts to render safe and pleasant the city within.

Do we fail to do this, we leave the young men and young women of this generation—our sons and our daughters—to stumble in darkness among the ruins we have made.

It is no use any longer covering life with the stained and torn rags of pretence of virtues we do not practice. Today we know too much. Our social conventions have become worm-eaten, and indeed, are crumbling into rottenness. We have found out the dark and unclean by-ways and corners of sexual conduct, and we want them to be spring-cleaned and made decent.

Never before have we needed so urgently to put our house in order. We must begin to tidy up, and begin soon.

Matters are likely to get worse, and not better. There is, whether we like it or not, a new type of woman about, who is anxious to snatch from love the freedom that men have had. Many of these women want lovers, and do not want a husband; they make a surprisingly clear distinction between the two. As long as we force these pleasure-snatchers—men of course, as well as women—who are quite unsuited for faithful mating, into marriage, and hold them bound against their desire, the holiness of marriage will be dragged in the filth of hidden sin.

Sometimes there is the necessity of purifying by loss. And the final answer I would give to those who fear increase of vice by any openly recognized provision to meet the sex-needs (and we can cause nothing but evil by failing to meet them) of these women and men, without the gifts that make for successful parenthood and happy permanent marriage, is that no deliberate change made in the direction of regulation can conceivably make moral conditions in the future worse than they have been in the recent past. . . .

We have, then, to choose whether we will accept recognition and the regulation as the one possible way in which these unions can cease to be shameful unless, indeed, we prefer the continuance and increase of unregulated, secret vice.

Let us not make any mistake. There is no other choice—at least I can find none; no other way to health and right conduct except to establish responsibility in all sexual relationships.

* * *

[The response to this moderate call for a relaxation of the reproductive matrix was, to put it mildly, critical. The *Casket*, the Catholic newspaper in Antigonish, called upon loyal Catholics to boycott the sensationalist

Herald, which it suggested was the only way the newspaper would stop printing such materials. But the strongest response came in the *Herald* itself, from Mrs. Donald Shaw, who wrote a series of articles defending traditional morality.]

Mrs. Donald Shaw/ What Is The World Coming To? There Seems to be a Mad Desire Just Now on the Part of a Large Number of People To Tear Down and Cast Aside All the Creeds, Rules and Laws That Have In the Past Built Up Moral and Stable Nations

Halifax Herald, *5 April 1920*

The civilized world seems to passing through a wave of disorder and lawlessness. Scarcely a newspaper or a magazine appears that...does not...put into print a startling theory for the improvement—sic—of society. That most of these so-called improvement suggestions are actuated by one or two motives, viz., self-interest or self-advertisement, is fairly plainly evident to thinking people. But unfortunately the world is made up of people who do not think and who are apt to blindly accept any new idea that is made public without looking below the surface, and before pledging adoption, adherence, or advocacy of the newest craze in religion or morality, considering exactly from what foundations such theories are propagated, or what will be the result on the generations to come if they are carried out.

There seems to be a mad desire just now on the part of a large number of people to tear down and cast aside all the creeds, rules and laws that have in the past built up moral and stable Nations and to evolve a go-as-you-please system of living whereby every man, woman and child is a law unto themselves, and lives, thinks and acts exactly as he or she pleases without the slightest regard for the welfare or happiness of the rest of humanity.

Everything that does not permit of license, and self-indulgence to every human desire or passion, is scorned as old-fashioned and out-of-date, and those of us who take time to think occasionally, and who, moreover, have the awful responsibility of bringing up and preparing children to take their places in the world are apt now and then to feel overcome with a sensation of shuddering horror at the thought of what sort of a world it will be into which in a few years time their children may be launched if some of the "advanced theorists" have their way.

When, for instance, such ideas as are recently published in England entitled "Women's Wild Oats," extracts from which appeared in The Herald and The Mail a few days ago, reprinted from an article appearing in a London weekly newspaper, one is inclined to wonder whether after all it would not be really kinder to have smothered one's offspring at birth than to have allowed them to live at all.

To what a state public opinion has descended in England (once the strictest advocate of press purity) can only be appreciated when it is understood that the Weekly Despatch which published the article in question, is one of the most widely read Sunday Newspapers and one that goes into the homes of those who belong to the class whose means are limited and whose work is one of the practical order. It is not a paper that is read by the intellectual few but by the intelligent and unintellectual million; and, moreover, it is read by people of all ages and both sexes—in fact, it is, or always has been, essentially a home newspaper.

Nice homes they will be in days to come, if the writer of Women's Wild Oats has her way—pleasant, pure and happy homes for the future citizens of Great Britain, though no doubt the race suicide that would be the inevitable outcome of such unions would soon settle the question of posterity and there would be no future citizens for Britain and in a short time no Britain—which is one way of solving the problem of over-crowding and insufficient housing accommodation, no doubt, but it is hardly in accordance with generally accepted ideas of National stability.

Exactly how the writer of this charming book imagines that the "cause of morality and healthy living" would be benefited by the inculcation of his theories in the receptive minds of the adolescents of today it is a little difficult to deduce, since it would seem to have, according to the previous investigations as to national health and sanity, exactly the opposite outcome. If we are to adopt the morals of the dog kennel and the poultry yard, unless some system similar to that which regulates and restricts the breeding of domestic animals is instituted for human beings, how are the necessary restraints on unions of those related by blood to be placed on those who are following in our footsteps and if these restraints and regulations cannot be imposed, then, according to medical opinion, we shall speedily have a world composed entirely of institutions for the mentally deficient and the congenitally malformed and enfeebled.

We shall feel so pleased, too, when a few years hence our daughter takes unto herself a "temporary husband" with the cold-blooded intention of casting him off as soon as she finds that he is not entirely to her liking, and acquiring another and yet another, until, as middle age creeps on, her chances grow fewer and she is face to face with that most appalling prospect for any human being: to face a loveless old age and a lonely death.

Gone will be the sanctity of the home, which even with its incompatibilities, its natural frictions, and its daily trials, yet has an ennobling influence on nearly all who successfully navigate the early stages of married life and the difficulties of bringing up children to maturity and independence in a world that grows more extravagant and expensive every year. Gone will be the family re-unions which, when the children are grown up and out in the world keep the home lively, gone the interest in the grandchildren, the friendship and affections between cousins and relatives—and gone will be that tried and tested friendship and devotion so beautiful between those who have grown old together and fought life's battles shoulder to shoulder and side by side, which so often makes the declining years of people who are "strong" enough to face and carry out to the end, permanent and honorable monogamic unions.

As for the physical health of the people whose minds are in such a putrid condition that they can seriously contemplate "irregular unions," which are held together by no tie, legal, moral or religious—for one who would be healthy, it would seem that a dozen would be diseased in body and mind. When will people wake up and realize that sin and disease are synonymous terms, and that promiscuity between the sexes is a sin which carries its own natural punishment, and that there is no way of evading the consequences of self-indulgence and moral license[?] Whatever the "advanced theorists" may say or think or advocate, it is no use for them to try and overlook the fact that human nature and human beings are exactly the same now as they were two thousand years ago, and that the sins of the fathers will be visited upon the children to the third and fourth generation, today, in the same manner as they have always been visited upon those who willfully violated Divine and natural law since the world was made.

As I pointed out in dealing with the subject of Birth Control, the sole idea of some people today seems to be to make sin easy, to call sin by some other name and pretend by some twisted and crooked means that it is not vice but virtue. Adultery is an ugly word, so they cut it out of the vocabulary and call it "irregular alliances" or something of that sort. The term "Unmarried Wife" came into usage during the war, chiefly for convenience in handling the cases of these same irregular unions and the illegitimate offspring thereof; and it has since been adopted by people generally, and is likely to remain with us as a prettier and more delicate way of defining the woman who lives with a man who is not her legal husband, than the rather crude epithets which used to be bestowed upon her. And if some people have their way the "unmarried wife" will soon be raised to the same status as the woman who is honorably and legally married, if indeed she is not exalted above her, which will be a reversion to the ideals of Pagan Greece, where the legal wife was merely the household drudge and the illegal mistress held the place of honor and received the homage.

As to what the children of tomorrow will be if such theories are put into general practice, it is painful to think. Minus mother love, minus parental supervision, minus the security and protection of the permanent home life, minus everything in fact that makes up the life of a normal, healthy happy child, what is to be the fate of these unfortunates who by chance or accident are allowed to enter the world? The theorists talk vaguely of "the child being the property of the state" and about the child being brought up by the state. Perhaps only those who know the essential difference which exists between children who are compelled by fate or adversity to be brought up in institutions realize what sort of a society would be evolved—and into what a world will these machine built children be launched, a world given up to license, a world in which human passions are the only deity and self-indulgence the only law.

Truly it would seem that it is time some comet wandering off its beat collided with a world that seems to be rapidly entering upon its dotage and sent us all flying into space before any more harm is done.

* * *

Mrs. Donald Shaw/ The Right or Wrong of Birth Control

Halifax Herald, *6 April 1920*

A few years ago there lived in Ontario a gentleman well-known in political circles whose hobby it was to take the president's chair at missionary meetings. As the representative of a Toronto daily newspaper it happened that I frequently attended those meetings in order to report their events, and therefore heard the gentleman in question deliver his speech. Most of the remarks he made have vanished into oblivion, but one that he almost invariably brought in some where or other in the course of his address has always clung to me and I realize the truth of it more fully every day.

"The majority of people in this world," he used to say, "are so busy teaching the Almighty how he ought to manage the world that they will not give Him a chance to do anything in His way, but insist that it must be run in theirs."

Scarcely a year passes that some new movement is not started which in the loudly vociferated opinion of its enthusiastic and often biased and short sighted advocates is going to entirely re-adjust the social conditions of the world and make it at last the sort of world its Creator intended that it should be almost instantaneously. The movement finds favour at first with a few, and if it is sufficiently advertised and advocated eventually with the many, and in the end perhaps becomes concrete law. In a little while people wake up to find that after all no great and transcendental change has taken place, and that the world is still chugging along and adding its daily and weekly quota to the list of sins and crimes and sorrows with which the pages of its history are inscribed since the days of Adam.

There was, for instance, the Women's Suffrage campaign. We were assured that once let the women get a recognized voice in the management of the nation and there would be an end of labor unrest and social evils.

The power of women is now frankly and freely recognized, yet the strikes continue without intermission and prostitution is still rampant in all civilized countries, while never for many centuries has there been such a flagrant disregard of the moral laws, and never have women so outraged all the canons of decency and modesty in dress and dancing as at the present day. Never have the theatres been so blatantly and paganly immoral—never has literature or what passes for such been so broad, pornographic or so entirely lacking in the promulgation of the higher ideals.

Then we were told, and are still being assured in the face of statistics that prove the exact contrary, that if once we could have prohibition of intoxicating liquors the millennium would arrive—there would be no more disease and no more sin. We have prohibition and Disease and Sin stalk unabashedly in our midst and flap their wings derisively in the faces of those who shriek that they are being crushed out and exterminated. While Crime, especially juvenile crime, is assuming paralyzing proportions.

Now come the advocates of Organized Birth Control and legalized limitations of families and say "only make this legitimate and recognized and the world will be readjusted—there will be nation upon nation of healthy people, all happy"—and all superlatively supremely and absolutely selfish and self-satisfied, they might add, but do not.

If it were not for the fact that these violent movements are merely the froth on the surface of evolution the world would speedily develop into one vast lunatic asylum—were it not that underneath it all, deep down and scarcely noticeable from the top, the real leaven of balance is working, always working slowly but surely for the ultimate betterment of the world, we should all be whirled into space in the mad scramble to attain perfection by artificial and unnatural means.

Apart, therefore, from any actual moral or religious considerations as to the right and wrong of authorized control of families, it is well to consider calmly the actual facts presented by history and see if such a scheme of legalized restriction of childbirth is likely to benefit such countries as Great Britain, the United States or Canada. Germany had no birth control—hence her power in the recent war, and Germany is certainly not contemplating birth control now in spite of her impoverished condition. France led the world in the restriction of families, and France paid dearly for it in her shortage of men when her chance came to reclaim her lost provinces. Holland is pointed to always by those who advocate this system of solving the question of overcrowded cities and congested labor markets, but one has first to see whether Holland is a developing nation or a stagnant one before one accepts the fiat that Holland is gaining anything nationally by this method. What is the position of Holland today amongst the nations as compared to her position in the days when she poured her colonists into the state of New York?

We are told that the limitation of families amongst the poorer classes will bring us better citizens and healthier ones—could we not instead improve the housing conditions of these people, improve their environment, educate and assist them by other means, and so retain these citizens who are badly wanted to carry on the detail work of the world? What does limitation of families amongst the leisured and wealthier classes do towards improving the moral and social welfare of the world? Apparently not much if one is to judge from the list of cases down for hearing at all the divorce courts, or studies the annals of prostitution and venereal disease. One instance in my own experience comes prominently before me now— during the war I spent a few weeks with three women, all wives of officers in the Canadian army. None of these women—who were all young and well endowed with this world's goods, whose husbands were all good, all moral, all well-to-do, all young and physically sound—had any children, although all of them had been married several years. Of these three women, one has been through the divorce court, one is separated from her husband and one is frankly unhappy and dissatisfied. In all of these cases I know that the childlessness was caused by unnatural means. As an opposite instance to this, another case occurs to me of some relatives of my own, who have brought up five children under the most straitened and difficult circumstances, living penurious lives under cramped conditions.

Of these five children, two sons served throughout the war and won distinction, one is married and has two flourishing children, their daughter has been in government employ since women first responded to the nation's call for help, another son is launched into the world and another is just finishing his school days. Now, had these two people been of the "practical and sensible" type of "birth controllers," they would have limited their offspring to at the most one or two and lived in comparative comfort, but would they have done as much for the world as they have done by their self-sacrifice and devotion? That is the point. It is not the good of the individual but the good of the nation that we have to consider in questions of national import.

The fact is that in all the reforms of today their advocates begin at the top instead of at the bottom; they try to produce by drastic and sweeping methods what can only be done by slow and laborious ones. The only legitimate method of birth control is by self-control—the very, very last method which any reformer ever thinks of advocating. They want to achieve by law and artificial means what should only be accomplished by individual and natural means.

Everything nowadays that cannot be done at once by persuasion must be done by legislation—in seeking to exterminate sin and disease and sorrow impatient reformers want to make it easy for sin to continue, but the consequences of sin to be eliminated, just as some people want to teach children to read or to play the piano without causing them any mental or physical fatigue. We must have a pure world, a healthy world, a happy and a good world, but we must not ask people to put themselves individually to any trouble or discomfort or deprivation in order to attain it. We must deprive a man of alcoholic beverages because he might make a fool of himself, but we may let him kill himself and half a dozen others by drinking poisons instead, or sending himself semi-insane with drugs— we may compel people not to bring more children into the world than they can afford to bring up, but we must not expect them to accomplish this by any method of self-discipline or self-control.

Frankly, the whole principle of moral reform, as it appears on the surface today is to let human passions run riot, but to protect human beings from the consequences of their self-indulgence by artificial means—instead of by the slow, painful, improbable, almost invisible methods of gradual and universal upraising of humanity by instilling into the masses the necessity of observing the laws handed down to us through the ages since Moses brought the tables of stone to the Israelites—and at the same time improving the housing conditions and the educational methods and facilities—extending the education into the homes of the children and carrying it beyond the pages of arithmetics and grammars into the ethics and morals which alone produce real national health and prosperity.

* * *

Mrs. Donald Shaw/ Never Forget That Evils Flourish In Darkness And Germs Are Killed By Sunlight And Fresh Air

Halifax Herald, *3 May 1920*

The doors of the Augean Stables within which the vice and disease, which are as a festering sore in the heart of the great city of New York, are propagated and disseminated have been flung open, and the light of day has flooded into them. Those who were unaware of their existence or who, like so many, preferred to keep their eyes and senses closed to the idea that they existed have stood aghast at the revelations forced upon them. There are some people who will probably say that it would have been better to keep them closed, and to let people remain in ignorance of the fact that a canker was in their midst which was bound to sap the youth and strength and lifeblood of the nation which harbored it—there are others who, sickened though they may be, yet maintain that it is only by letting in day light, and by frank and undisguised exposure that there can be any hope of a real cleansing process being carried through.

It is as impossible, to my mind, to clean up the dens from which vice is spreading throughout the civilized world with its inevitable resultant of misery, suffering and disease without full exposure as it would be to attempt to scrub out a cellar in the dark, and horrible though it may and must be to many to have to face the realization of these...undesirable facts, it is yet absolutely necessary that they should be faced, and faced as FRANKLY by women as by men. . . .

Whether it is a phase of the aftermath of war or not, I cannot say, but since the actual cessation of hostilities there has certainly swept over the face of civilization an extraordinary wave of irresponsibility—an obstinate and determined refusal to take life seriously or see in it anything but a kaleidoscopic panorama from which each and every one must snatch as many of the cold fragments as possible in as short a time as possible—excitement, change of scene and of society, a restless craving for perpetual movement and a positive orgy of spending has engulfed us—and beneath it all lie the reeking cesspits of Sin and Vice sucking down into them every day, more and more lives that might otherwise be good and useful ones....[I]t IS NOT a fact that "goodness keeps women in a narrow cell of vain respect, and there are no good men."

...[T]he women whose lives are lived in narrow cells of vain regret are more often those who have misspent and despoiled youths to look back upon, than those who have been content to be "careful pale-faced women," preferring to grow their complexions by natural means rather than buy them in a drug store, and to utilize their brains to think with before it is too late and they are afraid to think.

[I]t rests with the REFORMERS and the WORKERS and the THINKERS of today to see that the Spirit of Youth is kept on its rightful path, and it is wise that the public should KNOW exactly how deep is the mire that has already accumulated—and into which the unwary steps of the young may lead them.

LEST WE FORGET—THAT EVIL FLOURISHES IN DARKNESS AND THAT GERMS ARE KILLED BY SUNLIGHT AND FRESH AIR.

* * *

Mrs. Donald Shaw/ The Ouija Board: "The Danger is a Hidden and Insidious One," Declares This Writer; It Looks Innocent, But———"

Halifax Herald, *25 May 1920*

...Five people have just lately been committed to lunatic asylums in California, their insanity being attributed to experimenting with the ouija board. In England, where at the present time, the craze is positively raging, an eminent authority on nervous disorders, Dr. Schofield, has given it as his opinion that the almost inevitable end of those who continue in the practice of Spiritism is possession by an evil spirit. Sooner or later, in his opinion and experience, every medium suffers serious consequences either mentally, morally or physically, the vast majority succumbing to vice or drugs. The doctor utters a sole note of warning to the public against dabbling in what he frankly proclaims to be a dangerous science, as he personally knows of many cases of insanity which were brought about by psychic experiments; in one case the patient required the services of a resident doctor and two male trained nurses, while the language used by the victim was so foul that "it seemed to come straight from the pit."

...Its advocates claim that they want to prove not only the continuity of existence, the possibility of communication between the living and the dead but also to obtain some definite knowledge of the conditions prevailing in the next world. What they really seem to want to do in many cases, and what appears to give them the most supreme satisfaction is not in proving any spiritual progress or of establishing genuine communication with the souls of the dead, but to prove as conclusively and satisfactorily to themselves as they can THE CONTINUITY OF PURELY MATERIAL AND CARNAL CONDITIONS, appetites and desires. . . .

FURTHER READINGS FOR TOPIC 6

Jay Cassel, *The Secret Plague: Venereal Disease in Canada, 1838–1939* (Toronto: University of Toronto Press, 1987).

Terry Crowley, "Madonnas before Magdalenes: Adelaide Hoodless and the Making of the Canadian Gibson Girl," *Canadian Historical Review*, 67, 4 (December 1986), 520–47.

John D'Emilio and Estelle B. Freedman, *Intimate Matters: A History of Sexuality in America* (New York: Harper and Row, 1988).

Gaston Desjardins, "La pédagogie du sexe: un aspect du discours catholique sur la sexualité au Québec (1930–1960)," *Revue d'histoire de l'Amérique Française*, 43, 3 (Hiver 1990), 381–401.

Dianne Dodd, "The Canadian Birth Control Movement on Trial, 1936–1937," *Histoire sociale/Social History*, 16, 32 (November 1983), 411–28.

Karen Dubinsky, "Improper Advances: Sexual Danger and Pleasure in Rural and Northern Ontario, 1880–1929," Ph.D. Thesis, Queen's University, 1990.

Judith Fingard, *The Dark Side of Life in Victorian Halifax* (Porters Lake, N.S.: Portersfield Press, 1989).

Andrée Lévesque, *Le norme et les déviantes: des femmes au Québec pendant l'entre-deux-guerres* (Montreal: Les Éditions du remue-ménage, 1989).

Angus McLaren, " 'What Has This to Do with Working Class Women?': Birth Control and the Canadian Left, 1900–1939," *Histoire sociale/Social History*, 14, 28 (November 1981), 435–54.

Angus McLaren, *Our Own Master Race: Eugenics in Canada, 1885–1945* (Toronto: McClelland and Stewart, 1990).

James G. Snell, " 'The White Life for Two': The Defence of Marriage and Sexual Morality in Canada, 1890–1914," *Histoire sociale/Social History*, 16, 31 (May 1983), 111–28.

Mariana Valverde, "The Rhetoric of Reform: Tropes and the Moral Subject," *International Journal of the Sociology of the Law*, 18, 1 (1990), 61–73.

T O P I C 7

*Quebec's
Great
Upheaval*

I n its narrowest sense, the Quiet Revolution refers to the policies enacted
by the Liberal government of Quebec between 1960 and 1966. The
government introduced a number of significant economic and social
changes, notably the creation of a modern educational system and the
nationalization of hydro-electricity. In its broader sense, the Quiet
Revolution refers to the rise of modern Québécois nationalism, to the
process of secularization, and to the transformation of the structures of the
state. How should this immense change be interpreted? Scores of books and
articles have been written on the subject of Quebec since 1945, and the
three following selections represent only a small portion of a very large
literature.

In the first reading, Marc Renaud distills and refines a widely held
theory about the Quiet Revolution, which holds that it reflected the cultural
and economic interests of a new middle class. He sees the distinctive state
interventions of the Quiet Revolution as answering to the cultural and
political needs of this class. The second reading focuses on the rise of the
feminist movement, which, with organized labour, played a key (if often
unheralded) role in the vibrant politics of Quebec in the 1960s and 1970s.
In the third reading, Pierre Vallières, who came to be identified as a
theorist of the FLQ, reflects on his childhood years in greater Montreal. His
memoir is a reminder that not everyone who contributed to the Quiet
Revolution, broadly defined, can be described as a member of the new
middle class: indeed, support for nationalism extends far beyond the
academics, public servants, and technocrats who have undoubtedly, to this
point, tended to chart its public course.

Quebec's New Middle Class in Search of Social Hegemony:

Causes and Political Consequences

MARC RENAUD

Introduction

In the last three decades, Quebec has experienced social change to an extent and with a depth perhaps unparalleled in western countries. As a Canadian ambassador to Paris suggested, the recent transformation of Quebec society seems to be "the most rapid industrial, social, educational and religious revolution in the Western world."[1]

An overview of the most often cited indicators will permit an appreciation of the thoroughness of this change.[2] While two-thirds of the Quebec population lived in cities in 1950, more than 80 percent did in 1971, with the largest increases in the Montreal region, which half the population now inhabits. The Catholic Church was in 1960 the key institution of social control well as the moral authority and often, indirectly, the political authority. It was also the power holder, if not always the owner, in health, education, and social-welfare organizations. Ten years afterwards, it had been almost totally relegated to its spiritual role, with a sharp decline in the number of people engaging in religious orders, a drastic drop in the level of religious practice, and the state takeover of the health, education, and social-welfare fields. While there were about 2,000 new sacerdotal vocations per year in the late 1940s, only about 100 were

Marc Renaud, "Quebec's New Middle Class in Search of Social Hegemony: Causes and Political Consequences," in Michael D. Behiels, ed., *Quebec Since 1945: Selected Readings* (Toronto: Copp Clark Pitman, 1987), 48–79. Originally published in the *International Review of Community Development*, New Series, 39/40 (1978), 1–36. By permission of the author, Sociology, University of Montreal, and Canadian Institute for Advanced Research.

1. Quoted in Edmond Orban, "Indicateurs, concepts et objectifs" in *La modernisation politique du Québec*, edited by Edmond Orban (Quebec: Boréal Express, 1976), 7.
2. Unless otherwise noted, these indicators are taken from the various essays in E. Orban, ed., *La modernisation politique du Québec* and from Gary Caldwell and B. Dan Czarnocki, "Un rattrapage raté: Le changement social dans le Québec d'après-guerre, 1950–1974: une comparaison Québec/Ontario," *Recherches Sociographiques* XVII, 1 (1977): 9–58.

recruited in 1970.[3] While roughly 80 percent of the population practised its religion in 1960, in urban areas only 15 percent to 35 percent still do so now. This was paralleled by a substantial and extremely brusque decline in the birth rate, moving from 30 births per 1,000 population to 28 in 1959, to 14 in 1974. During the same period (1950–1974), the divorce rate increased eighteenfold and the suicide rate increased to 4.4 times the 1950 rate!

The organization of the polity also profoundly changed. Provincial government expenditures multiplied by 32 during this period, with the most visible and important increments due to massive state interventions during the Quiet Revolution (1960–65).[4] The traditionally dominant political party, the Union Nationale—which held power from 1936 to 1939 and from 1944 to 1960—gradually lost its importance in the popular vote, to be replaced by the Parti Québécois, which with an entirely different political base took power in November 1976.[5] In the 1960s, public administration was totally reshaped: from parochial and paternalist in style and highly decentralized in its structures, it became centralized, bureaucratic, and typically "modern." A series of events accounts for this change: the growth of the human-service sectors (education, health, and welfare), the government takeover of these sectors, the reorganization of all ministries, the greater involvement of the state in the economy (for example, creation of state enterprises, government involvement in industrial sectors, and the creation of planning agencies), and the creation of a multitude of other government boards and agencies. In 1960 the Quebec provincial public sector employed 36,000 people, while in 1971 almost 350,000 people were employed in its administration, in public enterprises and in health and educational services—that is, an increase from 2 percent to 15 percent of the labour force. And this is a gross underestimate of the

---

3. Denis Monière, *Le développement des idéologies au Québec des origines à nos jours* (Montreal: Éditions Québec-Amérique, 1977), 328.

4. For a discussion of these expenditures consistent with the argument developed in this article, see Daniel Latouche, "La vraie nature...de la Révolution tranquille," *Revue Canadienne de Sciences Politiques* VII, 3 (Sept. 1974): 525–35.

5. Here is the share of popular vote for the Union Nationale and the Parti Québécois in the last seven elections: 1956 (UN: 51.5%); 1960 (UN: 46.6%); 1962 (UN: 42.1%); 1966 (UN: 40.9%); 1970 (UN: 20.0%; PQ: 23.6%); 1973 (UN: 5.0%; PQ: 30.2%); 1976 (UN: 18.2%; PQ 41.4%). For analyses of these elections, see for instance Vincent Lemieux, ed., *Quatre élections provinciales* (Quebec: Presses de l'Université Laval, 1969); V. Lemieux, M. Gilbert, and A. Blais, *Une élections de réalignement* (Montreal: Cahiers de Cité libre, Éd. du Jour, 1970); or Robert Boily, "Genèse et développement des partis politiques au Québec," in *La modernisation politique du Québec*, 79–100. For a somewhat positive history of the Union Nationale and its leader, Maurice Duplessis, see Conrad Black, *Duplessis* (Montreal: Les Éditions de l'Homme, 1977).

number of people paid by provincial tax money and by state enterprises. The expenditures of the federal, provincial, and municipal public sectors in Quebec have grown, according to recent estimates, from 33.4 percent of the Quebec GNP at market prices in 1961 to 45.8 percent in 1970, with the Quebec public sector accounting for 31.8 percent of the GNP in 1970 as compared to 17.9 percent in 1961.[6] The most noticed result of this febrile growth has been a democratization of the access to the previously Church-controlled and highly elitist educational system and a substantial improvement in the access of poorer strata to health services,[7] along with an extremely intense, although not necessarily successful, reshuffling of jobs, personnel, and organizations.

Position of the Question

Except for the brusque character of these changes and the dramatic downfall of the Catholic Church, Ontario, the neighbouring and comparable province, has experienced similar transformations. In particular, contrary to what is often believed, the expansion of the provincial and municipal public sectors for the economy has followed quite similar paths in all provinces and has meant a similar quantitative development of the state. Further, this expansion was in all provinces associated with a change in the ideologically dominant institutions, from religious and rural ones to secular and urban-based political and social ones.

In general, however, in all provinces except Quebec, this expansion did not mean much more than a change in the organization of the economy linked to the worldwide transformation of capitalism into its "post-industrial" or "advanced" stages. The state directly employed many more people, social security policies were much more extensive and progres-

---

6. Given the available data, it is impossible to regionalize the effects of federal spending and to estimate with any precision the total amount of spending by the public sector in a given year in a province. Therefore, it is difficult to estimate the part of each province's GNP (or more precisely the Gross National Expenditure, which is equivalent) accounted for by government spending. For tentative estimates, see Kemal Wassef, "La situation du gouvernement du Québec dans les affaires économiques de la province" (unpublished manuscript, Confédération des Syndicats Nationaux, October 1971); and B. Roy-Lemoine, "The Growth of the State in Quebec" in *The Political Economy of the State: Quebec/Canada/U.S.A.*, edited by D. Roussopoulos (Montreal: Black Rose Books, 1973), 59–87.

7. For the health services, see A. D. McDonald, J. C. McDonald, and P. E. Enterline, "Études sur l'assurance-maladie du Québec," and André Billette, "Santé, classes sociales et politiques redistributive," both in *Sociologie et Sociétés: La gestion de la santé* IX, 1 (April 1977): 52–92.

sive, Keynesian economic policies became widespread, the state organizational apparatus was modernized, and the coercive legal and fiscal powers of the governments were increased. But, all things considered, this expansion did not fundamentally alter the basic matrix of interest groups and class relationships within each province. Therefore, it did not look "revolutionary," as it seemingly did in Quebec.

In fact, although the tangible outputs of governmental actions have not markedly differed among provinces, these same actions in Quebec have taken on a colouring that contrasts sharply with what has occurred in the Anglophone provinces. What is particular to Quebec is not the changes per se, but its style of problem solving. In other words, Quebec has evolved what may be termed its own distinctive strategy of reform. The growth of the presence of government in Quebec was accompanied by a rhetoric so strongly social democratic, stated objectives of reform so sweeping, and such legislative authoritarianism, that one is forced to recognize the distinctive character of government intervention in Quebec.

In all countries where the structure of the economy is monopolistic, the technocratic point of view that everything needs administrative rationalization is bound to emerge and to confront individualistic, entrepreneurial, or market-oriented points of view. As many have said, the state is bound to grow and to institutionalize more and more aspects of social relations. In Quebec after 1960, not only did the technocratic point of view emerge, but—contrary to elsewhere—it gradually totally dominated and penetrated the state along with social-democratic ideals. Reform after reform, the heralding of fundamental objectives, the systematic recourse to the powers of coercion, and reorganization of the state permitted this point of view of take over the political management of problems and crises, thus determining the emergence of unique political dynamics and of a distinctive political culture.

This strategy of reform boils down to a typical three-act play for government actions.[8] The characteristic initial reaction of the Quebec

---

8. I documented this scenario for health reforms in Marc Renaud, "Réforme ou illusion? Une analyse des interventions de l'État québécois dans le domaine de la santé," *Sociologie et Sociétés: La gestion de la santé* IX, 1 (April 1977): 127–52. Further evidence of the omnipresence of this scenario can be found in a variety of publications. See, for instance, *Une certaine révolution tranquille* (Montreal: Éd. La Presse, 1975); Kenneth McRoberts and Dale Posgate, *Quebec: Social Change and Political Crisis* (Toronto: McClelland and Stewart, 1976); Pierre Doray, "Une pyramide tronquée: les politiques de sécurité du revenu pour les retraités" (M.Sc. thesis, Département de sociologie, Université de Montréal, 1978); Diane Poliquin-Bourassa, "La réforme de l'éducation: phase II" in *Premier mandat*, edited by Daniel Latouche, vol. II (Montreal: Éditions de l'Aurore, 1977): 15–26; and Michel Pelletier

government to the various social ills or to heavy public pressure has almost always been to arouse seemingly boundless hopes and expectations. Unlike the other Canadian provinces, Quebec has summoned numerous commissions of inquiry and policy-making bodies to elaborate, often in enough detail to be convincing, policies inspired by the desire to rationalize the allocation of resources and by the great social-democratic ideals of our times—equality of opportunity, heritage preservation, collective ownership of natural resources, democratization and regionalization of decision-making, comprehensive medical care, and so on.

The second step in government action, following the policy recommendations and the resulting expectations and co-optations, consists in implementing with lightning speed extremely ambitious plans of total reorganization, restructuring, and reshuffling. This has been done almost solely through the coercive mechanisms of legislation, without extended public debate, pilot projects, or other unsual procedures for gradual change. . . .

According to the scenario, the third act opens a few years later, when it turns out that the reforms have fallen short of their objectives, not only because they bore few solutions to the social problems they were supposed to solve, but also because they were far removed from the many social-democratic ideals they promised to fulfill. The often gaping void separating the ideal from the actual objectives and their operationalization would then become the yeast for the increasingly complex crises to come.

Clearly, this is what happened for the reforms in the education, health, and welfare fields. Whatever the political party in power, the same technocratic and highly ambitious, yet only partially successful, crisis-solving style has by and large pervaded government actions in these fields. The story is different for economic reforms. During the Quiet Revolution, exactly the same scenario was followed. Electric-power companies were nationalized. State financial enterprises were created, along with many public enterprises in the productive sectors. And central and regional planning agencies were set up—all of this in a context of profound economic reform. Afterwards, with the Johnson, Bertrand, and Bourassa administrations (1966–76), these organizations, except for a few, received much less support from government officials. A move away from the development of an indigenous state capitalism seems to have

---

and Yves Vaillancourt, *Les politiques sociales et les travailleurs, Les années 60* (Montreal: available from the authors, 1974).

occurred: the overall government strategy shifted back to subsidizing foreign-owned enterprises, as incentives for their investments, thus lending credence to the hypothesis that the political base of these administrations was quite different from the one that supported the Liberal Party in the early 1960s and the Parti Québécois in the 1970s.

If this analysis is correct, the important question is the following: how can we explain the distinctive character of Quebec state interventions? How can we understand that, in general, technocratic elites and ideologies have had in Quebec an unparalleled status and legitimacy? How does one explain that, after so many years of passivity and conservatism, the Quebec state suddenly decided with such determination to pursue social-democratic objectives that undoubtedly present a leftist outlook by North American political standards?

There is an emerging consensus among Quebec sociologists to view the Quiet Revolution and later government reforms as the result of two interacting factors. First, there was the deeply felt need in various segments of the population to upgrade Quebec infra- and superstructures to catch up with the rest of North America economically, politically, and culturally. The 1957 economic depression, combined with the political pressures emerging from a structurally rapidly changing population, forced the Quebec government to modernize society to insure economic growth, full employment, and social peace. Second, a newly formed petty bourgeoisie could take advantage of this situation and more or less consciously manoeuvre to replace the Church as the locally dominant hegemonic group.[9] This search for hegemony would be the key feature of class relationships in Quebec in the 1960s and the 1970s. Within this new petty bourgeoisie, two segments are often distinguished: one, the neo-capitalist faction, is linked to private capital and is represented by the

9. Although present in the literature for a long time (e.g., Hubert Guindon, "Social Unrest, Social Class and Quebec's Bureaucratic Revolution" in *Social Stratification in Canada*, edited by J. E. Curtis and W. G. Scott (Toronto: Prentice-Hall, 1973), this hypothesis has been systematized by Gilles Bourque and Nicole Frenette in "La structure nationale québécoise," *Socialisme québécois* 21, 2 (1970): 109–56. A similar hypothesis has simultaneously been developed in Luc Racine and Roch Denis, "La conjoncture politique depuis 1960," ibid.: 17–78. Using different paradigms (in the sense of Robert R. Alford, "Towards a Critical Sociology of Political Power" in *Stress and Contradictions in Modern Capitalism*, edited by Léon Lindberg (Lexington, 1975): 145–60) a vast series of authors have expanded on a similar hypothesis. See, for instance, Anne Legaré, *Les classes sociales au Québec* (Montreal: Presses de l'Université du Québec, 1977); Pierre Fournier, *The Quebec Establishment: The Ruling Class and the State* (Montreal: Black Rose Books, 1976); Marcel Fournier, "La question nationale: les enjeux," *Possibles* 1, 2 (Winter 1977): 7–18; Daniel Latouche, "La vraie nature"; Denis Monière, *Le développement des idéologies au Québec*.

Liberal Party in the 1970s; the other, the technocratic faction, is tied to the new managerial roles in a monopolistic economy and can be found in Quebec especially in the top echelons of the public sector. The Parti Québécois is its political representative.

The purpose of this paper is to further specify this hypothesis, especially for understanding the distinctive reform strategy of the Quebec government. For reasons of conceptual clarity,[10] I prefer the term, "new middle class" to "new petty bourgeoisie." Needless to say, my argument here will be a highly tentative one. As Barrington Moore has stated, "All that the social historian can do is point to a contingent connection among changes in the structure of society." And, given the complexity of the issues to be addressed, their contemporary character and the lack of systematically gathered data, we can only hope to develop a plausible interpretation of the exceptional dominance of technocratic ideologies and elite groups, coloured as they are by social democratic ideas, in Quebec's political arena.

SUMMARY OF THE ARGUMENT

The most plausible and all-embracing hypothesis to explain the distinctive problem-solving style of the Quebec state during the 1960s and 1970s is the emergence of a new middle class with a definite stake in the expansion of the state apparatus and the latter's legitimacy in society. The following summarizes this hypothesis.

Contrary to Anglophone provinces, the expansion of the state in Quebec occurred in a political and economic context that radically altered the pattern of class relations. Quebec's political economy can be schematically characterized by the following idiosyncratic elements.

First, there have been profound structural changes in Quebec's economy since the end of the Second World War, with the numbers of white-collar workers and skilled manual labourers growing in leaps and bounds compared to the number of unskilled and agricultural jobs. The result has been an impressive surge in the upward mobility of the French-speaking segment of the Quebec population, and an equally impressive increase in the college and university enrolment figures. This trend gathered momen-

---

10. For a discussion of these terms, see Anthony Giddens, *The Class Structure of Advanced Societies* (New York: Harper and Row, 1973).

tum and, by the mid-1960s, thousands and thousands of young graduates were out looking for jobs.

Second, the private sector of the Quebec economy is less dynamic than in Ontario or British Columbia in terms of productivity, ability to attract new investment, and job-generating power. There is a general agreement among economists[11] to say that the Quebec economy has suffered a relative decline since the Second World War, compared to other Canadian provinces, especially because of this weak manufacturing sector and its heavy reliance on the primary and tertiary sectors for economic growth.

Third, the doors to upper and middle management in the largely English-Canadian and American private corporate world have remained for the most part shut for those who are of French origin, even when they have the same qualifications as their English-speaking colleagues. Several reasons have been suggested for this: the private economy was not expanding quickly enough, many enterprises were absentee owned and controlled, and the institutionalized networks of the business community systematically favoured the recruitment of people speaking the language of the incoming capital.

Unlike most other Canadians, French-speaking Quebeckers have been determined to work in their own province whatever the job situation may be. The politico-economic conjuncture in the 1960s and 1970s consequently conferred on the growth of the state apparatus in Quebec dynamics that are distinctive in the Canadian context. Given that the state turned out to be one of the only sources of job openings for the growing proportion of university graduates among the French-speaking population, had the civil service and public sector not expanded, the gap between English- and French-speaking Quebeckers would have continued to widen, since the already scarce upper- and middle-echelon jobs of the private economy were closed to the Francophones. The Quebec state was therefore the only institutional base capable of providing prestigious and well-paid jobs for educated French-speaking Quebeckers. In other words, these people had no choice but to orient themselves toward the state sector of the economy—that is, government, government-owned

---

11. See, for instance, Pierre-Paul Proulx, ed., *Vers une problématique globale du développement de la région de Montréal* (Montreal: CRDE, June 1976); P. Fréchette, R. Jouandet-Bernadat, and J. P. Vézina, *L'économie du Québec* (Montreal: Les Éditions HRW Ltée, 1975); Ministère de l'Industrie et du Commerce, *Une politique économique québécoise* (Quebec, Jan. 1974). This is also confirmed by the study of G. Caldwell and B. D. Czarnocki, "Un rattrapage raté."

corporations and autonomous state-managed agencies, and industries or organizations directly or indirectly dependent on the state. In the other Canadian provinces, more and more individuals also became university educated, but, contrary to Quebec, the state was not the almost sole purveyor of jobs for them. They could also work in the private sector of the economy and, if they could not find job satisfaction within their native province, they could always go elsewhere in English-speaking North America.

University- or technically-trained Francophones can in fact be said to constitute a class in the sense that their academic capital provides them with commonly shared levels of market capacity and with a set of objective common interests in seeing the state evolve, by various means, interesting (i.e., prestigious, powerful, and well-paid) jobs for them. Although this class is by and large composed of the people classified by census statisticians as "professional and technical labour," it is not merely a statistical aggregate. It is not simply the addition of individuals with certain attributes, such as a certain level of education, certain types of occupations, a given level of income, and so on. It is in fact a social collectivity grounded in the material order in a fairly identifiable fashion: specifically, by the similar symbolic skills brought by its members to the labour marketplace. Such a new middle class exists in all Canadian provinces, but in Quebec it has the supplementary cohesiveness-inducing constraints of a relatively closed and declining private economy. That is, contrary to its English-speaking counterpart, it is bound to view and use the Quebec state as its only leverage for survival.

The Quebec new middle class is not a "ruling class" or a "bourgeoisie" in the Marxist sense. That is, it is not part of this core group of families who own not only the larger part, but also the socially and culturally most determinant part of the world economy, the monopoly sector. It does not own the means of production in the private economy. The ruling class is for the most part foreign in origin, either English Canadian or American, and its enterprises often are absentee-owned and controlled.

The Quebec state with varying intensity throughout its history has had to act in ways that support foreign dominance, either directly (for example, subsidization of multinational enterprises for their investments) or indirectly (socialization of certain costs of production on public works, for example, to compensate for the lack of dynamism of the private economy). State spending has to behave in such a way in order to maintain the growth of the economy and low levels of unemployment.

This reality is undoubtedly harmful for the immediate interest of most of the fractions of the new middle class, but the latter are hard pressed to express their opposition lest they undermine the Quebec state itself. From time to time, when the economic context permits, some of these factions succeed in manoeuvring themselves into the position of being able to allocate resources in the manufacturing or the financing sectors of the economy, by socializing the purchase price or the investment capital necessary for creating this or that enterprise and nationalizing its profits. Such state actions may have the effect both of providing some new-middle-class elites with the power to allocate resources and of stimulating employment and economic growth to the satisfaction of both the general population and of the capitalist bourgeois class. Generally speaking, however, the new middle class most forcibly seeks to acquire real (if limited) hegemony at the local level in those sectors—especially human services—where the state has the freest hand.

Any action that has the effect of extending the quantitative and qualitative influence of the state serves the interests of this class. The new middle class has consequently produced a political culture that favours high-profile wide-ranging reorganizations that draw on, in the highly politicized context of Quebec, broad social-democratic and nationalist aspirations. Even though state intervention sometimes provokes short-term conflicts among petty-bourgeois factions (among "technocrats," "professionals," and "neo-capitalists," for instance), there is a common class interest in the self-preservative and self-promoting virtues of increased state initiative, and they spare no pains to impress on the population the idea that the Quebec state is the only collective lever it has. As an ex-Minister of Industry and Commerce said, given the weakness of the private economy and the general leverage of the Quebec state, Quebec would now be on the verge of creating a "socialism by default." This means the appropriation of key economic enterprises by the state and the enactment of thorough bureaucratic reforms aimed at equalizing the distribution of wealth and income in the society.

Against such a backdrop, when technocratic elite groups such as the dominant members of the Parent (education reform) or Castonguay-Nepveu (health and social-welfare reforms) commissions appear for one reason or another on the scene and formulate policies involving highly visible organizational shakeups, premised on larger social-democratic policies for Quebec society, they are automatically greeted with broad social support and open arms in civil service circles. No matter what short-term tensions these elite groups may cause, general class interest dictates that they be provided sweeping power and the legitimacy they need, inasmuch as they contribute to the quantitative *and* qualitative expansion of the state apparatus. This is why these groups have little trouble in obtaining broad cabinet and National Assembly approval for speedy and far-reaching reform, however authoritarian the legislation and regulations enacted may be.

In the very different context of Ontario, for instance, comparable groups have not been legitimized in this way nor received comparable powers. Of course, a new middle class also exists in Ontario, but the state apparatus is not its only means of survival and thus there are no social forces that push for unconditional support to technocratic elites whose aim is to extend state control. To put it another way, it is inconceivable, in a context like that of Ontario, that an elite group like the Castonguay-Nepveu Commission could succeed in completely controlling an entire sector of government activity and imposing its own blueprint for change and its own way of doing things. Again, this is not to say that such groups do not exist in Ontario—quite the contrary. But, given the politico-economic conjuncture in this province, their social status could not be as high and their ideologies could not penetrate the state as thoroughly as they have in Quebec. . . .

THE EVOLUTION OF QUEBEC'S POLITICAL ECONOMY

The discussion of the evolution of Quebec's economy will use the classification categories developed by James O'Connor in *Fiscal Crisis of the State*.[12] I will distinguish among the *monopolistic* sector, the market or competitive sector, and the state sector. The first sector is highly monopolistic in concentration of ownership and in economic behaviour (for example, price fixing). It requires large amounts of fixed capital invested per worker and it is involved in wide-scale markets. Important features of this sector are the high wages and salaries paid, the stable levels of employment, and the tendency toward vertical as well as horizontal integration of production and distribution processes. The market or *competitive* sector was once the largest economic sector, but it is now declining in importance. It is characterized by its lower levels of productivity, smaller-scale production, local or regional markets, lower ratios of capital invested per worker, lower unionization rate, lower wages and salaries, and more unstable levels of employment. Agriculture, construction, retail-trade, and personal-service enterprises are typically part of this sector of the economy. O'Connor also divides up the *state* sector into two categories:

---

12. James O'Connor, *The Fiscal Crisis of the State* (New York: St. Martin's Press, 1973); for further conceptual development, see his *The Corporations and the State: Essays in the Theory of Capitalism and Imperialism* (New York: Harper and Row, 1975).

production of goods and services organized by the state itself (for instance, mail, education, public health, welfare, and other social services) and production organized by industries owned by the state (state industrial enterprises) or under contract with the state (such as military equipment and supplies, highway construction).

1920–1945: COMPETITIVE CAPITALISM AND THE ARRIVAL OF FOREIGN INDUSTRY

It was not until the end of the Second World War that fundamental changes in the Quebec economy began. After the war, a massive migration took place to the major cities and foreign—especially American—monopoly capital moved in at an accelerated speed causing the occupational structure to change considerably. Quebec history from about 1900 to the mid-1940s has been thoroughly described elsewhere[13] and there is no need for us to discuss it in other than outline form.

This period was characterized by the fact that most French Canadians were engaged in petty commodity production, mostly in agriculture but also in small-scale industry. Priests, doctors, and lawyers were the local elites, in control of almost all the political, social, and cultural organizations of the community. During this period, foreign capital and its industries began to install themselves in Quebec, but this did not have any impact on the social organization of Quebec.

In fact, till the late 1940s, foreign and local capital largely remained two separate worlds, as they were fulfilling complementary functions. As Guindon has argued,[14] Anglo-Canadian and American industries moved into a society faced with the economic burden of the demographic surplus[15] of French-Canadian rural society. In relieving this acute pop-

---

13. See, for instance, the essays published in Marcel Rioux and Yves Martin, eds., *French-Canadian Society* (Toronto: McClelland and Stewart, 1964). See also Denis Monière, *Le développement des idéologies au Québec*, and Maurice Saint-Germain, *Une économie à libérer: le Québec analysé dans ses structures économiques* (Montreal: Presses de l'Université de Montréal, 1973).

14. Hubert Guindon, "The Social Evolution of Quebec Reconsidered" in *French-Canadian Society*, 137–61, and his "Social Unrest, Social Class and Quebec's Bureaucratic Revolution."

15. French Canadians had one of the highest birth rates in the industrialized world. Now it is among the lowest in Canada. See Jacques Henripin, "From Acceptance of Nature to Control: The Demography of the French Canadians since the Seventeenth Century," in *French-Canadian Society*, 204–15. See also Bureau de la statistique du Québec, *Tendances passées et perspectives d'évolution de la fécondité au Québec* (Quebec, 1976).

ulation surplus, they could accumulate capital by exploiting Quebec's natural-resource base and its cheap labour without encroaching on the traditional social organization of Quebec society or its traditional elites. Furthermore, the foreign group could itself fill the management and technical levels of industry with little conflict, for French Canadians provided only the semi-skilled and unskilled labour.[16] As for French-Canadian society, the absorption of surplus labour by foreign industry permitted its distinctive political and religious elite, its political and social institutions anchored to the rural parish, and its petty commodity-production economy to survive despite the changes in the surrounding material order.[17]

1945–1960: The Growth of the Monopoly Sector and its Consequences

With more and more Francophones working within foreign industry and with the increasing monopolistic characteristics of this industry, the complementarity of functions and the convergence of interests between Quebec's traditional elites and foreign entrepreneurs gradually disappeared. By the early 1950s, the Quebec economy had changed so much that the traditional social order had stopped being reproduced, despite the length of time it took for this fact to be politically and socially felt.

---

16. Some violent strikes have, however, occurred after the war. For a sociological analysis of these, see Hélène David, "La grève et le bon Dieu: la grève de l'amiante au Québec," *Sociologie et Société* I, 2 (Nov. 1969): 249–76, and "L'état des rapports de classe au Québec de 1945 à 1967," *Sociologie et Société* VII, 2: 33–66. On the beginnings of trade unionism, see Louis Maheau, "Problème social et naissance du syndicalisme catholique," *Sociologie et Société* I, 1 (May 1969), and Louis-Marie Tremblay, *Le syndicalisme québécois: idéologies de la CSN et de la FTQ 1940–1970* (Montreal: Presses de l'Université de Montréal, 1972).

17. Examples of the convergence of interests between the Church, political leaders, and "foreign" entrepreneurs abound. For instance, the Roman Catholic hierarchy supported simultaneously foreign corporations and French-Canadian workers in the development of trade unions. The actions of political leaders are even clearer as manifest in the proxy battle for the St-Lawrence Corporation, the 99-year leases to Iron Ore and others. For more examples, see the appendices to the manifestoes of the Quebec trade unions (translated in Daniel Drache, ed., *Quebec: Only the Beginning* (Toronto: New Press, 1972), and in *Quebec Labour* (Montreal: Black Rose Books, 1972). On the relations between political leaders and the corporate world, the most systematic study is Pierre Fournier, *The Quebec Establishment*. See also Union des Travailleurs du Papier et du Carton Façonnés, *Les Tigres de Carton* (Montreal: Éditions Québécoises, n.d.); Groupe de Recherches Économiques, *Les Compagnies de Finance* (Montreal: Éditions Québécoises, n.d.).

By the early 1960s, while French Canadians comprised more than 80 percent of Quebec's population and owned 50 percent of the enterprises, they controlled only 15 percent of the value added in Quebec industry while some of the 13 percent of English Canadians and a few Americans controlled 85 percent.[18] In other words, French-Canadian ownership and control was almost entirely limited to the much less profitable competitive sector of the economy, while English-Canadian and other foreign interests owned and controlled the profitable monopolistic sector.

The ex-president of the Economic Council of Canada, André Raynauld, has done research on industrial enterprises in Quebec in 1961. His results confirm that the Quebec economy is characterized by a French-Canadian competitive sector and a foreign monopolistic sector. He writes:

> French-Canadian establishments were at the one extreme in every respect. Foreign establishments were at the other extreme in every respect and Other Canadian establishments were in between. With regard to *size*, Foreign establishments were seven times larger than French Canadian, and four times larger than Other Canadian by *value added*. The *average output* per man was 6500, 8400, and 12000 dollars respectively for French-Canadian, Other Canadian and Foreign establishments. *Wages and salaries* in French-Canadian establishments were 30 percent below those in Foreign, and 12 percent below those in Other Canadian establishments. . . .[19]

French-Canadian-owned enterprises, with few exceptions in 1961, were within the competitive or market sector. French-Canadian ownership was concentrated in agriculture, construction, retail trade, and services. According to the Royal Commission on Bilingualism and Biculturalism:

> Francophones are owners and proprietors in large proportions in agriculture and to a lesser degree in the service fields and retail trade. In wholesale they play a still smaller role, while in finance and manufacturing they account for about one-fourth of the total. Moreover, within manufacturing itself, the pattern of ownership is also uneven. In small-scale manufacturing, such as the production of wood products, Francophones predominate; but in fields requiring large capital investment and highly advanced technology, such as the manufacture of chemicals

18. André Raynauld, *La propriété des entreprises au Québec* (Montreal: Presses de l'Université de Montréal, 1974), 78.
19. André Raynauld, "The Quebec Economy: A General Assessment" in *Quebec Society and Politics: Views from the Inside*, edited by Dale C. Thomson (Toronto: McClelland and Stewart, 1973), 152, my emphasis.

and petroleum products, they play virtually no role in ownership or control.[20]

Foreign-owned enterprises constituted Quebec's major enterprises, in terms of value added and outputs. These enterprises can be classified in three main categories. First, from this earlier phase of industrialization, largely created by the National Policy of the federal government in the 1870s, Quebec has inherited secondary industries in labour-intensive sectors (textile, wood, shoes, and other finished products). Second, in the mid-1930s, primary industries began to appear exploiting Quebec's natural resources (pulp and paper, primary metallic industries). Finally, later on, some large American high-technology enterprises (automobile, electrical equipment) came in, but at an extremely slow pace compared to Ontario.[21] Almost all these enterprises are owned and controlled by American and English-Canadian interests.[22] The second and third categories are largely part of the American monopolistic sector. The first category shows to a lesser extent similar monopolistic features.

Weakness of this Economy

This general structure of the economy in the early 1960s (much of it is still the same) had key economic and social consequences. The economy had

---

20. Report of the Royal Commission on Bilingualism and Biculturalism, Book III, *The Work World* (Ottawa: Queen's Printer, 1969), 447.

21. For descriptions of this industrial structure, see Gilles Lebel, *Horizon 1980: une étude sur l'évolution de l'économie du Québec de 1946 à 1968 et sur ses perspectives d'avenir* (Quebec: Ministère de l'Industrie et du Commerce, 1970); and P. Fréchette et al., *L'économie du Québec.*

22. For an examination of foreign dominance over the Canadian economy, see Kari Levitt, *Silent Surrender* (Toronto: Macmillan, 1970); R. Laxer, ed., *Canada Ltd., The Political Economy of Dependency* (Toronto: McClelland and Stewart, 1973); Wallace Clement, *Continental Corporate Power* (Toronto: McClelland and Stewart, 1977); T. Naylor, *The History of Canadian Business* (Toronto: Lorimer, 1975). For an examination of foreign dominance over the Quebec economy, see André Raynauld, *La propriété des entreprises au Québec*; Jorge Niosi, "Le gouvernement du PQ, le capital américain et le contrôle canadien" (unpublished paper, Département de sociologie, Université du Québec à Montréal, 1978); and Arnaud Sales, "La différenciation nationale et ethnique de la bourgeoisie industrielle au Québec," and "Le gouvernement du Parti Québécois et les pouvoirs économiques" (unpublished papers, Département de sociologie, Université de Montréal, 1978). As Niosi and Sales have convincingly shown, despite foreign dominance, an identifiable *grande* bourgeoisie exists among the Francophone segment of the Quebec population, but it is comparatively small and concentrated in specific economic sectors.

two overwhelming characteristics. In the first place, as just seen, the profitable monopolistic sector was almost entirely owned by foreign interests, while the fairly large and unprofitable competitive sector was French-Canadian owned. Second, since the monopolistic sector, with the complicity of Quebec traditional elites, was built on the requirements of foreign interests and their industries, it appeared almost only where high profits could be made. Foreign enterprises therefore exploited Quebec's natural-resource base and cheap labour. In those industrial sectors where labour was abundant and therefore cheap, labour-intensive light consumer-goods industries developed. The dynamism of these enterprises has now considerably declined. Extremely few durable-goods and producer-goods industries have replaced them, even though such enterprises would have been necessary to generate new investments and create new jobs. The combination of a fairly large competitive sector and a partially weak monopolistic sector in light consumer-goods industries means that a relatively large proportion of workers are employed in slow-growth and low productivity industries.

This situation accounts for the general weakness of Quebec's economy in contrast to that of Ontario. Here are a few indices of this relative decline of Quebec's economy. Fewer people worked in the Quebec manufacturing sector in 1971 than in 1961, while this number has increased on the average all over Canada.[23] In fact, as a task force to the Department of Industry and Commerce recently noted, new jobs in Quebec tend to be created in the nonvalue-producing tertiary sector alone, contrary to Ontario:

> About 230,000 jobs have been created between 1966 and 1971, among which 133,000 are in "personal social service- and others" and 22,000 in the public administration. More than 90 percent of the new jobs are due to the growth of the tertiary sector. During the same period, approximately 50,000 jobs have disappeared in equal parts in construction and in the primary sector, in particular forestry and mining. This means a net creation of 180,000 jobs; that is 36,000 on the average each year in comparison with 85,600 for Ontario (428,000 total for this five-year period).[24]

Further, Quebec consistently had 50 percent of the bankruptcies in

---

23. *Canadian Census*, 1961, vol. III, part 2, table 9; *Canadian Census*, 1971, vol. III, part 4, table 10.
24. Ministère de l'Industrie et du Commerce, *Une Politique Économique Québécoise* (mimeographed, 1974), 18.

Canada, while its GNP accounted for only 25 percent of Canada's GNP.[25] Quebec always had a 20 percent to 50 percent higher unemployment rate than the Canadian average, usually twice as high as Ontario. Over the last two decades, the personal income per capita in Quebec has been 12 percent to 15 percent lower than the Canadian mean, and between 23 percent to 30 percent lower in Ontario. The discrepancies between Quebec and English Canada are even clearer if we disaggregate according to ethnicity. André Raynauld has shown that French Canadians were among the most poorly paid workers in Quebec in 1961, ranking twelfth in labour income in a list of 14 ethnic groups. He writes: "The most remarkable fact. . .is that French-Canadian labour income was 12 percent below the overall average in every province except Quebec, where it was 40 percent below the overall provincial average. In absolute terms, the gap was about 1000 dollars a year in Canada as a whole, and 2000 dollars in Quebec."[26]

Eliminating the effects of several factors (age, sex composition of labour force, education, occupation, employment status, region, and labour-force participation) on this discrepancy, he found that ethnicity still accounted for more than 50 percent of the income differential. French Canadians, because they are French Canadians and for no other reason, earn much less than their English-Canadian counterparts in Quebec.

THE CLOSURE OF THE TOP CORPORATE WORLD TO FRENCH CANADIANS AND THE CLOSED NATURE OF QUEBEC SOCIETY

Not only was this structure of the economy weak for generating investments and for creating employment, but is also did not provide employment for university- or technically trained Francophones. On the one hand, the competitive sector does not possess high-income, high-prestige, and high-power jobs. The competitive sector is largely composed of small enterprises of self-employed individuals and a few workers. On the other hand, the top corporate world was and is closed to Francophones. Entries at the top of the occupational hierarchy were and are blocked to French Canadians, whatever their level of education. This has both historical and sociological grounds.

Both because of the "language" of the incoming capital and in view of

25. Ibid., 9.
26. André Raynauld, *La propriété des entreprises au Québec*, 147.

their earlier higher levels of education, successive English-Canadian generations have always been better placed in the occupational hierarchy. As a consequence, they are still at an advantage over French Canadians for high-income and high-power jobs in the monopolistic sector. English Canadians have systematically preceded French Canadians in their patterns of social mobility, thus blocking the entry of French Canadians in the top jobs of the private economy. Whatever the levels of education now achieved by French Canadians, the institutionalized networks of the big-business community tend to omit French Canadians. Examples of these networks are the well-known links between Anglophone universities and enterprises in the monopoly sector. The Royal Commission on Bilingualism and Biculturalism has noted:

> Because of their higher educational level, their position in the occupational structure, and their original position as leaders of Quebec's industrialization, the Anglophones have always been better prepared than the Francophones to enjoy the benefits of the province's economic development. Once socio-economic patterns have been established, they tend to be self-perpetuating; the momentum favouring the Anglophones was never matched in the Francophone community.[27]

As a consequence, very few French Canadians could be considered part of a corporate elite. Porter[28] estimated this group to be 51 persons in 1951 (or 6.7 percent of the Canadian corporate elite at that time). Milner and Milner[29] and Clement[30] estimate that in 1971, while French Canadians constituted a third of the Canadian population, this group included only 65 persons (or 8.4 percent of the Canadian corporate elite). In Milner and Milner's words:

> We looked at those Quebec firms controlled by French Canadians, borrowing the results of a study[31] which selected from these firms a sample of the two largest banks, the two largest trust companies, the six largest industries, the three largest insurance companies, and the three largest finance companies. There are 216 positions on the boards of directors of these enterprises held by 163 persons. Of these 163 persons,

---

27. Report of the Royal Commission on Bilingualism and Biculturalism, 81.
28. John Porter, "The Economic Elite and the Social Structure in Canada" in *Canadian Society*, edited by B. R. Blishen, F. E. Jones, K. D. Naegele and J. Porter (Toronto: Macmillan, 1961), 486–500.
29. Sheilagh Hodgins Milner and Henry Milner, *The Decolonization of Quebec: An Analysis of Left-Wing Nationalism* (Toronto: McClelland and Stewart, 1973).
30. Wallace Clement, *The Canadian Corporate Elite: An Analysis of Economic Power* (Toronto: McClelland and Stewart, 1975).
31. André Raynauld, *La Propriété des entreprises au Québec.*

65 (40%) hold 118 (54%) of the 216 positions. These men hold among themselves 50% of the directorships of the insurance companies, 68% of the trust companies, 43% of the six industries, and 72% of the banks. These 65 persons thus are a good approximation of the French-Canadian economic elite....Over half of this elite was educated in two schools: Collège Sainte-Marie and Jean de Brébeuf.[32]

It is important to add here that, notwithstanding the enormous fiscal and legal efforts of the Quebec state in the late 1960s to raise the level of education among Francophones and to enforce French as the language of work in Quebec, the private economy remained closed to Francophones. This runs counter to the popular belief that, with the increased levels of educational attainments of the Quebec population and the corollary rejection of the self-defeating rural and Catholic ideology, French Canadians could be in a position to make significant inroads into the private monopolistic economy.

Wallace Clement has presented convincing evidence to counter this belief. Noticing that the number of French Canadians in the economic elite had risen only from 51 to 65 from 1951 to 1971, he writes:

This means a net increase of only 14 more French Canadians or 1.7 percent more of the elite population over the last 20 years. These have not been uneventful years in French-Anglo relations; quite the contrary, they were supposed to contain the "new awakening" (a loaded phrase which somehow assumes the French have themselves been their own barrier to gaining equality and not their position vis-à-vis the dominant Anglos) and the "quiet revolution" of the 1960s and the not-so-quiet revolution of recent years. In spite of ideological statements to the contrary, the French have not made significant inroads into the economic world.[33]

He then cites the research of Presthus[34] to show that not only have the French not made it to the very top of the corporate world, but they also did not make gains in the middle range and smaller corporations:

A recent study based on 12,741 names of executives from some 2,400 companies operating in Canada listed in the 1971 *Directory of Directors* found only 9.4 percent to be French Canadians. This is only about one

---

32. Milner and Milner, *The Decolonization of Quebec*, 71.
33. Clement, *The Canadian Corporate Elite*, 233–34.
34. Robert Presthus, *Elite Accommodation in Canadian Politics* (Cambridge: Cambridge University Press, 1973).

percent more than are to be found in the economic elite and includes many corporations much smaller than the 113 dominant ones which are the basis of this study.[35]

Further evidence of the restricted mobility of Francophones into the private economy is provided by a study of the Institut International d'Économie Quantitative. It shows that, in 1971, 28 percent of the top management jobs in the private economy earning above $20,000, 28 percent of the middle management occupations earning between $15,000 and $19,999, and 48 percent of lower-level management positions earning between $5,000 and $14,999 were held by Francophones, while French Canadians constituted 75 percent of the labour force in 1971.[36] In other words, the proportion of Francophones occupying any level of management in the private economy is considerably smaller than the proportion of Francophones in the overall labour force. An analysis of the 1971 census has even shown that, at a same level of managerial occupation, French Canadians earn 11 percent less than their English-Canadian counterparts.[37]

To sum up, university- and technically trained Francophones were in the early 1960s and still by the mid-1970s confronted with the following situation: a fairly large competitive economy with practically no appropriate job for their training and a monopolistic economy with only a few job outlets, either because enterprises are absentee owned and controlled or because some of them are in such obsolete industrial sectors that they do not expand enough to provide new jobs. When a position does open up, because of the historically determined linkages between the Anglophones and the business community, it tends to be given to an Anglophone.

---

35. Clement, *The Canadian Corporate Elite*, 234. As Pierre Fournier has argued in "Les tendances nouvelles du pouvoir économique au Québec," *Le Devoir*, 9 and 10 juin 1976, there is something intrinsically misleading in this approach. Generally, it tends to underestimate the importance of the French-Canadian bourgeoisie because it computes only the number of persons on corporate boards, a number likely to be substantially increased by legislation forcing French as the language of work in Quebec. Further, since these data are limited to the corporate world, they do not include this segment of the Quebec bourgeoisie linked to the co-operative movement (Mouvement Desjardins, Coopérative Fédérée, Coopérative agricole de Granby) and to state enterprises (like Sidbec, Dosco, and the Société Générale de Financement).

36. Tore Thonstad with C. Fluet and C. Ross, *Simulations de la pénétration des francophones parmi les cadres du secteur privé au Québec, 1971–1986*, Études réalisées pour le compte de la Commission d'enquête sur la situation de la langue française et sur les droits linguistiques au Québec (L'éditeur officiel du Québec, February 1974).

37. Dominique Clift, "French Elite Lags in Salary Scale," *La Presse* (1975).

Almost the only job outlets therefore seem in the state sector of the economy.

One could object that, given this situation, French Canadians have incentives to go to work elsewhere in Canada or North America, as was the case for many French-Canadian unskilled labourers during the 1920s and the Depression years, but the situation was quite different then. In the 1920s and 1930s, the surplus labour of rural Quebec was such that it could not be entirely absorbed by incoming industry. In the 1960s and 1970s, we are talking about a different kind of people, individuals who have over 15 years of formal education and who correctly believe that they have the skills necessary for the top jobs at least as much as their Anglophone counterparts. In such cases, cultural barriers impose considerable restrictions on geographic mobility much more than they did in the 1920s or 1930s. The French-Canadian situation is different from that experienced by Canadians in the poorer Atlantic provinces. Maritimers who do not find jobs in their native province will tend to look for jobs anywhere on the North American continent. A corresponding Québécois, unless he or she accepts the disturbing emotional consequences of becoming an expatriate, is almost glued to Quebec's territory, whatever the job outlets.

Evidence for this phenomenon is overwhelming. For instance, reporting on a study of Quebec engineers, the Royal Commission on Bilingualism and Biculturalism wrote:

> Although 80 percent of the Francophone engineers in our Montreal sample thought Quebec offered them the best opportunities, only nine percent of the Anglophones agreed with them; almost half the Anglophone engineers named the United States instead. There are indications that the situation is changing, but the evidence is consistent in showing a lower mobility rate and a lesser willingness to move on the part of Francophone engineers and their wives. If they work for a large corporation, the consequence of this difference is the same for the managers—a slower rate of promotion. For those who work in small firms of Francophone-owned institutions, this effect, though not as pronounced, is still at work.[38]

Further, if we look at some aggregated migration statistics,[39] the same phenomenon is visible: Quebec loses proportionally fewer inhabitants than any other province and received the smallest relative proportion of

---

38. Report of the Royal Commission on Bilingualism and Biculturalism, 488.
39. M. V. George, *Internal Migration in Canada: Demographic Analyses* (Ottawa: Statistics Canada, 1970).

internal migrants. Ontario receives many more internal migrants and few leave the province, because of the economic wealth and immense job opportunities it offers. If these data could be analysed by ethnic origin, it is probable that even fewer Québécois would appear to be leaving the province.

In this sense, Quebec is a closed society for the Francophone segment of its population. However unfulfilling the job opportunities and whatever one's political opinions, Quebec, in a real sense, is a nation, the borders of which are not easily passed.

THE STRUCTURAL MOBILITY OF FRENCH CANADIANS AND THE INCREASED LEVELS OF EDUCATION

After the war, the politico-economic situation in Quebec changed somewhat. A great number of French Canadians had left the agricultural rural world to become unskilled or semi-skilled labourers in foreign industry. Many of the small commodity producers who in a former era had derived quite a good standard of living from their farms, retail stores, or crafts shops also joined the ranks of the increasingly urban working class. None of them was educated enough to occupy managerial, professional, or technical positions. During this period, English Canadians occupied the entire top managerial, professional, and technical occupations within industry.

From the 1930s to the early 1960s, two parallel phenomena took place. On the one hand, since Francophones increasingly filled the bottom positions of the occupational hierarchy and since more and more Anglophones filled the top positions of this hierarchy, French Canadians as an ethnic group were in fact getting proletarianized, in the sense of increasingly having nothing else to sell but their labour power. On the other hand, with the expansion of the monopoly sector and the corollary changes in the occupational structure (technical, clerical, and skilled tasks becoming quantitatively more important than unskilled and primary labour) came a structural mobility of French Canadians. That is, quite independently of their own volition and uniquely because of changes in the structure of the demand for labour, many French Canadians began to perform better-paid and somewhat more prestigious tasks. With such a structural mobility, French Canadians began to enjoy better standards of living and began to aspire for better jobs for themselves and their children. More and more people enrolled in school and great pressure was put on the state to facilitate the financial and geographical access to education.

The data that follow are unsatisfying because of the varying definitions of occupational categories used in different research studies and because of the lack of built-in comparability between the studies; however, they are the only published data available. However crude, they provide approximate empirical evidence for the phenomena just described.

The widening of the gap in the occupational hierarchy between Anglophones and Francophones in Quebec is well illustrated by an analysis performed by John Porter.[40] He compared the percentage of over- or underrepresentation of French and British males in various occupational categories, according to census data in 1931, 1951, and 1961. I have corrected for some slight computational errors in Porter's results and I have computed the same information for 1971. Because census statisticians have redefined certain occupational categories during this period, the results have only an indicative value.[41]

These data show that from 1931 to 1961 Quebeckers of British origin have increasingly been overrepresented at the professional and technical levels, moving from +5 percent to +7.2 percent. Conversely, the French have become more and more underrepresented in this group, moving from −0.9 percent to −1.5 percent. A similar evolution also seems to have occurred in the category "manager" between 1951 and 1961. For primary and unskilled jobs, although the gap has not been widened as much between 1931 and 1961, French Canadians have been constantly overrepresented, moving from 0.3 percent to 1.1 percent in 1961, to 1.3 percent in 1971. For the other occupational levels, there seems to have been a levelling off of the differences between the two groups, both increasingly tending towards the overall male labour-force distribution.

In other words, between 1931 and 1961, there seems to have been a widening gap between Anglophones and Francophones. This view is also confirmed by Rocher and de Jocas' analysis[42] of intergenerational mobility of sons in 1954. It showed that the relative proportion of English Canadians was increasing in nonmanual tasks and decreasing in manual jobs. In Rocher and de Jocas' sample, the gap in the top two categories (liberal professions and high management; semi-professionals and middle management) was, in 1954, increasing from 9.5 percent for the father to 15.2

40. John Porter, *The Vertical Mosaic: An Analysis of Social Class and Power in Canada* (Toronto: University of Toronto Press, 1965).

41. For reasons of space, all tables have been dropped from this article. For further detail, see Marc Renaud, "The Political Economy of the Quebec Health-Care Reforms" (Ph.D. thesis, University of Wisconsin, Madison, 1976), 411–28.

42. Guy Rocher and Yves de Jocas, "Inter-Generation Occupational Mobility in the Province of Quebec," *The Canadian Journal of Economics and Political Science* 23, 1 (Feb. 1957).

percent for the sons, in favour of the Anglophones, while manual workers were increasingly French in origin, the gap moving from 14.3 percent to 29.3 percent.

In the 1971 census, the overall picture changed considerably. For all the occupational categories listed, the distribution of Anglophones and Francophones tended towards the overall labour-force distribution. While the gap for "professionals and technicians" had been widening between 1931 and 1961, it is reduced by more than a half in 1971, the British moving from an overrepresentation of +7.2 percent in 1961 to only +3.2 percent in 1971, the French moving from an underrepresentation of −1.5 percent to −0.8 percent, for a reduction of the difference from 8.7 percent in 1961 to 4.0 percent in 1971. Although this might only be an artifact of the census redefinitions, a similar, yet less drastic, phenomenon seems to have occurred for "managers." The gap between Francophones and Anglophones in primary and unskilled jobs diminished from 7.0 percent to 3.6 percent.

The same phenomenon has been noticed by Jacques Dofny and Muriel Garon-Audy,[43] who studied the intergenerational mobility of sons in 1964, which they compared with the identical study of Rocher and de Jocas for sons in 1954. In 1964, the gap between Anglophones and Francophones was significantly reduced for all categories except "semi-professionals and middle managers," for "skilled and semi-skilled workers," and for "personal services." They concluded:

> In summary, for reduction of the gaps between French Canadians and English Canadians from the generation of fathers to the generation of sons in contrast to what was observed in 1954 (in 1954, in 6/8 cases the gap was increasing between the two ethnic groups; in 1964, on the contrary, the gap is decreased in 5/8 cases) would underline an acceleration of mobility for French Canadians.[44]

Sociologists call this phenomenon "structural" mobility, as opposed to "individual" mobility. Dofny and Garon-Audy have attempted to quantify its importance. French Canadians have recently experienced an enormous social mobility, much more so than the French Canadians studied in 1954 by Rocher and de Jocas or the English Canadians surveyed in 1964: 75.1 percent of the French Canadians studied in 1964 (with 50 percent upwardly mobile, 15 percent downwardly mobile, and 10 percent mobile

---

43. Jacques Dofny and Muriel Garon-Audy, "Mobilités Professionnelles au Québec," *Sociologie et Societé* I, 2 (Nov. 1969): 277–302.
44. Ibid., 287.

to approximately equivalent jobs) have been mobile with respect to their fathers' occupational status, as compared to 64.1 percent in 1954 (35 percent upwardly mobile, 20 percent downwardly mobile, and 10 percent mobile to equivalent jobs) and to 66.0 percent of the Anglo-Canadians in 1964. Yet, this recent social mobility of French Canadians is to an important extent solely attributable to changes in the occupational structure—from primary and unskilled labour to skilled and white-collar tasks—that is, the mobility was structural rather than individual. Nearly half (45.0 percent) of the observed mobility among French Canadians in 1964 is structural, compared to a fourth (27.6 percent) of the observed mobility in 1954.

The Porter, Rocher/de Jocas, and Dofny/Garon-Audy data underline a key phenomenon. They seem to show that the gap between Anglophones and Francophones, which had been widening between 1930 and 1960, was transferred during the 1960s to higher levels in the occupational hierarchy because of the structural changes in the economy. The 1971 census data indicate that this gap has perhaps even begun to diminish, with proportionally more French Canadians entering managerial, professional, and technical jobs. In other words, while for a long time it looked as if the whole French-Canadian ethnic group was being increasingly proletarianized, the 1971 census shows, it seems, that an important class cleavage is appearing within the Francophone community in Quebec. Given the closure of the private monopolistic economy to French Canadians, this can only be attributable to the expansion of the Quebec state sector of the economy. The expansion of the state sector opened up new possibilities for mobility and thus probably did reduce the income, prestige, and power gap between Anglophones and Francophones.

But before we examine this specific issue, let us consider an important correlate of the structural changes in the economy: the rise of education among French Canadians. This phenomenon explains why proportionally more Francophones could by the 1960s aspire to professional, managerial, or technical jobs.

The transition of capitalism into its monopolistic advanced stages is associated with increased levels of education in the population. The increasing complexity of industrial tasks, the expanding needs for regulatory jobs, the growth of the human service sector, and so on all demand high levels of formal training. It took Quebec Francophones a decade or two longer than Anglophones to realize this, partly because their low-level jobs did not require many years in school; partly because it was culturally assumed that academic studies were valuable only to those who wished to become priests, doctors, or lawyers; and partly because of the extremely elitist structure of the Church-controlled educational system. In the 1950s, with the increasingly individually felt changes in the economy, things began to change.

Jacques Brazeau[45] has noted that between 1950 and 1960 the percentage of the population between the ages of five and twenty-four who attended school rose from 53 to 62; attendance in grades 9 to 12 more than doubled and, beyond Grade 12, it increased by more than 50 percent. Yet, the educational sector was incapable of coping with demands for massive school enrolment, as a consequence of the high costs and maldistribution of educational facilities. In 1960, Quebec had the tenth rank among Canadian provinces in secondary schooling (actually, one out of two Quebec adults had less than seven years of school), but it had the fourth rank for the proportion of its population holding a university diploma. That this system was ill equipped to fit the needs of children from low-income families is manifested by the fact that the retention rate in Quebec—defined as the enrolment in Grade 11 as a percentage of Grade 2 nine years earlier—was the lowest in Canada (33 percent).[46] The educational reforms of the 1960s resulted from such pressures and the retention rate jumped to 70 percent in 1967, placing Quebec in the fifth-highest rank among the ten Canadian provinces. Furthermore, while the Quebec education sector had been oriented for generations towards training in the liberal professions and in the humanities, proportionally more students now enrol in those fields that were not so long ago reserved for Anglophones (sciences, engineering, and the like), so that the overall school enrolment picture for Francophones increasingly tends to look more like Ontario's.[47]

To sum up, by the early 1960s, quite a few French Canadians had the formal training enabling them to fulfill top managerial, professional, and technical jobs in the economy and, after the educational reforms of the mid-1960s, their number considerably increased. In effect, a new middle class was born—that is, a social collectivity characterized by the fact that only the certified academic capital of its members, as opposed to the classical monetary capital provides them with bargaining powers on the

45. Jacques Brazeau, "Quebec's Emerging Middle Class" in *French Canadian Society*, 296–306.

46. Ian Adams, William Cameron, Brian Hill, and Peter Penz, *The Real Poverty Report* (Edmonton: Hurtig, 1971), 219.

47. See Hélène Ostiguy, "Statistiques détaillées relatives à l'enseignement supérieur" (unpublished manuscript, Université de Montréal, Département de Sociologie, September 1971).

labour market. This new middle class is, in essence, different from Quebec's old middle class and traditional elites whose power and status derived above all from their position vis-à-vis the religious order.

In the early 1960s, this new middle class was confronted with a private economy quite incapable of generating new job outlets and quite inhospitable to certified French-Canadian skills. The expansion of the state in this context came as a miracle. It provided job outlets to university- and technically-trained French Canadians, thus securing the survival of that class within Quebec.

THE EXPANSION OF THE STATE SECTOR OF THE ECONOMY

As we have seen, all over Canada, the 1950s and the 1960s witnessed an enormous expansion of the state sector of the economy. This expansion is mainly the expansion of the provincial and local state sectors. Both the provincial and the municipal governments have enormously increased their gross general expenditures[48] in comparison with the federal government: from $101.35 per capita on the average in 1954–55 to $802.54 in 1971–72 for the provinces; from $58.37 in 1952 to $437.64 in 1971 for municipalities; and from $314.99 in 1954–55 to $844.65 in 1971–72 for the federal government.[49] Provincial and municipal expenditures took an increasing share of personal income, while federal expenditures remained fairly constant. In seventeen years, the provinces and the municipalities increased their gross general expenditures by 800 percent, while the federal increased its by less than 300 percent.

The growth of the provincial level of administration is largely attributable to the expansion of state-controlled social services, which are taking an increasing share (from a half in 1950 to two-thirds in 1970) of an otherwise rapidly increasing total budget. In fact, the administration

---

48. Gross general expenditures reflect the administrative burden of a given level of government. Net general expenditures reflect the fiscal burden. From an accounting point of view, the difference is constituted by the following items: (1) All revenues of institutions coming under the government; (2) revenues in the form of interests, premiums, and discounts; (3) grants-in-aid and shared-cost contributions; (4) all capital revenue. These revenues are deducted from the corresponding gross expenditures to obtain the net general expenditures.

49. Statistics Canada, *Federal Government Finance, Revenue and Expenditure Assets and Liabilities* (Catalogue no. 68–211), *Provincial Government Finance, Revenue and Expenditure* (Catalogue no. 68–207), *Local Government Finance, Revenue and Expenditure, Assets and Liabilities* (Catalogue no. 68–204).

responsibility for social-welfare services has shifted almost entirely to provinces. While 34 percent of consolidated expenditures for health (after elimination of transfer payments between administrations) was assumed by the federal administration in 1947–48, only 2.8 per cent was in 1970–71. The situation is identical for education (2.8 percent in 1970–71) but differs for welfare expenditures (where 73.4 percent were federal).[50] Overall, the priorities for provincial expenditures have shifted from roads and agriculture to health and education.

There is, besides governmental administrations, a second important element in the state sector: state enterprises. While the gross general expenditures per capita at the provincial level of government have expanded on the average in Canada by five times during the 1960s, the assets per capita of state enterprises have increased on the average in all Canadian provinces by four times during the same period.[51]

In general, these statistics underestimate the importance and the rate of expansion of the state sector of the economy, for they only partially include the economic activity derived from contracts of various private enterprises with the state. For instance, in Quebec, the economic activity—linked to Expo '67, to the massive construction of schools in the 1960s, hospitals, nursing homes, the Manic and James Bay projects, and the Olympics—is only partially accounted for in the previously presented statistics.

Now, if we compare the evolution of provincial finances, Quebec is strikingly different in three respects. First, because of Quebec's weaker economic structure, the share of provincial and municipal expenditures within personal income is considerably higher than in Ontario and in the other provinces on the average.[52] The consolidated provincial-municipal expenditures represented a relatively equivalent per capita expenditure, but 34.9 percent of Quebec personal income in 1971, as compared to 27.5 percent in Ontario and 30.9 percent across Canada.

Second, the growth of the state sector in Quebec has really only begun in 1960 with the Liberal party administration, while the 1950s had

50. Research and Statistics Division, Department of National Health and Welfare, *Government Expenditures on Health and Social Welfare—Canada, 1927-1959* (Social Security Series, memorandum no. 16, Ottawa, 1961), 45; and Canadian Tax Foundation, *The National Finance 1973-74*, 24.

51. Statistics Canada, *Provincial Government Enterprise Finance* (Catalogue no. 61-204); *Federal Government Enterprise Finance* (Catalogue no. 61-203).

52. Statistics Canada, *Consolidated Government Finance—Federal, Provincial and Local Governments, Revenue and Expenditures* (Catalogue no. 68-202).

been the takeoff point for Ontario.[53] This is evident in the evolution of provincial and municipal expenditures. It is also evident in the growth of the assets of provincial state enterprises. In the 1960s, there was a sevenfold increase of these assets in Quebec, as compared with a threefold increase in Ontario and a fourfold increase on the average among Canadian provinces, so that these assets represented $6,604,432,000 in 1971 in Quebec (or $1095.63 per capita) and $6,443,001,000 in Ontario (or $836.43 per capita). As a result of this febrile creation and expansion of state enterprises in Quebec, their assets as of 1971, both in absolute terms and per capita, were the highest among all Canadian provinces.

Third, because the growth of the state sector in Quebec gained momentum only in the 1960s, the current public debt in Quebec is much higher than in Ontario. From 1960 to 1968, Quebec's direct debt (the government's) has increased by five times (Ontario, about 1.5 times) and the indirect debt (debt guaranteed to other parts of the state, such as state enterprises) by three times (while in Ontario it remained about the same).[54] In other words, the fiscal efforts were spread out over the 1950s and 1960s in Ontario, but they were condensed into the 1960s for Quebec.

These differences boil down to one sociological observation: the state sector of the economy is qualitatively, if not in strictly quantifiable fiscal terms, more important in Quebec than in the other provinces. Since its expansion has been more sudden in its timing, more extensive in its nationalization and creation of enterprises, and more costly to its taxpayers, the state inevitably achieved a much greater presence in people's minds than anywhere else in Canada. This is to say that the state has expanded not only quantitatively, but also qualitatively. This has been well expressed by Claude Morin, a former high state official and minister of intergovernmental affairs in the Parti Québécois government:

> In the eyes of French-speaking Quebeckers, Ottawa and Quebec have no authority over each other; each administration is autonomous in its areas of jurisdictions; sometimes their activities are complementary, and if conflicts arise, the Government of Quebec is *a priori* in the right....The common denominator of views in the other provinces is that the federal government is the "national" government; neither the Newfoundlander nor British Columbian questions this basic postu-

---

53. For systematic summaries of the evolution of Ontario, see a series of publications issued by the Ontario Economic Council and entitled *The Evolution of Policy in Contemporary Ontario.*
54. *Annuaire du Québec* (1971), 733.

late. . . .An English-speaking provincial political figure, even a Premier, is considered to have received a promotion if he becomes a federal Cabinet minister. In Quebec, for a politician to move from the Quebec to the federal arena is no longer necessarily a promotion; the two are considered of similar significance.[55]

Because of this, the intensity of the feelings towards the actions of the Quebec government is incomparably higher in Quebec than elsewhere in Canada, as indicated by such things as the virulence of public debates, the much higher amount of press coverage, or the popular imagery surrounding political figures. In this context, given the general ideology surrounding this expansion—which we will describe later—the Quebec state can easily appear as the collective lever for the upward mobility of all the Québécois people, independently of who in fact most tangibly benefits from this expansion of the state.

THE QUEBEC STATE AS THE INSTITUTIONAL BASIS FOR THE NEW MIDDLE CLASS

With more and more French Canadians being university educated but incapable of finding appropriate jobs, the gap between Anglophones and Francophones would have widened to a historically unparalleled, socially explosive proportion. But the state sector did expand and did provide job outlets for a vast proportion of the new middle class. In so doing, it became the institutional basis for the existence of this class.

The available evidence to support this hypothesis is quite scattered and unsystematic. Yet it describes the issue from so many different angles that it makes a rather convincing case for the assertion that the Quebec state has evolved into the main locus for the local hegemony of a Quebec Francophone new middle class.

A first line of evidence is the following. If we break down the 1971 census category "professional and technical" into occupational specialities, we notice that Anglophones are overrepresented in the natural sciences, engineering, architecture, mathematics, and related fields (+ 18.8 percent); the Francophones, underrepresented (− 6.8 percent). Health and education are, however, significantly overrepresented by

---

55. Claude Morin, "The Gospel According to Holy Ottawa" in *Quebec Society and Politics: Views from the Inside*, edited by Dale C. Thomson (Toronto: McClelland and Stewart, 1973), 210.

Francophones (+ 1.9 percent and + 3.3 percent, respectively, for French Canadians; − 7.6 percent and − 8.4 percent, respectively, for Anglophones).[56] Because census statisticians presented disaggregated data of this sort only in 1971, longitudinal data are unavailable.

This pattern of over- and underrepresentation is not surprising. Health, education, and religion have traditionally been the only institutional sectors where mobility from bottom to top was conceivable for French Canadians. Similarly, because of their earlier association with monopolistic enterprises, Anglophones have until recently been more prone to specialize in and to work in hard-science fields.

What is important, however, is that the health and education fields are now almost totally under the jurisdiction of the Quebec state. With the hospitalization insurance plan, the educational reforms, the medical-insurance plan, and the reorganization of welfare services, almost all of the social services have become part of the state sector of the economy. The same has not occurred for the hard-science field. Further, the majority of the new jobs created within Quebec during the 1960s have been in social services. Health, education, and welfare employment has almost doubled, while the absolute number of people employed in manufacturing has slightly diminished. Making the reasonable assumption that the growth of employment in the state-controlled social services occurred for Anglophones and Francophones in proportion to their relative number in the overall population, this would mean that a large proportion of the Quebec new middle class went to work in these areas and thus in the state sector of the economy. In other words, the emergence of Quebec's new middle class was directly associated with the growth of the state's social-services agencies and departments.

A second line of evidence comes from the comparative examination of the location of work of various professional groupings of both ethnic origins. The Royal Commission on Bilingualism and Biculturalism investigated this question in the mid-1960s. It writes:

> Even among candidates with the educational qualifications suited to careers in industrial management, there appear to be substantial differences between Francophones and Anglophones as to where they actually choose, or are chosen to work. For instance, in 1964, commerce graduates of McGill were employed in industry to a greater extent than graduates of the École des Hautes Études Commerciales. . . . The mem-

---

56. *Canadian Census,* 1971, vol. 3, part III, table 5.

bership list of the Institute of Chartered Accountants of Quebec showed a similar pattern of employment. More than 90 percent of the chartered accountants employed by the provincial and municipal government were Francophones; in industry and commerce less than 40 percent were Francophones. Among both commerce graduates and chartered accountants, however, there was a trend among the younger Francophones towards greater participation in the private sector. Even so, Anglophones still outnumbered Francophones to a considerable extent among the younger employees.

The same is true for engineers and scientists:

The proportion of Francophone engineers working in private industry in 1963 was similarly low; only 25% of Francophone engineers compared with 78% of Anglophone engineers, were employed in this sector.... The pattern of employment of science graduates from Francophone universities among industrial sectors has many of the same features as that of Francophone engineers. Among scientists employed by provincial and municipal governments, 85% were Francophones. Their proportion was much lower in teaching (43%), the federal government (39%) and non-salaried professional services (32%). Like the engineers, they had low proportions in the large mining and manufacturing sectors (14%) and in construction, transportation, and communication (13%).[57]

The engineers' situation could be looked at from another angle. While one of the biggest electrical power companies employed only 20 Francophone engineers out of 175 in 1963 prior to being nationalized, Montreal Quebec Hydro (nationalized in 1944) had 190 Francophone engineers out of 243 at the same date.[58] We can reasonably assume that the nationalization of all electrical power companies has been conducive to the hiring of Francophone as opposed to Anglophone engineers. The situation in Montreal Quebec Hydro in 1963 has probably gradually been extended to the entire hydro field after nationalization. Again, this would show that the expansion of the state has served Quebec's new middle class.

This observation is strengthened by a third piece of evidence. The Centre de Sondage of the Université de Montréal conducted a study in 1973 on behalf of the Commission d'Enquête sur la situation de la langue française et sur les droits linguistiques au Québec (Gendron Commission). In this study, an inquiry was made into the location of work in a stratified

---

57. Report of the Royal Commission on Bilingualism and Biculturalism, 474–75.
58. Pierre-Paul Gagné, "L'Hydro et les Québécois: l'histoire d'amour achève," *La Presse* (13 June 1975), A-8.

random sample of Quebec university graduates. It showed that, on the aggregate, 25.6 percent of Anglophone university graduates in all fields worked for the Quebec government,[59] while 53.8 percent of Francophones did. In younger cohorts, the proportion is even higher: 65.3 percent of Francophone graduates and 33.8 percent of Anglophones work for the Quebec government. In other words, two-thirds of Francophones who graduated from university in the 1960s worked in the Quebec state sector of the economy, while one-third of Anglophones did. For those who had graduated from university before the early 1960s, the comparable figures were: about one-half of Francophones and one-fifth of Anglophones worked for the government.

Finally, not only has the expansion of the state provided, in gigantic proportions, job outlets to university-trained Francophones, but it also seems to have provided them with high incomes, perhaps even more so than if they had worked in a comparable job in the private sector of the economy. The relative income position of workers in the state sector considerably increased in the 1960s, while the income status of workers in the private sector either remained stable or decreased. It is remarkable that the entrance of a given occupational category in the state sector (for Quebec, physicians and surgeons in 1970, teachers in 1964, employees of institutions in 1961 for the most part) has meant a considerable amelioration of their relative income status in the following years. While workers in the state sector over the decade increased their declared incomes by at least one and a half times in constant dollars (two and one-third in current dollars), workers in the private sector have only very slightly increased their incomes.[60] Exactly the same phenomena occurred in Ontario, but, contrary to Quebec, they did not almost exclusively apply to a social collectivity whose survival depended on state expansion.

In short, all the evidence seems to point to the fact that state expansion has provided job outlets to the majority of educated Francophones within Quebec. It has created jobs that presumably were much more powerful, prestigious, and well-paid than the jobs the same individuals could have found in the private sector of the economy. To repeat, the expansion of the state and the creation of new job outlets within it are not unique to

---

59. The Quebec state is here defined as the provincial and municipal governmental bureaucracies as well as the electricity and the relevant parts of the education and health-care fields. It does not include state enterprises other than Hydro-Québec.

60. Department of National Revenue, *Taxation Statistics, Analysing the Returns of Individuals for the 1960, 1965, 1970, 1972, 1974, Taxation Year and Miscellaneous Statistics*, table 9.

Quebec. The same phenomenon has occurred in all provinces and quantitatively perhaps to a comparable degree. What is peculiar to Quebec is that this expansion served as the almost sole institutional basis for the Francophone new middle class as a whole.

STATE INTERVENTIONS AND THEIR IDEOLOGY

It would be false to say that state expansion benefited only Quebec's new middle class. For one thing, it helped to modernize considerably the economic infrastructure, to the benefit mainly of the capitalist owning class. The Quiet Revolution can indeed be viewed partially as state interventions aimed at socializing the costs of production of the monopolistic sector, despite the fact that profits were to be privately appropriated in foreign hands. As Milner and Milner write:

> While the reforms of the period were genuine and did transform Quebec society, they operated only at the middle level. The basic pattern of economic control, investment, and development was, except for a few adjustments, basically left untouched. Foreign interests were dominant and indeed many of the reforms were designed to encourage even further foreign takeover by providing the owning class with a modern economic infrastructure. As such there was a definite limit on the changes which the architects of the Quiet Revolution could accomplish, beyond what meant attacking the basic economic system root and branch. For the Liberals, being as always a party supporting and supported by big business, such a possibility was dismissed out of hand.[61]

In fact, never was this Quiet Revolution intended to go to the root economic causes of social inequalities between Anglophones and Francophones and among the Francophone population:

> From our vantage point today, we can make out the significant weaknesses at the base of Quiet Revolution. While it opened up the world of ideas to all possibilities, it limited changes in structure to those which meant catching up with North America. Those spheres of society which had been held back under the older order were permitted to expand and grow. The schools, the media, the arts, all experienced a renaissance and soon became the locus for the spread and discussion of the new ideas. The changes, though fundamental in relation to the older

---

61. Milner and Milner, *The Decolonization of Quebec*, 169.

order, did not at any point challenge the underlying economic structure of Quebec. And when some intellectuals and writers were no longer content to rail against Ottawa and devise even more complex constitutional schemata, but instead chose to attack the economic system head on; and when these new ideas began to receive attention and consideration among the students and trade unionists—then the authorities decided that things had simply gone too far. "Law and Order" came back into style.[62]

Furthermore, many state interventions only derived from the imperatives to strengthen the economy and to maintain full employment: the government simply had to do something about the high rates of unemployment, the lack of investment, the comparatively declining growth of Quebec total production, and so on. As many economists have indicated, the Quebec GNP has progressed at a high rate despite a relative decrease in private investments, because of massive public investments:

> Let us remember that, during the period 1961–67, public works such as Manic-Outardes (important dam construction), the construction of the Montreal subway, and the preparation of Expo '67 have sustained growth and carried along the private sector. The construction of schools and hospitals between 1967 and 1970 has permitted [Quebec] to escape catastrophe. Finally, since 1971, the preparation of the Olympic Games, the prolongation of the Montreal subway, the construction of Mirabel airport, and the James Bay project are above all responsible for economic growth. Consumption has also been largely sustained by governments. Subsidies of all kinds (transfer payments) have increased, over the last 10 years, at the annual rate of 20% and they now represent in Quebec more than 15% of personal income.[63]

In consequence, two journalists were able to write that "every new brick put up in Quebec costs as much to the taxpayer as it costs the private investor."[64] In fact, a task force to the Department of Industry and Commerce estimated that in Quebec over three-quarters of the jobs

---

62. Ibid., 191–92. A similar observation is expressed in Gérald Bernier, "Le cas québécois et les théories du développement politique et de la dépendance," in *La modernisation politique du Québec,* 19–54; and in Denis Monière, *Le développement des idéologies au Québec,* chap. 8.

63. Translated from Jean-P. Vézina, "Le développement économique: les enjeux en cause" in *Premier mandat,* 51.

64. Rhéal Bercier and Robert Pouliot, "Le pénible apprentissage de l'état québécois en matière de croissance: la charrue avant les boeufs…" *La Presse* (14 June 1975), A-7.

created between 1966 and 1972 were linked to government actions, while the proportion is much smaller in Ontario.

Yet, despite these imperatives to maintain the growth of the economy, certain government interventions seemed to be more directly aimed at correcting the social makeup of the Quebec private economy and at providing top control jobs to members of the new middle class.

James Iain Gow has noted that, while the Duplessis regime in nineteen years (1936–40, 1944–1960) had created only five new departments (among which only two remained stable), eight regulatory boards, and one state enterprise:

> The 1960s have seen a much more febrile activity as far as the creation of new administrative institutions is concerned. In six years, the Lesage administration has created six departments, three regulatory boards, eight state enterprises and nine consultative councils. The impetus was followed by the Union Nationale Administrations between 1966 and 1970, with the creation of five new departments, seven regulatory boards, five public enterprises and three consultative councils.[65]

Jean-Jacques Simard has likewise tried to compute the quantitative growth of the state apparatus. He writes:

> The Quebec government includes 23 departments among which only one, the Department of Revenue, has not changed vocation since 1960, 55 consultative boards which were nearly all born in the same period, nine judiciary institutions, and 63 organizations aimed at economic management and regulation. Of the 148 para-governmental organizations, 126 date back only 15 years. The growth of the 250 school boards, the CEGEP, universities and schools, the thousand and more municipal councils, the thousand health and social welfare institutions...brought about in the name of coordination and coherence, was proportional to the increase of the financial, administrative and political dependency of these organizations on the upper echelons of government.[66]

All these councils, departments, boards, and enterprises provided previously unexisting high-prestige and high-power jobs for university-trained Francophones. This is indicated, for instance, by the number of

---

65. Translated from James Iain Gow, "L'évolution de l'administration publique du Québec 1867–1970" (unpublished paper, Département de Sciences Politiques, Université de Montréal), 37. See also his "Modernisation et administration publique" in *La modernisation politique du Québec*, 157–86.
66. Translated from Jean-Jacques Simard, "La longue marche des technocrates," *Recherches Sociologiques* XVIII, 1 (1977), 119.

people involved in new managerial tasks in the Quebec civil service between 1964 and 1971 (economists, sociologists, social workers, psychologists): it increased by more than 400 percent, while the traditional professional personnel of the government (like doctors and engineers) increased only by 20 percent.[67]

A similar job-creating process seems to have occurred through the economic reforms. To sustain production in some declining French-Canadian industries and to encourage an indigenous capitalism, the Société Générale de Financement was created. Electrical power companies were bought up. To create a public fund out of individual savings, the Caisse de Dépôt et de Placement was created. New enterprises were created to venture into value-producing sectors, such as steel, mining, petroleum, forestry, and so on. In all these cases, the costs of maintaining, buying up, or creating enterprises have been socialized, the profits (if any) nationalized, and the high-power control jobs appropriated by members of the new middle class.

Economist Albert Breton suggested in 1964 that the creation of such jobs may well have been their sole purpose:

> The nationalization of private assets is aimed at providing high-income jobs for nationals, rather than at other objectives connected with raising social income, such as control of monopoly, increased investment in industries displaying external economies, or purchases of high-yielding public or social goods. This implication is borne out by the most important act of the new nationalist government of Quebec, namely, the nationalization of eleven private power companies.....This decision was not a decision about investing in electricity but one about investing in ethnicity. When the decision was made, it was not decided to consider the flow of rewards to society as a whole but only to a group within society...the new middle class in Quebec....[The same is true for the Société Générale de Financement where] the resources which could have been invested to increase the social income of the community have been used...to keep already existing high-income jobs for the same middle class.[68]

In retrospect, this view is clearly an overstatement. As Carol Jobin has shown, the main impetus behind the nationalization of Quebec private electrical power companies was the inability of these companies to

---

67. Ibid., 122.
68. Albert Breton, "The Economics of Nationalism," *The Journal of Political Economy* (1964), 382, 384, and 385.

expand in a way that would have been profitable to them.[69] And yet the growth of Quebec's economy required such as expansion. That the new middle class benefited from this nationalization is secondary to the economically determined constraints imposed on the government to further expand the hydro field.

The creation of planning agencies and programs has also provided new job openings and a new mystique about the role of the state. During the 1960s, Quebec evolved broad programs and instituted highly advertised supervisory agencies. Their impact seems to have been negligible as far as tangibly developing Quebec's economy and reducing regional disparities, but they were important for creating prestigious jobs for Francophones. As political scientist Jacques Benjamin has written:

> Everything that has been undertaken in the last twelve years in the field of planning has only an emotive value; Quebec, it seems to me, must first control its economy in one way or the other (directly or indirectly) before creating plans. To first instigate a mystique of the plan and then to control the economy is the same as putting the cart before the horse. For the last twelve years, we have been working backward. We have consciously put the emphasis on the concept of planning while it would have been more fruitful to pay attention to the instruments; the "fever from France" has invaded the offices of the first planners; we wanted to apply the French model integrally to Quebec, while Quebec did not even possess some of the instruments enabling it to operationalize its plans, especially the control of the economy, the coordination between state departments and even political stability in 1968–70.[70]

The reforms of health, education, and welfare displayed gigantic reorganizations but a comparable lack of tangible benefits to the overall population. Although they did considerably facilitate the financial and, to a certain extent, geographical access to medical and educational services, they did not achieve the far-reaching social-democratic ideals that had been put forward. The education reforms were to be conducive to an extensive democratization of education, with new pedagogical relationships, the suppression of class differentials between types of schooling, a decentralization of management to regions, and parents' involvement in decision making. The changes actually implemented have fallen considerably below expectations. The health and social-welfare reforms were to

---

69. Carol Jobin, "La nationalisation de l'électricité au Québec en 1962" (M.A. thesis, Université du Québec à Montréal, 1974).

70. Translated from Jacques Benjamin, *Planification et politique au Québec* (Montreal: Les Presses de l'Université de Montréal, 1974), 114.

institutionalize a new, more social approach to health and disease, decentralization of decision making to regions and institutions, and worker and consumer participation in the management of these institutions. The reality was again short of what had been promised. The net results of these reforms were huge reorganizations and administrative reshuffling that in a sense did rationalize the allocation of resources. But, above all, these reforms seem either to have maintained or reinforced the powers and privileges of various categories of Francophone professionals, or to have created new interesting jobs for university-trained individuals in the state bureaucracy.

THE UNPARALLELED STATUS AND LEGITIMACY OF TECHNOCRATIC ELITE GROUPS

This overview of the main interventions of the Quebec state during the 1960s and the 1970s is rapid and oversimplifies several points. Yet, it underlines a key phenomenon. Because the Quebec state is virtually the sole institutional basis for the new middle class, this class has evolved a unique nationalist and social-democratic political culture. The old all-encompassing rhetoric of bishops in the Church has been superseded by an equally far-reaching rhetoric of elite members of the new middle class in the state, but with a different content. As the religious symbols of the past have helped traditional elites maintain their social status in Quebec traditional society, the nationalist and social-democratic ideals of new-middle-class elites now legitimize and reinforce their recently acquired dominance over an increasingly unionized and politicized population. Nationalism is not new in Quebec politics, but its association with social-democratic ideals is. It is this association between nationalism and a mild form of socialism that characterizes the ideology of Quebec's new middle class. Under different forms and with different emphases, both the Liberal party and the Parti Québécois—at different points in its history for the former and more consistently for the latter—have put forward such an ideology.

Such a political culture camouflages the objective interest of this class while at the same time legitimates intervention into more and more aspects of social life through an administratively rational problem-solving approach, thereby furthering its hegemony as a class.

This is not to say that this class manoeuvres in some conspiratorial manner, as if totally conscious of its interests or unconstrained by larger social, political, and economic forces. This is not to say either that

administrative rationalization is useless. Quite the contrary: it is sometimes absolutely imperative. The point is that, because expansion of the
state serves its interests, the new middle class will support all actions that
will produce huge reorganizing, restructuring, reshuffling, *independently*
of the objective necessity and feasibility of such transformations. This is
so because both the quantitative (budget increase, growth of civil service
employees and of the assets of state enterprises, and so on) and the
qualitative (involvement in the greatest possible number of areas of social
life, increase in the prestige and importance of professional expertise in
the government, and increase of the visibility of the state) expansion of
the state serves its search for jobs and a local hegemony. In this context,
technocratic elite groups and ideologies that share the political culture of
the new middle class are bound to be endowed with a status, a legitimacy,
and political powers unseen in the rest of Canada, thus providing Quebec
with a distinctive strategy of social change.

CONCLUSION

The combination of the objective material interests of a class in seeing the
Quebec state sector of the economy expand quantitatively and qualitatively as well as its self-fulfilling ideological emphasis on nationalism and
social-democracy, as argued here, is the most plausible explanation for
the distinctive character of Quebec state interventions. There has developed in Quebec a systemic logic, so to speak, that has endowed the
inevitable expansion of the state with hopes and expectations far beyond
what could be delivered in a capitalist economy and under the present
system of national government. Yet it did introduce new political dynamics, the results of which one would be hard pressed to predict. It
introduced a new "social imagery" that could lead to a further technocratic and professional takeover or—because of the frustrations, inequi-
ties, and fiscal problems the reforms have brought on—it may lead to the
tangible implementation of the ideals as advertised. Under the guise of
deprofessionalizing through consumer and worker participation, of
debureaucratizing through decentralization of decision making, and of
repatriating the collective heritage and patrimony through nationalization
and creation of state enterprises, government actions have in fact led to a
further professionalization, bureaucratization, and concentration of
powers and privileges. This contradiction may be managed to the advantage of those who benefit from it, but it may also, in the long run, assume
a liberating character.

The Turbulent Years:

Feminism Ignites

MICHELINE DUMONT
MICHÈLE JEAN
MARIE LAVIGNE
JENNIFER STODDART

The 1970s were a time of protest and conflict in Quebec. In Montreal, the authorities attempted to stifle opposition; demonstrations on city streets were forbidden. In November 1969, close to two hundred women, activists from socialist and nationalist groups as well as women who advocated social change, staged a nighttime demonstration in which they paraded in chains. They thought police officers would not dare interfere with them; but the police packed the demonstrators into vans and took them to the police station, where they spent the night.

These demonstrators, whose previous experience had been in social movements defined and dominated by men, now felt the need to regroup as women. By their action that night, they heralded a new wave of feminism in Quebec. In five or six years, those women would radically change people's perceptions of women's position in society. For centuries, there had been solidarity amongst women during childbirth and when tending the sick and raising children. At the turn of the century, female political solidarity began to develop; its aim was to bring about changes for all women. The new solidarity of the Seventies went much further and led to the discovery of a new world, redefined by the experience of women.

Women were accustomed to seeing themselves through men's eyes, evaluating themselves according to male norms, perceiving their lives in terms of the absence or presence of a man. But during the Seventies, women discovered the new reality of female experience that only other women could really share.

The first phase of the new feminism was one of defiant protest: a radical, violent, even destructive questioning of women's lives. Everything was thrown into question: marriage, sexuality, the family, educa-

MICHELINE DUMONT, MICHÈLE JEAN, MARIE LAVIGNE, AND JENNIFER STODDART, "THE TURBULENT YEARS: FEMINISM IGNITES," *QUEBEC WOMEN: A HISTORY BY THE CLIO COLLECTIVE*, TRANSLATED BY ROGER GANNON AND ROSALIND GILL. TORONTO: WOMEN'S PRESS, 1987. THE WORK THAT APPEARS HERE IS AN ABRIDGED EXCEPT.

tion, the job market and stereotypes of beauty and behaviour. Beneath it all was a basic question: what was the relationship between women and men?

Taboos were shattered. Moral attitudes had broadened during the Sixties, and women were encouraged to speak publicly about their sexuality. They also began to ask questions. Why have a sexual relationship with a man if we get no pleasure from it? Why are children given only their father's name, when their mothers invest years of sacrifice and care? Why is this contribution not fully recognized? Isn't marriage economic servitude that uses the myth of romantic love to reduce women to working without pay? Their questions went beyond historical demands for political and legal equality; they would transform relationships between women and men, and, indeed, amongst women themselves.

Women were angry; they felt exploited by the male world. Their anger fueled female protest, but it also created change. Denunciations of the status quo were accompanied by new projects and new ways of living. Feminism attacked everything that had been thought, defined, controlled and used exclusively by men; but it also proposed a new equality defined by women. Women stopped thinking about what women should do for others and began thinking about what women wanted for themselves.

The feminist themes of the period were autonomy, self-definition and equality between the sexes. Many people thought sexual equality had been won with the right to vote in provincial elections in 1940 and the act respecting the legal capacity of married women in 1964. The new feminism exposed such "equality" for what it was: women had been granted rights, but there was no real equality. Economically, women were still wholly responsible for childrearing; they were underrepresented in the arts. Economically and socially, women were still dependent on men.

Feminist critiques revealed the extent of that dependence, and the degree to which women desired autonomy. This new concept of autonomy placed individual growth before self-sacrifice, a revolutionary idea in Quebec, where sacrifice was almost synonymous with femininity. Autonomy meant that a woman could plan her own life; it need not comprise only relationships with men, children and family. . . .

The Quebec women's liberation movement first emerged in 1969. A number of Anglophone women, in close contact with radical elements at Sir George Williams (later Concordia) and McGill universities were influenced by American feminists. (One of their spokespersons, Marlene Dixon, was teaching at McGill.) These women founded the Montreal Women's Liberation Movement in 1969. Also in 1969, two medical students published the *Birth-Control Handbook*, which sold more than two million copies. The Montreal Women's Liberation Movement opened a centre on Sainte-Famille Street with the financial help of Dr. Henry Morgentaler. (Morgentaler was one of the few doctors who performed abortions outside of a hospital—an illegal act, according to the Criminal Code, which, since 1968, had authorized "therapeutic" abortions performed in a hospital.)

Historian Martine Lanctôt describes how Anglophones tried to contact Francophone women, who were reluctant to respond because of their preoccupation with Quebec nationalism. The Francophone women admitted later that their reluctance to ally themselves with the Anglophones sprang from a fear of being ridiculed and of being accused of dividing the nationalist movement. But some became convinced that the nationalist and socialist movements should recognize the specific oppression of women. In January 1970, they founded the Front de libération des femmes du Québec (the Quebec Women's Liberation Front). The Front de libération des femmes (the FLF) was made up of Anglophone and Francophone activists. The Anglophones responded easily to American ideas and saw the oppression of women as a universal fact. The Francophones, whose political education had been the struggle for national liberation, were reluctant to collaborate with feminists from other provinces. They were looking for a way to reconcile three objectives: women's liberation, national liberation for Francophones and social liberation, which would lead to the overthrow of the existing class structure. Before long, the FLF expelled the Anglophones and moved into their own offices on Mentana Street in Montreal.

During the October Crisis, in 1970, nationalist and socialist groups were harassed by the police. This persecution sharpened feminists' awareness of oppression. In 1971, two militant feminists, copying the famous FLQ manifesto, published the *Manifeste des femmes québécoises* (The Quebec Women's Manifesto). They denounced the discrimination they experienced in left-wing groups and rejected national- and social-liberation projects that did not include women's liberation. They stated that women were victims of capitalist and patriarchal systems. They wanted to establish a militant movement specifically for women, but they also wanted to ally themselves with groups struggling for social change in general. Their feminism was closely linked to the fight for national liberation, as a popular slogan of the time indicated: *Pas de Québec libre sans libération des femmes! Pas de femmes libres sans libération du Québec!* (No Free Quebec without Freedom for Women! No Free Women without Freedom for Quebec!)

The FLF, which had only about sixty members, organized independent cells. The group protested the exclusion of women from the jury that was to try Paul Rose, a terrorist accused of killing a cabinet minister during the October Crisis. They denounced the Salon de la femme, an annual commercial fair held in Montreal, which they claimed strengthened the consumer society's paralyzing grip on women. One of the cells organized a public daycare centre. However, it was difficult to get a consensus among the various cells. One wanted to pursue women's liberation through revolutionary Marxist groups and published one issue of a newspaper called *Québécoises deboutte!* (Women of Quebec Arise!). Then, at the end of 1971, the FLF disbanded.

The formation of the FLF was an important event in the women's movement in Quebec: for the first time women had dared to dissociate themselves from left-wing movements dominated by men. The FLF introduced the idea of a revolutionary feminism—women could be liberated only if society fundamentally changed. But their ideological stance was not clearly formulated and members split into two groups: those with a Marxist background, who linked the oppression of women to the class struggle, and those who saw the source of their oppression in patriarchal female-male relations.

From 1972 to 1975, the Centre des femmes (the Women's Centre) on Sainte-Famille Street in downtown Montreal continued to operate, thanks to members of the FLF and women who had worked in left-wing movements. The centre was quickly perceived to be the base of the revolutionary feminist movement in the Francophone community. With the publication of *Québécoises deboutte!*, it became a place for exchanging ideas and making contacts. The centre attempted to produce a socialist feminism that integrated women's issues into the class struggle. However, the centre was outside the fashionable intellectual trends of nationalism and Marxism. It was also somewhat removed from broadly based feminist groups and women's groups, such as the Quebec Federation of Women and the AFEAS. Socialist groups remained hostile to the feminist ideology; but people began to talk about the centre, which was very active in the Comité de lutte pour l'avortement et la contraception libres et gratuits (Action Committee for Free Abortion and Contraception). The centre's objectives were: the analysis of the status of women, consciousness-raising, and the training of activists. Its aim was to set up small feminist community groups from which a women's liberation movement would eventually grow. Its activities included setting up an abortion service, which it hoped would politicize the issue, opening an information centre and the publication of eight issues of *Québécoises deboutte!*, which had more than two thousand subscribers.

Marxist feminists, socialist feminists and nationalist feminists found fertile ground in trade unions. At the Corporation des enseignants du Québec (CEQ), most of whose members were women, a committee was established in 1973 to study the status of women. The Gaudreault committee (named for the woman who introduced trade unionism to teachers) studied the link between the educational system and the status of women. The CEQ questioned the popular image of women as passive beings limited mainly to "women's" work, an image planted in the minds of very young children, through their school books.

Women constituted about a fifth of the members of the Fédération des travailleurs du Québec (FTQ)/Quebec Federation of Labour (QFL), but they had only a miniscule say in decision-making. In 1972, the QFL formed a study committee to look into the low participation rate by women in union decision-making. The committee's report, entitled *Travailleuses et syndiquées* (Women Workers and Unionists), drew attention to numerous aspects of a woman's life: family responsibilities, lack of day-care centres, and the burden of two jobs, which prevented women from participating in after-hours union activities.

In the Confédération des syndicats nationaux (CSN)/Confederation of National Trade Unions (CNTU), a third of the members were women. The CNTU, a federation of unions, had a women's committee, but it was dissolved in 1966, on the pretext that this would allow for more effective integration of women into the union. This neatly pushed the problems of women union members into the background. But the rise of the feminist movement in the Seventies forced the CNTU to see women's issues in a new light. In 1973, a new committee was formed which attempted to convince women union members that women's issues were important.

The three union centrals formed a committee to support Dr. Morgentaler. In the years that followed, the union's adoption of certain feminist demands—for maternity leave, child care centres and legislation guaranteeing equal pay for work of equal value—increased the credibility of these social goals. For example, women workers in the public and parapublic sectors obtained, in 1979, seventeen weeks' paid maternity leave at 93 percent of their salary.

The arrest, trial and imprisonment of Henry Morgentaler provided feminist and progressive forces with an opportunity to regroup. The feminist movement participated in the campaign to support Dr. Morgentaler, thus helping to publicize the feminists' position. The Comité de lutte pour l'avortement et la contraception libres et gratuits, comprising representatives from the Corporation des enseignants du Québec (Quebec Teachers' Association, known as "CEQ" in both French and English), the

Association pour la défense des droits sociaux (Association for the Protection of Social Rights) and the Centre des femmes saw the protests against laws restricting the practice of abortion and contraception as a stage in a long-term struggle. In 1974, the committee published a play by a feminist troupe, Théâtre des cuisines (Kitchen Theatre). Appended to the play was a manifesto entitled *Nous aurons les enfants que nous voulons* (We Shall Have the Children We Desire). It also published, in 1975, the *Dossier sur l'avortement et la contraception libres et gratuits* (Information Booklet on Free and Readily Available Abortion and Contraception).

Most women's groups in Quebec—although not those affiliated with the Catholic Church—supported Dr. Morgentaler. Marches were held; shows were organized; badges were sold. Morgentaler's trial demonstrated the difficulty encountered by women wanting therapeutic abortions. For an abortion to be legal, it had to be approved by a committee of doctors. In Catholic hospitals, doctors refused to set up therapeutic-abortion committees or refused to approve abortion requests. The doctors' actions were supported by the "pro-life" movement.

A jury found Dr. Morgentaler not guilty, but the Court of Appeal overturned the verdict; the appeal court's decision was upheld by the Supreme Court of Canada. Public opinion condemned the arrogance of judges who convicted a man already acquitted by a jury of his peers. As a result of this outcry, an amendment to the Criminal Code was introduced that would eliminate such judgements in the future, but Dr. Morgentaler served a prison sentence before he was freed to continue practising in Montreal.

During the Seventies, women in Quebec became familiar with feminist language. Although many did not identify with the feminists, whose revolutionary image frightened them, women in Quebec responded to the feminist message and incorporated it into their daily lives. When radical feminists said the family was exploitative and should be abolished, not many women agreed immediately; but they did begin to question their role in the family. Did they have a life of their own, outside of their family responsibilities? Did they have financial security? Why wasn't housework recognized or paid? What would they do when their children grew up? Marxist feminists argued that the production of goods and services, the daily work of housewives, was integral to the economy; why had no one recognized the value of their "invisible work"? When feminists pointed out that women who worked outside the home had two jobs, women began to ask their husbands to prepare supper or do the dishes. When Australian feminist Germaine Greer came to Montreal in 1971, she brought radical feminism into Francophone homes. A beautiful woman who spoke fluent French, she received a lot of media attention. Kate Millett visited Montreal in 1973. (In her autobiography, she recalls how the enthusiasm of the women of Montreal almost overwhelmed her.) But the process of consciousness-raising was a long one; ten years passed before some radical-feminist ideas were adopted, reworked and promoted by women in Quebec....

THE REALM OF CHILDHOOD

PIERRE VALLIÈRES

[This description of childhood in Quebec before the Quiet Revolution is drawn from *White Niggers of America*, a memoir written by Pierre Vallières, a political thinker linked to the FLQ. Born in 1938, Vallières spent the first seven years of his life in the working-class East End of Montreal.]

One of the most critical problems of the postwar period was housing. The poor French quarters of Montreal were overcrowded. Rents were going up while wages remained "stable." Many working-class families of the metropolis began to move to the suburbs: Montréal-Nord, Sainte-Rose, Sainte-Thérèse, Ville Saint-Michel, Pointe-aux-Trembles, L'Assomption, and that vast territory on the south bank of the St. Lawrence which was to become Ville Jacques-Cartier.

At Angus Shops, as in many other plants, the workers talked all day long about their housing problems. It was there that my father learned that at Longueuil-Annexe one could get a plot of land and even a house for a reasonable price. There was neither an aqueduct nor a sewage system, but that was only a question of time. A transportation company had bought a few buses and organized a regular service between Montreal and the South Shore. A few families from Montreal had already established themselves there and the children, it seemed, were blooming in the fresh air.

One weekend I went with my father to Longueuil-Annexe. For me it was a big adventure. We had to take the bus at the entrance to the Jacques-Cartier Bridge. We waited a long time before an old gray bus arrived. My father asked the driver if he knew Briggs and Saint-Thomas streets. The driver nodded and told my father he would let him know when we got there. "It's at the end of the line," he said.

The bus gradually filled with passengers and drove onto the bridge. I opened my eyes wide to stare at the river, the boats, St. Helen's Island. Then the bus reached the opposite bank. My father and I had never been

PIERRE VALLIÈRES, "THE REALM OF CHILDHOOD," *WHITE NIGGERS OF AMERICA* (TORONTO: MCCLELLAND AND STEWART, 1973), CHAPTER 2. USED BY PERMISSION OF THE CANADIAN PUBLISHERS, MCCLELLAND AND STEWART, TORONTO. U.S. RIGHTS © 1971 BY MONTHLY REVIEW PRESS. REPRINTED BY PERMISSION OF MONTHLY REVIEW FOUNDATION.

on that side of the river. We were in completely strange territory. The bus continued straight down Sainte-Hélène Street, then turned left on the Coteau-Rouge road. This was a real country road. Narrow, zigzag, bumpy, it crossed vast fields in which a few small houses of wood or sheet-metal appeared here and there. For quite a long time we saw only empty fields. Then we saw a farm with a poultry yard and a few cows by the roadside. Finally the bus entered a kind of village and a thick cloud of dust began to vibrate in the air. As most of the windows on the bus were open, we absorbed this dust, which smelled of dry earth, crumbled stone, and drought, through our noses, ears, eyes, and mouths. Turning toward my father, the driver shouted: "We're almost there!" The bus turned left and started down Briggs Street. The cloud of dust hid the houses and made the street disappear behind us as we advanced.

"Saint-Thomas!"

We got up. The bus stopped and the driver wished us luck the way a friend shakes your hand and says something encouraging when he thinks the adventure you are about to embark upon is sheer madness. We got off the bus, awkwardly; we were nervous, like travelers setting out into unknown territory.

Was it possible that freedom lay in this little village with dirt roads and scattered, dilapidated little houses, that it was to be found in this out-of-the-way place full of dust and dirty children?

There were only about ten houses on Saint-Thomas Street. On either side of the street and around each plot ran ditches filled with black, stagnant water that gave off a strong smell. "Tainted water," my father said to me. It was thick, sticky, covered with a cloud of flies and buzzing insects. We swallowed the dust that had stuck in our throats.

We walked for a while without hurrying. Then my father stopped in front of a little red and white house. "Eleven ninety-seven," he murmured. "This is it." A man came out of the house to meet us. He had the broad, toothy smile of a vegetable dealer who is about to cheat you. I didn't like his looks, but my father seemed to get on easily with him. The man said banal things to me: "How's it going, my little man? You go to school? You like the country?" etc. I did not answer. No, decidedly I did not like that man. But the impressions one has at the age of seven may not mean much.

I did not like the man, or his wife either, for that matter; she looked even more like a storekeeper than her husband. I saw that they wanted to sell their house and that they were only interested in us two as possible buyers of that house. I have never liked trade or tradesmen. For trade divides men into antagonistic groups, stimulates the exploitation of the weak and naive (the "pure," the simple), by the strong and "smart," constantly enriches some and constantly impoverishes others.

Nevertheless, I was happy to be in the country, and the smell rising from the ditches was less disgusting to me than the forced smiles of the man and woman. I stayed outside, gazing at the landscape (a grand word for such a shabby reality), while my father followed the couple into the house.

On the other side of the street there were only three houses, separated by fields. A little farther off were some woods. I imagined them full of Indians and wild animals. I began to hope my father would buy the house. I couldn't have cared less what the house would be like to live in. It was the woods and fields I was suddenly interested in. They would be much better than the sheds in the city.

When my father came out of the little red and white house, he seemed pleased.

"You know," said the owner, "there are no taxes to pay here. There's no mayor, no city hall, and nobody who gets political patronage. It's all bound to come some day, but in the meantime they leave you alone."

My father asked him why he had put his house up for sale.

"I've just built a bigger house on the Coteau-Rouge. I have five children now, you know. And then, I want to start a business around there, a grocery. The population is going to grow fast. Some plots have already been sold. They're talking about opening up several new streets next spring. I've always dreamed of working for myself. Sooner or later you've got to make up your mind to take a risk, no? Otherwise, you're just marking time....Right now I'm a longshoreman. It's irregular. In the winter there's no work. I'm fed up with that life. It's slavery, and I've put up with it for too long. And then, I want to send my children to the best *collèges*. I don't want them to have to do the same as me. I want them to have good jobs and an easy life. . . .Anyway, if I don't make it, we won't be any worse off than we are now."

My father listened to the man, devouring him with his eyes.

How long would *he* remain a slave of the CPR?

My father, who was then thirty-three, had been working since the age of fourteen. He had had to leave school in the fourth grade because his father, paralyzed by a serious illness, could no longer earn enough for his wife and fourteen children. "The oldest ones," and my father in particular, had had to resign themselves to taking over responsibility for the "Vallières tribe."

It was a few years before the crash of 1929. When the Great Depression came, the whole "tribe" had had to struggle in abject poverty, like most of the working-class families of Montreal. A few years later, the war and the draft were to increase their many difficulties by adding the fear of dying on a battlefield for a cause that was of no concern to the working class.

My father sometimes talked to me about those years of black misery. And from the things he told me, I have the impression that at that time the relations between one man and another, one beggar and another, were enveloped and steeped in a silent despair...silent because it was too profound for men to believe in the efficacy of cries and tears. Until the day when the anti-conscription movement reawakened the old revolt and set off the riots of 1917. But until the war, a despair like that of men condemned to death was the daily bread of the workers of Quebec....

My father and mother were both twenty-five when they were married, two years before the Second World War. My grandfathers had died almost at the same time, six months earlier, after very long illnesses. My parents had met in Lafontaine Park. They had decided almost at once to get married. They betook themselves to the church as soon as they had saved enough money to buy the essential furniture. There was no banquet on their wedding day and no honeymoon. They immediately installed themselves in a little house on Gilford Street. It was there that I was born in February 1938. A few months later, my father had managed to find a job at Angus Shops and we moved to Frontenac Park. And it was in that quarter, one of the many French-Canadian ghettos which the merchants call the "French East End," that our little family lived through the war and all the problems it created....

On the way back from Longueuil-Annexe, my father was not thinking either about God or politicians. He was dreaming of the house he would build out of this shack he had decided to buy. It remained only to convince my mother of the advantages of exile to the suburbs.

"If only Madeleine can agree to it," he said to himself. He was marshaling his arguments and silently preparing his case. "We'll be at peace. The children will have all the room they need to play. We'll be masters in our own house. There will be no more stairs to go up and down. André won't kill himself rolling downstairs. Pierre won't hang around the alleys and sheds any more...." My father tried to visualize the future: "The area is going to develop. The owner said so; the men at the shop say so too. There will be schools, stores, all the conveniences of the city. The slums will gradually disappear. They're going to install an aqueduct and a sewage system. They're going to pave the streets with asphalt and make sidewalks. They're going to plant trees. The government has already promised a hospital for the South Shore...."

The owner was prepared to stretch the payments out over many years....The union would soon obtain raises....Life would become easier....He would enlarge the house. A few years from now, Madeleine and the "little ones" would have peace and comfort. He could save a little money, and when the children grew up he would be able to allow himself to do a bit of traveling with Madeleine, a Madeleine relaxed, reassured, happy—they would take a vacation in the north country, see the Gaspé and the sea, and—who knows?—some day they might go to Vancouver, see the Rockies, the Pacific....

My father was building the future in his mind, trying to imagine his domain, which he would build patiently when he got home from the shop, on weekends, and during his annual two weeks' vacation. He would draw up the plan himself. He would do everything himself. Others were doing it, why not he?...

The bus, now on the bridge, had just passed St. Helen's Island. While I looked at the boats riding at anchor, I asked my father if we would be able to go hunting in the woods across the way, which I had spent part of the afternoon gazing at. He only replied: "First we have to persuade your mother."

For eight years my father had been dreaming of some day owning his own home. Of course, the shack was no castle, but it was still better than spending the rest of your life as a tenant in the damp apartments of the Royal Trust. "At least in Longueuil-Annexe," he said to himself, "there aren't any rats, or soot, or smoke....You've got fresh air." (He was forgetting the polluted water, the dust, the queer smells.)

And then, what did he know about people's habits, about their mentality?

When we got home at supper time, my father realized that he had forgotten to ask the owner of the shack if there were a few stores around, a doctor, a church, a school, etc.

All he knew was that there was regular bus service between Longueuil-Annexe and Montreal.

Madeleine said yes. And a month later we moved to Longueuil-Annexe.

The shack was made of wood covered with "*papier brique*," a kind of tarpaper designed to look like brick. In the center front was a little white porch. Inside, only three rooms: in the middle a kitchen, which also served as dining room, living room, bathroom, etc.; to the left, a large bedroom which my parents shared with Raymond (who was not yet walking); lastly, to the right, a tiny room with a double-decker bed and a chest of drawers: this was the room of the "two oldest," André and me.

The rooms were separated by walls of *"donnacona,"* a kind of hard, thick cardboard which could be bought quite cheaply from any dealer in building materials. Manufactured by Domtar in the Portneuf region (I think), *donnacona* was easy to cut up, install, and paint, and it was usually sold in panels four feet by eight. Many of the shacks that went up in Ville Jacques-Cartier in the years following our arrival were built entirely out of two-by-fours and broad panels of this economical cardboard, which was then covered with tarpaper. It was not exactly warm in winter, but it didn't cost much, and with this miraculous material you could build a little house in two days!

Our shack seemed almost luxurious compared to most of the hovels in Longueuil-Annexe, which were covered with black tarpaper and looked like sinister old shanties abandoned in a swamp. On rainy days especially, Longueuil-Annexe looked like a burnt-out shantytown. . . .

As can be seen, paper played an important role in the construction of the houses, which were also called "shit-houses." *Papier brique*, tarpaper, *donnacona*. . .From the surplus wood and paper they did not export back home, the Americans made cheap building materials to be sold to the cheap labor of Quebec to make them masters in their own houses!

Unlike most of the houses, our shack was located not at the back of the lot but at the front. There was a little hay growing around, which we were going to try to make into a lawn! To the right, between the street and the house, there was a cement well where you pumped water by hand. My father was supposed to install an electric pump soon, and he was already thinking about building on another room. He was forever making plans, while my mother scrubbed the floors and my brother and I went looking for Indians in the woods across the way.

In 1945 Longueuil-Annexe had a population of perhaps one or two thousand. There was no administration, and you had to go to Longueuil to obtain a building permit or any other such paper. But at that time Longueuil-Annexe was only the largest of an infinite number of little islands of houses springing up here, there, and everywhere out of the immense fields which in the space of a few years were to be transformed into a vast mushroom-city. These blocks of houses had not yet been named, and life there was, as my father said, "rather primitive." Longueuil-Annexe, a better-organized shantytown—it had four "main" streets and four cross streets, a grocery, a post office, bus stops, and even a little school run by nuns—was in the enviable position of having a chapel that served the surrounding area. Every Sunday a priest from Longueuil came to say Mass in the little wooden chapel at the corner of the Chambly and Coteau-Rouge roads. The bishop had promised the local "petty bourgeoisie"(the two old maids who ran the post office and the proprietors of the grocery store) that he would soon appoint a curé and grant Longueuil-Annexe the status of a parish. As soon as this news began to circulate, people said that soon they would have to pay for the construction of a luxurious presbytery (a curé is a personage who does not live any old place), when they themselves had to go into debt to pay for the cardboard to cover their houses. No one concealed his annoyance, but neither did anyone dare oppose the decision of the Bishop of Saint-Jean, who was the boss of the diocese. People said to themselves that the arrival of a curé heralded the arrival of the tax collectors. For the curé would surely create a cooperative savings bank and would want the assistance of a mayor to administer this new parish where there were no services of any kind. The administration would need revenues to pay a chief of police, a few firemen, a secretary, etc. Which meant that it would soon be necessary to pay higher and higher taxes. Most people did not suspect the scale of the coming invasion. They thought they were isolated, safe from outside interference, left in peace. They did not know that the owners of the abandoned fields were selling dozens of lots every month to workers who were only waiting to save up a few hundred dollars to move their wives, children, and furniture to the other side of the river.

The impending arrival of a curé disturbed them because most of the adult couples lived together without being married and practiced no religion; very often their children were not baptized. Furthermore, some of them dealt in petty crime and did not care to have a curé inquire into their affairs. A few families were like ours: good family, "hard-working" father, possessive mother, children clean though poorly dressed. My father was very surprised to learn that most of these "good neighbors" were, like himself, employees of the CPR. . . .

Some nights I went to bed not to sleep but to think. I was not yet ten, but I thought a great deal. I questioned everything I saw: things and men. (The philosophers call that "calling things into question.") Sometimes I felt sad and lonely. At other times, especially on days when school had been more trying than usual, I would clench my childish fists and dream of insulting my teachers in public, of humiliating *them* for a change, of throwing mud at them and shouting: "Hey! you, daughters of God, and you, *messieurs les abbés*, why don't you go do a little work building houses for 'your' poor that wouldn't be so cold and cramped, instead of teaching them to repent their sins. . . . Besides, if 'your' poor didn't sin, you'd be out of a job. What have you got to give us in exchange for everything you want to take away from us? Why don't you leave us our freedom, our sins, our filth, and our peace! Take your catechism, your good manners, and your holy water back to Longueuil! Isn't the important thing to be happy? And (except for a few 'converts') we're happy to remain savages and not have you trying to civilize us."

Of course I didn't say these things to myself in that style. My thoughts were not so well expressed. But I nonetheless felt a kind of wound inside me that penetrated the deepest recesses of my anguished mind.

Their ready contempt seared me; *their* habit of humiliating the "ill-dressed," "unkempt," "snot-nosed" children. . .the dirty children of the common people!

Oh! cursed masters of sacred *cleanliness!* Imbeciles with immaculate hands, projecting ears, pointed noses, disdainful mouths, glassy eyes, and sandpaper faces! Empty heads. . . .Deep inside, with all my heart, with all my intelligence, with all the hardness of a *degenerate* child, I proudly told you to go to the devil! If hell existed, it was your appointed residence. Imbeciles, you had everything it took to make "devilish" fine candidates for damnation! What did you expect out of this life? Why did you exist? Why were you our teachers?

In third and fourth grades, my hatred for school increased; for my mother forced me to continue my education with the nuns in Longueuil.

Bus service had just been inaugurated between Longueuil and Longueuil-Annexe, but it was very irregular. Often (especially in winter) I had to walk to school; it was hard going but "healthy exercise."

In Longueuil I made a few friends but I felt myself an outsider among these children who were "well dressed," "neatly combed," "cared for." Comparing myself with them, I became more and more ashamed of my milieu. I was alone, incapable of communicating what I felt. And the nuns who took pity on me made my existence even more painful.

Two years later, my mother went to see the Brothers of Christian Schools, who ran a big *collège* in Longueuil. This time, terror seized me. On registration day completely ignoring the arrangements my mother had made, I went to the wretched hovel on Briggs Street which had just been converted into a temporary schoolhouse: for two years families had been arriving by the hundreds in the still nameless town, and the government was in no hurry to build schools. Throughout the whole area shacks were being turned into schools overnight and muddy lots into "recreation grounds." But there, at least, I felt *at home*, with my own kind.

When I went back to school for the fifth time in my life, I had determined that henceforth it would be *I*, and not my mother, who would decide what school I went to. My mother resigned herself to my stubborn-ness, only muttering under her breath: "Damn pig-headed child! You'll regret it plenty later on."...

In the meantime, Longueuil-Annexe had ceased to be Longueuil-Annexe. Our quarter was part of a big city which the government had decided to name Jacques-Cartier. The first mayor and a few aldermen had been elected, all of them ignorant men of good will. It would not be long before they were eliminated or assimilated by the underworld. The deputy from the constituency kept making promises, but the government didn't do much. Every spring, as soon as the snow had melted, an army of bulldozers would lay out dirt roads between the houses. The shacks would be moved about, some backward, some forward, in a laughable attempt at town planning.

Everywhere, for miles around, mud streets full of puddles. When it didn't rain too often, the sun managed to dry up the puddles and the mud. Trucks came and poured tons of gravel on the streets. Bulldozers hastily spread the gravel out. The next time it rained the gravel sank into the mud, the puddles reappeared, and everything had to be started over again.

On dry days, in July and August, dust filled the air whenever automo-biles and trucks went by. Some families bought a few gallons of oil to spread on the streets and prevent the dust from poisoning the atmosphere. But that, too, often had to be done over. And even without dust, the smells that rose from the ditches and privies (commonly called "*bécosses*") were still as tenacious as poverty.*

When there was no oil on the streets and the dust hovered constantly in the air, the spaces between the black or multicolored shacks would turn yellow or gray, depending on whether the sky above was blue or dark with clouds.

On days when it rained hard, everything turned black. The houses, flattened and ashamed, took on a sinister, tormented look. The people picked their way through streets transformed into rivers of mud. The few puny trees, which each family had tried to preserve on its lot, bent their branches toward the wet earth. It was as if they wept at being powerless and ridiculous witnesses to all the misery that was obstinately trying to persuade itself the future would be better.

On these rainy days, if I wasn't sleeping in class, I would stand for hours at a time on the front porch of our shack watching the water trace figures

---

* The word "*bécosse*" is a Canadian-French corruption of the English "backhouse." (Trans.)

on the windowpanes. The neighboring houses, the streets, the sickly trees would seem to be transformed into a storybook landscape, and between reality and myself I would try to interpose one of the dreams my father sometimes talked to me about on weekends, his gentle eyes fixed on the yellow, limitless horizon beyond which there seemed to lie other worlds, less cruel than this one for men, for workers.

But the older I grew (for poor children grow old faster than they grow up), the more my dreams came to resemble those of a man condemned to death who cannot drive hope from his mind.

While my father was expanding the house, to make it more liveable, my mother hardly dared invite "the relatives" to visit us. She was so ashamed of "the surroundings," as she said. In spite of the misery that encircled and penetrated his domain, my father was happy to have something to build...even if it was only an extension to this jerry-built shack. But my mother dreaded letting others—city people—see our poverty.

It was as if our entire existence was nothing but a daily obscenity. We had to hide *that* from the people of the big city.

But the people of the big city and the rest of the province soon learned the truth...from the newspaper headlines in capital letters reading: "THE WHOLE TRUTH ABOUT VILLE JACQUES-CARTIER"—"BABIES DYING OF COLD IN COTEAU-ROUGE"—"TERRIBLE POVERTY ACROSS THE BRIDGE"—"A CITY OF SHEET-METAL"—etc. We would read these reports with rage in our hearts. What were we *guilty* of? Of having wanted freedom? We had never had it. Painfully, we were trying to achieve it. Why did these newspapers talk about us as if we were barbarians spewed out by Montreal, like bile spewed out by an unhealthy liver?

For some newspapers, which I need not name, we were not men but "the dirty masses" of Ville Jacques-Cartier, the human "scrap" of the biggest garbage dump in the metropolitan area.

After the stories in the newspapers came the "collections," the distributions of food and whatnot, the *charity* of all the people who had guilty consciences or who simply adored helping the poor. Fortunately, we were not armed; otherwise the Church would have acquired a few more martyrs and the statue manufacturers would have made money.

Everything was increasing: the population, the slums, the publicity, the taxes, the number of unemployed, of sick or crippled children and of unwed mothers, the churches, the thugs, the grocers, the thieves, the murderers, the drunks, the wretched...

Angus Shops, Vickers, Canada Cement, Canadair, etc., were laying off hundreds of workers every week. And each time the unions said it would only be temporary.

Some families converted their sheds into lodgings, moved into them, and rented out their shacks...so as to be able to buy enough "baloney" and Weston bread to feed the "little ones." Others sold their houses—because of the taxes—and went off to build others in Saint-Amable or Sainte-Julie, beyond Boucherville.

More than one mother tore her hair in despair, and more than one man thought of stealing, killing, or committing suicide. Some set fire to their houses in order to collect the insurance and try to start over again somewhere else. The Established Order declared that henceforth laziness and slovenliness would be forbidden in Ville Jacques-Cartier, that norms would be established, that those who did not meet them would be expelled and that taxes would be raised in order to force the "lazy" (that is, the unemployed) to leave the city. The underworld, which with the support of Duplessis controlled the city, tried to put up a respectable front and held numerous press conferences announcing reforms such as Quebec had never known. They began to build schools and distribute little gifts to their friends. Overnight, grocers, wrestlers, bandits became "entrepreneurs" and contractors for primary schools, churches, and administrative buildings. All this was financed with government subsidies or "Sunday collections"—in other words, with money stolen from the people, with the broad, hypocritical smile of a gentleman-thief. The purpose of building schools was not to educate children, but to grant "paying" contracts to supporters of the regime. So it was that Duplessis, financed by his friends on Wall Street, created his own class of petty bourgeois out of the very misery of the workers and farmers of Quebec who, taken in by a cunningly organized system of patronage, voted for him *en masse*—*against* their true interests and without quite realizing what was going on.

Around 1950, a vast, slow construction project was undertaken to provide a complete system of aqueducts and sewers for the "dirty masses" of Ville Jacques-Cartier. The underworld rubbed its hands at the thought of the enormous profits it would reap from this very humanitarian enterprise. They began by raising taxes. One after another, all the streets of the city were transformed into long trenches eight feet deep, with heaps of earth on either side about six feet high. Paths were improvised between the houses, piles of earth, trenches, sewer pipes, dynamite, steam shovels, etc. The daily dynamiting cracked the walls of the shacks and ruined the wells, which ran dry or filled with muddy water. A few public drinking fountains were installed here and there, on the privileged streets, which were served by the aqueduct from the first year on. But after a lightning beginning, the work slowed down. Everywhere there were trenches, unusable wells, and mud...mountains of mud. And the work did not progress: lack of funds, people said. But Quebec had put millions into the project. Where had the money gone? The people asked questions while the months and years passed. The work advanced at a snail's pace, a little here, a little there. In winter all the machines fell silent. The long trenches filled up with snow.

Most families had to collect rain water in huge barrels or buy water by the pail every day from a tradesman to whom the city authorities had granted a monopoly on the sale of water. Water cost five cents a pail. Many families, including mine, had to tighten their belts to buy water for cooking, bathing, doing laundry, etc.

That lasted for years, years during which Duplessis was letting the Americans loot the rich iron deposits of northern Quebec.

The Americans were making billions off *our* iron, Duplessis was making millions off the Americans, the political machine of the National Union Party was distributing its millions to the supporters and thugs of the regime...and we, poor starving wretches, we had to buy water!

Further Readings for Topic 7

Michael D. Behiels, *Prelude to the Quiet Revolution: Liberalism versus Neo-Nationalism, 1945–1960* (Kingston and Montreal: McGill-Queen's University Press, 1985).

Michael D. Behiels, ed., *Quebec Since 1945: Selected Readings* (Toronto: Copp Clark Pitman, 1987).

William D. Coleman, *The Independence Movement in Quebec, 1945–1980* (Toronto: University of Toronto Press, 1984).

Ramsay Cook, ed., *French Canadian Nationalism: An Anthology* (Toronto: Macmillan, 1969).

Alain C. Gagnon, ed., *Quebec: State and Society* (Toronto: Methuen, 1984).

Hubert Guindon, *Quebec Society: Tradition, Modernity, and Nationhood* (Toronto: University of Toronto Press, 1988).

Kenneth D. McRoberts, *Quebec: Social Change and Political Crisis*, 3rd ed. (Toronto: McClelland and Stewart, 1988).

S. M. Trofimenkoff, *The Dream of Nation: A Social and Intellectual History of Quebec* (Toronto: Gage, 1983).

TOPIC 8

The Shifting Boundaries of the Self: Transformations of Gender, 1940–1990

O*ur contemporary understanding of gender, indeed the way we use this word itself, reflects the impact of the Second World War. Once a modest little word, referring to the modifications of grammatical subjects according to distinctions of sex, "gender" has become a keyword of contemporary discourse, an analytical tool to distinguish between sexual difference on the one hand, and that which the culture makes of sexual difference on the other. The idea that "masculinity" and "femininity" are not "essences" or "things," but processes that are socially constructed and historically variable is explored in these three readings in an expanding branch of social history.*

Ruth Roach Pierson describes the ways "femininity" was both challenged and sustained in the armed forces of the 1940s; documents from the sensationalist press of Toronto and Montreal introduced by Steven Maynard suggest the pivotal role of the 1950s in gay and lesbian history; and Meg Luxton's study of Flin Flon, Manitoba, documents the ways working-class families are struggling to cope with the redefinition of gender roles, and of ideals of femininity and masculinity, in their daily lives. In the shifting boundaries of masculinity and femininity we find one of the most fascinating challenges of modern times.

"THEY'RE STILL WOMEN AFTER ALL":

Wartime Jitters over Femininity

RUTH ROACH PIERSON

"They're Still Women After All" was the title given, with an audible sigh of relief, by L. S. B. Shapiro, Canadian foreign correspondent and future novelist, to a piece he did for *Saturday Night* in September, 1942. In a light, jocular vein, the article expressed one man's fears, aroused by the British wartime sight of so many women stepping into formerly male jobs, that women might cease to be women, that is "feminine individuals," synonymous terms in Shapiro's vocabulary. Although closer observation convinced Shapiro that his fears were unfounded, similar fears continued to plague many other Canadians, male and female, as they viewed women entering the munitions plants and, what in the eyes of some was even worse, joining the armed forces.[1]

As the primary purpose of the services is the provision of the armed might of the state, their male exclusivity had been in keeping with a deeply rooted division of labour by sex that relegated women to nurture, men to combat, women to the creation and preservation of life, men, when necessary, to its destruction. Closely connected to the sexual division between arms bearers and non-arms bearers was a gendered dichotomy of attributes that identified as masculine the military traits of hardness, toughness, action, and brute force and as feminine the non-military traits of softness, fragility, passivity, and gentleness. Hence, the very entrance of women into the Army, Navy, and Air Force sharply challenged conventions respecting women's nature and place in Canadian society.

...Two specific sets of circumstances induced the Department of National Defence to admit women into the armed services: manpower shortages, felt first by the Canadian Army and the Royal Canadian Air Force, and a reserve of womanpower embodied in a Canada-wide paramilitary movement of women eager to serve. For the men in charge of Canada's military, efficient prosecution of the war was the reason for

---

RUTH ROACH PIERSON, "*THEY'RE STILL WOMEN AFTER ALL*": *THE SECOND WORLD WAR AND CANADIAN WOMANHOOD* (TORONTO: MCCLELLAND AND STEWART 1986), CHAPTER 4. USED BY PERMISSION OF THE CANADIAN PUBLISHERS, MCCLELLAND AND STEWART, TORONTO.
1. *Saturday Night*, September 26, 1942, p. 10.

putting women in uniform and under service discipline. They had no desire to tamper with existing gender relations by altering the sexual division of labour or the male-over-female hierarchy of authority. Obviously the members of the women's volunteer corps eager to become part of Canada's official forces wanted to end the male exclusivity of the military. But even they gave no indication of a desire to erase the demarcation line between male and female spheres. There was thus a tension inherent in the admission of women to the armed services: the tension between the Canadian state's wartime need for female labour within those pre-eminently masculine institutions and Canadian society's longer-term commitment to a masculine-feminine division of traits as well as separation of tasks. This tension was also apparent, albeit to a lesser degree, in the entrance of women into non-traditional trades in war industry. In both cases, under the pressure of the war emergency, women appeared to be breaking sex barriers on an alarming scale....

What were the reactions to women's entrance into the armed forces (as well as into non-traditional trades in war industry)?...

Recruitment propaganda, promotional newspaper stories, and patriotic advertising...reveal a deep ambivalence toward women's joining the armed forces. On the one hand was the celebration of the trailblazing and achievement of women in the services and, on the other, the assurance that joining the forces changed nothing in women's nature and place in Canadian society. In 1943 the ambivalence intensified as more and more women were needed but recruitment met resistance and monthly enlistment figures dropped. From the first enrolments in September, 1941, to July, 1942, 3,800 women had "stepped forward to serve" and been accepted into the Canadian Women's Army Corps.[2] Many of these came from the women's volunteer corps.[3] By March, 1943, the strength of the Canadian Women's Army Corps had risen to just over 10,000.[4] Although the CWAC's peak strength in 1945 would not exceed 14,000 (636 officers

---

2. *Women in Khaki*, n.d., but internal evidence places publication in second half of 1942, Department of National Defence (DND), DH, 164.069 (DI).

3. According to the nationwide survey of CWAC other ranks carried out in April–May, 1943, "about 20% of CWAC women belonged to a volunteer women's part-time service organization prior to enrolling in the CWAC. Most of these belonged to one of the unofficial uniformed women's corps or the Red Cross." *Report of Enquiry—Canadian Women's Army Corps: Why Women Join and How They Like It*, April–May, 1943, p. 23, copy at DND, DH, 168.009 (D91).

4. "Strength—Canadian Women's Army Corps as at 27 March 1943" was 354 officers plus 9,741 other ranks, totalling 10,095. PAC, RG 24, reel no. C-5303, file HQS 8984-2.

plus 13, 326 other ranks totalling 13, 962, on April 25, 1945),[5] military authorities in 1943 geared up for a considerable expansion of the women's forces on the assumption that "the Army, Navy and the Air Force urgently need 65,000 more service women to release men for combat duty."[6]

In February, National Selective Service began participating "in the recruiting of women for the Navy, the Army and the Air Force" by providing information to interested applicants and referring them to recruiting officers.[7] In March the Defence Council concurred in the recommendation of the National Campaign Committee for an intensive tri-service campaign to recruit women for the three armed services.[8] A Combined Services Committee was established to co-ordinate joint promotional and publicity endeavours for the CWAC, the WRCNS, and the RCAF (WD). The recruitment push coincided with the growing signs of opposition to women in the military.

The monthly enlistment figures for the women's services in late 1942 and early 1943 were disappointing.[9] Faced with this slowdown, the National Campaign Committee granted authorization to two opinion surveys in the first half of 1943.[10] The Combined Services Committee charged with joint recruitment endeavours for the three women's services proposed that a commercial market research agency conduct a general survey of public opinion. The firm of Elliott-Haynes Limited of Montreal and Toronto was retained to determine: (a) public awareness of the need for women in the armed forces; (b) factors believed to influence women in favour of joining the forces; (c) factors believed to influence women to

---

5. Weekly Strength Returns by D. Org. DND, DH, 113.3C1065 (D3) CWAC.

6. Letter of October 1, 1943, to newspaper editors from Captain T. H. Johnstone, Combined Services Committee, PAC, RG 24, reel no. C-5303, file HQS 8984-2. By July 1, 1943, 28,000 women had been accepted by the three services, 13,000 by the CWAC. *Report— C.W.A.C. : Why Women Join and How They Like It* (hereafter *C.W.A.C. Report*), p. 11.

7. Communication of January 30, 1943, to all regional superintendents, from R. G. Barclay, Assistant Director, Employment Service and Unemployment Insurance Branch, PAC, RG 24, reel no. C-5303, file HQS 8984-2.

8. Memorandum of March, 1943, to the Minister from Major-General H. F. G. Letson, PAC, RG 24, reel no. C-5303, file HQS 8984-2.

9. Comparative monthly enlistment figures for CWAC:

October, 1942	843
November, 1942	730
December, 1942	530
January, 1943	699
February (3 weeks)	570

10. Minutes of the 89th Meeting of the National Campaign Committee, February 22, 1943, PAC, RG 24, reel no. C-5303, file HQS 8984-2.

avoid joining the forces. The survey, which collected the opinions of 7,283 civilian adults from "56 Canadian centres and their surrounding areas," claimed to have covered "both sexes, all races, all geographical regions, all age levels, all economic levels, all occupations and all classes of conjugal condition."[11] Conducted in March and April of 1943, the results appeared under the title *Report: An Inquiry into the Attitude of the Canadian Civilian Public Towards the Women's Armed Forces.*

In April and May the Directorate of Army Recruiting carried out the second survey: a study of CWAC opinion. Based in part on the results of the first study insofar as they pertained to the CWAC, the in-house inquiry drew primarily on the "written answers to a questionnaire prepared by NDHQ in both English and French" and administered to a cross-section of 1,100 CWAC other ranks from all CWAC units, 18 per cent of whom were non-commissioned officers and 10 per cent French-Canadian women.[12] The secret and confidential report of the second inquiry, "Canadian Women's Army Corps: Why Women Join and How They Like It," was ready for limited distribution in July.

Both surveys revealed that there was widespread disapproval of women's joining the armed forces. The public opinion survey disclosed that few Canadians in the spring of 1943 gave high priority to enlistment in the armed forces as a way for women to contribute to the prosecution of the war. In answer to the question "How can women best serve Canada's war effort?" only 7 per cent replied "by joining the women's forces." Five other categories of work took precedence. "Maintaining home life" ranked first in importance for the highest proportion of Canadians (26 per cent), followed by "doing war work in factories" (23 per cent), "part-time voluntary relief work" (13 per cent), "conserving food, rationing" (11 per cent), and "buying war bonds, stamps" (8 per cent).[13] The ranking remained the same when the answers from French Canada were treated separately, the main difference being that an even higher proportion of French Canadians (40 per cent) thought "maintaining home life" was the most important job for women in wartime while only 18 per cent thought working in war industry was; a minuscule 3 per cent thought "joining women's forces" was most important. Separating out the answers from parents and from young men did not change the ranking either. Only the answers from young women showed a different order of priority: "main-

---

11. *Report: An Enquiry into the Attitude of the Canadian Civilian Public Towards the Women's Armed Forces* (Montreal/Toronto: Elliott-Haynes Limited, 1943), p. 3, hereafter cited as Elliott-Haynes, *An Enquiry.*
12. *C.W.A.C. Report*, pp. 3–4.
13. Elliott-Haynes, *An Enquiry*, p. 8.

taining home life" switched places with "doing war work in factories."[14] But the young women also placed ahead of "joining the forces" the same five kinds of war service as mentioned above. Furthermore, as "part-time voluntary relief work," "conserving food, rationing," and "buying war bonds, stamps" were all compatible with "maintaining home life," the inescapable conclusion is that an overwhelming majority of Canadians in 1943 saw women's place to be in the home, wartime or not.

Furthermore, according to the public opinion survey, among friends and relatives of young eligible women disapproval of their joining the forces ran higher than disapproval of their taking jobs in war industry. Of parents, husbands, boyfriends, and brothers, 39 per cent disapproved of their daughters, wives, girlfriends, and sisters joining the armed forces (43 per cent approved, and 18 per cent didn't know), while only 27 per cent disapproved of their female friends and relatives entering munitions factories (59 per cent approved and 14 per cent didn't know).[15] When the data for English and French Canada were segregated, the level of disapproval of women in the forces was found to be significantly higher in French Canada.[16] If one took the "don't know" as indifference or neutrality, a more negative construction could be put on the data, as was done in the report of the CWAC survey. "When pressed," it submitted, "57% of the public stated that they would not give open approval to their friends and relatives enrolling in the women's forces."[17] The public opinion survey highlighted another noteworthy contrast in level of disapproval. By separating mothers and fathers from boyfriends and brothers, it revealed that a higher proportion of young men objected to their girlfriends' and sisters' joining the forces than parents did to their daughters'.[18] . . .

Given the extent of the disapproval, it is not surprising that 61 per cent of the eligible women (56 per cent in English Canada, 72 per cent in French Canada) responded that they had never considered joining the armed forces.[19] Nor is it surprising that of the 39 per cent who did consider joining, about one-half finally abandoned the idea.[20] There was a connection between the disapproval of family and friends and the reluctance of

---

14. Ibid., p. 9.
15. Ibid., p. 12.
16. Ibid., p. 13.
17. C.W.A.C. *Report*, p. 28.
18. Elliott-Haynes, *An Enquiry*, p. 14.
19. Elliott-Haynes, *An Enquiry*, p. 15.
20. Ibid.

eligible women to join. Of those who entertained the idea of joining but ended up rejecting it, 33 per cent gave as their reason that the family objected (24 per cent of the English Canadians, 54 per cent of the French Canadians).[21]...

...According to the Elliott-Haynes survey, 20 per cent of the "young eligible women reported that they thought their parents, husbands, brothers, sisters," and male and female "friends would object to their joining the forces" on the grounds that "army life" was "unsuitable."[22]

In the hopes of dispelling that notion, speeches of recruitment officers, recruitment literature, sponsored advertising, and promotional news stories, even before but especially after the surveys, were full of assurances that membership in the CWAC—or RCAF (WD) or WRCNS—was not incompatible with femininity. "Our women in the Canadian Armed Forces are nothing if not thoroughly feminine in manner and appearance," recruiting officers instructed National Selective Service personnel being trained to help with servicewomen's recruitment in February, 1943.[23] Clearly, while the armed forces could persuade a male potential recruit that military service would make a man of him, they felt they had to do the reverse with a female prospective volunteer, that is, convince her that military life would not make her less of a woman.

From the start Army authorities assumed women in the services would be concerned about their appearance. Opposition to wearing a uniform *per se* was not anticipated from the women in the volunteer service corps (as many such corps sported their own uniforms), only opposition to a poorly designed one. In general, the planners of the CWAC calculated they would have a better chance of attracting volunteers the more attractive the uniform. The basic costume "underwent a considerable evolution before it settled into" the two-piece khaki suit identifiable as the CWAC uniform of World War II.[24] After National Defence Minister Colonel Ralston, his wife, the Master-General of the Ordnance, and a Toronto dress designer had all had a hand in the design, a committee at NDHQ produced the final model: the two-piece khaki ensemble of gored, slightly flared skirt and single-breasted tunic with hip pockets and one

21. Ibid. p. 25.
22. Elliott-Haynes, *An Enquiry*, p. 24.
23. Notes for the Assistance of Speakers for NSS Employment Personnel, February, 1943, PAC, RG 24, reel no. C-5303, file HQS 8984-2; NSS Representatives Conference, London, Ontario, February 15–17, 1943, PAC, RG 24, reel no. C-5322, file HQS 9011-11-5.
24. Director-General, CWAC, presumably Col. Margaret C. Eaton, "Preliminary Historical Narrative, History of the CWAC & Appendices" (n.d., but internal evidence suggests ca. mid-1945), p. 33, copy at DH, DND, 113.3CI(DI).

breast pocket, brown epaulets and brown CWAC and Canada badges, khaki shirt and brown tie, khaki peaked cap, and khaki hose and brown oxfords. According to the Director-General's preliminary history of the Corps, the CWAC uniform was "voted in some American and Canadian quarters to be the smartest of all women's service uniforms on this continent."[25] CWAC recruitment literature used this reputation to sell the Corps. The 1942 brochure *Women in Khaki* boasted: "C.W.A.C. uniforms have been acknowledged by leading dress designers to be the smartest in the world."[26] Enlistment ads sought to sell the wartime fashionableness of wearing the khaki with the line: "the C.W.A.C., the best dressed women of '43."[27] In addition, the Army went to greater and greater trouble to ensure a good fit in women's uniforms, much more so than in men's. In 1944 it was observed that "The equipping of C.W.A.C. personnel is considerably more complicated than this function for male personnel." And the evidence produced was that "C.W.A.C. clothing is supplied in as many as eighteen different sizes."[28] One ex-servicewoman of Prince Rupert, B.C., recalls that the colour and cut of the CWAC uniform led her to choose the Canadian Women's Army Corps over the WDs or the Wrens.

> Perhaps if I had had big baby blue eyes, I might have considered the blue uniforms of the R.C.A.F. or the Navy, but be that as it may, not only did the khaki match my brown eyes (used for coyly rolling and flirting in those days, besides the lesser use of just plain seeing); the trim, fitted tunic and the A-line skirt of the C.W.A.C.'s was known to be the most attractive of the three services. And the peaked cap fit nicely on the head to allow a modest fall of curls from under its back and sides.[29]

While only 5 per cent of the CWACs surveyed in 1943 mentioned wearing the uniform as a reason for joining, in answer to the further question of why they had selected the CWAC rather than the RCAF (WD) or the WRCNS, the highest proportion (37 per cent) gave "neat, smart uniform" as their reason.[30] On the other hand, only 13 per cent of the CWACs

---

25. Ibid., p. 34.
26. *Women in Khaki*, p. 20.
27. Cut-sheet of suggested sponsored ads for the CWAC, summer/autumn 1943, DH, DND, 164.069 (DI).
28. Minutes of meeting to discuss CWAC depot companies, February 10, 1944, in office of D. Org. (R), PAC, RG 24, reel no. C-8410, file HQS 9011-11-0-2-1.
29. Phylis Bowman, *We Skirted the War!* (n. p., 1975), p. 3.
30. C.W.A.C. *Report*, p. 24.

"stating likes" cited "wearing the uniform" as a "factor contributing to satisfaction" with life in the Corps.[31]

Certainly no one would have argued that pride in uniform was exclusively or particularly feminine, for men also took pride in their uniforms. There was, however, an important difference. A long association linked male with military uniform and military uniform with the masculine traits of forcefulness, toughness, and, in the case of an officer's uniform, commanding authority. When a man donned a uniform he stood to see his masculinity enhanced. Hence the popular notion that uniforms (on men implied) turned women's heads. Literary evidence exists that where the war effort was strongly supported and there were large concentrations of men in uniform (such as in London, England, or Ottawa, Ontario), men of military age not in uniform felt threatened not only by the possible charge of cowardice but by the possible loss of girlfriends to the soldiers, sailors, and airmen.[32]

Just the reverse was the fear in the case of servicewomen in uniform (or, for that matter, of women war workers in overalls and bandanas). Here reassurance was needed that such garb did not diminish femininity. For the January 1, 1943, issue of *Maclean's*, Lotta Dempsey contributed an article entitled "They're Still Feminine!," the point being to convince readers that "khaki, Air Force and Navy blue, or well-worn denim and slacks" had no lasting effect "on the softer side of Womanhood."

> Clothes don't make the man
> and uniforms and overalls
> don't seem to be unmaking
> the female of the species

was set out in bold print. And accompanying the article was a cartoon showing a CWAC, a Wren, and two women war workers congratulating a WD who blushingly holds out a diamond engagement ring for the others' admiration.[33]...

In the face of the persistent association of femininity with frills, fabrics soft to the touch, cheerful colours, and curving lines, Army authorities made concessions. The 1944 CWAC recruiting pamphlet announced that "recently silk stockings have been issued for off-duty wear.[34] In fact, they were made of rayon; nonetheless, they and their "happy neutral shade"

31. Ibid., pp. 33–34.
32. Lionel Shapiro, *The Sixth of June* (Garden City, N.Y.: Doubleday, 1955); Geoffrey Cotterell, *Westward the Sun* (London: Eyre & Spottiswoode, 1952).
33. *Maclean's*, January 1, 1943, p. 7.
34. 50 *Questions and Answers about CWAC* (Ottawa: King's Printer, 1944), p. 7.

received a warm greeting in the February, 1944, issue of the *C.W.A.C. News Letter*. The April, 1944, issue hailed the order allowing members of the CWAC in future to wear civilian clothes on any passover thirty-six hours as the "happiest new ruling" governing the Corps. This "weekend permission," the *News Letter* cheered, "will mean that twice a month girls will be able to cast aside the khaki for something more feminine."

Insofar as the four-square, drab and durable uniform resisted feminization, femininity could still find expression underneath the drill and serge. Already in the earliest draft of regulations and instructions for a women's army corps, it was arranged that the women who joined would not have to wear "issue" underclothing or lingerie. Instead each recruit would receive on enrolment (later enlistment) a dress allowance of $15 for "necessaries" and thereafter $3 every quarter for replacements and upkeep.[35] . . .

Even though the intent of the military was not to alter conceptions of femininity, the campaigns to promote women's uniformed service did have an effect on fashion. Hollywood, that powerful imagemaker, also helped to validate women's military service and the military look for women with such movies as *Here Come the Waves* (1945), starring Betty Hutton, and *Keep Your Powder Dry* (1945), in which heiress Lana Turner joined the U.S. Women's Army Corps. The fashionable "mannish" suit for civilian women, with its severe lines and padded shoulders, could be seen as partly in imitation of servicewomen's uniforms. The clothing regulations issued in 1942 by the Wartime Prices and Trade Board also had an impact. As Thelma LeCocq observed in *Maclean's*, all frills and furbelows, ruffles and ruchings were slashed. There were to be no more five-yard skirts or voluminous, bell sleeves.[36] With all excess yardage and detail shorn, fashions would be, as the *National Home Monthly* put it, "Streamlined for the Duration."[37]

It was also during the Second World War that the popularization of pants for women began. This was directly the result of women's recruitment into war industry as factory workers in armament, munitions, and aircraft assemblage plants. Although eventually the overalls and bandana or the slacks and turban of the woman war workers became symbols of service, in the early stages government officials were concerned that disapproving or ridiculing attitudes toward women wearing trousers

---

35. Draft copy of Regulations and Instructions for the Canadian Women's (Army) Service, June 23, 1941, PAC, RG 24, Vol. 2252, file HQ 54-27H1-2, Vol. 1.
36. Thelma LeCocq, "War Wear," *Maclean's*, August 15, 1942, p.15.
37. From Marjorie Winspear's column, "Beauty & Fashions," *National Home Monthly*, October, 1942, p.58.

would keep women from applying for essential jobs. The Department of Munitions and Supply for Canada considered it necessary to issue the message "PLEASE DON'T STARE AT MY PANTS" in March, 1942, and to illustrate it with the following picture: a middle-aged matron in hat, gloves, and furs has stopped to look disdainfully at a young woman in slacks, while a man in white collar and overcoat has a condescending smirk on his face. The fine print gives the supposed reply of the diffident object of all the attention: "Would you like to know why I wear trousers like the men when I go about the streets? Because I'm doing a man's job for my country's sake."[38] Just a year and a half later attitudes had changed enough that *National Home Monthly* could put on the cover of its September, 1943, issue a humorous drawing that reversed the roles depicted in the earlier poster. Now it is the female worker, swinging her lunch pail and striding along confidently in her slacks, who wheels around to take a second rather scornful look at a passing kilt-clad member of a Highland regiment.

The extension of slacks as wearing apparel for female military personnel, however, remained slow and restricted. Only in 1944 did the Navy's traditional bell bottoms begin to be issued for wear to members of the Women's Royal Canadian Naval Service, and then only to a select number of Wrens on coastal duty. To announce the new departure, a photograph was released to newspapers across Canada in June, 1944. When it appeared in the *Toronto Telegram* it carried the following caption:

> No wonder this husky sailor seems slightly puzzled. He has just spied a WREN wearing, of all things, bell-bottomed trousers! The once strictly male attire has recently been approved as official working uniform for Wrens on duty as signallers and (the Signalwoman shown here) is one of four west-coast Wrens who is entitled to wear them. She is stationed at a west coast Naval base, where she sends and receives important Navy messages in code and cypher.[39]

Similarly, in the Army, the wearing of trousers by women had to be justified by working conditions or by the task to be performed, but even then could still meet up with opposition. . . .

The "attractiveness" so central to the prevailing notion of femininity ultimately meant attractiveness to men. Heterosexuality was certainly one of the norms of femininity subscribed to in official publicity about the

---

38. *Maclean's*, March 1, 1942, p. 3.
39. RCN photo by Photographer Sheraton, RCNVR, *Telegram* Print Collection, York University Archives.

women's services. While advertisements acclaimed the good wholesome fun women could have together in the services, as in a shot of a Canadian Women's Army Corps Christmas party at Kildare Barracks in Ottawa in 1943,[40] celebrations of female camaraderie stopped far short of any suggestion of lesbianism. Under military law, after all, homosexuality could be constructed as grounds for discharge.[41]

The survey of CWAC other rank opinion had revealed that, after patriotism and the urge to travel, the third strongest motive for joining the service had been the desire "to be near family, friends in the forces." While 68 per cent had been influenced by having women friends in the forces, a larger proportion (77 per cent) had followed men friends into the military.[42] Recruitment propaganda, capitalizing on this information, came up with the poster: "Are you the girl he left behind?" In Army photo stories on life in the CWAC, public relations made a point of including material on dances and dates and boyfriends. The first photo in a series on Kildare Barracks showed three CWAC sergeants "with plans for a big evening ahead" approaching the company sergeant-major in the orderly room "on the subject of late passes." The caption to a later photo in the same series read: "There is no place for 'shop talk' in C.W.A.C. barracks after duty hours. Girls go typically feminine." Depicted as "typically feminine" was the one CWAC sergeant writing to a boyfriend in the RCAF while the two other CWAC sergeants looked "admiringly" (if not enviously) at his framed photograph. In the series' last photo the letter-writing sergeant had paused, pen in hand, to gaze dreamily at the photograph, which shows an Air Force officer clenching a pipe between his teeth and looking, even with the trim mustache, a lot like Henry Fonda.[43]. . .

One of the least examined and most unshakable notions of the time

40. PAC, National Photography Collection, Z-2405-3, December 27, 1943.
41. Rosamond "Fiddy" Greer's account of life in the Women's Royal Canadian Naval Service during World War II contains this personal recollection: "When two sisters slept together in a lower bunk across from mine, the thought of lesbianism never crossed my mind. This is not at all surprising, as I had never even heard of it. The more worldly-wise than I (which was probably almost everyone) may have known about 'it,' but none spoke the unmentionable word and for some time I thought how nice it was that the girls could comfort one another when they felt homesick. However, one day I heard that they had been 'found out': shortly afterwards they disappeared from *Stadacona*; and I surmised that 'something funny' had been going on. I was learning; although not too swiftly. . .for a long time after the incident I thought lesbians were rather peculiar sisters." Rosamond "Fiddy" Greer, *The Girls of the King's Navy* (Victoria, B.C.: Sono Nis Press, 1983), pp. 83–84.
42. *C.W.A.C. Report*, pp. 18, 24.
43. PAC, National Photography Collection, Army photos "In Barracks," negatives Z-1765-(1-9), July 7, 1943.

about women was that subordination and subservience to men were inherently female characteristics that dictated women's role and place in society. . . . This assumption converged with the real position of CWACs in relation to Army men, for in jobs, pay and benefits, and place in the command structure of the Army, the servicewomen were in general subordinate. As reflected in mottoes and enlistment slogans, the very function of the women's services was to subserve the primary purpose of the armed forces: the provision of an armed and fighting force. Having been excluded/exempted from combat, the women of the Canadian armed forces could adopt as their motto: "We Serve That Men May Fight."[44] That general motto had been adapted from the airwomen's "We Serve that Men May Fly." Even more expressive of the secondary status and supportive role assigned to Army women was a slogan used on enlistment ads: "The C.W.A.C. Girls—The Girls behind the Boys behind the Guns."[45] . . .

. . . The prevailing view was that men were by nature suited to dangerous, life-risking jobs while women were naturally adapted to monotony and behind-the-scenes support work. This view was reflected in the remarks of one Air Force officer on the suitability of airwomen for the trade of parachute rigger.

> Take parachute packing. To a man it's a dull, routine job. He doesn't want to pack parachutes. He wants to be up there with one strapped to his back. But to a woman it's an exciting job. She can imagine that someday a flier's life will be saved because she packed that parachute well. Maybe it will be her own husband's life or her boy-friend's. That makes parachute packing pretty exciting for her and she does a much more efficient and speedy job than an unhappy airman would.[46]

Deeply entrenched as the assumption was that the female was the second sex, there still surfaced from time to time the fear that women who were serving with the Army would lose their deference toward men and become "bossy." Mainly, it was the prospect of female officers that seems to have aroused this fear. When Jean Knox, Director of the British Army's Auxiliary Territorial Service, toured Canada in the fall of 1942, newspaper

44. NSS Representatives Conference re Recruitment of Women for Armed Services, London, Ontario, February 15, 16, 17, 1943, PAC, RG 24, reel no. C-5303, file HQS 8984-2.
45. CWAC Recruiting Pamphlet used in Military District No. 4 in January–March, 1943, campaign, DH, DND, 164.069(D1).
46. Mary Ziegler, *We Serve That Men May Fly: The Story of Women's Division Royal Canadian Air Force* (Hamilton, Ontario: R.C.A.F. (W.D.) Association, 1973), pp. 66–67.

coverage showed a preoccupation with the fact that she, the first female Major-General in the British Army, outranked her husband. As if looking for qualities to counter-balance her high military rank, news stories invariably described Knox as the "petite and pretty general" or "petite and completely feminine." Speaking of the women of the British Auxiliary Territorial Service and the Canadian Women's Army Corps, she herself remarked: "They're not an Army of Amazons doing men's work—they're still women...." In her view, "All women should share with men the experience of this war—but I would be violently displeased if in so doing, women lost their femininity."[47]...

...The overwhelming majority of uniformed women employed by the Army were assigned to jobs that had already become female niches in the civilian labour market or could be regarded as extensions of mothering or housework.[48] In propaganda and practice, a "woman's place" was created within the wartime armed services. Nonetheless, the very association of women with the military touched off fear of an impending breakdown of the sexual division of labour, akin to that triggered by the entrance of women on a massive scale into waged work. Under the anxiety over the changed appearance of women lay a more profound but less often articulated fear that women were invading male territory and becoming too independent. Humour of various sorts provided an outlet for these fears. In a 1942 article on "Woman Power" in *Maclean's*, for instance, Thelma LeCocq jokingly proposed a number of possibilities "that make strong men break out in a lather." What if, at war's end, she speculated, the thousands of war working women

> refuse to be stripped of the pants and deprived of the pay envelopes? What if they start looking round for some nice little chap who can cook and who'll meet them lovingly at the door with their slippers in hand? What if industry has to reorganize to give these women sabbatical years for having babies?[49]

---

47. *Globe and Mail*, September 9, 1942, p. 9; October 10, 1942, p. 11. Discussed in Marie T. Wadden, "Newspaper Response to Female War Employment: *The Globe and Mail* and *Le Devoir* May–October 1942" (History honours dissertation, Memorial University of Newfoundland, May, 1976), pp. 13–14. Statement of Major-General Knox quoted in W. Hugh Conrod, *Athene, Goddess of War: The Canadian Women's Army Corps, Their Story* (Dartmouth, 1983), p. 96.

48. See Chapter Three [Ruth Roach Pierson, *"They're Still Women After All": The Second World War and Canadian Womanhood* (Toronto: McClelland and Stewart, 1986)].

49. Thelma LeCocq, "Woman Power," *Maclean's*, June 15, 1942, pp. 10–11, 40.

These fears survived till the end of the war. In September, 1945, despite the fact that approximately 80,000 women war workers had already been laid off by then, *Maclean's* ran a cartoon by Vic Herman that derived its humour from the preposterous yet feared possibility of a reversal of the sexual division of labour between male breadwinner and dependent female domestic. A husband wearing an apron and standing with a mop in his hand and a bucket at his feet frowns in annoyance at his overalls- and bandana-clad wife who, home from the factory, has headed straight for the refrigerator, tracking muddy footprints across his nice, clean floor.[50] . . .

---

50. Drawn for *Maclean's* by Vic Herman, September 15, 1945, p. 32.

Mixed Messages:

Lesbians, Gay Men, and the Yellow Press in Quebec and Ontario During the 1950s–1960s

INTRODUCTION BY STEVEN MAYNARD

The recovery and writing of lesbian and gay histories in Canada is still in its infancy. The rise of the lesbian and gay liberation movement in Canada over the past twenty years has created the space and provided the motivation for individuals and groups to document Canada's lesbian and gay past. The mid-1980s were particularly busy years that saw the formation of such groups as the Canadian Lesbian and Gay History Network and the collective Lesbians Making History. Much of this research, based in grass-roots communities, has been written for the lesbian and gay press. Lesbians and gay men have received little attention from the mainstream historical profession. Like historians of women, people of colour, and the working class, lesbian and gay historians have had to struggle to broaden the definition of what is considered "legitimate" history.

The yellow press or scandal sheets of the 1950s and 1960s were newspapers not unlike today's tabloids such as *The National Enquirer* or *The Star*. As lesbian and gay historians have discovered, these early scandal sheets provide a wealth of information on gays and lesbians in the 1950s and 1960s. In the first article of this reading, Ross Higgins and Line Chamberland look at Montreal's yellow press and find that it reveals much about emerging lesbian and gay subcultures, including references to bar life and social/sexual networks, as well as general attitudes toward homosexuality. But as Higgins and Chamberland make clear, the most common references to gays and lesbians in the yellow press usually involved arrests and sexual scandals. In the second article of this reading, Robert Champagne introduces and interviews Jim Egan. During the 1950s and 1960s, Jim Egan embarked upon a prolific letter-writing campaign in

---

"Mixed Messages: Gays and Lesbians in Montreal Yellow Papers in the 1950s," by Ross Higgins and Line Chamberland was a paper presented to the international conference on gay and lesbian studies, Homosexuality, Which Homosexuality? (Amsterdam, December 1987).

"Interview with Jim Egan," by Robert Champagne is condensed from Robert Champagne, ed., *Jim Egan: Canada's Pioneer Gay Activist* (Toronto: Canadian Lesbian and Gay History Network Publication No. 1, 1987).

Toronto's scandal sheets to counter their inaccurate and homophobic accounts of gay and lesbian life.

The history of lesbians, gays, and the yellow press raises a number of important issues. In addition to giving us a glimpse into lesbian and gay life in the 1950s and 1960s, the yellow press reveals much about what we might call "heterosexual hegemony," or the ways in which heterosexuality is seen to be "natural" or given and other sexual identities and practices are defined as deviant, sick, or criminal. Certainly the sensational accounts of sex and crime carried in the yellow press must have done much to reinforce negative and homophobic attitudes toward lesbians and gay men. In this way, the tabloids indicate the important role played by the press or media in regulating the lives of lesbians and gay men and point to the central place of sexuality in the more general history of cultural hegemony in Canada. While heterosexual hegemony remained dominant during the 1950s and 1960s, it did not go unchallenged. The work of Jim Egan, in addition to the countless women and men who led everyday lesbian and gay lives, is evidence of the different levels of lesbian and gay resistance to heterosexual hegemony.

* * *

MIXED MESSAGES: GAYS AND LESBIANS IN MONTREAL YELLOW PAPERS IN THE 1950s

ROSS HIGGINS
LINE CHAMBERLAND

For Montreal, Canada's largest city with over one million inhabitants, the period following World War II was one of transition. The era of Mayor Camillien Houde and his "Ville ouverte" policy, under which the city was known far and wide for its wide open nightclubs, brothels and gambling joints, drew to a close under the scrutiny of a commission of enquiry into police and political corruption which saw the rise to prominence of Jean Drapeau, the commission's prosecutor, who won election as mayor on a morality platform in 1954. Whether the changes symbolized by Drapeau's election were real or merely cosmetic has been questioned.[1] Nonetheless, municipal politics were dominated by the morality crusade. The details of its impact on gay life will be a fertile field for study.

---

1. Jean-Paul Brodeau, *La délinquence de l'ordre: Recherches sur les commissions d'enquête*, Hurtubise HMH, Montréal, 1984, pp. 169–74.

In discussing French-speaking Quebec's consciousness of, and attitudes towards, homosexuality one must take into account the Latin heritage of tolerance, the puritanical Jansenist influence of the Catholic Church, the important role of homosexual writers such as Proust, Gide and Genêt, as well as the culturally filtered impact of currents from the English-speaking world from Oscar Wilde to Alfred Kinsey. Little work has yet been undertaken along these lines, though a few guideposts have been planted by writers like Brigitte Garneau and Guy Ménard.[2] Elsa Gidlow's autobiography provides a few clues to English artistic circles in the 1920s.[3] Echoes of homosexuality can be found in Quebec literature in French before the 1940s, but it is only in that decade that the trickle of more explicit works (which today has become a torrent) began.[4] Many areas of basic research are still uncharted. . . .

Although the earliest record of gay social life in Montreal is an account of outdoor cruising on the Champ-de-mars in the newspaper *La Presse*, June 30, 1886, few specific details are available before 1950. As in other cities, gay social life likely consisted of and relied mainly on private networks in which key individuals hosted periodic house parties. To find sexual partners, gay men relied mainly on outdoor cruising, with an occasional foray to the cafés and cabarets, some of which had gay sections, or to the sailors' bars on the waterfront. Turkish baths, locker rooms and movie theatres surely have a long history as cruising places. Newspaper ads for shared accommodation have no doubt long been used as well.[5]

By 1950 a few drinking establishments had a majority gay clientele, at least in the evening. For 1953, Leznoff[6] lists four bars and two restaurants, and other sources reveal that there were seven or eight others. These were all straight-run places—gay bar ownership does not enter the picture until after 1965. Nevertheless there was a visible gay culture in the form of Armand Monroe's drag shows at the Tropical Room on Peel Street and the Miss Montreal contests on the Main, in the milieu so eloquently evoked in the plays and novels of Michel Tremblay. In 1956, one of his predecessors

---

2. Brigitte Garneau, "L'homosexualité masculine au Québec," thèse de maîtrise, Dept. d'anthropologie, Université Laval, 1980, 118 pp.; Guy Ménard, "Du berdache au *Berdache*: lectures de l'homosexualité dans la culture québécoise," *Anthropologie et sociétés*, 9(3), 1985:115–138.
3. Elsa Gidlow, *Elsa, I Come with My Songs: The Autobiography of Elsa Gidlow*, Booklegger Press, San Francisco, 1986, 422 pp.
4. Early novels include André Béland, *Orage sur mon corps*, 1944, and Jacqueline Mabit, *La fin de la joie*, 1945.
5. Maurice Leznoff, "The Homosexual in Urban Society" (M.A. thesis, McGill University, 1954), p. 168.
6. Ibid., pp. 161–62.

published the first explicit Quebec gay novel in French, *Derrière le sang humain*, a turgid exercise in Catholic guilt.

General Description of the Yellow Newspapers: Format, Circulation, Readership

We use the term "yellow newspapers" to designate the least respectable type of publication, one which resorts to the most outrageous kind of sensationalism to sell papers and/or to transmit the image of society favoured by its publishers. Though the term is well-established in English (and "*jaune*" is used similarly in Quebec), it is sometimes not readily understood in common language. In the *Random House Dictionary* one definition for yellow is "offensively sensational as newspapers." This usage originated in the type of journalism practised by two rival New York newspapers at the end of the nineteenth century.[7]

...To the best of our knowledge, no public collections of the yellow press exist in the province. The approximately two hundred different issues of ten different periodicals which we acquired and which are now on deposit in the *Archives gaies du Québec* therefore constitute the only accessible collection. . . .

...Our work has thus far dealt almost entirely with *Ici Montréal*. A typical issue consisted of sheets of the cheapest newsprint, folded to form sixteen 8 1/2 by 11 inch pages. The cover almost always featured an alluring woman whose image had nothing to do with the provocative or comic headlines. Inside, there were few photos. The text was mainly composed of short two to four sentence "*potins*" or gossip tidbits, arranged under subject headings like agriculture, profiteers, morality or sports. Most issues have one or two longer articles, often relating details of sex trials or attacking political leaders. Every issue also had its lonely hearts ads, and just a few commercial ads, together with the occasional "lucky dollar" contest. . . .

Apparently the papers were widely sold in corner stores and on newsstands as well as being available for reading in barbershops, etc. They were distributed outside of Montreal, as attested by the lonely hearts ads from other regions and the coverage of provincial news stories reflecting input from readers elsewhere. The subscription prices are given

---

7. The name "Yellow Press" arose in the United States when W. R. Hearst's *Journal*, during the circulation battle with Pulitzer's *World*, introduced a comic picture feature called "The Yellow Kid." This rivalry was dubbed yellow journalism and came to be characterized by "scare headlines, sensational articles, lavish illustrations, comic features, Sunday supplements, etc." *Brewer's Dictionary of Phrase and Fable*, p. 1209.

in American funds as well as Canadian, suggesting the papers reached readers in the French-speaking areas of Vermont and New Hampshire and perhaps as far away as Massachusetts. The only indication of circulation is an estimate of 3,000 copies for the paper *Montréal-Confidentiel* (published in *L'Oeil en coulisse* 60:4—30/05/53). All together, the yellow papers probably never sold more than about 25,000 copies. In comparison, figures for the "respectable" weekly *Le Petit Journal* and for *La Presse*, the city's largest daily, were ten times greater.[8]

It is difficult to evaluate the readership in terms of sex, though it is clear that they were not exclusively aimed at either men or women. . . . It seems plausible to assume that readers were largely working class. Presumably most professionals would have sympathized with the mother of a friend who recounts that when, as a child in the mid-fifties, he brought one of these papers home, his mother grabbed it and tore it into tiny bits, telling him never to look at such garbage. This type of reaction was fostered by denunciations of these "immoral" papers from the pulpit and in a campaign conducted by the *Ligues du Sacré-Coeur*. Towards the end of the decade the clergy's campaign against the yellow papers was extended to include the "respectable" weekend press. Its failure, signalled by the rise in total circulation of these publications to the million mark around 1960,[9] is clear indication of the loss of ideological hegemony by the Church at this time.

The gay and lesbian content of the yellow press can be analyzed on several levels. To some extent, it provides factual information on bar life, cruising patterns, and social networks. It also reports on incidents in the lives of individuals, often involving arrests or scandals. More than specific facts however, the papers transmit values or attitudes. They were vehicles of social discourse, dealing with subjects other publications were reluctant to broach.

Though the emphasis of the Montreal papers was on stigmatizing non-conforming sexual practices, the attitudes they expressed towards gays and lesbians also include a more neutral approach and sometimes even positive support, or at least indulgent, humorous tolerance. A given

---

8. Elzéar Lavoie, "La constitution d'une modernité culturelle populaire dans les médias au Québec (1900–1950)," in Yvan Lamonde et Esther Trépannier (eds.), *L'avènement de la modernité culturelle au Québec*, Institut québécois de recherche sur la culture, Québec, 1986, pp. 261, 274.

9. Paul-André Linteau, et al., *Histoire du Québec contemporain*, vol. II *Le Québec depuis 1930*, Boréal Express, Montréal, 1986, p. 373.

publication could exhibit all of these variations in a single issue or over a short period of time. . . .

Items pertinent to gay men and lesbians include three major types: "*potins*," articles, and lonely hearts ads. We have completed a detailed study of fifteen issues of *Ici Montréal* dating from 1953, 1956 and 1957. We have also read another fourteen issues, up to 1960, but have not yet made a detailed analysis. Although this is a very small corpus, we have found in it a surprisingly large number of relevant items, and while it is too early for definitive conclusions, they seem to correspond to what we have seen in reading other parts of the collection.

In fifteen issues of *Ici Montréal*, we found a total of 92 relevant items, an average of over 6 per issue. Five items referred to both lesbians and gay men; eight to lesbians exclusively; and 79 to gay men only. This disproportion extended to the different item types. Reading the lonely hearts ads in these issues would have given lesbians only three chances at happiness, as compared to 21 for gay men. There were just four disparaging gossip tidbits about lesbians, but 51 on gays. Of the articles in which both were mentioned, one was a short section on homosexuals in a cabaret in a much more general article entitled "*Vice dans les cabarets*." The other was a brief reference to the presence of two lesbians at a New Year's party of gay men. . . .

Vocabulary

For a paper that delighted in coming up with front page headlines like "*40 Homos fêtent le Nouvel An dans une orgie inimaginable*" (January 1957) or "*Grande joie au pen: Un fifi de plus*" (March 1963), *Ici Montréal* turns out to be surprisingly tame in its use of vocabulary overall. The most common word for homosexual in its stories is "*homosexuel*," sometimes varied to "*homo-sexuel*," presumably to make it sound more "*sexuel*." Though the number of occurrences is much smaller, the same pattern can be discerned for women: the most common term is "*lesbienne*." There are three other terms for lesbians: the rather descriptive "*femme aux femmes*," the self-explanatory "*lesbienne-masculinisante*," and the uncertain reference "*fifille*," a term apparently sometimes used by older lesbians.

Slang terms for gay men are also quite common, with "*fifi*" in first place. The modern favourite "*tapette*" and the French "*pédé*" occur only once each. Québécois readers are clearly not expected to know "*pédé*," since it is followed by the suggestion "*faites-vous expliquer*." Feminine terms are extremely common, beginning with "*effeminé*" and including "*femme*," also spelled with a derogatory "*a*," and "*ma chère*." The ever-popular *"grande"* is used but its usual companion/synonym *"folle"* is strangely absent. The choice of words also brings out the tendency to emphasize youth and small size with "boy," *"imberbe,"* *"mignon"* and the much used *"petit monsieur"* and *"petit ami."* Finally, scientific terms are not neglected, as we find *"troisième sexe,"* a term still heard from older people in Quebec. Even the venerable *"inverti"* appears once.

As the language items suggest, the dominant stereotypes derived from nineteenth century pseudo-scientific discourse occupy a major place in the yellow newspapers' image of homosexuality. This is summed up in two humorous *"potins,"* one of which remarks how curious it is that the grammatical gender of *"homosexualité"* is feminine, while *"lesbianisme"* is masculine. The other asserts that a study of respiration has revealed that *"fifis"* breathe like women and *"lesbiennes"* like men.

Aside from their breathing, lesbians are also seen as predatory. Another yellow paper, *CanCan*, features a 1957 cover story: *"Les lesbiennes sont nombreuses à la campagne,"* claiming that there are more lesbians than gay men, based on a fifty year old comment from Havelock Ellis, and goes on to warn young girls against predatory women at Laurentian resorts. To build up the tough *"masculinisante"* image, *Ici Montréal* periodically gossips about one Ramona, who hangs out at the Café St-John on the Main (St-Laurent) and will take on all comers, male or female, who invade her turf. Another item assures readers that she "had more scars than a veteran of the Foreign Legion."

Gay male effeminacy is directly referred to in six items, and six others talk about men wearing dresses. On the other hand, one item says that a provincial police officer, with nothing effeminate about him, was seen going into a tavern that is seldom known to refuse gays. This is the only remark in the papers studied that directly counters the stereotype. Three items also imply that gays are small, physically weak or stupid. A 1963 cover story, *"Fifis versus homos,"* also in *Ici Montréal*, strongly makes the point that all gay men are not effeminate. This fairly positive article also informs us that the word *"fifi"* is short for *"effeminé."*

It must be remembered that the yellow newspapers were not fabricating these stereotypes. Stereotypes were based on the observable behaviour of the most visible members of the homosexual minority in the bar world. All the papers did was assume everyone was like that. . . .

Social Control

The "labelling" of "deviants" was a role the yellow paper played with relish, pointing a very public finger at those who had been discovered transgressing sexual norms. This sometimes led them to publish names or other identifying information about individuals, even when they were not accused of committing a crime. Gay men and lesbians were thus exposed to a wide range of social sanctions: job loss, expulsion from housing, ostracism by families and friends, physical violence or even murder.

In the fifteen issues of *Ici Montréal* analyzed, the names of three men not accused of a crime were printed in connection with homosexuality. One other might be deduced by people in the right circles and two had clues to their identity (i.e. place of residence) published. Two men convicted of sex crimes were also named. Three other items refer to an individual by first name only. Ramona has already been mentioned; another item wondered if perhaps "Paulo" was the leader of the lesbians in the city of Sherbrooke.

Homosexuality was frequently described as an "alarming problem," an "abnormal penchant" or simply as "vice." "Scandalous behaviour" was condemned and the "filthy proposals" that preceded it would "make the toughest sailor blush."

The yellow papers were also fond of making rather vague appeals to "the authorities" to act to clean up saunas or male prostitution or to stop "sick sadists" from seducing the young in movie houses. This recourse to political and police intervention seems out of step with their generally contemptuous attitude towards these "authorities" and their activism in favour of greater sexual openness.

The most prominent theme of social control found in the fifteen issues of *Ici Montréal* is that of assaults on or seduction of youth. A total of eleven items deal with this subject. Delivery boys were attacked by an "invert" who kept sending himself telegrams. Another, seen deep in conversation with a newspaper boy, had his license plate number printed. A clarinet teacher led his boy students into "vice." A doctor was warned the police had their eye on him after parents' complaints about his treatment of adolescents.

Moralizing was not the papers' true aim however—they merely wanted to sell papers. Taking a moral stand was a good cover for printing a lot of juicy details in order to give their readers a taste of forbidden worlds, a little vicarious adventure for only ten cents a week. A 1956 article on male prostitutes in *Ici Montréal* devotes most of its space to an interview in which a hustler defends his profession while the writer knowingly asserts that the young man was simply deluding himself when he claimed he only did it "*pour la business*." Anybody interested could also learn a trick by which to recognize a hustler in a gay tavern—watch for the ones who tear the beer bottle label down the middle. Somehow one feels that saving prostitutes from the "hellish nightmare" of their lives was less crucial to the writer than titillating his readers.

In the days before gay phone lines, with no gay papers listing the cruising spots, it was a major problem for those coming out to simply find the gay world. Here the yellow newspapers played a key role, all the while appearing to attack homosexuality.

An *Ici Montréal* account of the year's first gay arrest on Mount-Royal all but prints a guide map to mountain cruising spots. At the St-Moritz restaurant on Ste-Catherine St., a lot of *"petit messieurs"* can be found drinking Homo milk. Since his "A View from the Bridge" had its first version banned for homosexual allusions, it is suggested that Arthur Miller might be a relative of the author of *Derrière le sang humain*, the 1956 Quebec gay novel. Here both the film and the book are publicized.

In all, in the fifteen issues covered, we found six items giving direct, clear information about places frequented by gays, plus two that might be found with a little effort. Lesbians would have to be content with seeking out Ramona at the St-John Café. Twelve items pointed out pertinent books, films, physique magazines, and shows. . . .

Reference to places and cultural events were all very well, but what could be more direct than a personal ad in the lonely hearts columns? The openness of these seems somewhat surprising now. The men advertising fall into two main groups: the cultured and the sports-minded. Could readers of thirty years ago have wondered what this man was after? "38 year old, 5'6", curly brown hair, brown eyes, car, bilingual, all sports, would like correspondents of both sexes. I'm bored. Photo exchanged." A third of the men ask to meet people of both sexes. Some are not so ambiguous, though. One 26 year old would like to meet body builders. Photo appreciated. A couple of advertisers want to exchange ideas as well as photos. For women, the choice of ads was much more restricted, but there were a few. A good-looking widow who describes herself as *"gaie"* (in the old sense) with a nice home wants to meet *"une belle fille."* Another woman wants to *"égayer"* her *"soirées"* in female company.

These ads are few and far between compared to the vast number of people looking for serious Catholic partners with whom to start a family. There are quite a number that are ambiguous as well, and we have been fairly conservative in selecting the most obvious same-sex references. From these it is clear that this channel of communication was used by both lesbians and gay men to meet others like them, and in this capacity the yellow papers played an absolutely crucial role.

Aside from their importance in setting up contact between people and giving them access to bars, etc., the yellow papers occasionally took stands, or at least expressed attitudes, that were far from condemnatory. Sometimes this is simply a sort of complicit tolerance between writer and reader, sometimes it is more direct. Liberace is ridiculed in a story about him being stung by a wasp, but later his privacy is defended against an attack by a television personality.

A long article recounting the trial of a young man who tried to pick up a policeman in a gay tavern depicts him as effeminate and rather silly, but also good-looking and likeable; his behaviour is not considered particularly reprehensible. Even the gesture he made with a rolled-up newspaper (the closest he came to making explicit the sexual purpose of the trip to the rooming house) is considered something to laugh about. When he is acquitted because the judge finds he has been entrapped, the journalist reports that he left the courthouse puzzled but glad to be free.

A much more direct example of defense of gays is found in a September 1956 letters column in *Sentimental* where homosexuals are defended against a reader's charges of favoritism in hiring at Radio-Canada. The columnist answers that in Montreal, rightly or wrongly, and he believes it is wrongly, homosexuals are harassed by the police and despised by most people. Therefore it's understandable that they help each other out, but it's not the institutionalized system described by the reader. If left to themselves, and as long as they don't attack the young, there should be no problem.

The opportunities for contact and the somewhat favourable treatment sometimes accorded to gays and lesbians by the yellow press should not make us forget that their dominant message was quite negative. They exploited the subject of homosexuality in order to sell papers.

The yellow papers seem quite unconscious of changes occurring in the social pattern of homosexuality, even at a time when a major transformation was underway. We have as yet no Canadian studies comparable to Allan Bérubé's work in the United States on the impact of World War II on gay life.[10] It can be assumed, however, that the mobility and money given to thousands of young people had a similar, if smaller scale, effect here. Kinsey's study also had its impact on Montreal, bringing homosexuals in the city suddenly to the realization of their membership in a minority with substantial numbers. The yellow papers failed to recognize change despite the fact that their own emphasis on gay and lesbian themes, assumed to be quite unprecedented in Quebec publishing, was itself a symptom of the

10. Allan Bérubé "Marching to a Different Drummer: Lesbian and Gay GIs in World War II," in Ann Snitow et al. (eds.) *Powers of Desire: The Politics of Sexuality*, Monthly Review Press, New York, 1983, pp. 88–99.

change. In providing space for personal ads and supplying access information about the gay world, they could be described as predecessors of the later gay press. . . .

* * *

INTERVIEW WITH JIM EGAN

ROBERT CHAMPAGNE

[Jim Egan may have been the first public spokesperson in Canada for lesbian and gay rights. Starting in 1950, Egan began an energetic letter-writing campaign aimed at ending the "conspiracy of silence" regarding homosexuality and at removing the laws that made homosexual acts criminal offences. For fifteen years, Egan's work appeared in scandal sheets and mainstream newspapers. Public sentiment in Toronto seems to have changed at the end of the 1950s, when Egan's letters, which up to that point had often been rejected by the mainstream media, began appearing frequently in *Saturday Night* and the *Toronto Star*. A breakthrough to greater visibility was represented by Sydney Katz's two-part article on homosexuality in *Maclean's* magazine in 1964, with Egan serving as tour guide and "informant" in what was by then a well-established gay community in Toronto.]

Robert: *You began your letter-writing and publishing efforts in 1950. What motivated you to begin and how did you get started?*
Jim: Well, I've often thought about that. The truth of the matter is I cannot think what triggered off this idea because I certainly had no models to go by. It may well have been having read a great deal by some of the early people like John Addington Symonds and Edward Carpenter who wrote very positively on the subject—not in the name of god that I'm comparing myself to Symonds or Carpenter—but I felt that. . .I guess that the truth of the matter is I just felt somebody should be doing something about this.

The only place that you could get published information about homosexuality was in the scandal sheets. I would read those things and I would be absolutely outraged by most of the articles, if not all of them. If you didn't read those then there was very little opportunity to be exposed to it. Every once in a while in the local Toronto scandal sheets like *Tab*, *Flash*, *Hush*, or *Justice Weekly* you would be able to read about, for example, some unfortunate vicar who was convicted of "interfering with a boy-scout"—as they delicately termed it—or some unfortunate man who had been beaten up and robbed or murdered in Allen Gardens or Riverdale Park. The large newspapers like the *Star* and the *Telegram* did not give very much publicity to this sort of thing. Of course, there was absolutely nothing ever mentioned on a news broadcast.

So I just decided one day, "Well, this is preposterous—somebody's got to do something about this." So I sat down and started typing letters. Well, when I first started, and later...I did a great deal of letter writing which never saw the light of day. I didn't keep any carbons and many of them just perished into the waste basket. But at some point—and for reasons which I could not explain—suddenly the scandal sheets at least started publishing the letters. And they were all written under the *nom de plume* of "J.L.E." in the early writing. I'm not sure when I switched over and started using my own name.

Robert: *What did you hope to accomplish by writing those letters?*

Jim: I suppose the main thing was public awareness. I think that was my main motive. In many cases I took a positive delight in shattering the myths that were being promulgated. For instance, I had an exchange with a reader in *Saturday Night*. His letter referred to something about the scribblings of degenerates who didn't know how to keep their thoughts in line. I wrote a letter back and pointed out that among the degenerates who have done scribbling were Walt Whitman, Francis Bacon, Christopher Marlowe, and Shakespeare. I said, "It's unfortunate that your reader apparently derived his knowledge of homosexuality from reading graffiti on washroom walls." They published that letter and I got a great personal sense of satisfaction.

I have been told before now that it was a bit of an ego trip for me to do this, to see my name in print. Well, maybe there's a certain amount of truth to that, because I think if you don't have the egoists and the rebels you would have no progress at all in society. If you sit back and wait for the polite little ladies and gentlemen to do something they're going to take a long time to do it. I feel that rightly or wrongly, once I got that first letter published in the Toronto *Star*, and I wrote several letters to them before anything was published, once the first one was published it just seemed to open the door and they published every letter I wrote after that.

Robert: *And you don't know why these newspapers suddenly began to publish the letters?*

Jim: I don't know. Unless they just felt it would be acceptable, that maybe the time was here. It might have been that they felt they were creating a reader interest by printing provocative letters. And that's what they were, very provocative. I made no bones about it, defending the rights of gay men and women to live their lives as homosexuals, pointing out the injustice of the law. In all the letters that they published criticizing what I had written—and they published a fair few critical letters—there wasn't one of those letters that ever said, "Egan doesn't know what he's talking about. What do you mean unfair, unjust archaic laws, there's no such thing?" They never took that line—all of it was vague condemnation, for example, "How much longer do we have to read this nonsense from the pen of James Egan?" or "Why waste valuable space in the newspaper with this revolting defence of sick people." There was never any attempt to refute any of the things that I actually said in my letters. I think people were genuinely shocked at actually seeing, perhaps not so much a reference to homosexuality, but a defence of homosexuality. Saying in effect, that the homosexual was a victim of the ignorance and stupidity of society and that it was high time that archaic laws and unjust attitudes were changed. I think it was a real jolt to some of their sensibilities to see this.

Eventually, I wrote quite a lengthy article for the Toronto *Star* in 1963 which they published as part of a series called "Against the Grain." That was, I felt, a real breakthrough. It's one thing to write a letter to the editor and quite another to have a full fledged article published. Nathan Cohen at the time edited that particular series. What they did was they published a number of controversial views—legalizing marijuana, for example, although I don't know whether they actually published that, but that sort of thing. And Cohen did blue pencil it—took some of the kick out of it—but a sufficient amount was left that it did put up a rather spirited defence on the part of the homosexual and that drew a number of very critical letters from people. Much to my distress, there were very few letters of support that came in.

Robert: *Were you aware of any other individuals in Canada doing what you were doing either before or during the time that you were writing?*

Jim: No. Not one soul.

Robert: *So you saw yourself as the very first person to have done this kind of thing in Canada?*

Jim: As far as I was concerned, I was the first person in Canada to do the kind of thing that I did. To the best of my knowledge, when I started writing this stuff about 1949–1950, no one had ever made any prior attempts along those lines at all. If they did, certainly I was never able to find any record of it. It's not beyond the realms of possibility, of course, that there could have been somebody in Calgary or Vancouver who was writing letters to the editor, but I certainly did not know about them. My only prior knowledge of that kind of thing was, well, for example shortly after Oscar Wilde went to jail Lord Alfred Douglas wrote a number of very supportive letters about homosexuals. Later on, the sniveling hypocrite retracted everything he said. But at the time he did write them. In the United States, there was a man by the name of Henry Gerber. I carried on a correspondence with him. You come across references to him in some of the gay studies as being the first to organize or to try to organize the first gay organization in the United States back, it must have been around, it couldn't have been later than 1930.

Robert: *In addition to the many letters you had published in the tabloid press, you managed to have several series of columns on homosexuality published, including two quite lengthy series in* Justice Weekly *in 1954. How did this come about? Did Philip Daniels, the editor of* Justice Weekly, *persuade you to write the series?*

Jim: Well actually, Philip Daniels did not persuade me to do anything. I wrote letters to *Justice Weekly* because it was just one publication that I thought would perhaps publish something on homosexuality. The very first letter I wrote was published and, in fact, Daniels published everything I wrote to him. After I had written four or five letters, it occurred to me that perhaps he'd go for a series. It was my own idea, not actually his at all. And so I went down one day with what I saw as the first article in that "Homosexual Concepts" series.

Daniels was the absolute living caricature of the sleazy editor of a sleazy newspaper, with a cigar stuck in his mouth and the ashes dribbling down his vest. And when I first walked in there he says, "What's all this with you aping the male?" I said, "What do you mean 'aping the male'?" He says, "You know, You chaps don't grow beards." We got into quite a discussion and I pointed out to him that there were truck drivers and loggers and construction workers and all kinds of people who were gay and that all gay men did not have bleached blonde hair and tear-drop earrings. I think he was really serious about it. Daniels was motivated to publish the series by nothing more or less than the idea that it would sell copies of *Justice Weekly*. I sort of fed him that idea. I said, "There are thousands of gay people in Toronto and they would probably be interested in these articles. Who knows? Maybe your circulation and news-stand sales will increase." His old eyes lit up. . . .

Robert: *In the media in the 1950s, it seems that there was a lot of lumping together of various sexual categories and activities, like pedophilia, homosexuality and rape, under the generic term "sexual deviancy." In many of your letters and columns it seems to me that what you were trying to do in part was to separate those groups and categories, to say that they were not all the same.*

Jim: Yes. That's right. I can tell you that back in the 1950s it was quite common to refer to homosexuals as sexual deviants. That was a common synonym. Inverts, sexual deviants, perverts and a whole host of other unkind words like degenerates and this sort of thing. Sexual deviant was a common phrase, but it was a catchall phrase, it covered everything. If they said that such and such a bar was a hangout for sexual deviants you weren't quite sure what they meant. It probably included transvestites and gay men and god only knows what. They would be talking about "the problem of homosexuality" and the next thing you know they're talking about peeping Toms and voyeurs and child molesters and transvestites. And I argued that until you learn to separate and clarify what you are dealing with, you can't even define the problem that you keep on talking about. What is this problem? What is the problem of homosexuality? Describe the problem. Define it. I don't know, I don't know. I suppose in part it was sheer ignorance and stupidity that prompted them to do that. . . .

Robert: *Were there any individuals that you might want to mention who played a role in raising gay and lesbian issues in Canada in the period of the 1950s and 60s?*

Jim: I think in their own way, Rick and Sara at the Music Room did some heroic groundwork and may, for all I know, have prepared some of those younger ones for CHAT (Community Homophile Association of Toronto) when it finally came along. Some of them, perhaps, did benefit from listening to the discussions that we had there quite frequently on Thursday nights. They didn't last all that long, but for a while every Thursday at about nine o'clock they turned off the music and pulled out all the chairs and sat around in a big group and talked.

On one occasion, we had three or four psychiatrists from the Forensic Clinic come in and they had a lot to say. And I remember that this one psychiatrist was holding forth and one of the boys in the audience asked this doctor point blank, "Do you think all gay men are sick?" And he hedged a little bit about it and he said, "I think all gay men are by definition neurotic and in one sense of the word, yes, SICK, require treatment." And so the kid said, "Why do you think we're all sick?" And he said, "Because of your inability to engage in normal sexual intercourse with a woman." And so the kid says, "Well why do you think we do not engage in normal sexual intercourse?" And he said, "Because the homosexual male is afraid to make the effort for fear he fails. He fears failure in the act and doesn't try." So the kid thought about that and sat down and nobody else said anything. So I said, "Now, wait a minute. How could you possibly fear failure of an act you have not the slightest desire to commit?"

I said, "If I were sitting here drooling over girls and wishing I could go to bed with them but was afraid to make the effort, yeah. But, what if you don't have the faintest desire in the world to go to bed with a woman and you have no desire to succeed at all. How could I be afraid of failure?" And he didn't have much of an answer for it. I think his answer was that I had succeeded in convincing myself that I really wasn't interested. But that's just the sheerest sophistry, as far as I'm concerned.

And so, some of that talking may have helped. In fact, I feel reasonably sure it probably did help. But I don't know anybody else who was the least bit interested in doing anything or who did anything at the time. Given the atmosphere of the time, I can understand it. I can quite understand it.

Robert: *How did you become involved in helping Sydney Katz with his famous two-part 1964 article on homosexuality for* Macleans?

Jim: Well, by the time Sydney Katz had been assigned the task by his editor—don't know why the editor decided to do this—but by this time I was having quite a bit of stuff published in the papers and had written all those articles for *True News Times*, and *Justice Weekly*. So I just got a phone call from him one day and he introduced himself to me and said that he had been assigned to write this two-part article and would I be willing to cooperate with him and give him some guidelines.

He told me quite frankly, "I know nothing about homosexuality but from what I've read of your writings you seem to feel that everything that's written is negative and inaccurate and I don't want to produce an article like that. I would like to think that the article was as unbiased as possible and factual." So I said, "Sure, by all means, I'd be delighted to cooperate with you on it."

At that time, I was at the very peak of my activities and I had vast numbers of books and clippings and magazines relating to homosexuality and Katz came up one evening and we spent two or three hours talking about it. He left loaded down with books and pamphlets and material from *One* and *Mattachine* and so on.

I met Katz maybe five or six times and he roughed out the article and then came up one night and we went over the roughed out article and talked about this point and that point. I felt it was a very well done article. It's true he interviewed the police and the people at the Forensic Clinic. He interviewed both sides of the issue. I felt the article was very supportive of gay people, but it didn't bend over backwards to favour them. He did refer to the problem of school teachers molesting small boys, I think if I remember rightly, but he put it into a context. It wasn't as though this was common practice among homosexuals to go chasing boy scouts. He quoted the Chief of Police and I would say that any intelligent person who read the entire article would realize that the quotes from the Chief of Police showed just what an idiot he was. And Katz quoted him without comment.

Robert: *So you feel that you had a fair amount of influence over what he ended up publishing?*

Jim: Oh yes, a great deal. He quoted me extensively in the article under a false name, what was it, Baldwin...?

Robert: *Verne Baldwin.*

Jim: Verne Baldwin, yes. He relied heavily on what I told him and I really made a very, very special point at the time not to be unduly prejudiced. I didn't want to shade the thing in favour of gay people. I wanted to be as objective about it as I possibly could. I feel it was an objective article. I certainly got many important points across in the course of being quoted by him. Now true, nothing much ever happened as a result of those articles in *Justice Weekly* in the way of readership response. But after those two articles appeared in *Macleans* magazine there were about four or five letters that were published that were supportive of the article. And I, with downcast eyes and cheeks aflame with embarrassment, must admit that I wrote every one of them and sent them in under assumed names because I figured the magazine would be flooded with letters of protest and I figured nobody else would write in support. So I thought I would take advantage of this. So I just wrote all the letters and they published every damn one of them. And as I recall there were no negative letters received at all.

Robert: *Were there any other positive letters?*

Jim: No. Every one that was published was written by me.

Robert: *Did Katz know this?*

Jim: No. I never told him. . . .

Robert: *Looking back on your past activities, do you have any concluding comments to make about what you did and the value that you saw it having?*

Jim: Well, I suppose it would be difficult to evaluate what value if any it had. I like to think it provided some ground breaking for what came afterwards. . . . I will never know what influence if any I ever had on those parliamentary committees and on individual ministers. . . involved at the federal level. Who knows what influence I may have had on individuals like Pierre Berton or Nathan Cohen. God knows how many letters I wrote along those lines and I don't know what influence they had. I know I put a vast amount of time and energy into it and I don't regret one minute of it. I thoroughly enjoyed doing it. . . .

The labour is the important thing—how you do that. And if you can say afterwards, there was nothing more I could do, or even if you look back and say, "Jesus, I wish I'd have done it this way or I wish I'd have done it that way," that's alright because you didn't know at the time. You did the best you could do at the time. And the results, you cannot be held responsible for the results because there are so many other factors that are working, either for you or against you, that ultimately you cannot be held responsible. And I think that is something that people who are involved in these movements and become very discouraged because they don't see these great changes happening over night should realize....

...I don't think I said anything that was really outrageous or unreasonable. I think a demand for equality and justice under the law and acceptance as an equal, I don't see anything wrong with that at all. I don't see any reason why we should back down on any of those demands. I don't think any intelligent person knowing and understanding the facts would deny the rights of a gay person. And I think back in the 1950s and 60s the problem was that the average person had no opportunity to examine those facts.

TWO HANDS FOR THE CLOCK:

Changing Patterns in the Gendered Division of Labour in the Home

MEG LUXTON

When I first got a job, I just never had any time, what with looking after the children and the housework. But now my husband has started to help me. He cooks and picks up the kids and is even starting to do other stuff! What a difference! Before, I used to feel like the second hand on the clock—you know, always racing around. Now, with his help, it feels like there are two hands for the clock—his and mine—so I get to stop occasionally.

More and more married women with young dependent children are employed outside the home. Studies conducted in the early and mid-1970s suggested that when married women took on paid employment, their husbands did not respond by increasing the amount of time they spent on domestic labour. These studies reached the general conclusion that married women were bearing the burden of the double day of labour almost entirely by themselves.[1]

Underlying women's double day of labour is the larger question of the gendered division of labour itself. The gendered division of labour, and particularly women's responsibility for domestic labour, have been identified as central to women's oppression in the capitalist societies as a whole, and specifically to women's subordination to men within families.[2] Women's changing work patterns have posed sharply questions about

MEG LUXTON, "TWO HANDS FOR THE CLOCK: CHANGING PATTERNS IN THE GENDERED DIVISION OF LABOUR IN THE HOME," *STUDIES IN POLITICAL ECONOMY* 12 (FALL 1983), 27–44 BY PERMISSION OF THE JOURNAL AND AUTHOR.

THIS PAPER REPORTS THE RESULTS OF RESEARCH CARRIED OUT IN FLIN FLON, MANITOBA, IN 1981. ALL THE QUOTES CITED IN THE PAPER WITHOUT REFERENCES ARE FROM INTERVIEWS CONDUCTED AS PART OF THAT RESEARCH.

THE ARTICLE IS A REVISED VERSION OF A PAPER PRESENTED AT THE CANADIAN SOCIOLOGY AND ANTHROPOLOGY ASSOCIATION MEETING IN OTTAWA IN 1982. FOR CRITICAL COMMENTS I AM GRATEFUL TO MARGARET BENSTON, PAT CONNELLY, HEATHER JON MARONEY, PAT MARCHAK, ESTER REITER, HARRIET ROSENBERG AND WALLY SECCOMBE.

1. Heidi Hartmann, "The Family as the Locus of Gender, Class and Political Struggle; The Example of Housework," *Signs* 6:3 (Spring 1981), 377–86.
2. Rayna Rapp, "Family and Class in Contemporary America: Notes Towards an Understanding of Ideology," *Science and Society* 42 (Fall 1978), 278–301; Michelle Barrett, *Women's Oppression Today* (London 1980); Michelle Barrett and Mary MacIntosh, *The Anti-Social Family* (London 1983).

domestic labour—What is actually being done in the home? Is it sufficient? Who is actually doing it? Who should be doing it? This in turn has raised further questions about the existing unequal power relations between women and men.

In the paid labour force, some women's groups, particularly within the union movement, have organized campaigns centred on such specific issues as equal pay and equal access to jobs. Their efforts are a challenge to the existing divisions of work between women and men.[3] Such changes in the definition and distribution of women's work raise the question of whether or not attitudes toward the gendered division of labour in the family household are also being challenged. Has there been any comparable redefinition of men's work roles? And further, has there been any redistribution of work inside the family household? As women learn to drive electrohauls, shovel muck, and handle the heat of coke ovens, are men learning to change diapers, comfort an injured child, or plan a week's food within the limits imposed by a tight budget?

A recent Gallup poll on the sharing of general housework is suggestive. The poll, conducted across Canada in August 1981, reports that during the years 1976 to 1981, Canadians changed their opinions substantially about whether husbands should share in general housework. When asked the question, "In your opinion, should husbands be expected to share in the general housework or not?" 72 per cent responded "yes" in 1981 as compared with 57 per cent in 1976. Only 9 per cent (11 per cent of all men and 7 per cent of all women) replied that men should not share the work.

However, changes in attitudes do not necessarily indicate changes in behaviour. The Gallup poll goes on to suggest that there has apparently been little change in what husbands do. It also implies that women and men disagree on the extent to which men are helping regularly. In 1976, 44 per cent of men polled said they helped regularly with housework, while in 1981, 47 per cent said they did. By contrast, in 1976, 33 per cent of women polled said men regularly helped while in 1981, 37 per cent of women polled said men regularly helped.[4]

---

3. For example, see Deirdre Gallager, "Getting Organized in the CLC," and Debbie Field, "Rosie the Riveter Meets the Sexual Division of Labour," in *Still Ain't Satisfied: Canadian Feminism Today*, ed. Maureen Fitzgerald, Connie Guberman, and Margie Woolf (Toronto 1982).
4. Canadian Institute of Public Opinion, *The Gallup Report* (Toronto, 7 October 1981), 1–2.

FLIN FLON REVISITED

In 1976–77 I investigated women's work in the home through a case study of one hundred working class households in Flin Flon, a mining town in northern Manitoba.[5] Five years later, in 1981, I carried out a follow-up study to discover whether or not changes had occurred over the preceding five years. As Flin Flon is a small, fairly remote, single-industry town, it is not a Canadian pace setter. Changes occurring in Flin Flon probably indicate more widespread developments. While this case study does not dispute the finding of earlier studies (that when married women get paying jobs they continue to do most of the domestic labour), it does suggest that the situation is considerably more complex than had previously been perceived. It illustrates some of the factors underlying the emergence of the different patterns of attitudes and behaviours reflected in the Gallup poll. It also shows that in some working-class households, important changes in the division of labour are beginning to occur, as women exert pressure on their husbands to take on more domestic labour.

In the first study, I interviewed women of three generations. The first generation set up households in the 1920s and 1930s, the second in the 1940s and 1950s, and the third in the 1960s and 1970s. With just a few exceptions, women of the third generation were the ones with young children under the age of twelve. Just over half the women interviewed had held paid work outside the home for some period after their marriage. None of them, however, had worked outside the home while their children were young. Most had worked for pay before their children were born, but then had not worked for pay again until the children were of school-age. Regardless of whether or not they held paid jobs outside the home, these women identified themselves primarily as housewives and considered domestic labour their responsibility. They generally maintained that they did not expect their husbands to help with domestic labour. Those few men who did some work were praised as wonderful exceptions.

In the follow-up study I sought out only women of the third generation and was able to locate forty-nine of the original fifty-two. In striking contrast to the previous study, I found that these women, all of whom had children twelve years of age or less, were for the most part working outside the home for pay. Over half of these women had pre-school

---

5. Meg Luxton, *More than a Labour of Love: Three Generations of Women's Work in the Home* (Toronto 1980).

children, and nineteen had had another baby between 1976 and 1981. Despite their continued child care responsibilities, forty-four women had full-time employment. Of these, fourteen said they would prefer to be in the home full-time; nine said they would prefer part-time paid work; and almost half (21) said they were satisfied with the situation they were in. Four women had part-time paid work. Of these, two were satisfied while one wanted, but had not yet been able to find, a full-time paid job. One wanted to return to full-time domestic labour, but could not afford to quit her job. Only one woman was still working full-time in the home and she said she was there by choice.

What emerged from the interviews was that regardless of whether or not they wanted to be employed, these women were changing their identification of themselves as being primarily housewives. As one of the women who was working for pay full-time, but who wished she could stay at home, put it:

> I am a housewife. That's what I always wanted to be. But I have also been a clerk for four years so I guess I'm one of those working mothers— a housewife, a mother and a sales clerk.

Given the demands of their paid work, these women were forced to reorganize their domestic labour in some way. Both interviews and time budgets showed that the attitudes women have towards their work responsibilities (both paid and domestic) affect the way they reorganize domestic labour. A key factor was the extent to which they were willing to envisage a change in the gendered division of labour inside the family household.

Labour-force participation did not necessarily reflect their approval of "working mothers." In 1981 all of the women were asked what they thought about married women who had dependent children and who worked outside the home. Seven flatly opposed it under any circumstances, although all of them were in that situation. Nine did not think it was right for them personally, although they felt such a decision should be made on an individual basis. Eight women said it was fine if the woman needed the money, although they opposed mothers working outside the home for any other reasons.[6]

---

6. The problem here, however, lies in trying to determine what constitutes economic need. All of these women (24) maintained that they were working outside the home for economic reasons, because their families needed the money. In all likelihood, this is true. However, it may be that these women, like most employed housewives who have been studied, also have non-economic reasons for accepting paid employment. Economic

In contrast, over half of the women interviewed (25) maintained that mothers with dependent children had every right to work outside the home if they wanted to. Many of them (14) went further and argued that it was better for mothers to be working outside the home. For these women, economic need was only one of several valid reasons that women would take paid employment.

There was a direct correspondence between the attitudes these women expressed toward paid employment for mothers and their views on the gendered division of labour in the home. All of the women were asked who they thought should be responsible for domestic labour. Their responses show three distinct strategies in balancing the demands of domestic labour, paid employment and family. I have identified these distinct positions, based on their conceptualization of appropriate gender relations, as follows:

1. separate spheres and hierarchical relations;
2. separate spheres and co-operative relations;
3. shared spheres and changed relations.[7]

1. Separate Spheres and Hierarchical Relations

Seven respondents (14 per cent) advocated a strict gender-based division of labour. They flatly opposed women working outside the home because doing so would both violate women's proper role and detract from their ability to do domestic labour. These women argued that men, as males, were breadwinners and were "naturally" also household or family heads.

---

necessity is a more socially legitimated reason and some of these women may be dealing with the contradictory feeling they have toward their family obligations and their pleasure in employment by convincing themselves and others that they are only working because they "have to."

7. There were no obvious sociological factors that might explain the differences in opinion and behaviour. While a large-scale survey might reveal correlations between these different strategies and such factors as political or religious affiliation, ethnicity, and husbands' attitudes, at least among this group of women, and given the available data, no such patterns emerged.

It is also important to point out that while these three approaches are typical, they are not the only available options. Some women have fully egalitarian relations with the men they live with; others live alone or with other women.

A creative strategy was developed by one couple (not included in the study). The man worked a forty-hour week in the mines; the woman was a housewife. They determined mutually what work she was responsible for during a forty-hour week. She did child care while he was at work, as well as heavy cleaning and certain other chores. The rest of the domestic labour—child care, cooking, cleaning, laundry, shopping—they divided equally between them. As a result, each worked a forty-hour week at their own work and shared all remaining labour.

Women were to be subordinate to their husbands—this was described by several women as "taking second place to my husband." They argued that women's wifely duties included acquiescence in relation to their husbands' demands and putting their families' needs before their own. These women maintained that they themselves held paid jobs outside the home only because their earnings were crucial. They intended to stop work as soon as the "emergency" was over.

They insisted that their paid work must never interfere with their ability to care for their husbands and children or to run their households. Because they assumed that domestic labour was entirely women's responsibility, they did not expect their husbands to help. They maintained that boy children should not be expected to do anything at all around the house and argued that they were teaching their girl children domestic labour skills, not because the mothers needed help, but as training for the girls' future roles as wives and mothers. Accordingly, these women sustained the full double day of labour entirely by themselves.

To deal with the contradiction between their beliefs and their actions, these women worked even harder at their domestic labour. In what appears to be a rigorous overcompensation, they actually raised their standards for domestic labour. They were determined to behave as though paid work made no difference to their domestic performance. Many of them insisted, for example, that every evening meal include several courses made from scratch as well as home-made desserts.

As a result, these women set themselves up in a never-ending vicious circle and ran themselves ragged. Their fatigue and resulting irritability and occasional illnesses only served to convince them that their original prognosis was correct: paid employment is bad for women and harmful to their families.

2. Separate Spheres and Co-operative Relations

Seventeen women (35 per cent) said that women and men are different. Each gender moves in a separate sphere and marriage, in uniting a woman and man, requires co-operation between the two spheres, with each person pulling his or her own weight. These women considered it acceptable for women to "help out" by earning money when necessary but, they argued, women's real work was in the home.

There were two identifiable currents within this general position. Nine women advocated full-time domestic labour for themselves though they agreed that might not be the best option for all women. These women maintained that they should not be working outside the home because they thought it interfered with their family responsibilities. While they were more flexible in their attitudes than those in the first group of women, they argued generally for the maintenance of the gendered division of labour. Particularly in their childrearing attitudes and behaviour, they adhered to a strict notion that boys should not be expected to engage in domestic labours while girls should be encouraged to do so.

Like the first group of women, these women also did most of the domestic labour on their own. Their way of trying to cope with the enormous strain this created, however, was to ease up their standards for domestic labour. They were much more willing to purchase "convenience foods" or to eat in restaurants. They talked about doing less around the house and about feeling vaguely disappointed that they could not keep their place nicer. They were, however, prepared to accept that they could not work outside the home and continue to do full-time domestic labour as well.

Taking a slightly different approach, eight women stated that paid work was acceptable for women with children, if the woman's income was necessary for her household economy. While these women also indicated that they were in favour of maintaining a traditional gendered division of labour, they often engaged in contradictory practices. They would argue that domestic labour was women's work, but in day-to-day activities they frequently asked their husbands to lend a hand, and they all expected their boy children as well as the girls to learn and take on certain domestic tasks.

To a large extent, it appears that the discrepancy between their beliefs and their behaviour lies in an experienced necessity. Unlike those who argued for hierarchical relations, these women were unwilling to become "superwomen." They acknowledged the pressures on them and were willing to ask for help. The extent to which they asked for, and received, assistance varied from household to household. In most cases, children had assigned chores such as washing the dishes or setting the dinner table which they were expected to do on a regular basis. Husbands were not assigned regular jobs but were usually expected to "lend a hand" when they were specifically asked.

3. Towards Shared Spheres and Changing Relations

Twenty-five women—just over half the sample (51 per cent)—stated that regardless of necessity, women with young children had the right to paid employment if they wanted it. For them, wives and husbands were partners who should share the responsibilities for financial support and domestic labour. They supported the idea of changing the division of labour and in practice they were instituting such changes by exerting increasing pressure on their husbands and children to redistribute both the responsibility for, and the carrying out of, domestic labour. As it is these women who are challenging the existing ideology and practice of the gendered division of labour, and especially the place of women and men in the family home, I want to look more closely at the changes they have enacted in the last five years.

A REDISTRIBUTION OF LABOUR TIME

While the women who argued for separate spheres were defending a gendered division of labour within the household, statements made by the third group reflected the trends indicated in the Gallup poll. When these twenty-five women were asked in the 1976 study if they thought husbands should help with domestic labour, most agreed that they did not expect their husbands to do anything, although six said their husbands actually did help. By 1981, however, they unanimously insisted that husbands should help out and all said their husbands did some domestic labour on a regular basis.

An examination of time budgets for these households shows that men have in fact increased the amount of time they spend on domestic labour. By themselves, the figures seem to be quite impressive; men increased their domestic labour time from an average of 10.8 hours per week in 1976 to 19.1 hours in 1981—an increase of 8.3 hours.

By contrast, in 1976 full-time housewives spent an average of 63 hours per week on domestic labour while women working a double day spent an average of 87.2 hours per week working, of which 35.7 hours were spent on domestic labour. In 1981, women doing both jobs averaged 73.9 hours per week of which 31.4 hours were spent on domestic labour. This is a decrease of only 4.3 hours per week. While one would not expect a direct hour for hour substitution for one person's labour for another, there is a discrepancy between the increase in men's work and the relatively insignificant reduction in women's work. Women on an average were spending 12.3 hours a week more than men on domestic labour. Furthermore, there is a discrepancy between the women's insistence that domestic labour should be shared equally and the actual behaviour of household members. These discrepancies generate considerable tension between wives and husbands—tension which reflects the power struggle inherent in the redistribution of domestic labour.

WOMEN AND MEN'S DOMESTIC LABOUR

The women who want their husbands to be more involved have developed a variety of strategies and tactics with which to get the men to take on more work. These range from gentle appeals to fairness or requests for assistance to militant demands for greater (or equal) participation. In a few cases, women discussed the situation with their husbands and they mutually agreed on a sharing of tasks that both partners considered fair and reasonable. In the majority of cases, however, negotiations appeared to be out of the question. Instead the couples seemed locked into tension-generating, manipulative power struggles.

For the women, the impetus to change comes first from the pressures of their two jobs. It is fuelled further when they compare their experiences with those of their husbands. Some contrasted their own working time at home with their husband's leisure time.

> I come home from work dead tired and I still have to cook and be with the kids and clean up. And he just lies around, drinking beer, watching TV and I get so mad, I could kill him.

Others compared the standards their husbands expected from their wives with those the men held for themselves. They noted that when living alone, some men kept their households immaculately clean; others lived in a total mess. Whatever their standards for themselves, when the women were around, men changed their behaviour, altered their expectations and pressured the women to meet male standards.

> When my husband is on his own, he's quite happy to live in a pig sty. Mess doesn't bother him. But the minute I get back he insists that he can't live in the house unless it's spotless.
>
> Before we were married he lived on his own and his place was so clean and tidy. But as soon as we got married, he somehow never felt he could clean up. It was all up to me.

Despite the obvious interest these women have in redistributing domestic labour, and despite their motivating anger, there are numerous forces operating which make it difficult for women to insist that their spouses actually share the work.

Because inequalities in the division of labour are based on male power, when women demand equalization of the work, they are challenging that power. Some women were afraid that if they pushed for more male participation, they would provoke their husbands' anger and rage. At least one woman said her husband had beaten her for suggesting he help with domestic labour.

While there is evidence to suggest that when women have paid employment they increase their own power in marriage, all of these women earned considerably less than their husbands. As a result, the men retained economic power (bread-winner power). Men can also use their greater earnings as a justification for not doing domestic labour. They often argued that with their earnings they discharged the responsibility to the household. Under present circumstances it is up to the individual women to initiate changes in the patterns of domestic labour. For many, economic dependency makes it difficult to challenge their husbands.

Furthermore, the actual task of getting men to do domestic labour is often difficult. If women want their husbands to begin doing domestic labour, they must be prepared to take responsibility not only for overcoming male resistance but also for helping the men overcome both the accumulated years of inexperience and the weight of traditional assumptions about masculinity. Generally, the women assumed that their husbands were unfamiliar with domestic labour and therefore neither knew what needed doing nor had the necessary skills to carry out the work. Taking on this training of resisting and unskilled workers is often in itself an additional job.

When men do start doing domestic labour, women begin to lose control. Domestic labour has traditionally been the one sphere of female control and power. For most women, the kitchen is the closest they ever come to having a "room of one's own." It is difficult for many women to relinquish this, particularly if they are not compensated for that loss by gains made elsewhere—for example in their paid work. While the women were uniformly pleased that their husbands had increased their contribution, they were troubled by the way domestic labour was being redistributed.

MEN AND DOMESTIC LABOUR

That men increase the amount of time they spend on domestic labour does not in itself convey much about changing work patterns. Most significantly, it was still assumed that women were primarily responsible for domestic labour and that men were "helping out." When women do domestic labour they often juggle several tasks at once. One of the ways that men have increased the amount of time they spend on domestic labour is by taking over some of that simultaneous work. Many women reported that their husbands were willing to watch the children while the women prepared dinner or did other household chores. While such actions obviously relieved some of the pressures and tensions on women, they did not reduce the amount of time required of women for domestic labour.

Often when men (and children) took on certain tasks, they ended up generating even more domestic work. A number of women indicated that their husbands cooked, but when they did so they seriously disrupted the orderliness of the kitchen, emptying cupboards to find something and not putting things back or using an excessive number of dishes in the preparation. Another commonly cited example was that when men agreed to look after the children, they actually paid more attention to their visiting friends or the TV. Unattended, the children ran "wild" through the house so that when the woman returned she had to spend a great deal of time tidying the house and calming the children. Further, many women pointed out that getting their husbands to do domestic labour required a considerable amount of their time and energy. Sometimes, women argued, it took more work to get the man to do the work than it did to do the work themselves.

Furthermore, men tended to take over certain specific tasks which had clearly defined boundaries. They did not take on the more nebulous, on-going management tasks and they rarely took responsibility for pre-task planning. For example, a number of men did the grocery shopping on a regular basis but they insisted that the woman draw up the basic list of things needed. Some men would do the laundry, if all the dirty clothes were previously collected and sorted and if the necessary soap and bleach were already at hand. . . .

The redistribution that is occurring is selective. The husbands tend to take the path of least resistance. The trend has been for men to take on those tasks that are the most clearly defined, or sociable and pleasant ones, while leaving the more ill-defined or unpleasant ones to the women. Repeatedly women noted that their husbands had taken on reading the children a bedtime story and staying with them until they fell asleep, thus "freeing" the women to wash the dishes and tidy the kitchen. Men were often willing to feed their infant children or take older ones to the park, but on the whole they would not change soiled diapers or wash their children's hair. They would wash the dishes but not the kitchen floor or the toilet. One man would vacuum the living room rug but refused to do the stairs because they were too awkward.

A number of women expressed concern about this pattern. They noted that when men took on the more pleasant aspects of domestic labour, they were left with the most onerous and boring tasks. They were particularly concerned when the man took on more of the playtime with children. As one woman expressed it:

> I'm really glad he's spending more time with the children. They really enjoy it. But it's beginning to make me look like the meany. Daddy plays with them and tells them stories and other nice things while I do the disciplining, make them wash up, tidy their toys and never have time to play because I'm cooking supper.

One of the most significant transformations of men's involvement in domestic labour has been in the area of child care. While most fathers have always spent some time with their children, particularly with older children, increasingly they are doing more of the day-to-day caregiving, especially with younger children. Perhaps the most significant change of all has been with the birth process itself.[8] In 1976 only 4 out of 25 men had been present at the birth of at least one of their children. However, of the babies born between 1976–1981, 10 of the 19 new fathers had been present at the birth (and only 2 of these were of the original 4). The wives indicated that they felt very strongly that having their husbands involved in the birth also drew the men into the whole process of pregnancy, child birth and infant care. Men who were willing to attend the birth were subsequently more inclined to get up at night with the baby, to take over certain feedings and to be generally more involved with their small babies.

Despite this very promising shift, women were still responsible for overall child care. All twenty-five women said it was up to them to arrange day care for their children when they worked outside the home. If the child care arrangements fell through on any particular day, it was the woman who had to get time off work to stay home, although this can in part be explained by her lower pay and in part by his unavailability when underground.

Furthermore, men "babysat" their own children—something that women never did. The implication of this typical reference was that the children were the responsibility of the mother, and the father "helped out." This attitudinal difference was often carried out in behaviour as

---

8. It seems to me that the involvement of men in the actual birth of their children is of enormous significance—something which has not yet been appreciated, or studied.

well. Women repeatedly described situations where men would agree to watch the children, but would then get involved in some other activity and would ignore the children. As children grew up, they learned from experience that their mothers were more likely to be helpful, and so they would turn to the woman rather than the man for assistance, thus actively perpetuating the traditional division of labour.

The ambivalent and often reluctant way in which these men have moved into domestic labour reflects a combination of valid reasons and invalid excuses. In "The Politics of Housework," Pat Maindari describes with biting sarcasm the various forms of male resistance developed in response to a wife's attempt to share housework:

> (Husband): "I don't mind sharing the work, but you'll have to show me how to do it." Meaning: I'll ask a lot of questions and you'll have to show me everything every time I do it because I don't remember so good. And don't try to sit down and read while I'm doing my jobs because I'm going to annoy the hell out of you until it's easier to do them yourself.[9]

Flin Flon women described various forms of male behaviour that were obviously intended to resist attempts to draw them into domestic labour. The majority of resisters took a subtle approach (passive resistance) similar to the ones satirized by Maindari. One woman described how their kitchen sink was directly in the centre of the kitchen counter. Normally the draining board sat on the left-hand side and the dirty dishes were stacked on the right. Her husband maintained he was unable to do the dishes as he was left-handed and the sink was designed for right-handed people. Some women talked suspiciously of the way household machinery "broke down" when their husbands tried to use it. Several women told of incidents where their husbands agreed to do the work but then repeatedly "forgot" to do it, complained when the women "nagged" them about it, and finally told the women to do it themselves if they did not like the way the men did it. One man explained his position quite clearly:

> Look, I'm not interested in doing stuff around the house. I think that's her job, but since she's working she's been on my back to get me to help out so I say "sure I'll do it." It shuts her up for a while and sometimes I do a few things just to keep her quiet. But really, I don't intend to do it, but it prevents a row if I don't say that.

For men to take on domestic labour meant that they had to give up some

---

9. Pat Maindari, "The Politics of Housework," in *Sisterhood is Powerful*, ed. Robin Morgan (New York 1970), 449–51.

of the time they had previously spent on their own enjoyments. Within certain limits this may not be much of a sacrifice, but at some point a man's increasing involvement in domestic labour starts eroding his ability to engage in other activities he values highly. There is a substantial difference between washing dishes and watching TV, and in having to come home early from drinking with one's mates at the pub because one has to cook dinner.

Because the majority of men have, until recently, not been expected to do domestic labour, they have not been taught either implicitly, the way girls learn via their dolls and play kitchens, or explicitly, through "helping" mother or in home economics classes. As a result, they often lack knowledge and are unskilled and awkward. Working at a job for which one is ill-prepared often generates feelings of anxiety, inadequacy and incompetence which are easily translated into a generalized reluctance to continue the job.

Some men expressed a willingness to do domestic labour but they were afraid that if it were publicly known that they did "women's work," they would be subjected to teasing and ridicule. One man, for example, quite enjoyed doing the vacuuming. However, there were no curtains on the windows, so the interior of the house was visible from the street. As a result, he did the vacuuming on his knees so that no one would see him! Other men were willing to do tasks inside the house but steadfastly refused to do those tasks that were "women's work" outside in public (hanging washing on the line, for example).

This fear of public ridicule was illustrated by two neighbours. Both families visited together frequently, and the men were friends. They also did a considerable amount of cooking and cleaning. Both, however, insisted that their wives not let the other couple know of the extent to which the men did domestic labour. The fear of public ridicule may reflect a deeper fear. When wives insist that men move into an area that has traditionally been defined as "women's work," men face a challenge to their conventional notions of femininity and masculinity. This may arouse deep psychological and emotional resistances, and stimulate anxiety and fear. . . .

CONCLUSION

This case study suggests that changing patterns of paid employment are creating a crisis in the way labour is currently distributed and accomplished in the family household. It illustrates the ambiguities reflected in the Gallup poll findings and shows that these ambiguities arise from serious problems in the way domestic labour is changing. It also suggests that ideologies of "family" are very strong and play a central part in the way most people organize their interpersonal relationships and their domestic lives.

Because people tend to evaluate their experiences in light of existing social explanations and ideologies, the response of Flin Flon women can be set in a broader context. The three perspectives expressed reflect ideologies which are currently prominent.

Those women who put forward a "separate spheres and hierarchical relations" position were defending the traditional conservative view which locates women inside the family, subordinates women's interests to men's, and places priority above all on the preservation of the bread-winner husband/dependent wife nuclear family.

Because the beliefs these Flin Flon women held conflicted directly with the activities they engaged in, they were compelled to mediate the contradiction. Their attempts to defend a strict gendered division of labour forced them deeper into the hardship of the double day. Their actual experiences highlight the conditions under which support for right-wing "pro-family" reform movements is generated, for in their opinion, it is their paid work that creates the problem.

Those women who argued for "separate spheres and co-operative relations" were expressing a classic liberal view of appropriate female/male relations in the family. This "different but equal" perspective echoes the maternal feminism of some early twentieth-century theorists. It is also found in many sociologists of the family such as Young and Wilmott, who argue that marriages are now symmetrical or com-panionate.[10]

Those women who argued for "shared spheres and changing relations" were expressing contemporary feminist views which hold that the existing gendered division of labour is a major factor in women's oppression. In challenging the way work is divided in the home, they are questioning the existing relationships between women and men, and between children and adults. Discussing existing family relationships, Hartmann has argued that "Because of the division of labour among family members, disunity is thus inherent in the 'unity' of the family."[11]

This study suggests that a large-scale social transformation is occurring

---

10. Nellie McClung, *In Times Like These* (1915; Toronto 1972); Michael Young and Peter Willmott, *The Symmetrical Family* (London 1973).
11. Hartmann, "Family as the Locus," 379. (See n. 1 above.)

as traditional patterns are eroding and new ones are emerging, but to date the change has been acted out on the level of the individual household, and may, in the short run, be intensifying family disunity. What emerged from these interviews was the total isolation both women and men felt. Women involved in active, collective organizing to change the division of labour in the paid workforce have the women's liberation movement, the trade union movement, Status of Women committees, and sometimes the law and other organizations or institutions such as the Human Rights Commissions, to back them up. In contrast, women challenging the gendered division of labour in the home do so on an individual basis. Similarly, there is a complete lack of social and material support for men with regard to domestic labour. Very few unions have won paternity leave, for example, so it is very difficult for new fathers to get time off work to be with their new children. This makes it very difficult for men actually to take equal responsibility for their infants.[12] Accordingly, any man who takes on domestic labour places himself at odds with current social practices. It takes a certain amount of self-confidence and courage to do so.

As a result, the majority of respondents implied that they considered that the changes in their domestic division of labour were specific to their individual households. They perceived these changes not as part of a large-scale transformation in the patterns of work and family life, but as a personal struggle between them and their spouse. Such a perception only exacerbated the tensions between women and men.

As material conditions change and new ideologies emerge, many individuals and families are floundering, trying to decide what they want, how to get it, and most problematically, how to resolve conflicts between various possibilities and needs. There are currently no social policies or clear-cut, developing social norms to provide a context in which individuals can evaluate their own actions. Instead, there are several contending ideologies and related social movements, such as the "pro-family" movement and the women's liberation movement.[13] While these movements articulate positions on what female/male relations should entail, they rarely organize to provide support for women to achieve the desired end. The current situation is thereby generating a great deal of confusion and

---

12. In Québec the unions of CEGEP teachers have won paternity leave. This has made it possible for some men to take equal responsibility for infant care.
13. Susan Harding, "Family Reform Movements: Recent Feminism and its Opposition," *Feminist Studies* 7:1 (Spring 1981), 57–75.

often pain and interpersonal conflict, especially between women and men.

Finally, this study demonstrates that until the exclusive identification of women with domestic labour is broken, there is no possibility of achieving any kind of equality between women and men. If the necessary labour is not redistributed, women end up with a dramatically increased work load. Unlike earlier studies, the findings of this research suggest, that despite all the problems, some working-class women are contesting male power and challenging male privilege and some men are responding by assuming more responsibility for domestic labour.

FURTHER READINGS FOR TOPIC 8

John D'Emilio, *Sexual Politics, Sexual Communities: The Making of a Homosexual Minority in the United States, 1940–1970* (Chicago and London: University of Chicago Press, 1983).

Gary Kinsman, *The Regulation of Desire: Sexuality in Canada* (Montreal: Black Rose Books, 1987).

Meg Luxton, *More Than a Labour Of Love: Three Generations of Women's Work in the Home* (Toronto: The Women's Press, 1980).

Joy Parr, *The Gender of Breadwinners: Women, Men, and Change in Two Industrial Towns, 1880–1950* (Toronto: University of Toronto Press, 1990).

Ruth Roach Pierson, *"They're Still Women After All": The Second World War and Canadian Womanhood* (Toronto: McClelland and Stewart, 1986).

Joan Wallach Scott, *Gender and the Politics of History* (New York: Columbia University Press, 1988).

Veronica Strong-Boag and Anita Clair Fellman, eds., *Rethinking Canada: The Promise of Women's History*, 2nd ed. (Toronto: Copp Clark Pitman, 1991).

Jeffrey Weeks, *Sex, Politics and Society: The Regulation of Sexuality Since 1800* (London and New York: Longman, 1981).

TOPIC 9

Storms Ahead

"There can be few countries in which scholars. . .have been so preoccupied with 'nationhood,' 'national identity,' and 'national unity,'" Margaret Prang remarked in 1977. A decade later, that seemed like an understatement. The Free Trade Agreement and the failure of the Meech Lake Accord placed the questions of identity and survival at the centre of all talk about Canada. Free Trade, the demolition of the CBC, the attacks on VIA Rail, the virtual termination of regional development, rumours of the end of the Canada Council: the neo-conservative era of the 1980s has been a harsh one indeed for Canadian nationalism. What will remain of Canada if Quebec leaves Confederation? For some scholars, not much. Whatever distinctiveness Canada retained after the Free Trade Agreement, argues J. L. Granatstein in Nation: Canada Since Confederation, resides in "the bilingual character of the nation," and every effort thus has to be made to make Québécois feel like full partners in Confederation. Others disagree. Some, like the critic Linda Hutcheon, note the special Canadian sense of irony; others emphasize such traditions as North America's strongest social democratic movement, the distinctive radicalism of the United Church of Canada, and the welfare state—which has thus far survived, albeit in battered condition, the neo-conservative wave.

This is one of the issues discussed by Philip Resnick and Daniel Latouche in their 1990 commentaries, which represent updated versions of Resnick's Letters to a Québécois Friend, which was printed, along with a rebuttal by Latouche, in 1989. We conclude with David Cameron's appeal for clarity and calm in dealing with the constitutional crisis. Dusk or dawn? It may be earlier than we think.

Free Trade, Meech Lake, and the Two Nationalisms

PHILIP RESNICK

In a strange way, the Free Trade Agreement has helped to trigger a crisis between English Canada and Quebec that is potentially as serious as the one provoked by the emergence of a new Quebec nationalism in the aftermath of the Quiet Revolution. This crisis gave rise to anguished questions ("What Does Quebec Want?") and to a series of policy initiatives including the Official Languages Act, Bills 22 and 101, the Quebec referendum of 1980, and the constitutional patriation of 1981–82, which included the Charter of Rights. The current crisis has such benchmarks as the Meech Lake Accord, the Free Trade Agreement, and Bill 178.

Before I examine the relationship between free trade, Meech Lake, and the current impasse between our two nations and nationalisms, let me raise the question of responsibility. Should we be pointing fingers as we begin this discussion, and, if so, at whom? At Robert Bourassa, for example, for his cynical betrayal of his 1985 election promise to Quebec anglophones regarding amendments to Bill 101 and his subsequent override of the Supreme Court judgement on signs; for his blatant support both for free trade and for Brian Mulroney during the 1988 election, when what many in English Canada perceived to be our own future as a "distinct society" was on the line? At Mulroney, whose decision to foist free trade onto the political agenda has left many wounds across English Canada and whose relative silence over Bill 178 has helped spark some of the backlash against Meech Lake and the distinct society clause? At Pierre Elliott Trudeau, whose referendum-eve promise of change to the electors of Quebec gave rise to a Charter from which all reference to group rights or national rights was studiously omitted? We would be justified at pointing at each of these in turn.

Yet there is a group that bears even greater responsibility—big business, both in English Canada and in Quebec. If the chickens of nationalism are coming home to roost in 1990, it is in good part because Canadian big business and its allies—the Economic Council of Canada, the Macdonald

Philip Resnick is a professor in the Department of Political Science, University of British Columbia.
Reprinted with permission from *Queen's Quarterly*, 97, 2 (Summer 1990), 355–60.

Commission—managed to wrest a stranglehold over the political agenda in the 1980s, the high point of neo-conservatism throughout the English-speaking world. Free trade was a crucial ingredient in the attempted turn to more market-oriented values and in the downplaying of the role of the state. The Business Council on National Issues had little use for sentimental arguments about defensive nationalism and even less for the communitarian values which large sections of Canadian society—labour, women, environmental groups, anti-poverty coalitions—might advance. In the relentless search for greater market share and for more rigidly market-driven social and industrial policies, big business was prepared to force free trade down our collective throats. And in the process, it helped foster a new wave of English-Canadian nationalism, which has suddenly become a good deal more sensitive to measures which threaten our sense of national identity.

In my *Letters to a Québécois Friend*, I suggest that there are two key elements that have characterized English-Canadian nationalism since Confederation. One of these is our love-hate relationship with the U.S., characterized by simultaneous attraction and fear of engulfment. The other is an identification with a reasonably strong central government, which from the time of the National Policy, through two world wars and the Depression, and a host of initiatives in the cultural, economic, and social fields, has done much to foster the degree of national identity that we have in this country. It is the first element, the fear of being engulfed by the U.S., that was stirred to life during the free trade debate, and that plant closures and cut-backs to key cultural institutions like the CBC and to social programs have helped keep alive since. It is the second element, the commitment to a reasonably strong central government, that suddenly, in the aftermath of free trade, is perceived to be threatened by various components of Meech Lake—provincial lists for Senate and Supreme Court appointments, opting-out provisions for all provinces from future federal-provincial programs, the unanimity requirement for future constitutional change.

I spent the year 1987–88 on a sabbatical from the University of British Columbia in the Political Science Department at the Université de Montréal, and I had several occasions to be back in Quebec during the 1988 election campaign. As a result, I have a reasonable sense of what Quebec attitudes towards the free trade agreement were and of Quebec reaction to some of the concerns being voiced in English Canada. Before I explore these reactions, however, let me go back a little further in time and address the nature of Quebec's attitude towards the U.S.

In my *Letters*, I refer briefly to an elective affinity in Quebec political culture for the U.S. over English Canada. This is neither new nor entirely surprising for anyone with a sense of Canadian history. How could French Canadians identify with English Canadians through the long decades after 1867 when English-Canadian identity was defined first and foremost in terms of Britain and the British Empire? French-Canadian attitudes during the Boer War, WWI, and WWII reflected a resistance to the British connection, even though France herself was allied with Britain in 1914 and again in 1939. At the same time, French Canadians feared the assimilationist attitudes that Loyalists and Orangemen might have. Overall, French Canadians—in their view of the outside world—were therefore closer to Americans, with their isolationist attitude towards the Old World, than they were to their English-speaking countrymen.

In the more recent period, however, as English Canada has grown away from Britain and even fitfully attempted to put some small distance between itself and the U.S. there has not been a corresponding shift inside Quebec. In one way this is understandable. Quebec has been absorbed with its own internal transformations in the decades since 1960—first the Quiet Revolution, then battles over language and constitutional status, and side by side with all this, the development of its own bourgeoisie. Yet, at another level, the new Quebec nationalism, as it has come to push for ever greater autonomy from federal institutions or for out-and-out independence, has been driven to take a quite different position on the U.S. than the new English-Canadian nationalism that developed in the late 1960s and beyond.

Some Québécois nationalists of the left might denounce American imperialism, alongside Canadian federalism, in their manifestos and broadsides: René Lévesque was never of this persuasion. Indeed, there was a certain logic from the *indépendantiste* point of view to try to outflank Ottawa and Toronto by appealing directly to New York and Washington. Hence, the attempts of Lévesque and Jacques Parizeau to woo American businessmen in the late 1970s in the lead-up to the referendum. The argument, moreover, would be repeatedly made that because of language and culture Quebec had less to fear from the American colossus than might English Canada.

What was striking, therefore, in the year preceding the 1988 federal election was the near unanimity of Quebec's political and business élites in support of free trade. While the political forces of English Canada were split, with the left and liberal centre generally opposed and the right favouring free trade, Quebec—once Parizeau had replaced Pierre-Marc Johnson as leader of the Parti Québécois—projected a very different image. At the same time, Quebec intellectuals and journalists, so strident in their support for sovereignty in the 1960s and 1970s, were either openly supportive of the free trade initiative or strangely silent. Only the trade union movement and a small number of other popular movements, for example, women's organizations, voiced any opposition.

Speaking personally, I can say that a number of Québécois intellectuals went one step further in their support for free trade. As I heard on a number of occasions in 1988, it was only right that English-Canadian nationalists experience the bitter fruit of defeat that their Québécois counterparts had experienced in the referendum of 1980. If independence was ruled out for Quebec, why should it be any more legitimate for English Canada?

Now as one of that handful of English-Canadian intellectuals who supported Quebec nationalism through thick and thin in the 1960s and 1970s and into the referendum battle, I must confess to a sense of personal betrayal when I found myself faced with such arguments. And I must confess to a feeling of chagrin when I heard Quebec's demands for recognition of its status as a distinct society and could not get across the point that for English Canada our relationship with the U.S. posed very similar problems. I suspect the genesis of my *Letters* does go back to my experience in Montreal, coupled with the evidence that on 21 November 1988 it was the 63 Tory seats from Quebec (out of 75) that had given Mulroney the majority needed to make free trade possible.

For English-Canadian nationalists the support shown both by Bourassa and Parizeau for free trade could not but provoke a very strong backlash against a constitutional accord that would simultaneously weaken the central government. After 21 November 1989, therefore, many of those who might have held their noses and supported Meech Lake on the grounds that it undid Trudeau's "humiliation" of Quebec in 1981 found themselves taking a very different position. Bourassa's override of the Supreme Court judgement in December 1988 and the passage of Bill 178 added further fuel to the fire, making English Canadians who were favourably disposed to bilingualism sharply aware of the double standard now entering the politics of Quebec nationalism.

There is yet a further element that colours the views of nationalists on the left in English Canada as we view Quebec in 1990. Quebec nationalism is no longer a force necessarily linked to the left. Indeed, its staunchest supporters at the moment, as journalist Lise Bissonnette correctly pointed out, are the new entrepreneurs, the much praised heroes of Bourassa's and Parizeau's Quebec. Now I am the last person to begrudge Quebec its capitalists or its accession to capitalist modernity. But I have no apologies to make to Daniel Latouche or to any of my other nationalist friends in

Quebec when I tell them that I find the Michel Gauchers of this world, with their patter about nationalism, competition, and markets, no more worthy of support than I would Conrad Black or Jimmy Pattison, were they suddenly leading the forces of English-Canadian nationalism. I think Quebec intellectuals of the left have got to rethink their position and ask themselves seriously whether they really have more in common with their capitalist entrepreneurs than with their confrères and consoeurs in English Canada. For the important battle, I am convinced, must be waged against the ascendancy of neo-conservative values.

I also think—and here I have re-thought my position *vis-à-vis* the 1960s and 1970s—that federalism has more to offer both Quebec and English Canada than would the emergence of two independent states. For one, federalism can help soften the extreme edges of nationalism. If we are concerned about the intolerance we have recently seen in Sault Ste Marie or earlier in Bill 178, let us just imagine what would follow the breakup of this country. I do not need to invoke Kosovo or Azerbijan in order to suggest that the lot of francophones outside Quebec and anglophones within Quebec will be a lot less enviable, that the nasties of APEC and the Mouvement Québec Français will vent their anger on their respective minorities. Secondly, I am profoundly convinced as a *francophile* who happens to live in Vancouver that the cause of French (both in Quebec and the world) will be much better served by the continuation of a Canada in which French is one of our two official languages, in which the federal government puts our collective resources behind bilingualism and behind *la francophonie*, in which Quebec can continue to take reasonable measures to enhance and preserve the French language in Quebec, than would be the case in a small, independent Quebec. François Mitterrand, in this regard, sees things more clearly than did Charles de Gaulle—and so should the Quebec left. Thirdly, I think Québécois significantly underestimate the danger which the U.S. represents for them, no less than for ourselves. Do Bombardier et al. really think they will beat the Americans at the capitalist game? Robert Campeau has already learned his lesson. Is Quebec popular culture any more insulated from American films, rock music, or television programmes than our own? Are Quebec's social programmes or taxation policies immune from pressures for harmonization with those of the U.S.? Is an independent Quebec more likely to resist the blandishments and pressures of the U.S. in defence or in foreign policy than a united Canada?

Where do we go from here? Into a new and uncertain round of wrangling between our two nationalisms, particularly when Meech Lake goes down the tube as it almost inevitably must? I am less fearful of the consequences of a Meech breakdown than are our élites, whose attitude, in typical Canadian fashion, is to try to sweep any and all conflicts under the rug, or better yet drown them in gobs of maple syrup. We need frank talking between English Canadians and Québécois, not because we will have a perfect meeting of two minds or easy agreement, but because it may allow us to separate out the essential from the inessential, the things on which we may well have common interests as we enter on the 1990s, and others on which our interests or analyses may diverge. But even when they diverge, I think we need to show respect and understanding for each other's nationalism. We need a willingness to recognize that making our relationship work—whether an ongoing federal relationship, as I would prefer, or a second-best arrangement like sovereignty-association— requires reciprocity in the way we relate to one another. Beyond free trade and Meech Lake, the two nationalisms that make up the northern part of this continent are condemned to continue to live side by side with one another. And it is my fervent hope that we can do so by sharing strong progressive values, communitarian and egalitarian ones, rather than the neo-conservative ones adhered to at the moment by our political and corporate élites.

Quebec and Canada: The Last Rejoinder

DANIEL LATOUCHE

Quebec is out of "rejoinders" to offer. This Québécois certainly is.

What else is there to say? We are guilty of voting conservative when it is no longer appropriate to do so. We supported Free Trade and we should have known better. We were happy with Bill 101, but that was before the Supreme Court's action. We made use of the "Notwithstanding Clause," although it is illegitimate to do so.

We are permanently out of bounds, outside the rules, out of touch, and out of our senses. But rest assured; very soon we'll be out of Canada.

I sympathize with English Canadian intellectuals and with the Toronto intelligentsia—not to mention the literati of Vancouver and Kingston. They never really had their day in court, while we had more than our fifteen minutes of fame. Life is unfair and certainly no bowl of cherries. But don't take it out on us.

It would have been good for all of us if all of you had been able to convince all of them that Free Trade was indeed a danger to the survival of the country. You almost did it, or more precisely John Turner almost did it for you. Mind you, this alliance with a reactionary party, a party that had taken the lead in putting Quebec in its place, did not seem to bother you at the time. Nor did you bother to consult with us as to the best way to oppose this measure. You simply assumed that if Free Trade was bad for your Canada, it also had to be bad for Quebec.

What about the argument that Free Trade could jeopardize Quebec's right to self-determination and would constitute another stumbling block on Quebec's road to sovereignty? We would have loved to hear you make use of this argument. You would have made a killing in Montreal. Too far-fetched? You could have pointed out instead that Free Trade posed a threat to Quebec culture and to the predominance of the French language.

But this is an old story. A new one is in the making, more interesting because it's yet to be articulated. Soon now, probably before the turn of the century, Quebec will be a country, just like the others. It's getting boring to talk about it. Will it have its own army? What about passports and the exchange rate? Is a Quebec dollar a good idea? All these questions

Daniel Latouche, "Quebec and Canada: The Last Rejoinder," *Queen's Quarterly*, 97, 4(Winter 1990), 700–703. By permission of the author.

are now being debated with the passion of undergraduates discovering the real world out there.

These days I find the rest of Canada more interesting than Quebec. Of course, its newly discovered sense of national identity is taking us for a ride (and what a ride), but the feeling is great. Stick to it. You have only begun to explore the many possibilities of a Canada without Quebec.

Allow me to join in your conversation. I promise that I won't impose myself and will leave if required. If we ever decide to reject federalism, will Canada necessarily disintegrate—as provinces and regions seek to profit from Quebec's departure, while the central government sits power-less, without the legitimacy or the will to regroup the federation as Pakistan was able to do after the secession of Bangladesh?

The disintegration hypothesis has a number of variants, all centred on whether or not some or all the provinces decide to cast their lot with the U.S. Until now no provincial or federal political party has advocated such a union, and at least one premier, John Buchanan of Nova Scotia, raised a storm when he first suggested that Quebec's independence would leave the Maritimes with no other choice than to join the U.S. He was ready for the Senate.

There is no doubt that logical reasoning as well as a conjuncture of events could lead you to accept and even seek such a union, but the drama surrounding the rejection of the Meech Lake Accord would seem to indicate that such a disintegration is not likely. It assumes that Quebec is such a necessary component—politically, economically, and psychologi-cally—of Canada that its departure would make it impossible for Canadi-ans to want to live together or would make the annexation hypothesis suddenly more attractive. I don't believe so, neither do you, and it's about time that you start saying so. Don't be afraid: such a statement will not create a self-fulfilling prophecy. The example of East Germany, one of few states able to willingly disappear from the map, illustrates how different the Canadian case is and the unlikelihood that it would follow the same path. Sweden and Malaysia, both of which underwent similar traumas, have adapted well to their new borders. You and I know very well that you will do the same and that you won't necessarily be a poorer country for having done so. Don't forget: it's not Canada and Canadians that have failed but federalism; and what is federalism but a constitutional formula?

The combination of Free Trade and the Meech Lake debate has revealed the existence of an English-Canadian public opinion that transcends the traditional regional and provincial differences. A decade ago, the mere hint of an English-Canadian national identity was cause for suspicion, since it assumed the existence of a bi-national fabric. But now a similar reaction is encountered whenever it is suggested that English-Canadians are merely Americans-in-disguise or show little disposition for a national identity of their own. It's about time.

With Ontario possessing 49 per cent of the population and 54 per cent of the GNP, the new Canada will undoubtedly have to be reorganized to prevent such imbalance from paralysing the country. The creation of new provinces in the North, the partition of Ontario itself, and the regionalization of Western and Atlantic Canada are possible ways of correcting this imbalance. But by itself an Ontario-dominated Canada is not an unworkable outcome and would not necessarily further exacerbate the regional frustrations coming out of the West and East. After all, these tensions owe much of their acrimony to the perturbing impact of the "Quebec Problem," which always seems to monopolize everyone's attention. This is not to say that such domination would go unchallenged. On the contrary. But the resolution of this imbalance will be facilitated, not hindered, by the absence of Quebec. As we get out of your way, the level of loyalty to the rest of the country is bound to increase.

No single province or region of Canada would benefit or suffer more than the others (provided they suffered at all), were Quebec to leave the Canadian federation or ask for a reorganization of such magnitude that it would be tantamount to departure. Relative to one another, the position and the economic endowment of the other four regions of the country, including the North, would not be modified in the least. Over the years Quebec has sought to build a diversified and export-oriented economy. In no area does it control strategic natural or human resources that the rest of the country cannot do without. The St Lawrence Seaway comes to mind, but, as in the case with other such links, the Seaway is of value to Quebec if and only if it is used by others. The same reasoning applies to energy export, where both New England and Quebec have locked themselves into a situation of mutual dependency.

For a generation Quebec has been in the curious position of being both at the receiving end of a number of equalization and regional development programmes while being considered part of the richest and the best-taken-care-of region of the country. Because of its large and "poor" population—relative to Ontario, that is—Quebec takes in a large share of all such programmes, much to the chagrin of the rest of the country. On a per capita basis, though, its share is significantly lower than the Atlantic provinces, where approximately 25 per cent of all personal income is achieved through redistributive schemas. Furthermore, because such programmes are based on the economic situation of each province taken as a whole, Quebec, which is really two provinces in one (Montreal and *la province*), qualifies as a poor province while others (those in the West, for example) do not, although their resource-based economies make them particularly susceptible to boom-and-bust cycles. Clearly, if Quebec had not been a "different" province such programmes would have been redesigned a long time ago, and they undoubtedly will if Quebec leaves.

Undoubtedly, the departure of Quebec would affect Canada's international standing, notably as an already fringe member of the select group of most industrialized countries. Its reputation as an oasis of peace and harmony and as the land where complex problems are always resolved through complex solutions would also suffer. Though harsh for Canadians, such a penalty would barely be noticed in today's turbulent international environment.

I will probably sound paternalistic—and, as you know, this is a sound I don't particularly appreciate—but you're almost there. *Encore un petit effort.*

Let's go, Canada!

Lord Durham Then and Now[*]

DAVID R. CAMERON

ROYAL OBSERVATIONS ON THE LORD

Queen Beatrix of the Netherlands visited Canada a year ago [1988]. While she was here, Her Majesty gave an address before both Houses of Parliament in Ottawa. Figuring largely in her remarks, along with William of Orange, Mary Stuart and the Glorious Revolution of 1688, was Lord Durham, of whom the Queen said:

> In Canada in 1839 Lord Durham laid the foundations for a democratic form of government in his *Report on the Affairs of British North America*. On the basis of the "responsible government" principle he entrusted the government of the colony to the colonists themselves. The policy of placing the responsibility for government with the people was thereby extended to Canada[1]

It is not hard to understand the *frisson* of anxiety that started up in the breasts of those listening to the Queen's address, for she had touched a nerve in the Canadian body politic by mentioning Durham at all on a ceremonial occasion of this kind, and—worse still—by mentioning him *favourably*.

It would, I presume, be *lèse majesté* to suggest that Queen Beatrix had been maladroit and undiplomatic in making this comment, so I will simply say that her advisors, Dutch and Canadian, failed her by not expunging the Durham reference, in order to ensure that the address was kept as anodyne as these addresses are meant to be.

Both the Queen's statement and the *frisson* which followed contain within them the seeds of much of what I have to say....For the Queen may have been ill advised in what she said, but she was not wrong; the Durham *Report*[2] did stoutly affirm the principles of responsible govern-

---

DAVID R. CAMERON, "LORD DURHAM THEN AND NOW," *JOURNAL OF CANADIAN STUDIES*, 25, 1 (SPRING 1990), 5–23. REPRINTED WITH THE PERMISSION OF THE *JOURNAL OF CANADIAN STUDIES/REVUE D'ÉTUDES CANADIENNES*.

[*] As a public servant I should say that the views expressed in this paper are my own, not those of the Government which I serve.

1. House of Commons, *Debates*, May 10, 1988.

2. The edition of Lord Durham's *Report* to which I refer in the text is that of G. M. Craig, ed., *An Abridgement of the Report on the Affairs of British North America by Lord Durham* (Ottawa: Carleton University Press, 1982).

ment as the way to compose the ills common to all five of Britain's North American possessions, if not the disease specially afflicting Lower Canada. What Queen Beatrix did *not* mention about the Durham *Report* is the other thing Lord Durham said, the thing which made the Queen's Canadian listeners uneasy, namely, that the French in North America had to be obliterated as a nationality if peace, progress and social equality were to prevail. The anxiety occasioned by the Queen's remarks is a good indication that the *Report's* currency continues, that it is a document of contemporary significance, at the very least at the level of political folklore.

My purpose here is to begin with an assessment of Lord Durham's diagnosis and prescription, then to offer some thoughts about the evolution of English–French relations in Canada and about the increasingly important phenomenon of multiculturalism. That context will provide the occasion to reflect on some of the conceptual and practical issues that attend the attempt to find a happy home for both liberal principles and cultural pluralism within the framework of a single political community.

The Canadas in Lordly Perspective

To put it mildly, there have never been many fans of Lord Durham in French-speaking Canada, and it is not hard to see why. Radical Jack Durham was an uncomfortable colleague even for many of his British aristocratic associates, not only because of his gritty and unbending commitment to advanced social and political views, but also because of his prickly, austere and, at times, arrogant demeanour. Indeed, for some of his British colleagues, one of the not inconsiderable advantages of Durham taking on his commission in British North America was that it would keep him out of Britain for a while. With his own political allies feeling this way about him, it is not, perhaps, surprising that he did not go down well with the French Canadians of Lower Canada either.

But, more to the point, Durham was an enthusiastic British imperialist who saw the hand of God and destiny in the ultimate domination of the entire North American continent by the English people, "the great race which must, in the lapse of no long period of time, be predominant over the whole North American Continent." The resources of British North America, Durham declared, "are the rightful patrimony of the English people, the ample appanage which God and Nature have set aside in the New World for those whose lot has assigned them but insufficient portions in the Old."[3] Hardly a reassuring point of view for the French community which had inhabited the banks of the St. Lawrence for more than a century by the time he visited British North America.

In addition, with a candour characteristic of an earlier age, Lord Durham launched a merciless and scathing attack on the French Canadians, who clung "to ancient prejudices, ancient customs and ancient laws, not from any strong sense of their beneficial effects, but with the unreasoning tenacity of an uneducated and unprogressive people." Retaining "their peculiar language and manners," they were a people with no history and no literature, "an old and stationary society in a new and progressive world."[4] These powerful, declarative statements have echoed down the years on both sides of the language divide, shaping prejudices and perceptions through the generations. Small wonder that French-speaking Canadians have customarily remembered Durham for his English ethnocentrism, not for his liberalism, and have regarded him warily as a kind of pit-bull terrier of the British imperial establishment.

Yet these two convictions, namely, his belief in the superiority and mission of the English race and his commitment to the progress of liberty in the world, co-existed without apparent difficulty in Lord Durham's mind and received synthetic expression in the pages of his *Report*.

Living, as we do, in a more relativistic and culturally sensitive age, we find Durham's comfortable reconciliation of liberalism, cultural superiority and empire to be a good deal more problematic than he did, and his confident assertion that God Himself has had a hand in establishing the dominion of the English-speaking people in North America more a rationalization than an argument. But anyone who consults the political literature of Victorian England will be aware that Lord Durham was far from unusual in holding this combination of opinions. He is not the only Englishman of enlightened views to break his liberal lance on the tough hide of empire.

Durham's views place him squarely in the John Stuart Mill camp as far as the relationship between cultural pluralism and liberty is concerned. "Free institutions," Mill wrote, "are next to impossible in a country made up of different nationalities."[5] The diversity which Mill so avidly sought in

---

3. *Report*, pp. 146, 20.
4. Ibid., pp. 28, 150.
5. John Stuart Mill, *Considerations on Representative Government*, ed. Currin V. Shields (Indianapolis: Bobbs-Merrill, 1958), ch. 16.

his liberal philosophy was a diversity of belief and ideas, not a diversity of ethnic origin, language or culture.

The contrary view was ably stated by another famous Victorian liberal, Lord Acton, who, in a celebrated essay, wrote: "The co-existence of several nations under the same State is a test, as well as the best security of its freedom. It is also one of the chief instruments of civilization...and indicates a state of greater advancement than the national unity which is the ideal of modern liberalism."[6]

For Canadians, who have been living à la Lord Acton both in freedom and in two national communities for more than a century, the contention of Lord Durham and John Stuart Mill is empirically doubtful and conceptually flawed. It is easy, then, for us to say that Lord Durham got it wrong. In the years since Durham's *Report* appeared people have been saying just that—in the brutally frank characterization of the French-Canadian community which he found, or thought he found, on the shores of the St. Lawrence, and in his prescription for its assimilation into the English community, Lord Durham blotted an otherwise masterful report to his Sovereign on the affairs of British North America. Indeed, I think it is fair to identify this as the conventional historical understanding of Lord Durham and his *Report*. But if we are not to inflict Whig history on a prominent nineteenth-century liberal—something, I suspect, which Lord Durham himself would not have hesitated to do to his own intellectual ancestors—we would do well to consider carefully why Lord Durham adopted such—from our point of view—wrong-headed views. He was, after all, a cultured intellectual of advanced social opinions, an able politician if a discomfiting cabinet colleague, a man with international experience, and a militant and uncompromising liberal, in both thought and action. In addition, despite its signal flaw, his *Report* is acknowledged to be one of the great state papers in the English language.

Why, then, did he get the French-Canadian issue wrong? The question is worth asking, I think, not simply as a matter of antiquarian interest, but because the answer may illuminate vexing issues which we continue to wrestle with in our national life. Durham's line of reasoning, I would suggest, can be summarized in a series of propositions.

1. French Canadians, while currently more numerous in Lower Canada than their English-Canadian compatriots, were destined with the pass-

---

6. Lord Acton, "Nationality," in his *Essays on Freedom and Power* (Cleveland: World Publishing, 1964).

ing of the years to be submerged numerically by the growing population of British settlers.

2. French Canadians were an amiable but backward people, quite incapable, with the existing constitution of their society and culture, of competing with the socially advanced and commercially competitive English community.

3. The organization and assignment of power in British North America, especially in Lower Canada, had to be made with a view to ensuring that stable government was established, social and economic progress was made possible, and liberal political principles were advanced.

4. This meant that a limited form of representative government had to be introduced, specifically, that the domestic affairs of the colonies had to become the responsibility of the colonists themselves. Thus, the advisors of the Queen's representative in Canada had themselves to be responsible in these matters to the popularly elected assembly.

5. This meant further that in Lower Canada the legislative assembly to which the executive had to be responsible had itself to be dominated by English-speaking Canadians, not by the French—hence the proposal of legislative union of Lower and Upper Canada which would give the English a clear majority in the single assembly.

These are, I think, the key points of Lord Durham's argument. Taken together, they fulfil his commission in British North America "for the adjustment of certain important questions depending in the Provinces of Lower and Upper Canada, respecting the form and future Government of the said Provinces." His recommendations set the stage, he thought, for achieving a critical long-term objective, namely, the gradual assimilation of the French Canadians into the English community and, with that done, the receipt by the French Canadians of all the benefits of social and economic progress, English style.

THE FAULT LINE IN CANADIAN LIFE

At the beginning of his *Report*, Lord Durham wrote that he had expected to find "a contest between a government and a people," of a sort familiar to the English for many generations. Instead, he found in Lower Canada "a struggle, not of principles, but of races,"[7] and recognized in consequence that a simple legal or constitutional reform that left the elements of society unaltered would fail of its purpose. It is for this reason that the union of the two Canadas was so critical; while admittedly a constitutional change in form, its object was to compose Lower Canadian society differently. Durham's proposal, in response to the 1837 troubles in Lower Canada, was to offer resolution by dissolution; he resolved the problem of two warring nations by dissolving one into the other.

This was undoubtedly a recommendation based on *realpolitik* and on Durham's assessment of how best to protect and advance British imperial interests in North America. It was also clearly grounded in an effort to meet the needs and aspirations of the British colonists in North America, even if it was not warmly received by all of them. But it is a recommendation which is rooted in yet another species of rationale and justification, less frequently observed and remarked on, but conceptually more interesting. Lord Durham proposed the assimilation of French Canada into British North American nationality in part because he believed that, in the final analysis, this was the best route to follow to secure the interests, well-being, and future prospects of the French Canadians themselves. It is my impression that this was a genuine consideration, although by no means the dominant one, in the framing of his analysis and recommendations.

Any other approach, in his view, was likely to consign the French in British North America to a status of perpetual inferiority, constrained by increasingly antiquated social, cultural, and religious institutions, forced either to remain in stagnant backwaters while the real life of North America went on all about them or, alternatively, to seek escape from the increasingly untenable conditions of rural life by entering the cities and commercial establishments dominated by the English, and doing so at the most inferior level.

Consider Lord Durham's comment on what he deemed to be a relevant parallel in the United States. He wrote favourably of the experience of the French in Louisiana who, gradually adjusting themselves to the reality of life in English North America, learned to compete effectively—but in English—in the wider field of commerce and politics presented by the American union. An implicit bargain was struck, according to Lord Durham, decidedly to the advantage of the Acadians of Louisiana. They agreed to give up, over time, most of the active features of their national-

---

7. *Report*, p. 23.

ity; in return, they received the opportunity of full and equal participation in the life and affairs of the American union. A choice as fateful presented itself to the French Canadians of British North America, and the moral and prudential calculus led, in his opinion, to the same conclusion. What are we to make of all this?

The troubles which brought Lord Durham to Lower Canada were social and cultural in character and went to the core, not only of British North America's relatively brief history, but of whatever future it could construct for itself as well. That Durham saw the character and seriousness of the crisis is evident in his observation that a response which left the elements of society unaltered would fail. The relatively simple introduction of limited representative government in the other colonies would be sufficient to relieve the tensions there, but in Lower Canada that would not suffice. He saw the seriousness of the crisis clearly, but did not appreciate that it was in fact too serious—too structural—in its character to be successfully addressed by the means he suggested.

Without perhaps fully appreciating it, Durham was acting as a kind of social geologist, exploring the great fault line of British North America and of Canada itself as it emerged. The line dividing English and French was as primordial in the social geology of British North America in 1839 as it is in Canada today. If the society forming itself on the northern half of the continent were to crack, it would crack along that line. The point, then and now, is not to make futile efforts to erase the fault line, but to learn to live with it, and to render the social and political institutions of the country, as far as possible, earthquake proof. In the 1830s, the ancillary controversy over representative government was a problem that could, in principle, be solved; the relationship between French and English in North America was not. Indeed, it was not, in the same sense, a problem at all, but an existential reality to be acknowledged and accommodated, one which spawned a slew of problems, admittedly, but which was too intimately related to existence and identity to be considered a problem like the others.

It was this, I think, that Lord Durham failed to appreciate, probably because, like many another nineteenth-century liberal, he was insensitive to the power and durability of culture and nationality. By using the yardstick of progress to find French Canada grievously wanting and, therefore, of relatively little account, Durham allowed his analysis to lead him to a flawed conclusion, namely, that a society which he judged to be backward was, therefore, weak and without significant defense, and could be dismantled through peaceful and political means. He did not realize that territory would not be won easily, if at all.

Indeed, it was the very effort to reconcile political liberty and cultural assimilation that was doomed to failure. A sufficient exercise of power may well keep the national sentiments of a subject people in check, at least for a time, although Mikhail Gorbachev, now struggling with the powerful expression of Georgian and other forms of nationalism in the Soviet Union, would no doubt have a rueful word to say about just how long that power has to be applied to ensure that the job of assimilation is done.

In the absence of that power, and in fact with the specific intent of establishing government based on consent, the notion that a numerically powerful minority could be assimilated through constitutional means—at least in the context of British North America—was doubtful in the extreme. The point was not that a free society was impossible *without* assimilation, but that, in Canada at least, it was impossible *with* it.

Not Mill and not Durham, but Lord Acton was the thinker who provided the intellectual foundation for the direction which British North America—despite Durham's *Report*—was already destined to take. The course British North America was set upon was not the suppression of one national community but the mutual accommodation of two, a development which was ultimately to play a key role in the fashioning of a federal system and the establishment of Canada.

It would be quite inaccurate to imply that the evolution of Canada in this way was the expression of some explicit collective preference. Certainly, on the part of the British in North America, it was more a matter of circumstance than volition. The capacity of the colonies scattered along the northern edge of the United States to do otherwise than they did was ultimately recognized to be fairly limited. The mutual accommodation of French and English, then, was a necessity, and, for many, a regrettable necessity. One might characterize a good deal of the history of French–English relations since that time, especially recent history, as an attempt to make a virtue of necessity. It is an enterprise that is still underway.

MAKING A VIRTUE OF NECESSITY

If Lord Durham failed to appreciate the fact that British North America had, tacitly, settled on the path of cultural duality and accommodation between French and English, he was accurate beyond a shadow of a doubt in his sense of just how difficult that path, if taken, would be. As we have seen, one of his reasons for advocating assimilation was his belief that any other course would condemn French Canadians to perpetual inequality vis-à-vis their English-speaking compatriots. In this he was for a great many years substantially correct, for the effort to secure and maintain a settlement between French and English in Canada depended for more than a century on the existence of what might be called mutually compatible solitudes. On the French-Canadian side, this meant that the social and economic circumstances of French Canadians for generations appear not to have been materially different from those which Durham had predicted for them in the absence of integration into English-speaking North America.

By "mutually compatible solitudes," I mean to refer to the fact that the character and values of French-Canadian society were sufficiently different from those of English Canada that the scope for direct conflict and competition between the two was more restricted than it otherwise would have been. At the risk of over simplification, one might point to an important dimension of the situation by saying that the English could get on with commerce and industry in the cities and the westward expansion of Canada if the French were prepared to satisfy themselves with a substantially agrarian lifestyle on the banks of the St. Lawrence. If a French Canadian during this period were to break out of the cycle of economic disadvantage, social inequality, and political weakness to which his community had been largely consigned, it could normally be done only with great difficulty and only if he were prepared to play the game *à l'anglais* and to leave his cultural baggage at the door before entering the trading halls of prosperity.

One would be hard pressed to describe this as an arrangement which was the product of free choice on the part of French Canadians. It was rather the situation as it emerged, but as such it constituted the terms of accommodation that were to govern French–English relations in Canada for more than a hundred years and that allowed two different communities (should I say "distinct societies"?) to live side by side within one country. Clearly, it was not ideology or culture, but circumstance and opportunity that tied French and English together.

The post-war period, and particularly the years since 1960, have seen French Canada's approach to ensuring its survival in North America evolve very rapidly. This has led both Quebec and the country as a whole to engage in fundamental reflection upon the destiny of Canada. Social and economic forces had been pushing Quebec towards the adoption of a new collective cultural strategy for generations, but the political and attitudinal transformation was substantial when it came, and it brought the two linguistic communities much more directly into contact and competition with each other. From a condition of mutually compatible solitudes, we moved to a condition in which the aspirations of the francophones of Quebec came directly into conflict with the English minority of the province and the assumptions of the rest of the country. With respect to a number of central public policy matters, such as the language regime in Quebec, it became a zero-sum game, for what the Québécois sought necessarily involved the denial of practices, assumptions and prerogatives that English Quebec had enjoyed for generations.

The irony is that it is at least in part the fact that French Quebec's values and aspirations have become more like those of English Canada, which has contributed to the conflict and tension that has marked much of our last thirty years. Quebecers have become the modern, secular, commercial, bustling society that Lord Durham thought they were incapable of. But they have done it *en français* and collectively, not by assimilation.

Quebec's rapid evolution has been a major factor in the remarkable transformation of English-Canadian thinking about national identity. Several decades ago it would have been common ground for anglophones to think of Canada as an English-speaking country, a member of the family of British Commonwealth countries which happened to have a substantial French-speaking minority within its borders. It would have been understood that it was up to the minority to learn the language of the majority, even in the Province of Quebec where the numbers told a different story. Today, the conventional English-Canadian understanding of Canada is that it is a country composed of two linguistic communities with two official languages. This is understood to imply that the country's common institutions will function in both official languages, will serve citizens in either language, and will offer career opportunities equally to members of both language communities. It has also produced a further, but far from complete, understanding of the duty to protect linguistic minorities. Bilingualism is now an acquirement of the professionally ambitious. The powerful and distinctively Canadian movement in favour of French-language immersion education is evidence of the degree to which these views have implanted themselves in the minds of many English-speaking Canadians. For many, historical necessity has become a contemporary virtue and the French–English fact is celebrated as a defining characteristic of Canadian society.

While Québécois welcome both the institutional expression of Canadian official-language policy and its growing acceptance on the part of English Canadians, they would insist that this addresses but one dimension of the many-faceted reality they are confronting. In the final analysis, it is not the dimension most intimately related to the survival of French in North America.

The recognition of the equality of two official languages and the policy of institutional bilingualism in the organization and operations of the Canadian government is appropriate and necessary, given that the government serves two language communities. But that, for French-speaking Quebecers, does not imply that the institutions of Quebec society should equally reflect the two Canadian official languages.

During the past twenty-five years Québécois have aggressively used their control of the provincial government to establish a language regime which has significantly altered the face of Quebec. The object is to establish conditions in which French will survive and flourish as the dominant language in Quebec. The pursuit of linguistic dominance has involved confining the use of English and placing limits on the rights of the English-speaking minority in the province. The resurgence of linguistic conflict and an unfortunate increase in linguistic intolerance in Canada today suggests that the two language communities may be tragically "out of synch" with one another yet again, as they have been on several occasions in the past.

French-speaking Canadians discern at times a double standard and a generous dollop of hypocrisy in English Canada's outbursts about language. They could more readily accept the severe criticism of Quebec's Bill 178 and the use of the notwithstanding clause if it had been matched by equally severe criticism of Alberta and Saskatchewan. A few months before, both had acted to restrict the rights of the francophone minorities in their provinces which had just been confirmed by a decision of the Supreme Court.

Many English-speaking Canadians find Quebec's language policies incomprehensible and objectionable. Given the confidence and energy displayed by Quebec society today, English-speaking Canadians outside Quebec find it very difficult to appreciate how deeply seated Quebec's feelings of cultural insecurity continue to be. French is now an official language in Canada, English Canadians are fighting to get their children into immersion classes, francophones make up the vast majority of Quebec's population and the proportion is growing. English Canadians are inclined to ask, "How can they feel insecure about their language situation?"

The fact is that they do, and for a number of reasons. Their long struggle to endure in an indifferent or hostile environment, the galloping assimilation of most francophone minorities outside of Quebec, the dwindling population base in the Province, their tiny minority status in North America (about 2% of the total continental population), the impact of American television and music on their young people, the English language's dominion over the computer and scientific worlds—all these factors play to Quebecers' sense of vulnerability and feed each successive language crisis as it arises.

I suspect we may not be far from the time when we will need, as a country, to establish a new basis of accommodation of our two national tongues. During the past twenty-five years, the English-Canadian sense of identity has increasingly encompassed the concept of cultural duality. In what direction have the Québécois been moving? A country whose two great language communities do not share a common sense of civic identity is unlikely, in the modern era, to remain tranquil and stable for long. What we have now is not simply differing language regimes animated by rather different values, but mutual incomprehension; Canadians, in many cases, honestly do not understand the reasons for what is happening linguistically in other parts of the country.

More generally, we have yet to achieve a settled and enduring answer to the issue Lord Durham raised 150 years ago—how can French-speaking Canadians exist on a footing of genuine equality with their fellow inhabitants of this vast continent and still remain true to themselves and their culture? Durham's flinty answer was that they cannot do both, and he was prepared, on their behalf, to have them give up culture for the sake of equality. Canadians rejected this prescription and have tried since that time to reconcile the two.

IMMIGRATION AND CANADIAN SOCIETY

In his examination of the troublesome co-existence of two national communities within British North America, Lord Durham was tackling, as we have seen, large questions relating to the foundations of liberty and culture. Multiculturalism in Canada raises a parallel set of issues concerning the interplay between cultural pluralism and liberalism in modern societies and it is to that matter I should like to turn. Cultural pluralism is now thoroughly entangled in our history, it is a rising force in our contemporary life, and it will most assuredly be central to our future destiny as a nation.

If one considers the non-native population of the country at the time of Confederation, it is a fair generalization to say that Canada was bicultural in its social composition. With the successive waves of immigration during the late nineteenth and twentieth centuries, Canada has become a multicultural society. In the 1986 Census, 40% of Canadians reported that their culture or ancestry was other than totally French or British.[8]

Three points are germane to our story at this stage. First, immigration to Canada has benefited the English side of the French–English equation disproportionately. From Confederation until just after the Second World War, the high fertility rate of French-speaking Canadians counterbalanced the benefits that the English-speaking community derived from immigration and assimilation; at the same time it allowed the French to preserve their relative population position in the country at about 30%. The situation has radically changed, to Quebec's disadvantage, since the 1960s. For the last twenty years, the fertility rate of Quebecers has been the lowest in the country, thus turning the "revenge of the cradles" argument on its head. Quebec's acute interest in immigration policy and its government's introduction in May 1988 of a $3,000 allowance for the third child in a family, now increased to $4,500, can be readily understood with these demographic facts in mind. They also explain, to an extent often not realized by Canadians living outside of Quebec, the Québécois preoccupation with language policy; from this perspective it is not so much the English minority in Quebec, but the immigrant population which is the crucial target of policies to give French clear predominance within the province.

The second point to underline is the shift in the parts of the world from which our immigrants have come. The regional origins of Canada's immigrants have altered substantially since Confederation, from Western Europe at the beginning, to Southern and Eastern Europe in the 1950s and 1960s, to Third World countries in the last two decades. With the introduction in 1967 of an immigration policy that eliminated preferences for particular national groups, there has been a dramatic change in the composition of Canadian immigration: 80% of Canada's immigrants used to come from Europe or from countries of European heritage (like the U.S.A.); now almost 75% come from Asia, Africa, Latin America, and the Caribbean. Currently, Asian immigration accounts for about half the annual total. The size of the Canadian population born in Asia, Latin America and Africa increased by 340% between 1971 and 1986.

The third point concerns the destination of immigrants arriving in Canada. Historically, a substantial proportion of Canada's immigrants

---

8. The data on immigration and multiculturalism in Canada are drawn from *The Review of Demography and its Implications for Economic and Social Policy*, Update Number 5, Health and Welfare Canada, Winter 1988.

came to make a better life for themselves in the rich and relatively undeveloped farmlands of the country. Today the situation is profoundly different. For one thing, post-war immigration has focused in particular on the provinces of Ontario and British Columbia to the disadvantage of Quebec and the Atlantic provinces. Less than 5% of the population of the Atlantic provinces is foreign-born, and 8% of Quebec's, as compared to 23% of Ontario's and 22% of B.C.'s. If one looks exclusively at the size of Ontario's Canadian-born population, it is only 17% larger than that of Quebec; if one adds in the foreign-born, Ontario is 30% larger. For another thing, immigrants now come overwhelmingly to cities rather than to rural areas, and particularly to the larger metropolitan centres. Toronto, which for thirty years has received nearly twice its share of immigrants, has demonstrated the most rapid increase in ethnic diversity. Vancouver is the only other metropolitan area which consistently attracts more than its share of immigrants. Between 1976 and 1986 90% of Canada's immigration went to the country's eight largest metropolitan areas.

These, then, are some key facts about post-war Canadian immigration; it has benefited English Canada far more than Quebec; Canadian immigration now comes chiefly from Third-World countries; and immigrants typically go to just a few Canadian provinces and almost exclusively to large metropolitan centres. In conjunction with this rapidly emerging demographic reality, there has been, for the past twenty-five years, a gradually expanding consciousness among Canadians of the importance of cultural pluralism. Along with that, both at the federal level and in the immigrant-receiving provinces, a chain of policy initiatives has attempted to recognize that growing reality and work it into our national life.

A concentration on ethnocultural traditions and folklore has been supplemented by a recognition of the necessity to establish conditions of equality and fair treatment in the workplace, in government and in the common institutions of society, whatever a person's cultural origin may be. Multiculturalism, which had historically been a relatively marginal feature of our cultural landscape, has, within the past twenty-five years, become a central force in Canadian life. A number of policy matters which will call for attention in the future are discernible in the forces at work at present.

With a low birth rate and an aging population in Canada, immigration becomes a strategic component of any national effort at population planning. Since its foundation, Canada has shaped its development and continually replenished its ranks by welcoming people from other lands, and assuming the country is capable of absorbing newcomers adequately, immigration levels will likely need to be increased substantially in coming years if the country is to stave off population stagnation or decline. We have noted that immigration consistently favours the English-language community over the French-language community. That, combined with Quebec's extraordinarily low birth rate, is a rivetting reality for Quebec's francophones, but I would argue that it should be a matter of concern for English-speaking Canada as well.

Canadian society is constructed on the basis of the two great language communities. A serious weakening of one or the other should worry both. Who we are and what we stand for are in no small measure defined by the French–English fault line of which I spoke earlier, and by the ongoing accommodation of two language communities within a single state. If the French community in Quebec is seriously weakened over time by a low birth rate and only feeble replenishment of its population by immigration, it is likely that its self-perceived capacity to function effectively within Confederation will be called increasingly into question and more protective measures will be sought. All Canadians have an interest in the preservation within Confederation of a strong and confident Quebec. This being so, it seems clear to me that there is a concomitant interest in supporting Quebec's efforts to attract substantial numbers of immigrants who will integrate themselves into the francophone community.

For the Québécois there is some difficult terrain to traverse. Immigration has to be regarded not as a threat but as one of the keys to their cultural health and vitality. They face all the challenges any other part of the country faces with immigration—plus one, namely, language. Language not only acts as an impediment to increased levels of immigration, reducing the attractiveness of Quebec as a destination, but it is also an indispensable dimension of the integration process, if that process is to be accounted a success. The natural flow in the rest of the country, and, in the absence of government policy, even in Quebec, is towards English; no special effort is necessary to make sure that English will be the language of choice for immigrants in the rest of Canada. Not so in Quebec, which must fashion policies and arrangements to ensure that her immigrants adhere to the French community, if a potentially beneficial instrument is not to be turned back against the community as a destructive agent.

Another observation can be made on the basis of the aforementioned data. Without quite realizing it, Canadians are in the process of building a new country within the old one. The new country is composed of the large cities, especially the great metropolitan centres of Montreal, Toronto and

Vancouver. The old country is all the rest. Life in the former bears little resemblance to life in the latter, whether with regard to cultural expression, crime, the sense of neighbourhood, price and income levels, traffic, or the pace of life.

What has a small community like Peterborough, Ontario got to do with Toronto, except for the fact that it too is finally being caught in the jet-stream of development radiating from the greater metropolitan area? I often think of the sentiments that must be aroused in the breast of an Ontarian who has lived his or her life in a small community and who visits Toronto periodically. There must be a sense of loss mixed with a feeling of wonderment—the loss of an urban centre you once knew and understood, and wonderment in the face of an urban landscape and mix of lifestyles that have become quite alien. It must be a bit like being a foreigner in your own country, with the underlying, disquieting realization that what you are visiting used to, in some greater sense, belong to you.

In Canada, one of the most significant agents of change is immigration, and its role in the transformation of our large cities is unlikely to abate. What this will probably mean is that Canada will increasingly be composed of a few, vast metropolitan centres which are riotously multicultural, surrounded by hinterlands where "old style" Canadians continue to live. And some parts of the country, such as most of Canada east of Montreal, will be virtually passed by in the process. The Canadian Human Rights Commissioner recently gave a speech on multiculturalism in which he spoke of federal employment-equity legislation and the importance of achieving non-discriminatory employment practices and equitable representation of ethnocultural groups in the Canadian workplace. The speech was given in Montreal. Consider just how remote the message would have been had the speech been given in Chicoutimi, where well over nine out of ten residents are French in origin, or in St. John's, Newfoundland, which is 93% British.

If, as seems likely, we continue to be a country with a low birth rate and high immigration levels, and we decline to engage in aggressive efforts to disperse newcomers to Canada over a wide geographical area, Canadians and their governments will need to prepare themselves to tackle the stresses and strains that are bound to arise more acutely in our large cities. We will also have to learn to cope with the increasing gulf between city and country-side and the fact that multicultural forces will likely become elements in the expression of Canadian regionalism in ways that they have never been before. The social and cultural character of Canada in the twenty-first century is likely to be determined as much by how we respond to immigration and cultural pluralism as by any other single factor.[9]. . .

CONCLUSION

The issue Lord Durham was commissioned to address is still with us today: How can two national communities be accommodated within a single state? The route we have followed is not Durham's, but the enterprise of working out the relationship between French and English has become an inescapable part of Canada's identity. The conceptual questions which formed the backdrop to Durham's analysis are alive today as well. While we may criticize Lord Durham's approach to reconciling the demands of liberalism with the more intimate affiliations of nationality, it would be folly to think that we've got that all sorted out. Far from it.

French–English relations in Canada are, in significant degree, a continuing dialogue about the terms of this on-going reconciliation. In addition, our recent experience of multiculturalism, which has emerged as an increasingly insistent overlay on the country's fundamental duality, suggests that there is much practical and conceptual work to be done before we can say that the legitimate requirements of liberalism and cultural pluralism have been adequately addressed.

A few years ago many people argued that, at least for a time, Canada's eternal verities of language and culture would recede in importance, to be replaced by a preoccupation with the economy and questions of interna-

---

9. Interestingly enough, most of the policy fields relevant to multiculturalism lie principally within the jurisdiction of provincial governments and their municipalities which are responsible for housing and municipal planning, immigrant settlement, education, social services, most workplace regulation, and so on. This raises nice questions about the role of the federal government. The Government of Canada shares jurisdiction for immigration with the provinces, and traditionally it has played a leadership role in most of the nation-building projects and nation-threatening crises of our past. Unless we are witnessing a fundamental shift in the nature of Ottawa's responsibilities and its chosen role, it would be surprising if the federal government did not seek—or was not offered by some provinces—active participation of some kind in these fields. The reverse may be true as well. Immigration is the source which feeds multiculturalism; as the size and the composition of the flow become more critical to the life of the receiving provinces we may find that jurisdictions other than Quebec begin to express an active interest and a desire to participate in the country's immigration policy and programs.

tional trade and industrial development. I suspect that this assertion would be made with more circumspection today. I have the growing conviction that we are entering a new and difficult period in the building of our country, a period in which questions of language and culture will play a central part.

I am fond of Ernest Renan's definition of a nation—"une plébiscite de tous les jours," a daily plebiscite. For me, it calls to mind the importance of time, and the importance of the affirmation and re-affirmation of a will to perpetuate a common existence. The act of living together one day after another, solving problems, making things work, is after all how most free societies hang together. And time, well used, is the best negotiator. With time we adapt, we enlarge our views, we accommodate ourselves to new situations; with time we domesticate what initially seemed to be alien and troublesome forces; with time we make friends.

One of the ingredients in using time well is the spirit of compromise.... Reaching a compromise between people who are free and equal and who hold strong opinions and well-developed views is difficult, not easy. And it has more of nobility about it than it has of a tawdry diminution of the human spirit. Successful compromise requires an effort to understand the other person's position and point of view, and it requires an honest search for a resolution or a common interest around which both can rally. It implies a relationship "de tous les jours," for it leaves each person with dignity and each in a position to approach the next round—for a next round there will certainly be—not in a spirit of revenge or conquest, but in a spirit of good faith and mutual respect.

Canadians, at critical moments in their history, have shown that they have learned this lesson well. We will, I think, have need of it again. Indeed, I think we need to remember it daily.

FURTHER READINGS FOR TOPIC 9

Keith Banting and Richard Simeon, *And No One Cheered: Federalism, Democracy and the Constitution Act* (Toronto: Methuen, 1983).

Michael Behiels, ed., *The Meech Lake Primer: Conflicting Views of the 1987 Constitutional Accord* (Ottawa: University of Ottawa Press, 1989).

Christian Dufour, *A Canadian Challenge/Le défi québécois* (Lantzville, B.C.: Oolichan, and Halifax: Institute for Research on Public Policy, 1990).

Peter C. Emberley, ed., *By Loving Our Own: George Grant and the Legacy of Lament for a Nation* (Ottawa: Carleton University Press, 1990).

Linda Hutcheon, *As Canadian as...possible...under the circumstances!* (Toronto: York University and ECW Press, 1990).

Robin Mathews, *Canadian Identity: Major Forces Shaping the Life of a People* (Ottawa: Steel Rail, 1988).